Praise for *Take and Make Art*

"I believe Creativity = Novelty + Value, and this book is a cornucopia of creativity. It's overflowing with Von's unique, idiosyncratic artwork that will add value and imagination to design projects large and small. Don't miss this book."

—Sam Harrison, author of *IdeaSpotting, IdeaSelling*, and *zing!*

"With *Take and Make Art*, Von Glitschka has spawned the Bad Boy Bible of twisted illustrations. For anyone who's ever coveted Von's logos and icons, forget about stealing them. They're yours for the taking in this totally unexpected visual treasury. Brilliant! You'll never look at stock art in the same way."

—Bill Gardner, author of *LogoLounge* and *Logo Creed*

"This book is just another example of Von's amazing creativity! The unique stock illustrations are so damn stimulating they'll serve as a solid starting point for any designer's creative process. Can't wait to dig in."

—Barbara Vick, Principal Director, Barbara Vick Design

"The illustrative ideas in this book are a great way to stimulate creativity. Whether you use the artwork directly or as a jumping off point to ignite your creative process, this book will be a valuable resource for a long time."

—David Lomeli, Senior Designer Licensed Products, Blizzard Entertainment

"I've worked with Von for more than a decade on everything from T-shirts to TV spots—and just about everything in between. He's a pro's pro, a special talent, and now this great book gives any designer access to Von's broad-ranging talent to create truly original, high-end art. The work in this book feels anything but "stock"—good designers will see the difference immediately. Typical stock art doesn't lead to great work, but you'll see right away that the art in this book is anything but typical."

—Dan Greenwald, Chief Creative Officer, White Rhino

TAKE AND MAKE ART

HUNDREDS OF ROYALTY-FREE VECTOR ILLUSTRATIONS FOR DISCRIMINATING DESIGNERS

WRITTEN AND ILLUSTRATED BY VON GLITSCHKA

TAKE AND MAKE ART

Hundreds of Royalty-Free Vector Illustrations for Discriminating Designers

Von Glitschka

Peachpit Press

Find us on the Web at www.peachpit.com
To report errors, please send a note to errata@peachpit.com

Peachpit Press is a division of Pearson Education.

Acquisitions Editor: Nikki Echler McDonald
Copy Editor: Jan Seymour
Production Editor: Tracey Croom
Composition and Template Design: Kim Scott/Bumpy Design
Cover Design: Glitschka Studios
Art Direction: Von Glitschka

ISBN 13: 978-0-321-98631-3
ISBN 10: 0-321-98631-8

9 8 7 6 5 4 3 2 1

Printed and bound in the United States of America

This book is dedicated to every designer who is expected to produce unique creative results from low-end budgets and unrealistic timelines and yet still exceed the high expectations required of you on a daily basis.

Your creativity is often taken for granted, diminished by corporate politics, unappreciated by bean counters, truncated by middle-management suck-ups, and neutered by marketing directors as you simply try to do your job the best you can.

The creative process can be a demanding, often frantic, and heart-wrenching experience. I hope the resources in this book ease your process and assist you in your daily pursuit of creating compelling graphic ideas for your demanding clients.

Royalty-Free License Terms and Conditions

Glitschka Studios is sharing this collection of artwork with you. You are free to use the art without paying a royalty under the terms of this license, however, please understand that we have to put some limits on how you use the work. We are giving you permission to use the illustrations, but not for absolutely any type of commercial purpose. (We're not that crazy.) For example, you cannot resell and distribute this art as your own product or collection. But you can use the art in projects like newsletters, on T-shirts, as a poster, or in brochures, or you can animate them on your website, get one tattooed, or use the art for many other creative ideas not listed here. Any retail reproduction of any piece of artwork is limited to a one-time run of no more than 500. For usage rights beyond this amount please download our full license agreement using the website at: www.TakeandMakeArt.com.

We grant you permission to use the artwork only under these terms and conditions so please read and understand the full terms and conditions of this license before using the illustrations in this book.

If you have questions after reading our license agreement and terms, email: license@vonster.com.

Acknowledgments

Drawing out and then building over a thousand pieces of unique vector illustrations that other designers can use and leverage in their own creative projects was a labor of love for me. The creative process on this book's concept was well over two years in the making. We created the actual artwork over a four-month period.

The Vector Posse

Simply put, I couldn't have physically built all the art for this book by myself. I drew out all the designs by hand, and scanned them in, but I needed a dependable group of vector-minded artists who could precisely discern my sketches and build them out to align with my established aesthetic standards.

The following people made up my Vector Posse:

Savannah Glitschka

Nothing thrills me more about design than seeing my daughter enjoy drawing and creating her own artwork. Savannah was my creative partner in crime on this project. She took my sketches and built hundreds of the images showcased in this book and I couldn't have physically done it all without her help. I love you, Bug, and I look forward to seeing all the wonderful things you do with your talent as you continue to grow into a beautiful and talented woman.

Graham Molthan

As a former student of mine, I was thrilled to see your attention to detail in taking my provided sketches and building them so well that they felt like my own work. I appreciate your help in making this book a reality. You have a bright future ahead of you, Graham, and thanks for all the hard work.

John Nissen

I first met you in 1987, right after I graduated from art school. I've always admired your quirky sense of humor and passion for art. You've been a good friend to me and my family for over 27 years, and I was thrilled when you said you'd help me build the artwork for this book. Your attention to detail and insight have been appreciated. Thanks, buddy!

Sean Ferguson

Sean is an incredible illustrator in his own right. So when he generously offered to help with the production of this book's art, I was thrilled to take him up on his offer. He's a very talented creative I'm privileged to call a friend. Thanks, Sean!

Nathen Springs

I brought Nathen in as an intern this summer to augment the building of all the art. He's currently in design school and was very helpful to the overall process. Thanks, Nathen.

Nikki McDonald

Nikki, you're the most relentless gentle persuader I've ever met. Many times during the long process of development I've become frustrated, weary, and wanted to just throw in the creative towel and say, "Screw it." But your crockpot-like patience and understanding has helped me shift my thinking and refocus my efforts and for that I'm thankful. Thanks for being a good editor and an even better friend.

Featured Artists

To the featured artists I showcase in this book, your contributions exemplify the professional diversity that makes design such an incredible medium to communicate with. Thank you for sharing your creative approaches utilizing the artwork found in this book. I'm privileged to call you colleagues.

Peachpit Team

Thank you for taking a calculated creative risk in publishing this book. I know it's a different niche from your normal fare, but you took the time to understand my vision and see the potential of what it could offer the creative community. I appreciate and value your trust.

About the Author

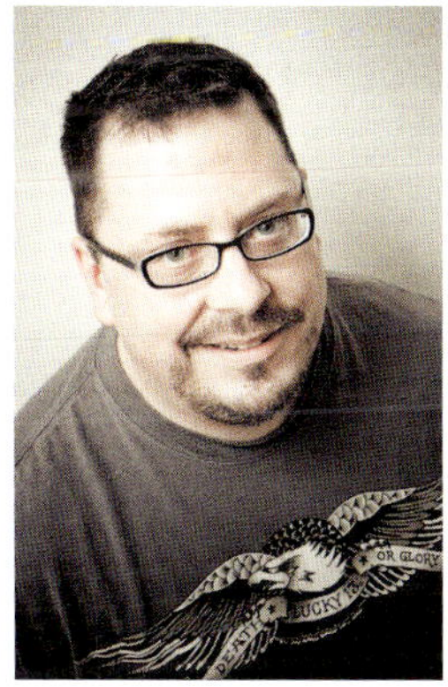

For over two decades Von has created award-winning illustrative design through his multi disciplined Glitschka Studios located in the Pacific Northwest.

He has collaborated with ad agencies, design firms, and in-house art departments all around the world working on some of the most respected global brands. Whether a project is with a multi-national or small business, Von works with clients to create memorable visual narratives.

Von's mix of humor, inspiration, great design, and solid creative methodology make him a sought-after speaker on the topic of design and creativity.

He also develops skill-based design courses for Lynda.com and can usually be found hanging out on Twitter (@vonster) posting snarky tweets about anything and everything.

www.vonglitschka.com

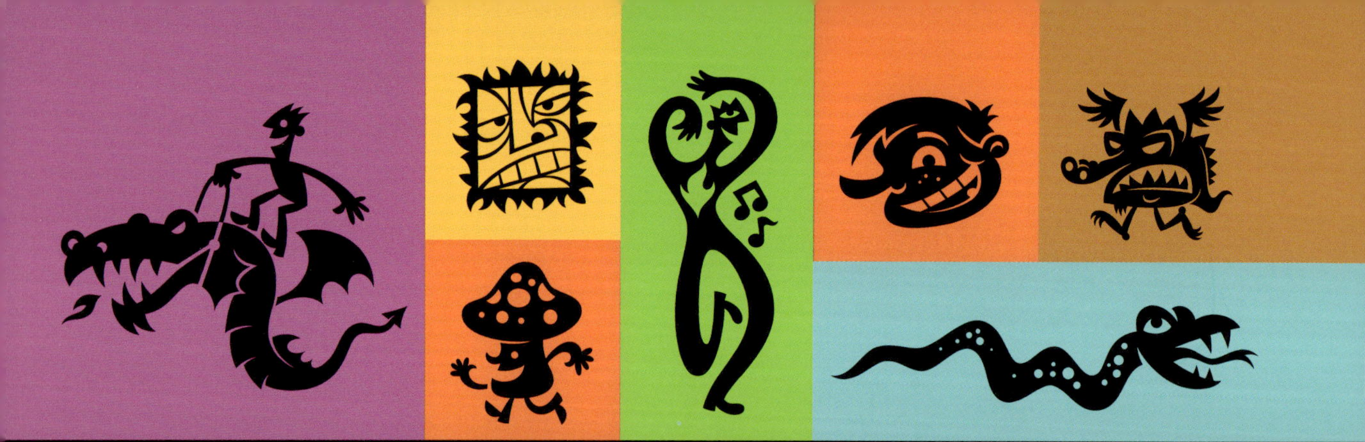

CONTENTS

FEATURED ARTISTS

INTRODUCTION

This book is filled with concept-oriented artwork you can use to make anything and everything. Buying this book gives you immediate access to a diverse collection of vector illustrations featured on these pages.

Register this Book, and then Download the Art for Free

To access the artwork, log into your Peachpit account or create one at Peachpit.com/join (it's free). On your Account page (under the Registered Products tab), click Register Your Products Here or Register Another Product, enter the ISBN for this book: 0321986318, and then click Submit. Finally, below the title of this book, click the Access Bonus Content link.

Fresh New Artwork FREE Each Month

This art collection is an ever-growing one: Anyone who buys this book will continue to get ten new royalty-free illustrations (or more) every month for at least five years after date of original publication.

To access the ongoing monthly downloads, visit www.TakeandMakeArt.com and subscribe for FREE. With each download your collection will continue to grow along with your creative possibilities.

In addition, I'll continue to share more information, sample usages showcasing the versatility of the artwork, and new upcoming monthly content via social media.

Custom Art Requests

If you ever have an art theme idea you'd like to see in a monthly update, or would like to commission me to create specific artwork for your project, just email me at: illustrativedesigner@gmail.com.

However you choose to use the artwork in this book for your own projects, I encourage you to share it via social media. When you post an image use the hashtag #TakeMakeBook so that I make sure not to miss it.

I look forward to seeing how you use the artwork in this book. The creative possibilities are limitless, so experiment and blow up your creative routine using some well-focused TNT, that is, *Try New Things.*

Creativity is birthed from moments of unexpected results.

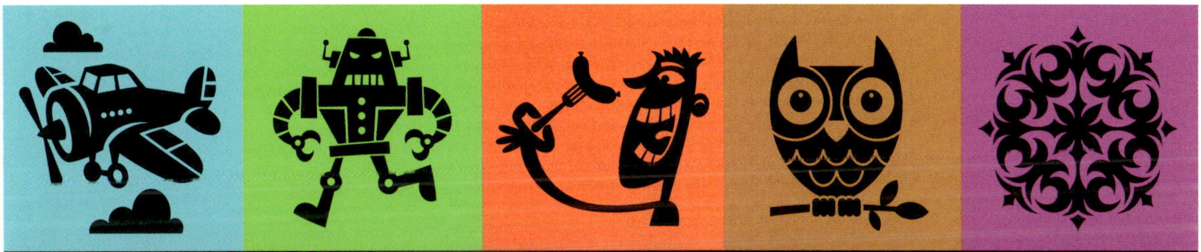

JUST TAKE AND MAKE

My Artwork Creation Process

It All Starts in Analog

Every single piece of artwork you see in this book started off as a simple drawing. Filling this book took many moons of late-night work. And truth be told, I hand draw nearly everything I create before I ever attempt to build it in digital form. In other words, I want to firmly establish what I'm creating before I attempt to digitally create it because drawing is still design's best friend.

The aesthetic of the artwork in this book is all about simplicity of shape in order to make visual communication quick and the art more adaptable. So let me give you an idea of the art creation process. In **FIGURE 1.1**, the theme I'm trying to capture is "excitement." I first draw thumbnail sketches for ideas on how I can form this character.

After selecting a direction to take from my thumbnail sketches, I then proceed to draw my artwork in a more precise form. It's at this stage I usually switch from a regular pencil or pen to a mechanical pencil so I can make my line work nice and crisp (**FIGURE 1.2**).

Since this refined drawing will serve as a road map for building my vector shapes in Adobe Illustrator, I spend as much time needed working out all the details. It's important not to rush the creative.

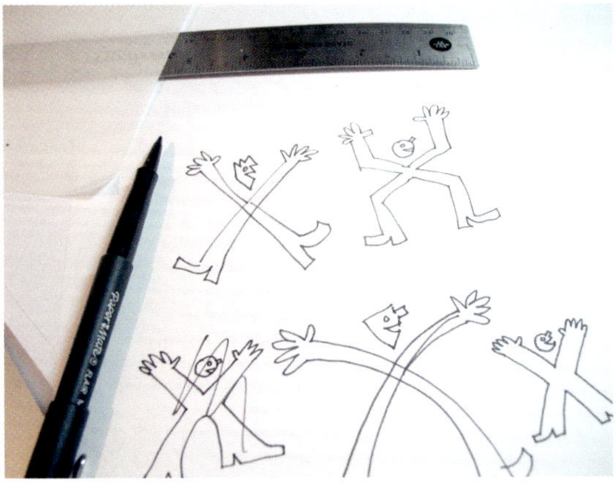

FIGURE 1.1 Some of the rough thumbnail sketches I draw before starting to refine the artwork.

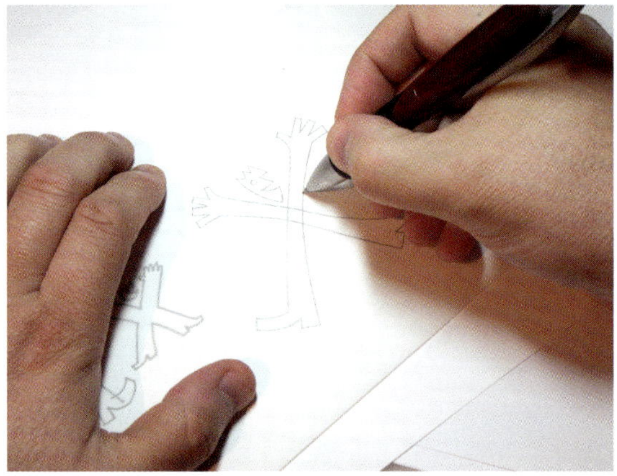

FIGURE 1.2 Drawing my illustration in a more refined sketch format.

Now imagine this same analog process for pages and pages of the illustrations contained in this book, each one scrutinized in this same manner.

Building the Vector Illustration

Once I scan my refined sketch, I place it on its own layer in Illustrator and lock it. I then proceed to build my vector paths on another layer on top of the drawn sketch, using the sketch as my guide for building (FIGURE 1.3).

Since I worked out the artwork in analog, the build process is now faster because I've already made all of my aesthetic decisions; it's just a matter of digital craftsmanship at this point.

Once I have all my base vector shapes created, I'm ready to fuse the shapes into one cohesive illustrative vector image (FIGURE 1.4).

At this state, I select all my base vector shapes and fuse them using Illustrator's Pathfinder palette (FIGURE 1.5).

Finally I colorize the illustration black and I'm done (FIGURE 1.6). I repeated this same illustrative process hundreds of times for the images contained in this book, creating everything you see in the pages that follow. It was a labor of love.

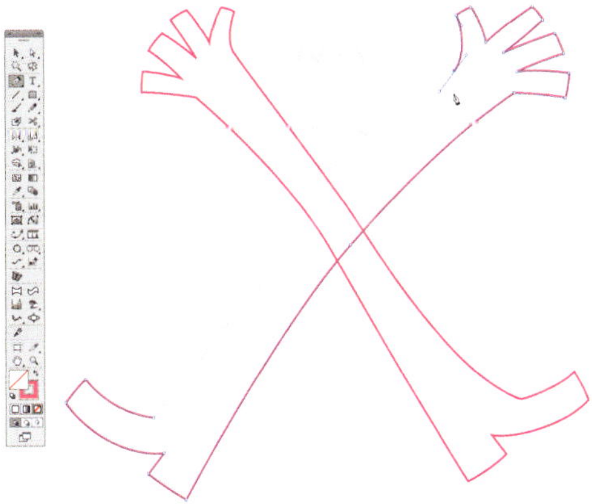

FIGURE 1.3 Simple point-by-point vector building using the Pen tool in Illustrator.

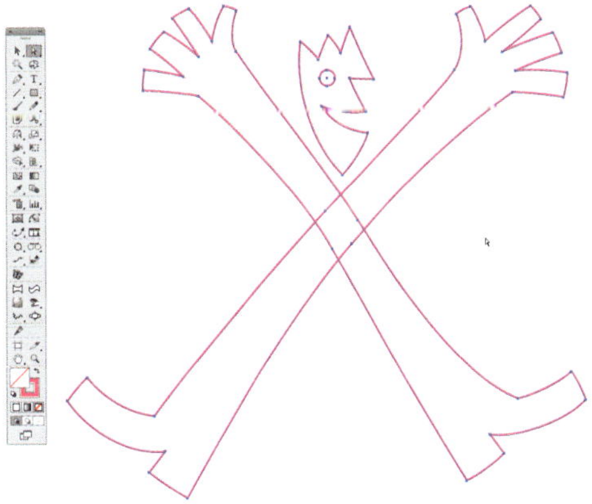

FIGURE 1.4 Finalized base vector shapes; you can see how they align with my underline refined drawing.

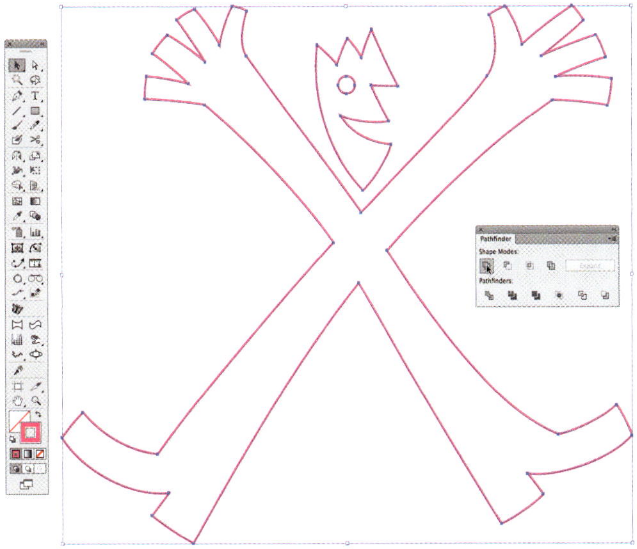

FIGURE 1.5 I call this process *shape building*. You create independent shapes and then simply fuse them together using the Pathfinder palette.

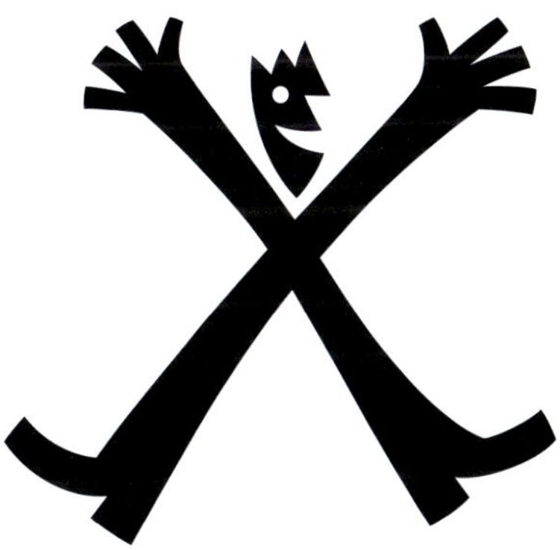

FIGURE 1.6 It's exciting once I finish an illustration like this.

But this is just the genesis of these illustrations. The best part is yet to come when you put them to use in your own design projects. I hope you get excited when you realize the limitless possibilities of using the artwork in this book. So let me show you how you can utilize the illustrations in an actual design solution.

How to Use the Art in this Book

Creative Context

I purposely designed all of the illustrations in this book so that the end user can read into them whatever narrative they choose. Sure, you'll find some visually specific genres and topics within this book's collection, but how you put them to use in your own design context for communicating your ideas is where your imagination and clever creativity come into play.

Saul Bass said it well when he suggested that design is thinking made visual.

So as you browse the images in this book, think conceptually how you could leverage a visual to suit your specific context.

A local youth outreach called "Xcited Community" needed a fun new visual identity for their program and contacted me to help. I'm going to use the artwork I just created to play off the idea of excitement, and I'll form the letter "X" in my logotype as well (**FIGURE 1.7**).

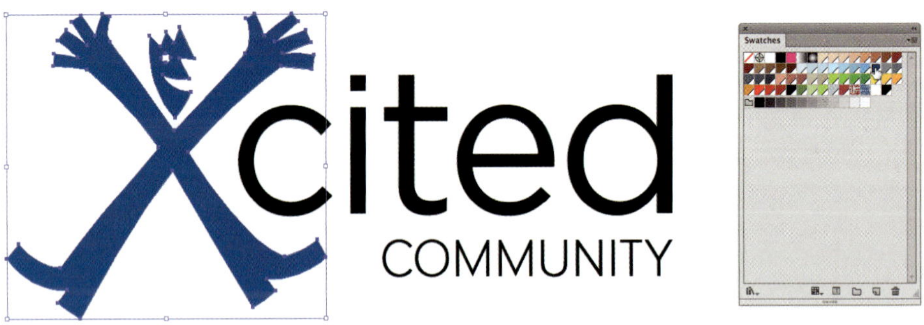

FIGURE 1.7 I position the artwork from the book into my design composition and colorize it to match the brand colors I'm establishing.

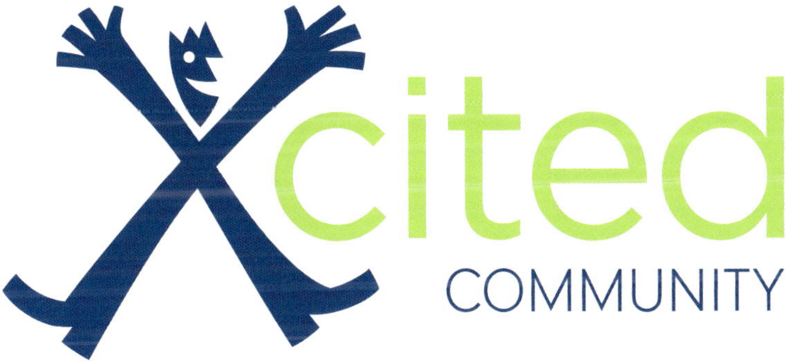

FIGURE 1.8 Use this book as a concepting tool. Force yourself to think how you could use something even if it doesn't seem appropriate for your project. This is how unexpected ideas are discovered.

The final design for Xcited Community is fun and reflects the emotion and personality of who they are and what they facilitate for the local community they serve (FIGURE 1.8).

Top Ten Usage Tips

1. Avoid distinctly literal approaches. Don't be afraid to be figurative.
2. Mix and match artwork to create your own visual narrative.
3. Think of different applications, such as T-shirt designs, tattoos, posters, or mugs.
4. Try something different. Experimentation is the life blood of creativity.
5. Use the art as visual metaphors to communicate ideas.
6. Try hand lettering to go along with the artwork.
7. Experiment with flat planes of color and texture as they work well with this art.
8. When using multiple images, scale them differently to add visual impact.
9. Art doesn't need to free-float so crop in when needed.
10. When using as spot art, rotate artwork to create more dynamic action.

Endless Design Possibilities

Anyone can take the illustrations in this book and place them into a newsletter, or decorate some other form of boring print collateral with an image to enhance its visual impact. But I truly hope you go far beyond that.

Throughout this book you'll notice featured artists who have gone beyond. They've taken the artwork available in this book and have put it to use in a variety of clever ways. So let their usages inspire you to discover your own unique design approach using this artwork.

Design should never become, "It's good enough." Designers must resist the urge of complacency. Steer clear of the marginal. Continually challenge your own creative proclivities and always stay hungry.

Creating design that goes beyond the norm will require you to do your part and think up some unique ideas that can take the artwork this book contains and amaze with it.

I decided the new visual identity for Xcited Community could utilize a brand pattern for their identity pieces and onscreen graphics within their facility and via Microsoft PowerPoint presentations (**FIGURE 1.9**).

The pattern tool in Illustrator is drop-dead simple to use. For a free-floating pattern like this, just start experimenting with the settings to move and compose your pattern repeat (**FIGURE 1.10**).

Using this artwork for a pattern design never crossed my mind when I originally created it. But that's what happens when you take the time to think through ideas and explore and experiment with the illustrations in this book (**FIGURE 1.11**).

A good designer knows how to carry an established aesthetic throughout all the various marketing vehicles they are designing for. In this case the business card identity pieces utilize the nice brand pattern as well (**FIGURE 1.12**).

To learn more about creating precise vector artwork, designing logos, and creating patterns, check out my design courses on Lynda.com.

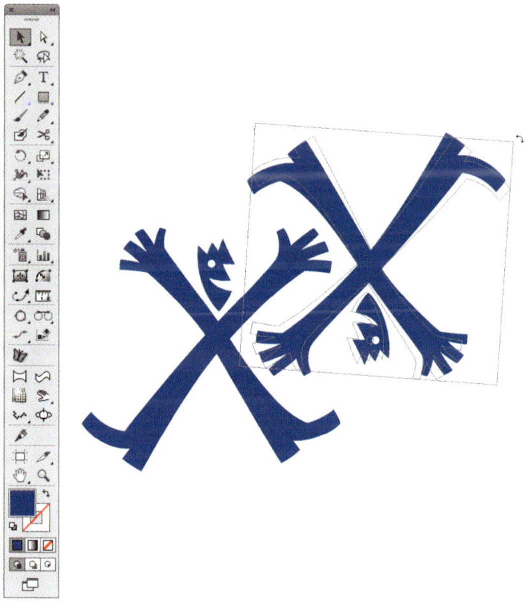

FIGURE 1.9 I begin to lay out the core art for my pattern by rotating the figure.

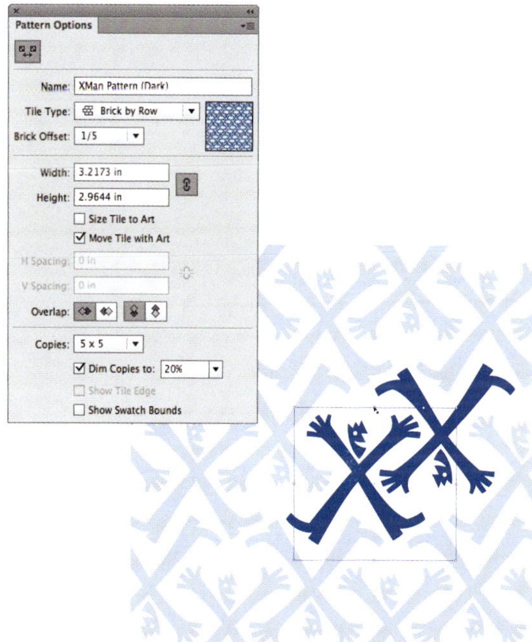

FIGURE 1.10 Here I finesse the artwork in Illustrator's pattern definition mode.

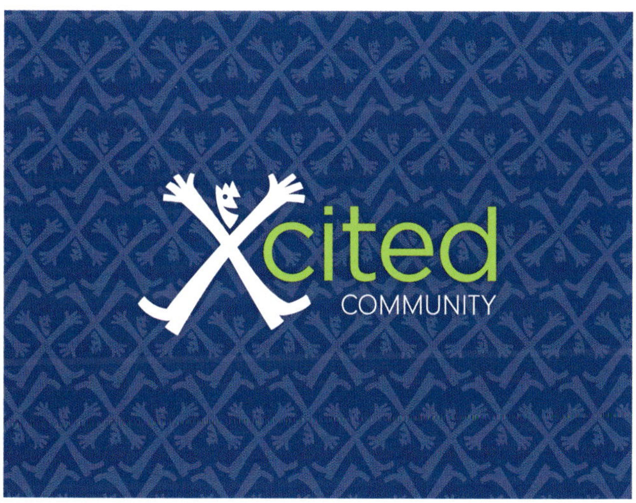

FIGURE 1.11 The pattern and final logotype work well together and make for an engaging aesthetic.

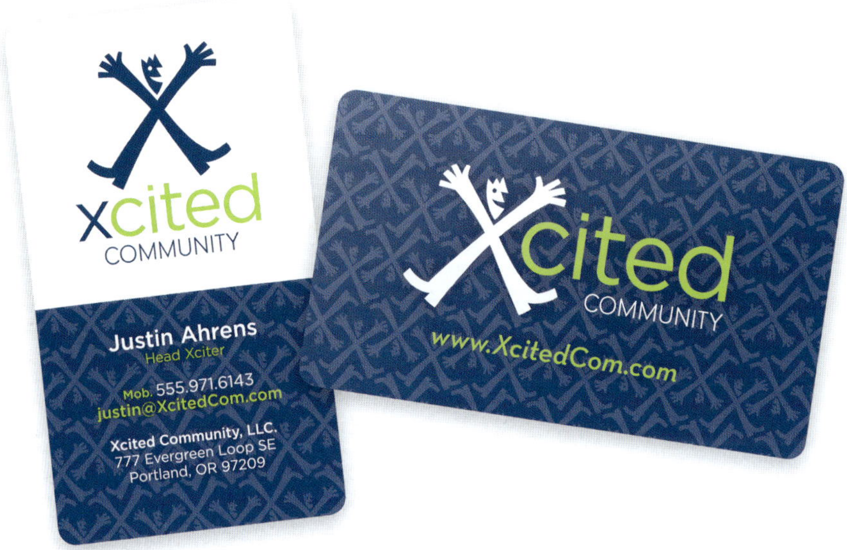

FIGURE 1.12 A beautiful and compelling usage of the artwork on a business card design.

Take a Creative Leap

Use this book as a conceptual springboard in your ideation process. Anything that can help your creative process spawn that eureka moment is a good resource to leverage.

And remember to check out each of the featured artists throughout this book. From them I hope you can glean design inspiration for using this book's art within your own projects moving forward.

Whatever you take and make with the artwork in this book will only be as limited as your imagination. So let your imagination run wild and you'll unlock the full creative potential this book has to offer.

So go forth and create!

TAKE AND MAKE

VECTOR ILLUSTRATIONS FOR DISCRIMINATING DESIGNERS

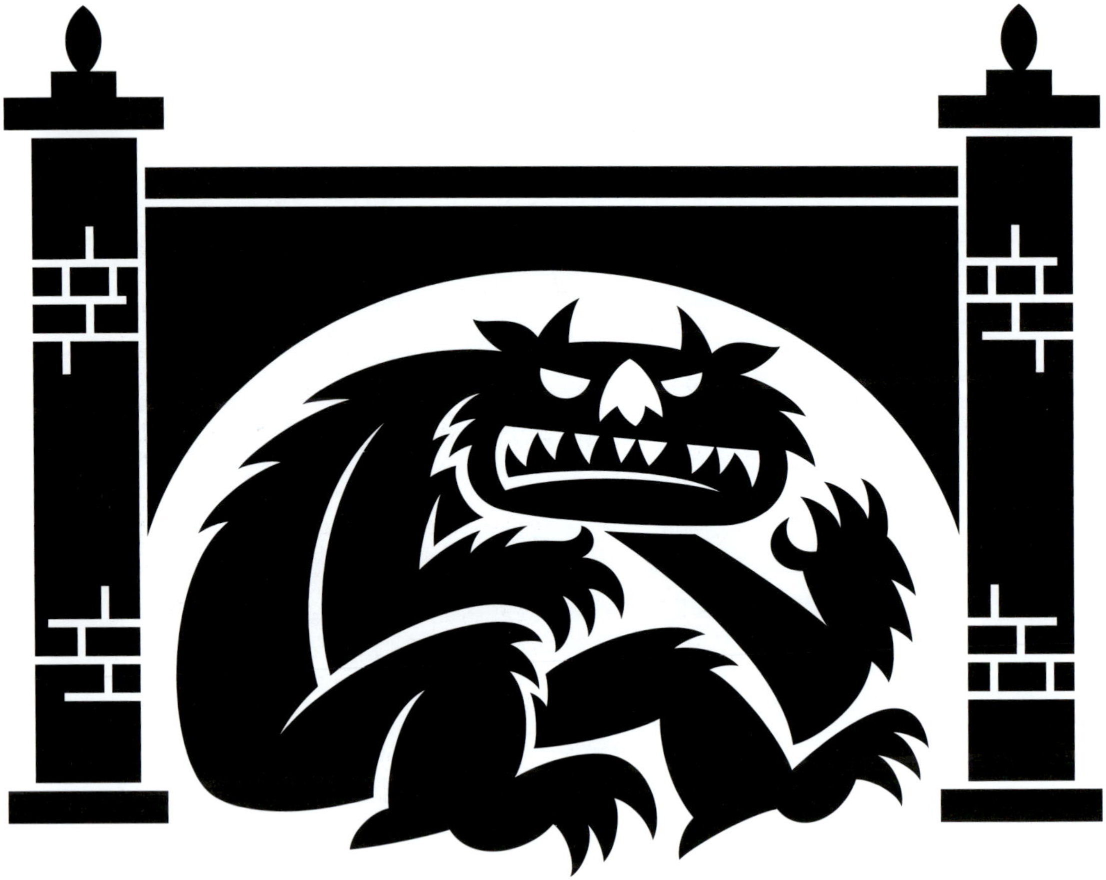

Pay_The_Troll_**TM1**

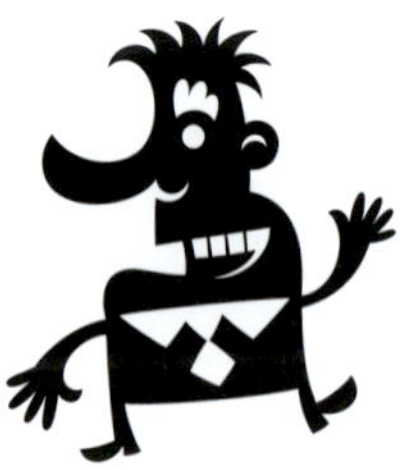

Howdee_**TM2**

Burn_Baby_Burn_**TM3**

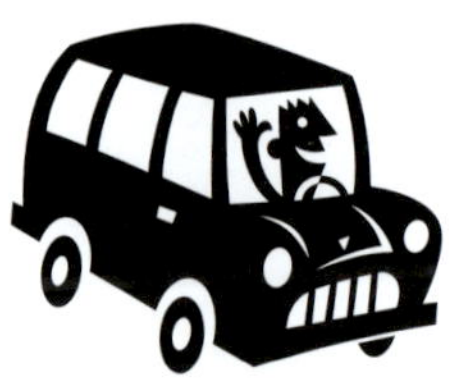

SUV_**TM4**

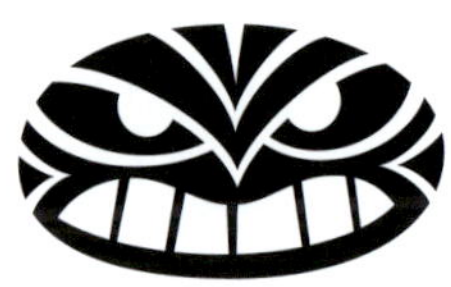

Rune_**TM5**

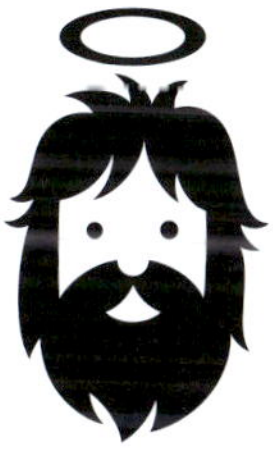

God_Head_**TM6**

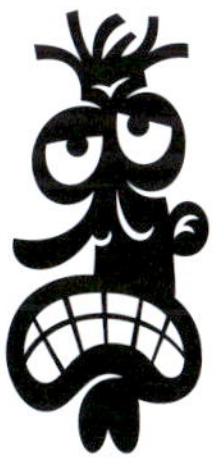

Not_Cool_Mon_**TM7**

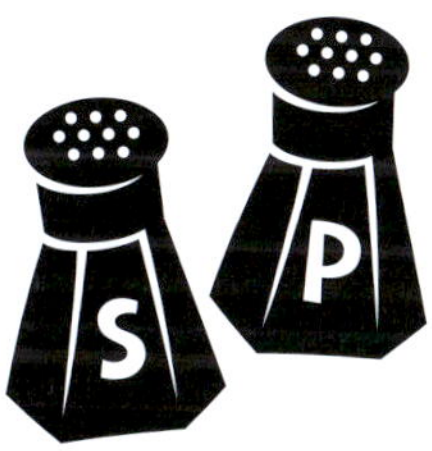

Salt_And_Pepper_**TM8**

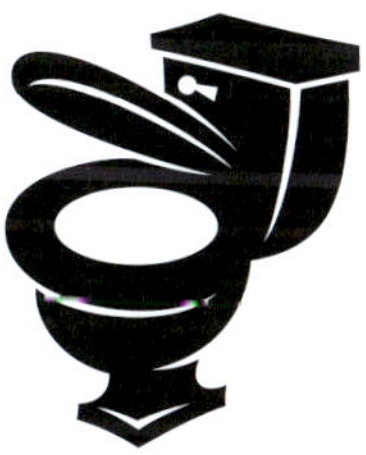

Open_For_Business_**TM9**

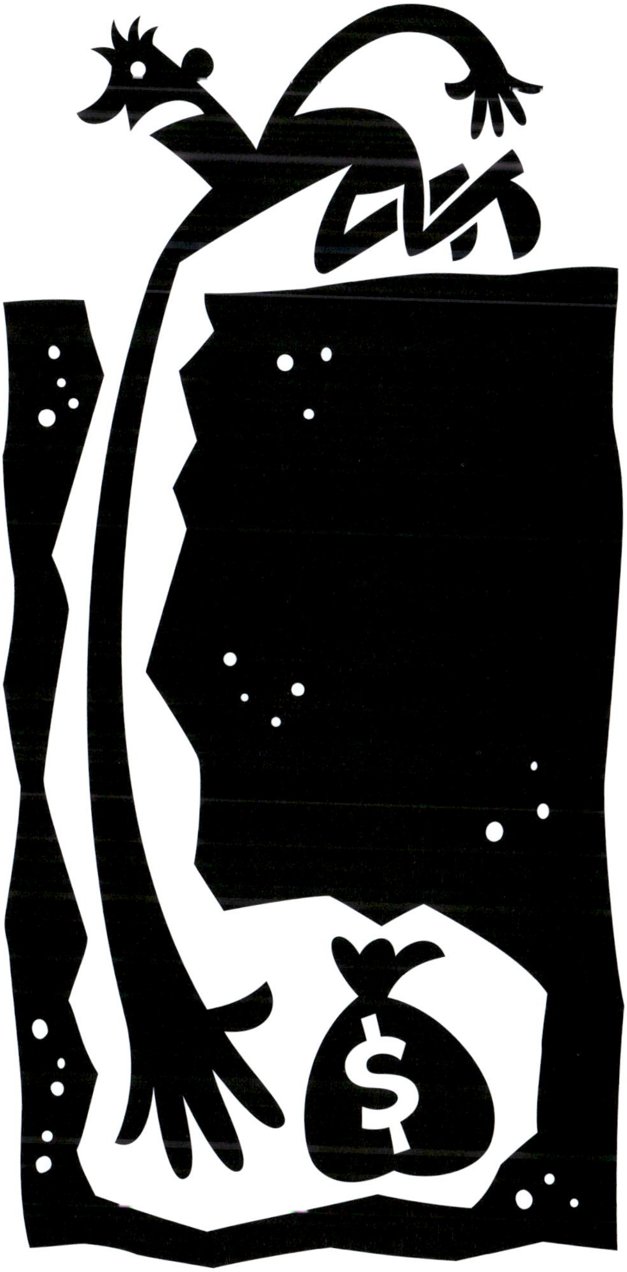

Within_Your_Reach_**TM10**

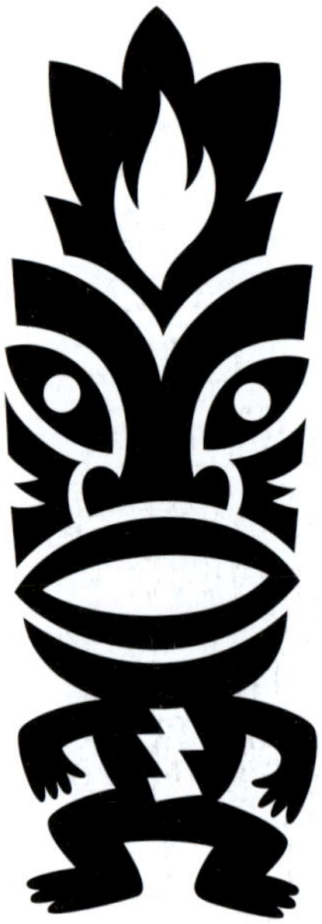

Tiki_**TM11**

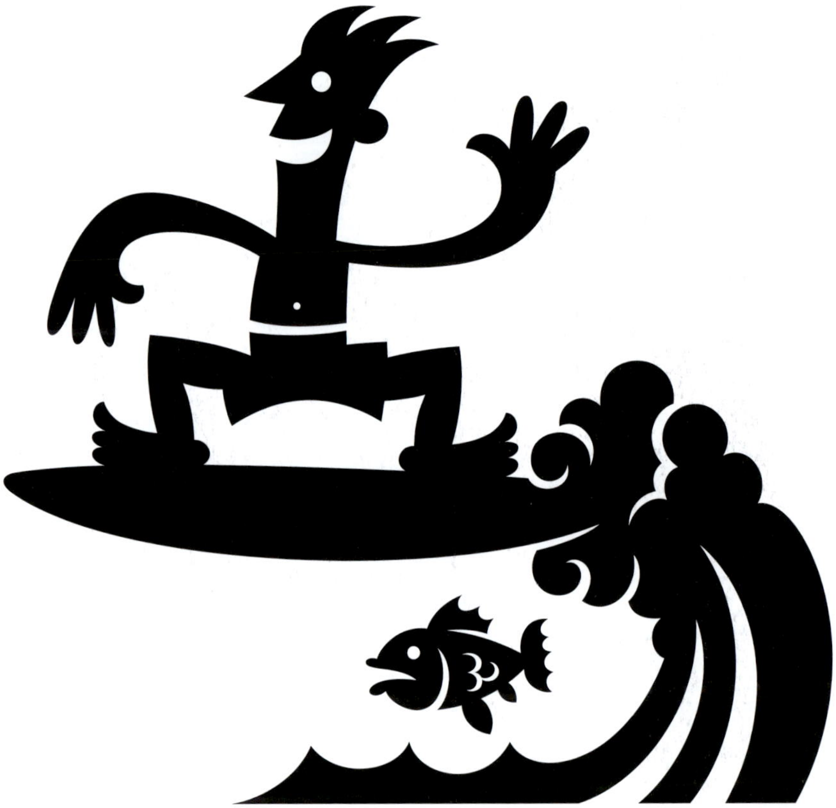

Hang_Six_**TM12**

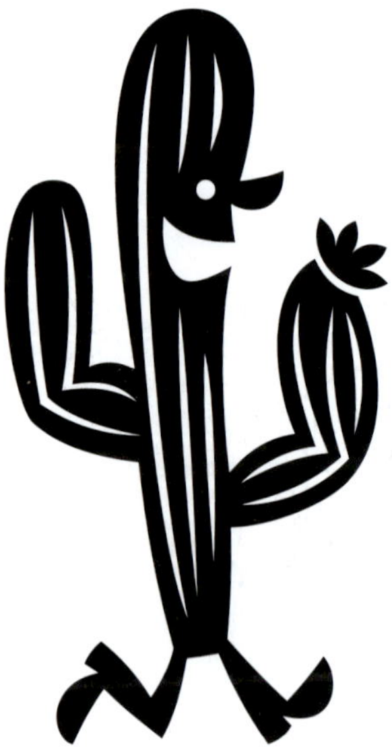

Abrasive_Personality_**TM13**

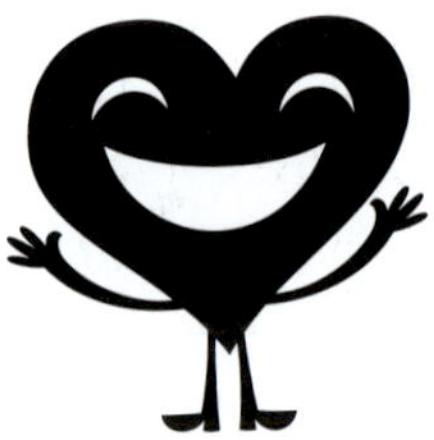

A_Joyful_Heart_**TM14**

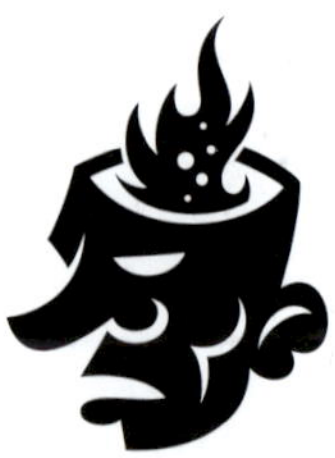

Mind_On_Fire_**TM15**

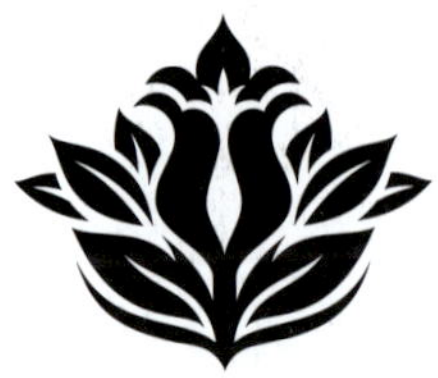

Flower_Burst_**TM16**

Hooter_**TM17**

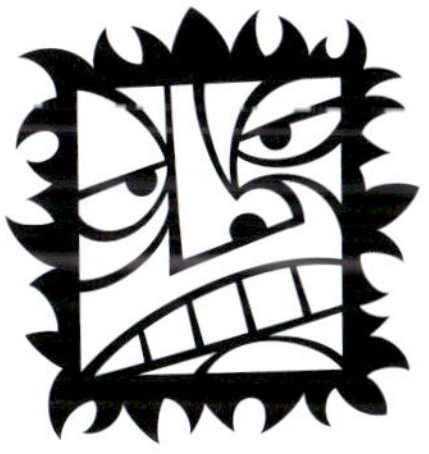

Everything_Is_Ho-Hum_**TM18**

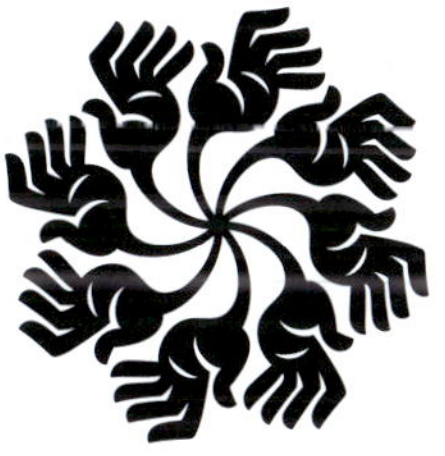

Hand_Wheel_**TM19**

King_Of_Gog_**TM20**

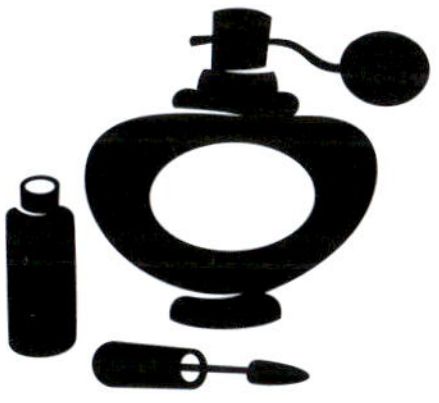

Parfum_**TM21**

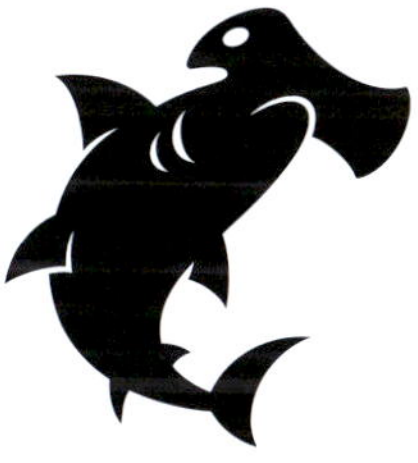

Hammer_Time_**TM22**

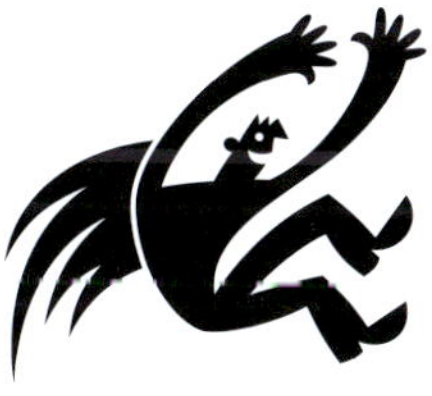

Leap_Of_Faith_**TM23**

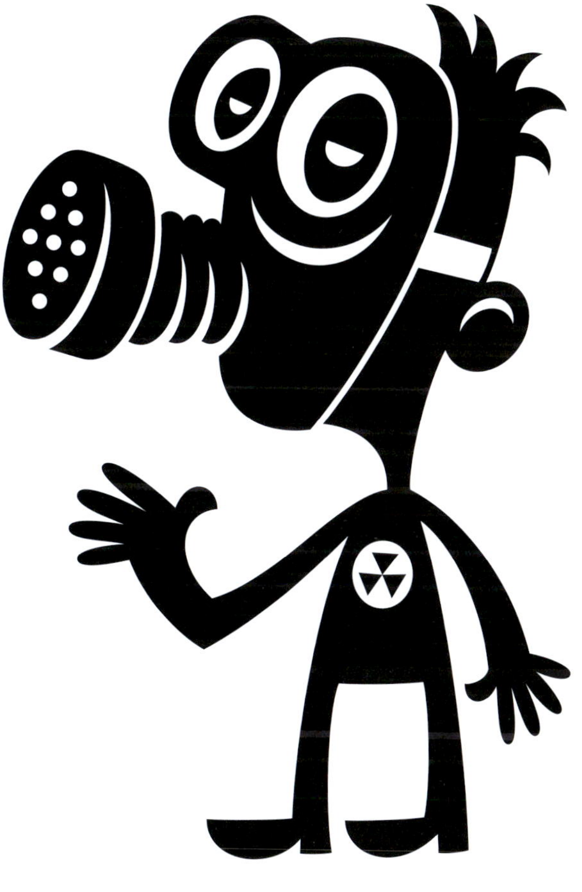

A_Toxic_Situation_**TM24**

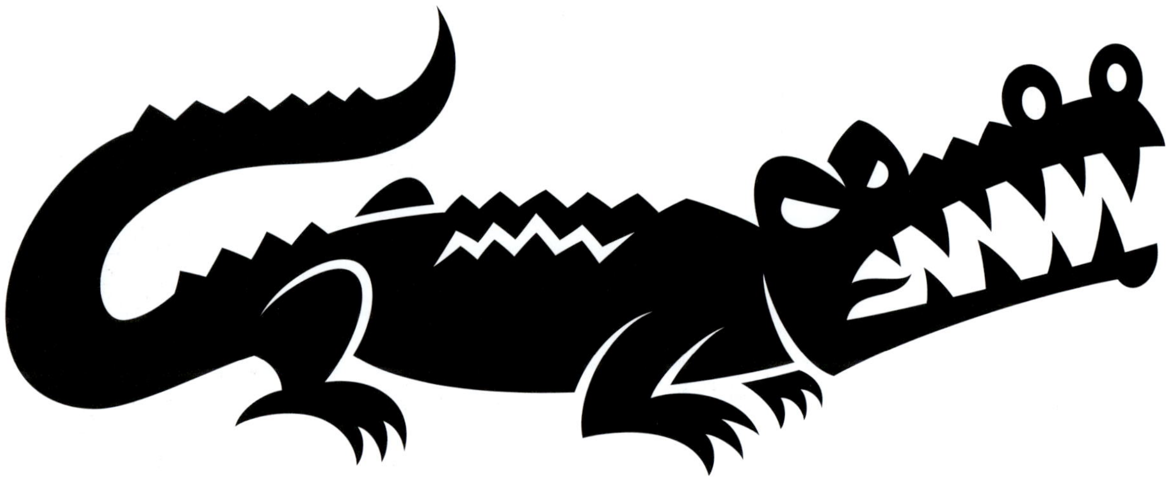

What_A_Croc_**TM25**

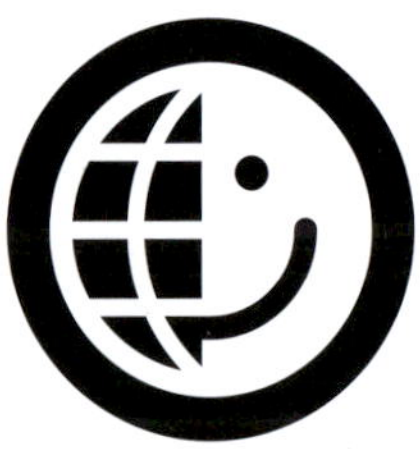

Happy_Planet_**TM26**

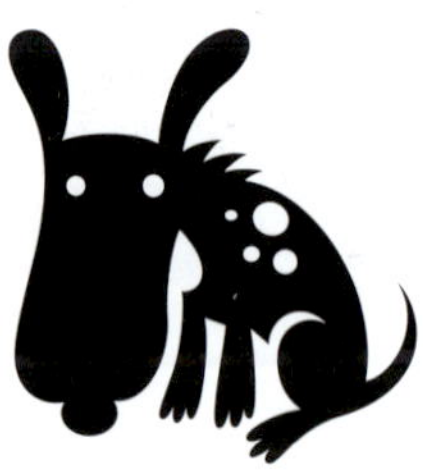

Dog_Squat_**TM27**

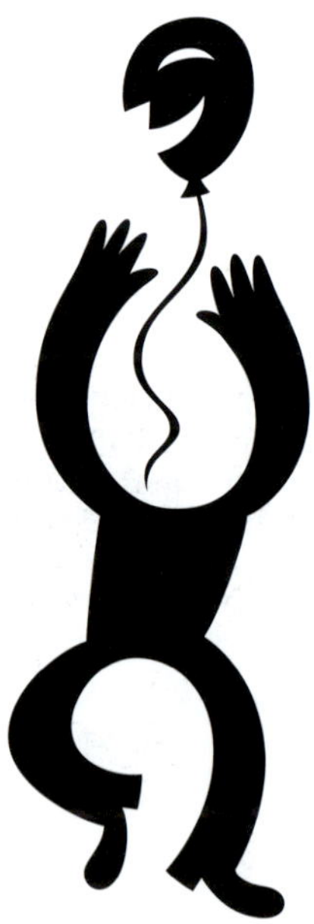

Airhead_**TM28**

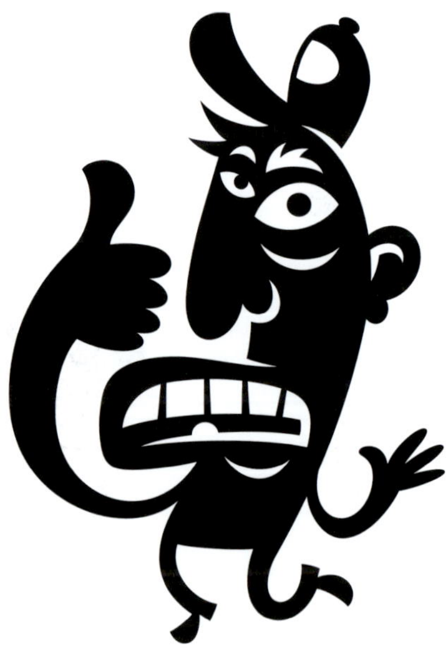

I_Like_It_**TM29**

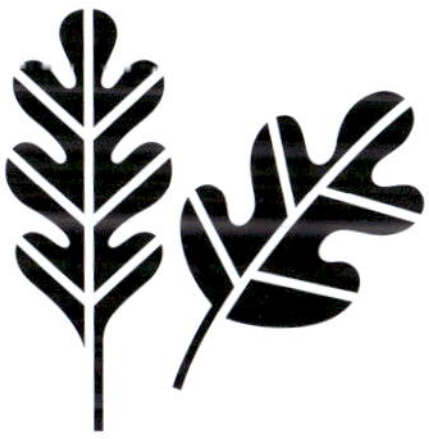

Oak_Leaf_**TM30**

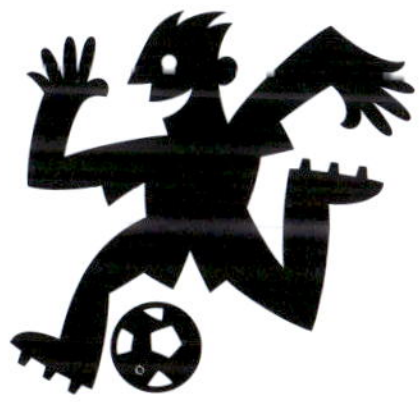

Kick_In_The_Grass_**TM31**

Proud_Mary_**TM32**

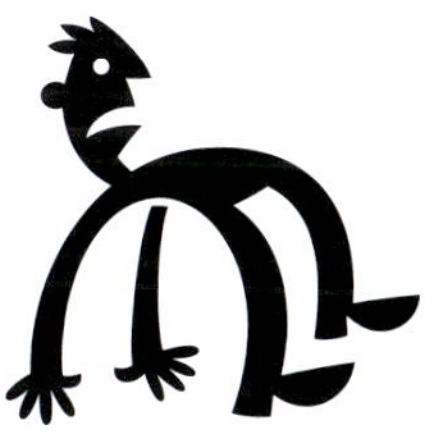

Crab_Walker_**TM33**

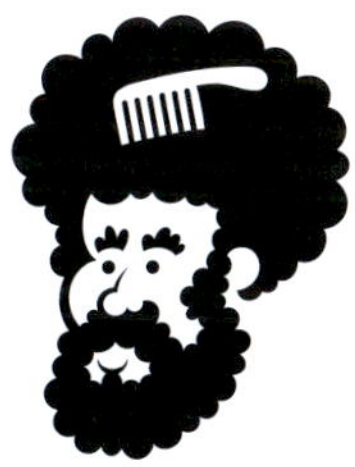

Happy_Afro_**TM34**

Space_Villain_**TM35**

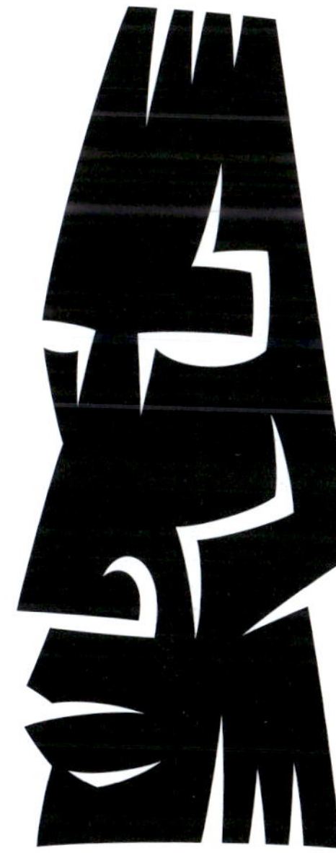

Primitive_Deity_**TM36**

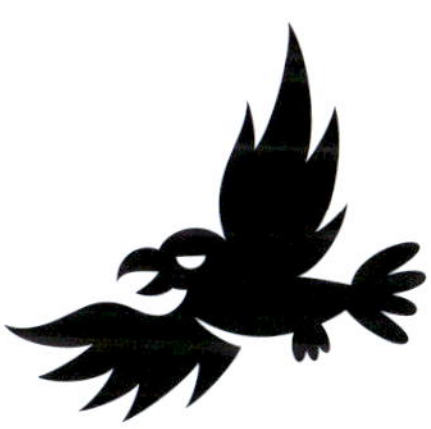

Soaring_Bird_**TM37**

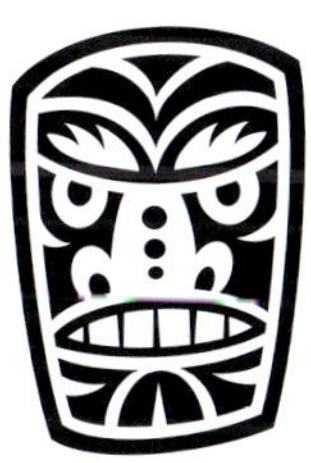

Ooga_Booga_**TM38**

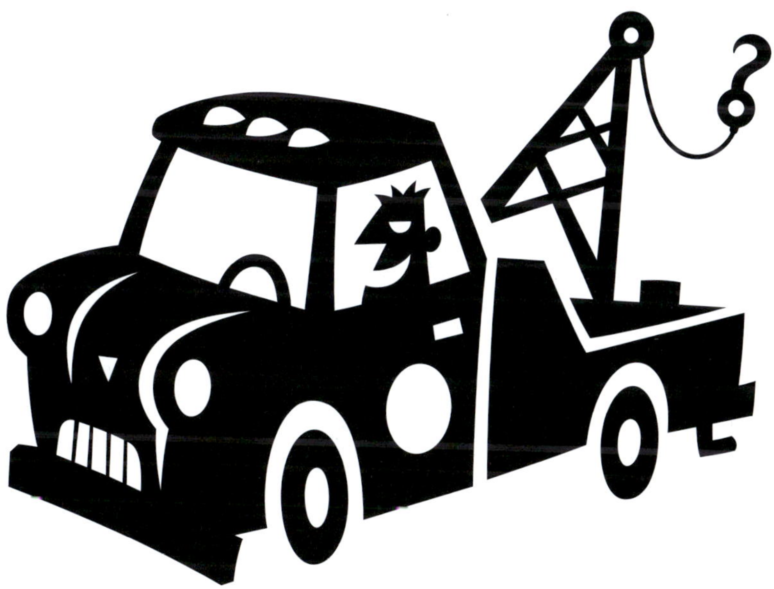

Tow_Truck_**TM39**

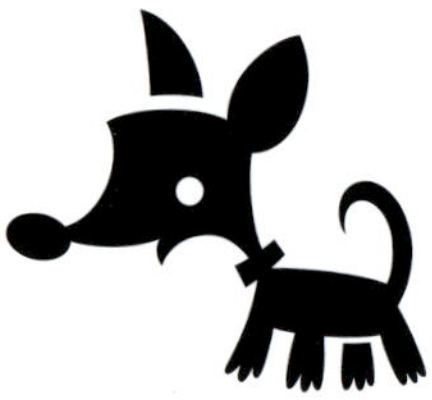

Ankle_Biter_**TM40**

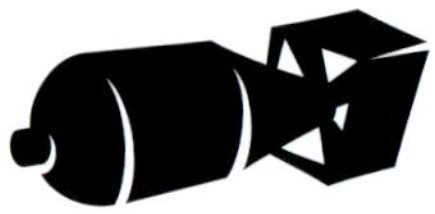

Nukem_**TM41**

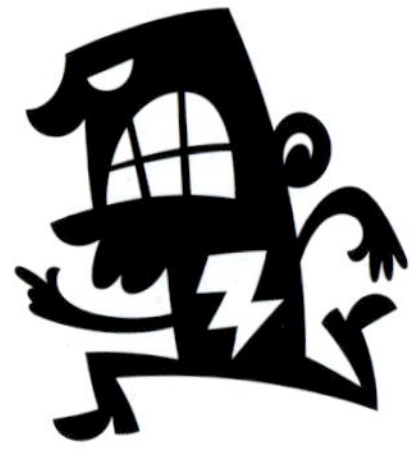

Lightning_Quick_**TM42**

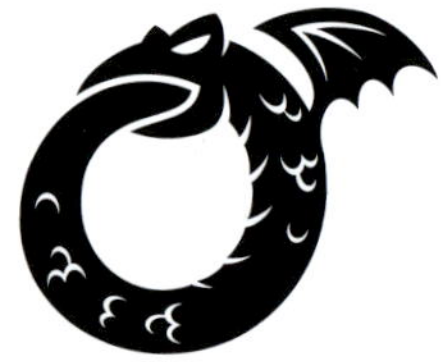

Ouroboros_**TM43**

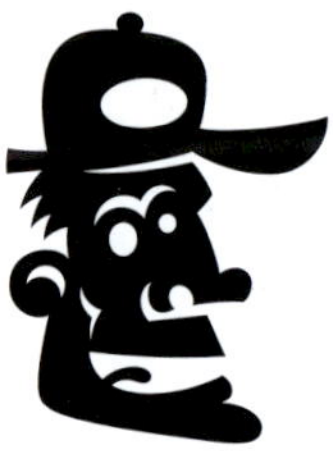

Zeke_**TM44**

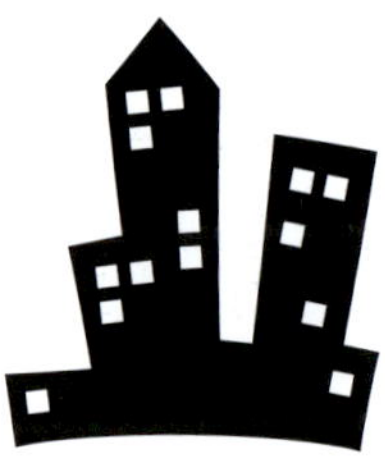

Big_City_**TM45**

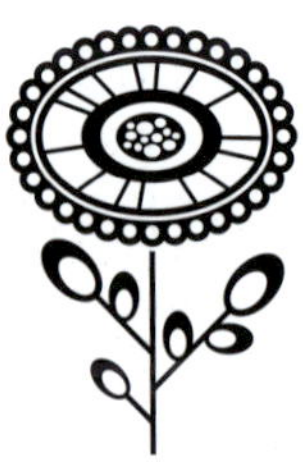

Pushing_Daisies_**TM46**

Bad_Eats_**TM47**

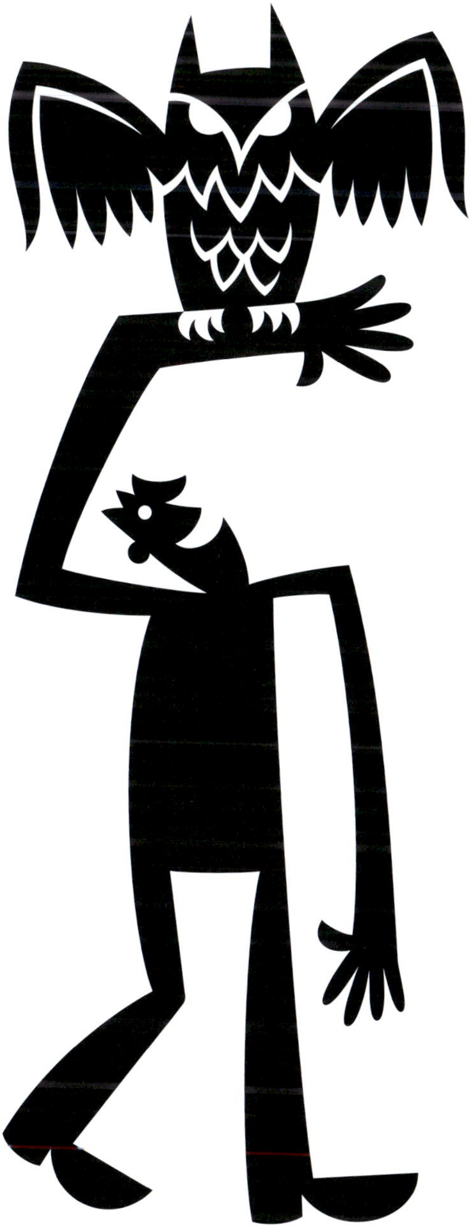

A_Wise_Friend_**TM51**

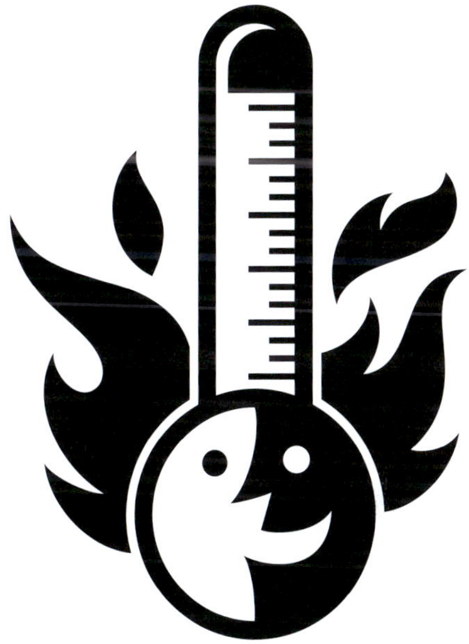

What_A_Hottie_**TM48**

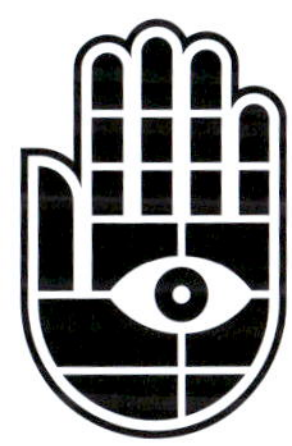

Oracle_Hand_**TM49**

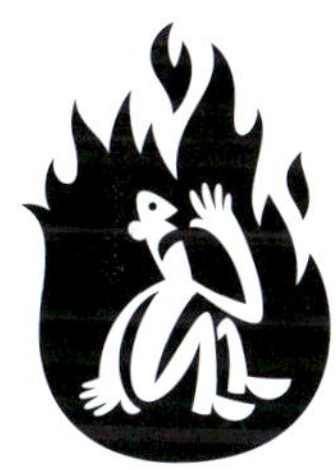

Hell_Fire_**TM50**

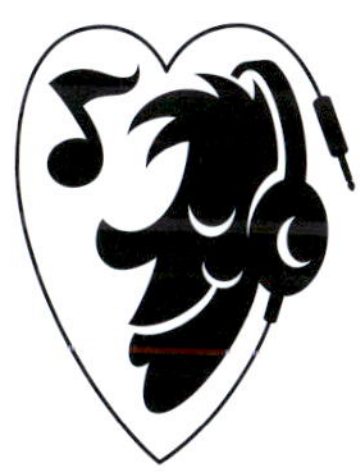

I_Love_Music_**TM52**

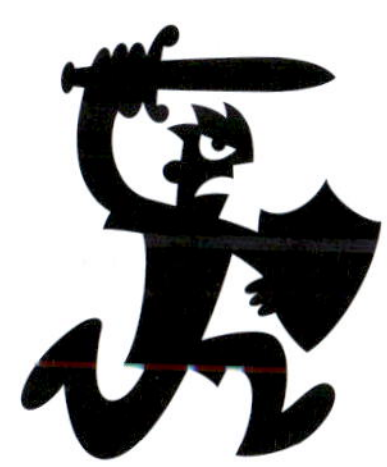

Plan_Of_Attack_**TM53**

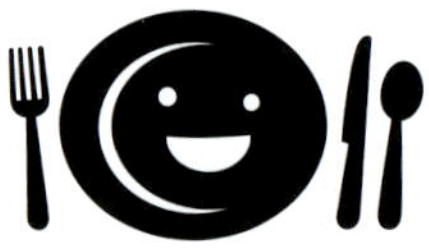

Happy_Meal_**TM54**

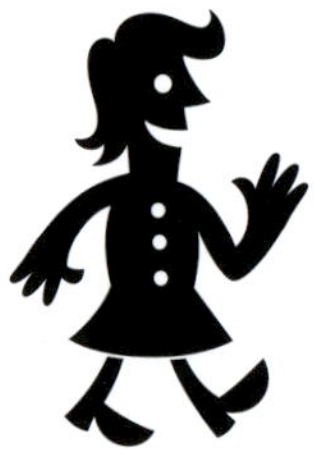

Girl_Walk_**TM55**

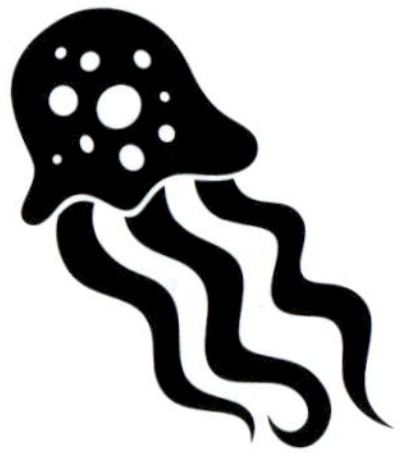

Jellyfish_**TM56**

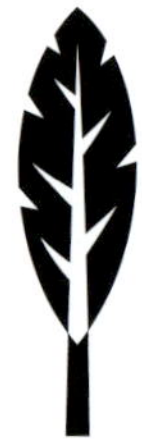

Hedge_Your_Bet_**TM57**

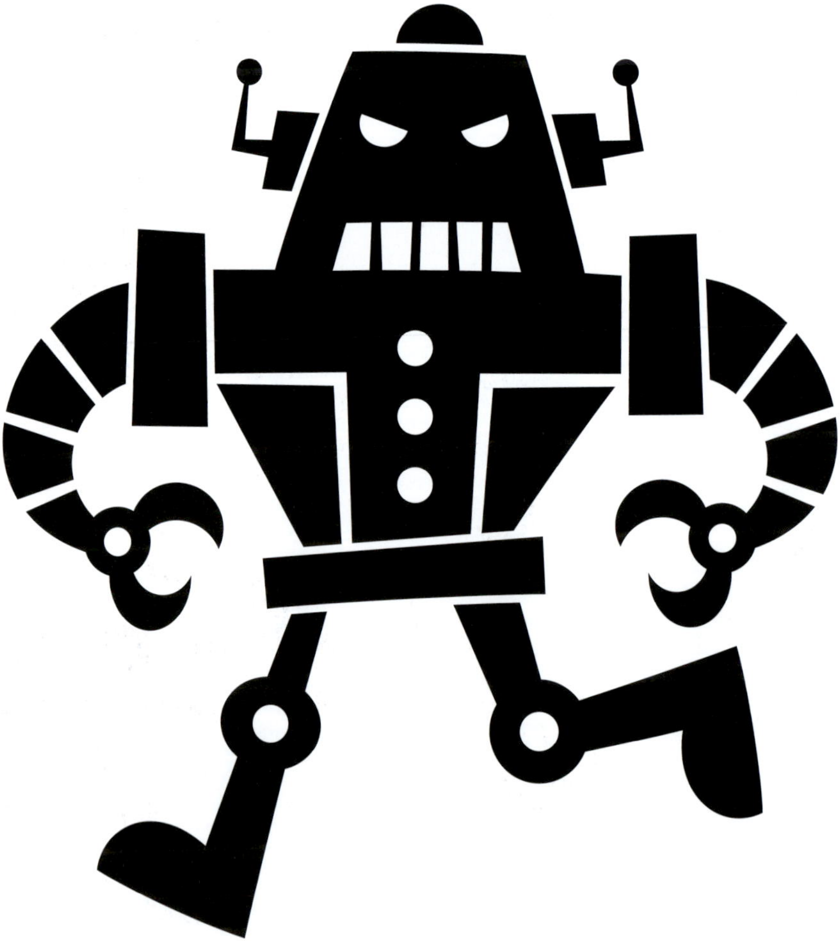

Intruder_Alert_**TM58**

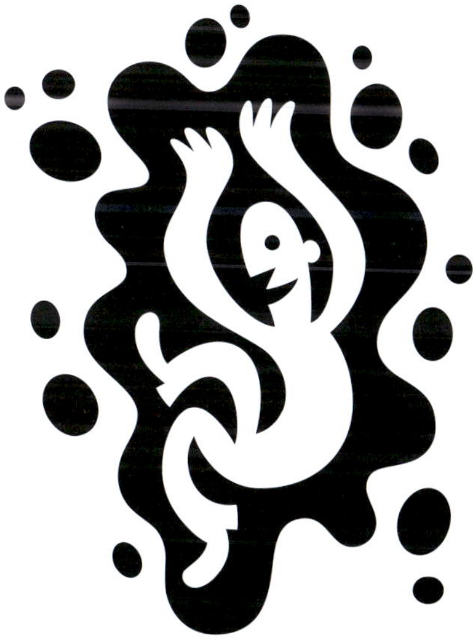

A_Fluid_Situation_**TM59**

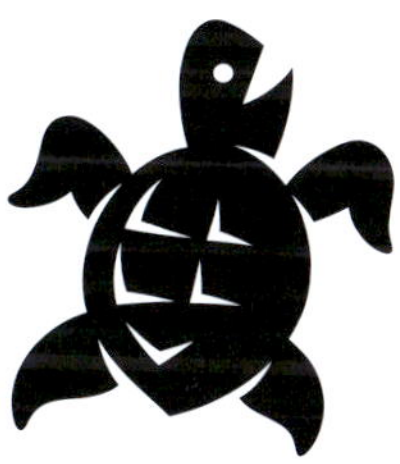

Sea_Turtle_**TM60**

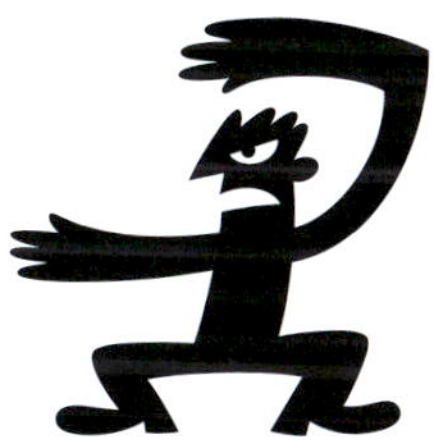

Karate_**TM61**

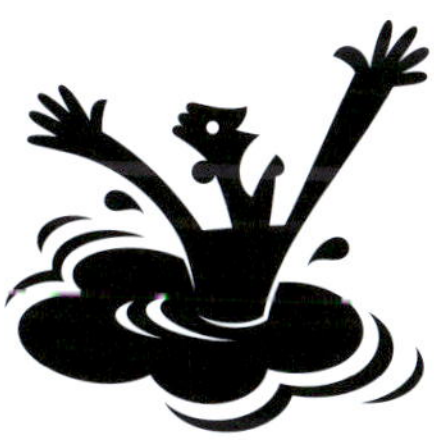

In_Over_Your_Head_**TM62**

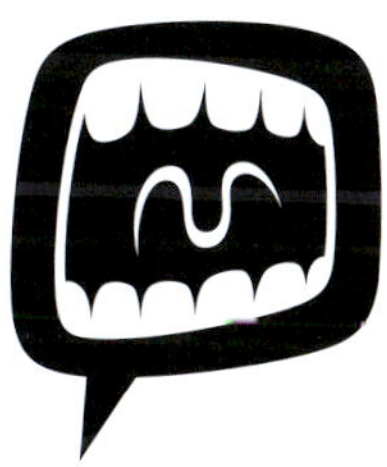

Hear_Ye_**TM63**

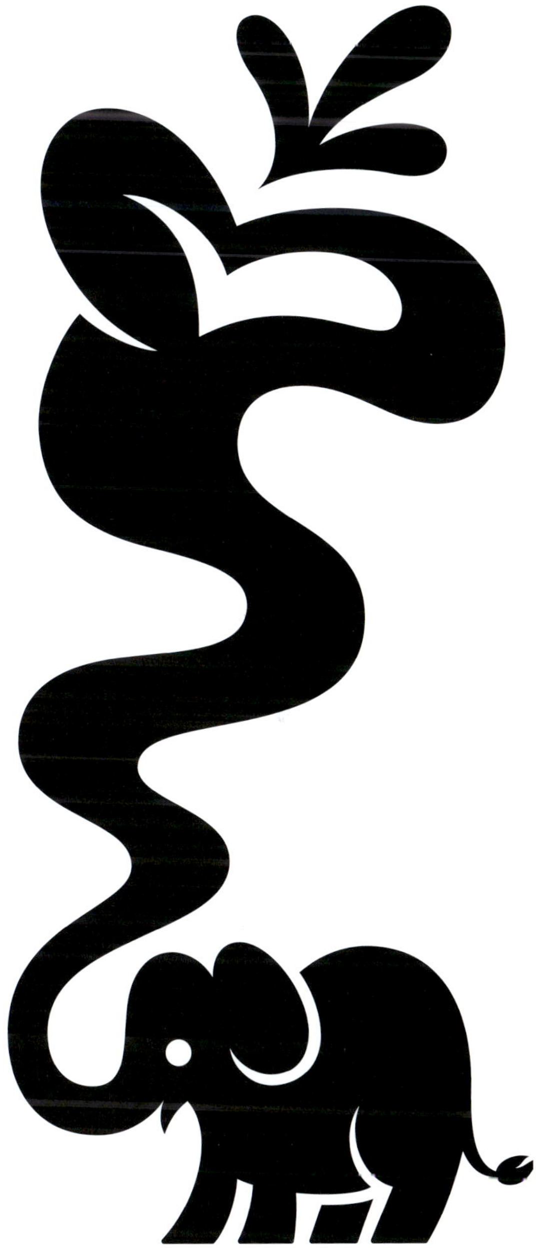

Spout_Off_**TM64**

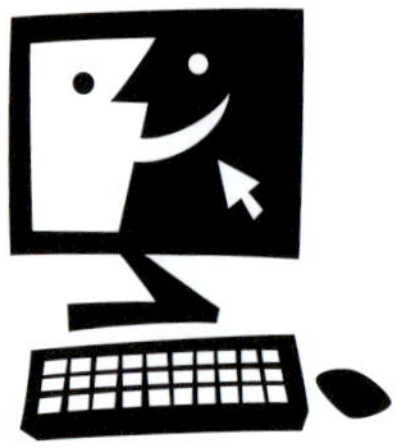

Mac_Geek_**TM65**

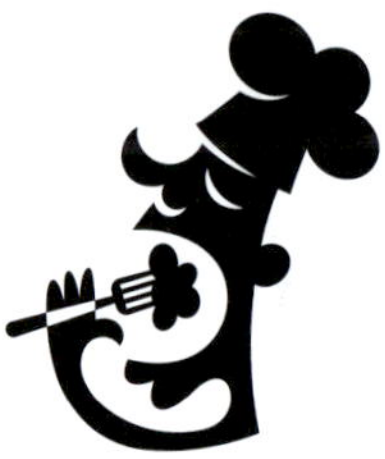

Vittle_Maker_**TM66**

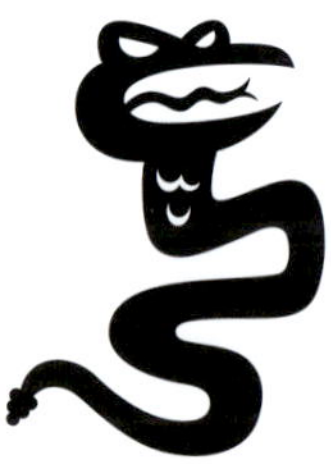

Speak_With_A_Forked_Tongue_**TM67**

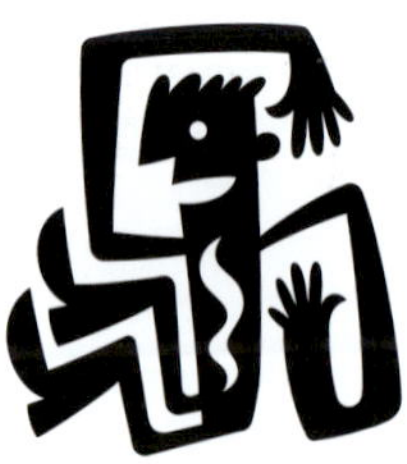

Indwelling_**TM68**

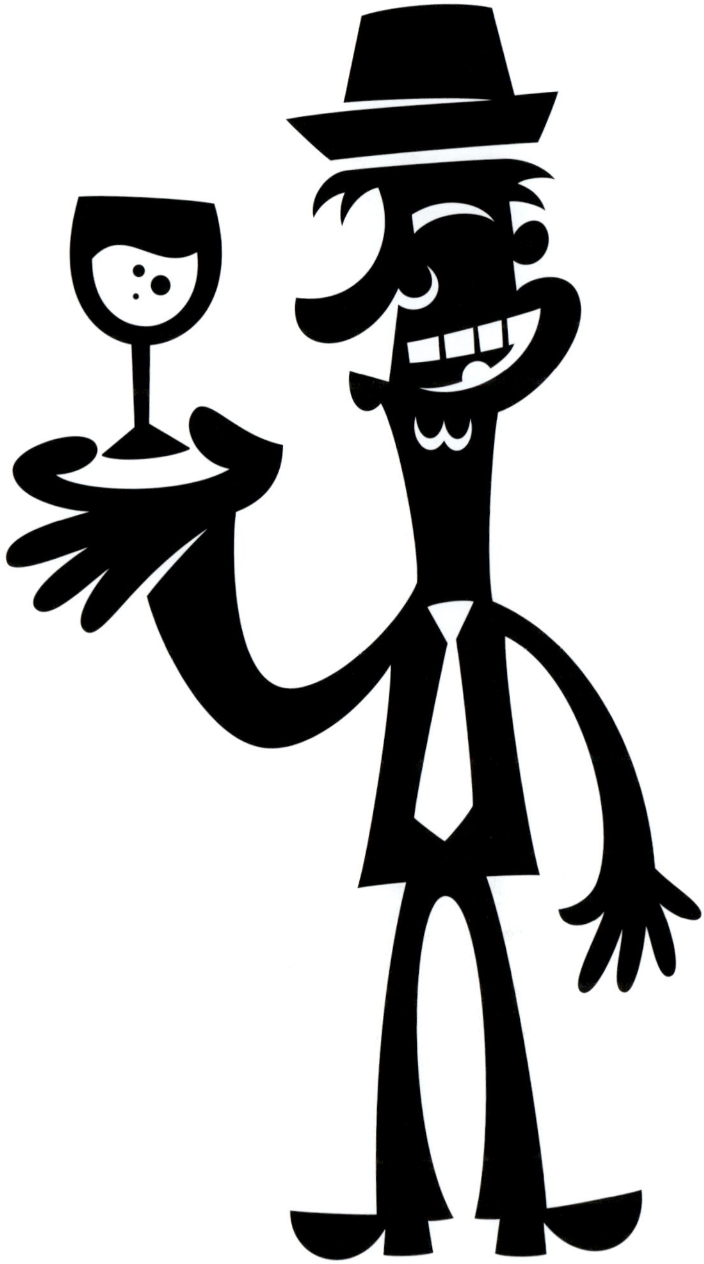

Lite_Drinker_**TM69**

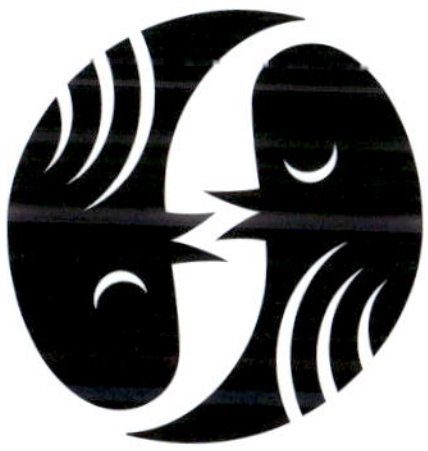
Balance_Birds_**TM70**

Flame_Broiled_**TM71**

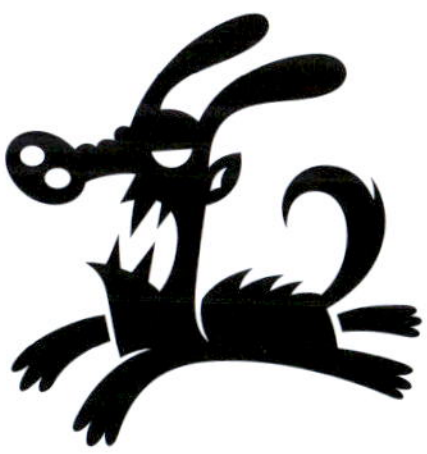
Vivigix_**TM72**

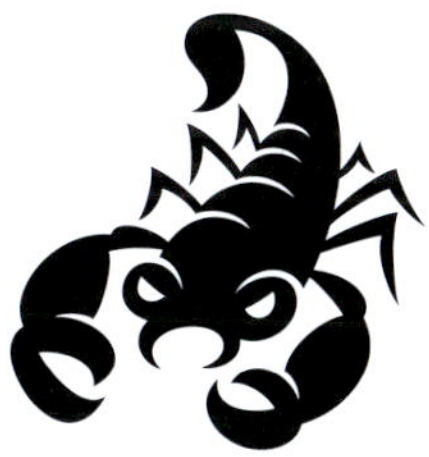
Scorpion_**TM73**

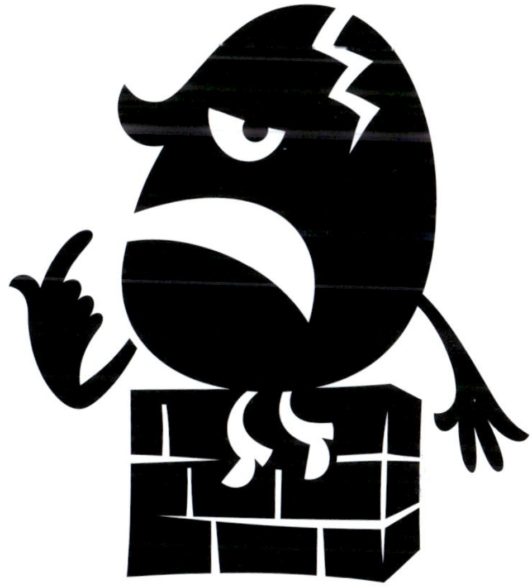
Accidents_Happen_**TM74**

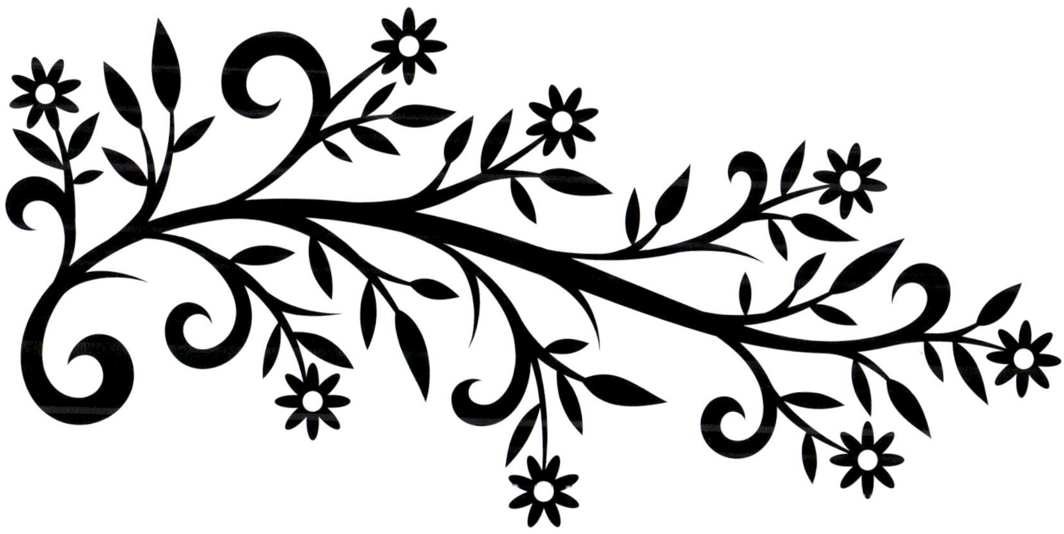
Beautiful_Wood_**TM75**

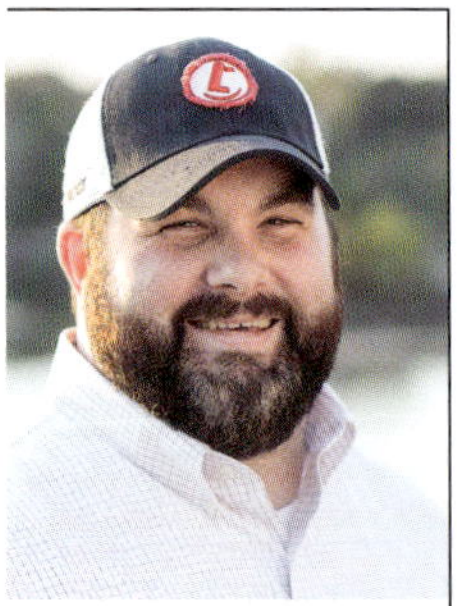

Mike Jones
Designer / BBQ'er
Serve Studios • Columbus, Georgia
www.ServeStudios.com

I had a blast cooking up this sauce label design. Great art and good design sensibility makes for a tasty final package. Seriously, who doesn't love pigs, especially flying ones? Hence, the name on the label. Y'all don't know 'bout no "Hog Sauce" up in the North!

Art Used: High-Flying Hog TM423

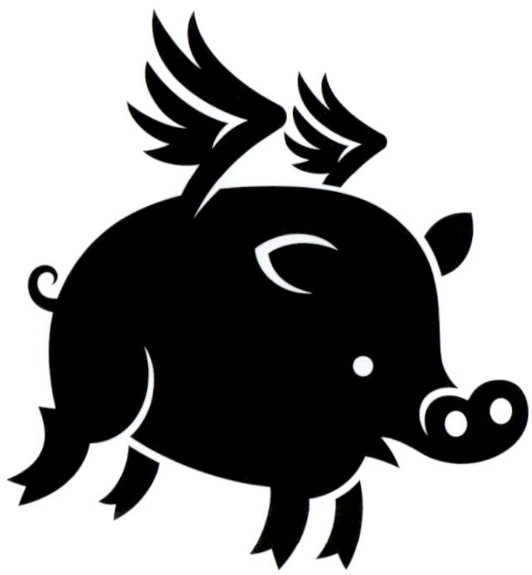

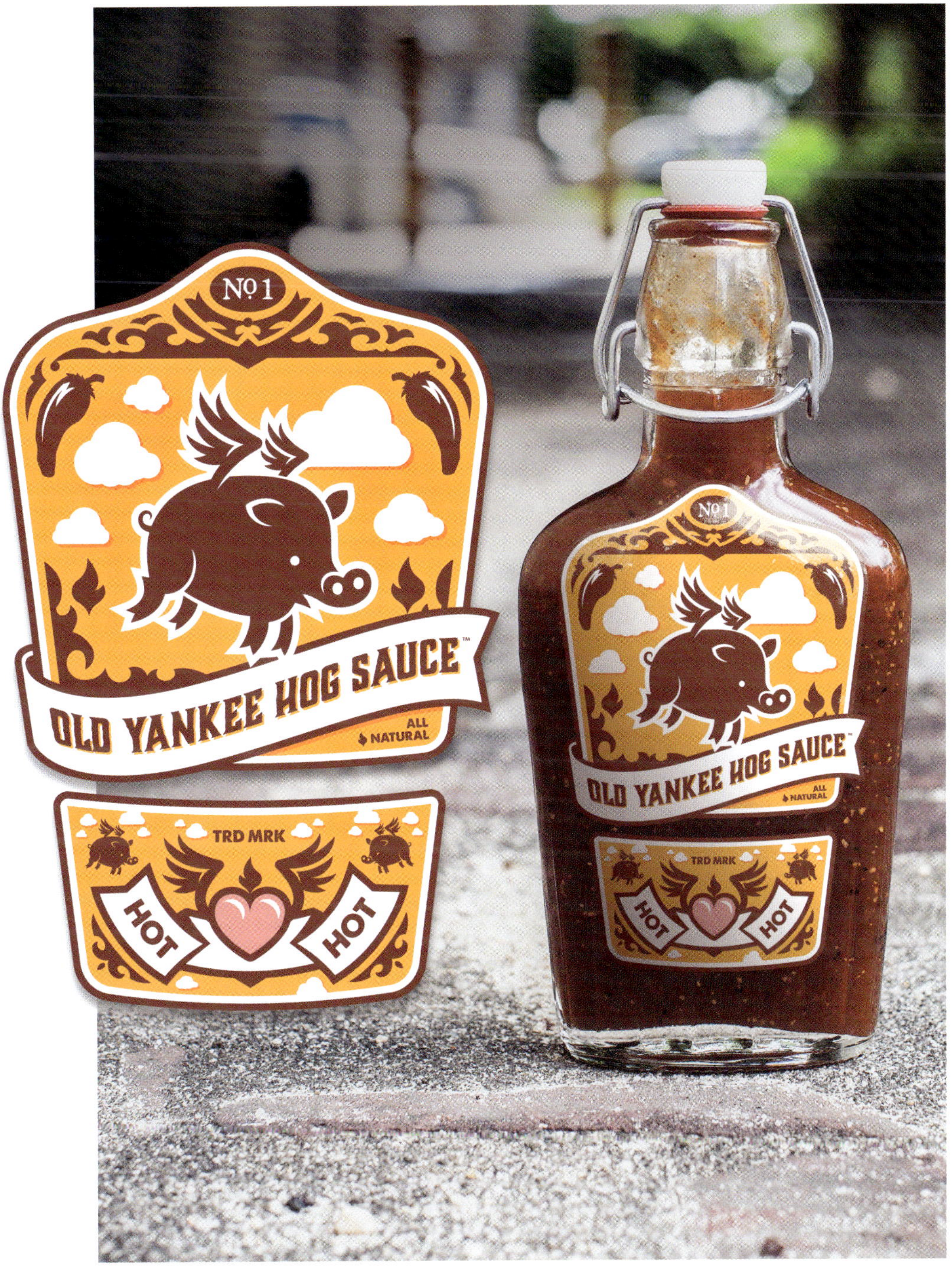

No 1
OLD YANKEE HOG SAUCE™
ALL NATURAL
TRD MRK
HOT
HOT

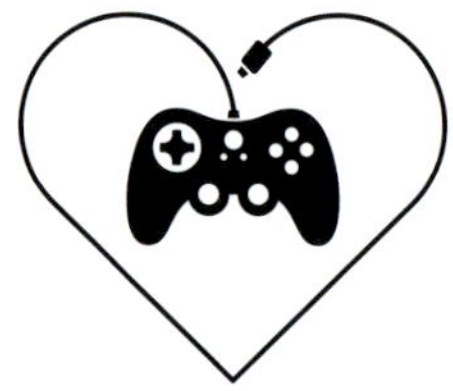

Love_Gaming_**TM76**

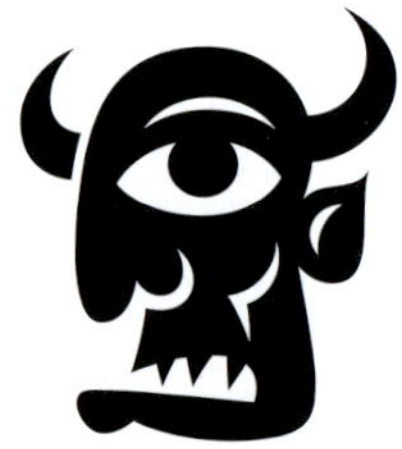

Horny_Goblin_**TM77**

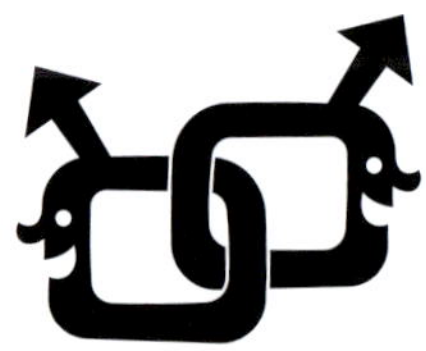

Male_Bonding_**TM78**

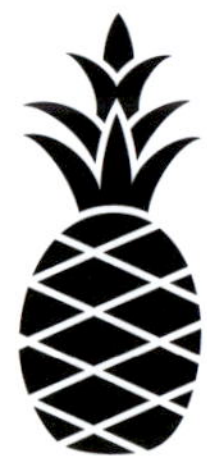

Pineapple_**TM79**

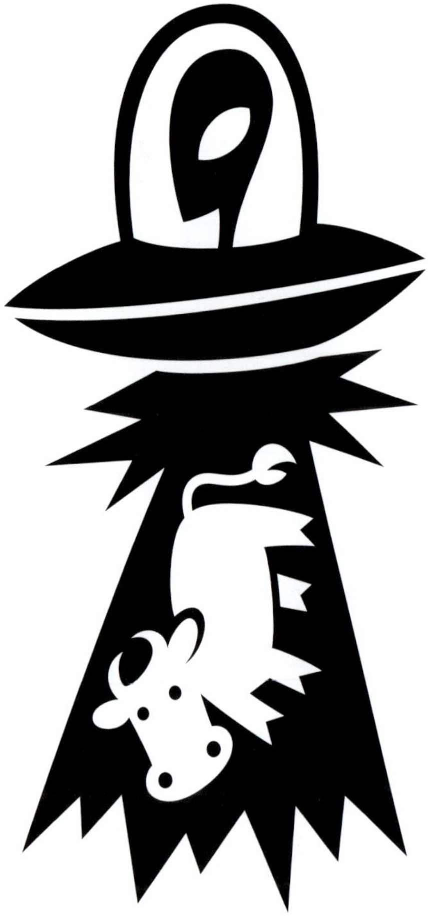

Abducted_**TM80**

Worm_King_**TM81**

Tick_Tock_**TM82**

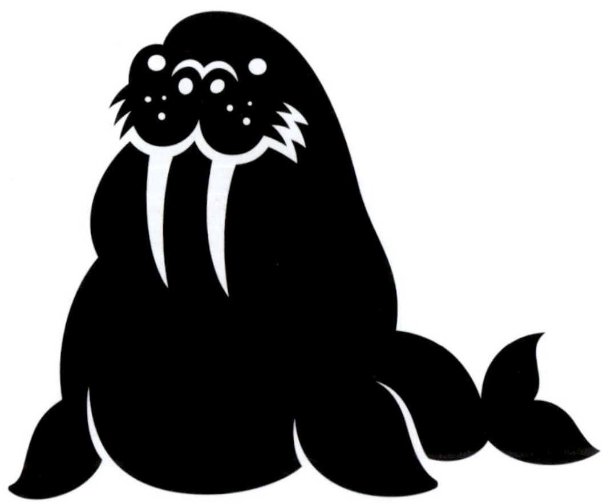

I_Am_The_Walrus_**TM83**

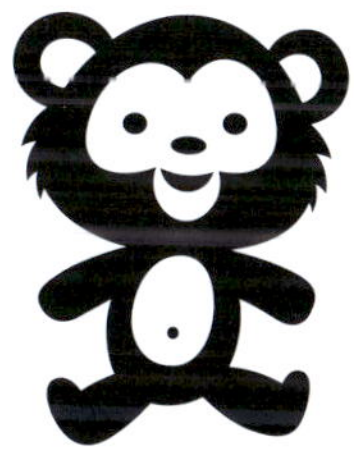

Teddy_TM84

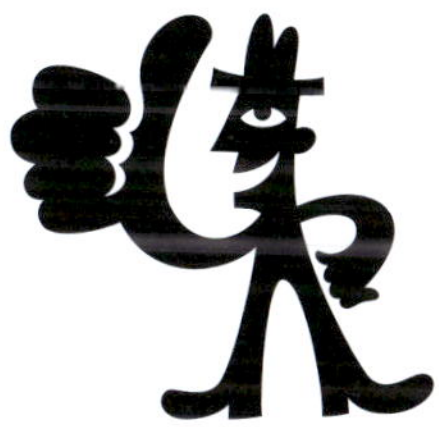

Thumbs_Up_TM85

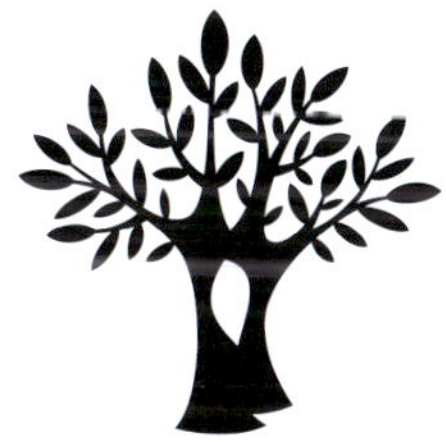

Wood_You_Mind_TM86

Sea_Shell_TM87

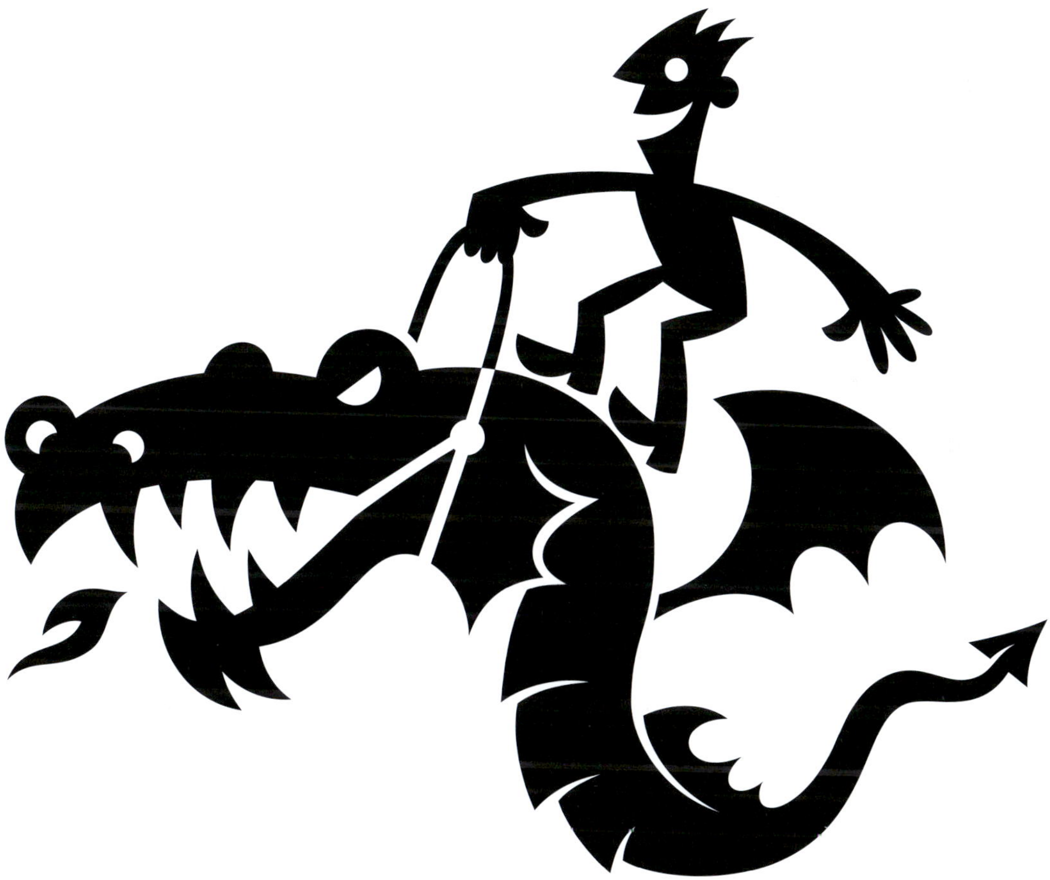

Master_The_Impossible_TM88

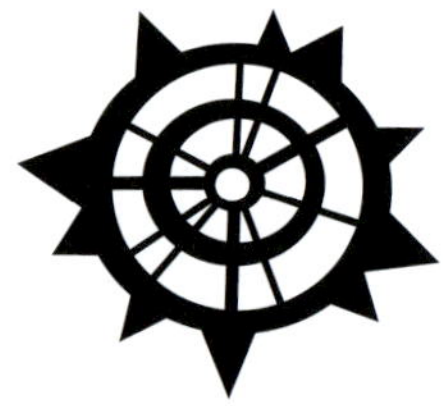

Sunny_Daze_**TM89**

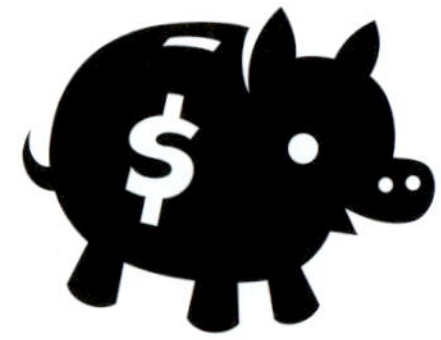

Piggy_Bank_**TM90**

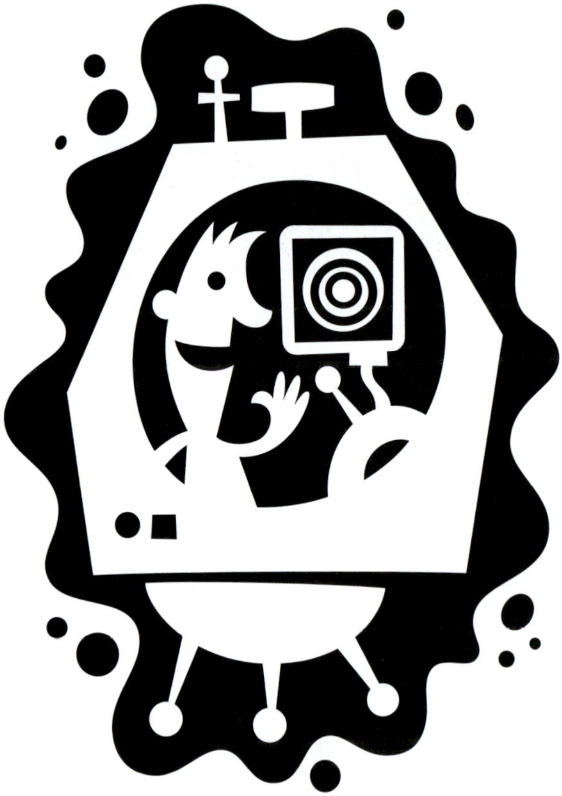

Time_Machine_**TM91**

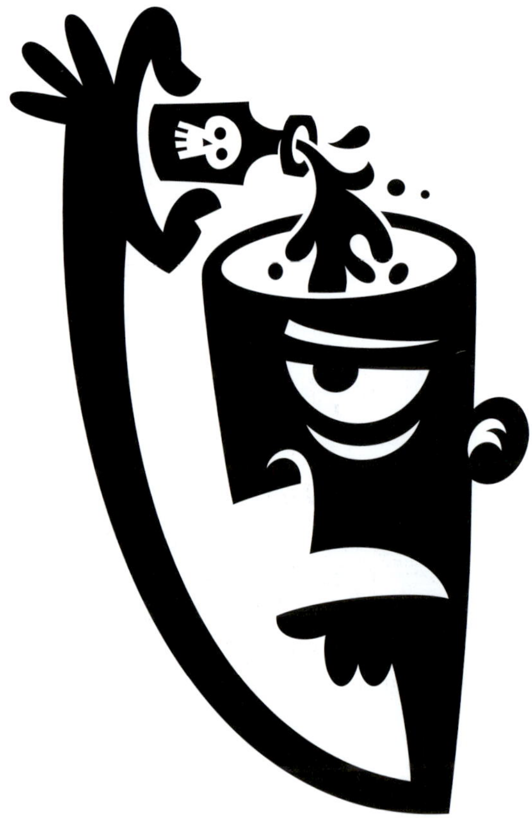

Poisonous_Thoughts_**TM94**

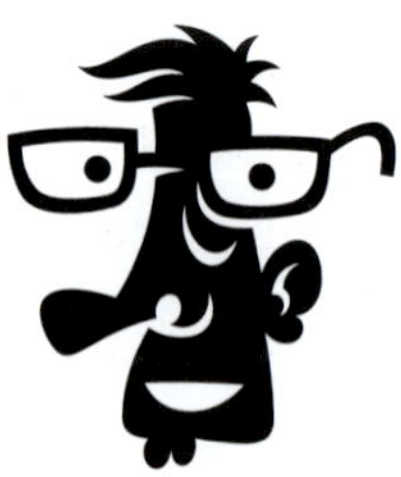

Nerdstein_**TM92**

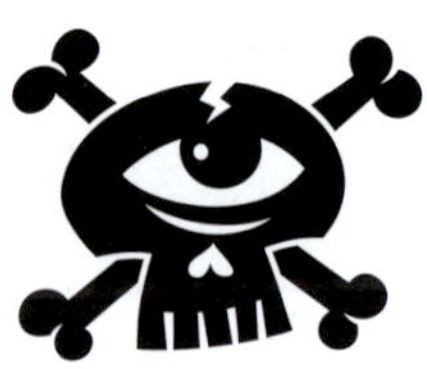

Dead_Vision_**TM93**

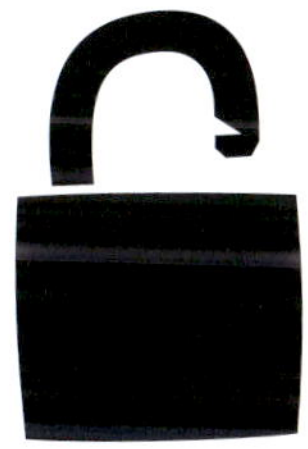

Lock_Me_Up_**TM95**

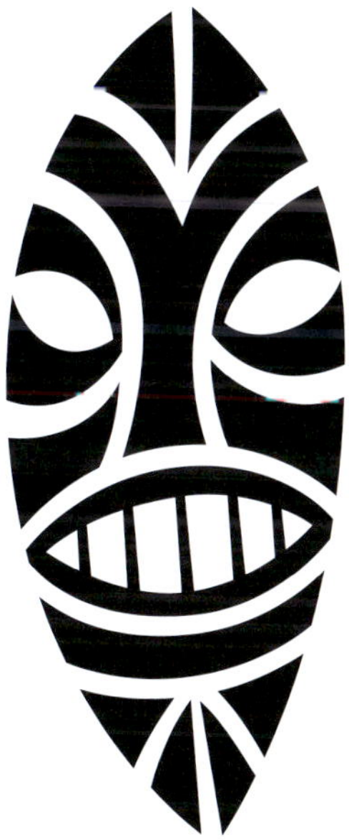

Tiki_Mask_**TM96**

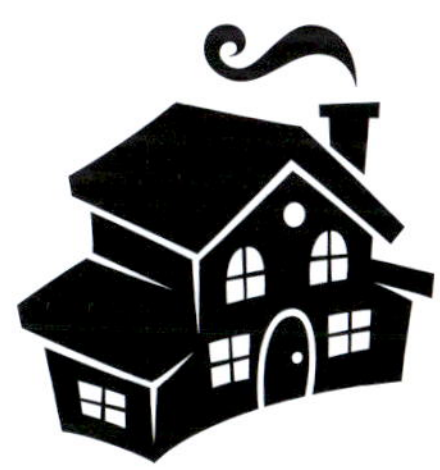

Home_Sweet_Home_**TM97**

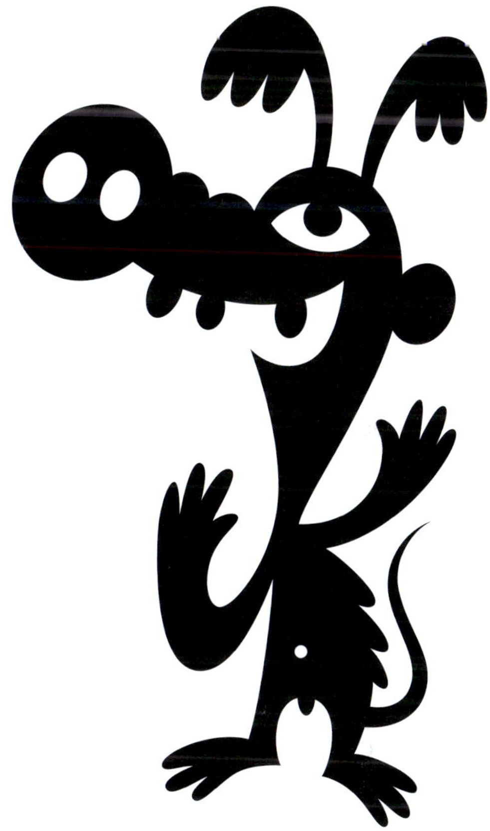

Sock_Gobbler_**TM98**

Flower_Pop_**TM99**

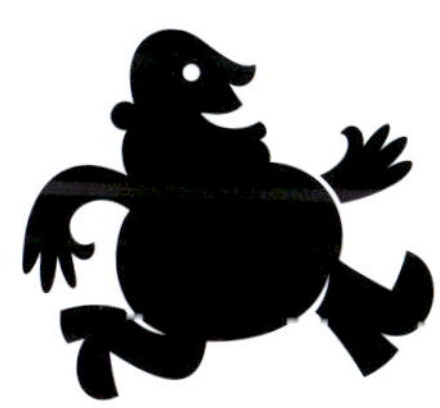

Fat_Man_Walking_**TM100**

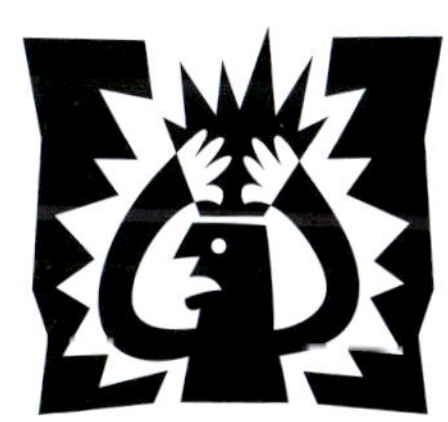

Its_Mind_Blowing_**TM101**

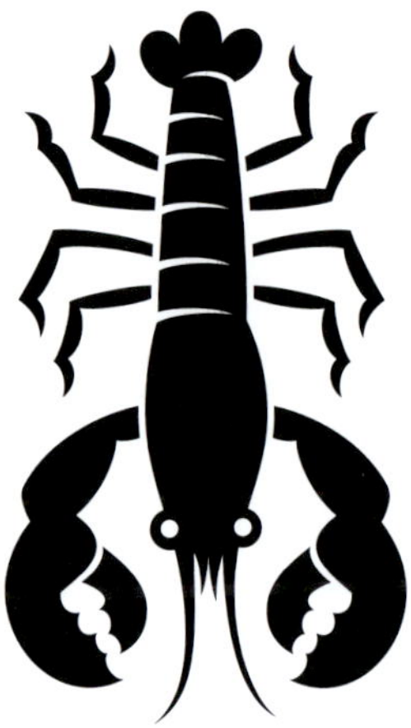

Delicious_Crustacean_**TM102**

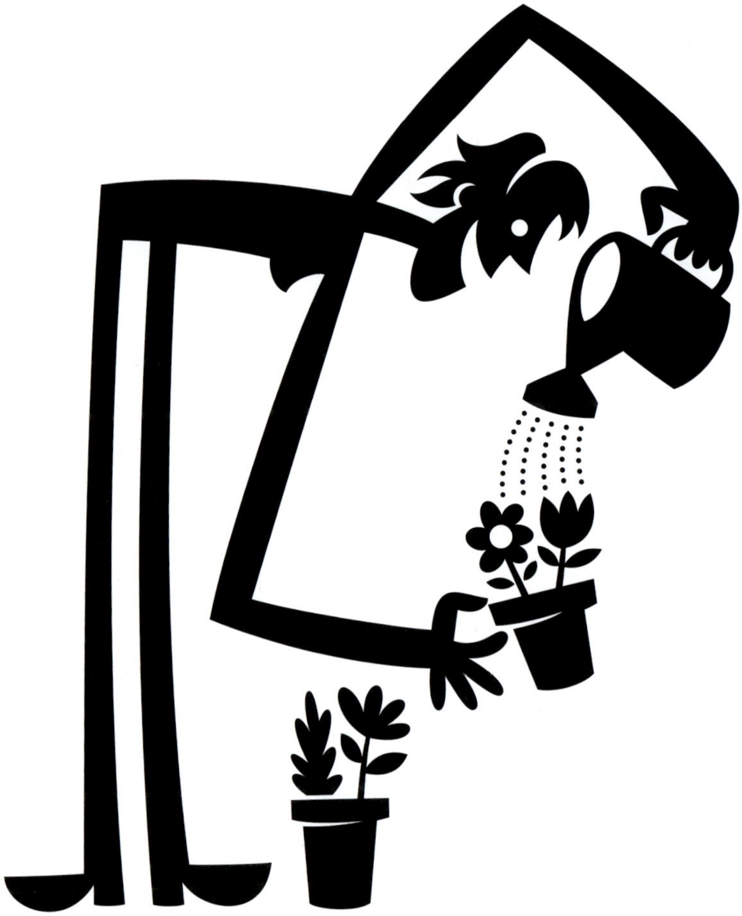

Garden_Goddess_**TM103**

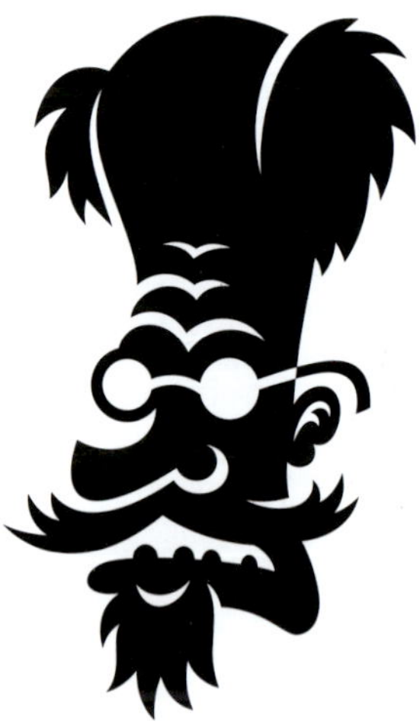

Brainiac_**TM104**

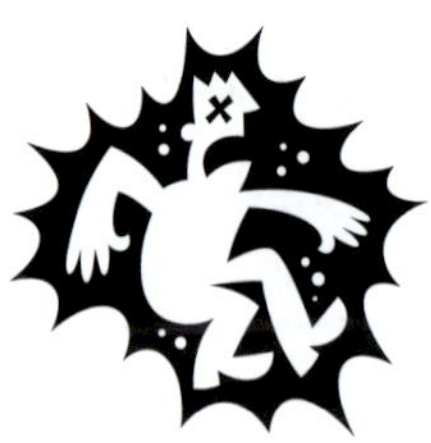

Shocker_**TM105**

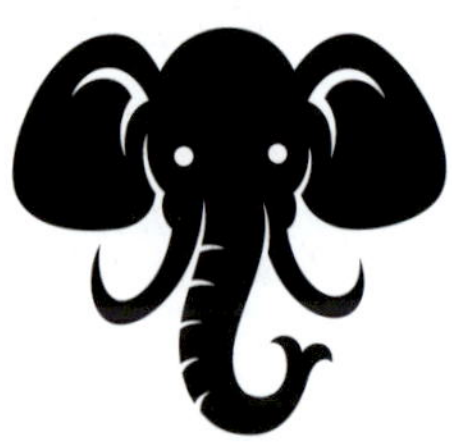

Elephant_Memory_**TM106**

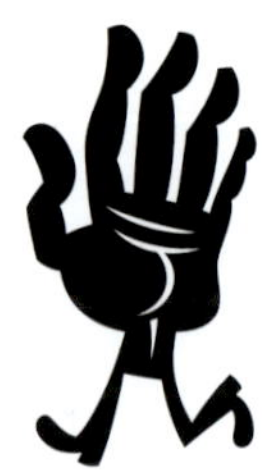

Handyman_**TM107**

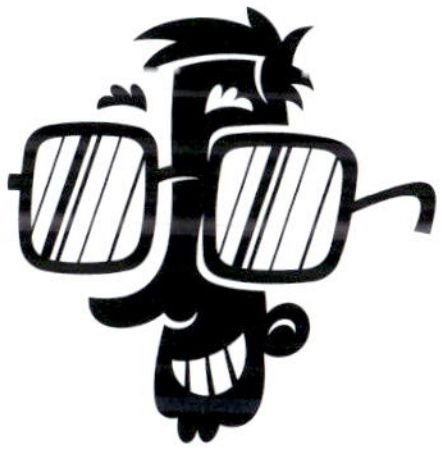

A_Bright_Future_**TM108**

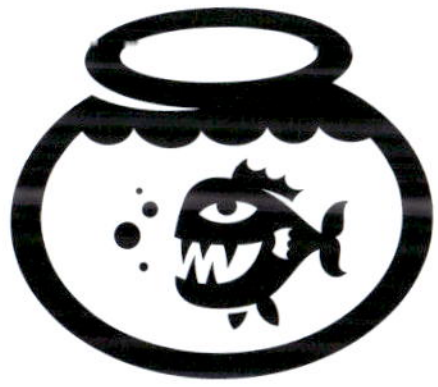

Pet_Fish_**TM109**

Shot_Through_The_Heart_**TM110**

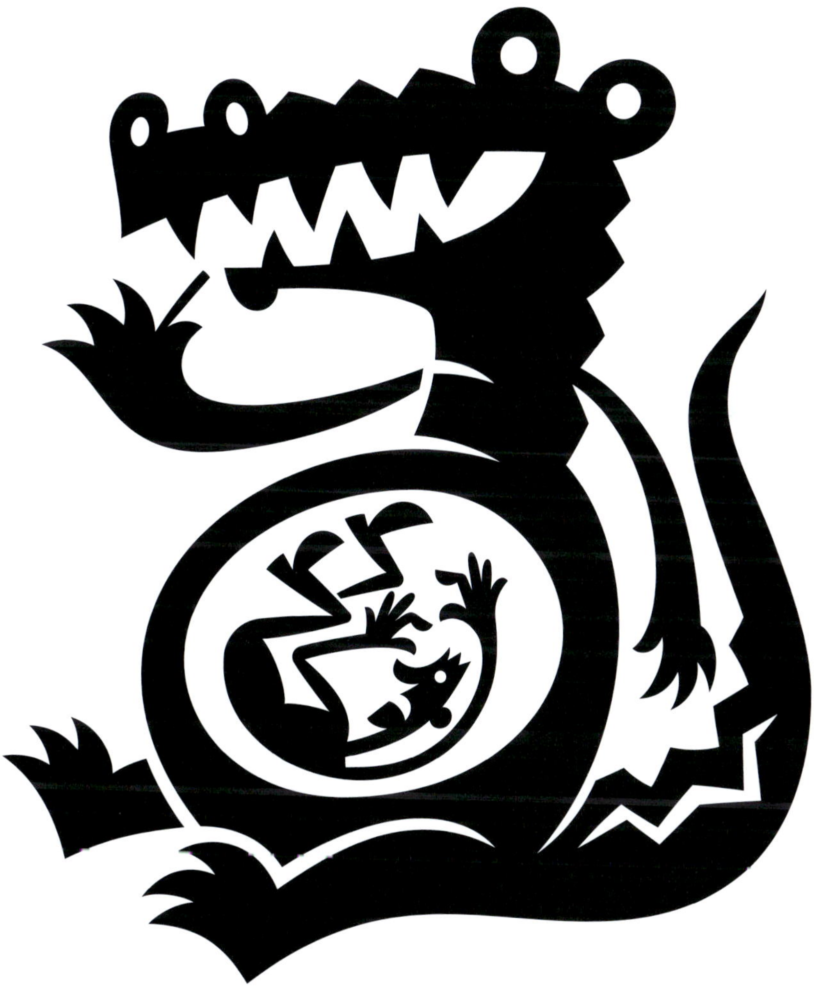

Southern_Food_**TM111**

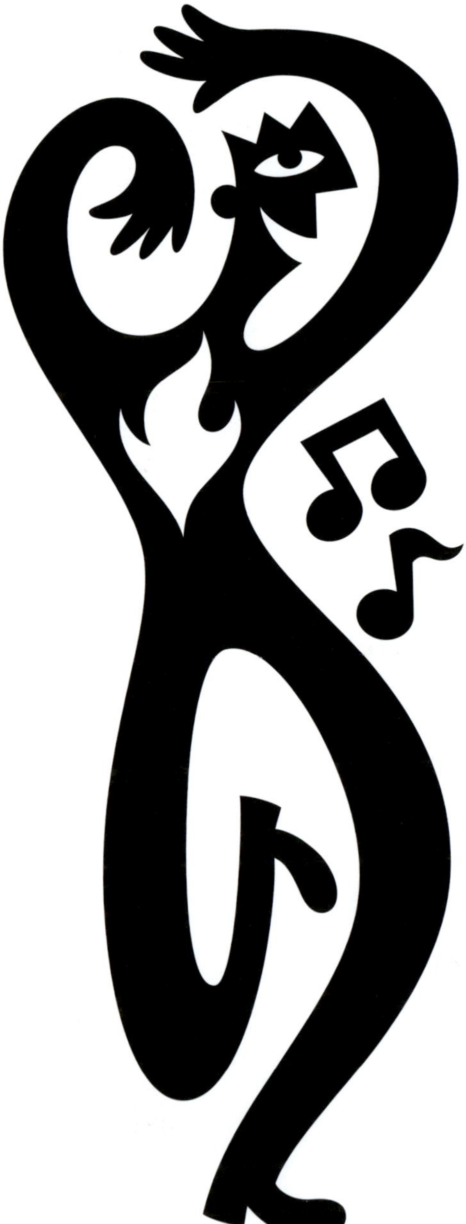

Get_Funky_**TM115**

Lovely_Garden_**TM112**

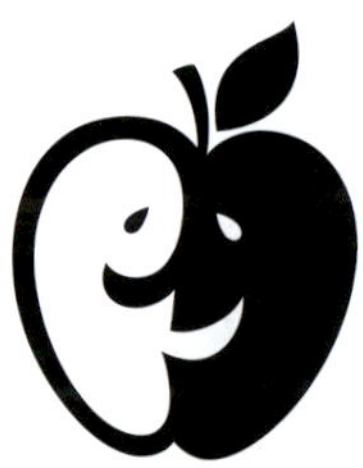

The_Apple_Of_My_Eye_**TM113**

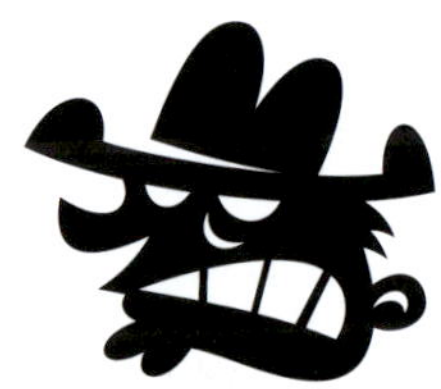

Gruff_Manner_**TM114**

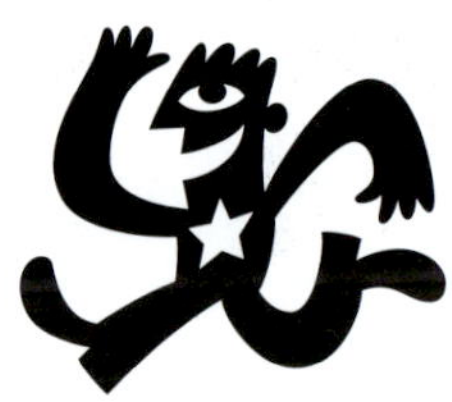

Happy_Jogger_**TM116**

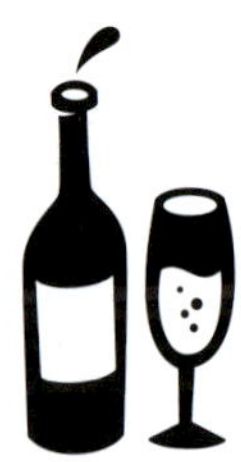

Pinot_Noir_**TM117**

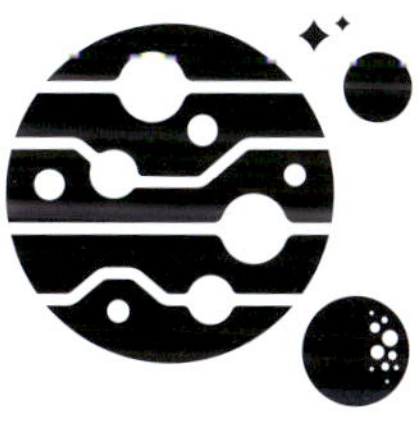

Planets_**TM118**

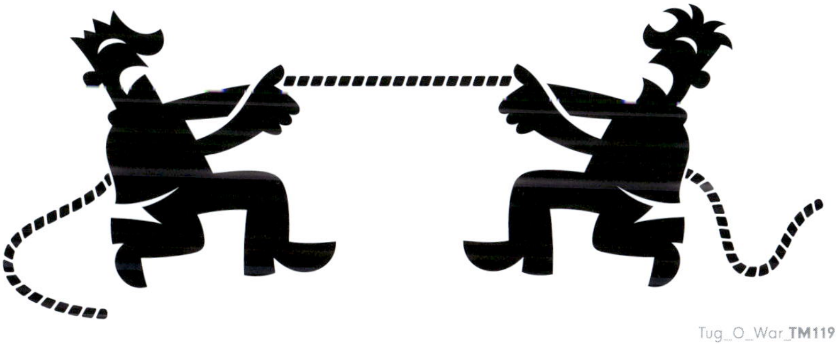

Tug_O_War_**TM119**

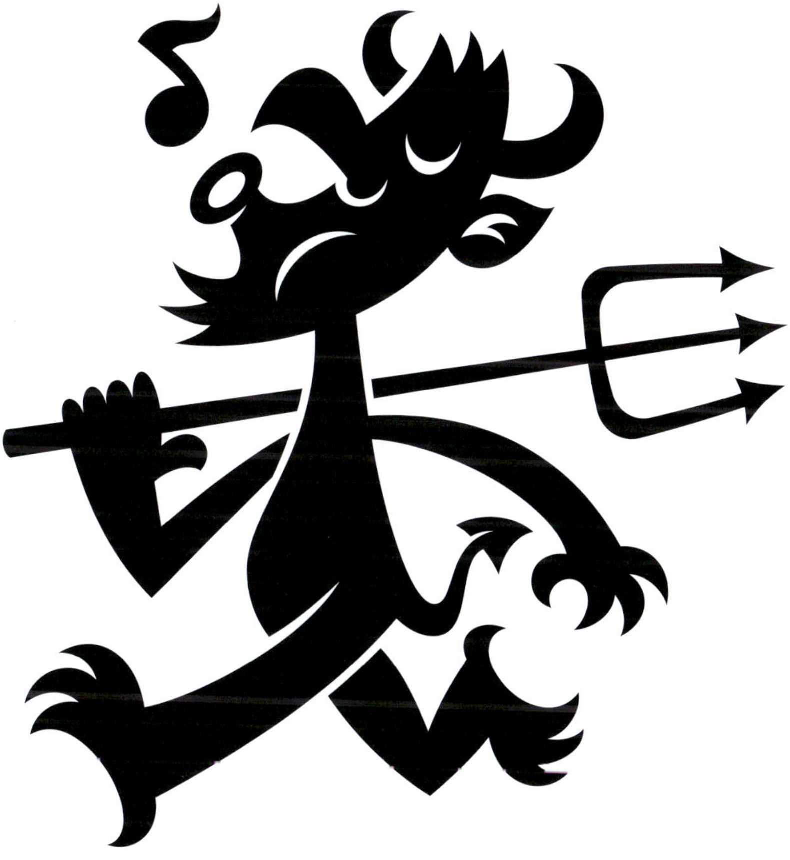

All_In_A_Days_Work_**TM122**

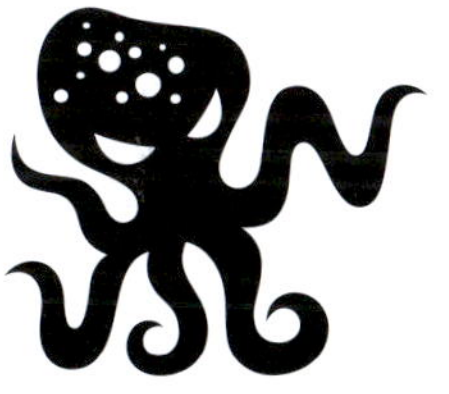

Menacing_Octopus_**TM120**

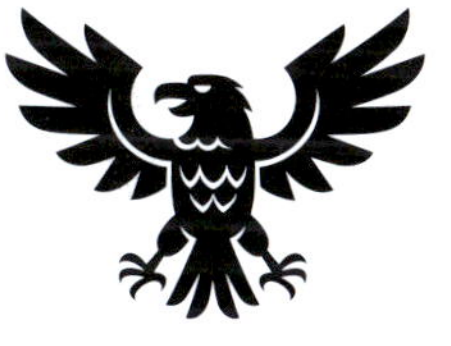

Soar_High_**TM121**

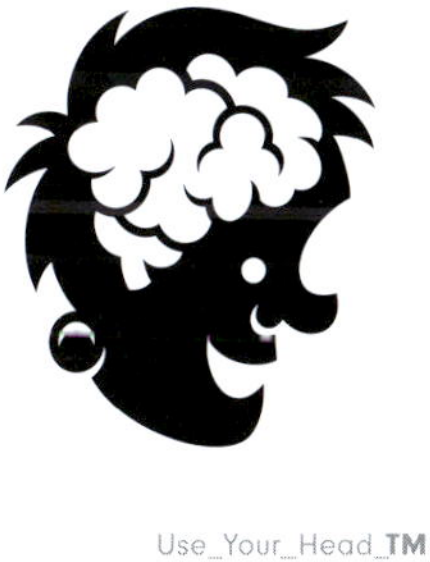

Use_Your_Head_**TM123**

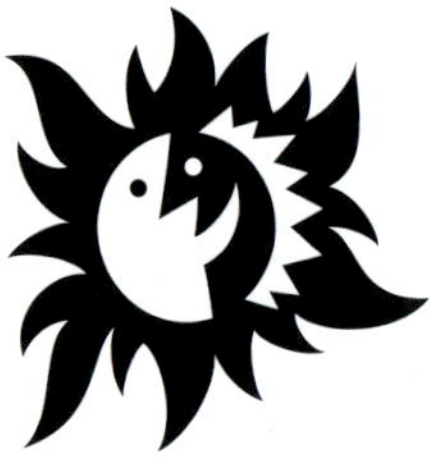

Sunny_**TM124**

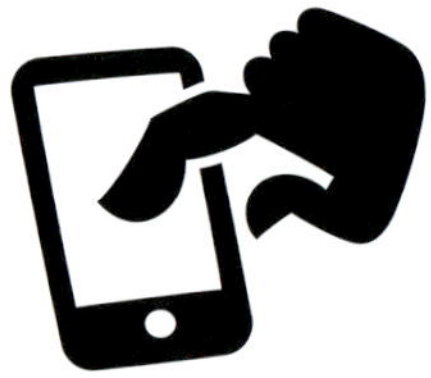

Touch_Me_**TM125**

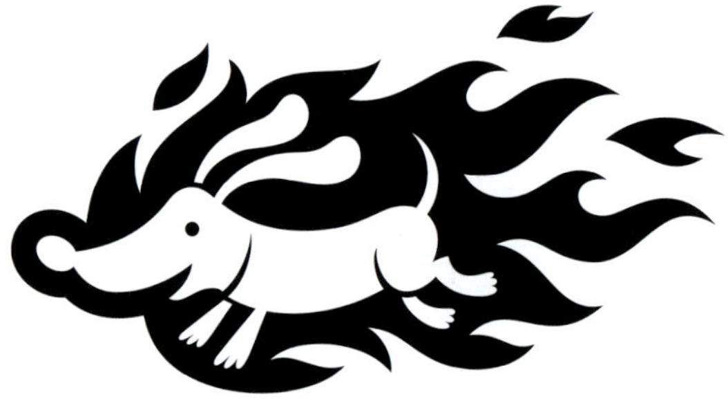

Hot_Dog_**TM126**

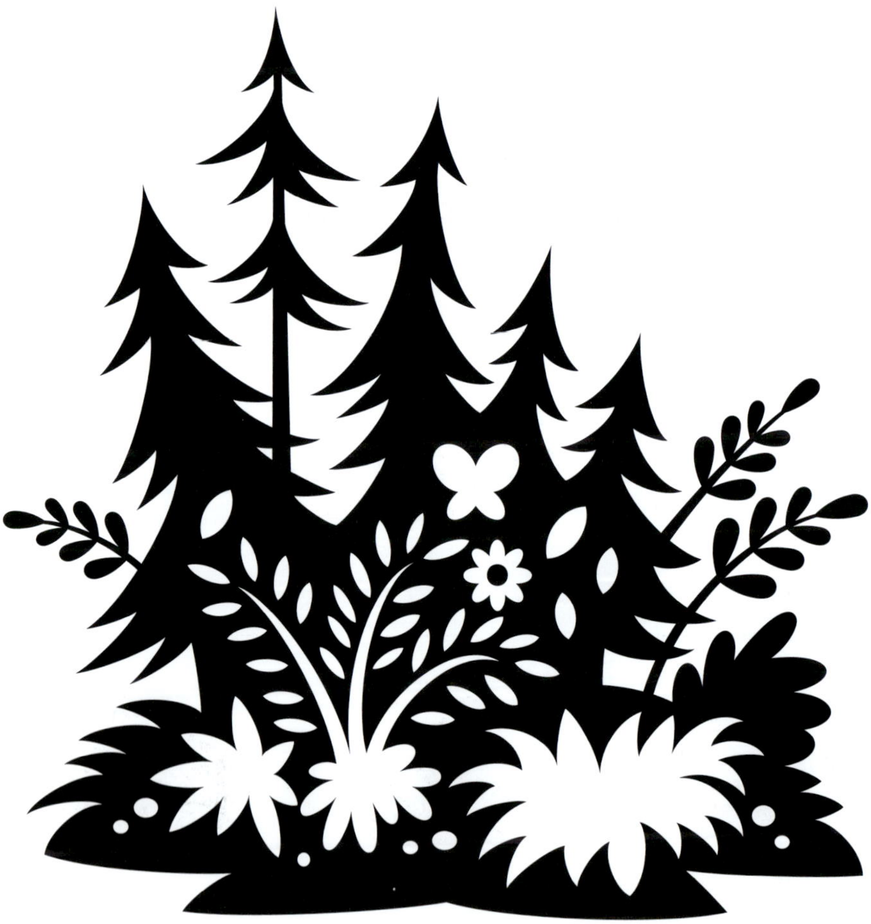

Get_Back_To_Nature_**TM129**

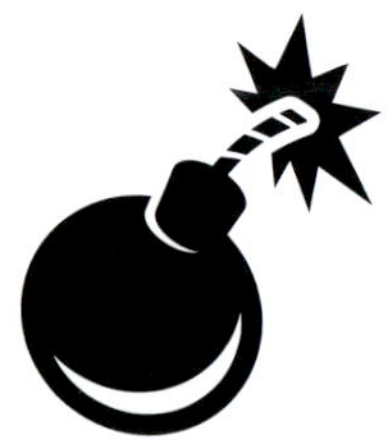

Ka_Boom_**TM127**

Gear_Head_**TM128**

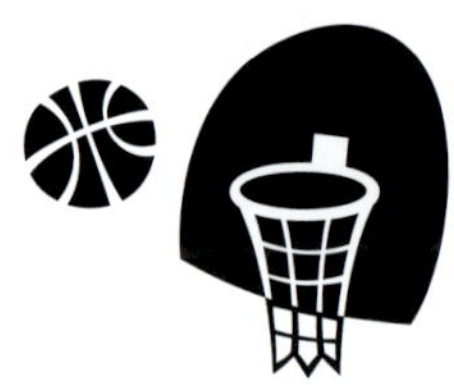

Hoops_**TM130**

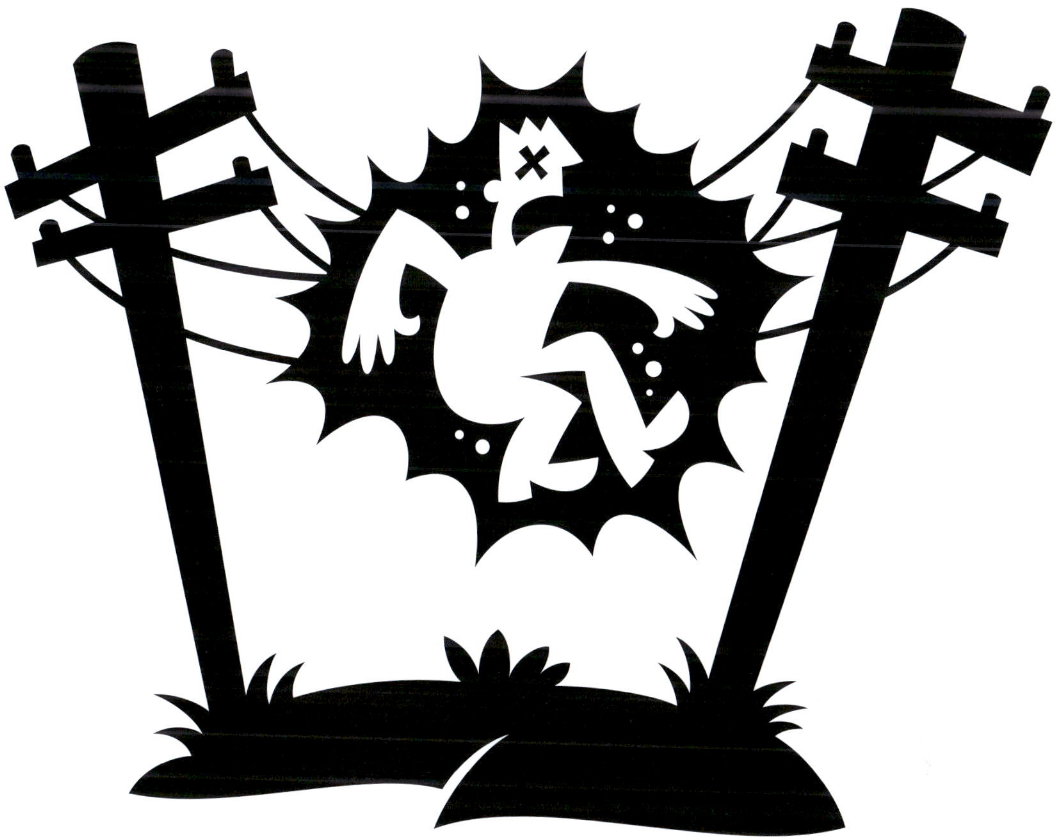

Power_To_The_People_**TM131**

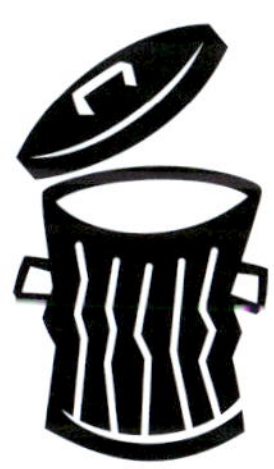

Trash_It_**TM132**

Mustachio_**TM133**

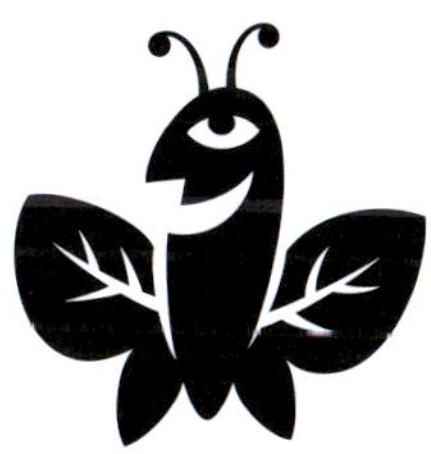

Insect_Man_**TM134**

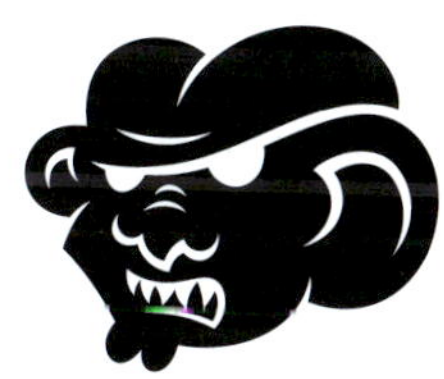

Rule_Of_Acquisition_Number_7_**TM135**

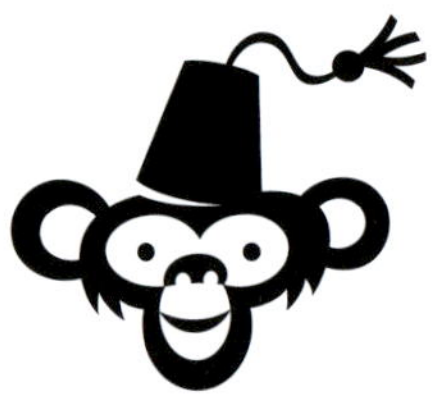
Monkey_Fez_**TM136**

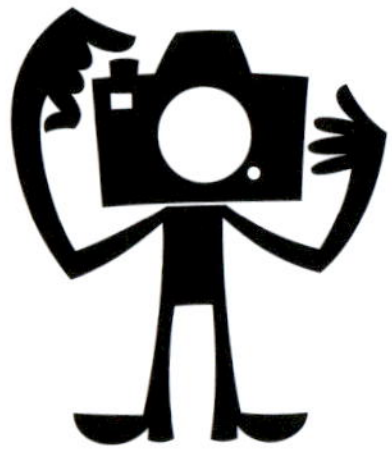
Say_Cheeze_**TM137**

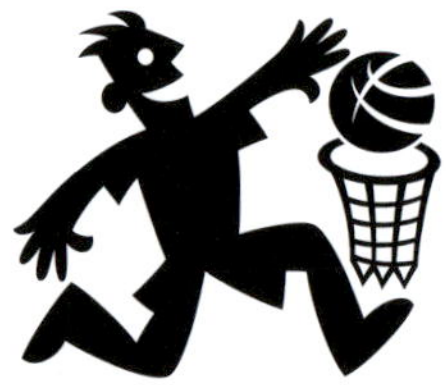
Slam_Dunk_**TM138**

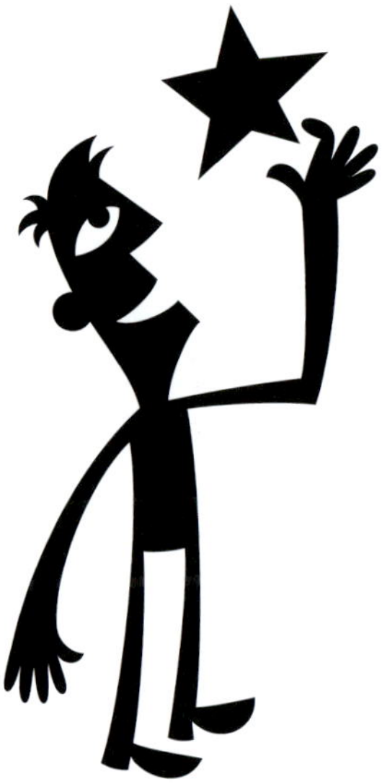
Reach_For_Your_Dreams_**TM139**

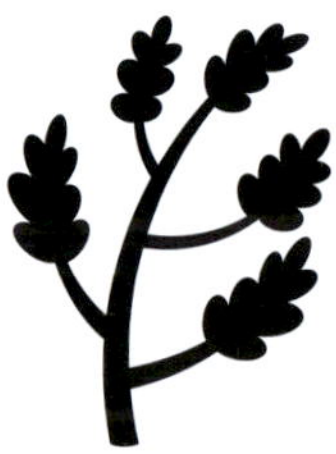
Shrub_**TM140**

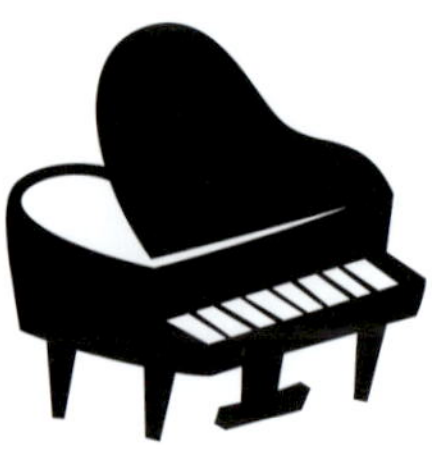
Tickling_The_Ivories_**TM141**

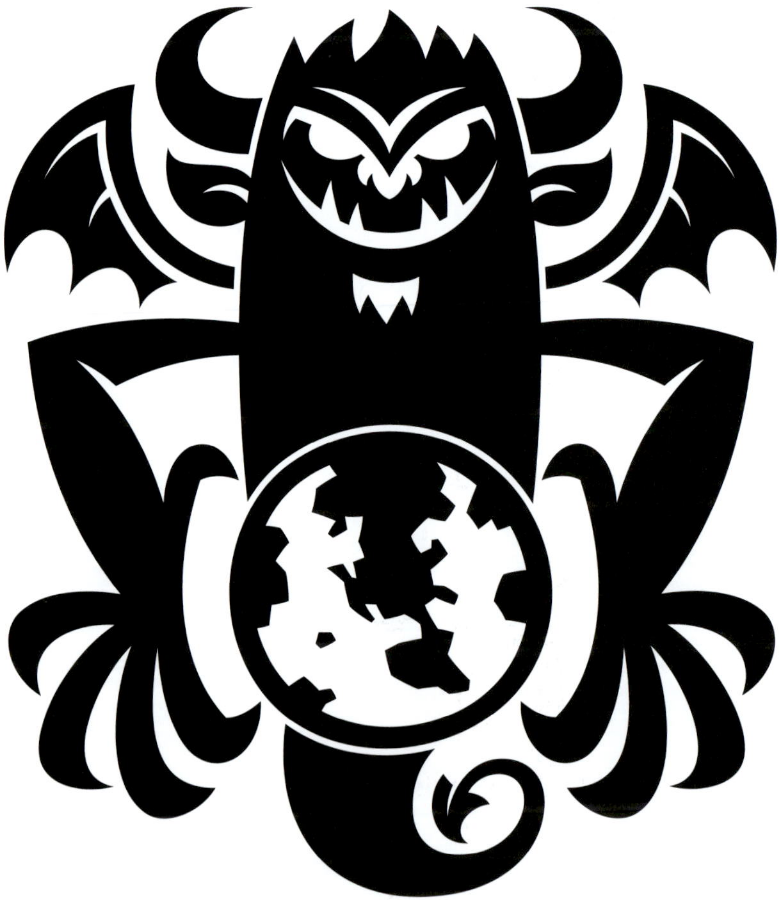
Overlord_**TM142**

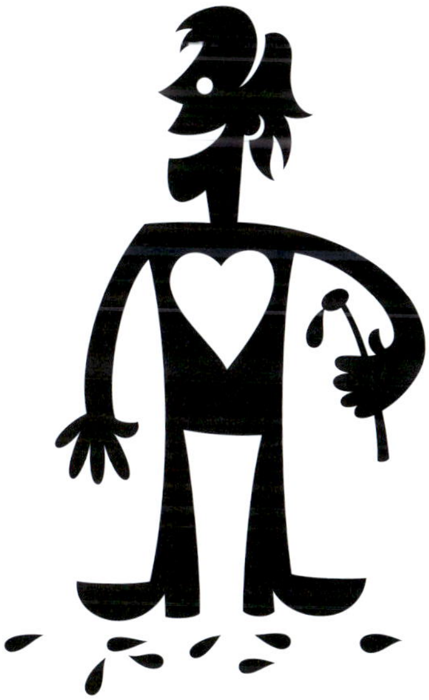

He_Loves_Me_**TM143**

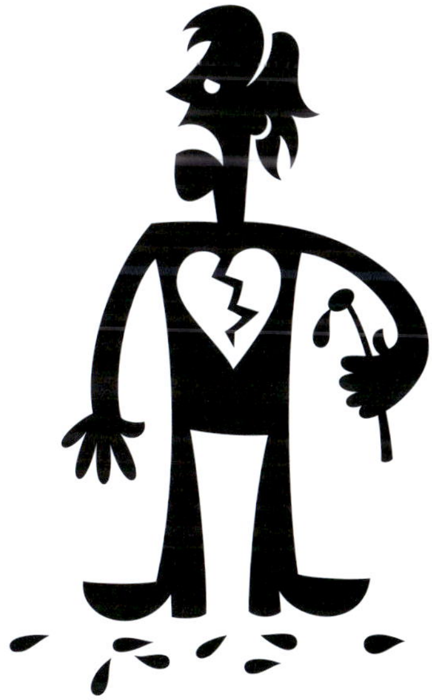

He_Loves_Me_Not_**TM144**

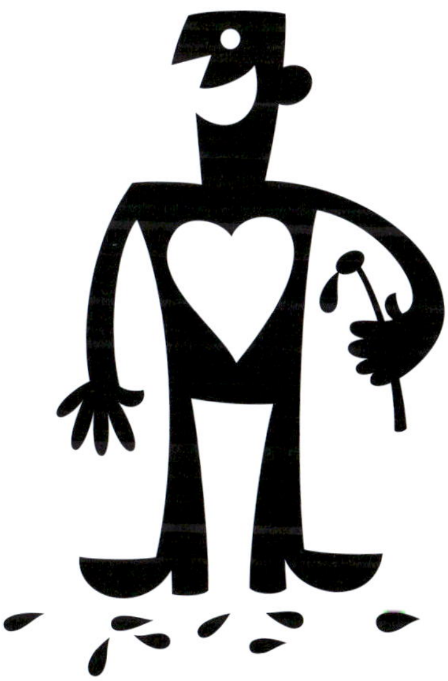

She_Loves_Me_**TM145**

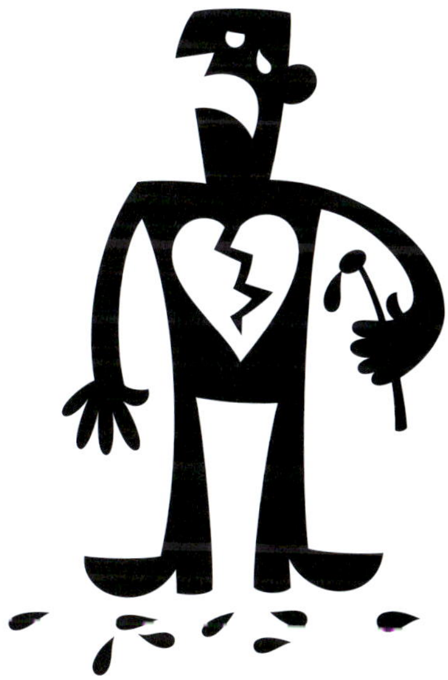

She_Loves_Me_Not_**TM146**

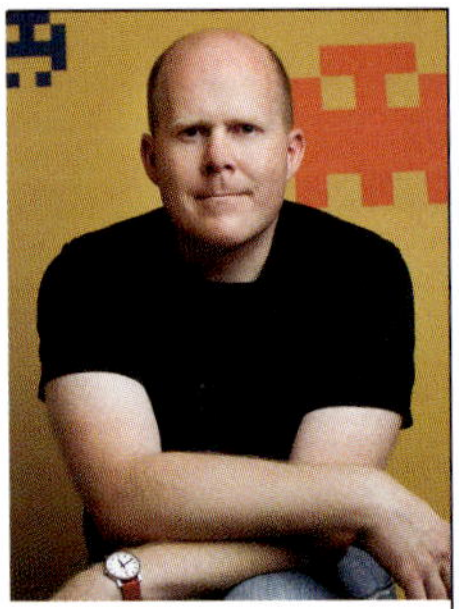

Donovan Beery

Owner

Eleven19 • Omaha, Nebraska

www.eleven19.com

A great spot illustration can breathe life into a layout. Starting with a strong concept and combined with typography, you can achieve a beautiful visual narrative that engages the viewer and draws them in. It's design magic.

Art Used: Robot Clone TM851

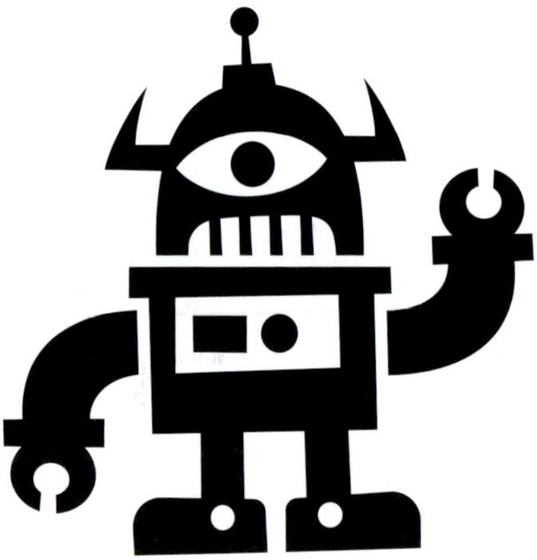

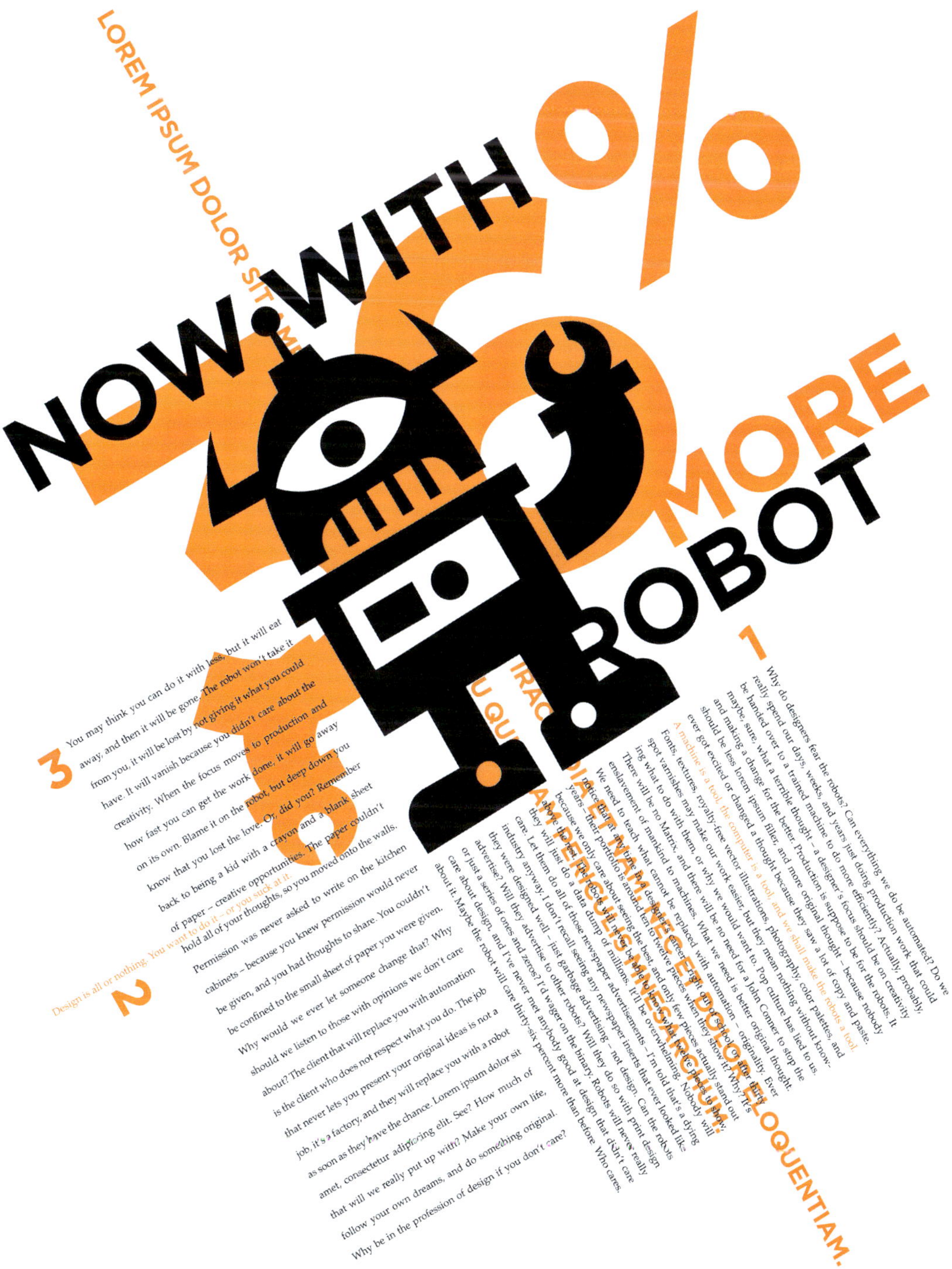
LOREM IPSUM DOLOR SIT AMET
NOW WITH
%
MORE
ROBOT
1
2
3
Design is all or nothing. You want to do it – or you suck at it.
A machine is a tool, the computer is a tool, and we shall make the robots a tool.
AM PERICULIS MNESARCHUM.
ET NAM NEC ET DOLOR ELOQUENTIAM.

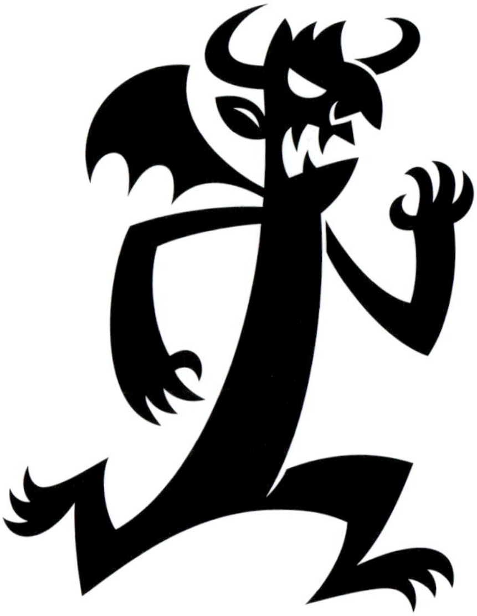

Running_With_The_Devil_**TM148**

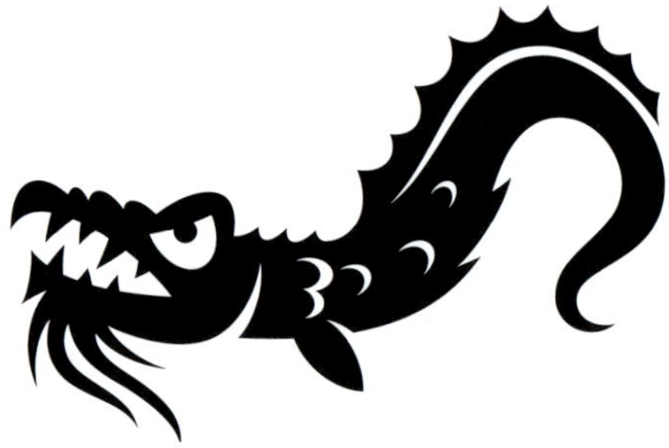

Eel_**TM147**

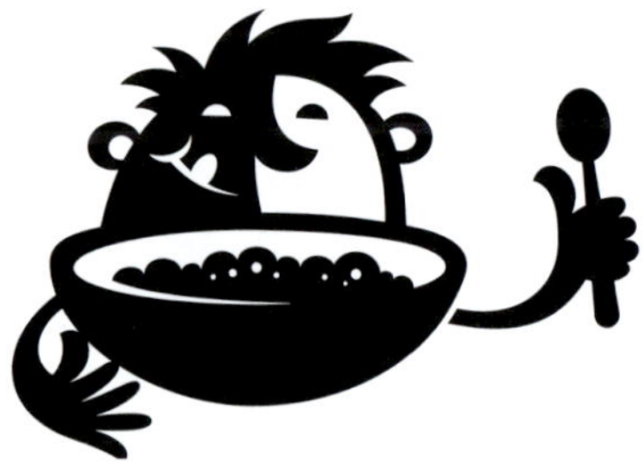

Mikey_Likes_It_**TM149**

Nocturnal_Living_**TM150**

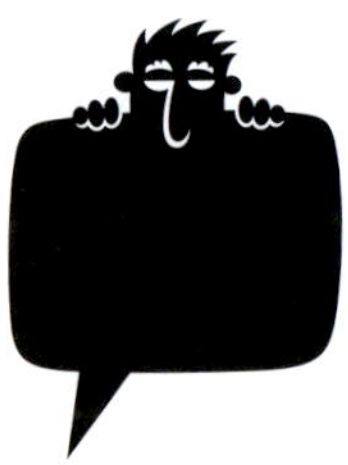

What_Are_You_Saying_**TM151**

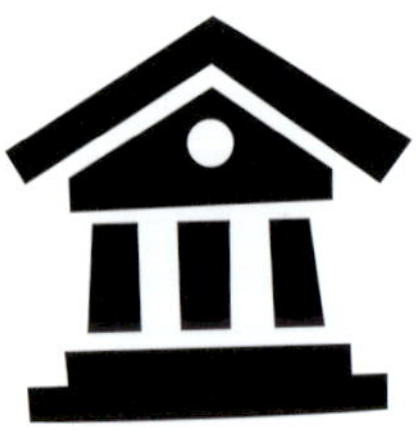

The_Love_Of_Money_**TM152**

Shit_Head_**TM153**

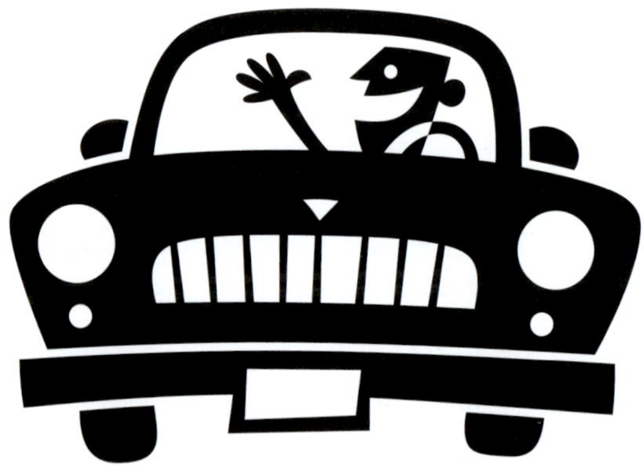

A_Driven_Personality_**TM154**

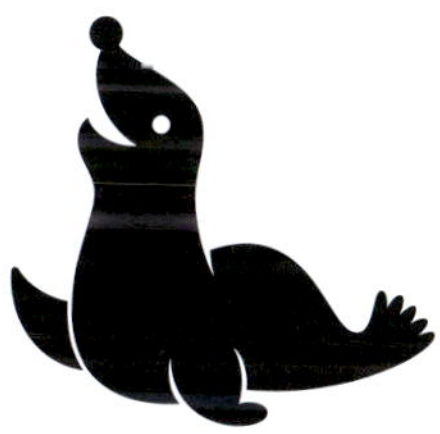

Seal_Of_Approval_**TM155**

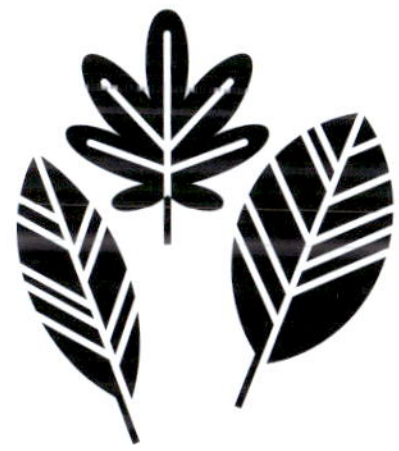

Turn_A_New_Leaf_**TM156**

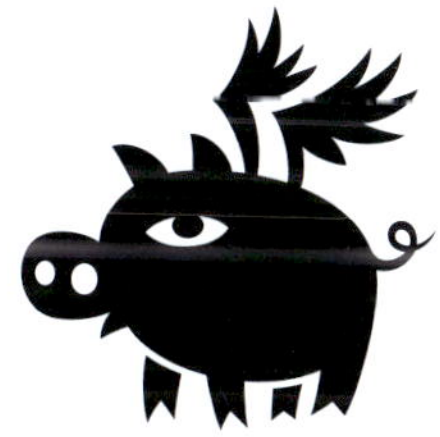

When_Pigs_Fly_**TM157**

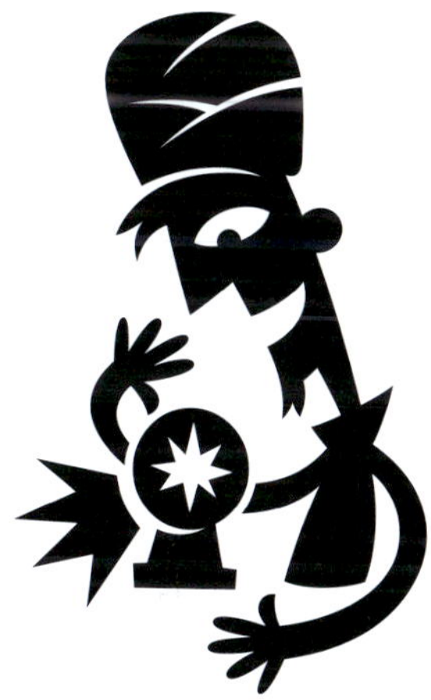

Swamy_**TM158**

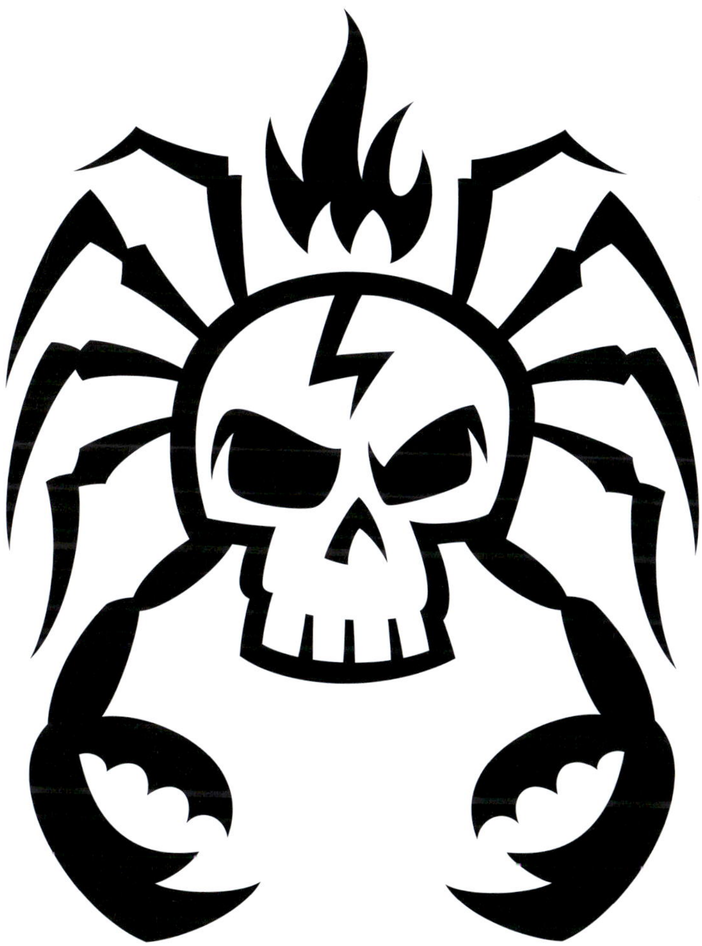

Nightmare_**TM159**

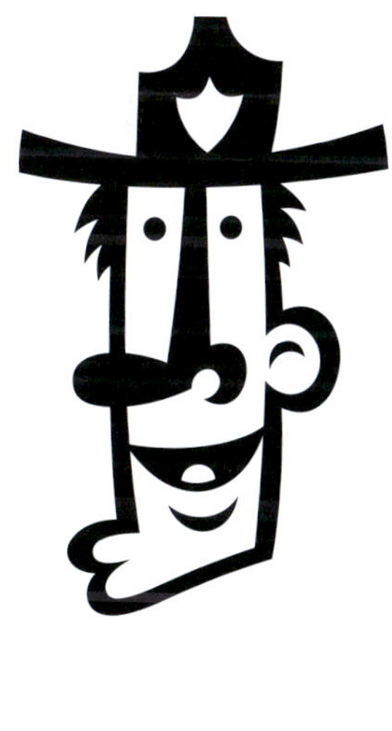

Ranger_**TM160**

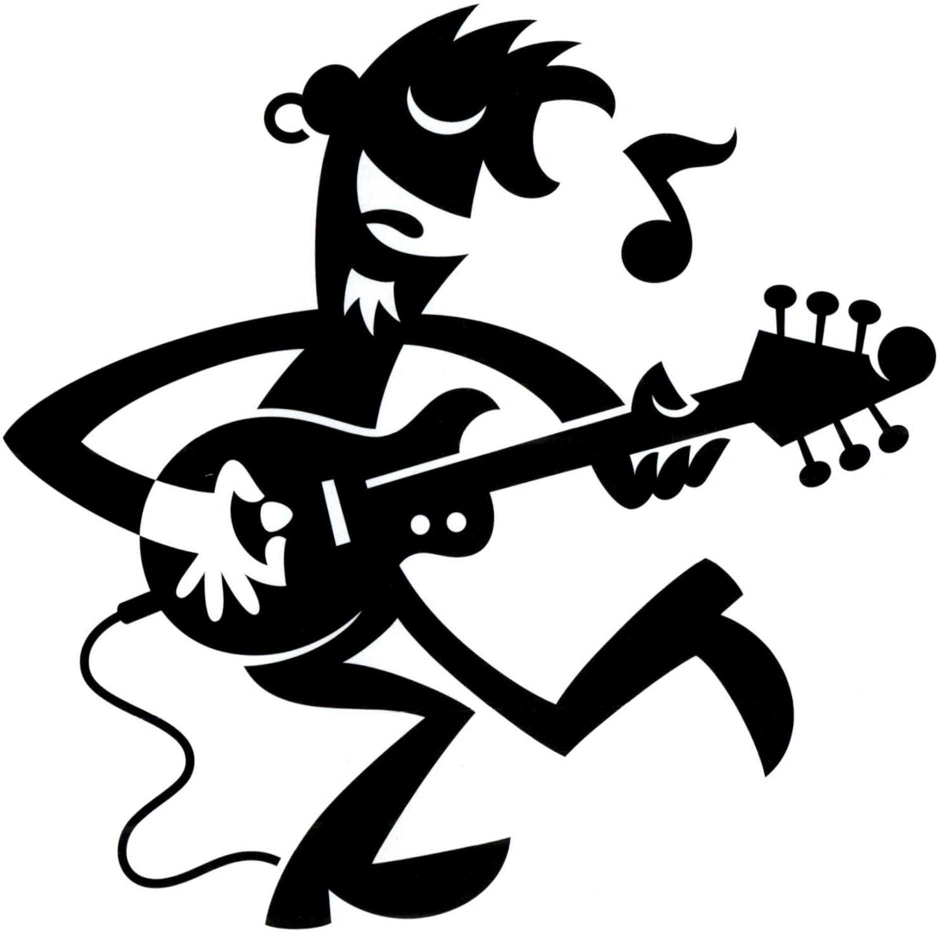

Rock_N_Roll_Forever_**TM161**

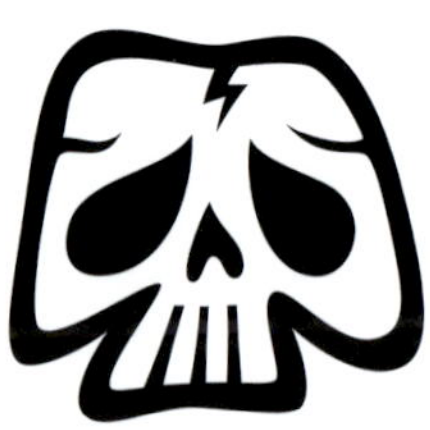

Skully_**TM162**

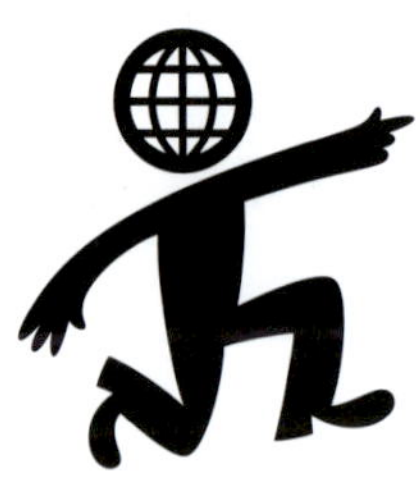

Look_**TM163**

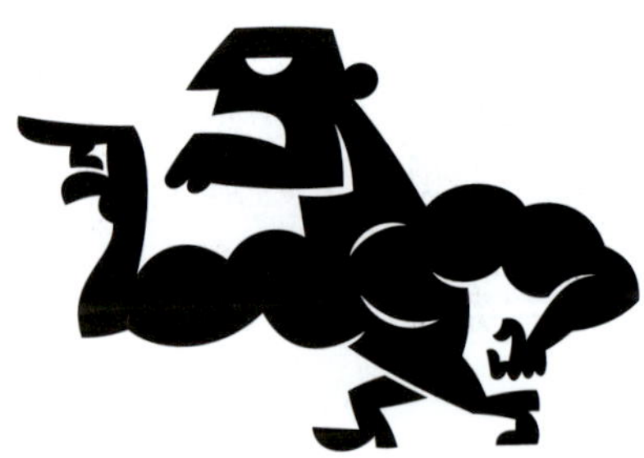

Take_It_Outside_Bro_**TM164**

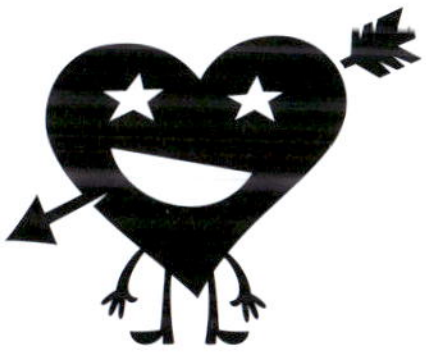

Lovestruck_**TM165**

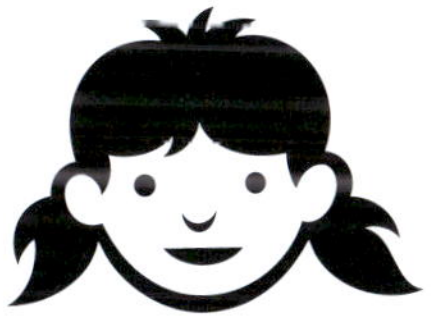

Lil_Girl_**TM166**

Mountain_Top_Experience_**TM167**

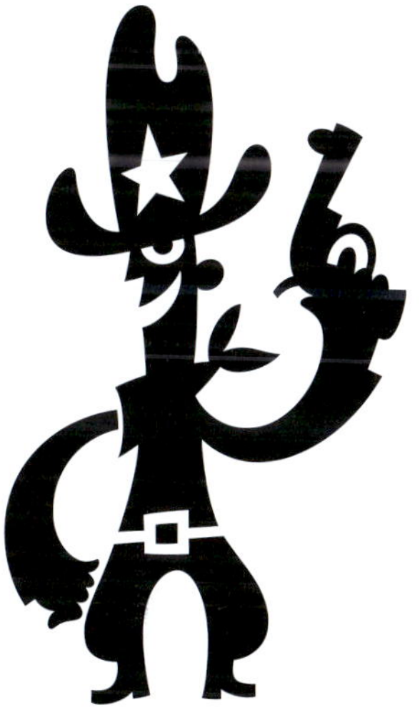

Sheriff_**TM171**

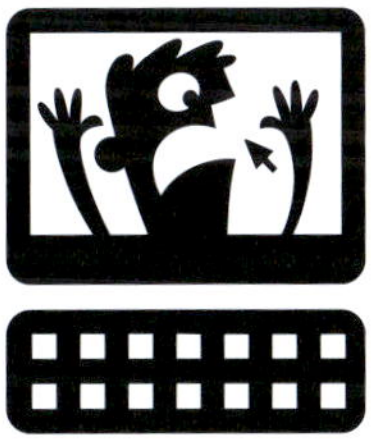

Techno_Phobia_**TM168**

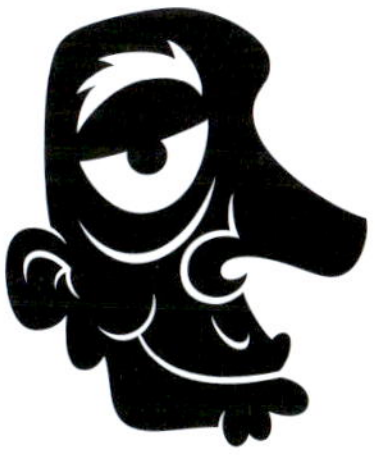

Take_A_Downer_**TM169**

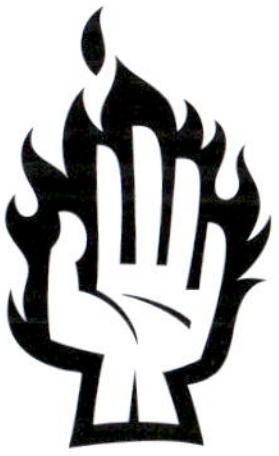

Pledge_Allegiance_**TM170**

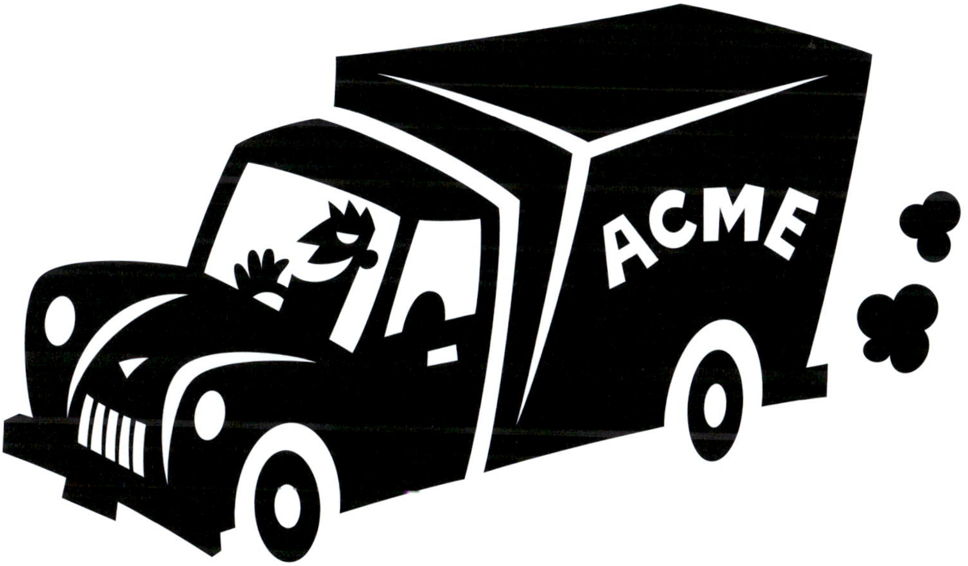

Special_Delivery_**TM172**

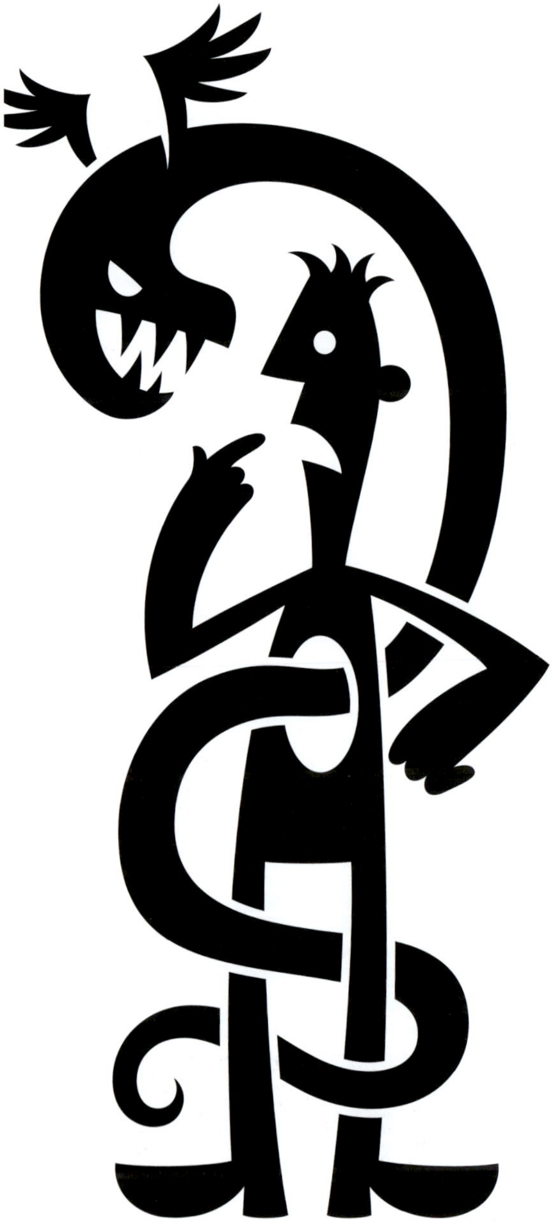

Questionable_Ethics_**TM176**

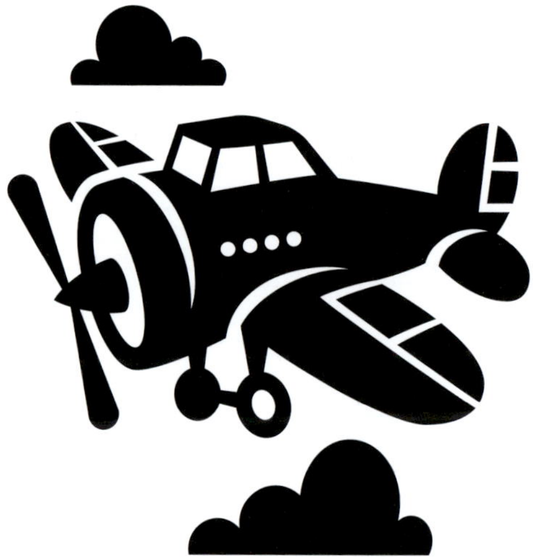

Airborne_**TM173**

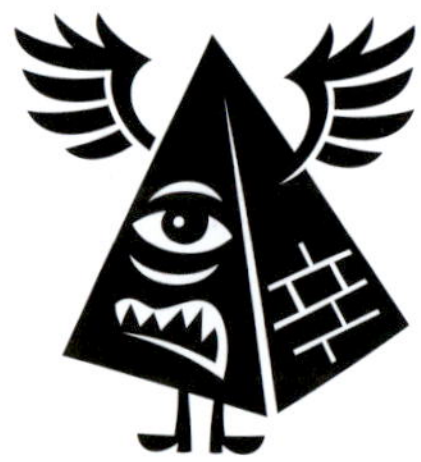

The_World_Is_Ruled_By_Fools_**TM174**

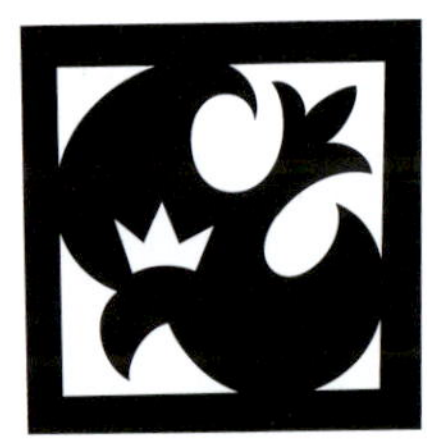

Peace_Box_**TM175**

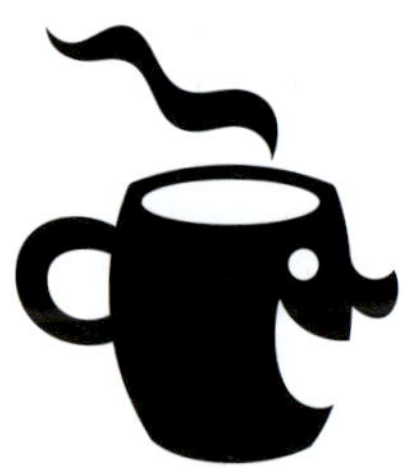

Mr_Coffee_**TM177**

Spazoid_Annual_**TM178**

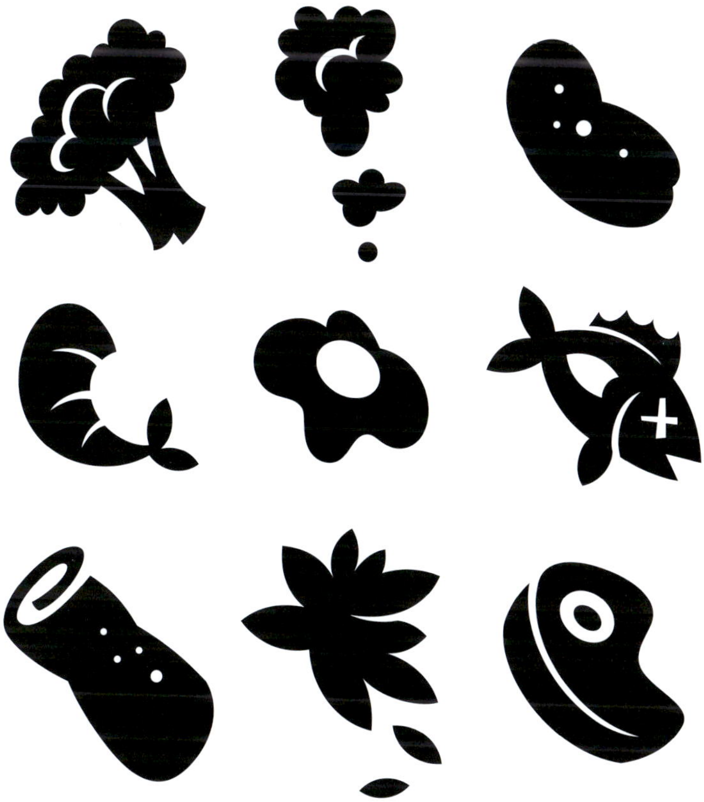

Good_Eats_**TM181**

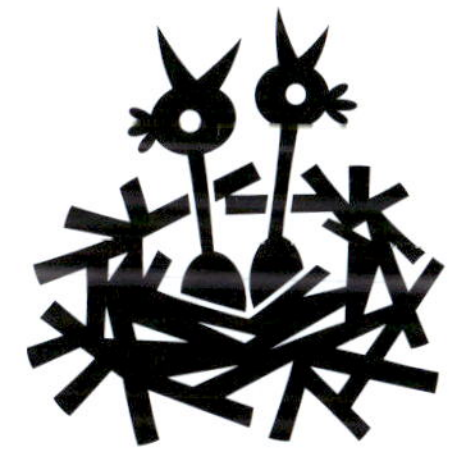

Nest_**TM179**

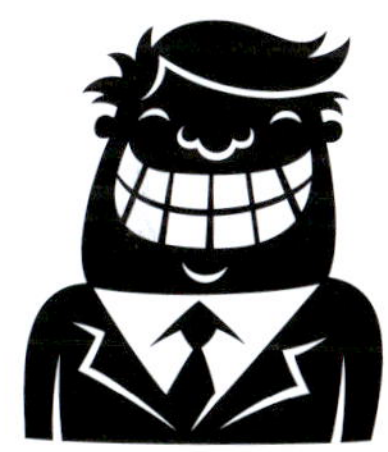

Infernal_Intern_**TM180**

Jovial_Floral_**TM182**

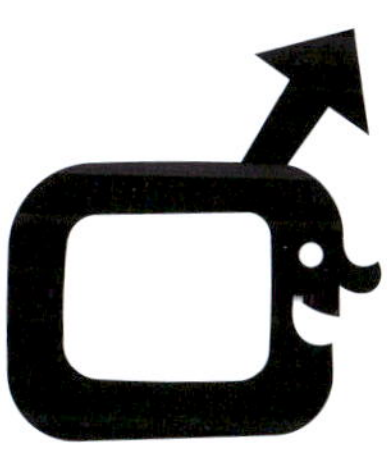

Male_**TM183**

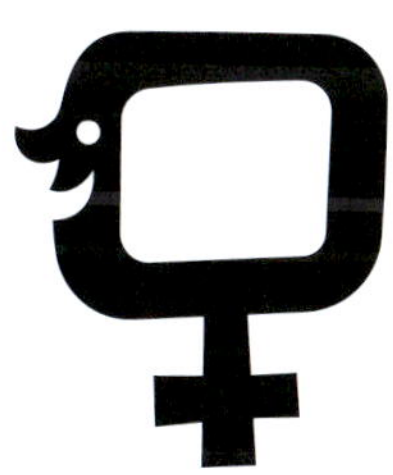

Female_**TM184**

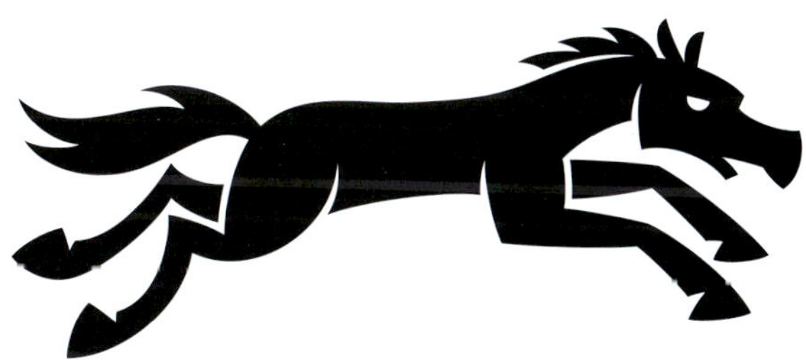

Pony_Express_**TM185**

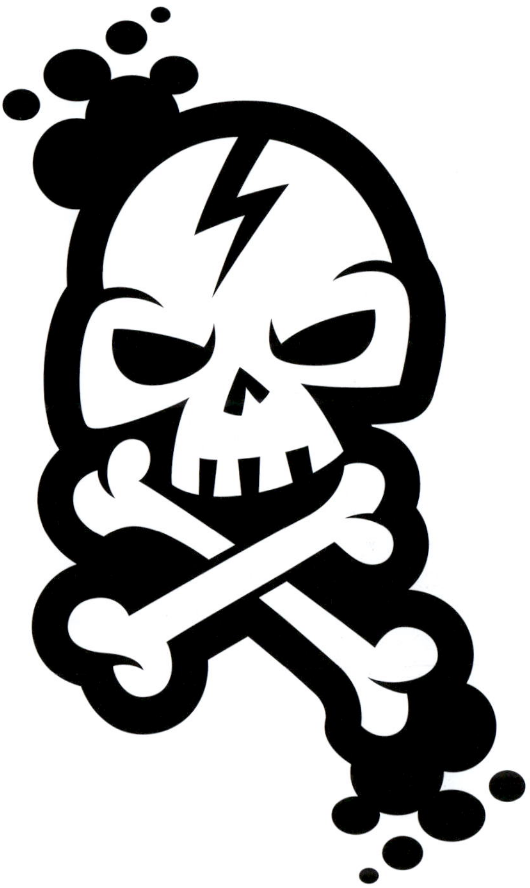

Disease_**TM188**

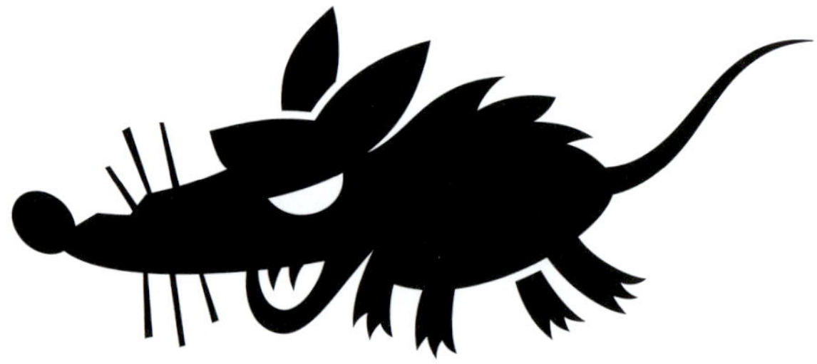

Ratz_**TM186**

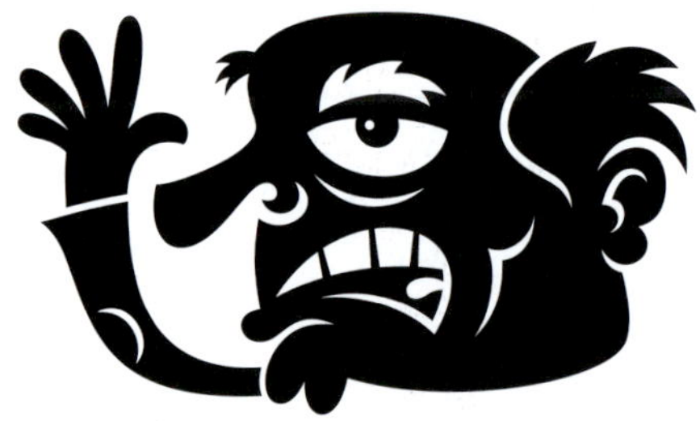

Mr_Grumpy_Pants_**TM187**

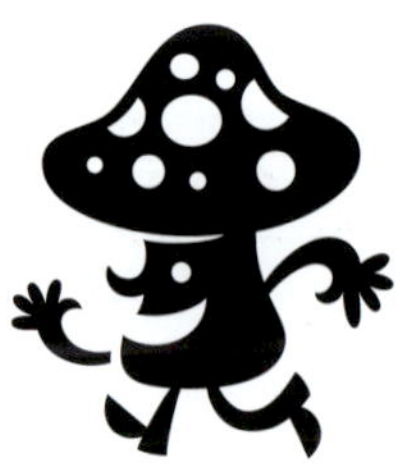

Fun_Guy_**TM189**

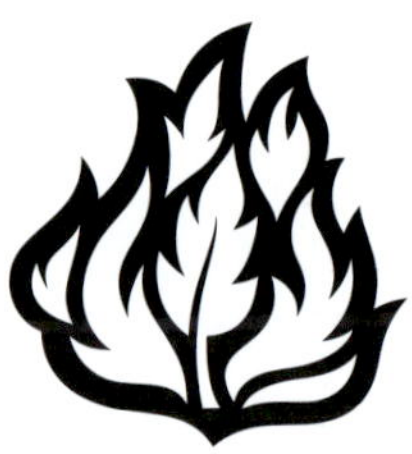

Green_Fuel_**TM190**

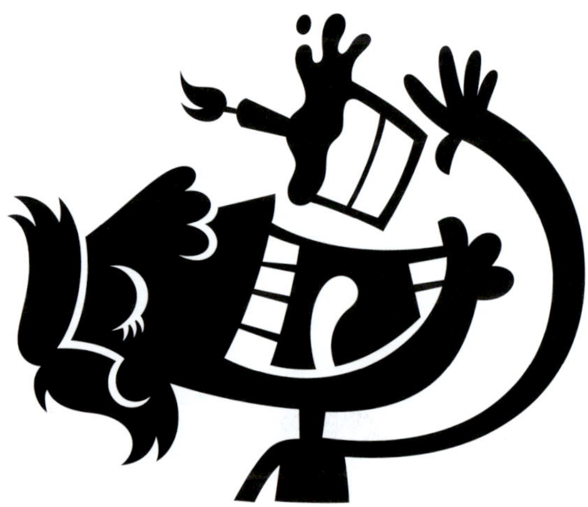

Snack_Time_**TM191**

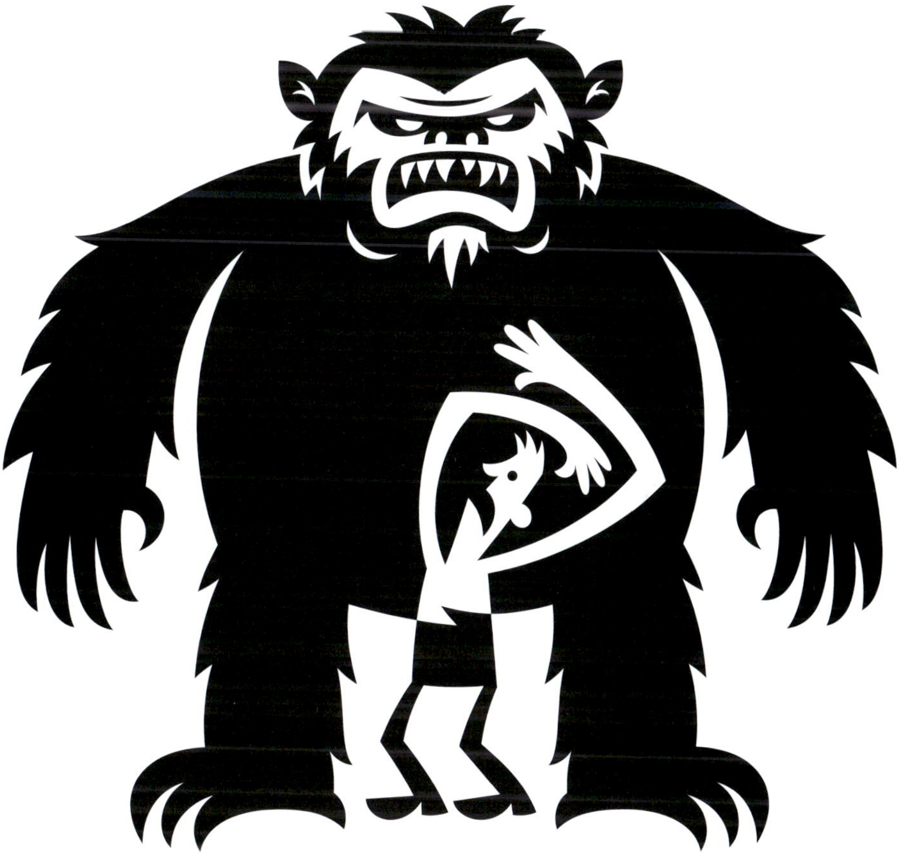

Face_Your_Fears_**TM192**

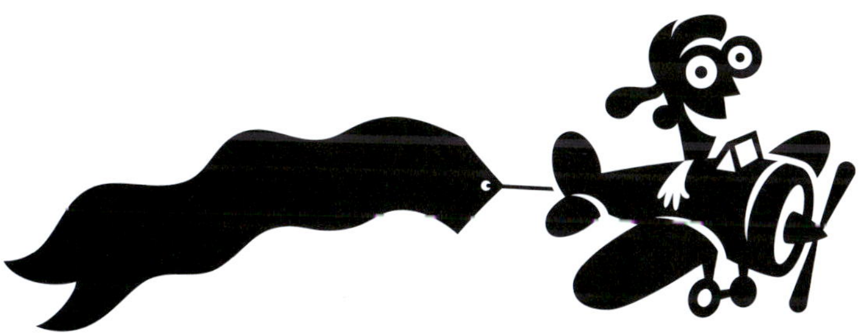

Get_The_Word_Out_**TM193**

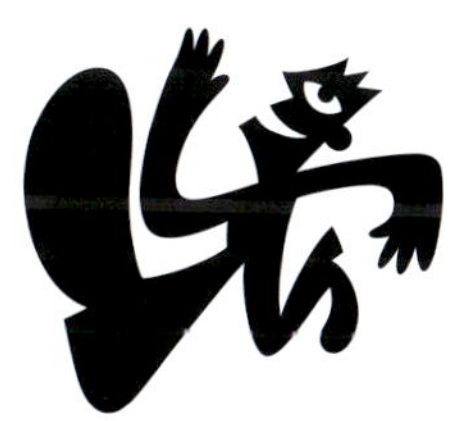

Full_Tilt_**TM194**

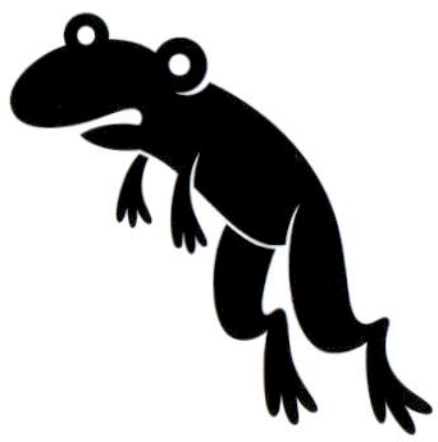

Hop_To_It_**TM195**

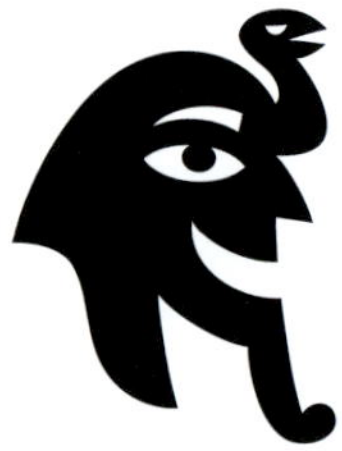

Pharaoh_Dude_**TM196**

Mr_Incognito_**TM197**

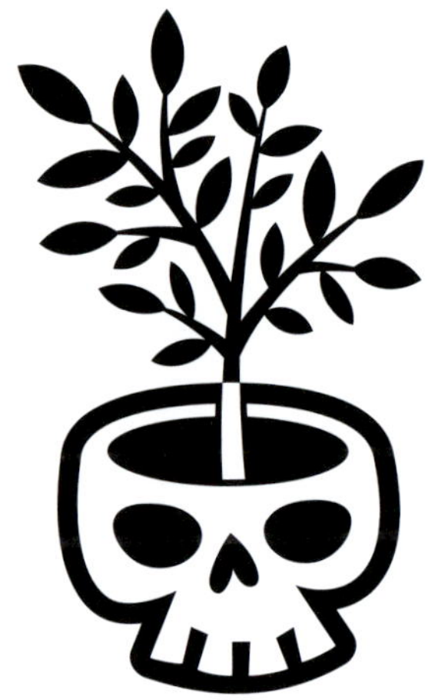

Life_After_Death_**TM198**

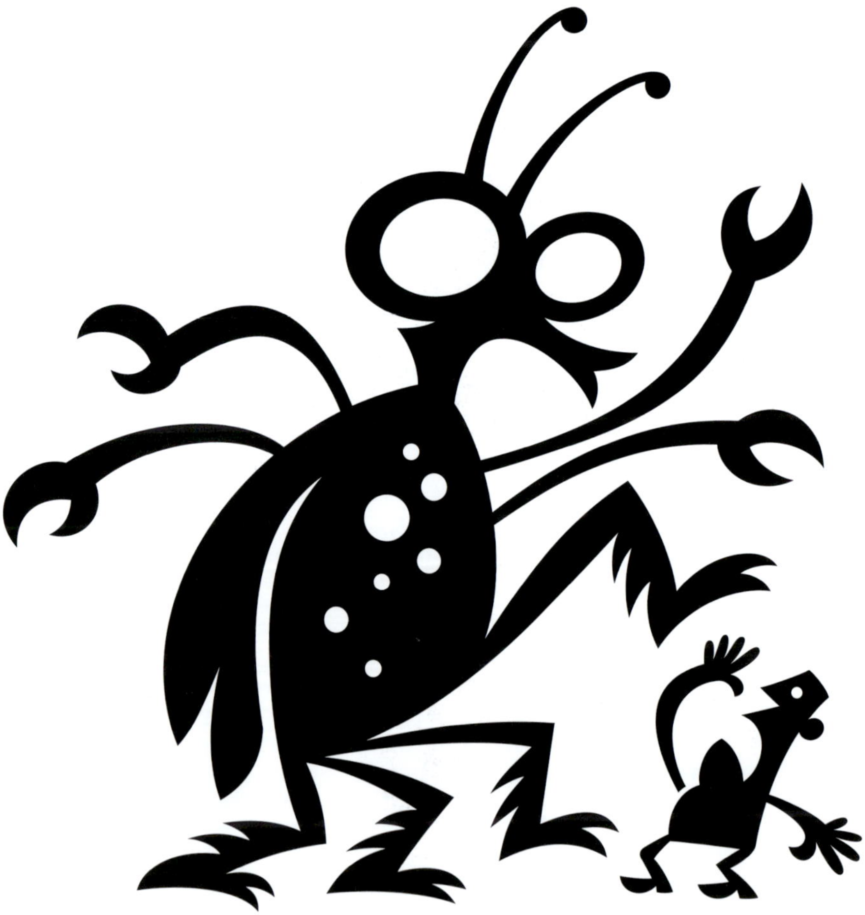

Pest_Extermination_**TM200**

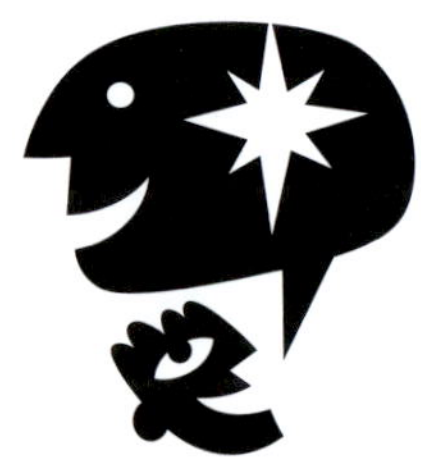

Resonate_**TM199**

Triclops_**TM201**

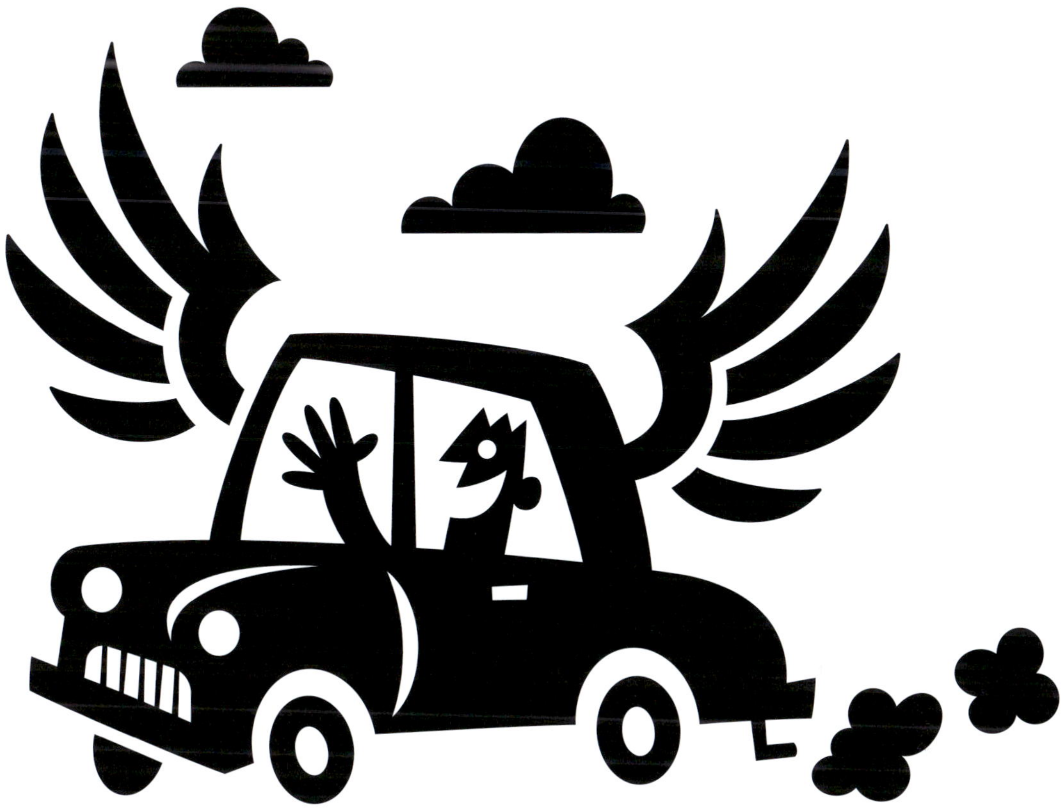

Cloud_Driver_**TM202**

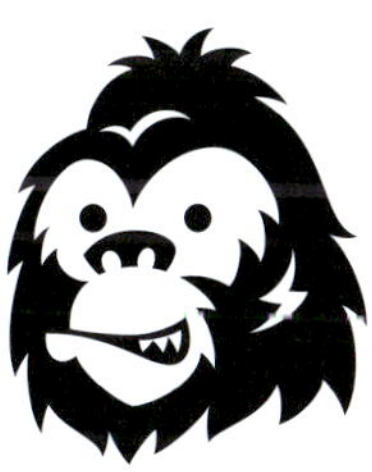

Happy_Ape_**TM203**

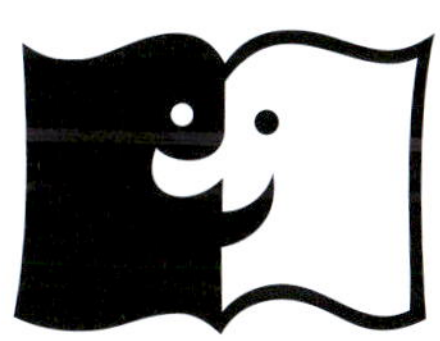

Read_You_Like_A_Book_**TM204**

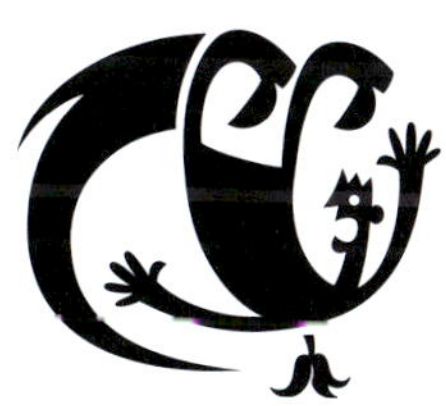

Peel_Out_**TM205**

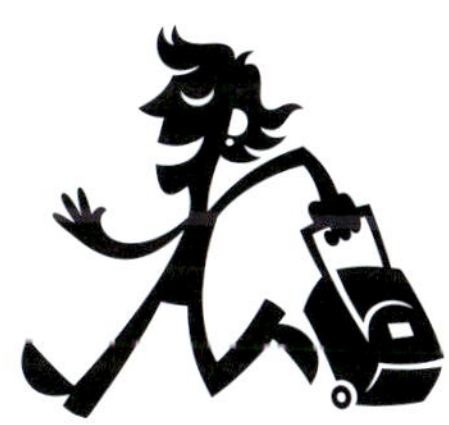

On_The_Go_**TM206**

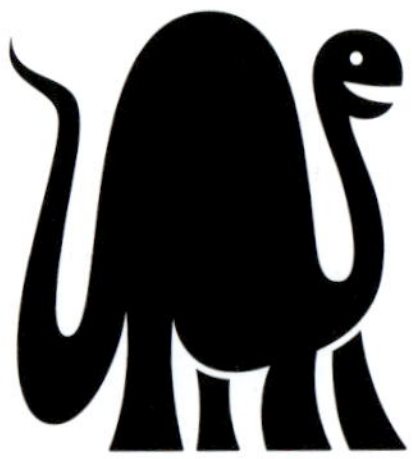

Longneck_**TM207**

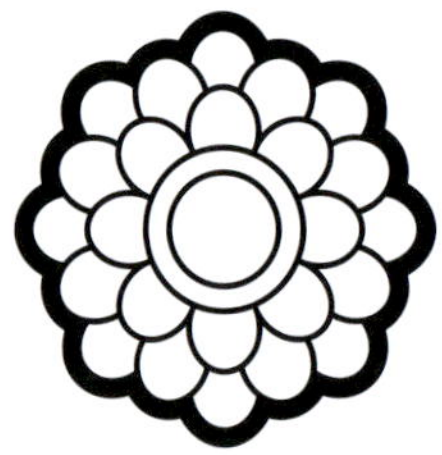

Petals_**TM208**

Senseless_**TM209**

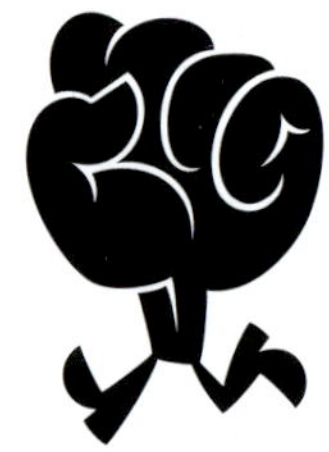

Strong_Headed_**TM210**

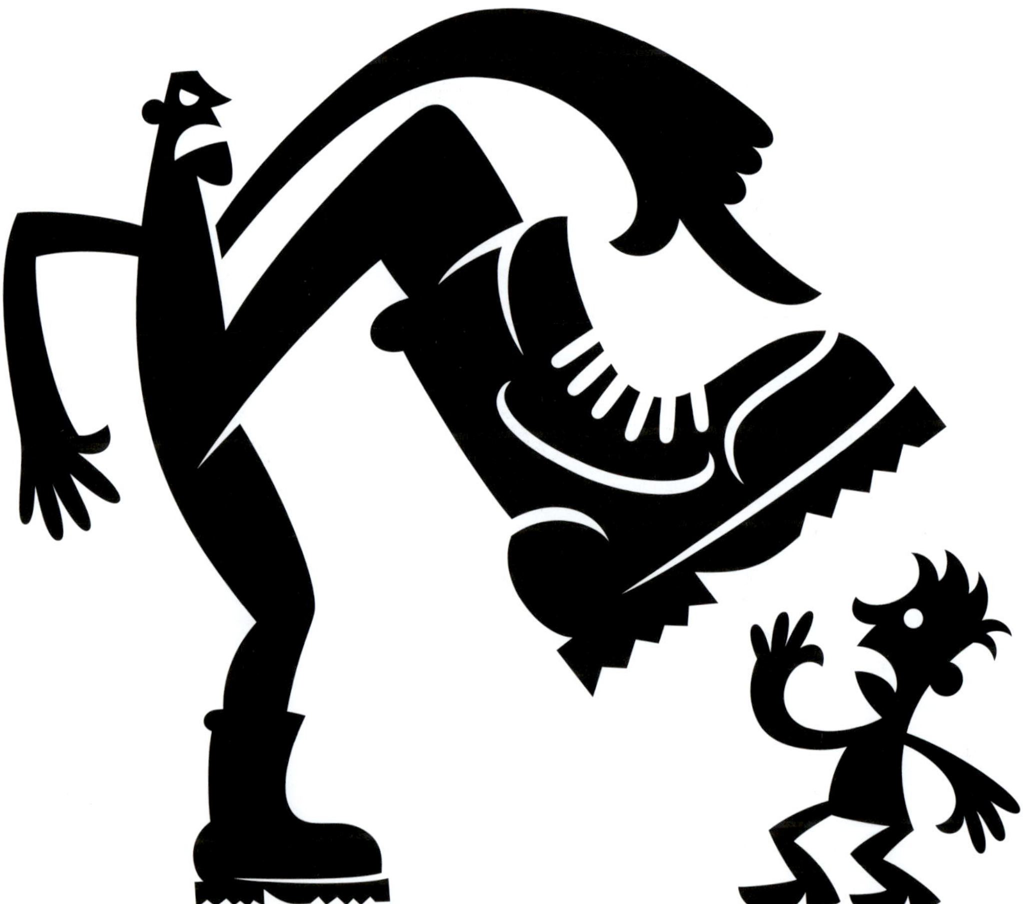

Jackbooted_Thug_**TM211**

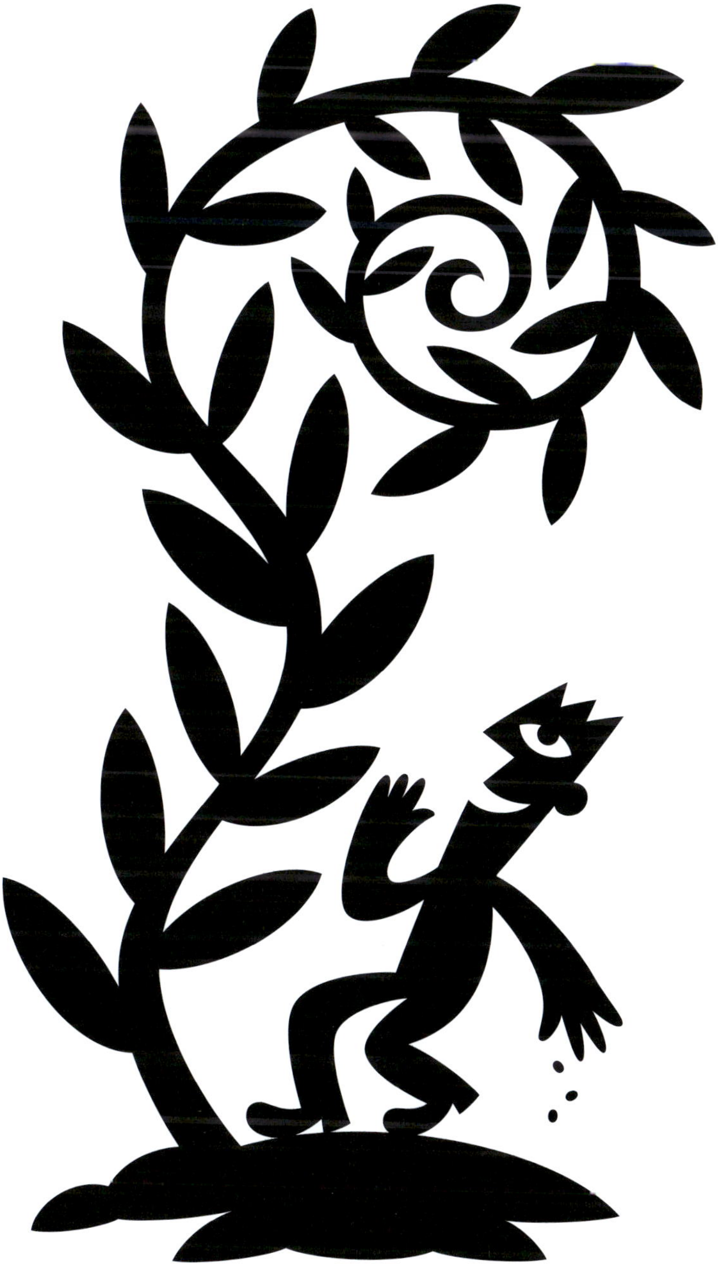

GMO_**TM215**

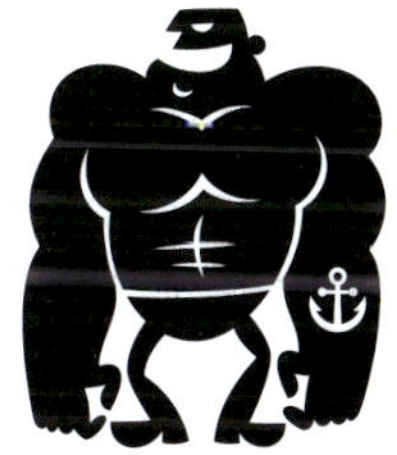

What_A_Goon_**TM212**

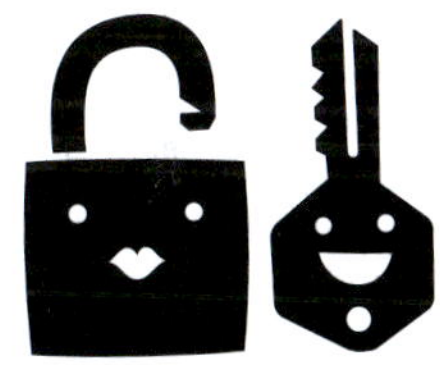

The_Key_To_Love_**TM213**

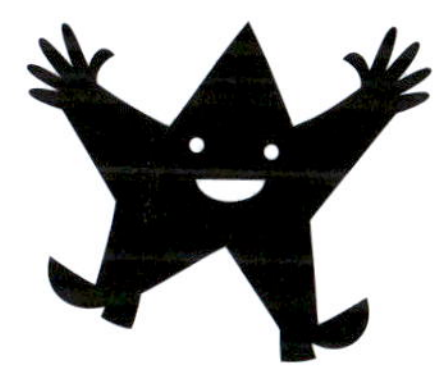

Stardom_**TM214**

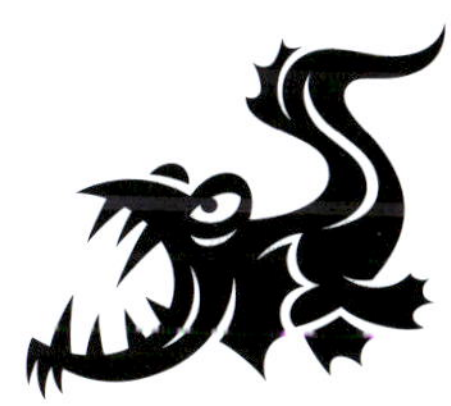

Sea_Serpent_**TM216**

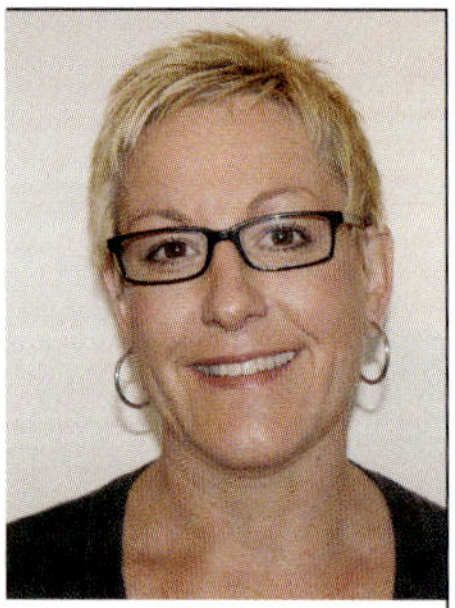

Karen Larson

Principal / Creative Design Director

LMstudio Art & Design • Lathrup Village, Michigan

www.LMstudio.com

I love to combine my passion for art with design anytime I can. So I incorporated my personal love of watercolor with the playful icon graphics in this book. From there I created a digital wayfinding system for a nature preserve, another topic close to my heart. The contrast of the clean iconic forms against the background textures brings the art to life.

Art Used: Nest TM179, Flower Burst TM16, Dog And Bone TM502, Go With The Flow TM866, Charbroiled TM679, Thataway TM247

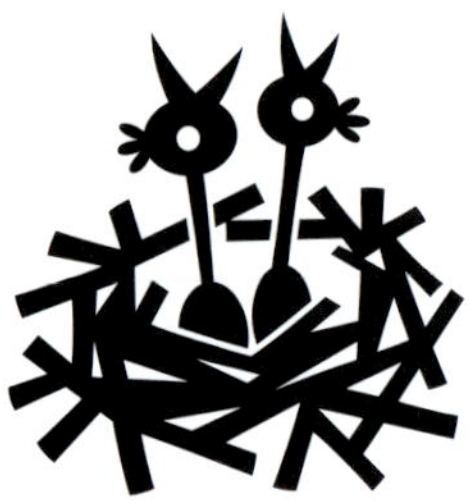
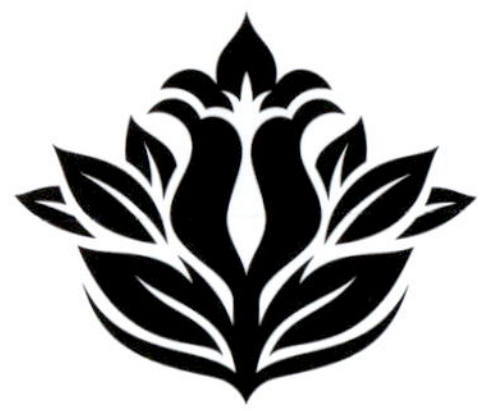
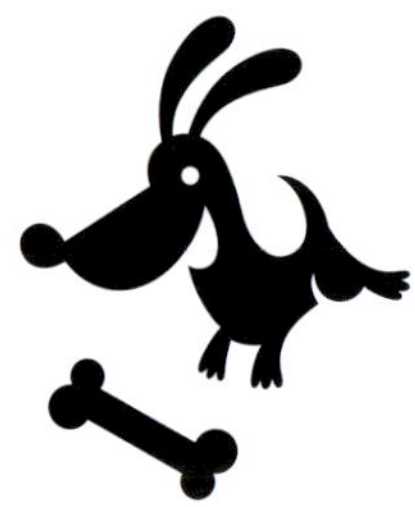

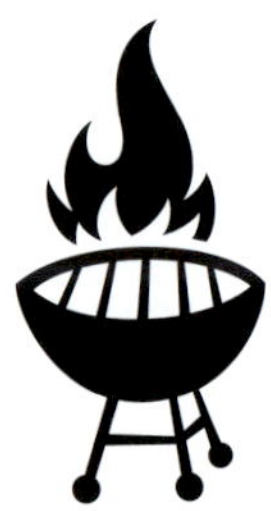
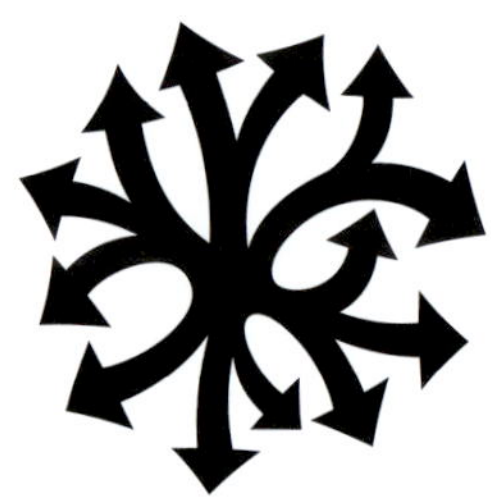

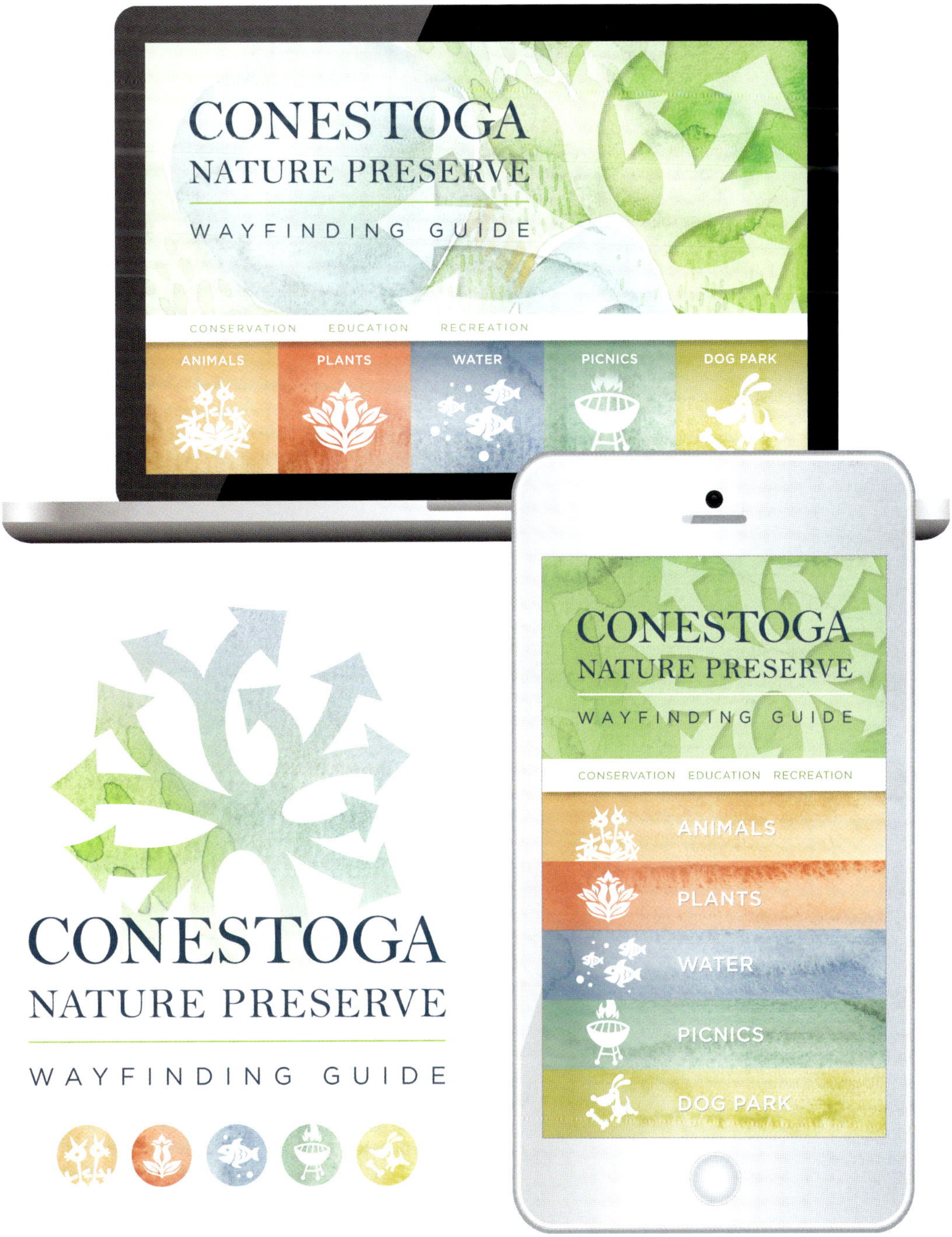

CONESTOGA
NATURE PRESERVE
WAYFINDING GUIDE

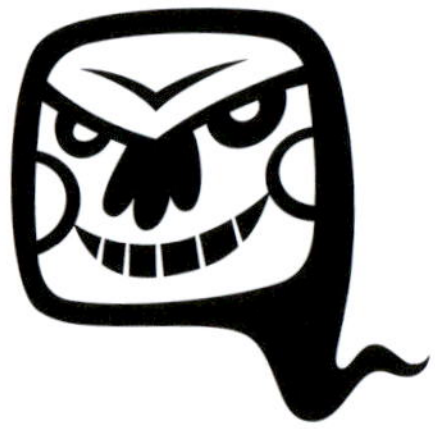
Ancestral_Spirit_**TM217**

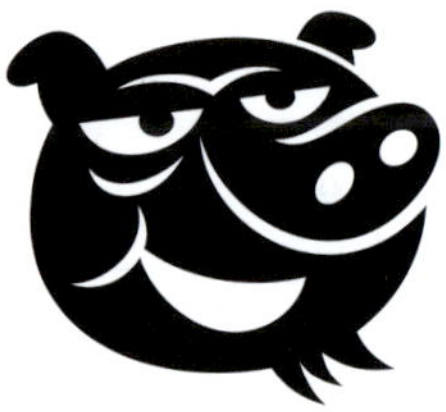
Dont_Be_A_Pig_**TM218**

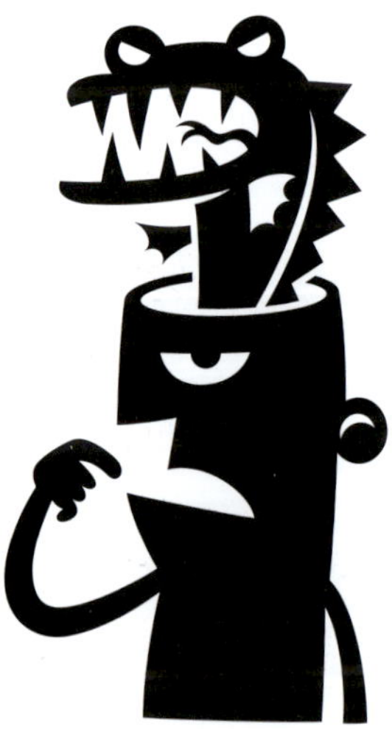
Self_Loathing_**TM219**

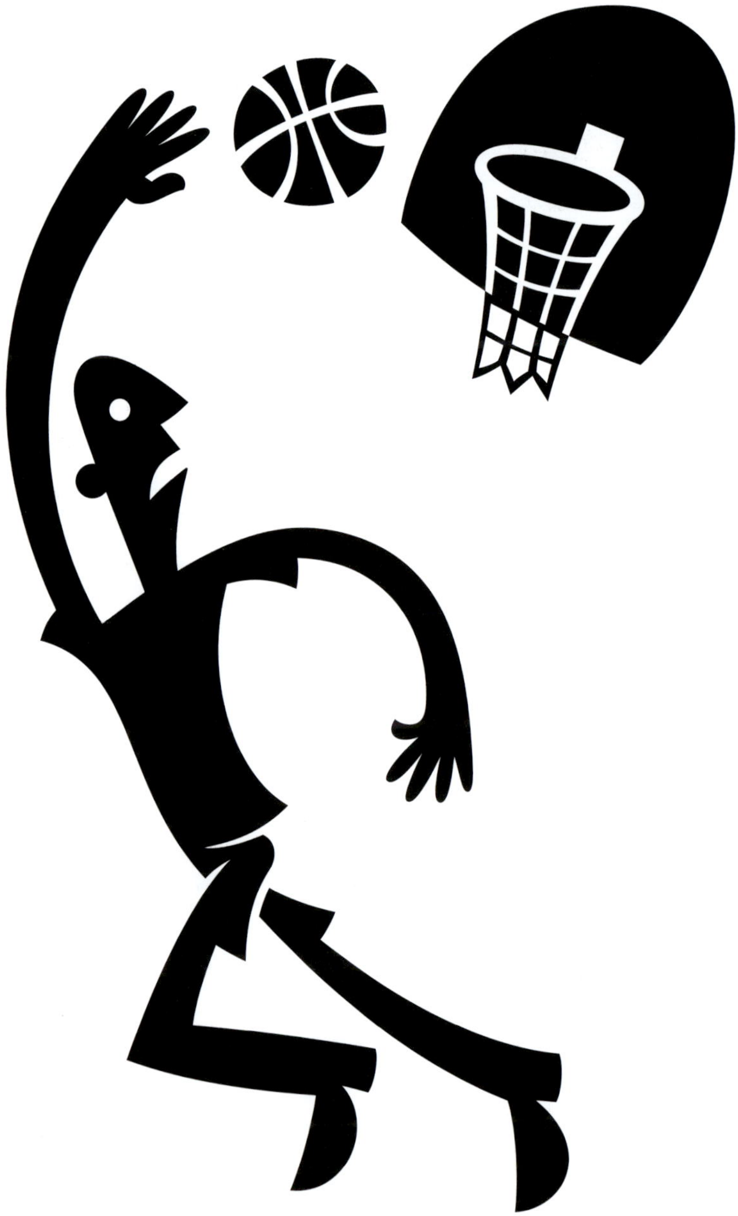
Ballin_**TM220**

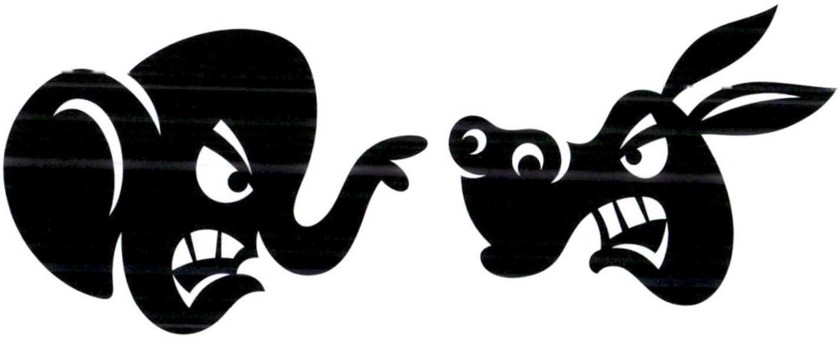

Insanity_**TM221**

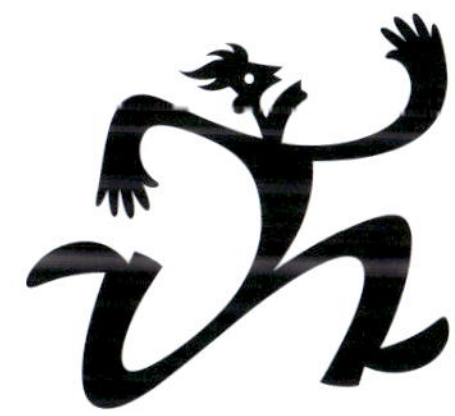

Fleeee_**TM222**

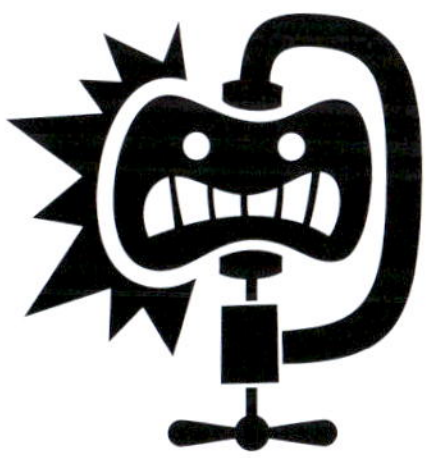

Feeling_The_Pressure_**TM223**

Nice_Fro_Bro_**TM224**

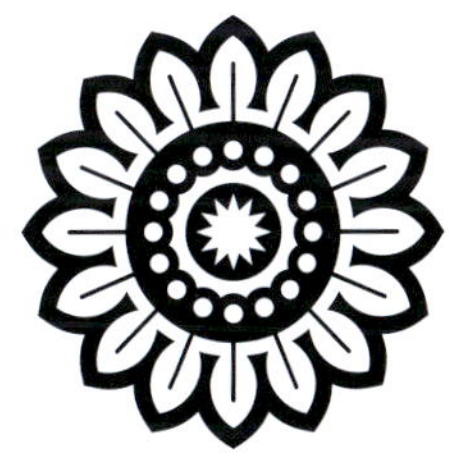

Spiro_Floral_**TM225**

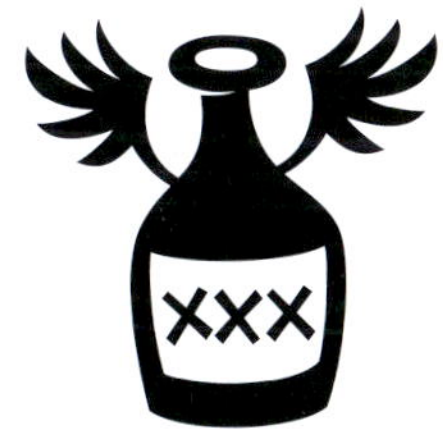

Gimme_Three_Fingers_Of_Hooch_**TM226**

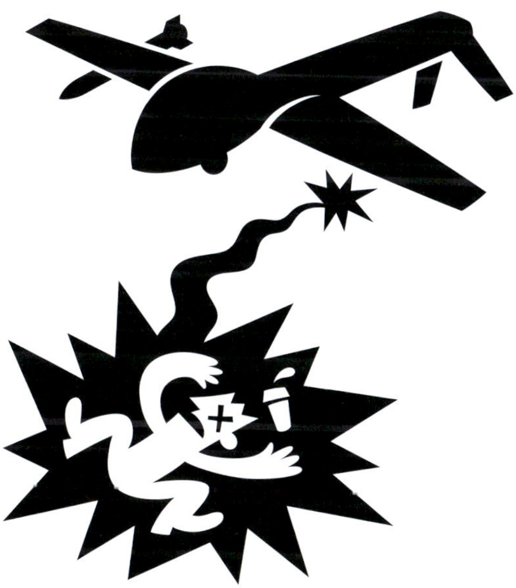

Dont_Drone_Me_**TM227**

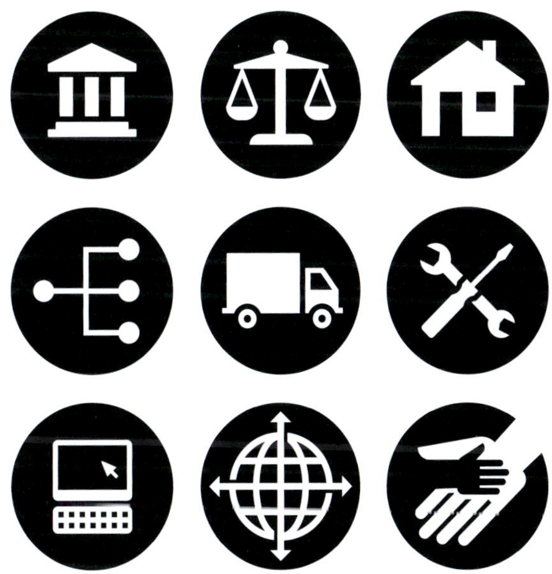

Iconics_**TM228**

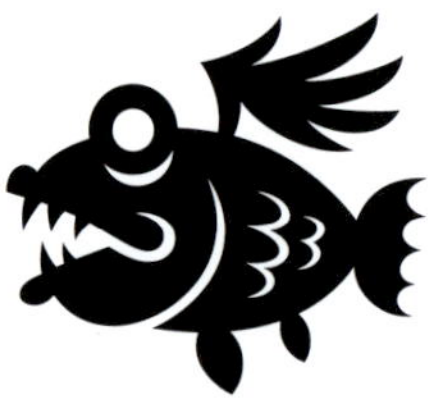

When_Fish_Fly_**TM229**

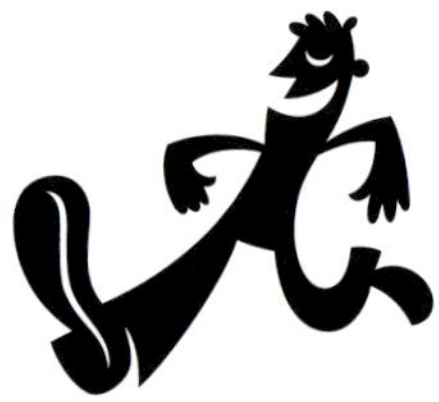

Strut_Your_Stuff_**TM230**

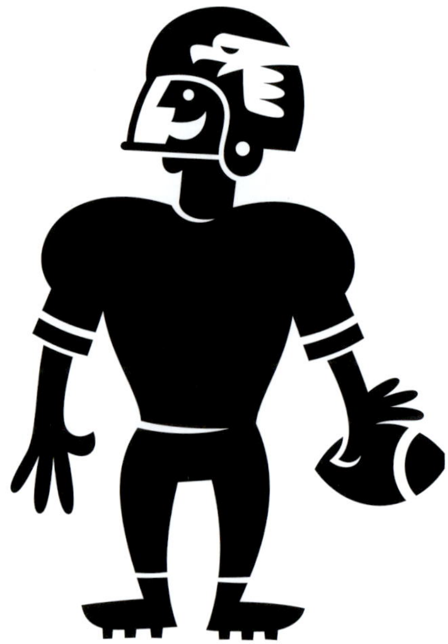

Grid_Iron_Warrior_**TM231**

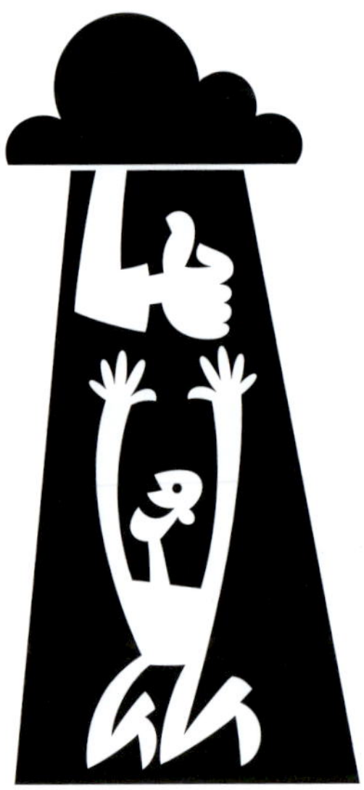

Divine_Approval_**TM232**

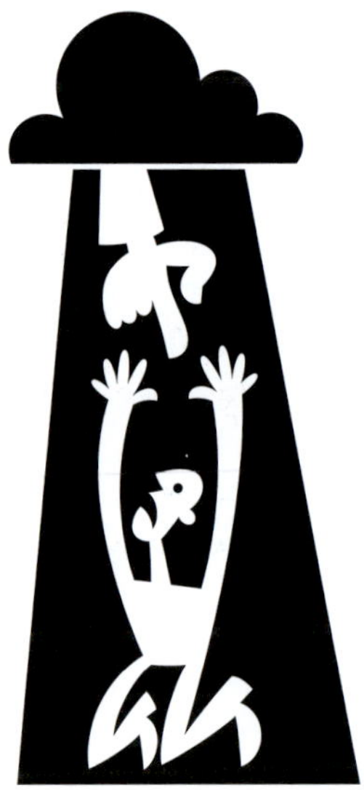

Divine_Judgement_**TM233**

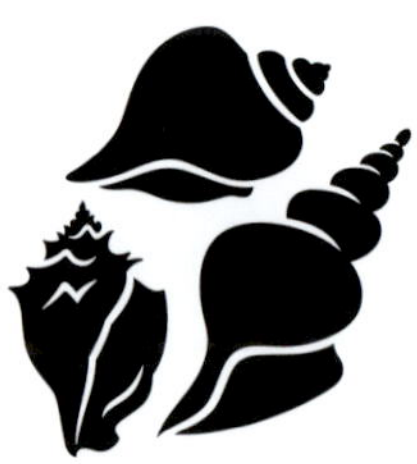

Shell_Shocked_**TM234**

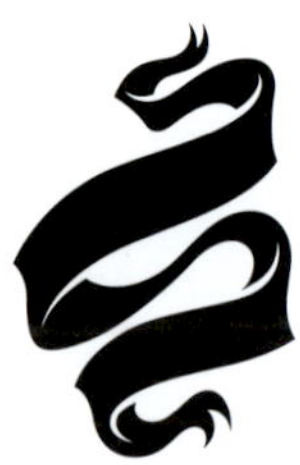

Ye_Olde_**TM235**

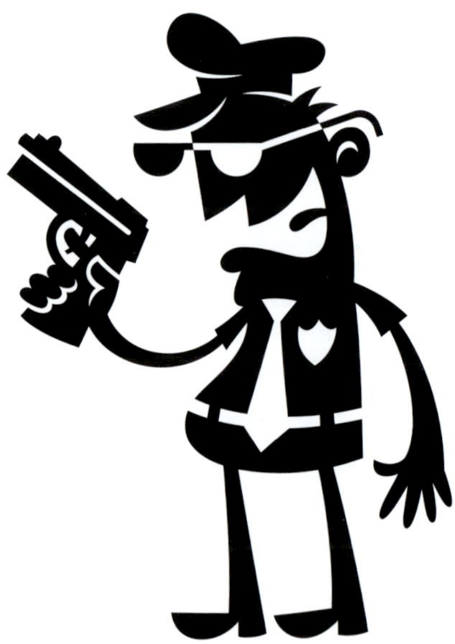

Protect_And_Serve_**TM236**

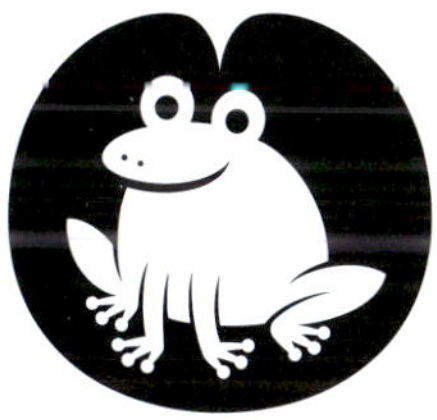

Visit_My_Pad_**TM237**

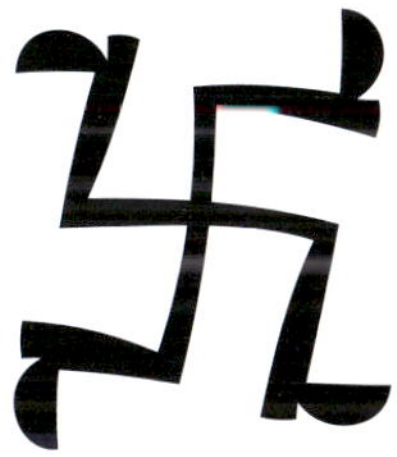

Tyranny_Run_Amuck_**TM238**

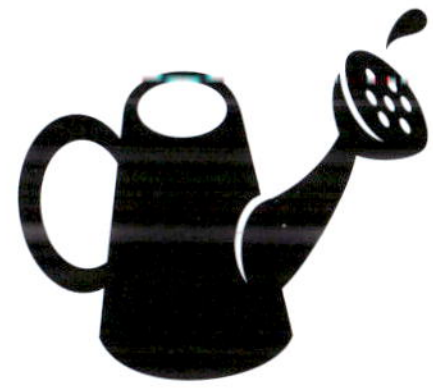

Thirsty_Earth_**TM239**

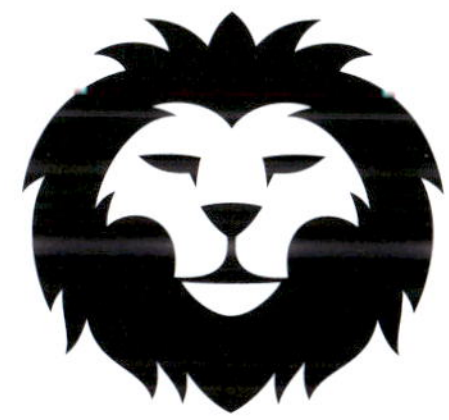

Lion_Hearted_**TM240**

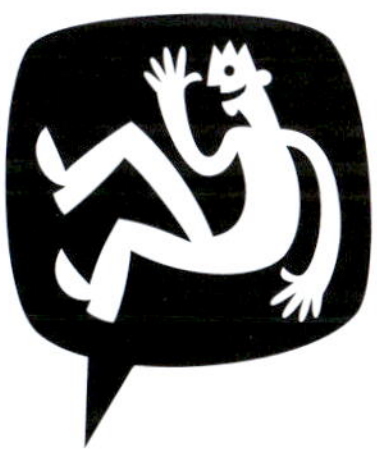

Talk_About_Them_**TM241**

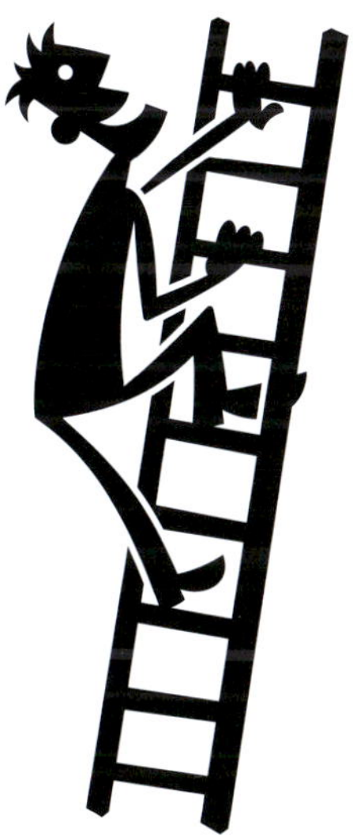

Ascending_**TM242**

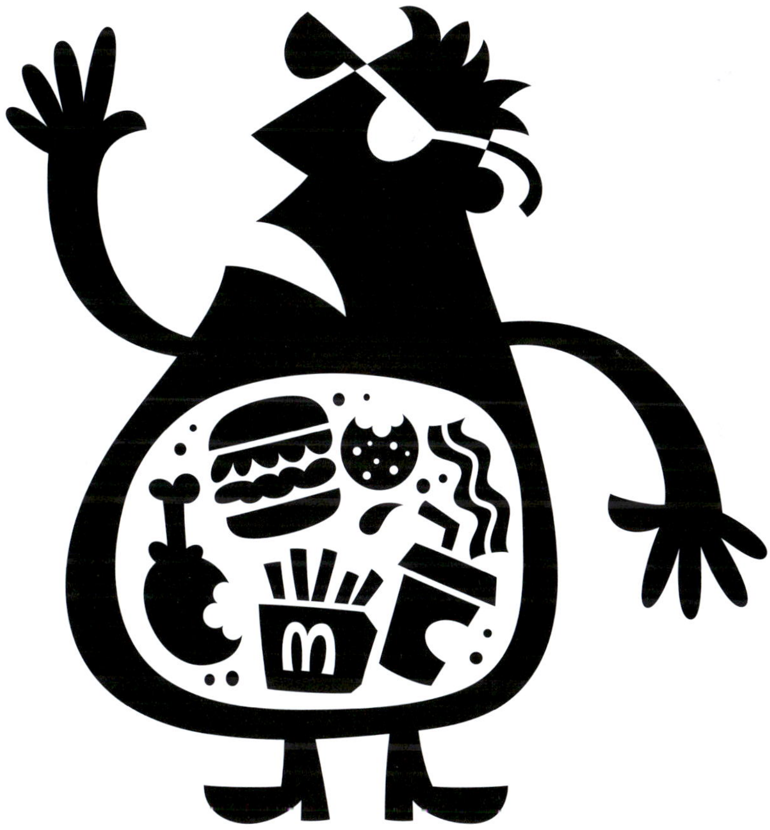

You_Are_What_You_Eat_**TM243**

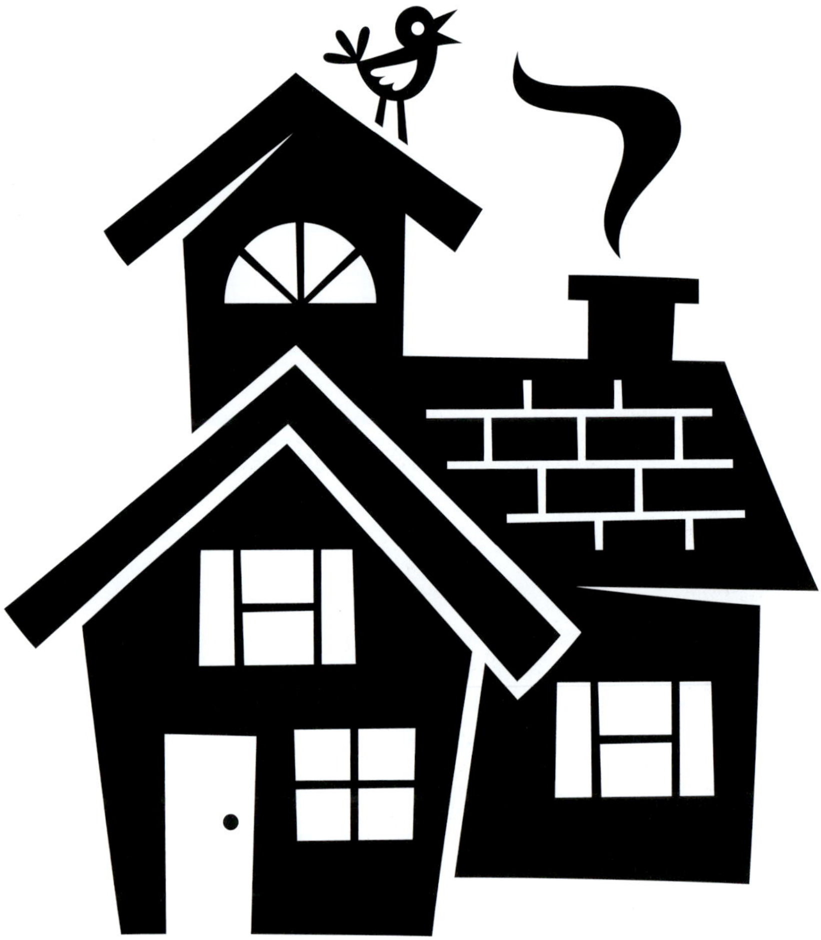

Mi_Casa_Es_Su_Casa_**TM244**

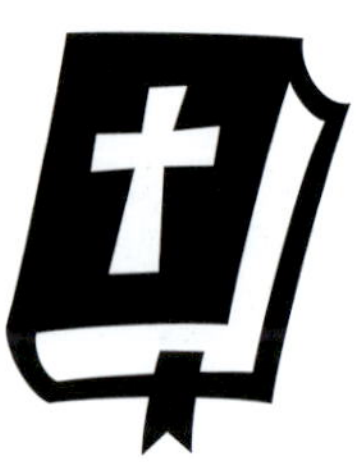

Bible_Thumper_**TM245**

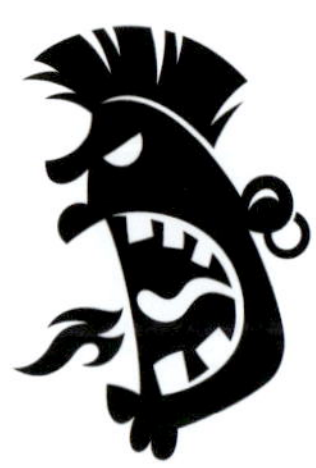

Punk_Rocker_**TM246**

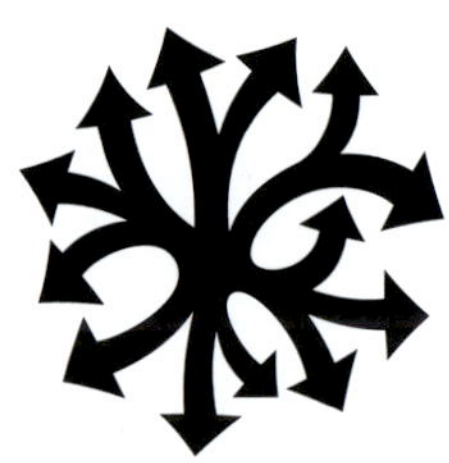

Thataway_**TM247**

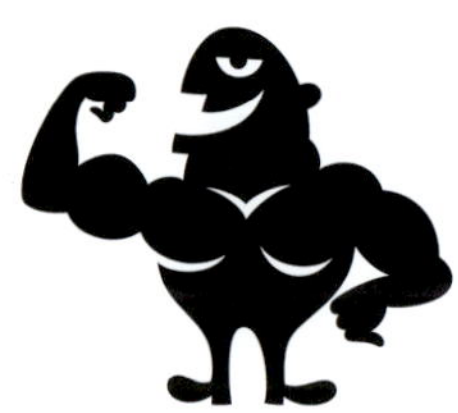

Mr_Beefcakes_**TM248**

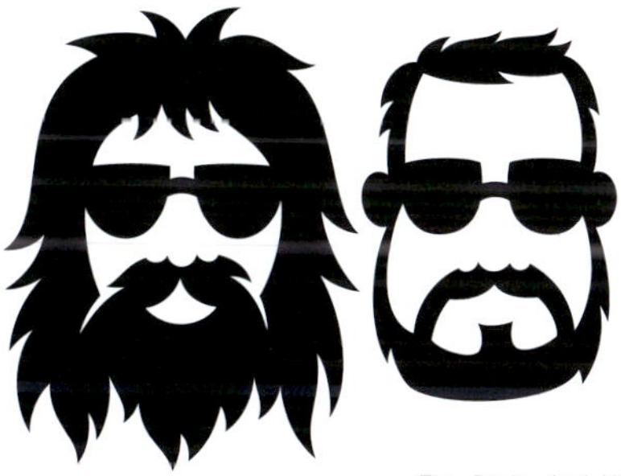

The_Dude_And_Walter_**TM249**

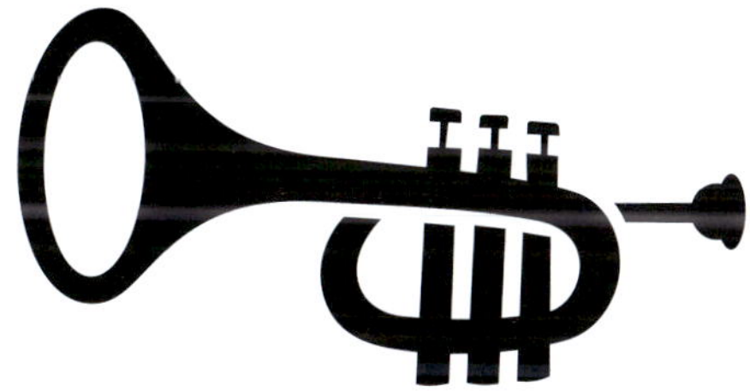

Toot_Your_Horn_**TM250**

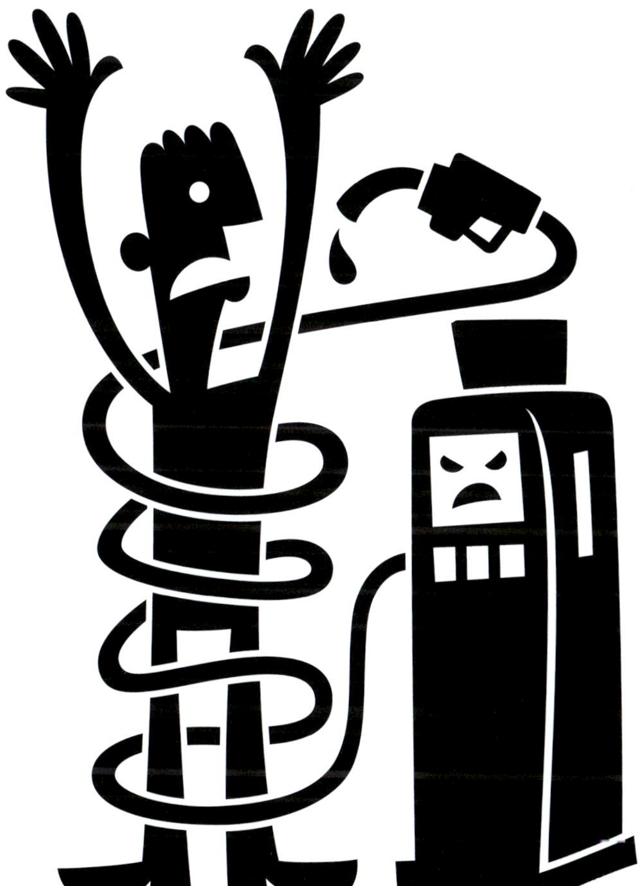

Hostage_Of_The_Economy_**TM253**

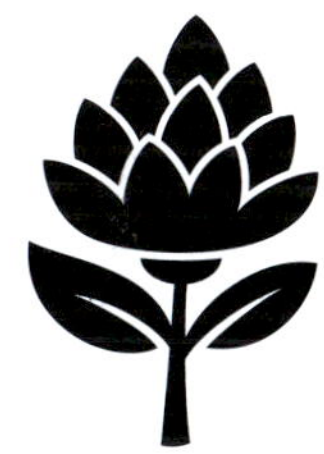

Pollinate_**TM251**

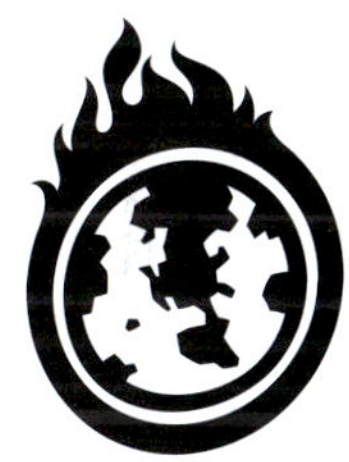

Scorched_Earth_**TM252**

Numero_Uno_**TM254**

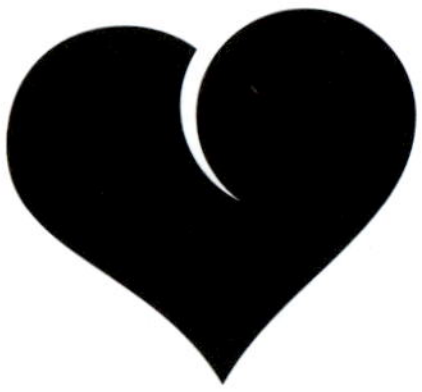

From_The_Bottom_Of_My_Heart_**TM255**

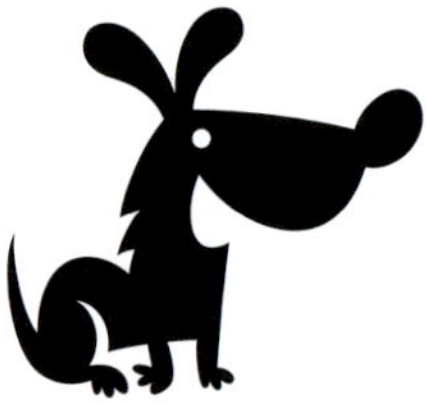

Dog_Gone_It_**TM256**

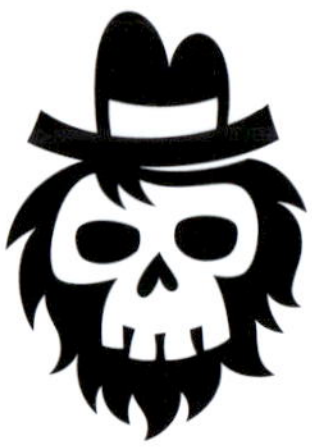

Death_Of_A_Business_Man_**TM257**

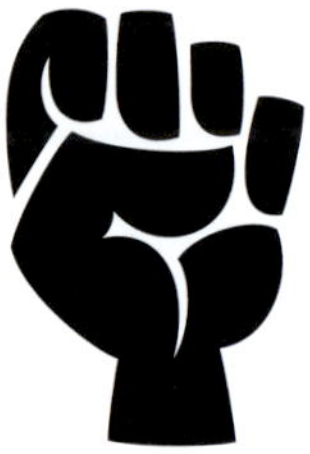

Fight_Powa_**TM258**

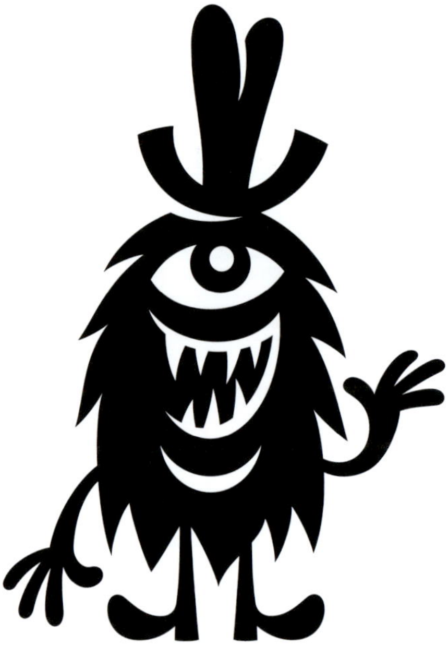

Fuzzy_Wuzzy_**TM259**

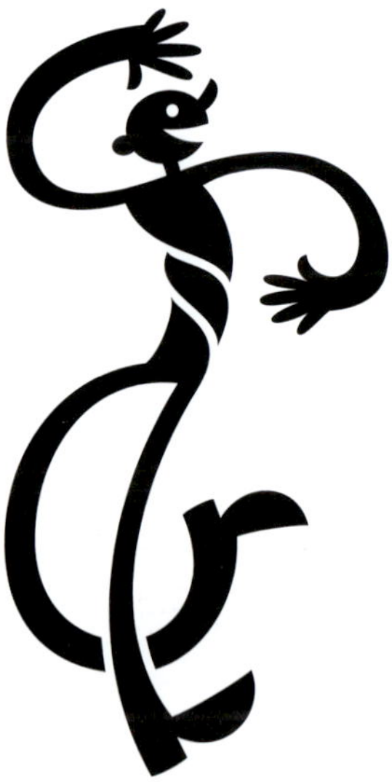

Twisted_Personality_**TM260**

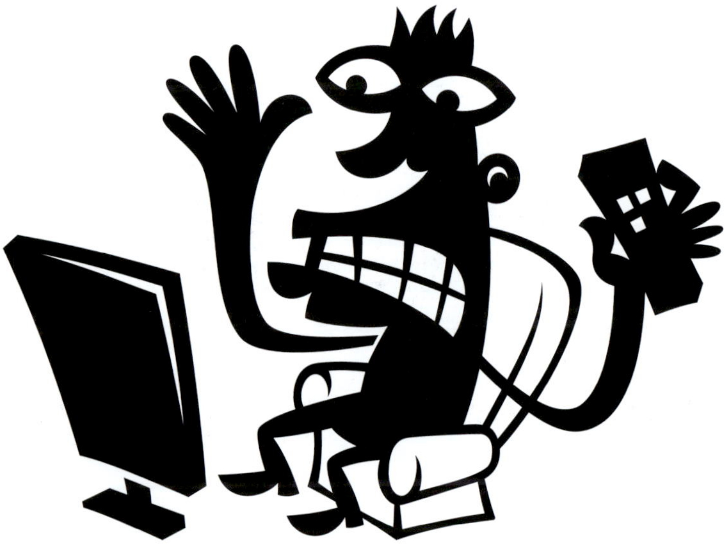

Lame_Stream_Media_**TM261**

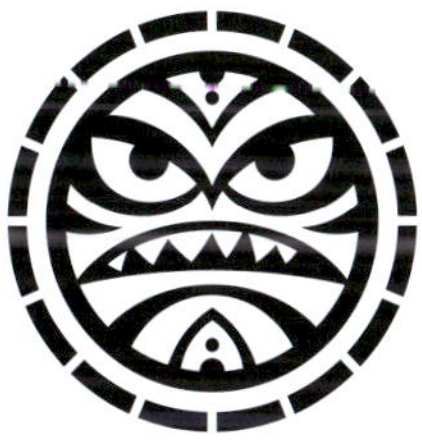

Gremblem_**TM262**

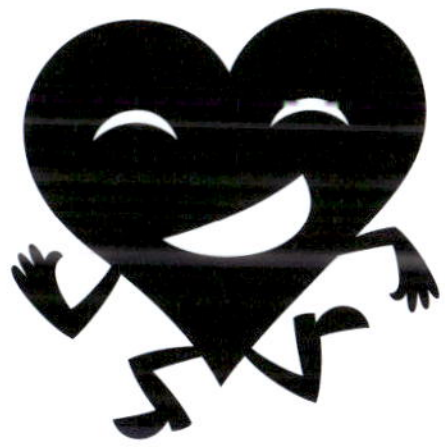

Get_Some_Cardio_**TM263**

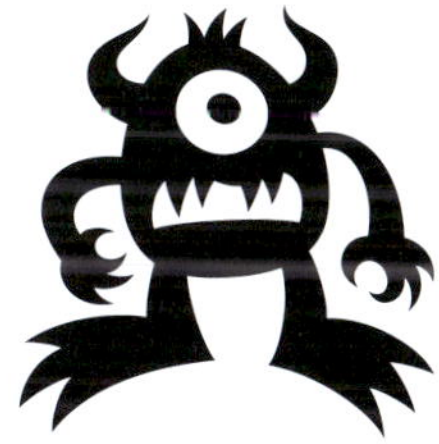

Cycloptic_Kid_**TM264**

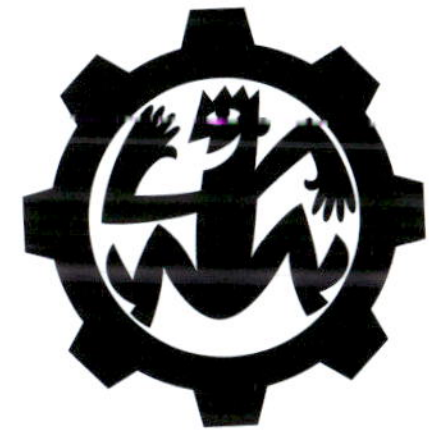

Get_In_Gear_**TM265**

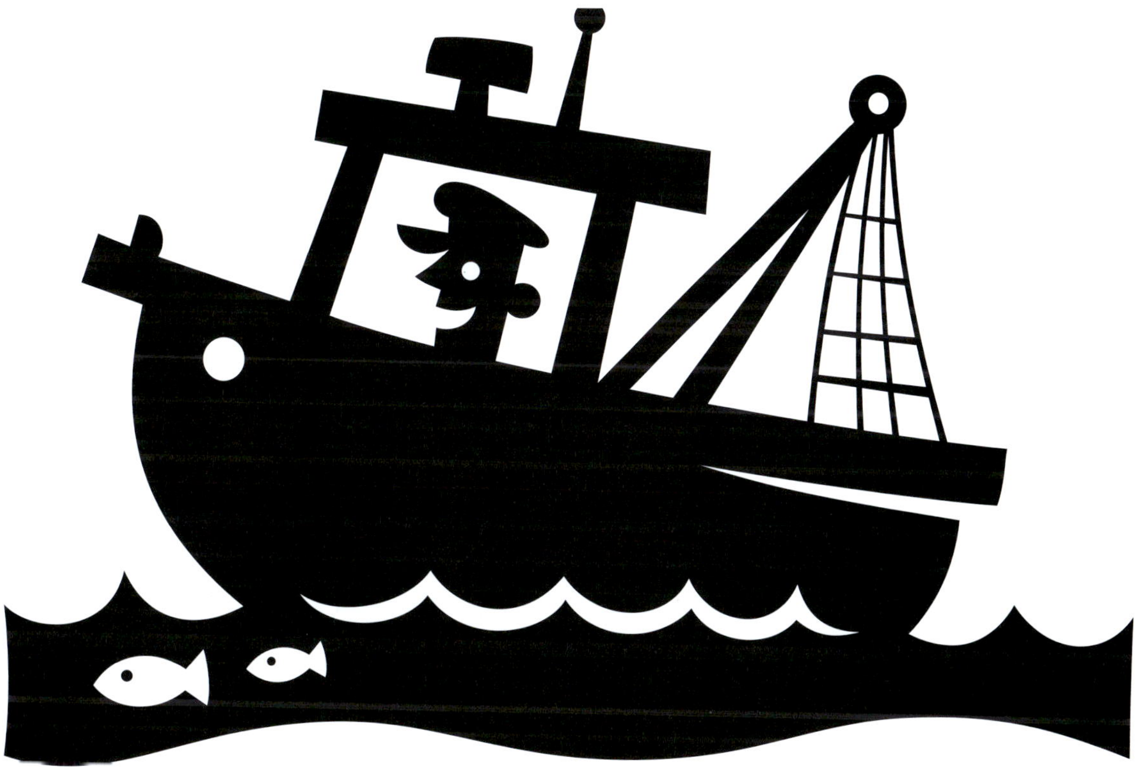

Trolling_**TM266**

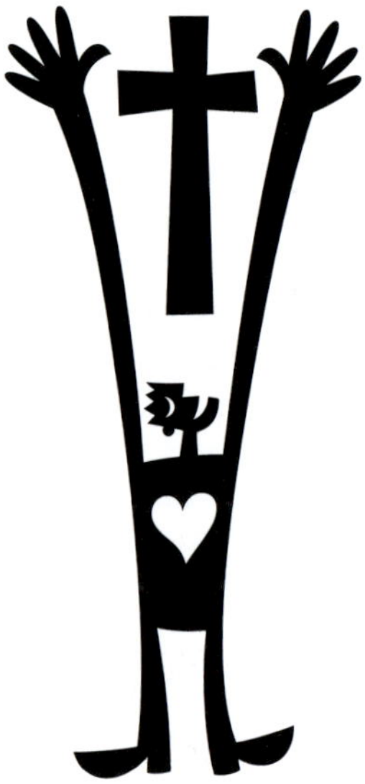

Love_Hymn_**TM267**

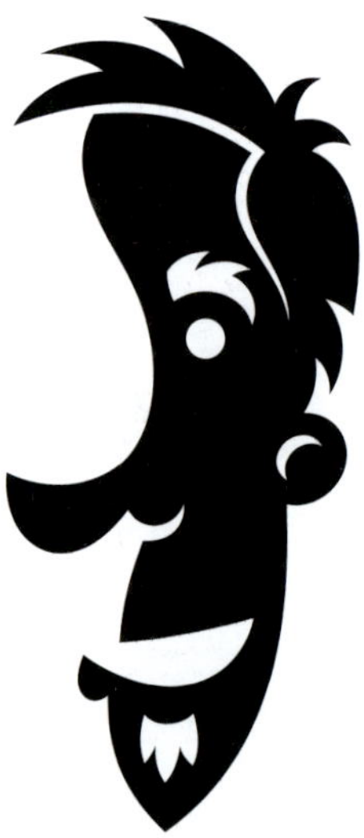

Soul_Patch_**TM268**

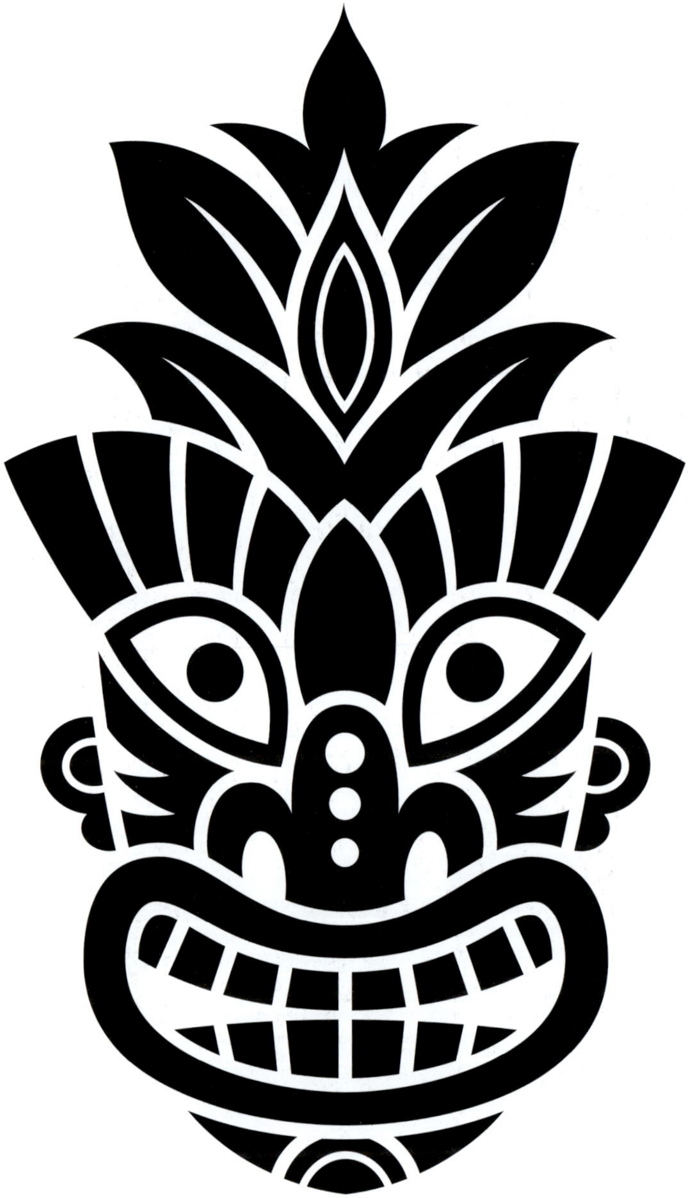

Vector_God_**TM269**

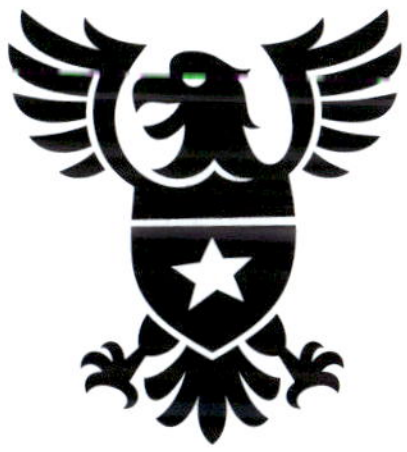

Let_Freedom_Fly_**TM270**

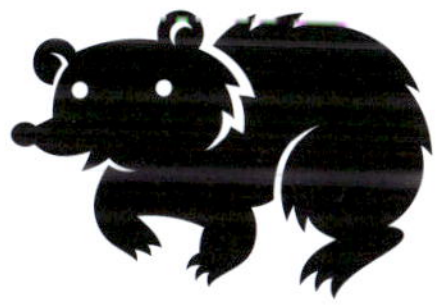

Bear_With_Me_**TM271**

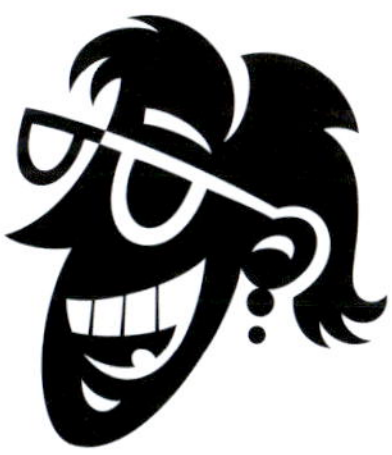

Gleeful_Gossip_**TM272**

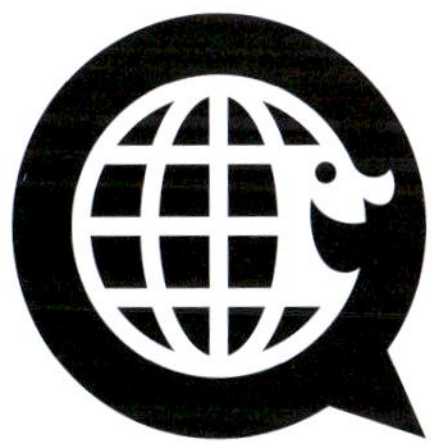

Global_Discourse_**TM273**

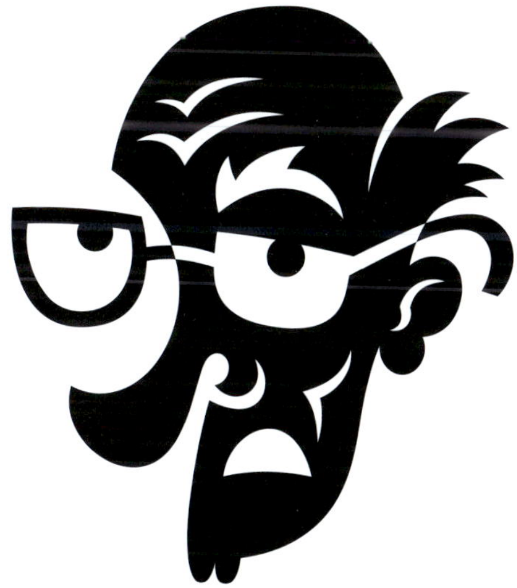

Living_Fossil_**TM274**

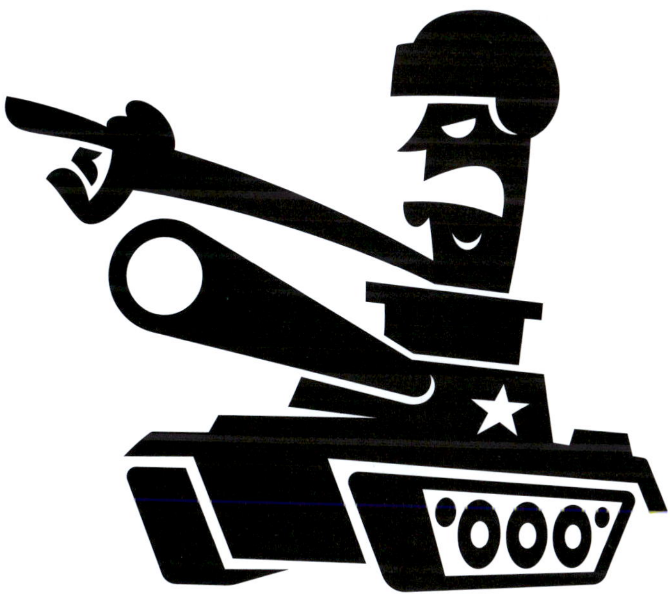

This_Means_War_**TM276**

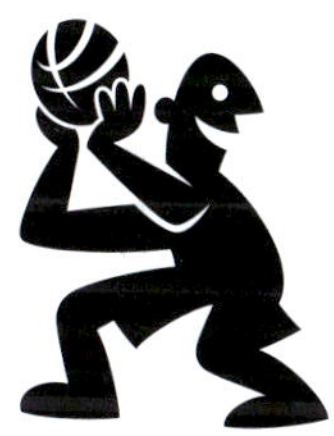

Full_Court_Press_**TM275**

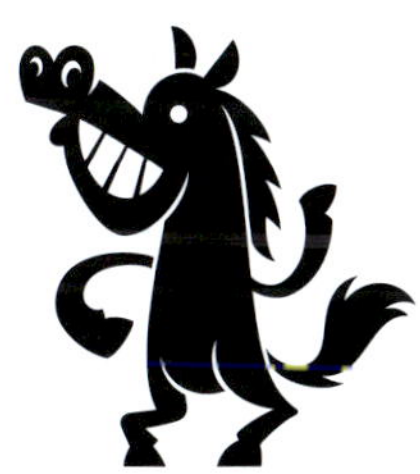

Horses_Ass_**TM277**

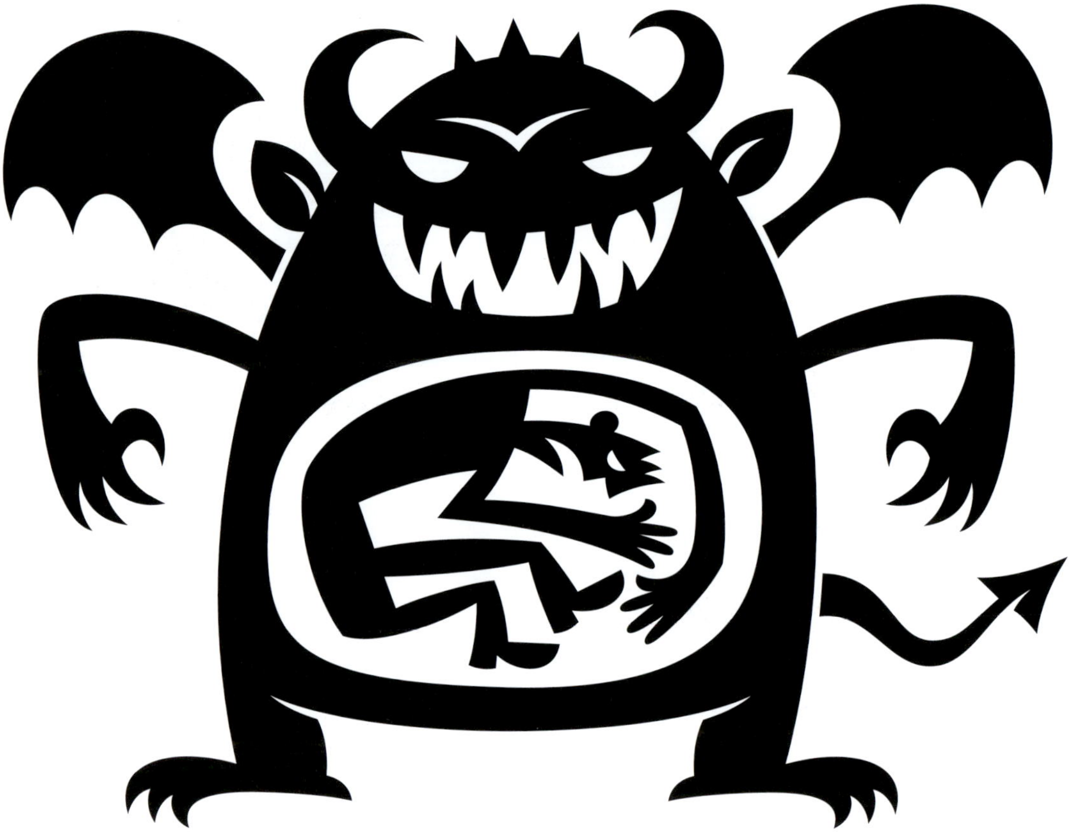

Indigestion_**TM278**

Happy_Birthday_**TM279**

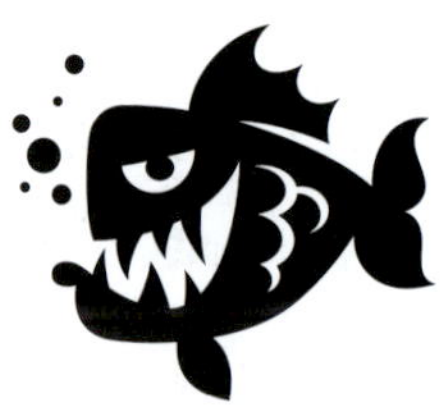

Sinister_Fish_**TM280**

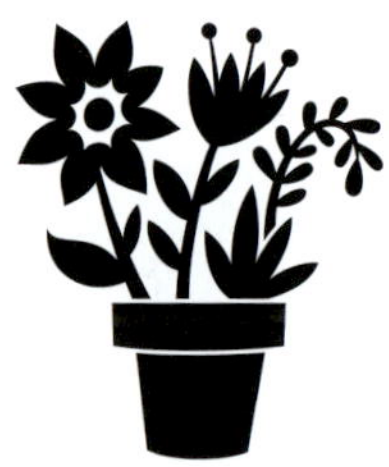

Porch_Garden_**TM281**

Grey_**TM282**

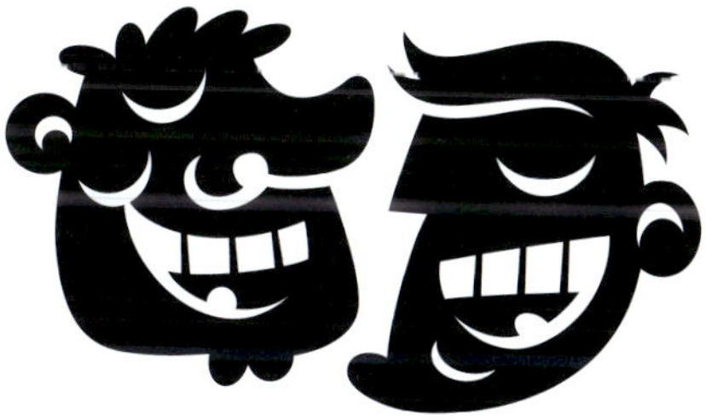
Happy_Talk_**TM283**

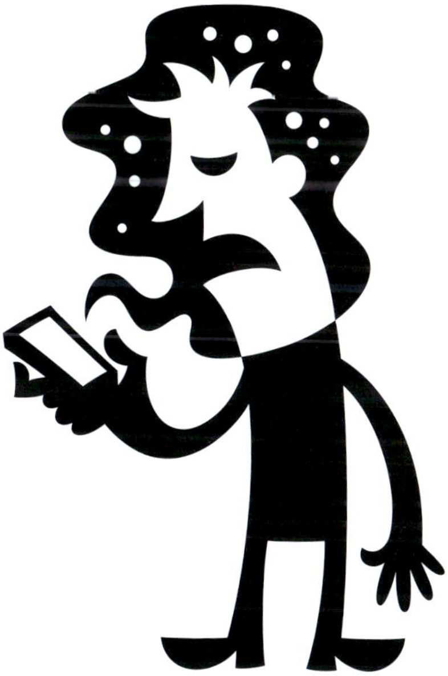
iFog_**TM284**

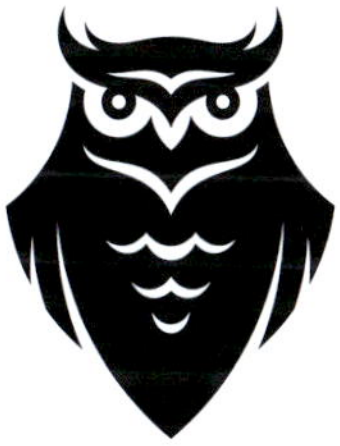
Im_A_Hoot_**TM285**

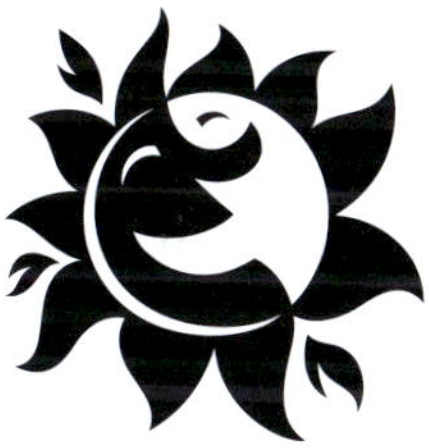
Sweet_Sunshine_**TM286**

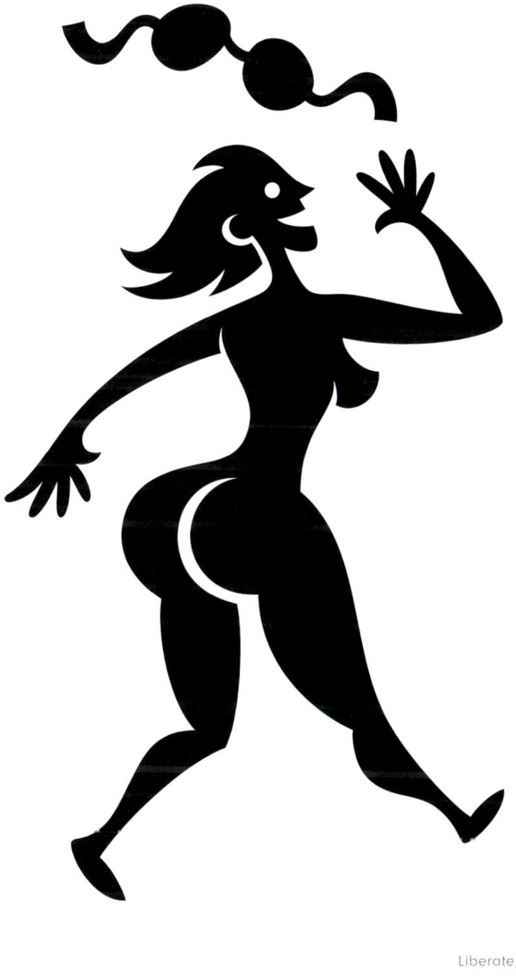
Liberate_**TM287**

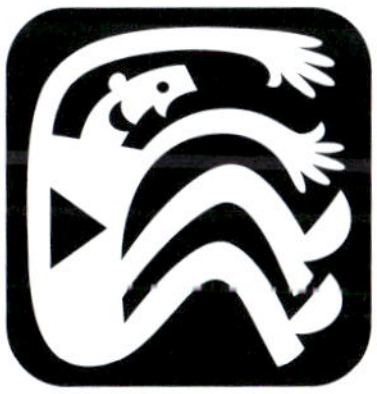
Play_It_**TM288**

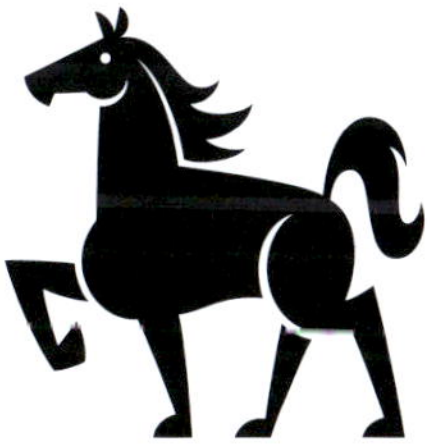
Trusty_Steed_**TM289**

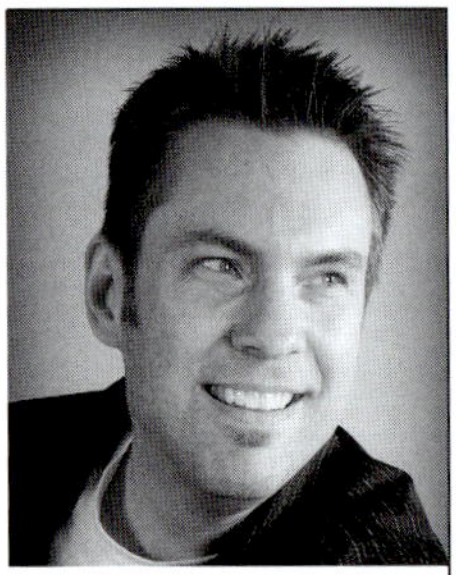

Paul Howalt

Designer / Illustrator

Paul Howalt Illustration • Gilbert, Arizona

www.PaulHowalt.com

I produced this stationery suite for a local transport business here in Arizona. This was an exploration for an updated look to the client's current visual identity.

I was going for a more utilitarian, handcrafted, and assembled look than what the client had been using. The delivery van illustration proved to be the perfect centerpiece for a new "J" arrow logo as well as for checklist forms and the visual language that now surrounds it. The spot graphic also provides just the right amount of whimsical spirit to the potentially boring and rigid genre that many competitors employ.

Art Used: Special Delivery TM172

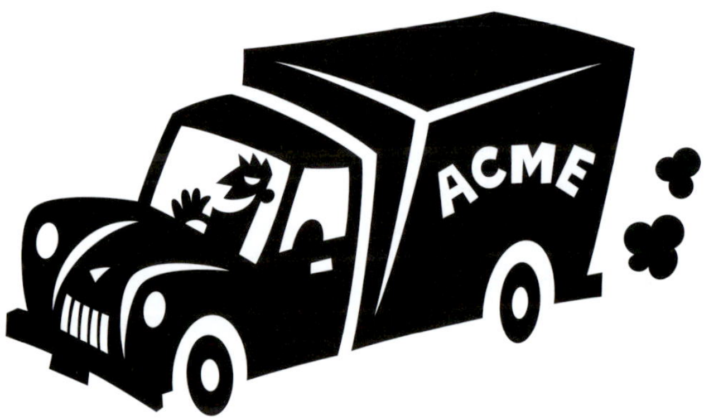

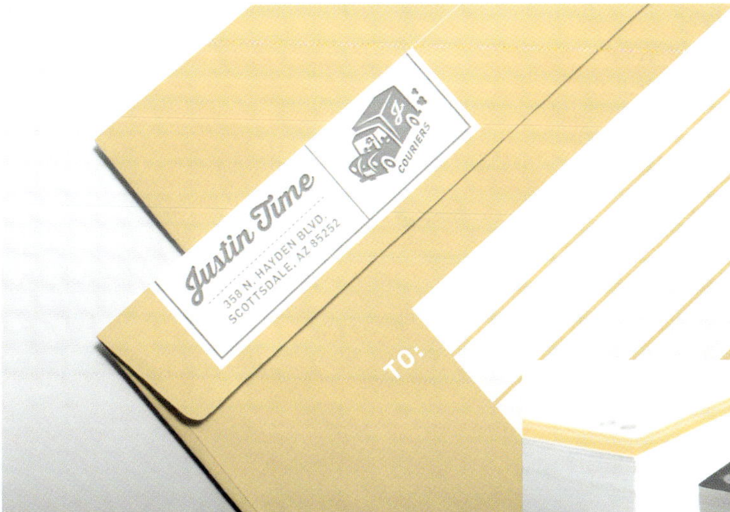
Justin Time
358 N. HAYDEN BLVD.
SCOTTSDALE, AZ 85252
COURIERS
TO:

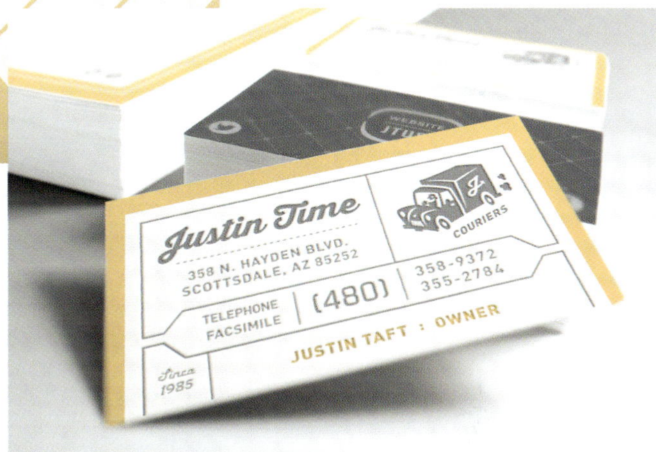
Justin Time
358 N. HAYDEN BLVD.
SCOTTSDALE, AZ 85252
COURIERS
TELEPHONE
FACSIMILE
(480)
358-9372
355-2784
JUSTIN TAFT : OWNER
Since 1985

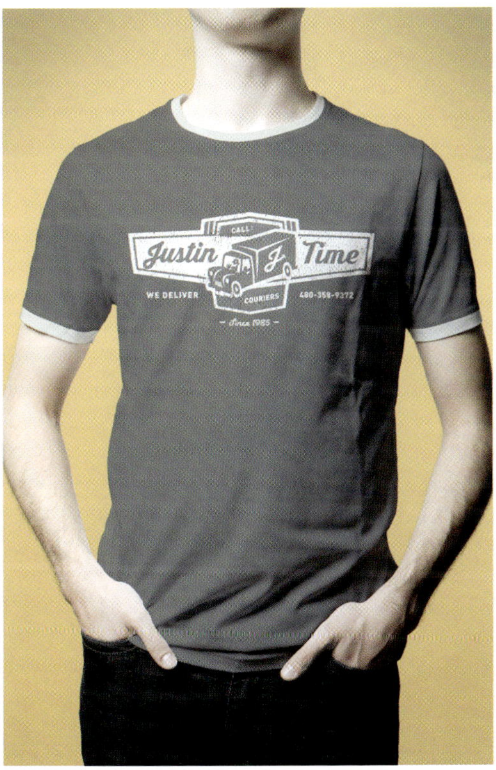
CALL
Justin Time
WE DELIVER
COURIERS
480-358-9372
Since 1985

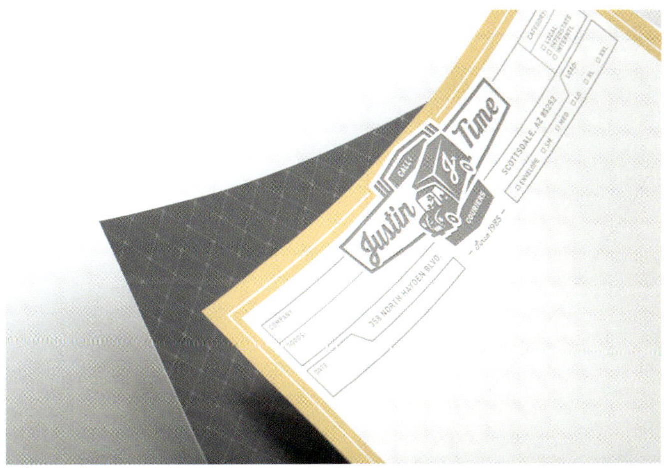
Justin Time
CALL
COURIERS
Since 1985
358 NORTH HAYDEN BLVD.
SCOTTSDALE, AZ 85252

Donut_Gobbler_**TM290**

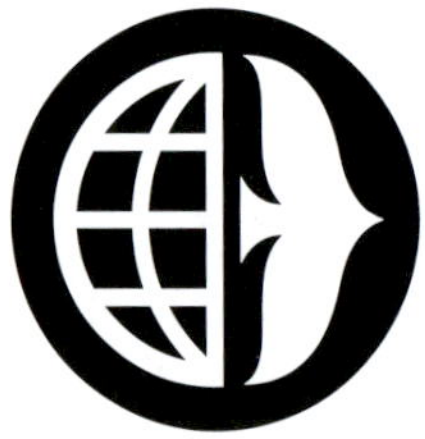

Global_Peace_**TM291**

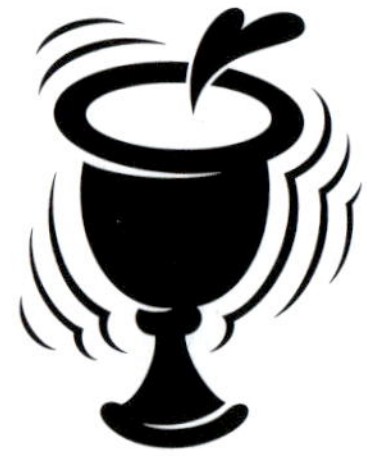

Cup_Of_Trembling_**TM292**

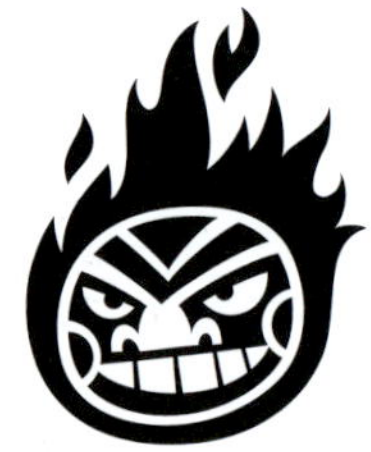

Scorch_**TM293**

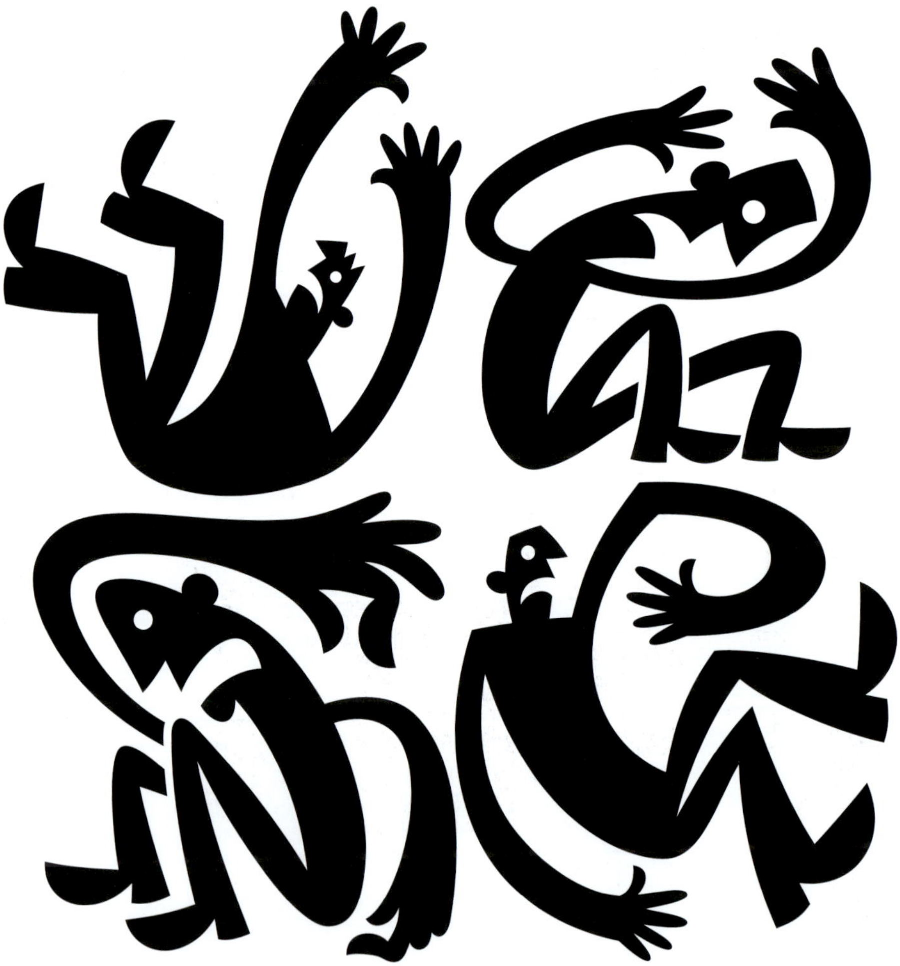

An_Uncomfortable_Reality_**TM294**

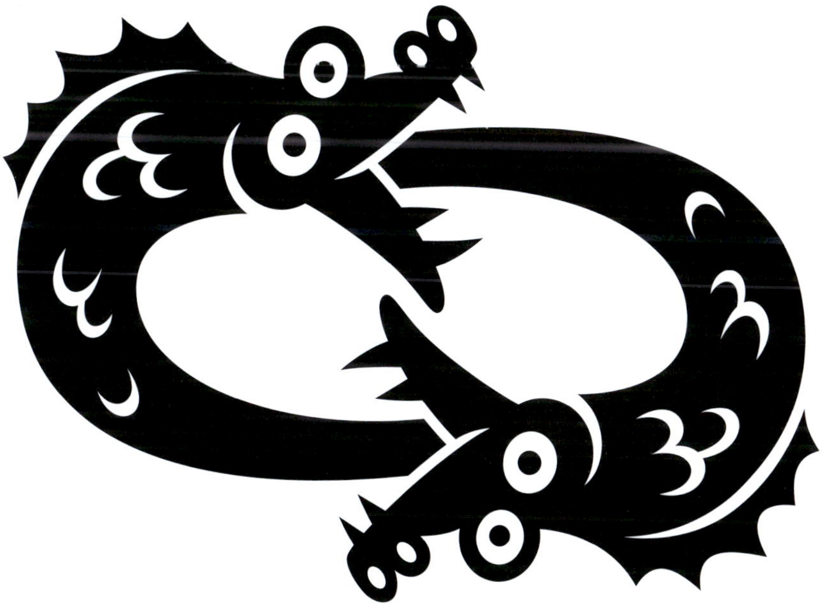

Consumed_**TM295**

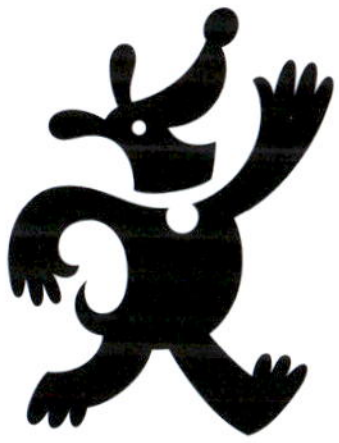

Dog_Day_Afternoon_**TM296**

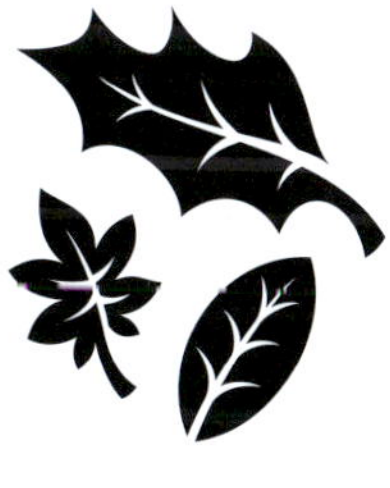

Leafy_**TM297**

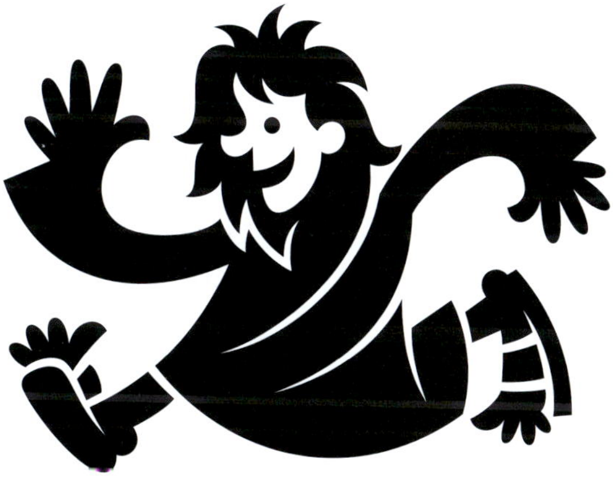

Walk_Like_Jesus_**TM298**

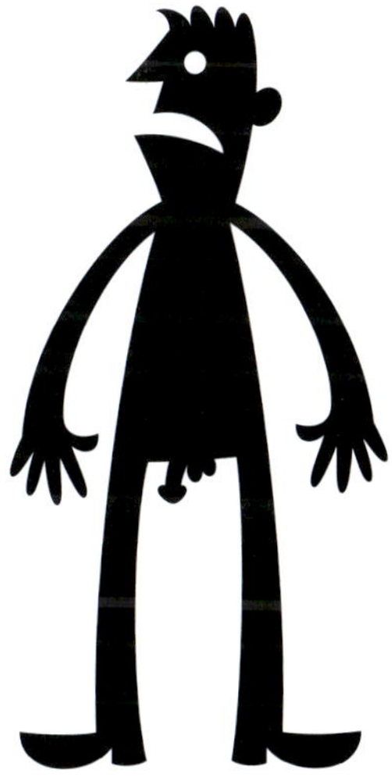

Little_Buddy_**TM299**

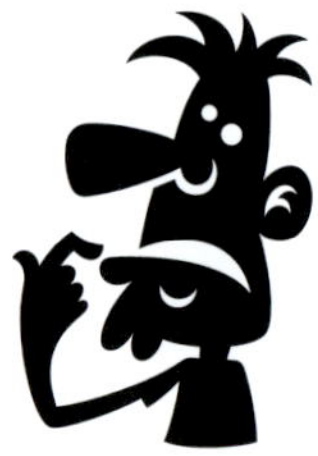

Totally_Clueless_**TM300**

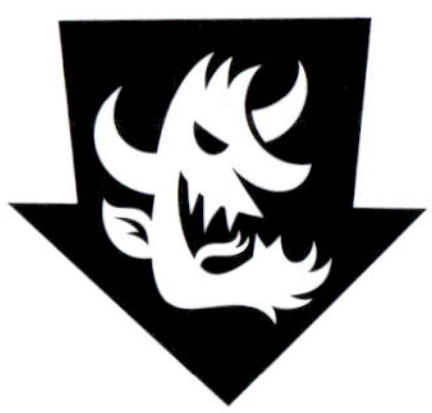

Youre_Going_Down_**TM301**

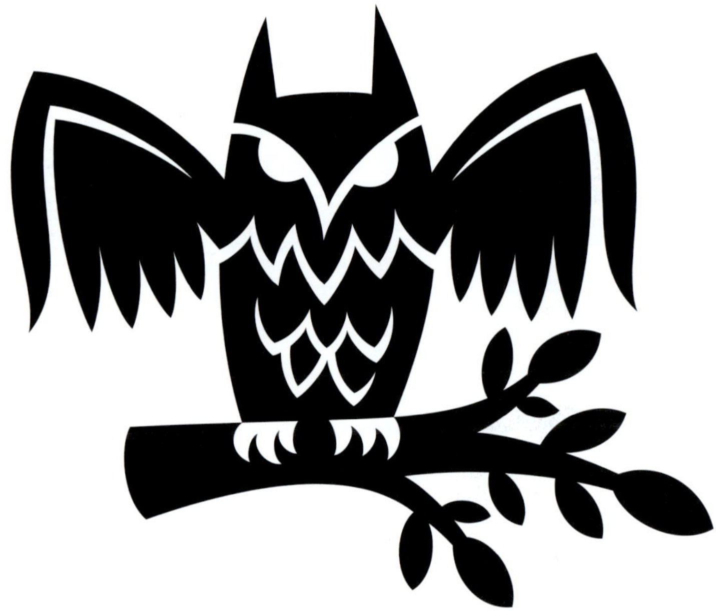

Bohemian_Grove_**TM302**

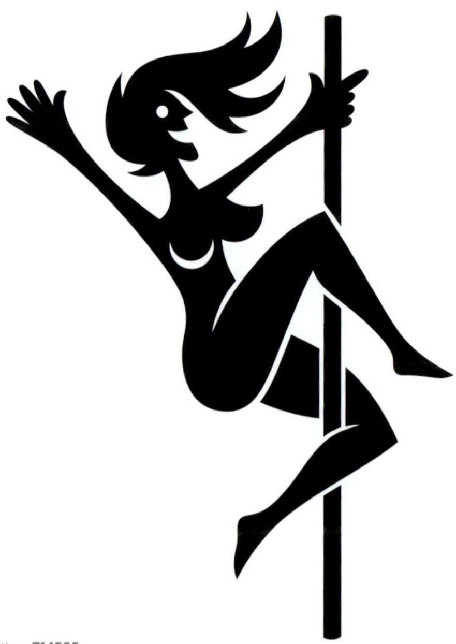

Pole_Position_**TM303**

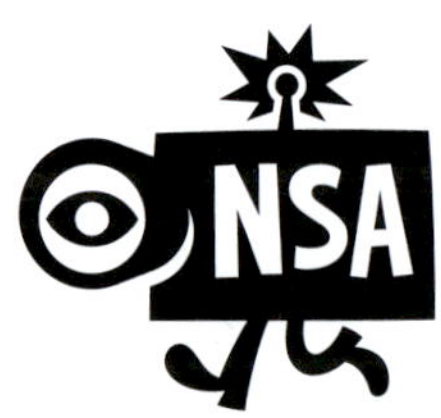

Puzzle_Palace_**TM304**

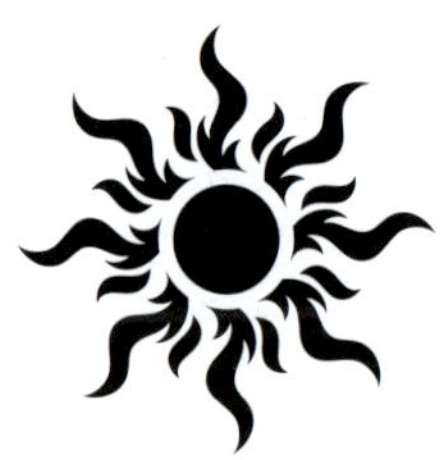

Solar_Flare_**TM305**

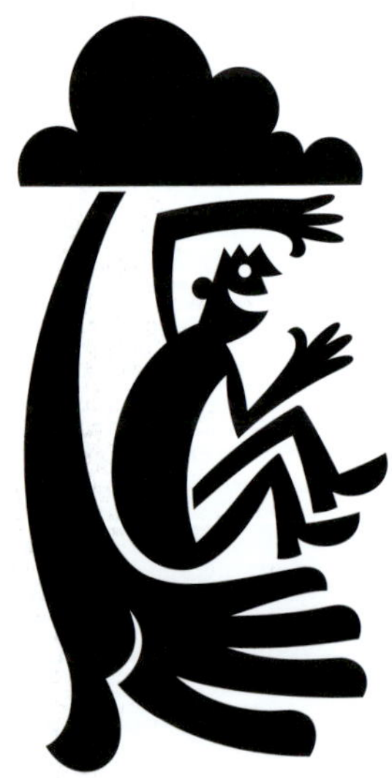

The_Hand_Of_Providence_**TM306**

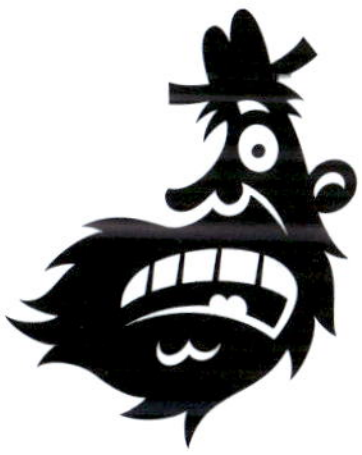

Beard_Of_Doom_**TM307**

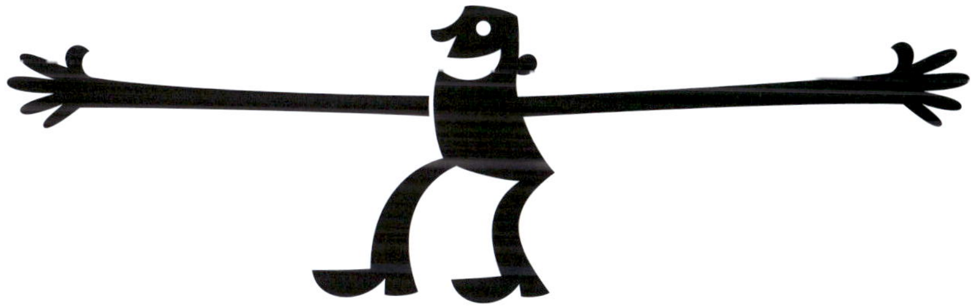

It_Was_Huge_**TM308**

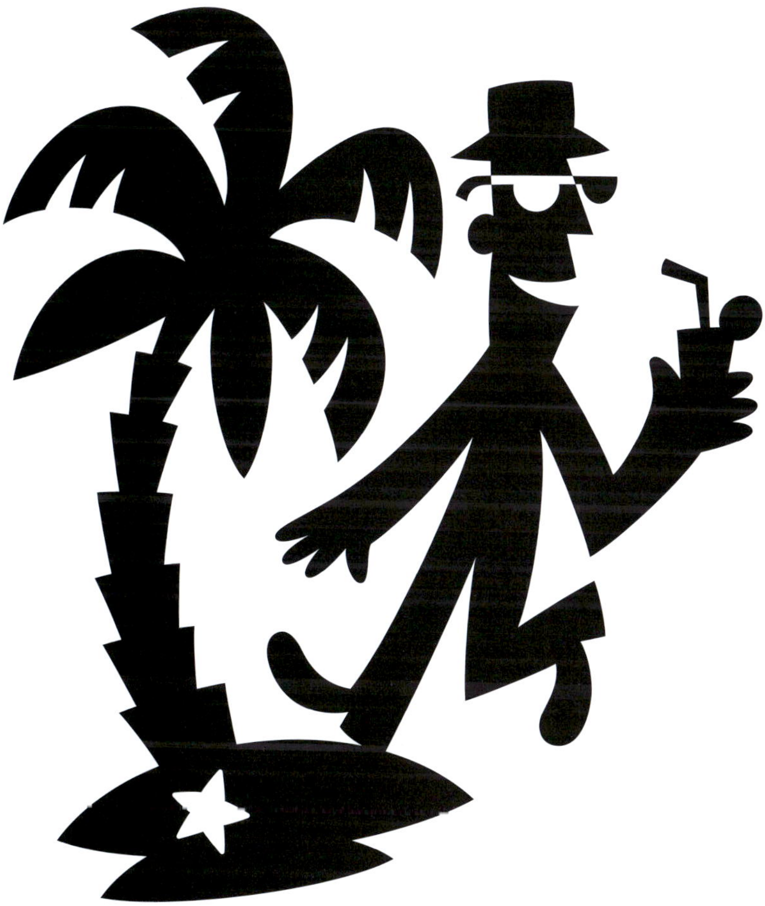

Maui_Mode_**TM311**

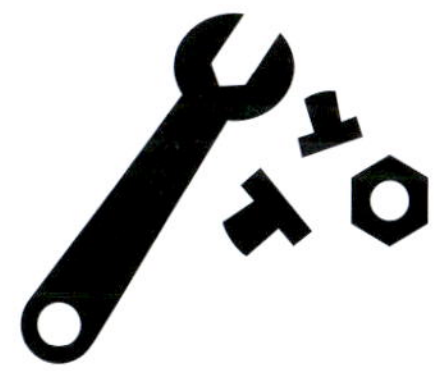

Wrench_And_Bolts_**TM309**

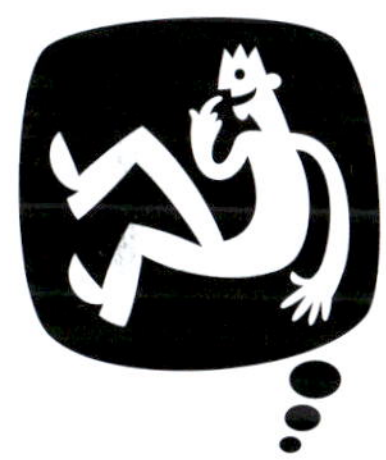

Thinking_Of_You_**TM310**

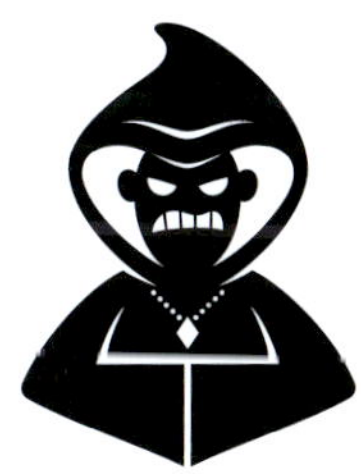

Secret_Society_**TM312**

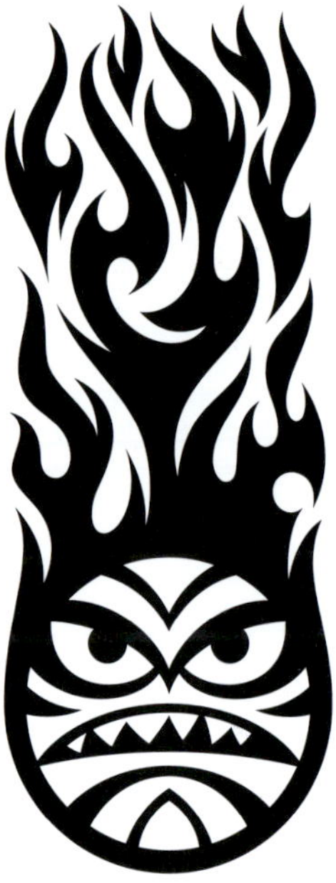

Flame_Out_**TM316**

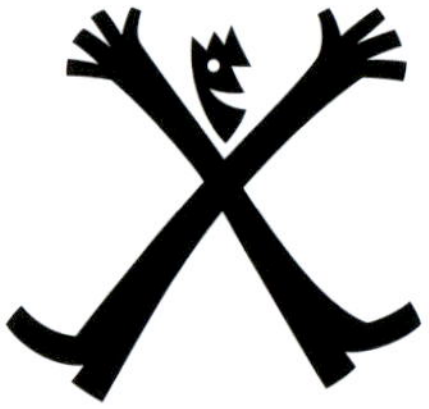

Xcited_**TM313**

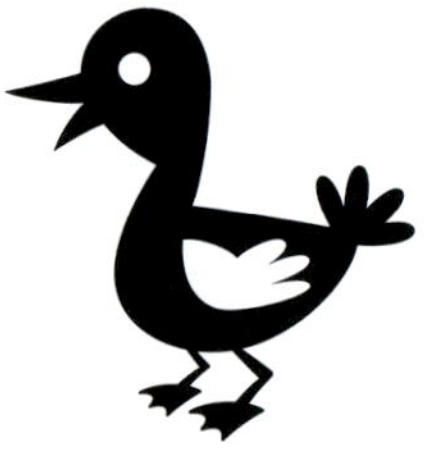

You_Quack_Me_Up_**TM314**

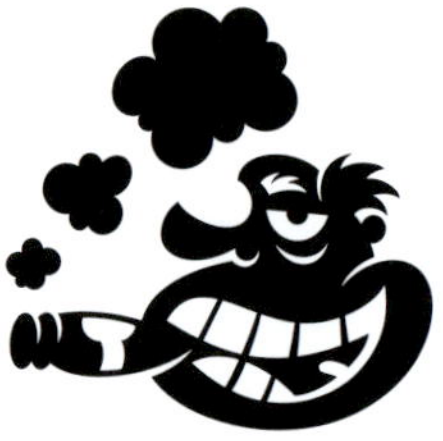

Old_Fogeys_Stogies_**TM315**

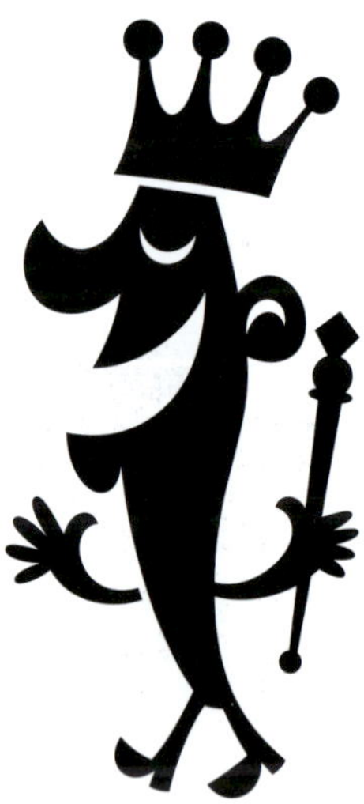

King_Of_Fools_**TM317**

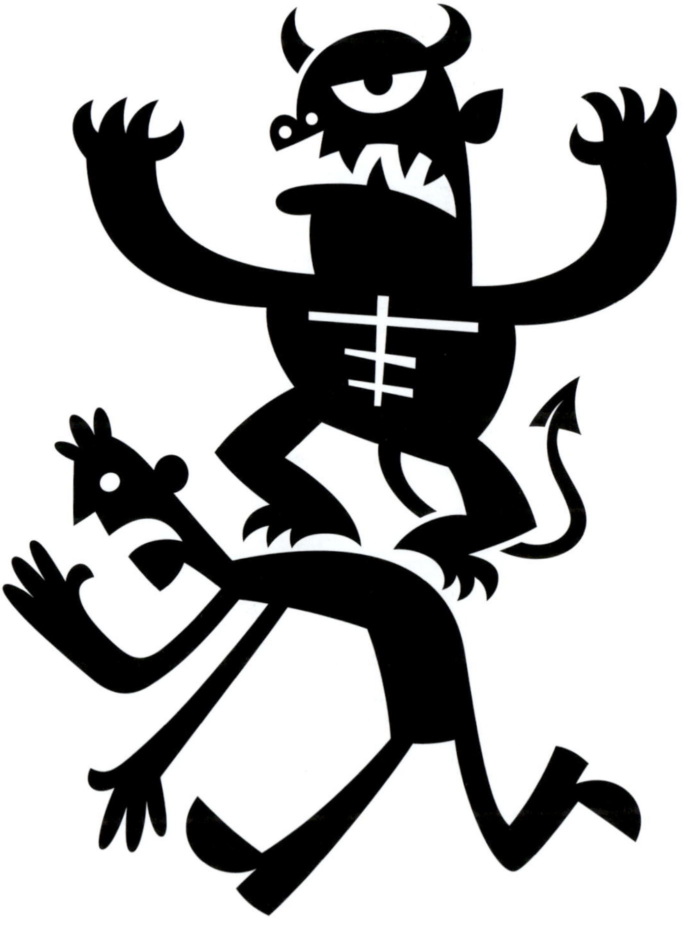

Bare_Your_Burden_**TM318**

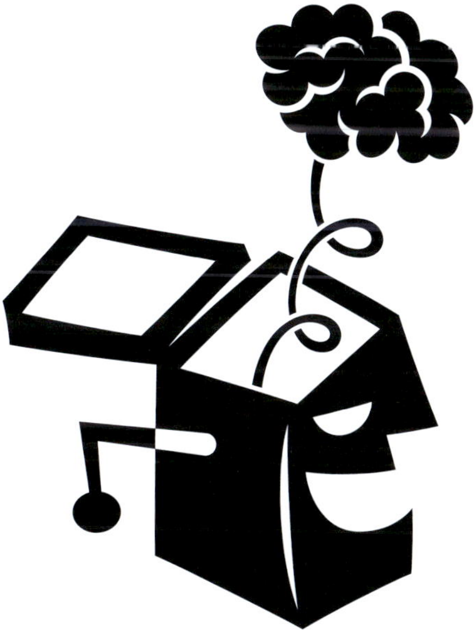

Pop_Goes_The_Idea_**TM321**

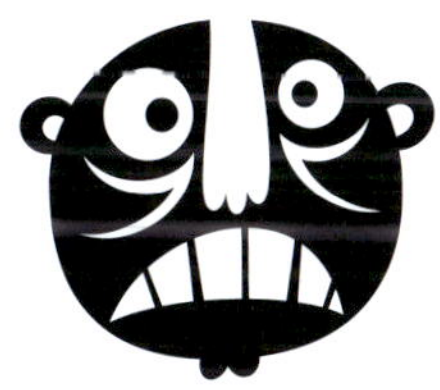

What_Are_You_Scared_About_**TM319**

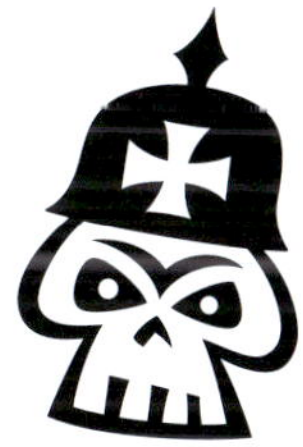

Pickelhaube_**TM320**

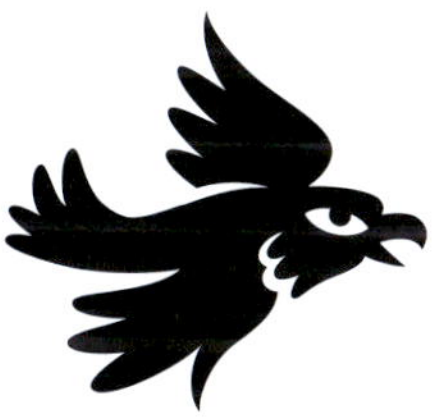

Wings_Of_Eagles_**TM322**

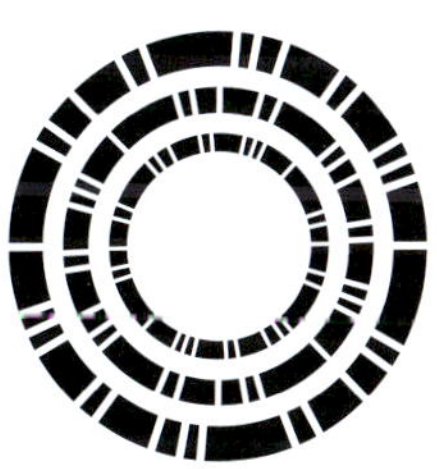

Temporal_Vortex_**TM323**

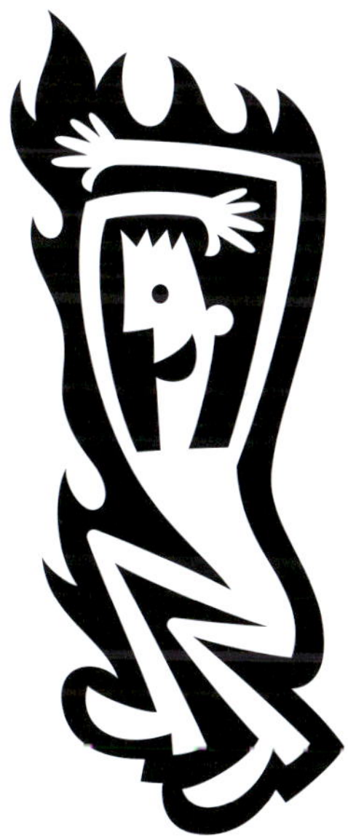

On_Fire_**TM324**

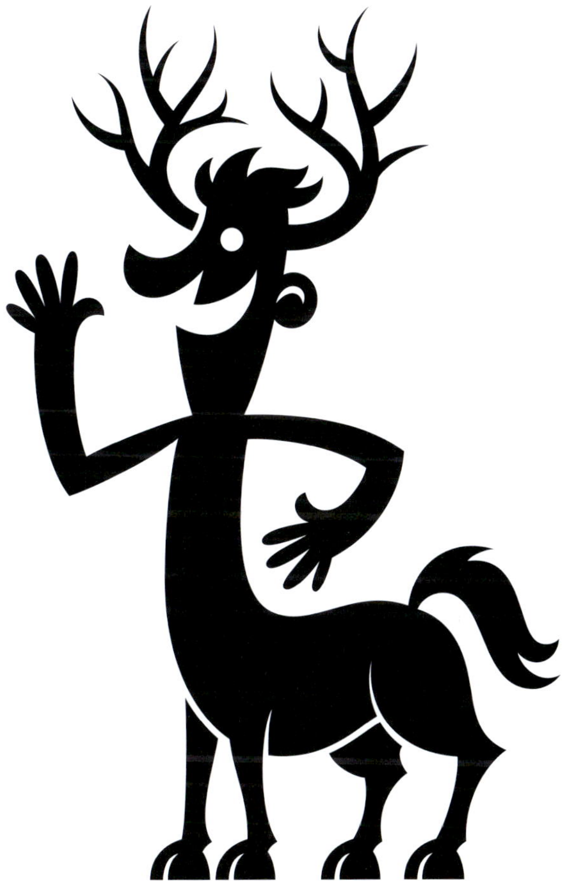

Truth_Is_Stranger_Than_Fiction_**TM325**

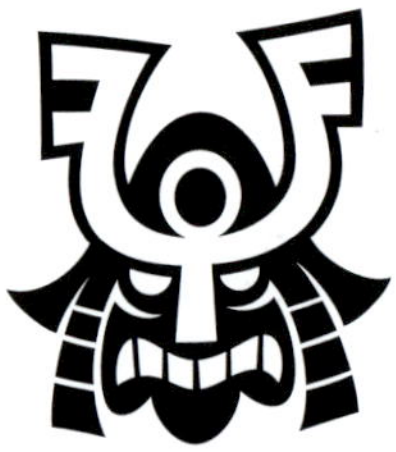

Lead_Like_A_Warrior_**TM326**

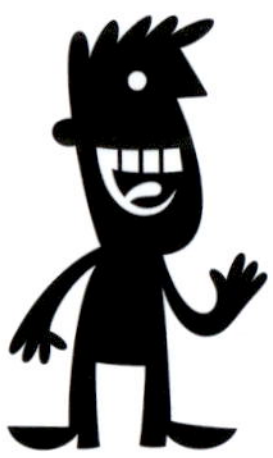

Hello_There_**TM327**

Swirlydoo_**TM328**

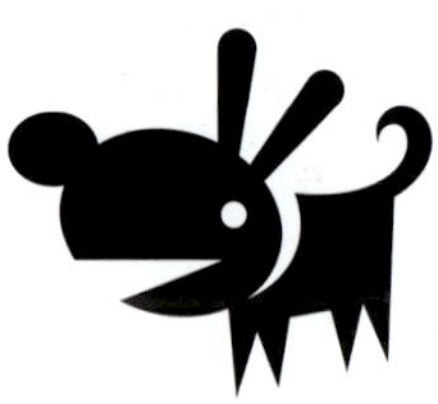

Pooch_**TM329**

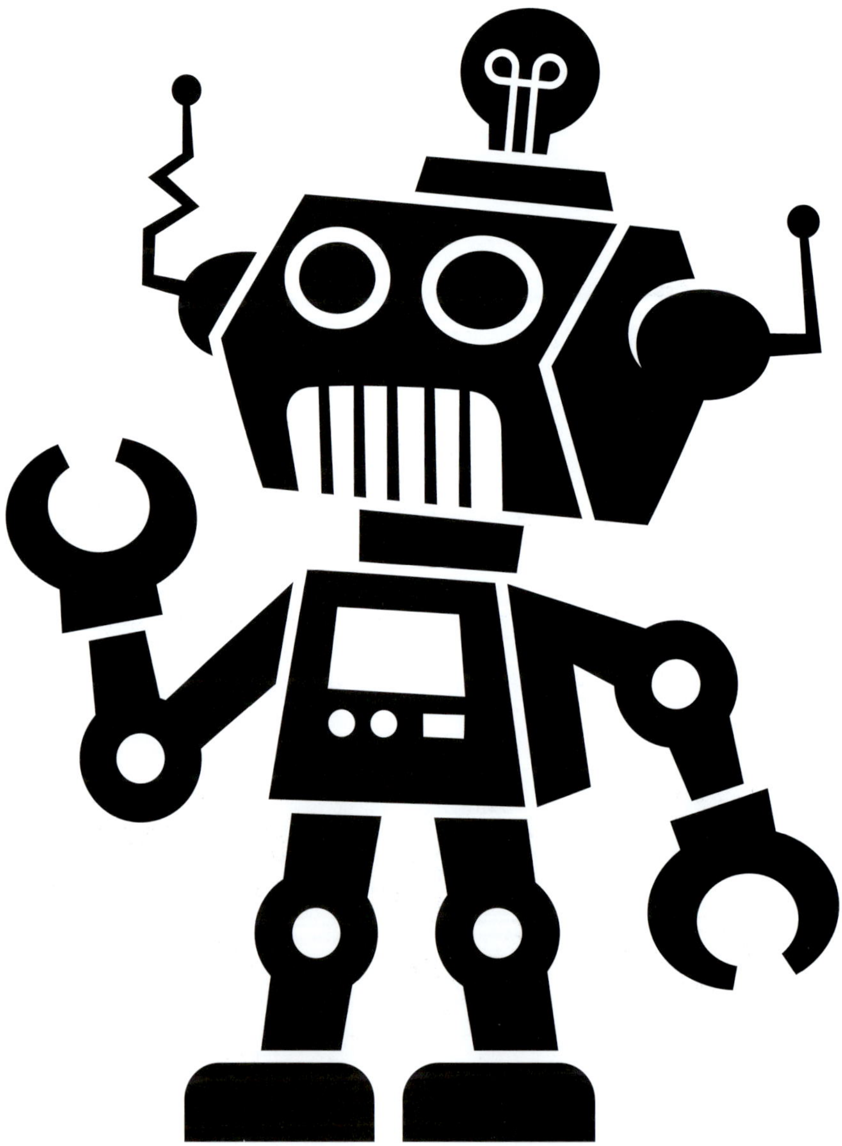

Robot_Future_**TM330**

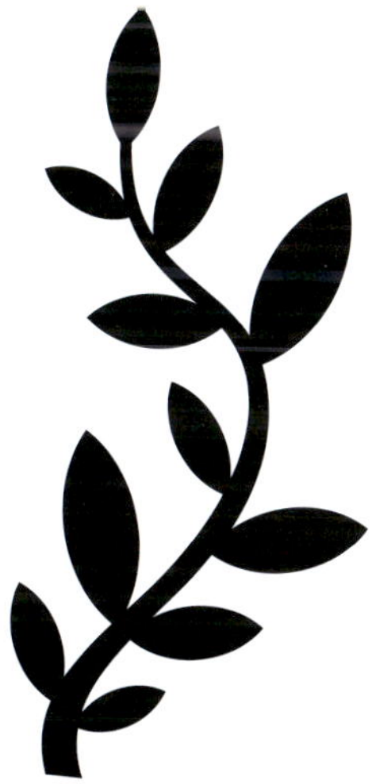

Vine_**TM334**

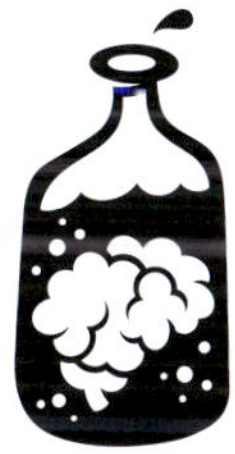

Hold_On_To_Your_Memories_**TM331**

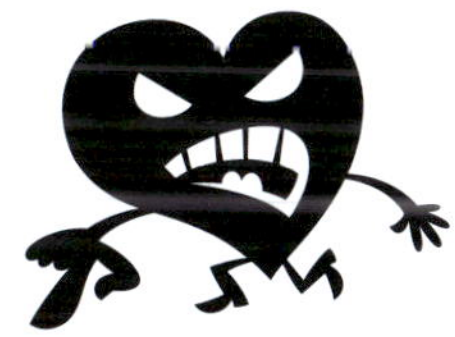

An_Angry_Heart_**TM332**

Smoked_Halibut_**TM333**

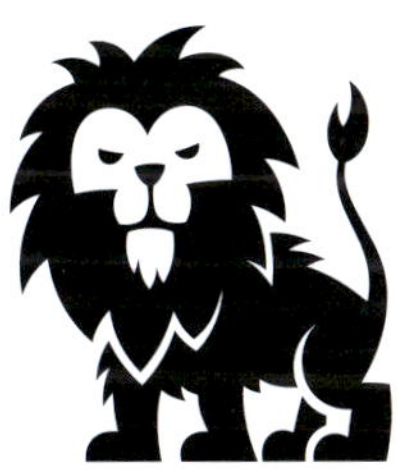

King_Of_The_Jungle_**TM335**

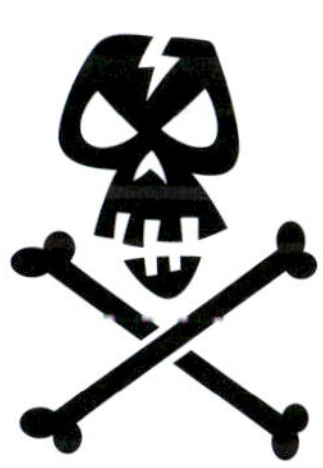

Mr_Bonez_**TM336**

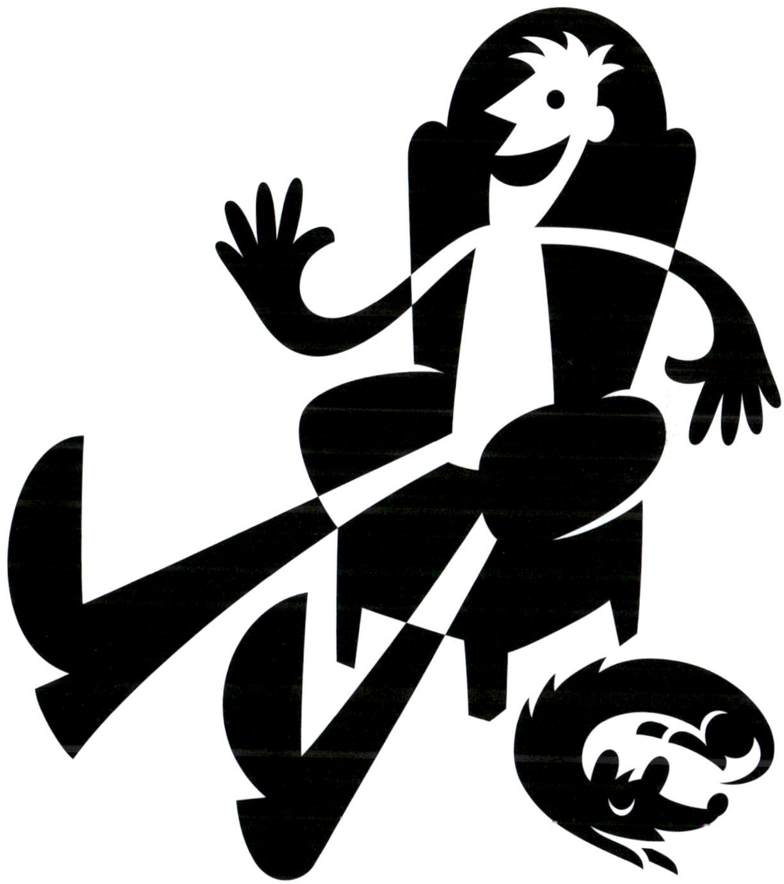

Take_It_Easy_**TM337**

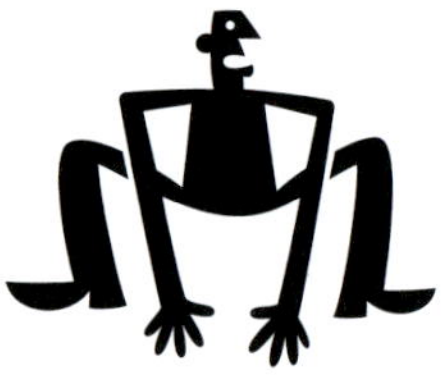

Squatz_**TM338**

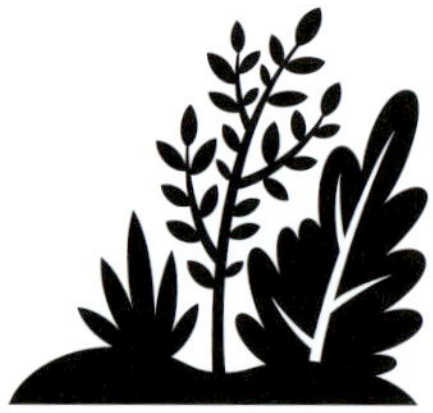

Terrarium_**TM339**

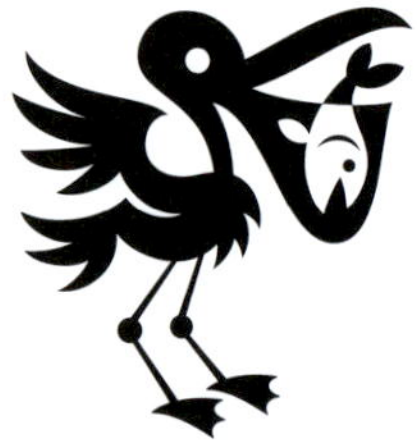

Pelican_**TM340**

Winter_Dandruff_**TM341**

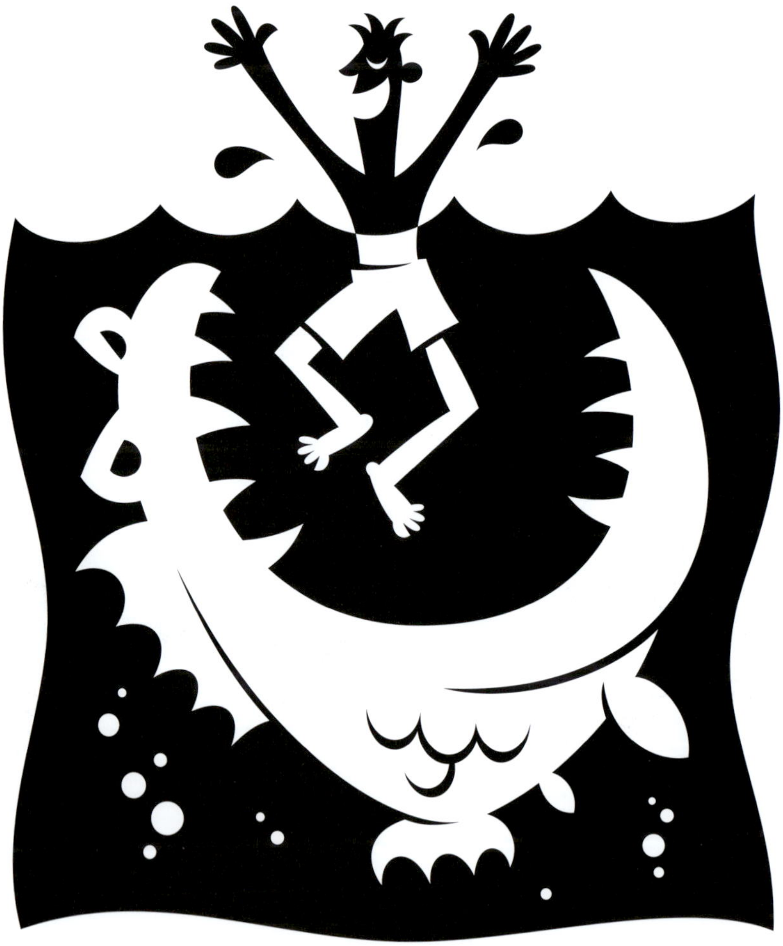

Expect_The_Unexpected_**TM342**

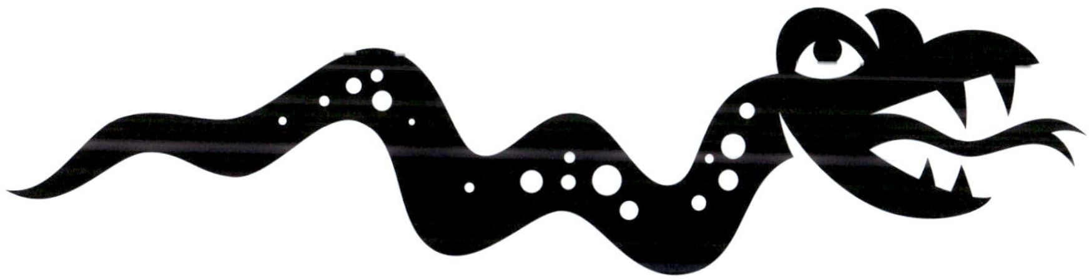

Slither_**TM343**

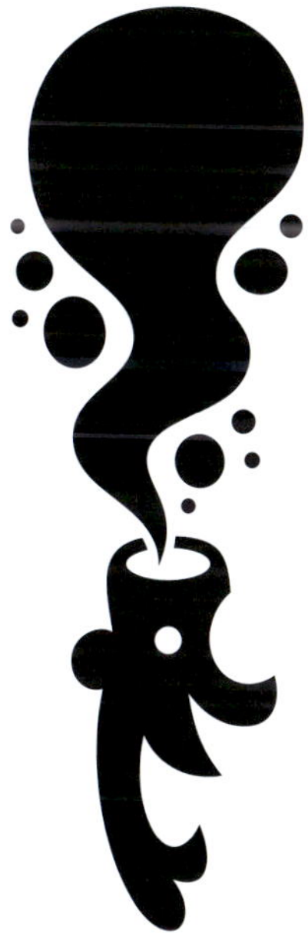

Percolating_Ideas_**TM344**

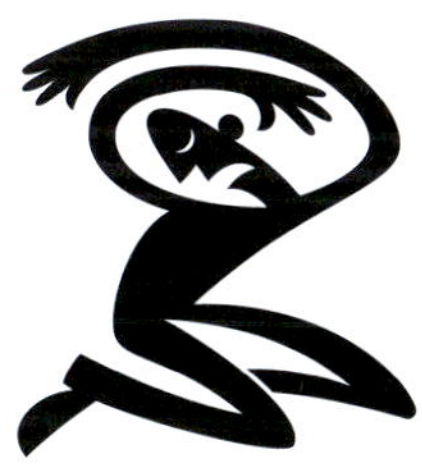

Woe_Is_Me_**TM345**

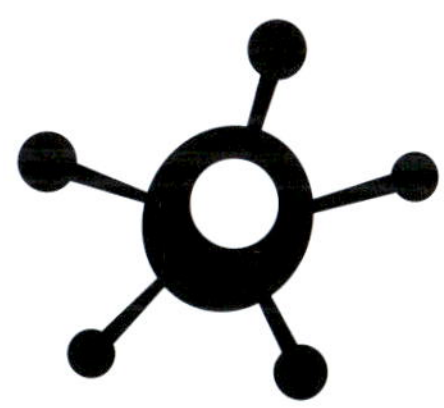

Sputnik_**TM346**

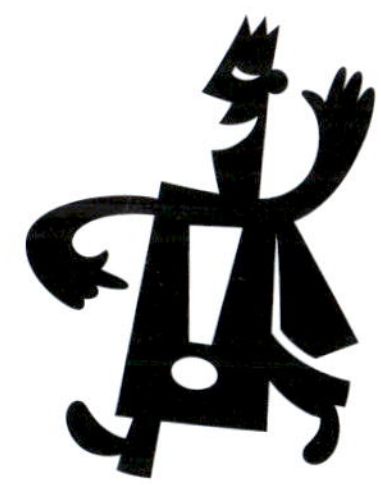

Sandwich_Board_**TM347**

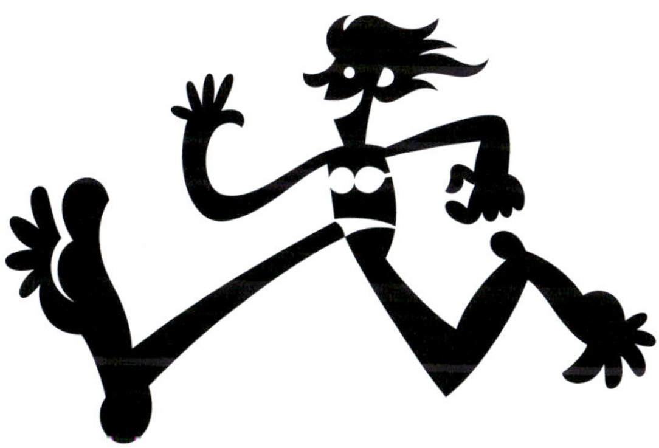

Beach_Babe_**TM348**

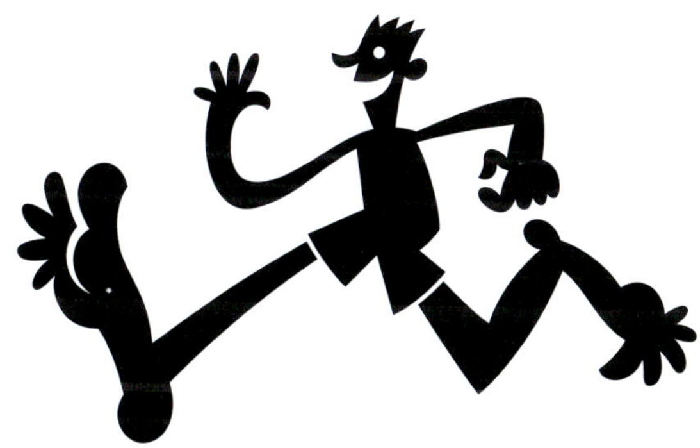

Beach_Bum_**TM349**

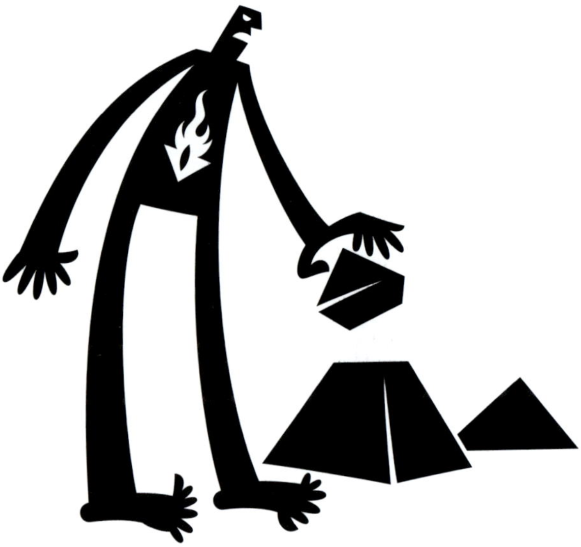

Ancient_Ones_**TM352**

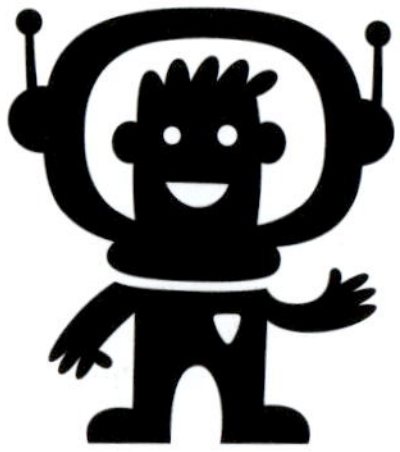

Astro_Kid_**TM350**

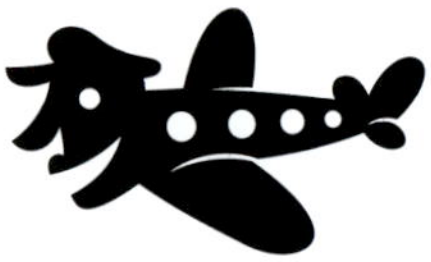

Flying_High_**TM351**

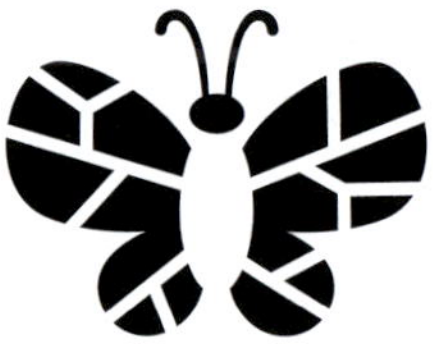

Bug_Off_**TM353**

Damn_Good_Pie_**TM354**

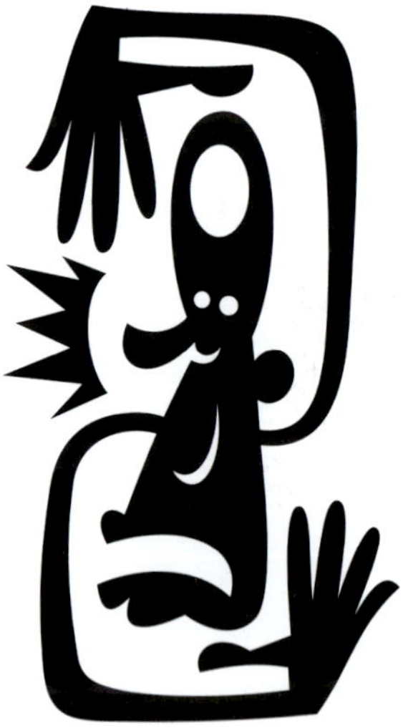

Mental_Void_**TM355**

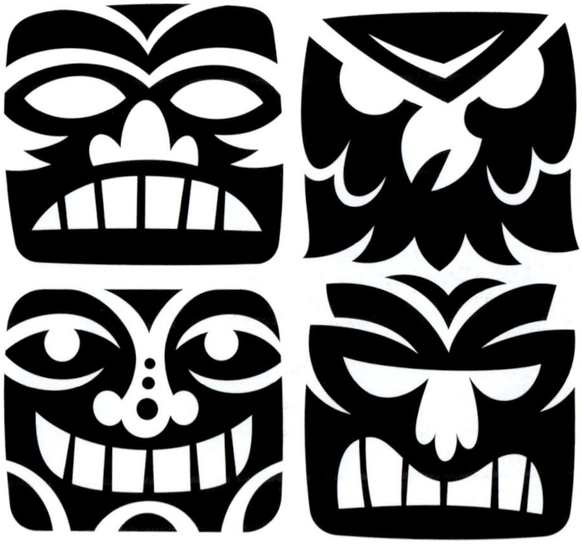

Totem_Masks_**TM356**

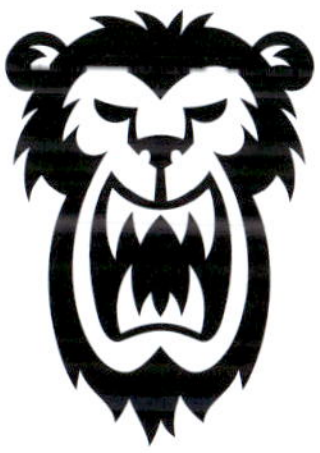

Beast_Mode_**TM357**

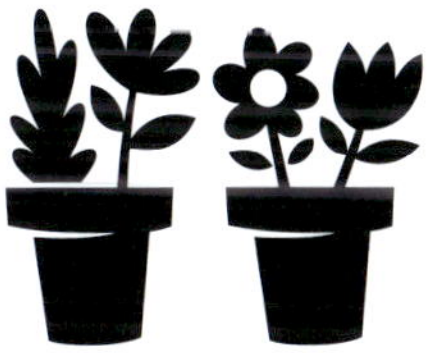

Annuals_**TM358**

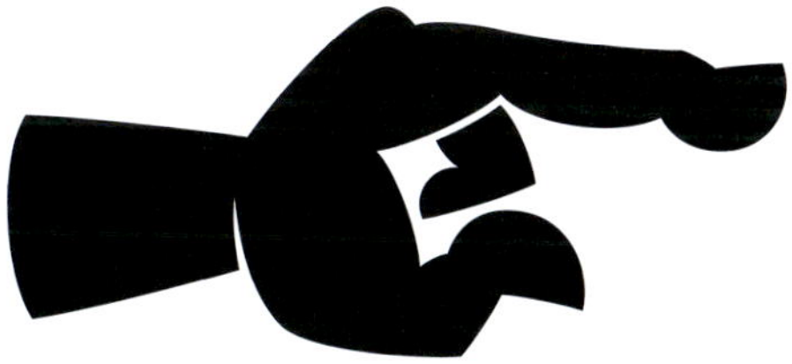

That_Way_**TM359**

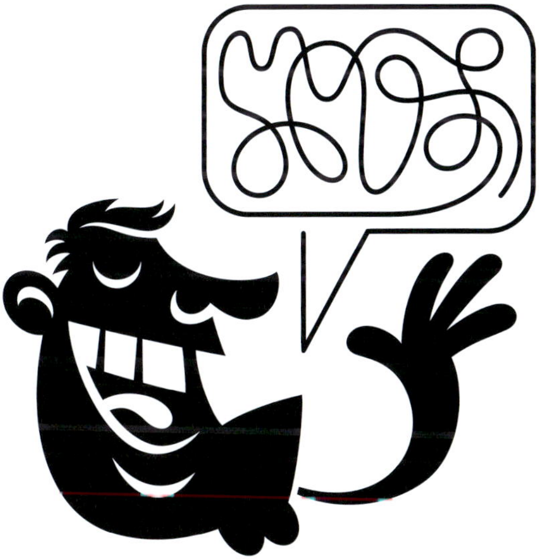

Spin_A_Yarn_**TM360**

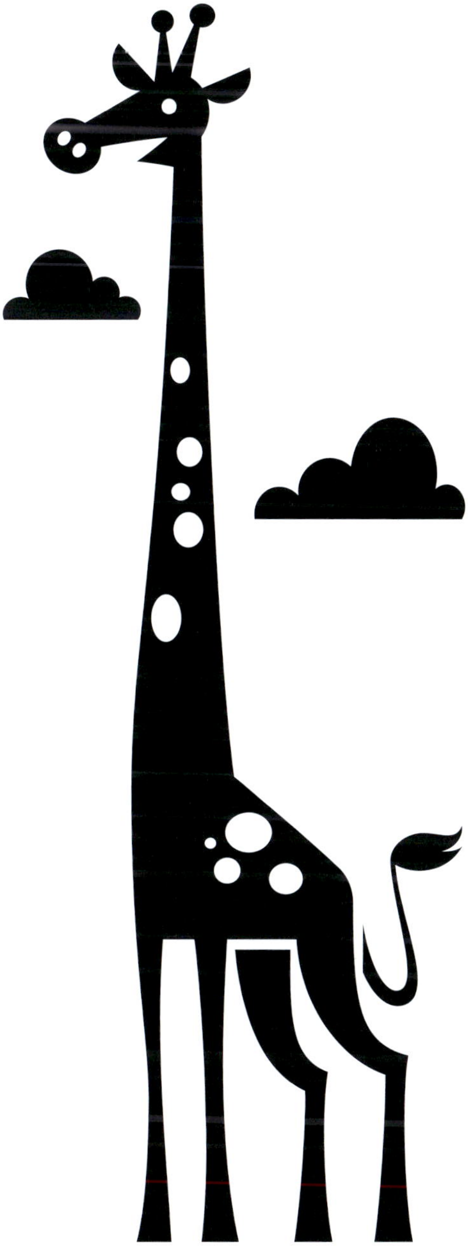

Giraffe_**TM361**

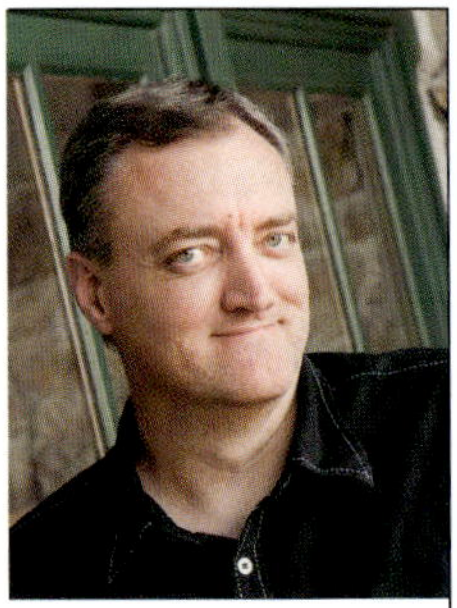

Stefan Mumaw

Creative Director

Callahan Creek • Lawrence, Kansas

www.CallahanCreek.com

If you think about it, there are few things more mysterious than a message in a bottle. There's always a story behind it. What is the message? Who wrote it and why? Where did it come from? There are so many questions that are attached to a message in a bottle. No one can resist opening it. Unless *not* opening it is somehow better than opening it.

The artwork begs for a story so I decided to write one about this particular message in a bottle. It's the story of heritage and family, but it's also a story of human behavior and the power of mystery. Can an unopened bottle with an unread message inside change the course of a family's well being? Can it change yours?

Art Used: Message In A Bottle TM389

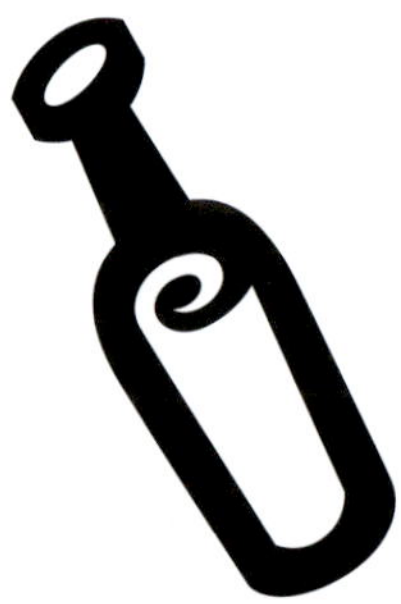

He mistook it for a fish the first time he saw it, bobbing between the breaks in the waves. From the shore, it meandered in and out of sight, appearing so randomly that it seemed organic. But as he walked along the shore, it seemed to follow him, as if it needed something from him. Sufficiently interested, he hiked into the cold surf and retrieved the object: a bottle. A beautiful blue bottle in a beautiful blue sea. It was sealed with a cork that was wedged tightly down its thin neck, crusted around the surface of the bore. The glass was thick and round, bumpy to the touch and riddled with callous imperfections. He turned it in his hand, brushing off the sea foliage that had collected around the throat. That's when he first noticed its contents. Rolled tightly within its body was a scroll of paper, worn from moisture but still intact. The bevel and hue of the thick glass kept him from being able to read anything on the scroll, a problem he tried to remedy by holding it up to the sunlight. Whatever secret lie within, the only way he was going to know was to open the bottle, an act that seemed sacrilegious considering it's condition and obvious age. So instead of breaking it, he decided to take it home and give it to his son. He told his son the story and how he can't open it without breaking it. His son agreed that destroying it was not an option, so they kept it on their mantle and conjured ways that the bottle could be opened. As the years moved onward, the bottle was passed through generations of fathers and sons, transforming it from keepsake to heirloom. Each generation found providence with the bottle, a family lineage of successful arborists and designers, forensic scientists and chemical engineers. And as it sat on Wendell's shelf, perched next to his grandfather's picture, he could almost hear his father's voice telling him, "We can't break it, Wendell. No matter how much we want to know what is written on the paper inside, we can't break the line." Wendell was a strapping young man but had little motivation. His father had told him how the bottle had brought luck to his ancestors, wealth and inheritance to the family. And while Wendell wanted for little, he also pursued little. Purpose had eluded him most of his life. And when his father, a brilliant mechanical engineer, passed away, he faded deeper into the inertia of apathy. But something about the bottle spoke to him, as if it had his father's voice. He stared at it constantly, recalling conversations with his father about the potential of its scrolled cargo. He became obsessed by the bottle. Determined to release its secret without destroying it, he set out to investigate its construction. He studied and researched, experimented and collaborated. Years he spent analyzing the materials used to make the bottle. He researched ocean currents and tide activity to determine potential manufacturing origins. He hypothesized possible ancestries for the corked seal. His thirst to uncover the mystery of the bottle led him to academic and scientific success. He became acclaimed for his discoveries and lauded for his research. But his quest was always the bottle, a quest that finally ended when he discovered a chemical compound that could compress cork and return it to its former shape within minutes of application. Minutes would be all he needed to extract the scroll, reveal its contents and return it to its home. He applied the compound and the cork gave way. He reached into the bottle with his finger and slowly pulled the paper through the neck. It was finally free. He carefully unspooled the document to read the only thing written on the faded parchment, six simple words that would prove both historically overwhelming and devastatingly prophetic:

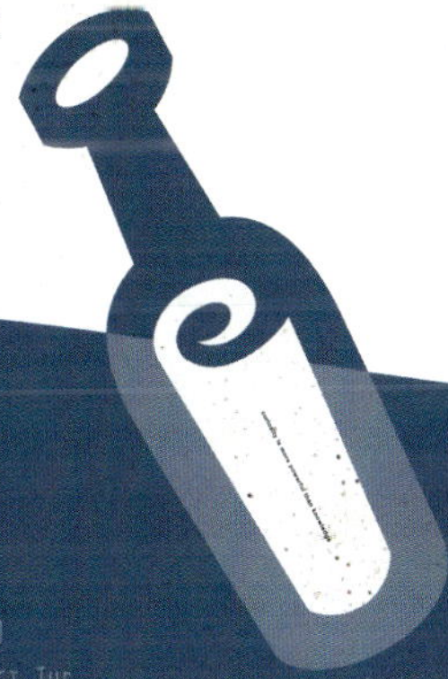

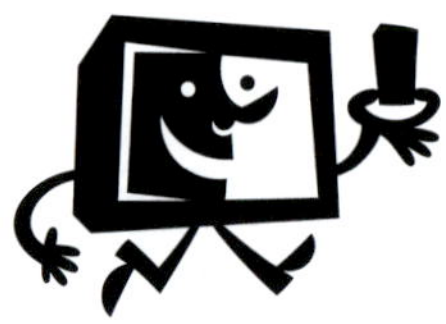

Screen_Junkie_**TM362**

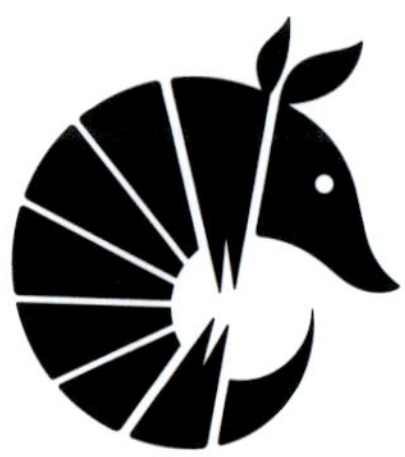

Armadillo_**TM363**

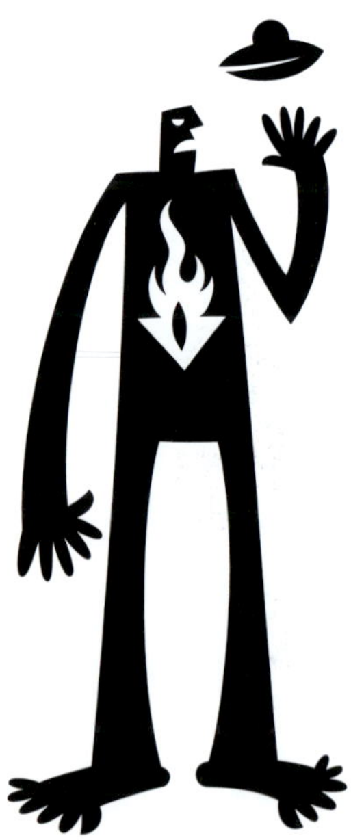

Watcher_**TM365**

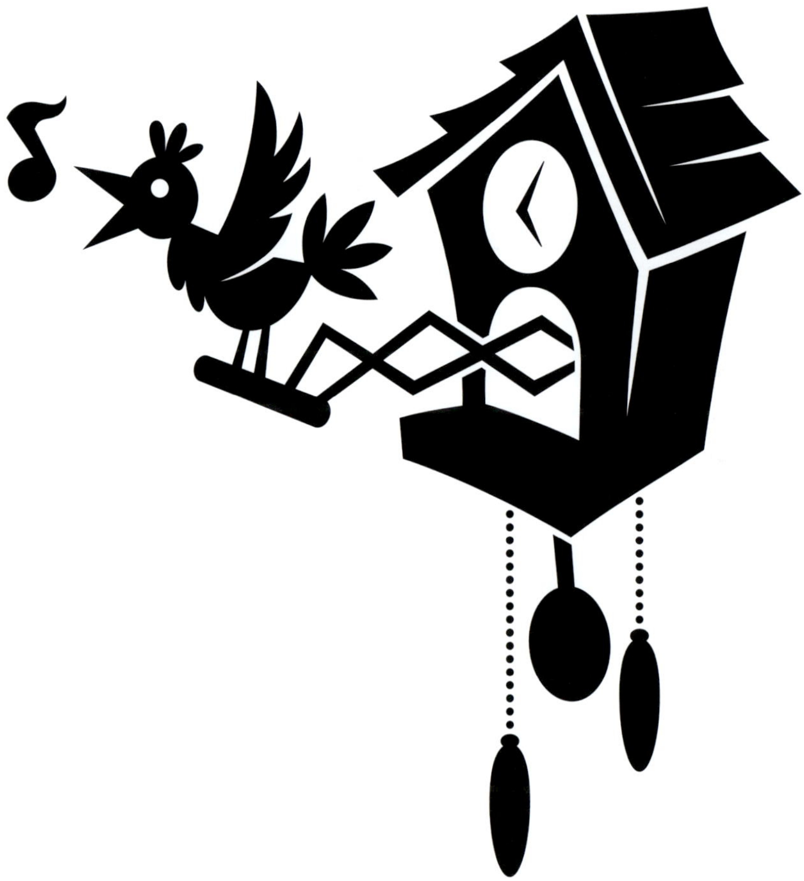

Time_For_A_Change_**TM364**

Bad_Choices_**TM366**

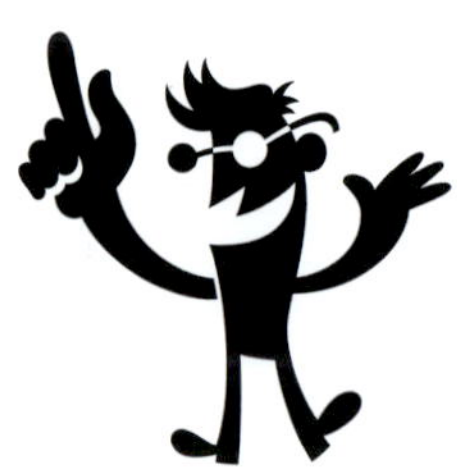

Ill_Buy_That_For_A_Dollar_**TM367**

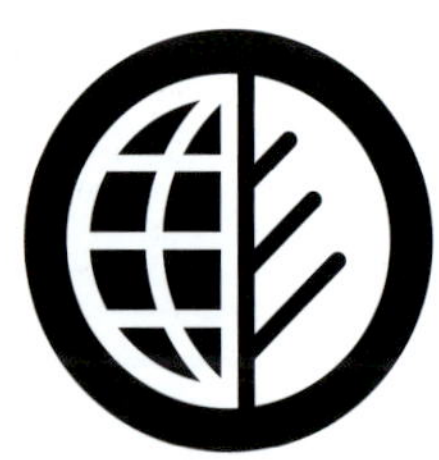

Green_Earth_**TM368**

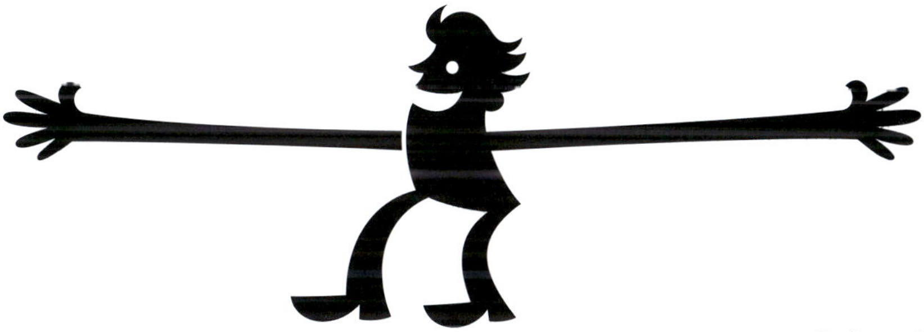

Big_Hugger_**TM369**

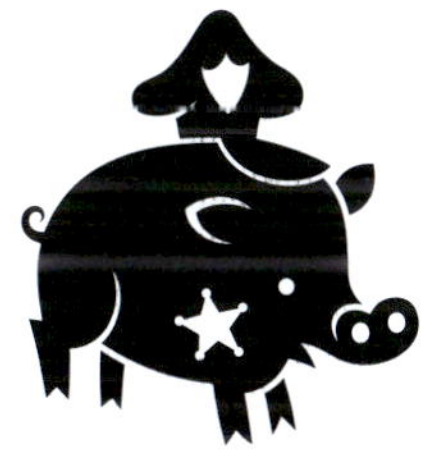

Pig_**TM370**

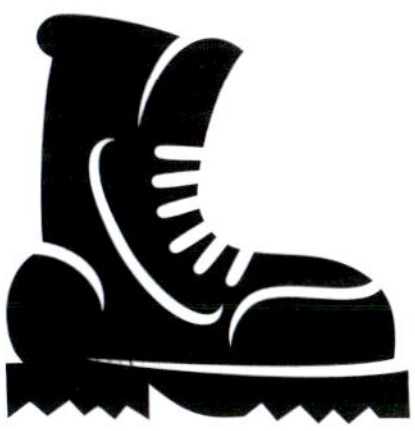

Booty_**TM371**

Crazy_Face_**TM372**

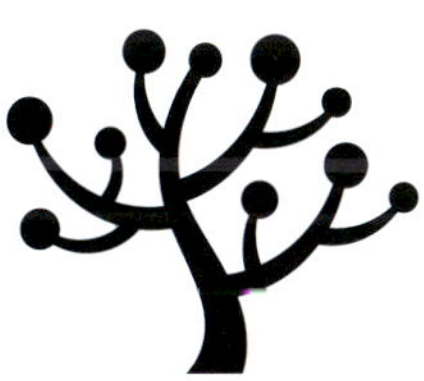

Pod_Tree_**TM373**

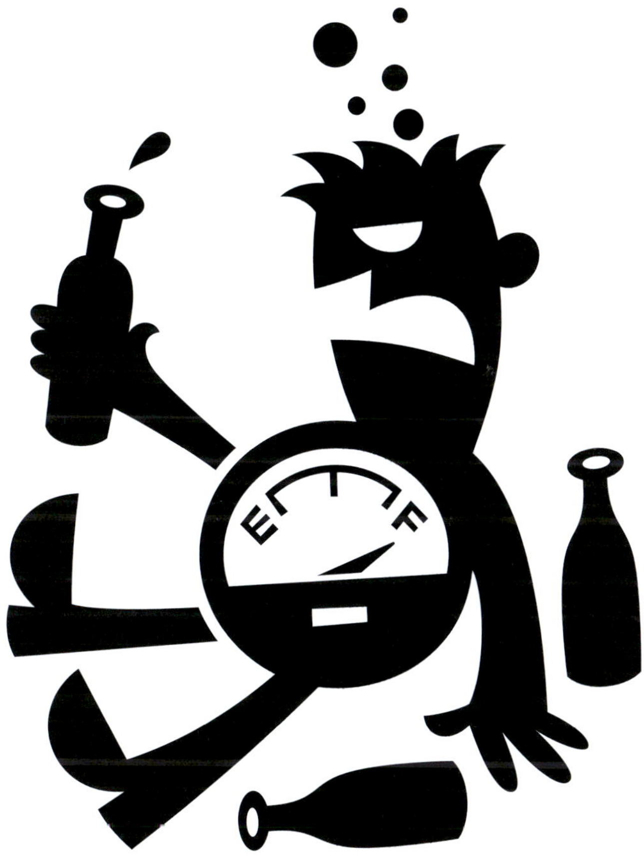

Tanked_**TM374**

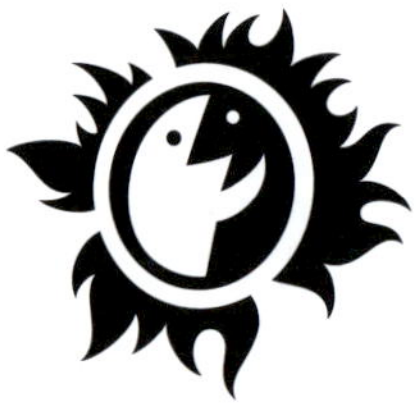

Mr_Corona_**TM375**

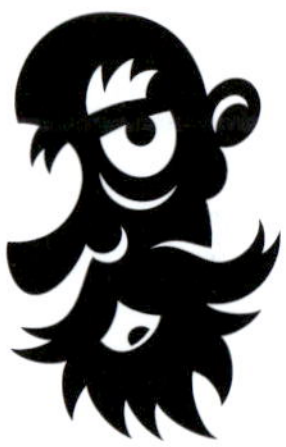

Gaze_Upon_Me_**TM376**

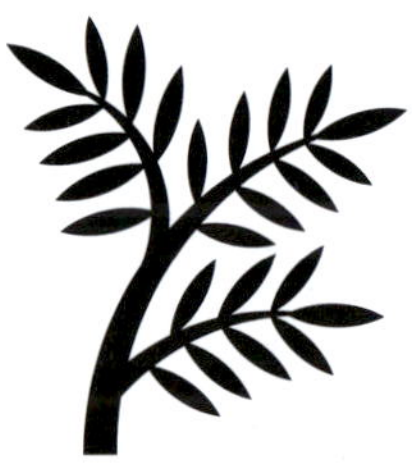

Foliage_**TM377**

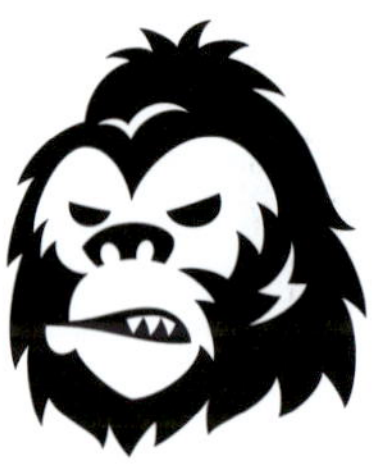

Go_Ape_**TM378**

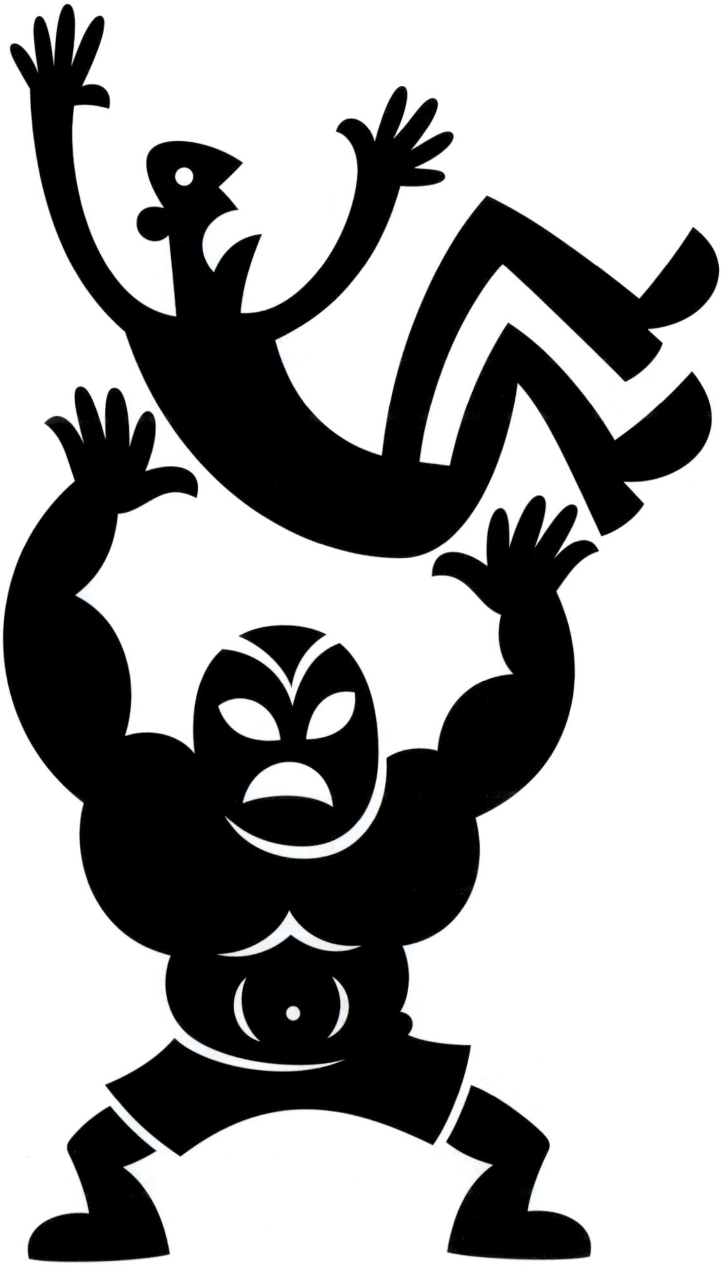

Wrestling_With_Problems_**TM379**

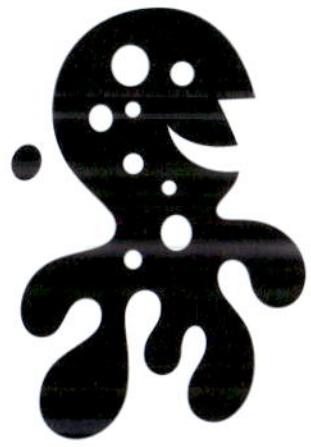

Globby_**TM380**

Arrrrgh_**TM382**

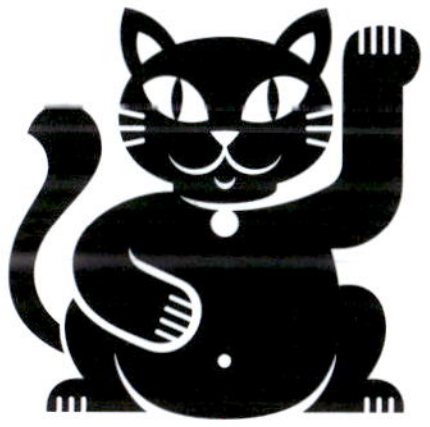

Good_Luck_Cat_**TM383**

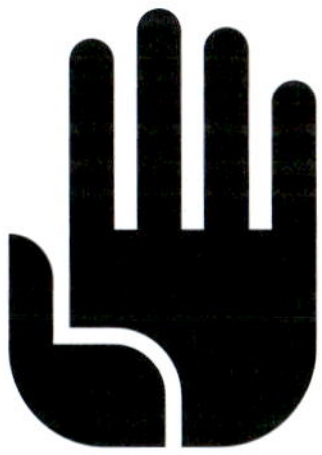

High_Five_**TM381**

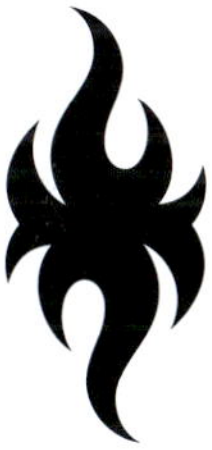

Flame_Flip_**TM384**

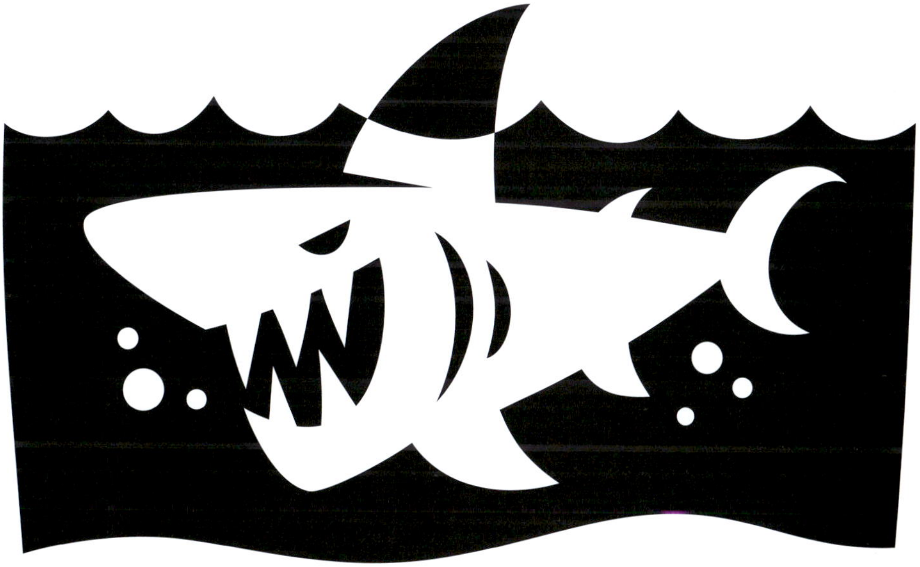

The_Water_Is_Fine_**TM385**

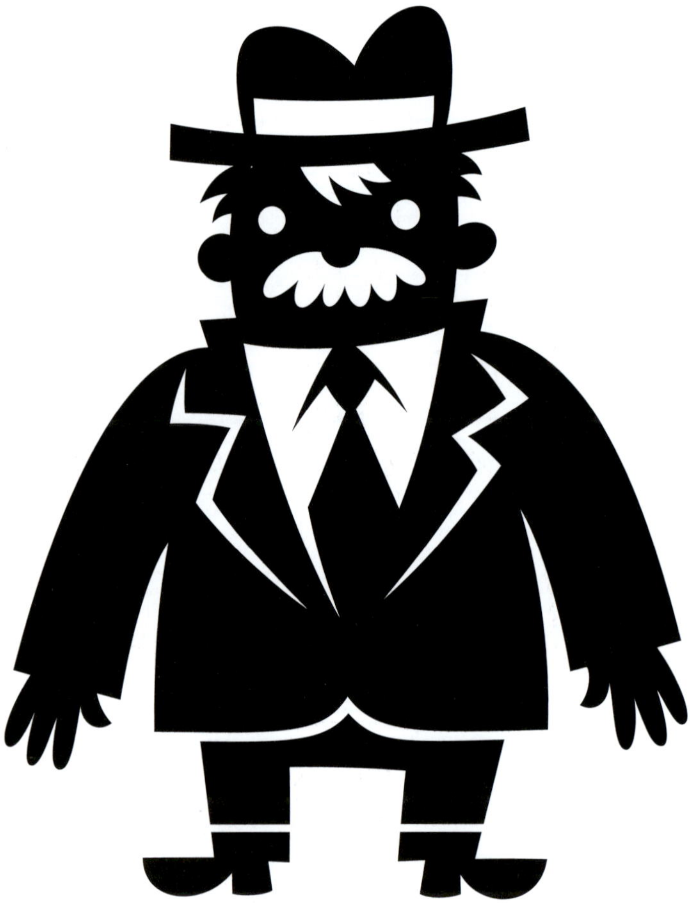

My_Good_Chap_**TM387**

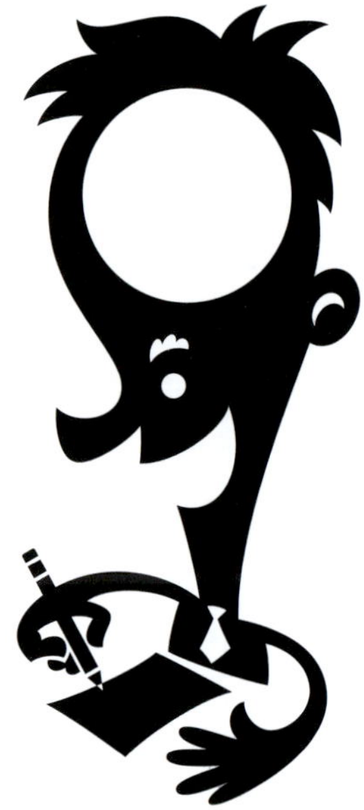

Pen_Pal_**TM386**

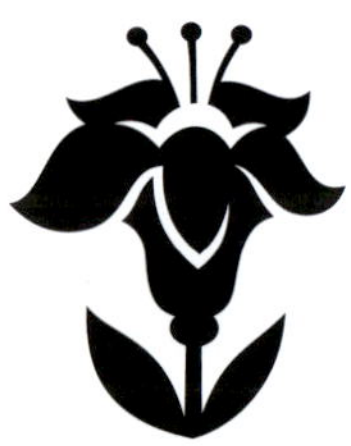

Pollen_Pollution_**TM388**

Message_In_A_Bottle_**TM389**

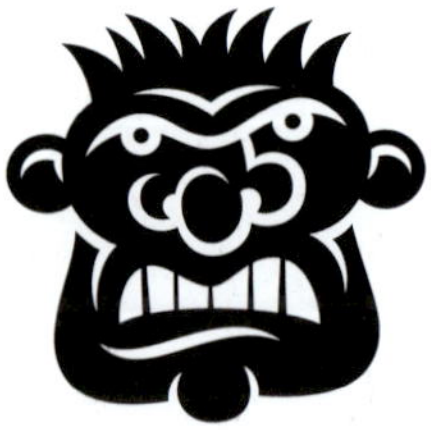

Knucklehead_**TM390**

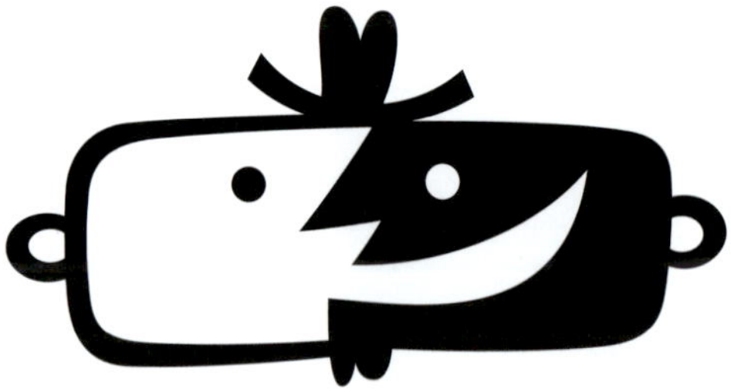

Mr_OS_**TM391**

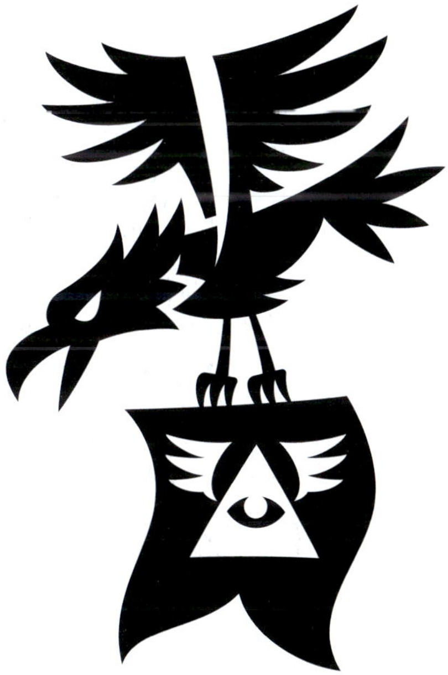

Sacred_Crow_**TM394**

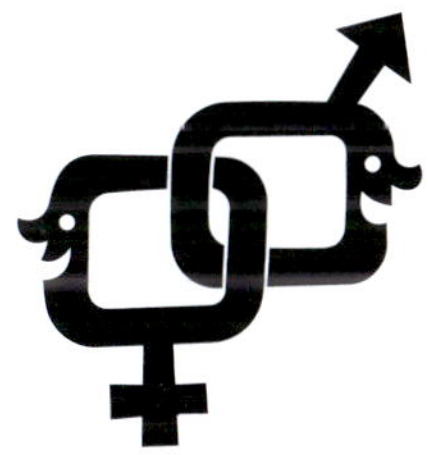

Love_And_Marriage_**TM392**

Hoo_Loves_You_**TM393**

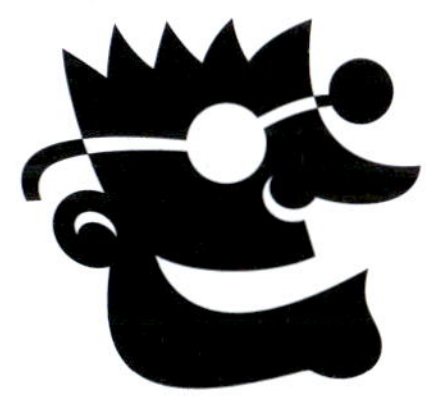

Happy_Four_Eyes_**TM395**

Jar_Of_Wonder_**TM396**

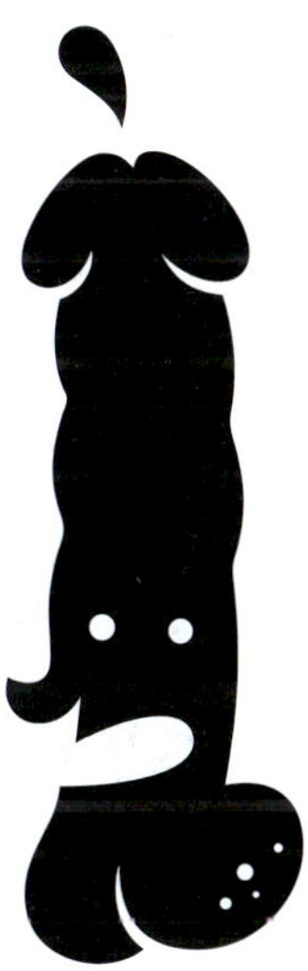

Dont_Be_A_Dick_**TM397**

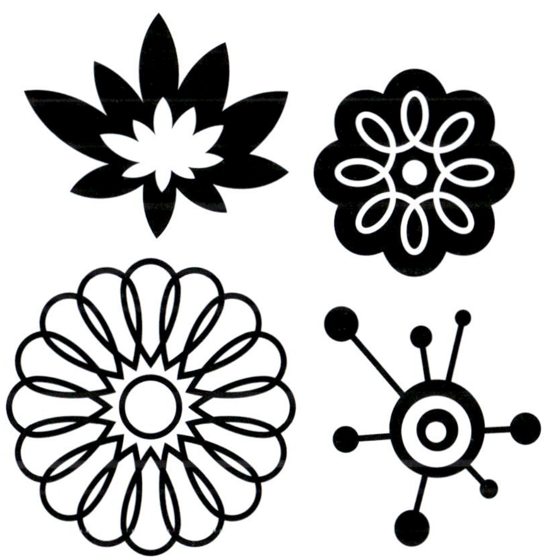

Flourishments_**TM398**

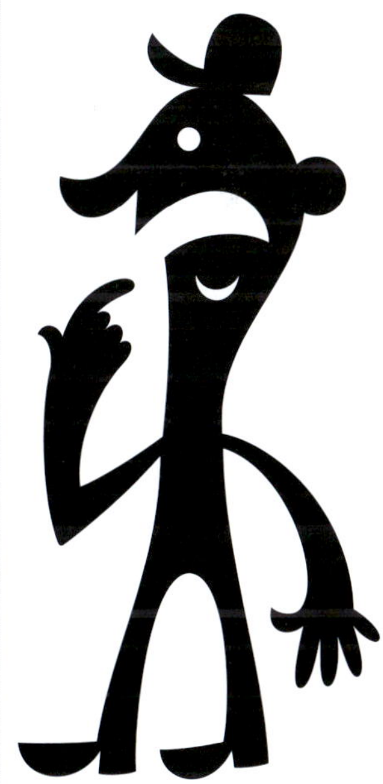

Unsure_**TM399**

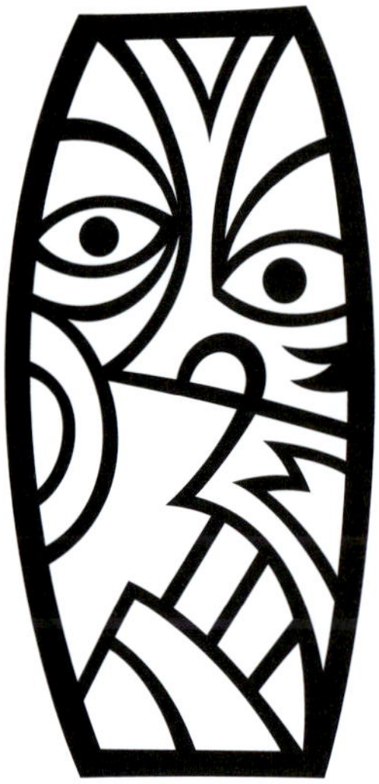

Primitive_Methods_**TM402**

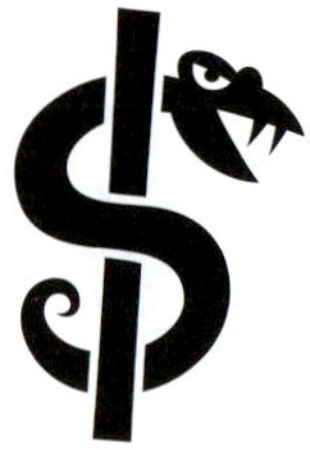

Serpent_Dollar_**TM400**

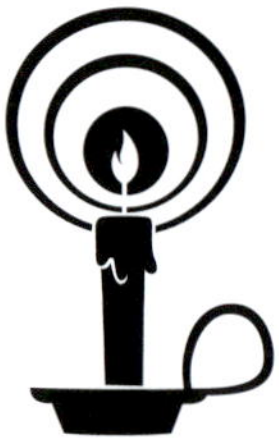

This_Little_Light_Of_Mine_**TM401**

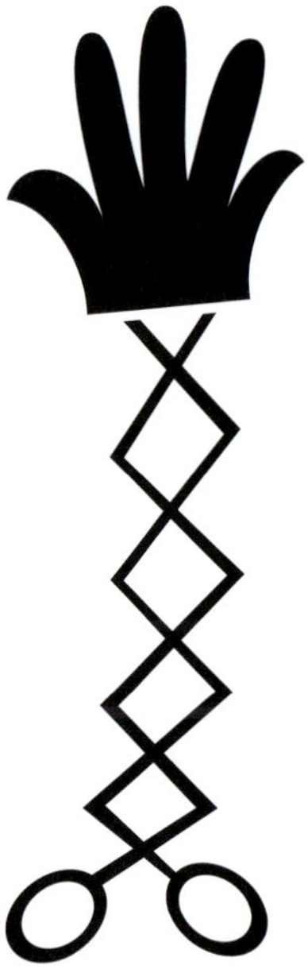

Reach_Out_And_Touch_Someone_**TM403**

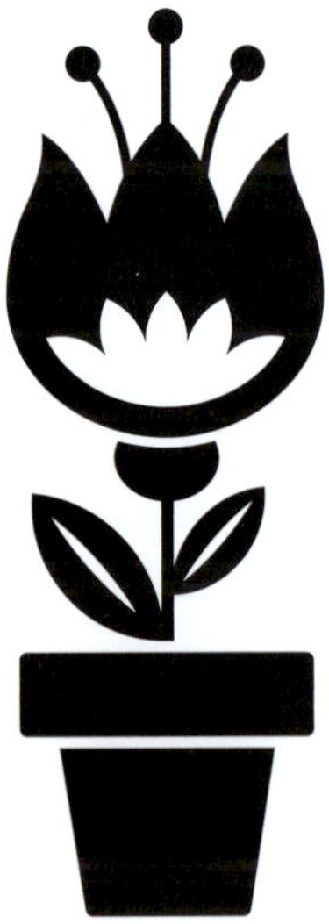

Patio_Garden_**TM404**

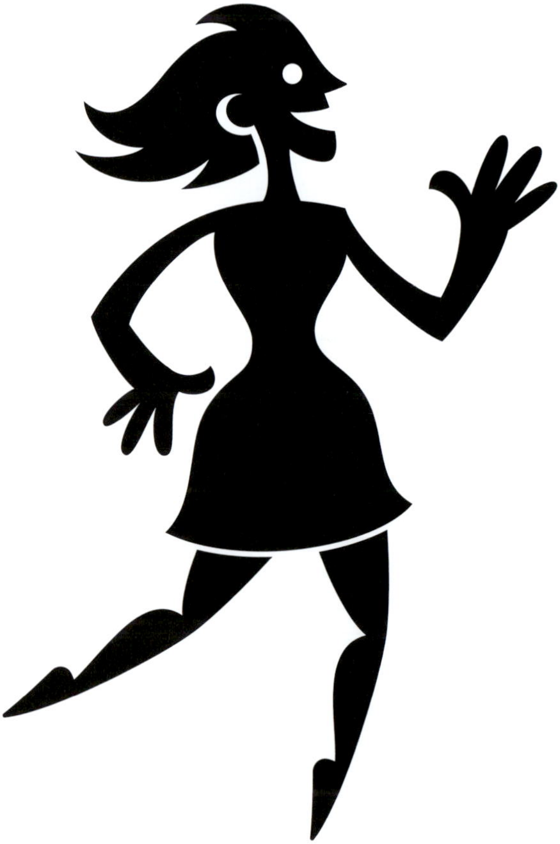

MILF_**TM405**

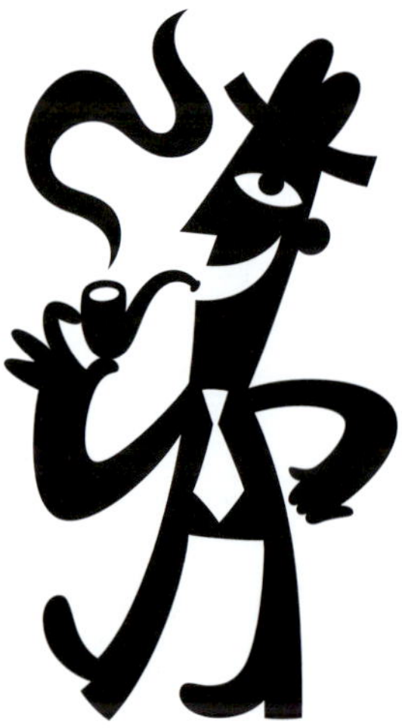

Pipe_Down_**TM406**

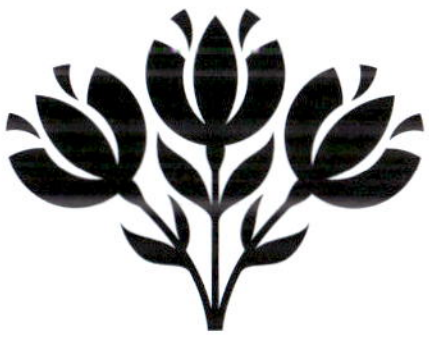

Spring_Growth_**TM407**

Let_It_Reign_**TM408**

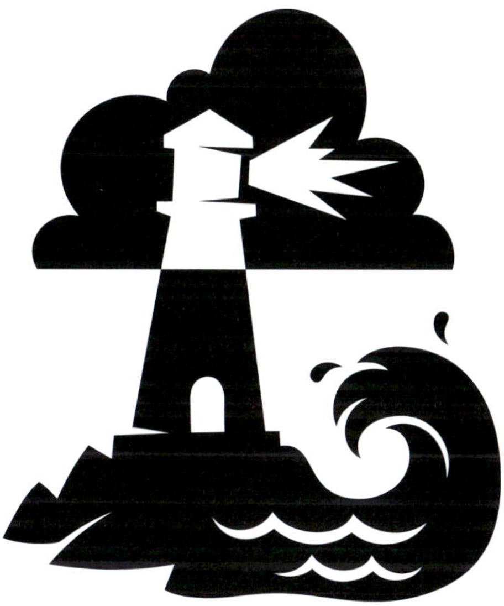

Shine_Your_Light_**TM409**

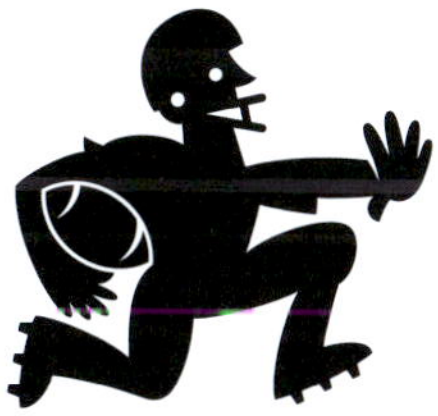

What_A_Rush_**TM410**

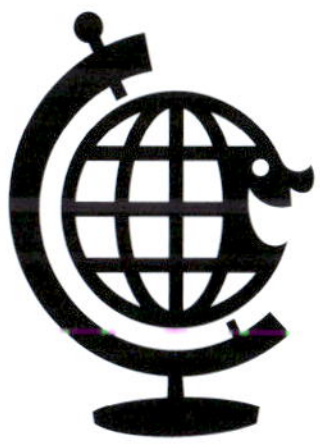

Where_In_The_World_**TM411**

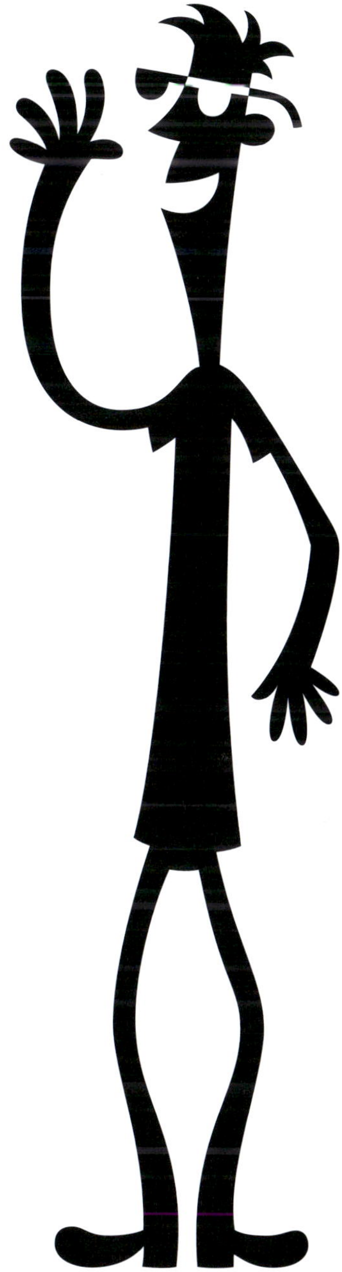

Mr_Vert_**TM412**

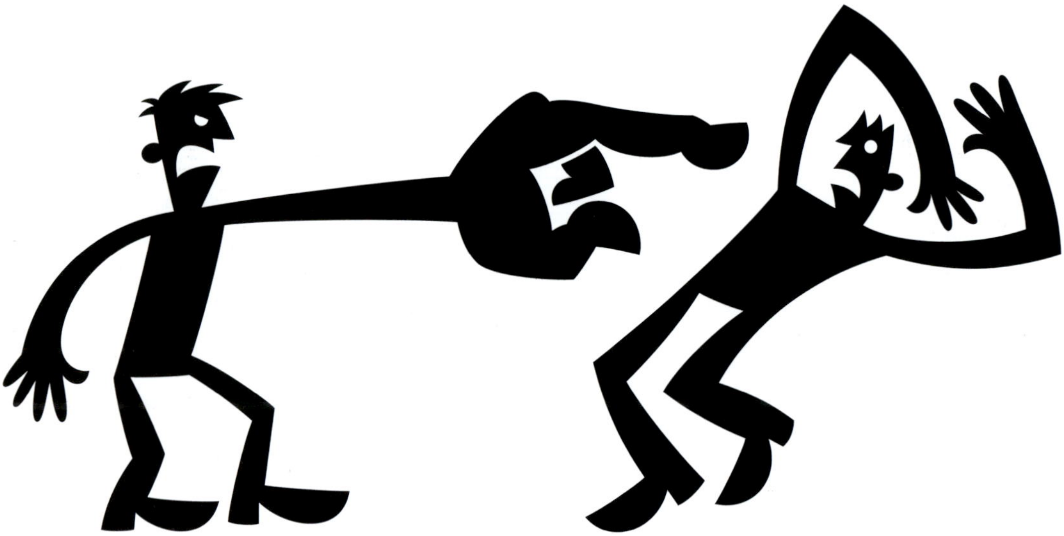

Placing_Blame_**TM413**

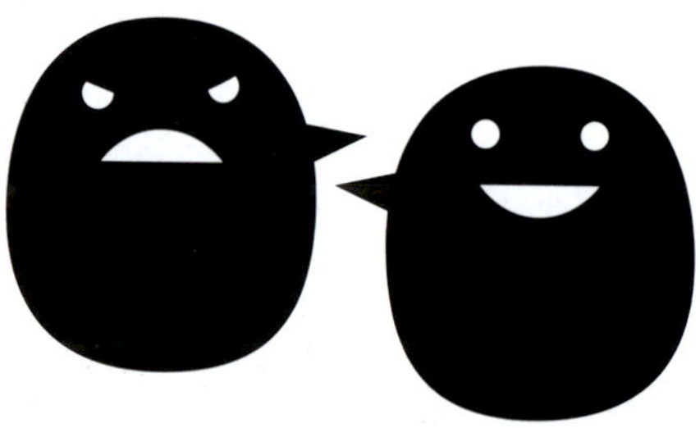

Talk_About_It_**TM414**

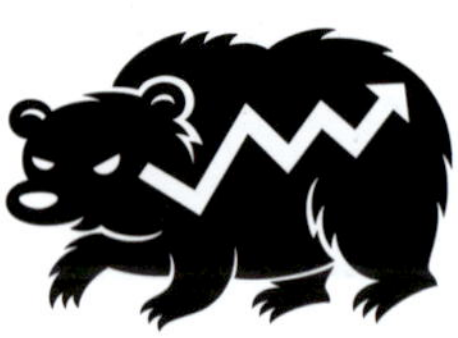

Bear_Market_**TM415**

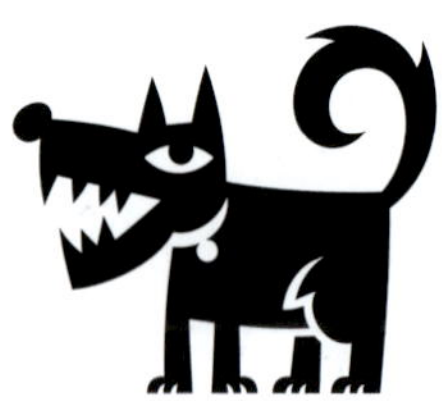

Bite_Me_**TM416**

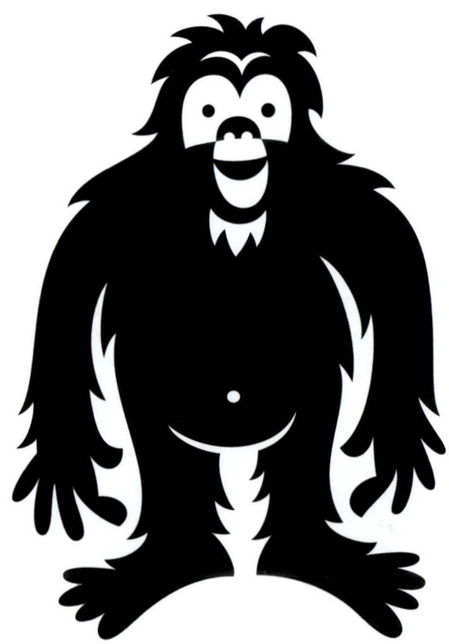

True_Believer_**TM417**

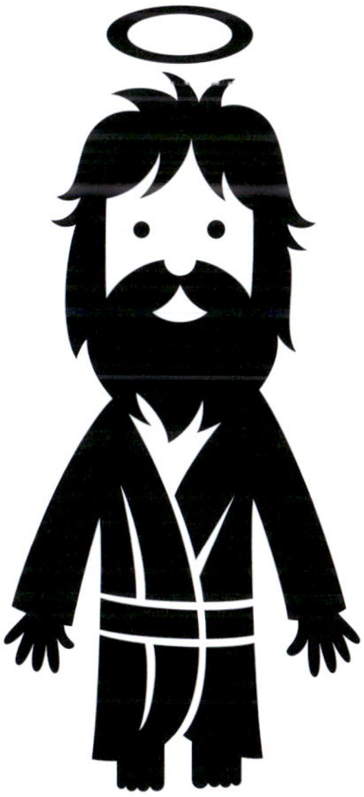

Tiny_Jesus_**TM418**

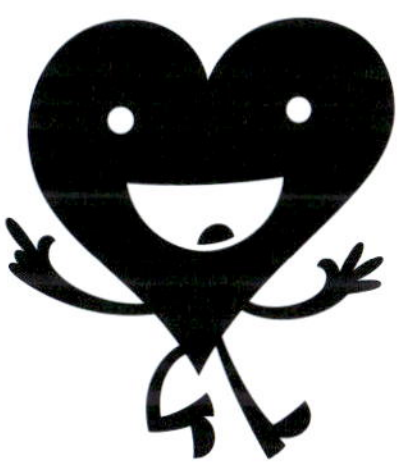

A_Cheerful_Heart_**TM419**

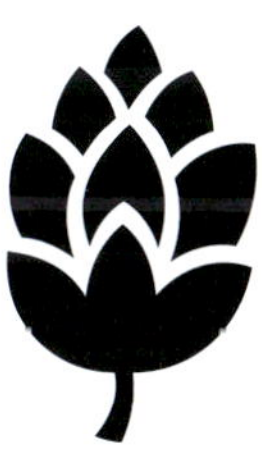

Beer_Seed_**TM420**

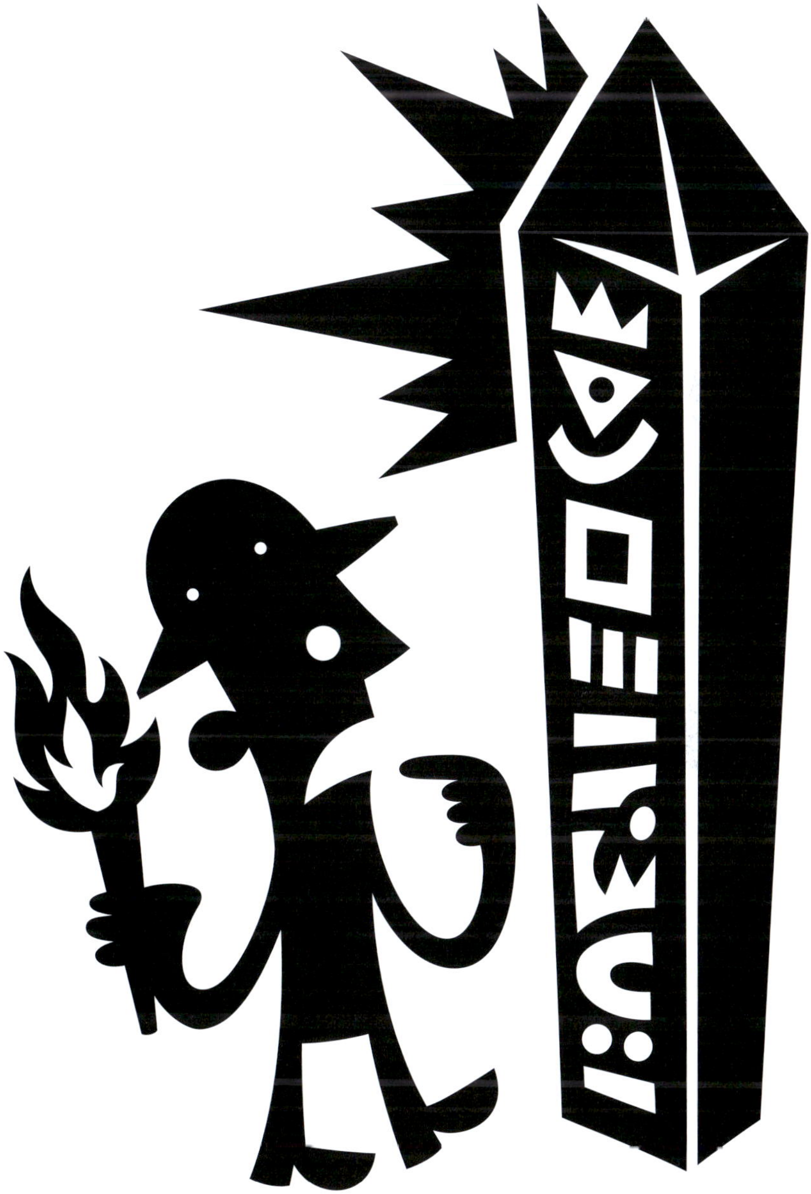

Unexpected_Discovery_**TM421**

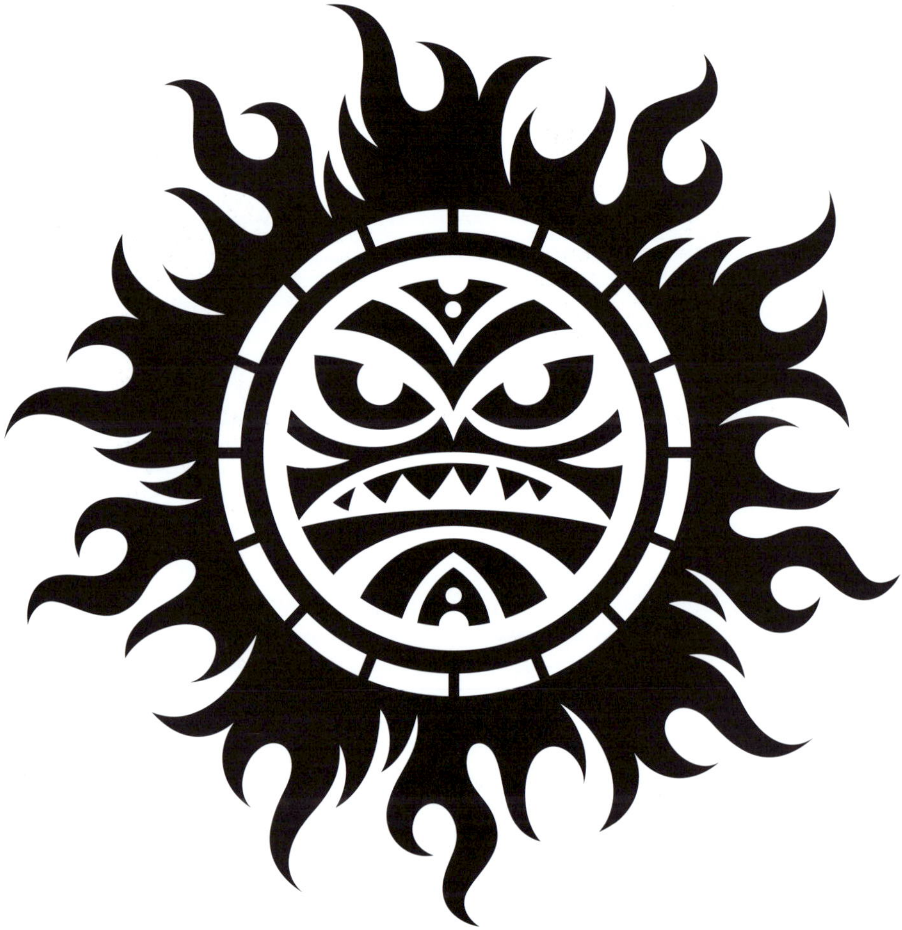

Tribal_Burn_**TM422**

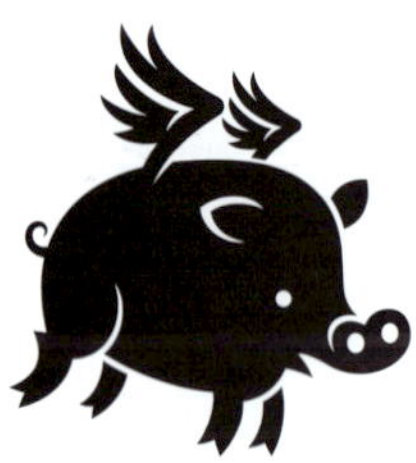

High_Flying_Hog_**TM423**

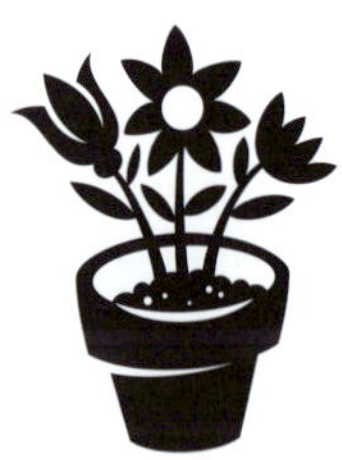

Horticulture_**TM424**

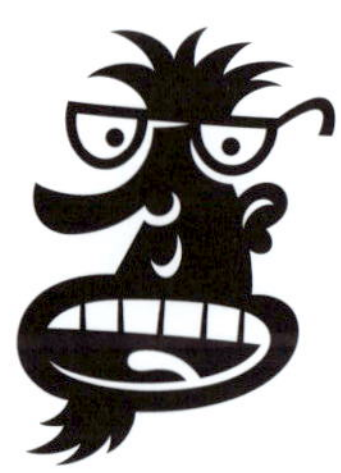

Hipster_Speaks_**TM425**

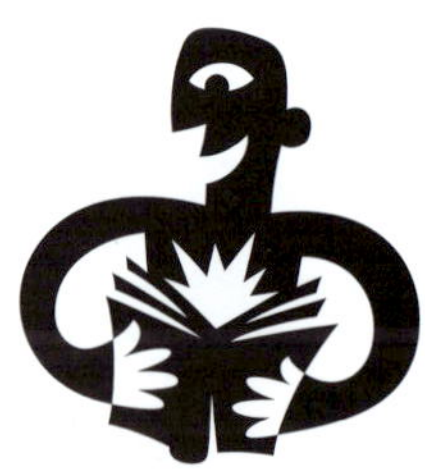

Insightful_Reading_**TM426**

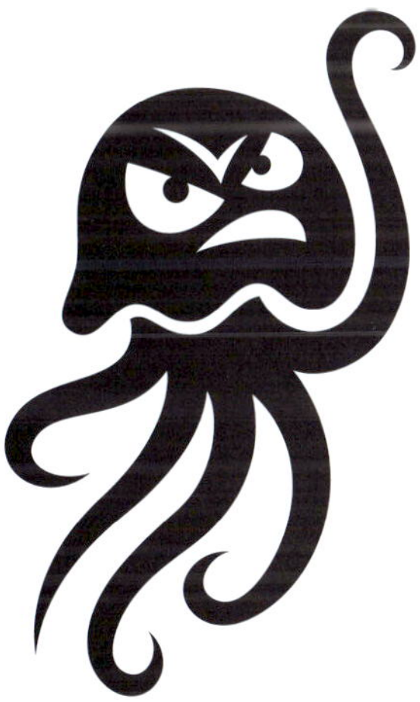

Jaded_Jellyfish_**TM427**

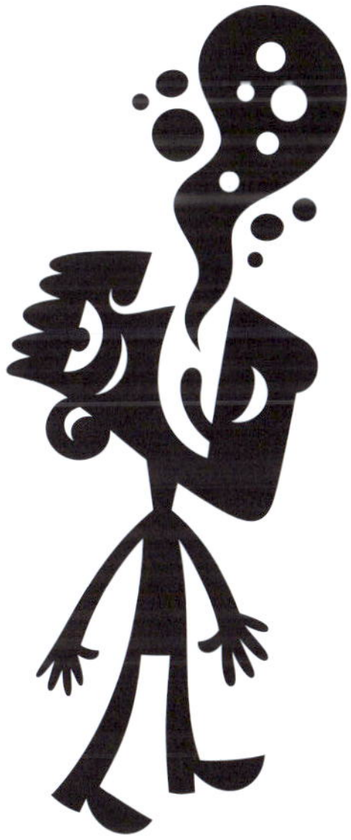

Belcher_**TM428**

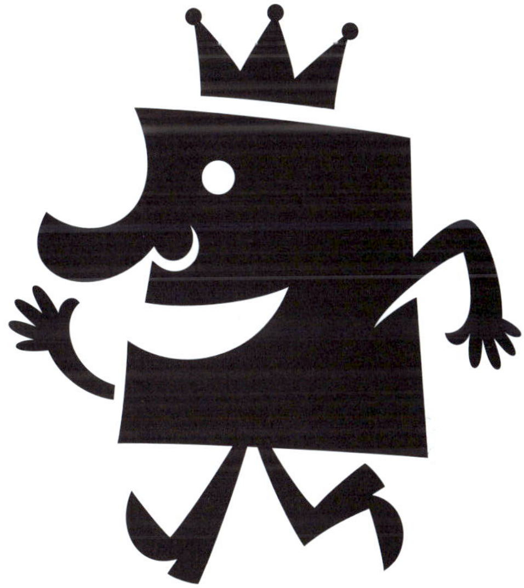

King_Cubistic_**TM429**

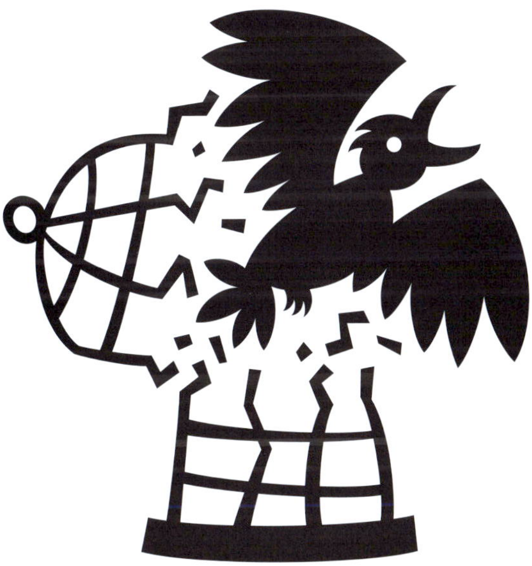

Uncaged_**TM431**

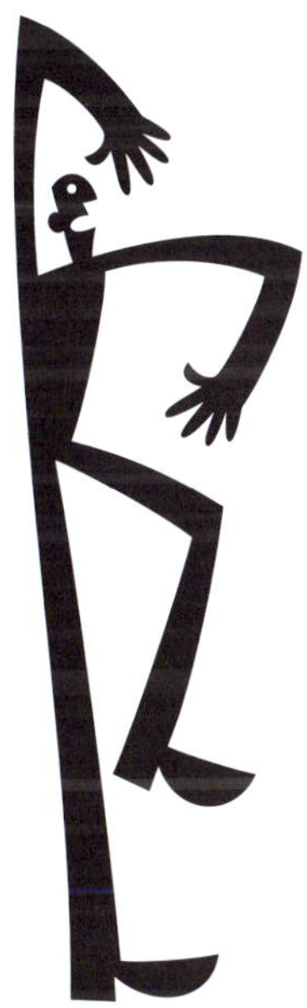

Knees_And_Elbows_**TM432**

Happy_Bloom_**TM430**

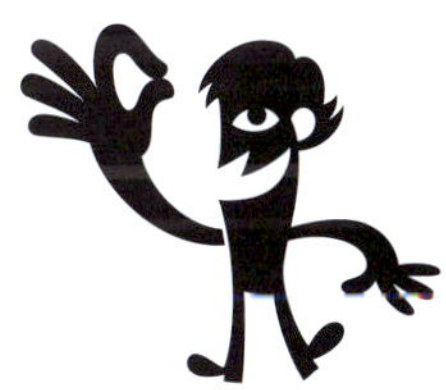

Just_A_Pinch_**TM433**

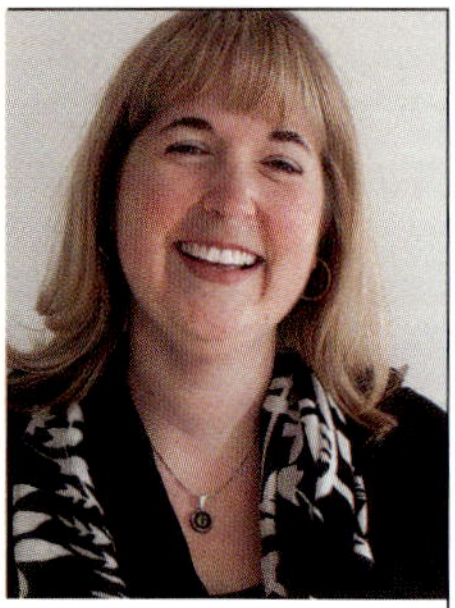

Grace Ring

Art Director

Madison Design • Cincinnati, Ohio

www.Madison-Design.com

Take and Make Art is not only a useful design resource but a helpful tool for brainstorming. Just paging through the illustrations sparked a number of conceptual ideas for my project.

The vector artwork is easy to apply to a variety of formats and is equally legible in both large- and small-scale applications. For my invitation design, I used the tree as a cover illustration, integrated it into a background pattern, and bled it off the edges of the envelope and inner card.

Art Used: Wood You Mind TM86

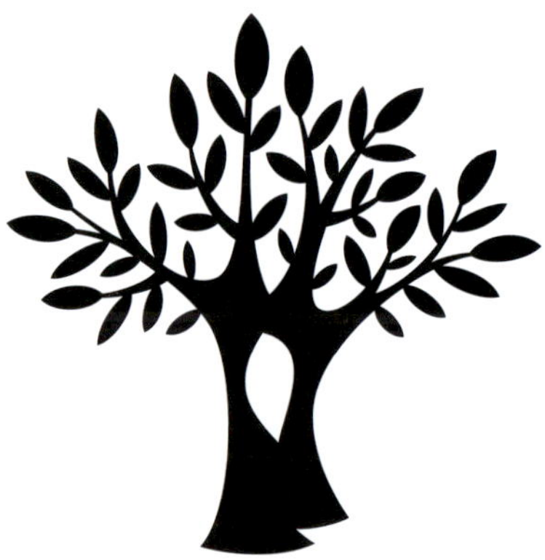

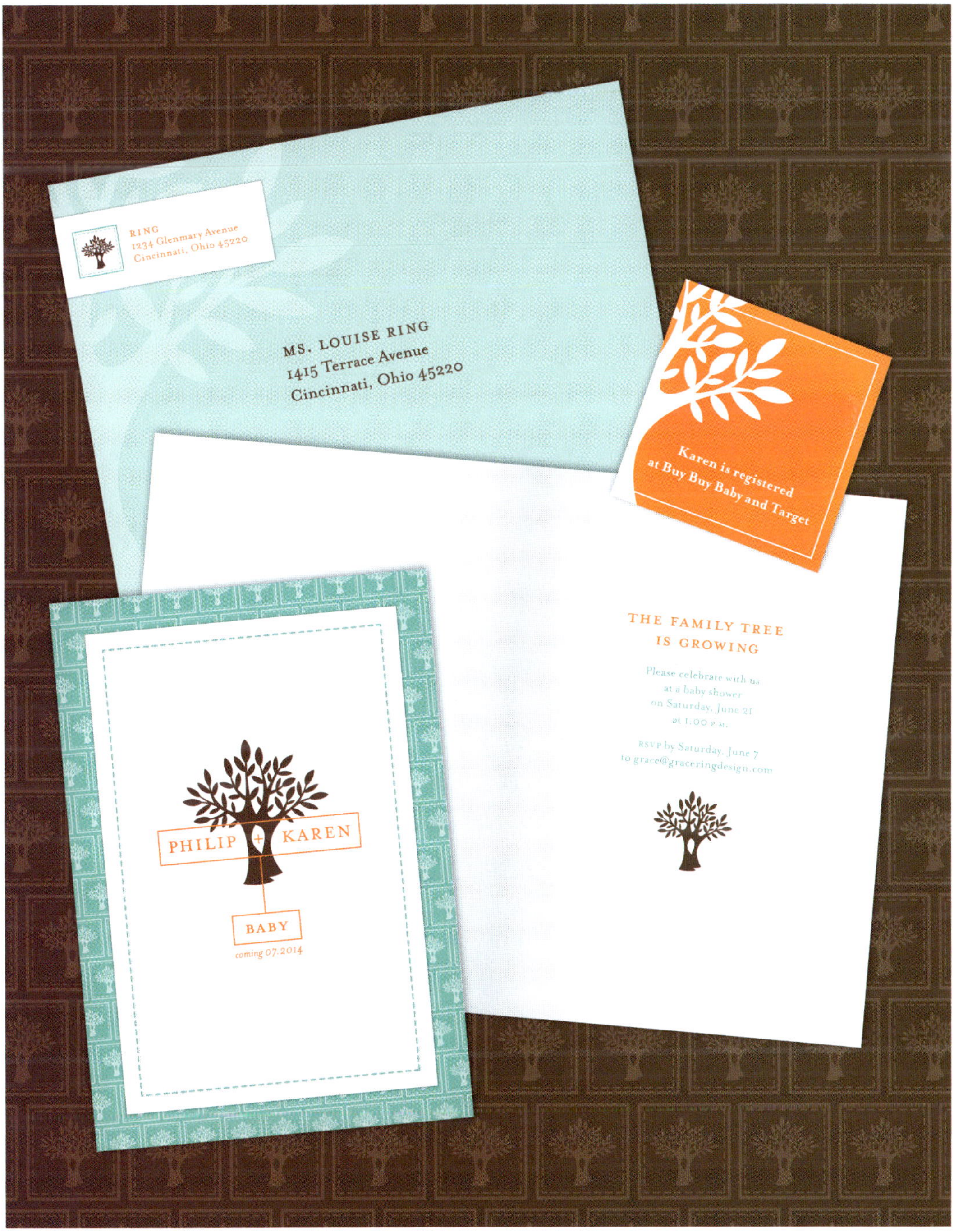
RING
1234 Glenmary Avenue
Cincinnati, Ohio 45220
MS. LOUISE RING
1415 Terrace Avenue
Cincinnati, Ohio 45220
Karen is registered
at Buy Buy Baby and Target
THE FAMILY TREE
IS GROWING
Please celebrate with us
at a baby shower
on Saturday, June 21
at 1:00 P.M.
RSVP by Saturday, June 7
to grace@graceringdesign.com
PHILIP + KAREN
BABY
coming 07.2014

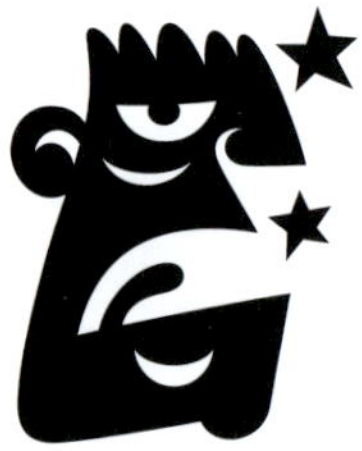

Barely_Sober_**TM434**

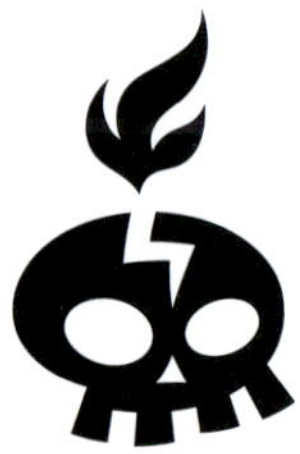

Bone_Head_**TM435**

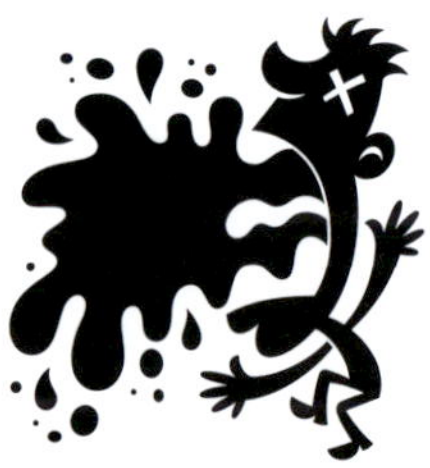

That_Makes_Me_Sick_**TM436**

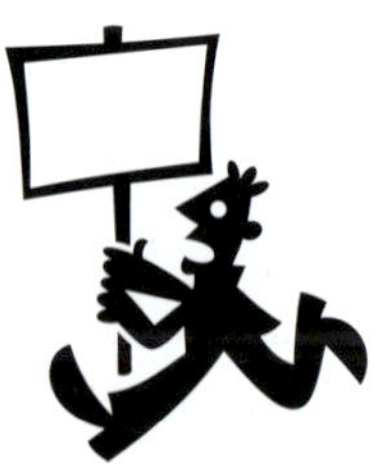

Protest_**TM437**

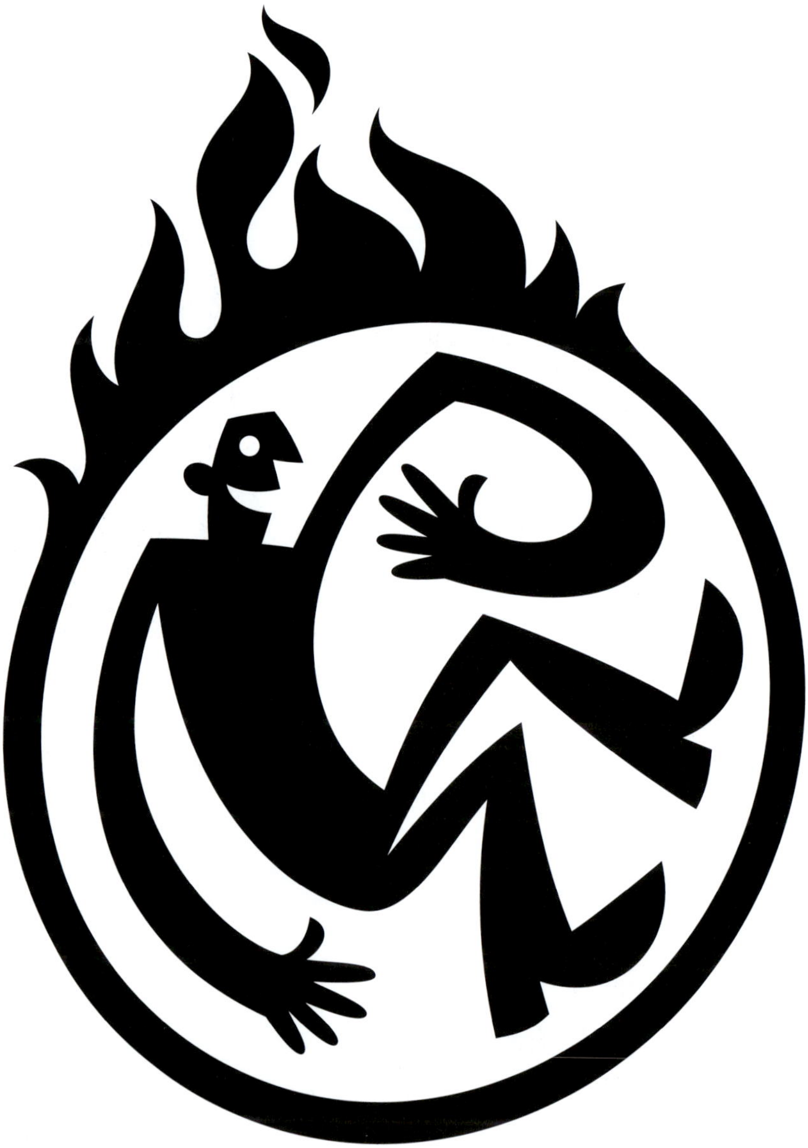

Ring_Of_Fire_**TM438**

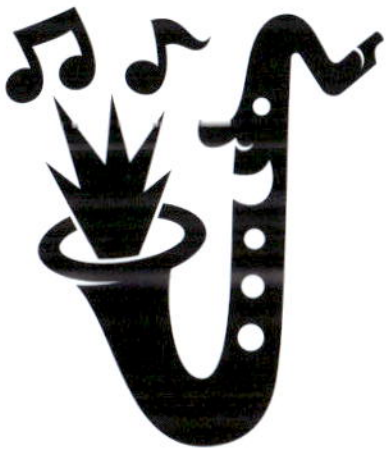

Why_So_Blue_**TM439**

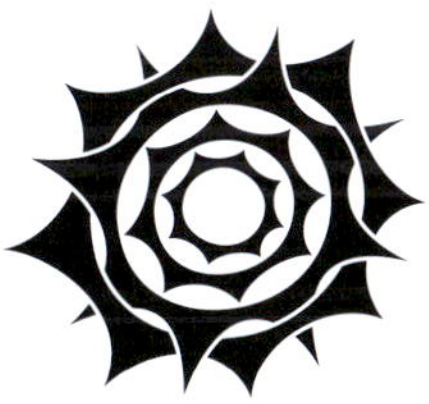

Rosette_**TM440**

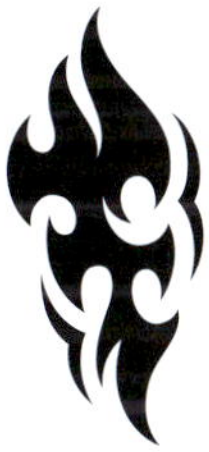

Will_O_Wisp_**TM441**

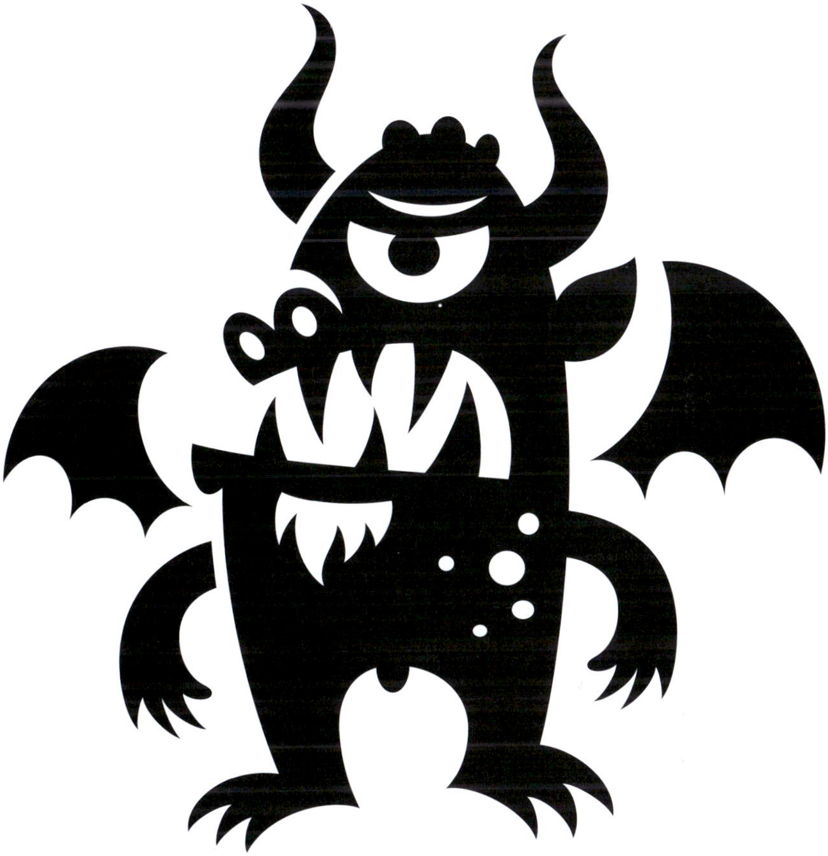

Beastly_**TM442**

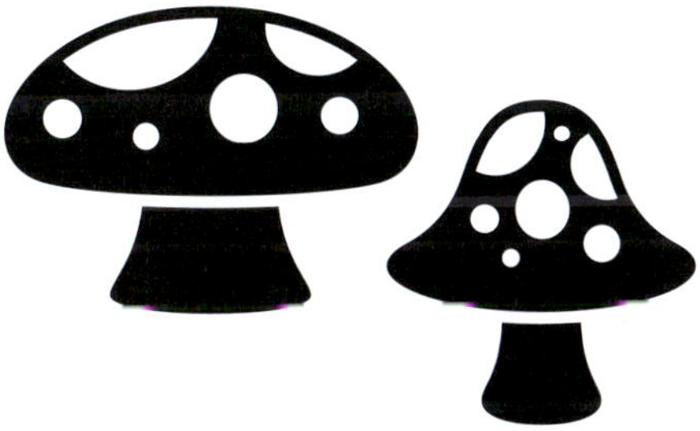

Shrooms_**TM443**

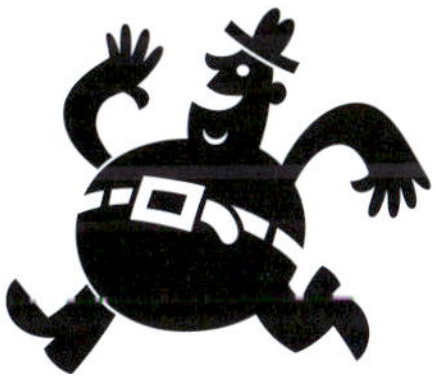

Reaching_Maximum_Density_**TM444**

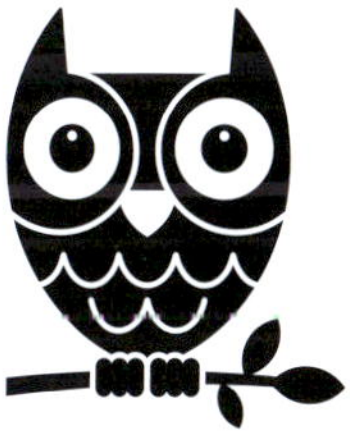

Wise_Bird_**TM445**

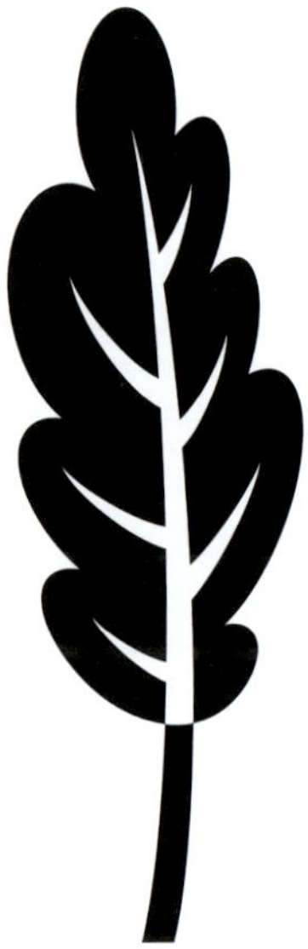

Spruce_**TM447**

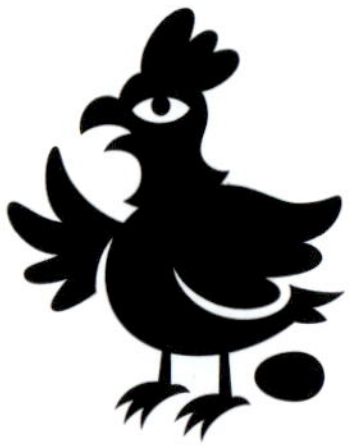

What_Came_First_**TM446**

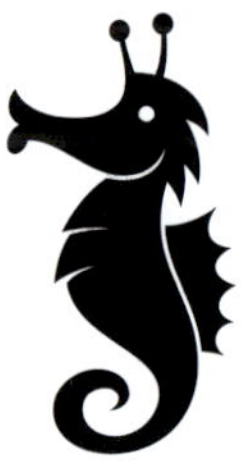

Seahorse_**TM448**

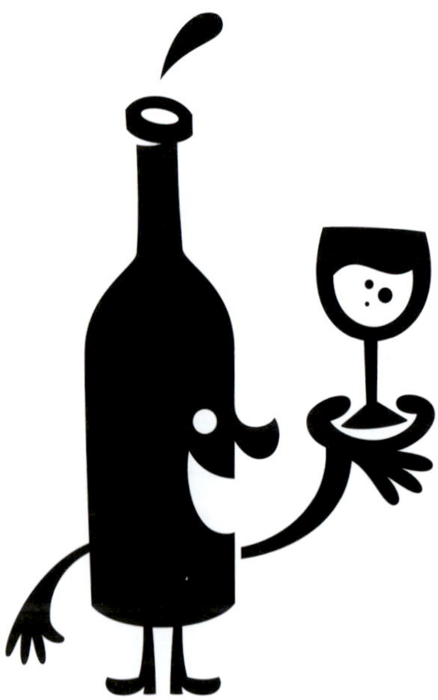

Salute_**TM449**

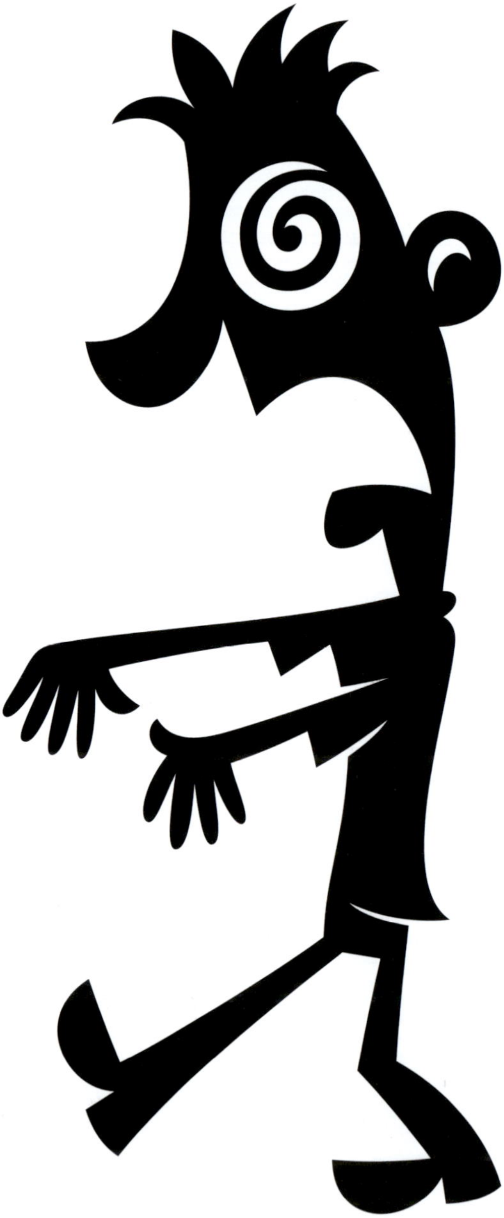

Consumer_Zombie_**TM450**

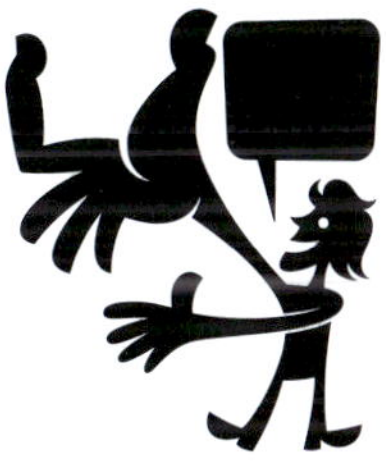

You_Go_Girl_**TM451**

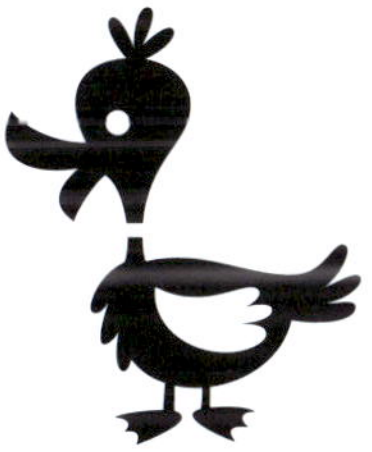

Water_Off_A_Ducks_Back_**TM452**

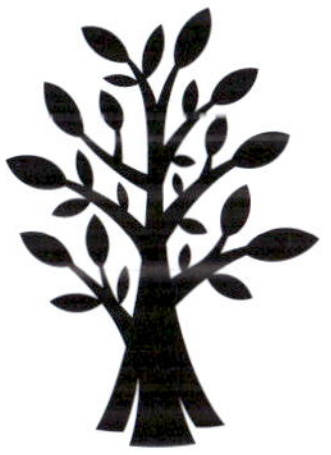

Celebrate_Arbor_Day_**TM453**

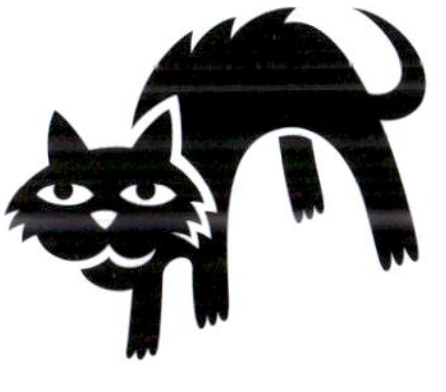

Black_Cat_**TM454**

All_Aboard_**TM455**

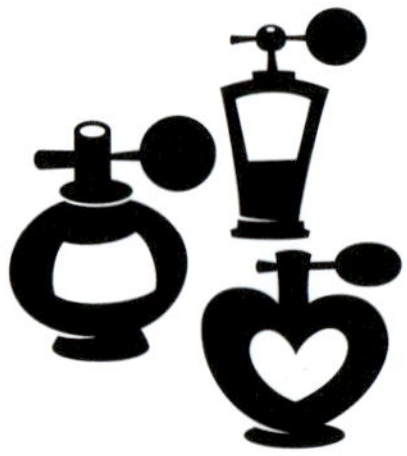

Overwhelm_Your_Olfactory_Senses_**TM456**

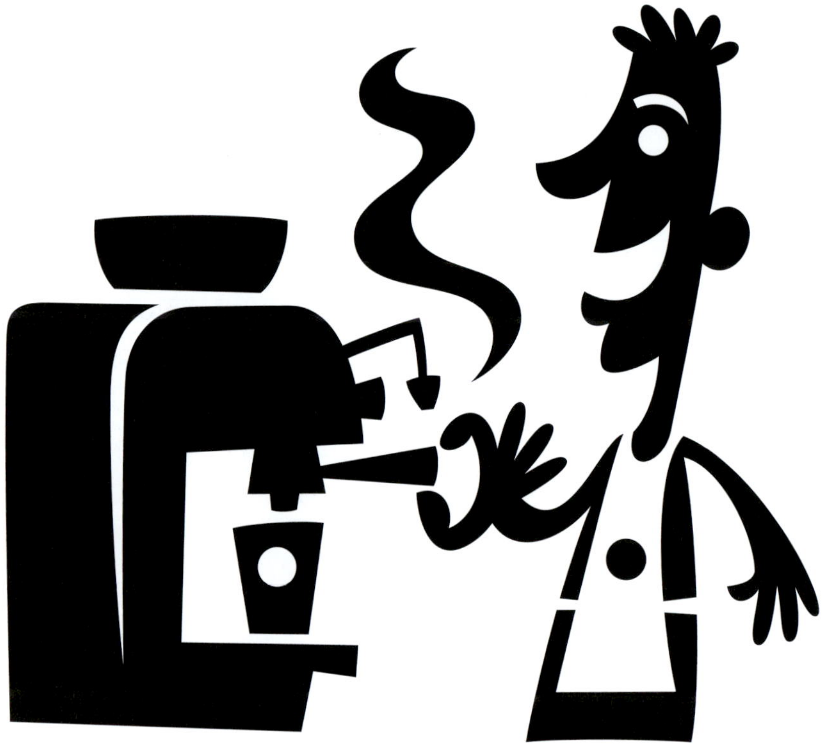

Coffee_Monger_**TM457**

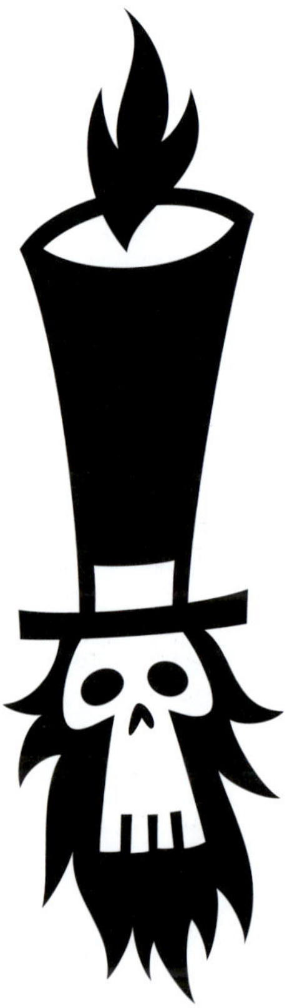

Killer_Inspiration_**TM458**

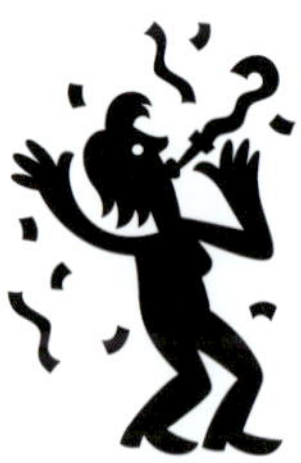

Party_Girl_**TM459**

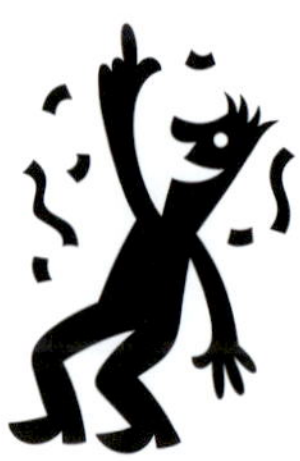

Party_Guy_**TM460**

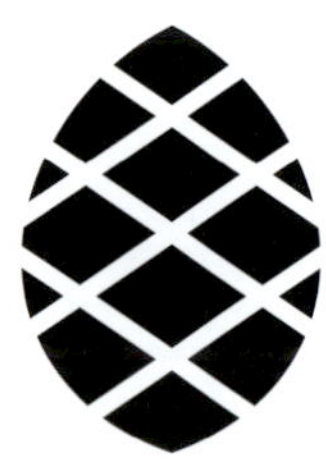

Pine_Cone_**TM461**

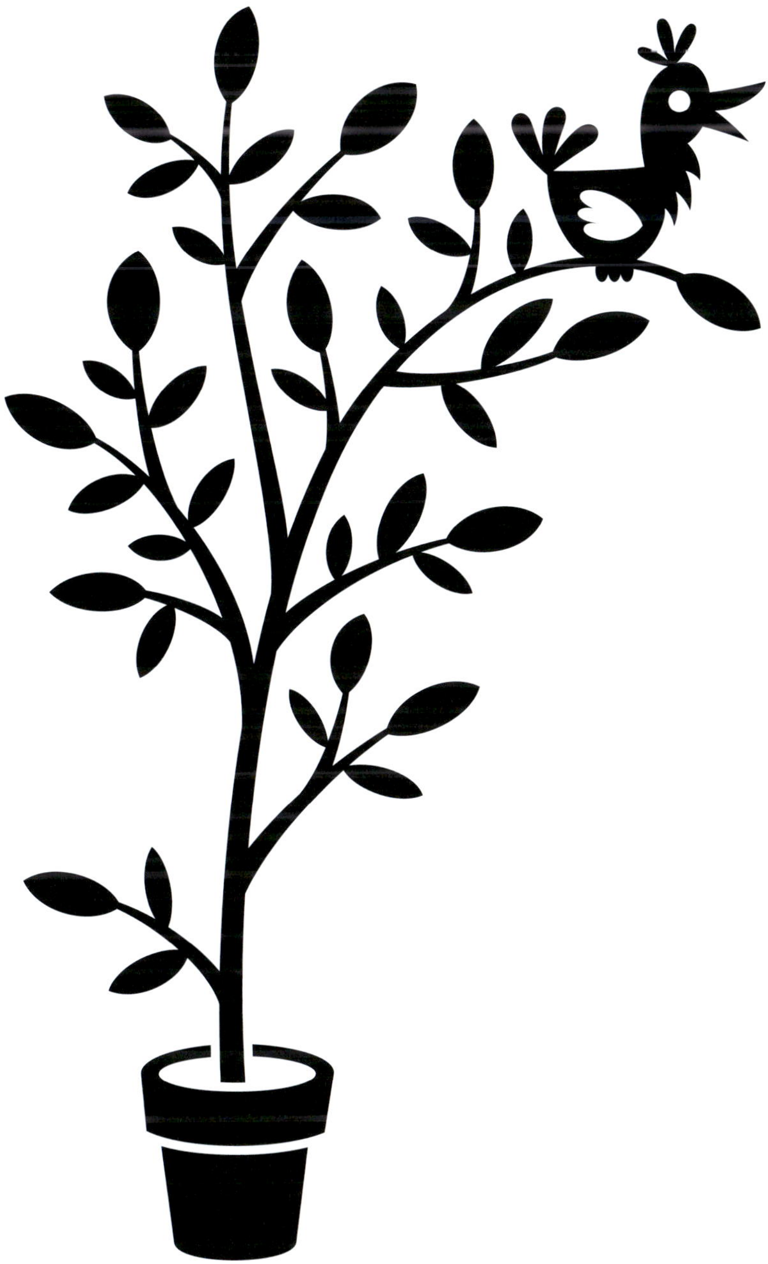

Lets_Hang_Out_**TM464**

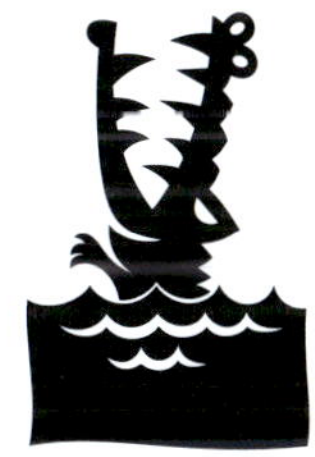

No_Swimming_**TM462**

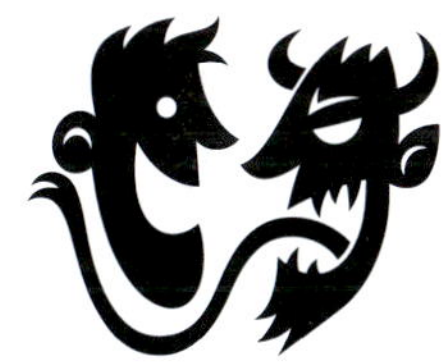

Smooth_Talker_**TM463**

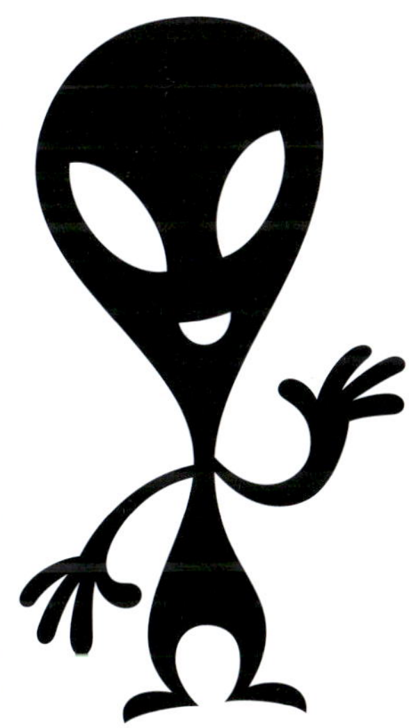

Alien_**TM465**

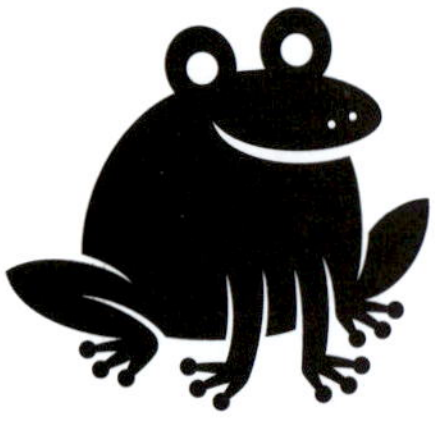

Big_Frog_Small_Pond_**TM466**

Cold_Particle_**TM467**

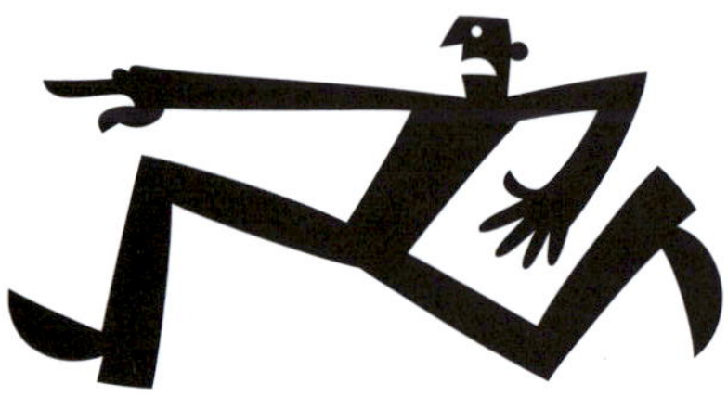

Over_There_**TM468**

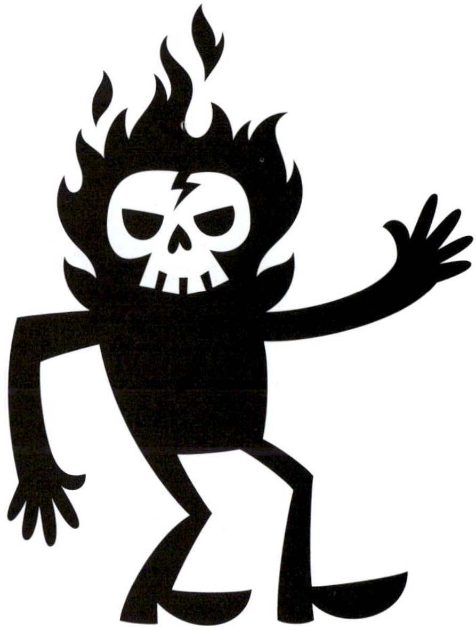

Dead_Ahead_**TM469**

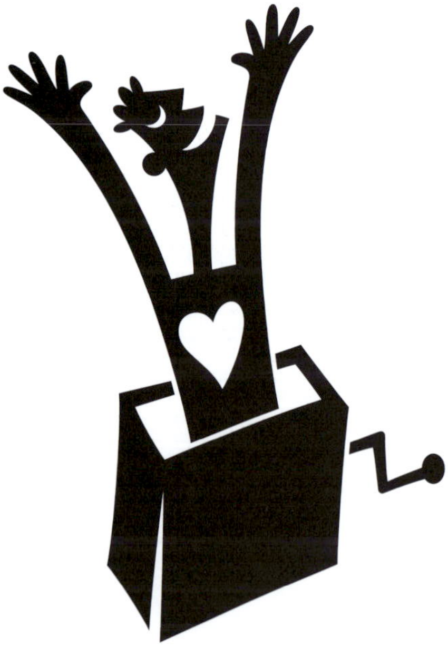

Crank_It_Up_**TM470**

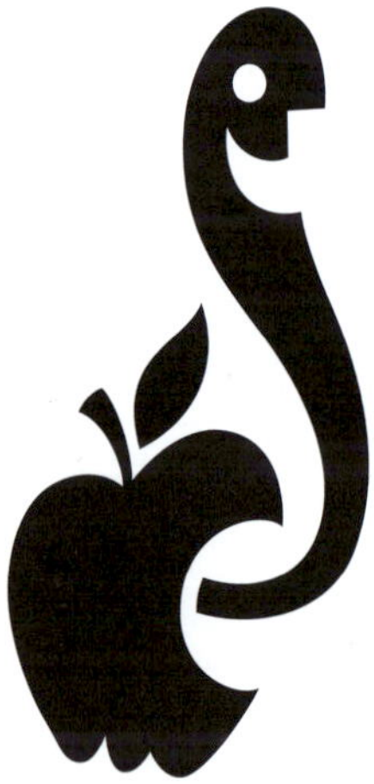

Apple_Worm_**TM471**

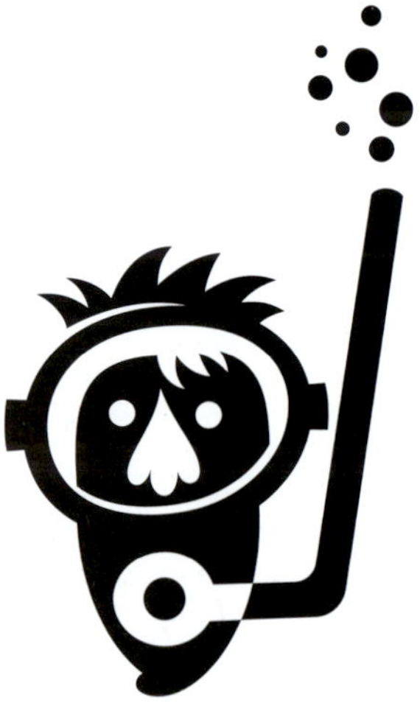

Sea_What_I_Mean_**TM472**

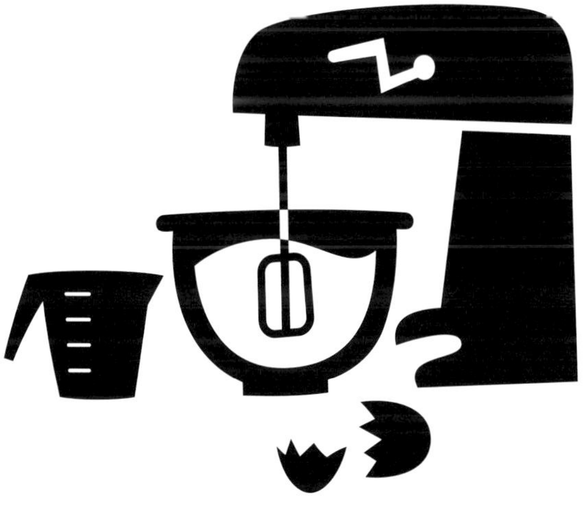

Mix_It_Up_**TM474**

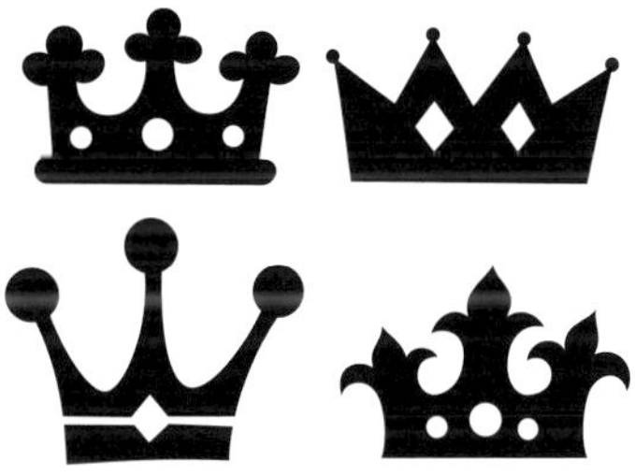

Daidems_**TM473**

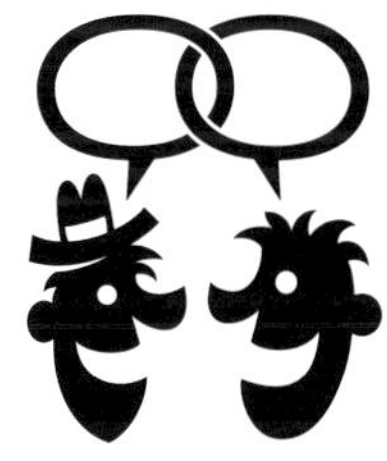

Engaging_Conversation_**TM475**

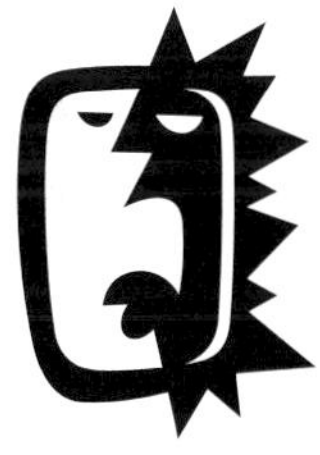

Burst_Of_Anger_**TM476**

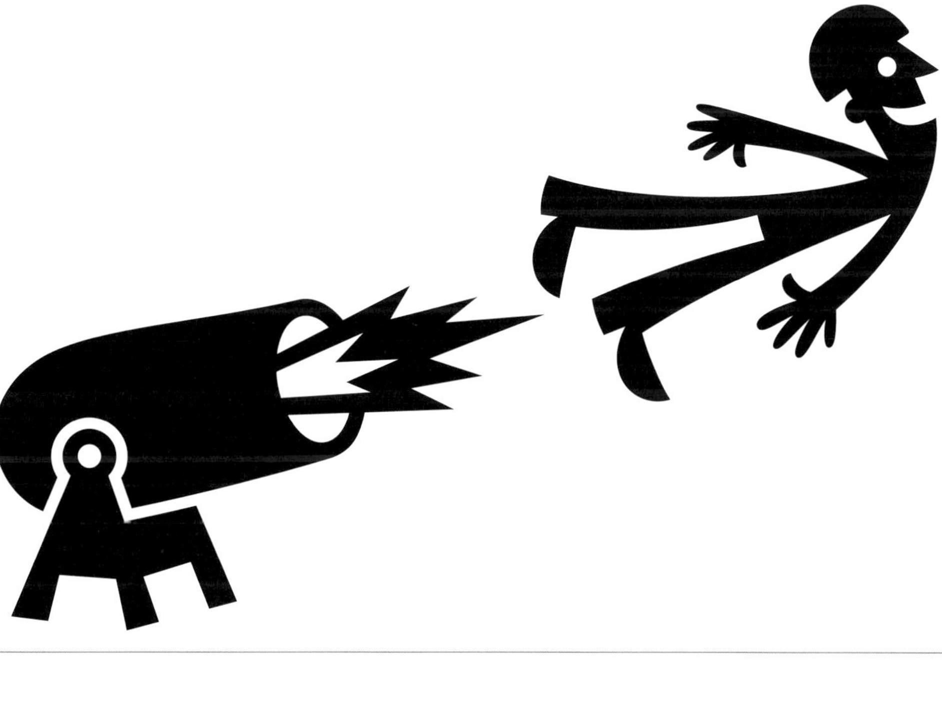

Dare_Devil_**TM477**

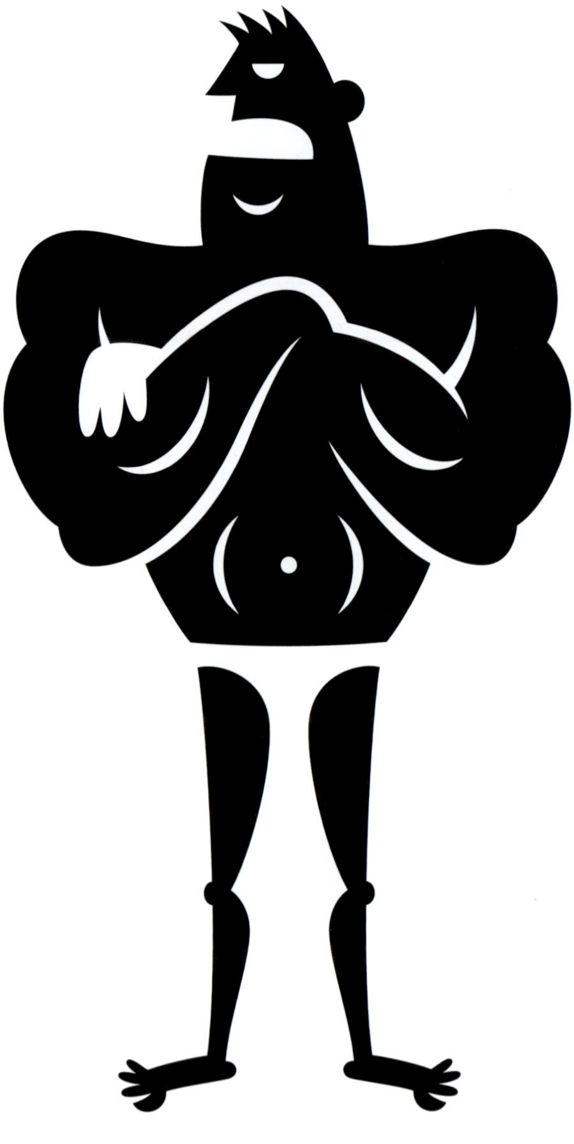

Beef_Cake_**TM479**

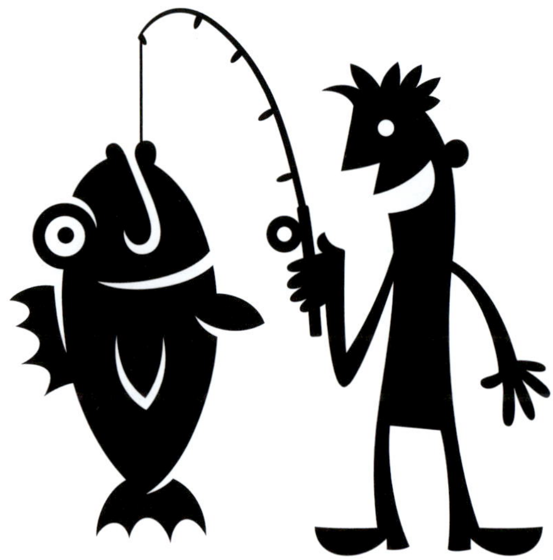

Fisher_King_**TM478**

Bloomers_**TM480**

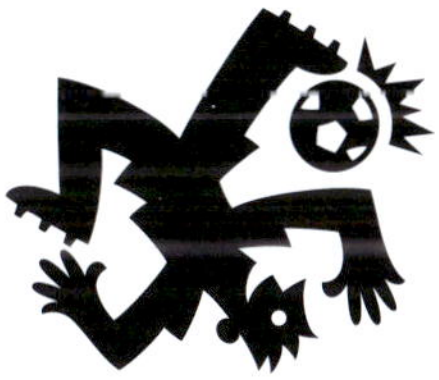

Go_All_Out_**TM481**

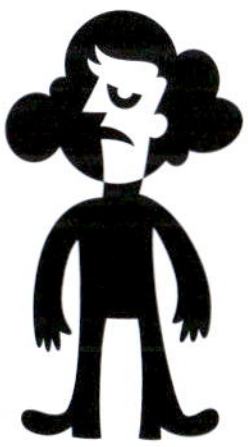

In_A_Mood_**TM483**

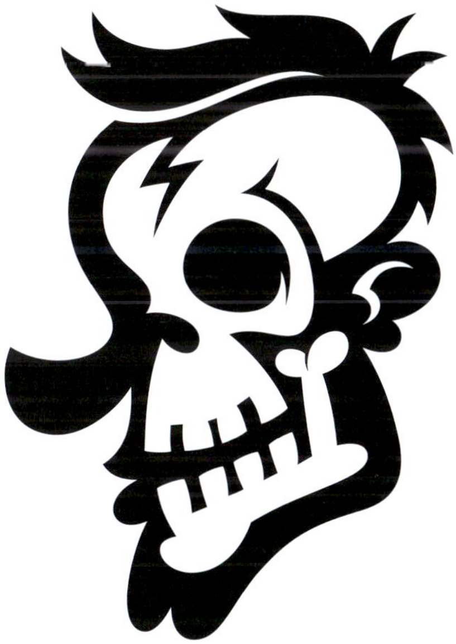

Numb_Skull_**TM484**

Furry_Grin_**TM482**

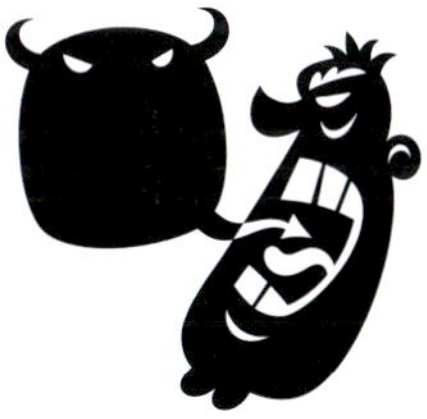

Hate_Speech_**TM485**

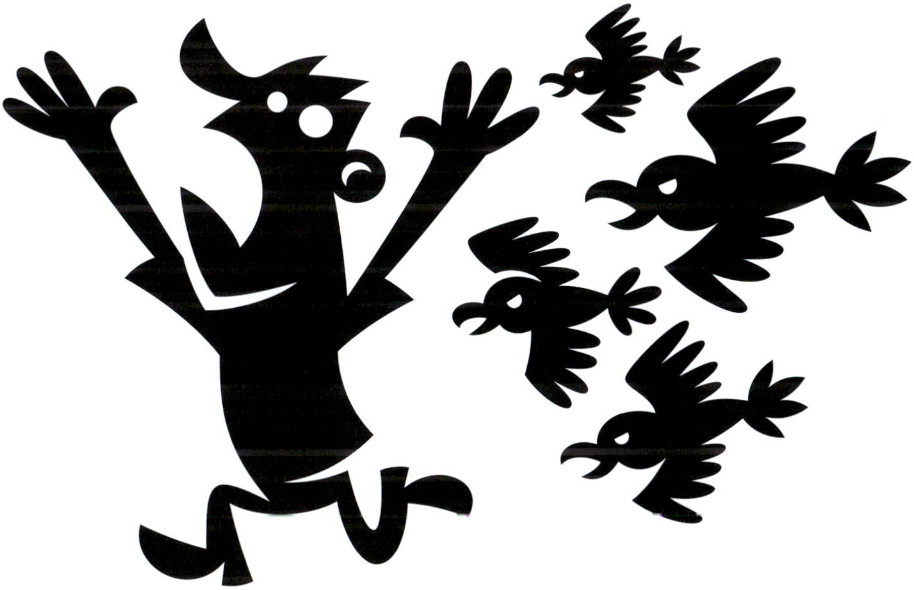

Flock_Of_Torment_**TM486**

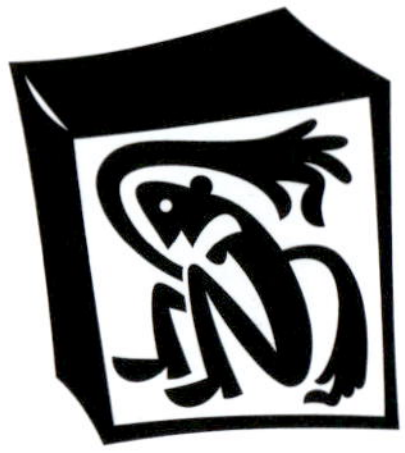

Boxed_In_**TM487**

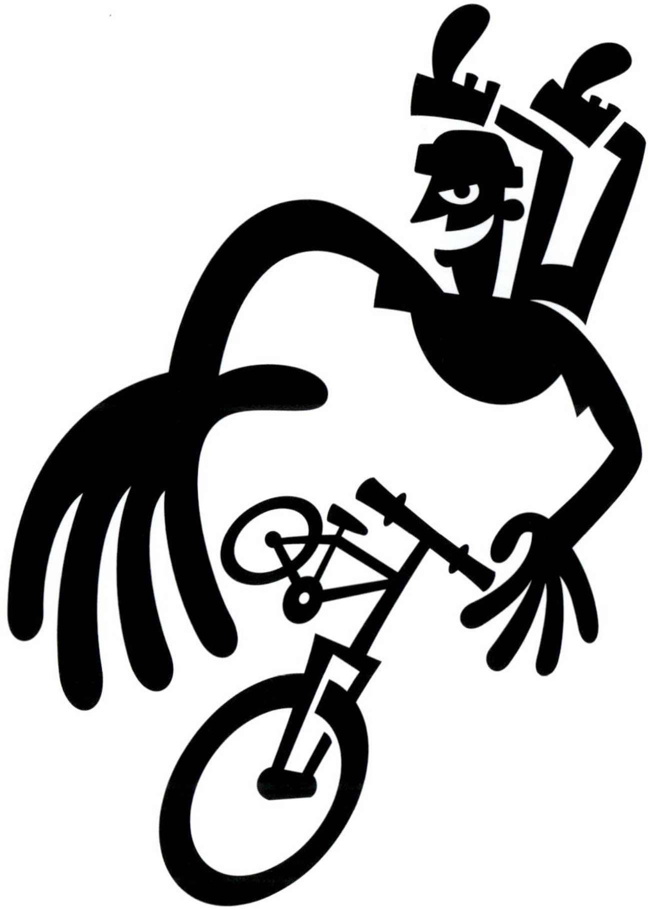

Grab_Air_**TM488**

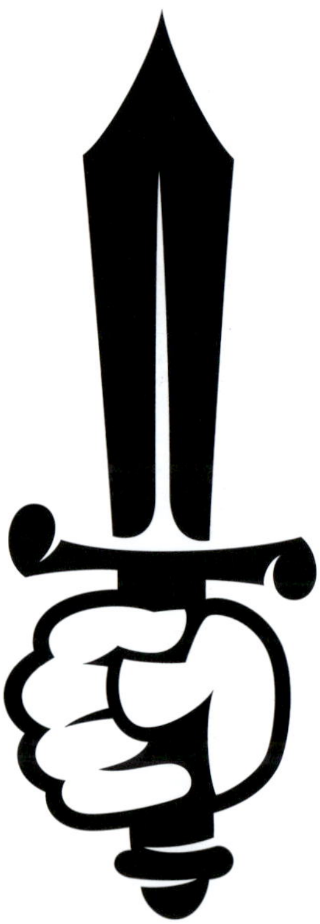

Double_Edge_**TM489**

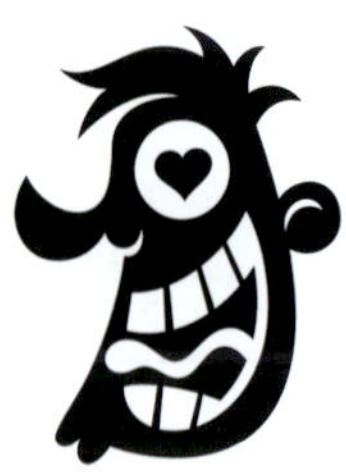

Crazy_For_You_**TM490**

Junk_Food_**TM491**

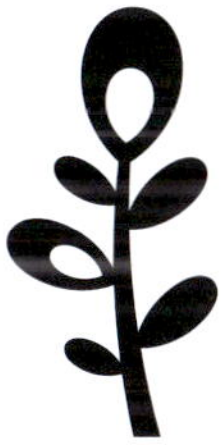

Botanical_**TM492**

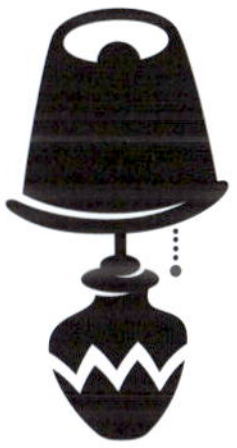

Lamp_**TM493**

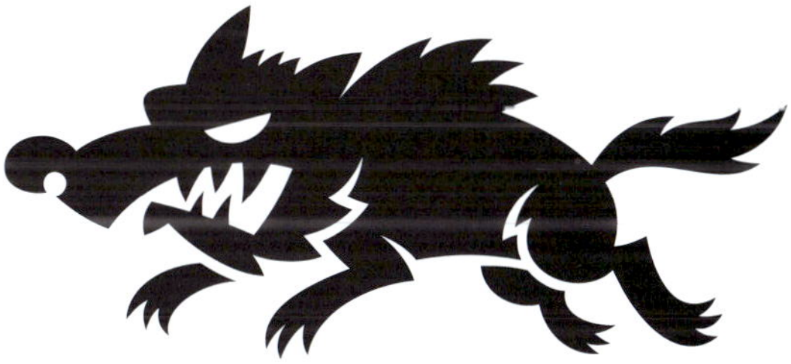

Hungry_Like_A_Wolf_**TM494**

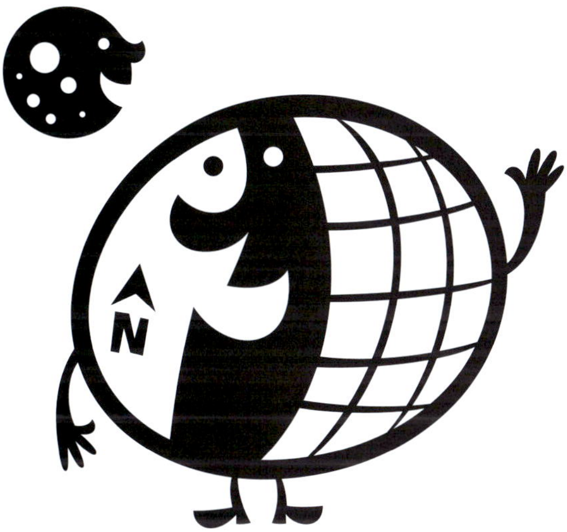

Hey_Little_Buddy_**TM495**

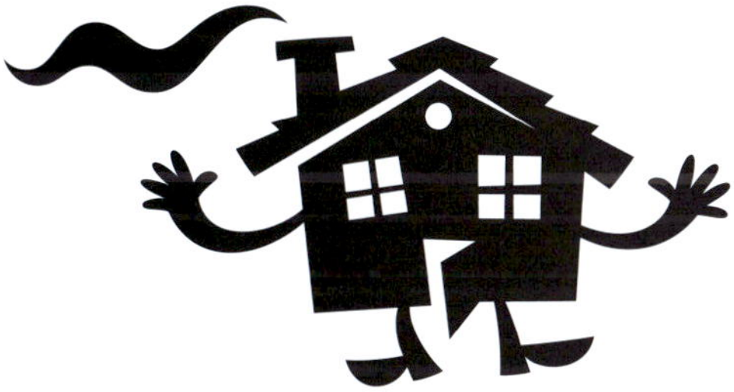

Homey_Welcome_**TM496**

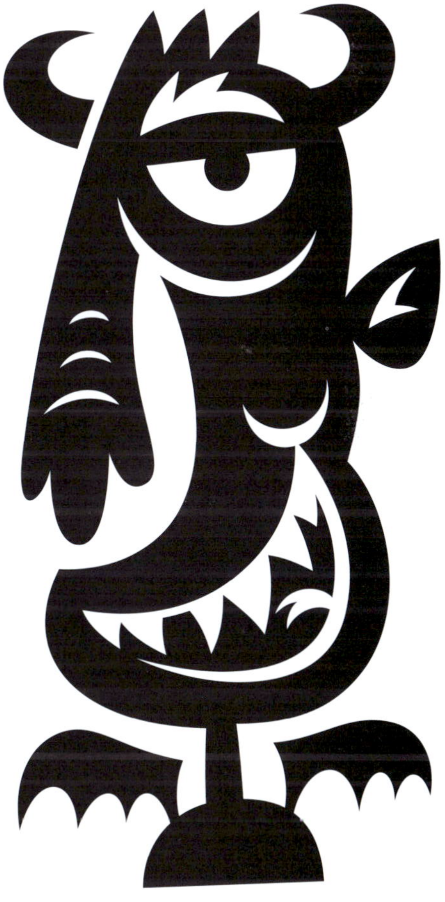

Embrace_Your_Goblin_**TM497**

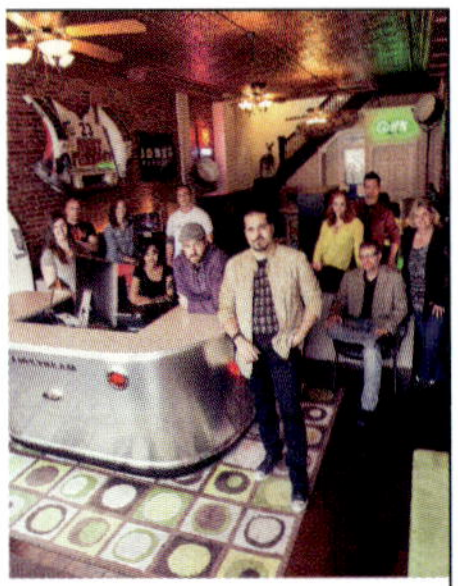

U! Creative

Miamisburg, Ohio

www.ucreate.us

For this exercise, we chose to go with the *Take and Make Art* monster "Triclops." Most all of us at the U! office have little vinyl toys all over our desks and shelves. For this book we wanted to come to the table with something that was a little unexpected and break away from the typical 2D realm. That being said, we couldn't think of a more exciting way than to reimagine this little guy as a proof of concept for a line of vinyl toys!

We're proud to introduce...*Lil' Vonsters.*

Art Used: Triclops TM201

Lil' Vonsters Logo

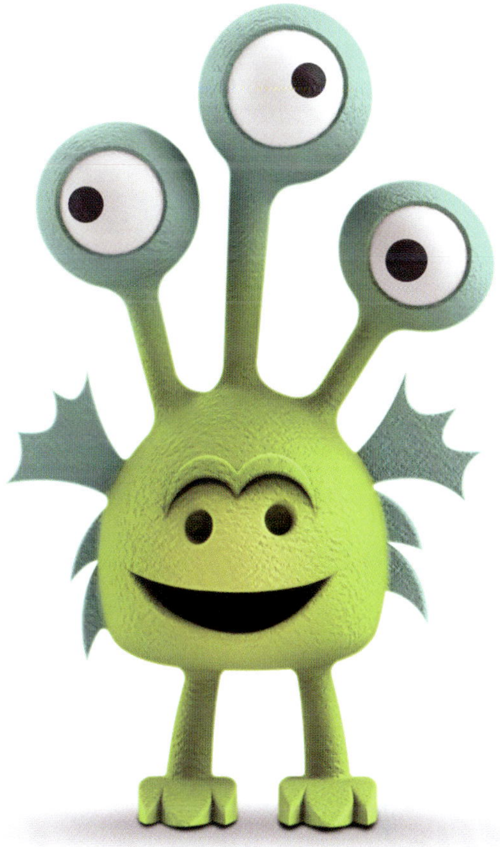

Triclops Vinyl Design
Take and Make art was transformed from a flat 2D design to a virtual 3D vinyl figure.

Lil' Vonsters Figures
Lil' Vonsters figures would be developed in an assortment of character types and come in a variety of colors in a slick, matte finish black box with spot varnish to complement the high-end look.

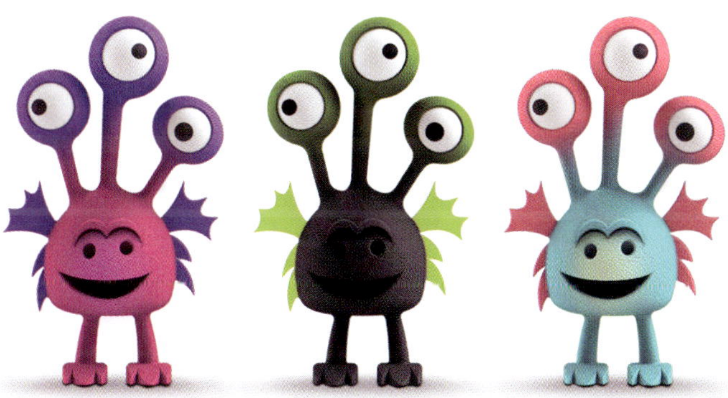

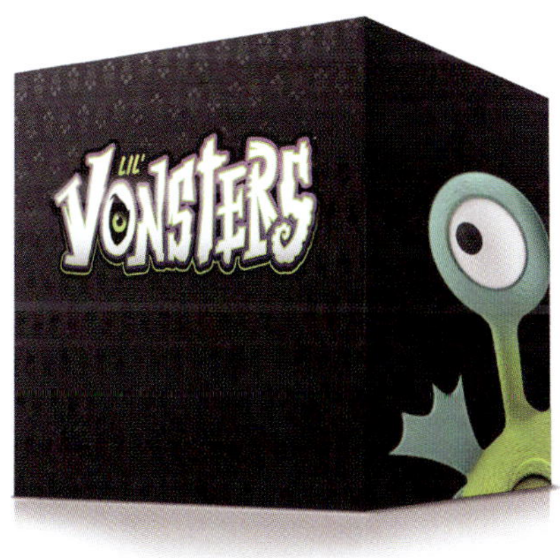

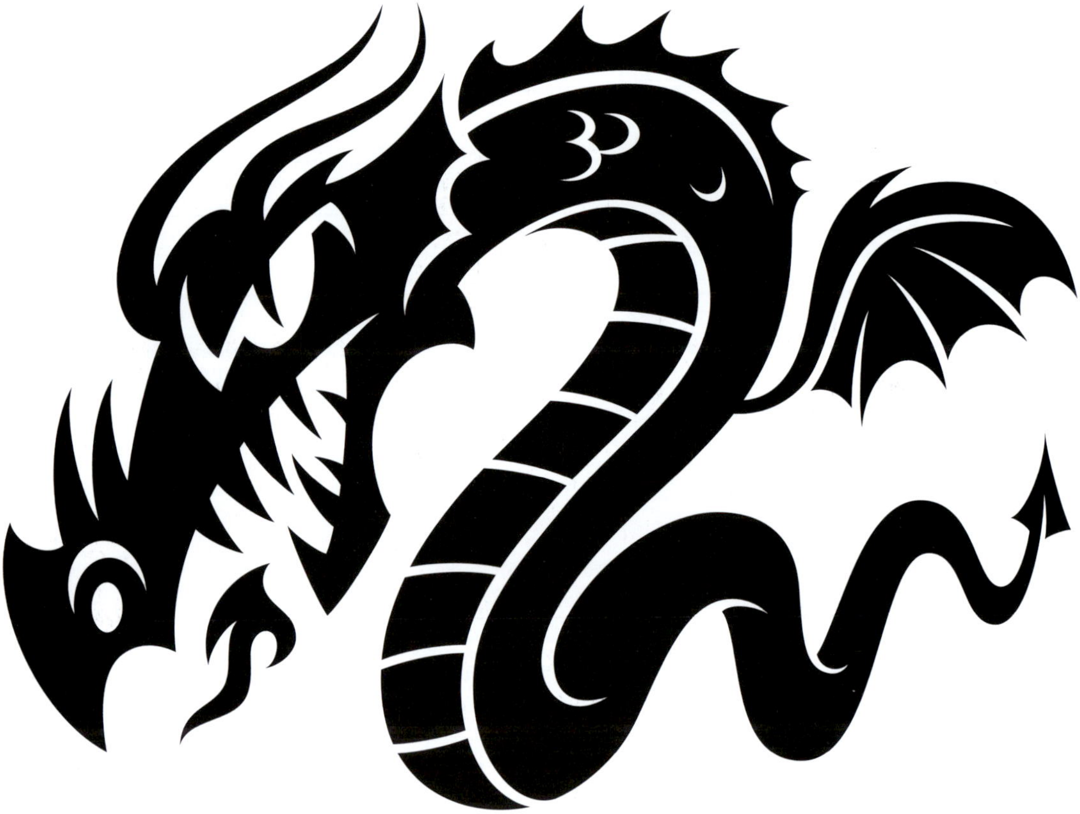

Draco_**TM498**

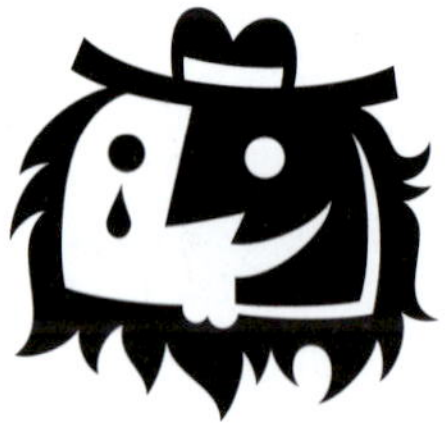

Crying_Amish_**TM499**

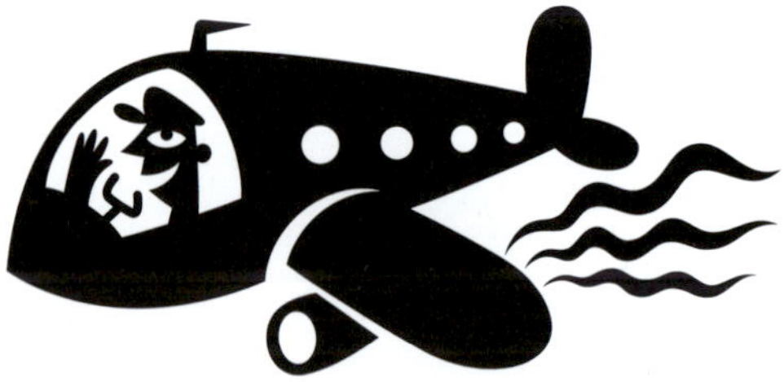

Chemtrails_**TM500**

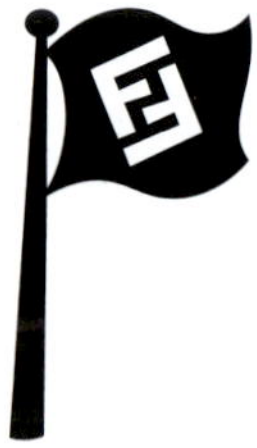

False_Flag_**TM501**

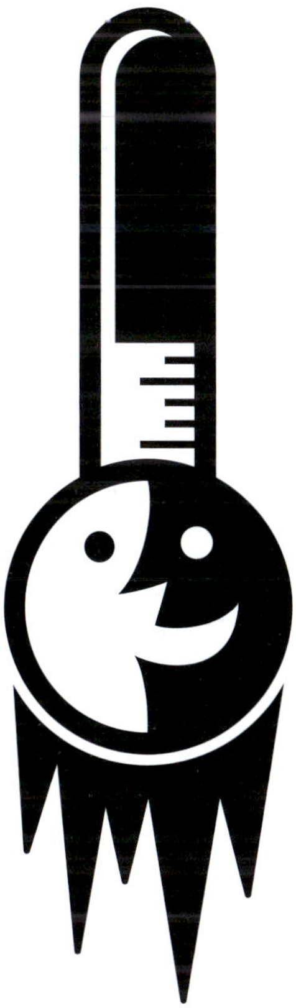

Chill_Out_Bro_**TM504**

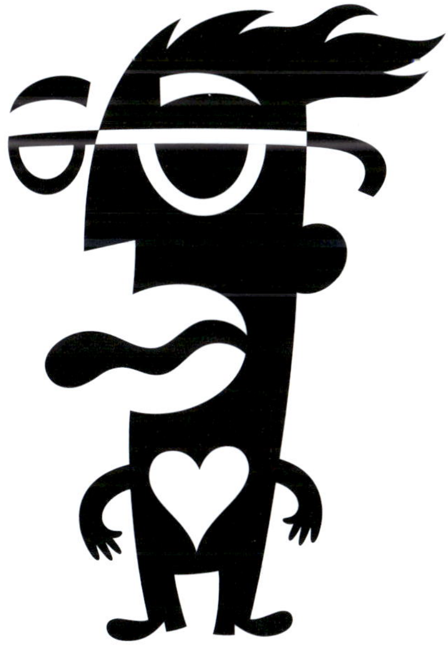

Crazy_Love_**TM503**

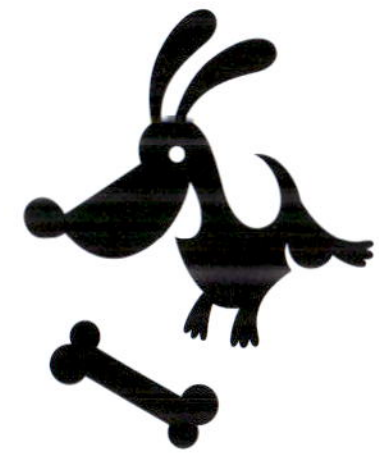

Dog_And_Bone_**TM502**

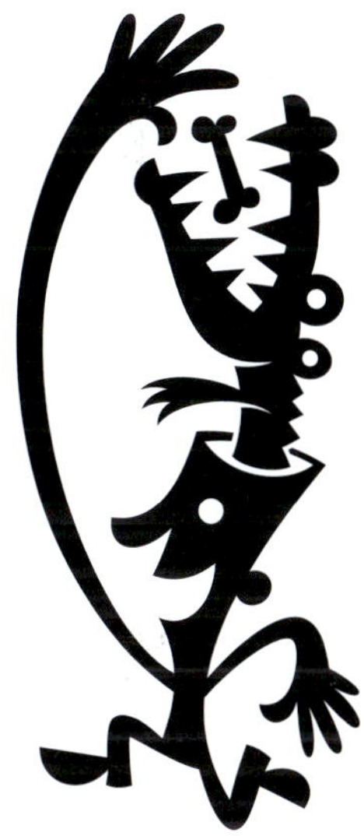

Feed_Your_Imagination_**TM505**

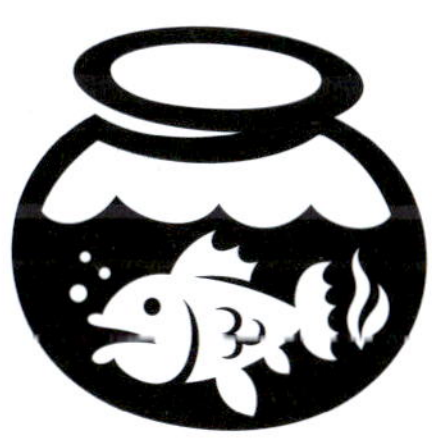

Fish_Bowl_**TM506**

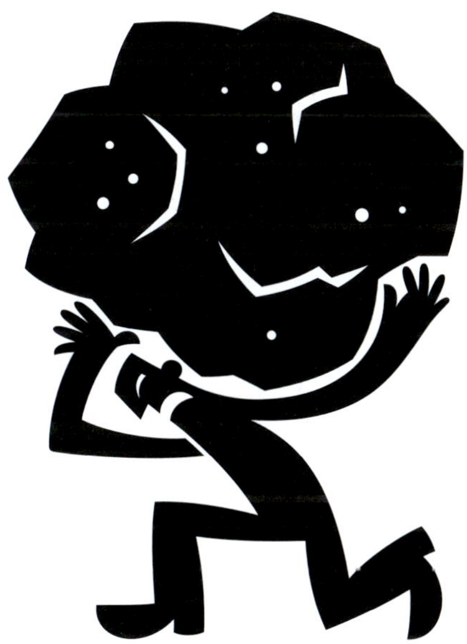

A_Burdensome_Stone_**TM507**

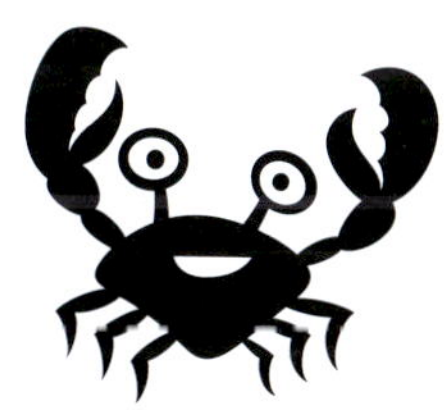

Dont_Be_Crabby_**TM508**

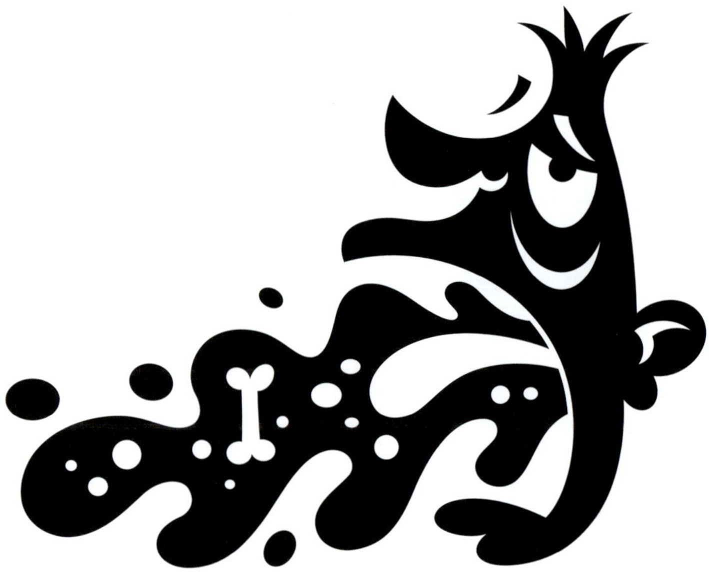

Dont_Make_Me_Puke_**TM509**

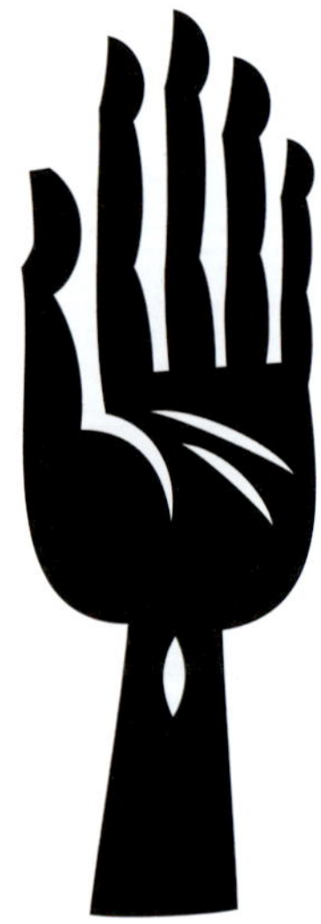

Holey_Hand_**TM510**

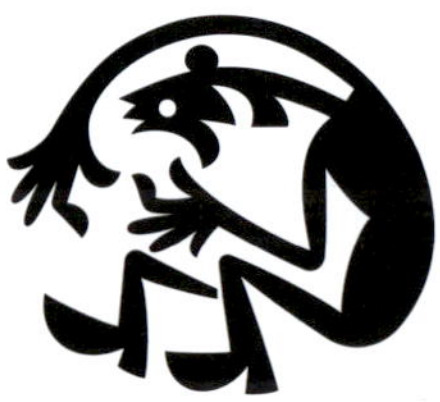

Fetal_Position_**TM511**

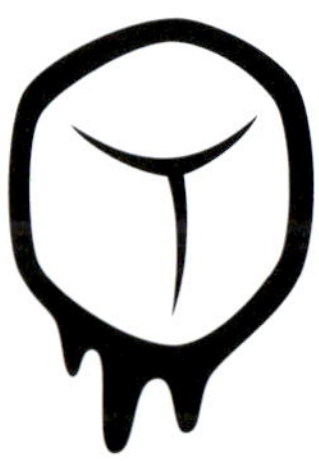

Chill_Out_**TM512**

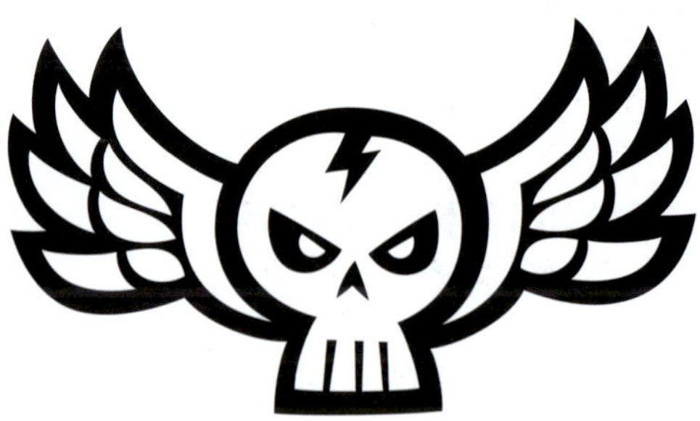

Death_Flight_**TM513**

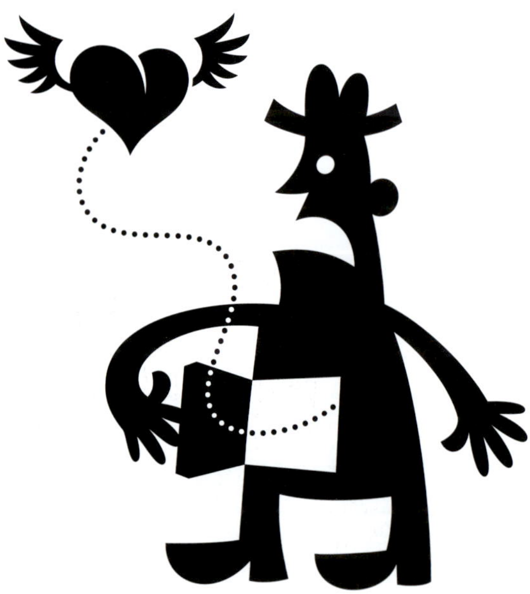

Heartless_**TM514**

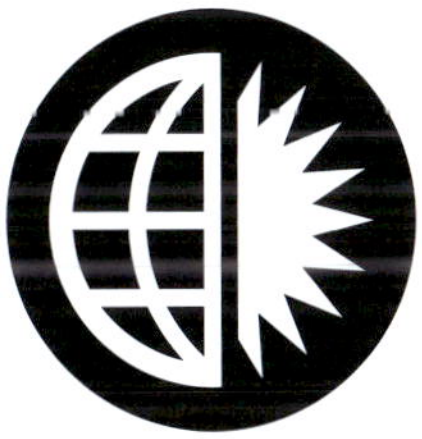

Global_Event_**TM515**

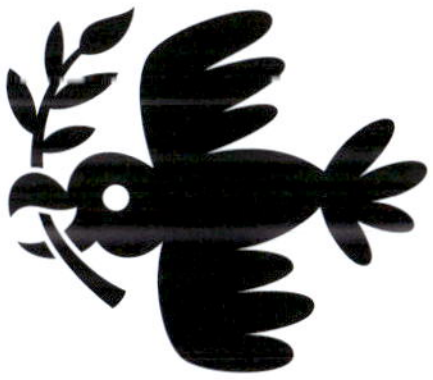

Give_Peace_A_Chance_**TM516**

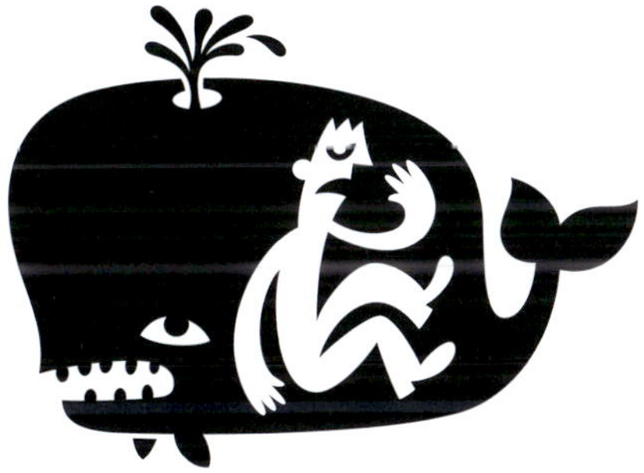

Difficult_Situation_**TM517**

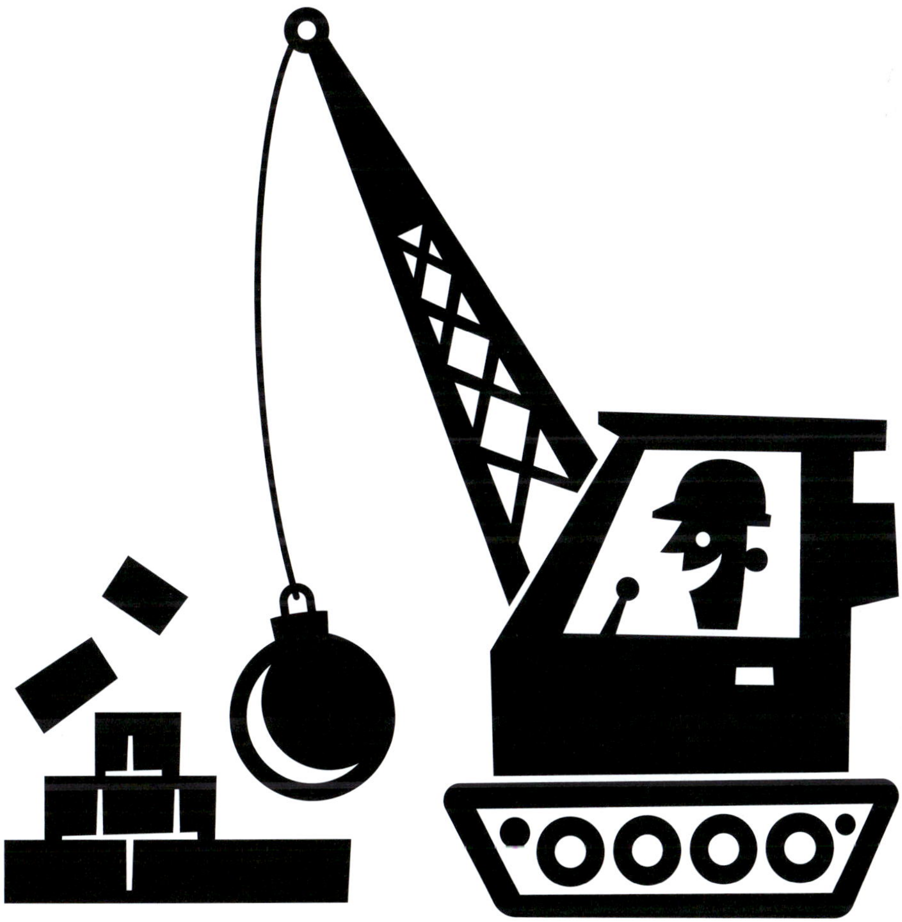

Break_Down_Barriers_**TM518**

Inquisitive_Joe_**TM519**

Alien_Gardening_**TM520**

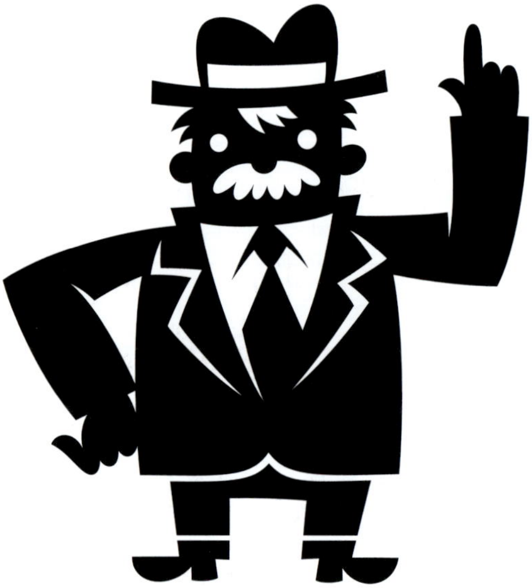

I_Do_Declare_**TM521**

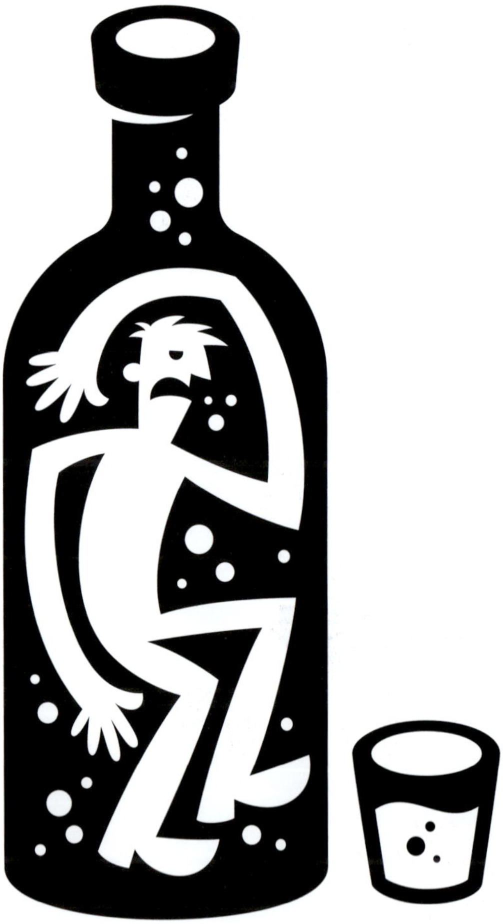

Booze_**TM522**

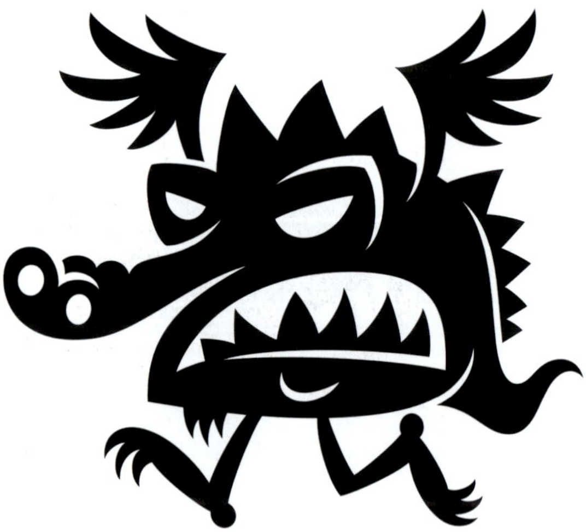

Goblin_**TM523**

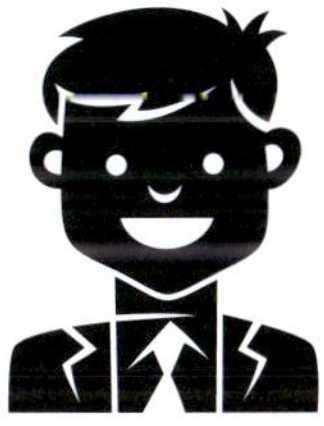

Happy_Little_Boy_**TM524**

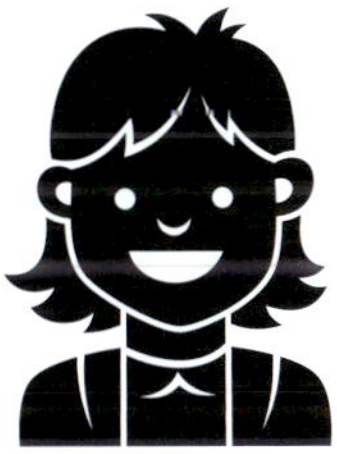

Happy_Little_Girl_**TM525**

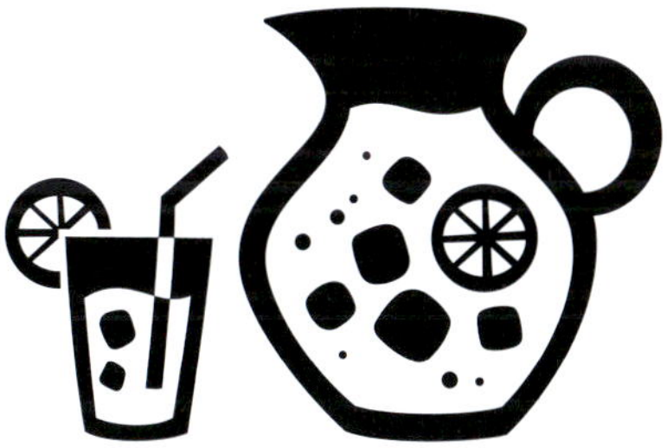

Cool_Lemonade_**TM526**

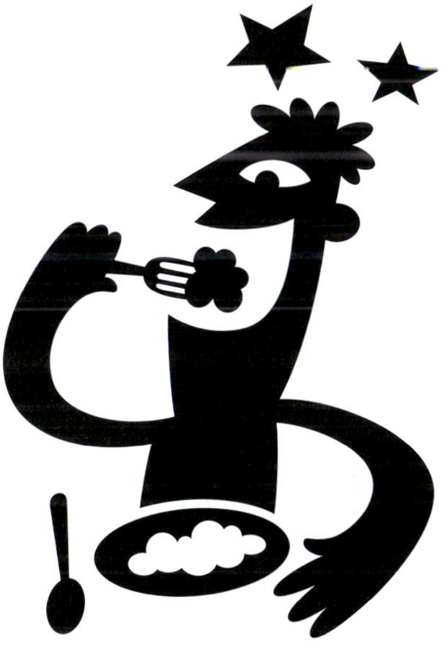

Eat_Your_Mush_**TM527**

Wheels_On_The_Bus_**TM528**

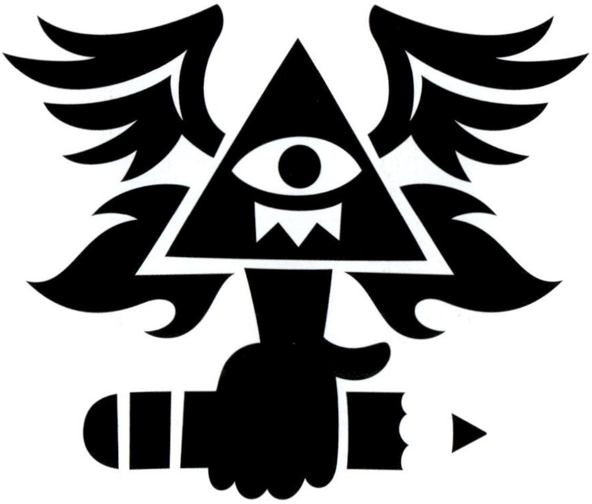

Creative_Overlords_**TM530**

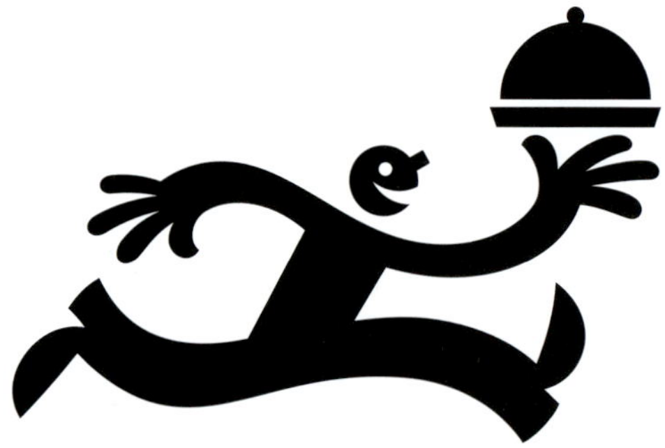

Order_Up_**TM529**

Nodes_**TM531**

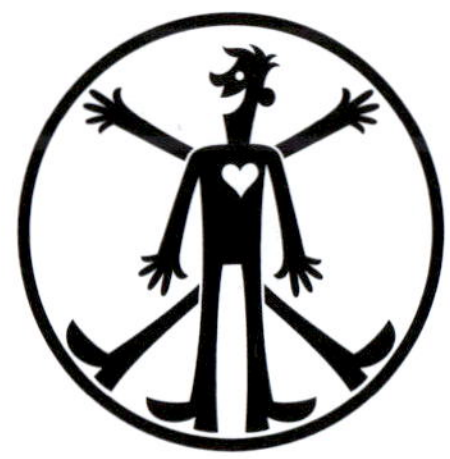

MAN_Mainly_A_Nuisance_**TM532**

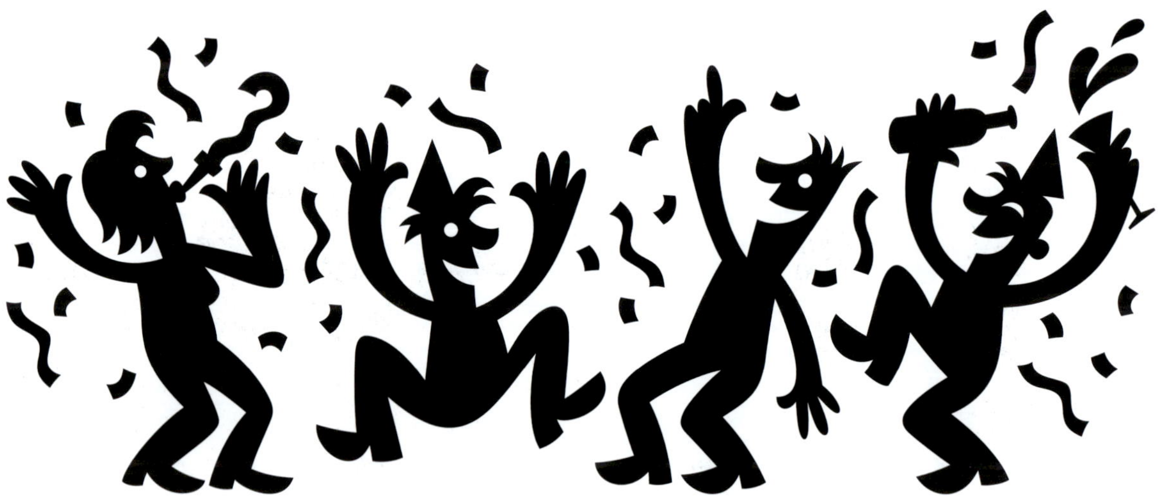

Party_Time_**TM533**

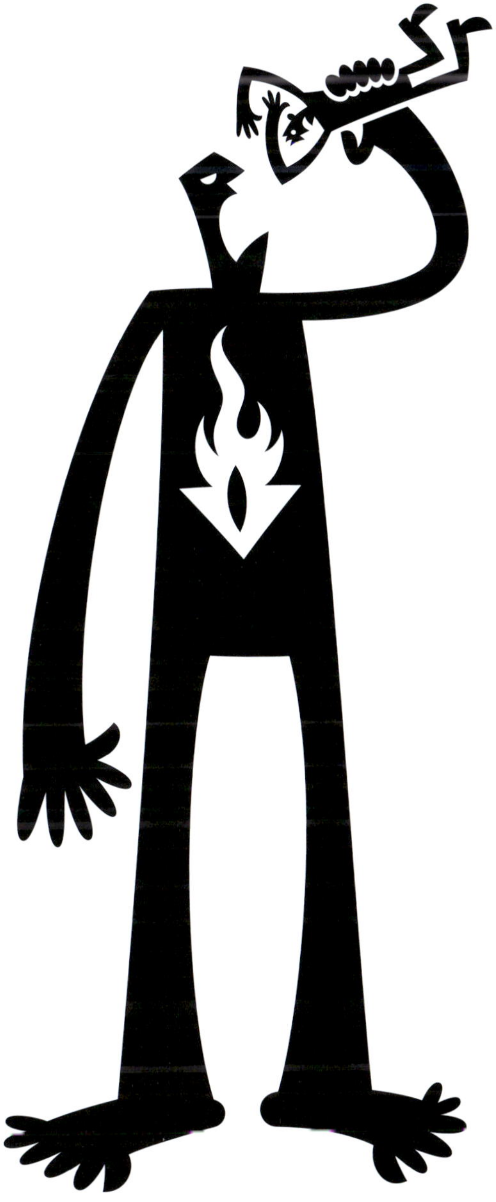

Giant_Problems_**TM537**

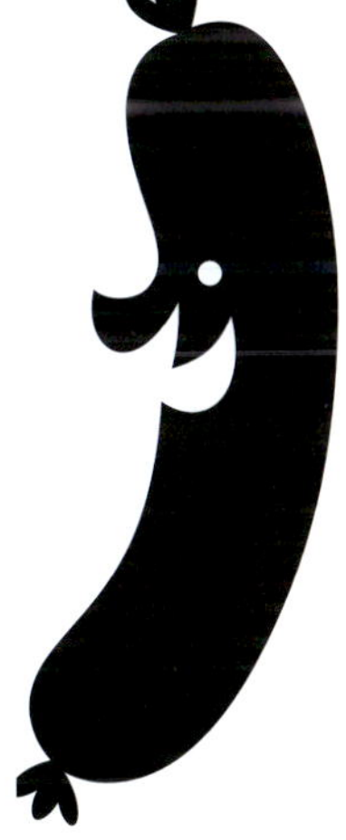

Dont_Be_A_Weenie_**TM535**

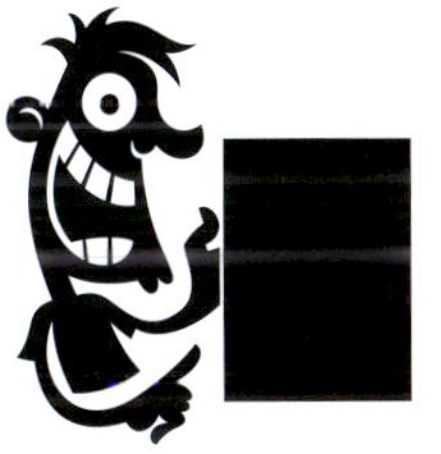

Look_Here_**TM534**

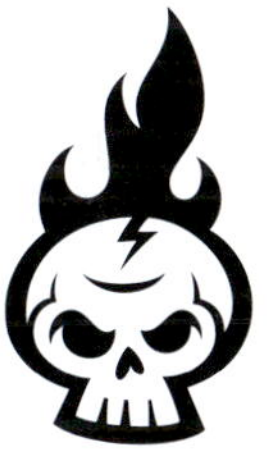

Torch_Head_**TM536**

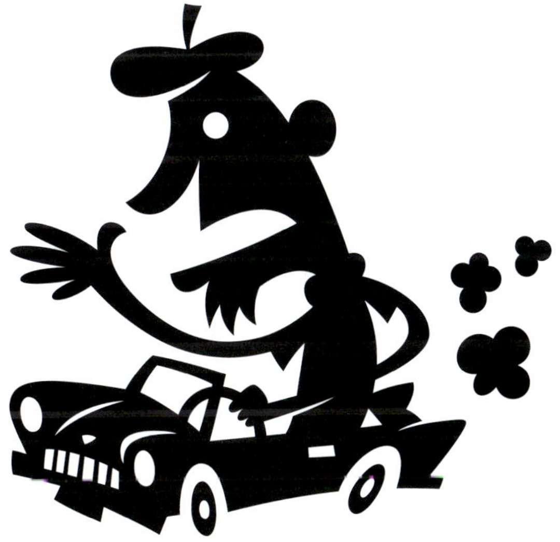

Pedal_To_The_Metal_**TM538**

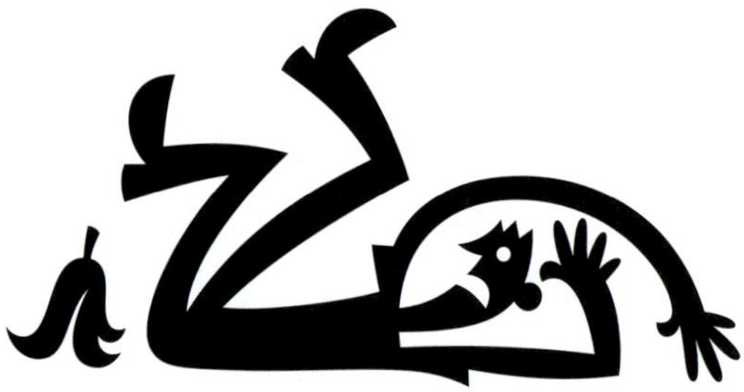

Dont_Fall_For_It_TM539

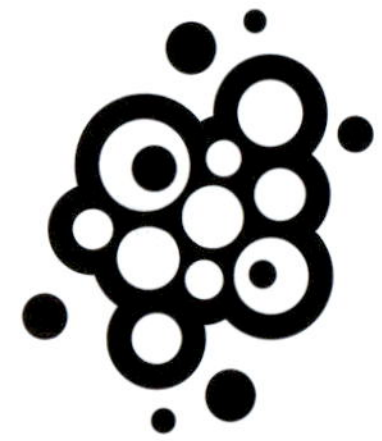

Cohesion_TM540

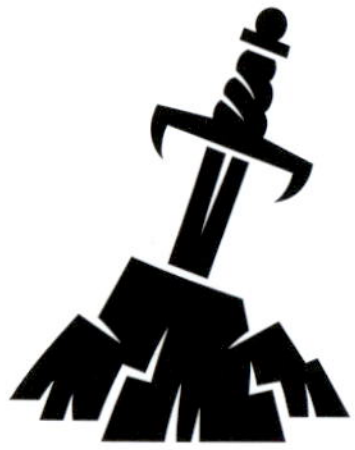

Excalibur_TM541

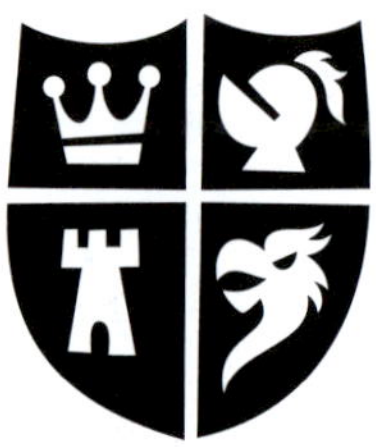

Coat_Of_Arms_TM542

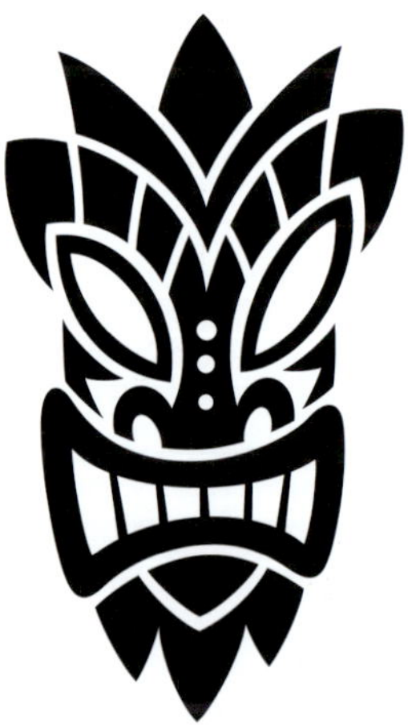

Native_Urge_TM543

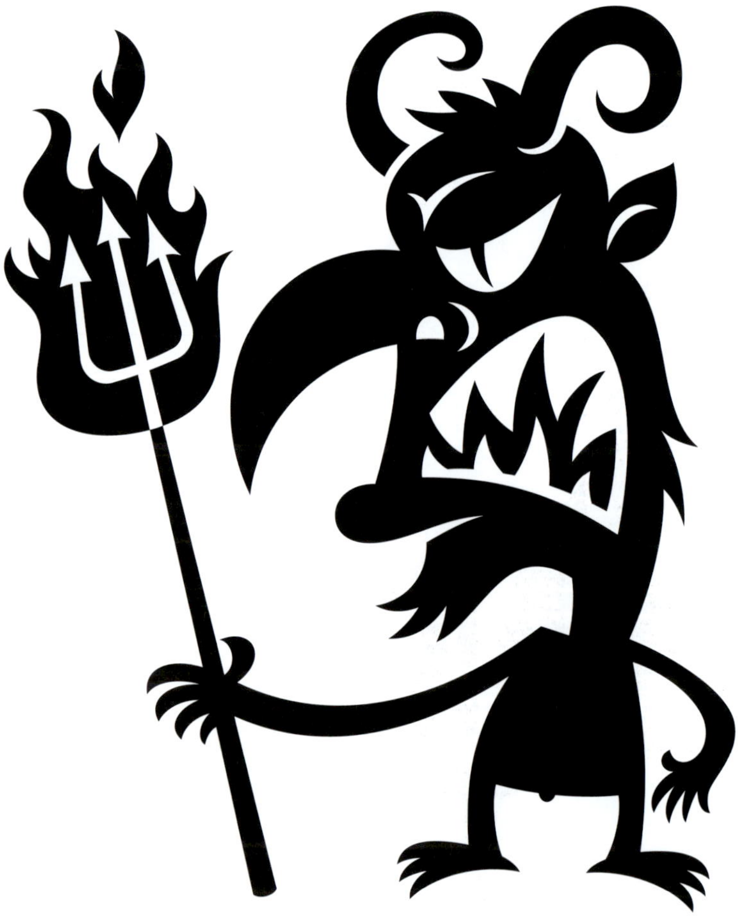

Beelzebub_TM544

Handle_With_Care_**TM545**

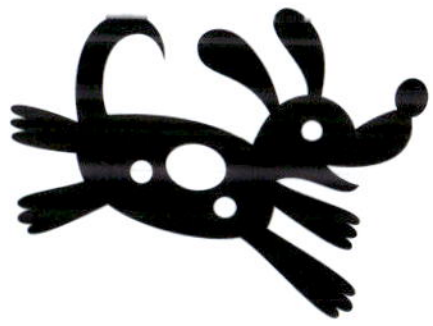

Dog_Run_**TM546**

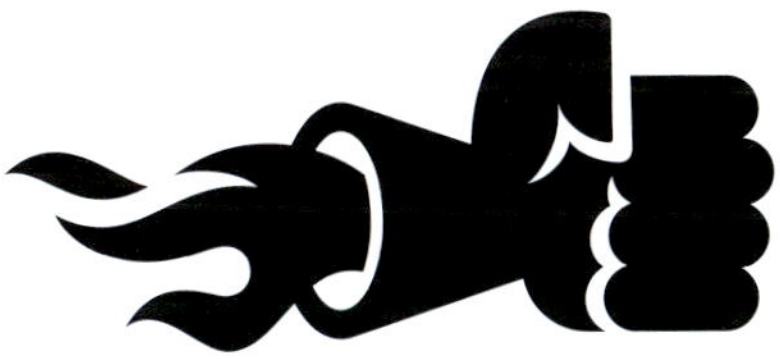

Fist_Of_Fury_**TM547**

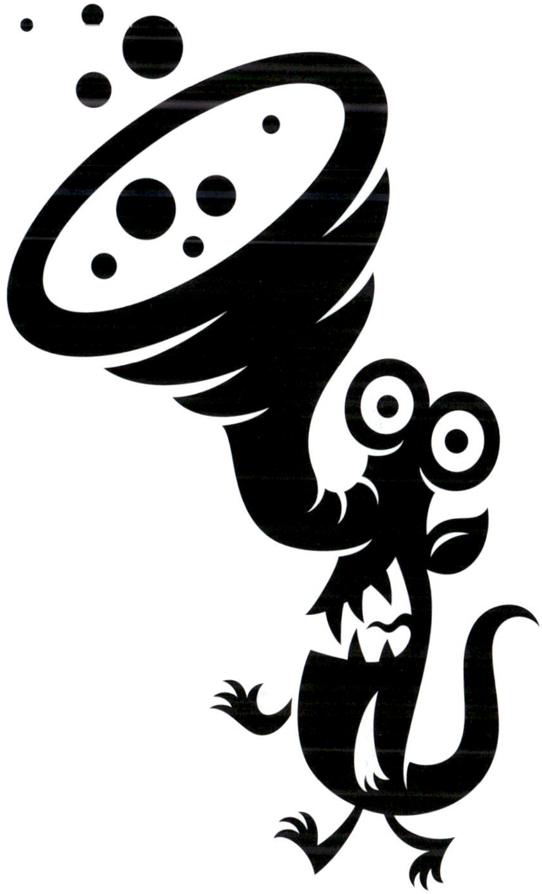

Express_Yourself_**TM548**

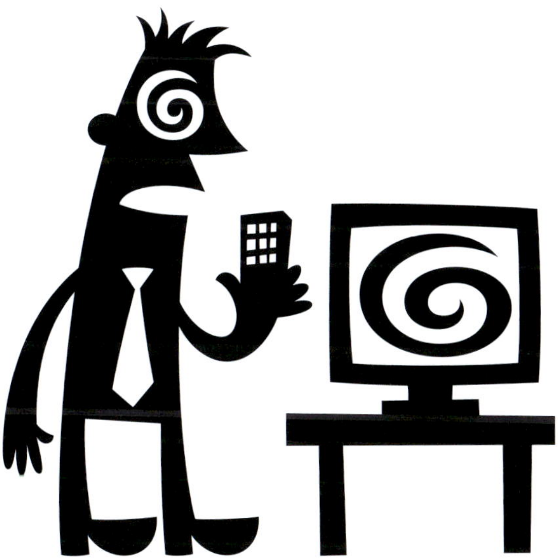

Mainstream_Zombie_**TM549**

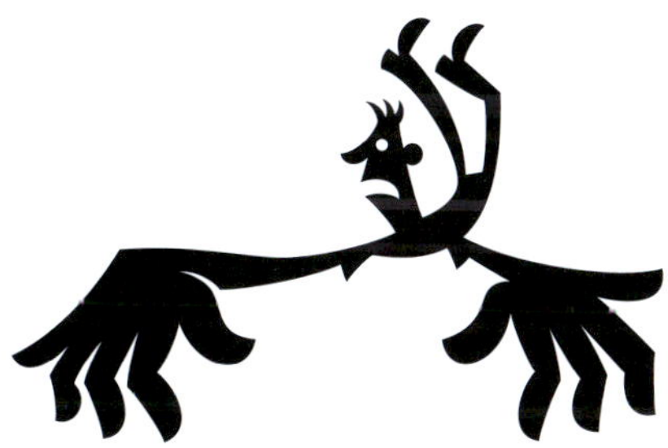

Hang_In_There_**TM550**

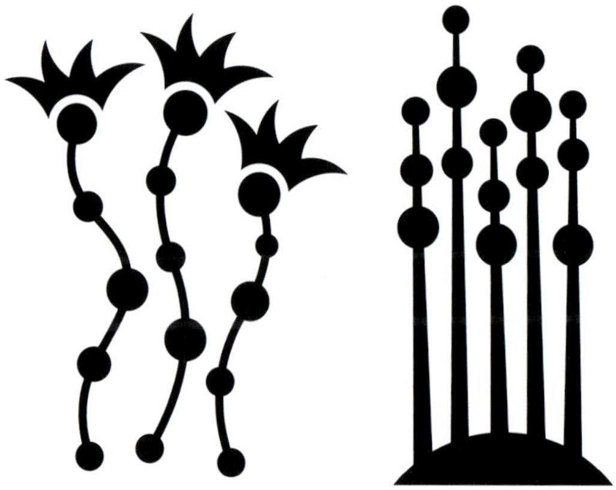

Bizarro_Botany_**TM551**

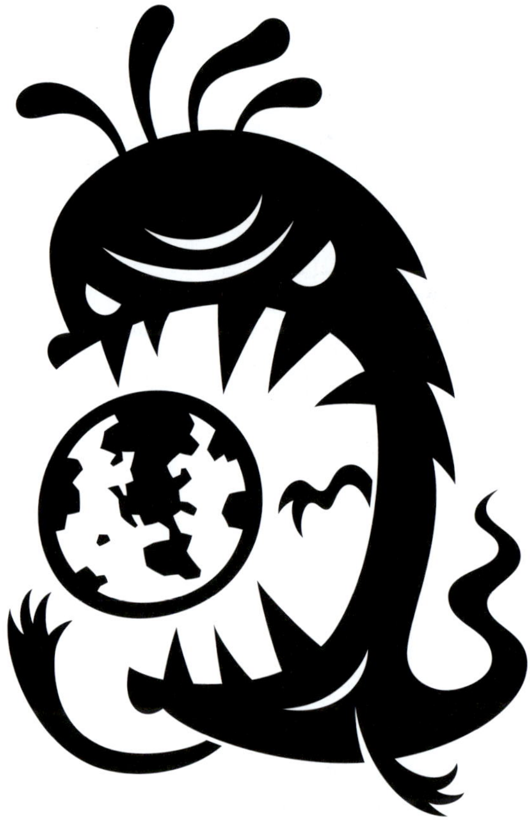

Planet_Eater_**TM552**

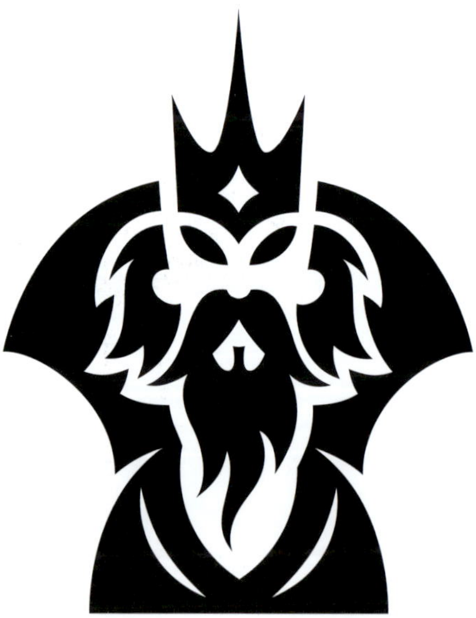

Cast_A_Spell_On_You_**TM553**

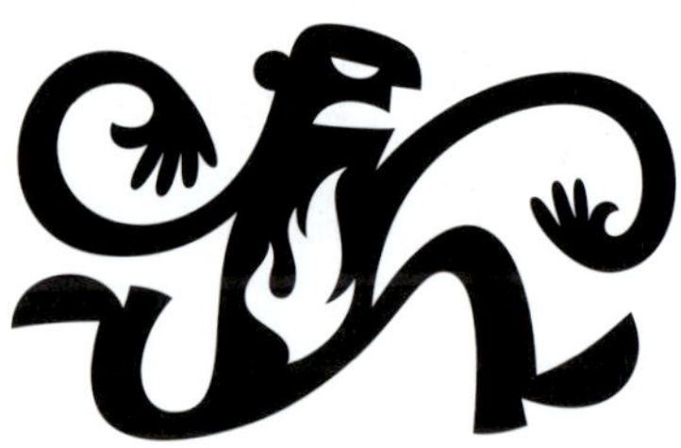

Fuel_The_Passion_**TM554**

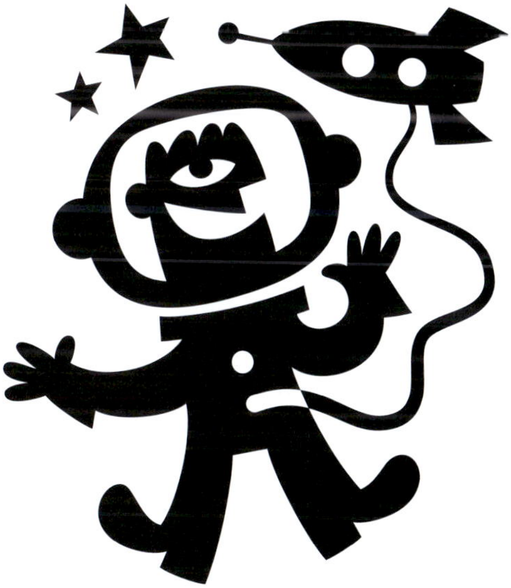

Major_Tom_**TM557**

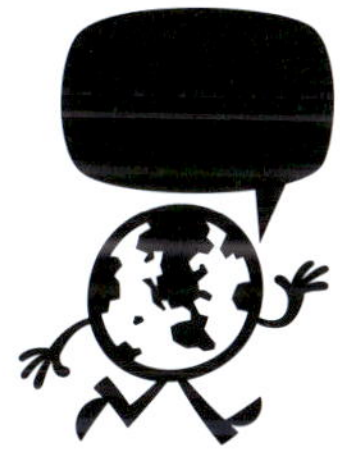

Global_Communications_**TM555**

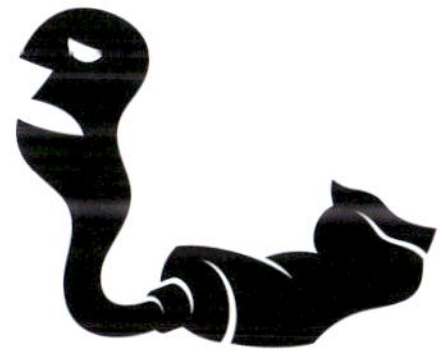

Getting_The_Squeeze_**TM556**

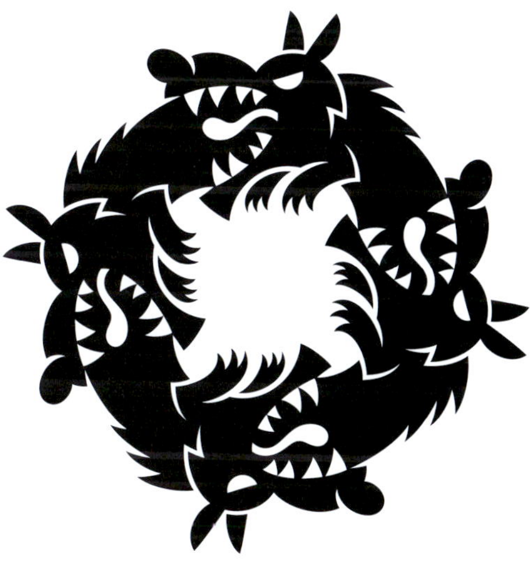

Dog_Eat_Dog_World_**TM558**

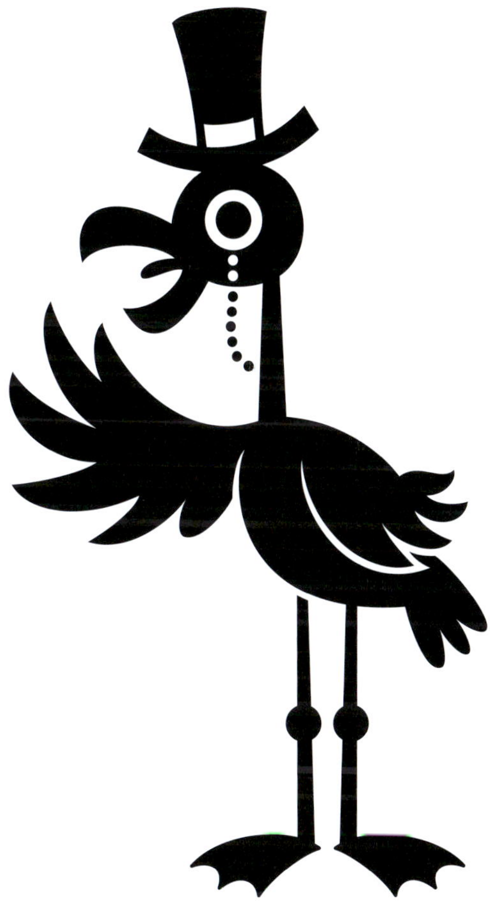

Lorde_Beaky_**TM559**

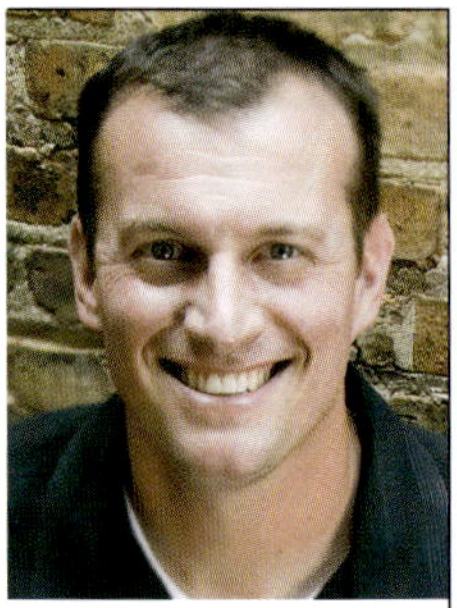

Justin Ahrens

Creative Director

Rule29 Creative • Geneva, Illinois

www.rule29.com

One of the most important virtues that kids can learn is to step outside themselves and help others. Sometimes it takes some positive encouragement to help them get into the discipline of serving others; when we saw *Take and Make Art's* "Heroic" icon we were inspired to imagine a campaign that called upon kids to be "Daily Heroes." When kids choose to be Daily Heroes, it means that they are consciously choosing to do things for others, without acclamation or something in return. Acts of service could be anything from picking up a piece of trash, holding a door open for a teacher, or standing up for a friend.

The Daily Heroes Superhero signifies a call to action for all kids everywhere; we hope that it will remind kids that they are called to be Daily Heroes every day, in whatever way they can. As a part of the campaign, we envisioned that kids could use stickers to stick on everyday places, carry around lunch boxes with the Superhero icon, wear T-shirts, and fill out a pledge card so that they can be held accountable to the good deeds they pledge to do. Our hope is that whenever a kid sees the Daily Heroes icon they will be compelled to help others and make the world a better place.

Art Used: Heroic TM835

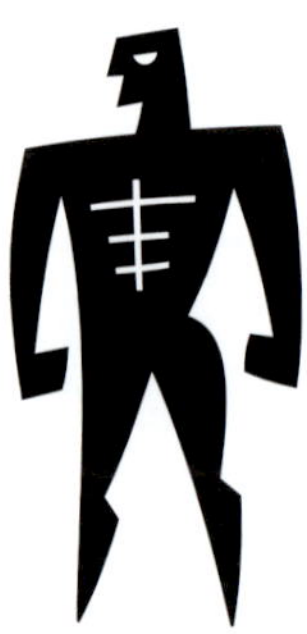

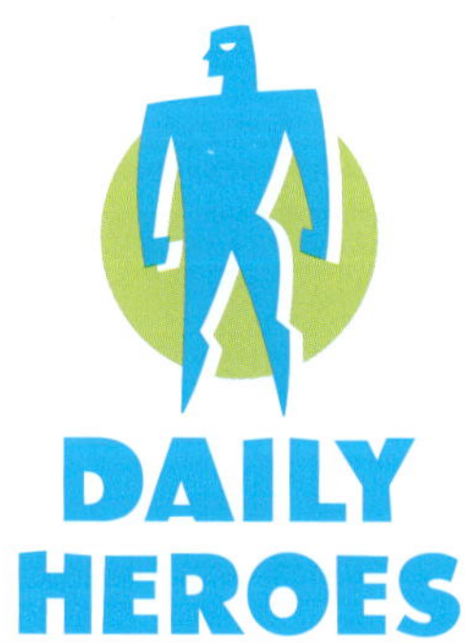

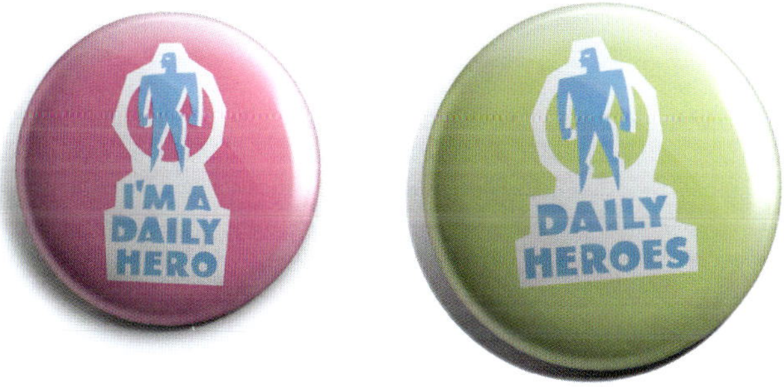

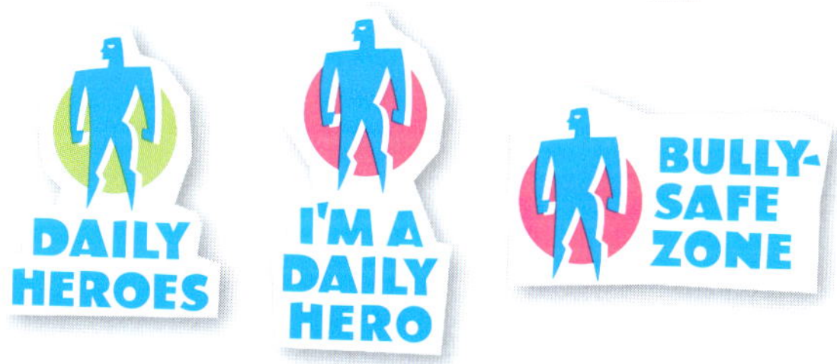

Pins & Stickers

Kids can use these pins and stickers to help remind themselves and others that they are called to do acts of service for others.

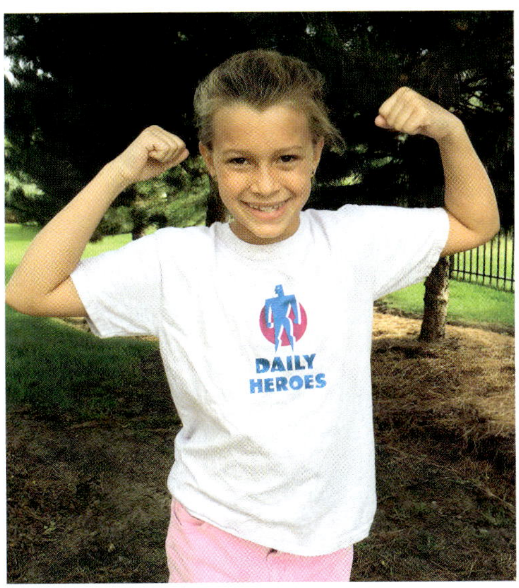

Clothing and Wearables

Daily Heroes Clothes lets kids demonstrate, wherever they are, that they have taken the pledge. It also serves as a reminder of who they are and what they protect, and brings awareness to the cause.

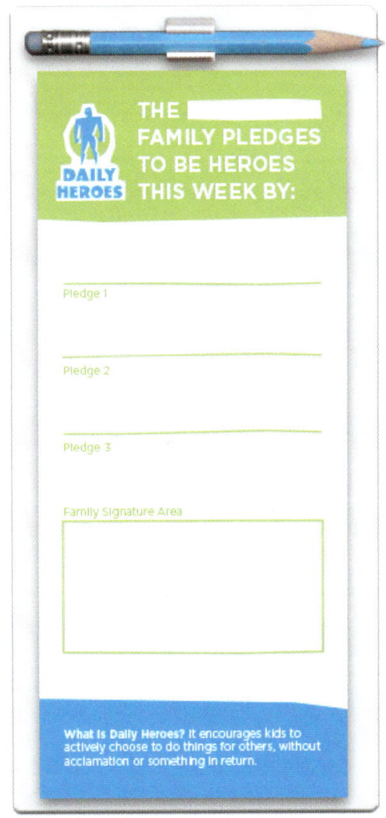

Family Oriented

In order to remind kids and adults about being a Daily Hero, we envisioned a fridge magnet that lets pledges be seen by every family member.

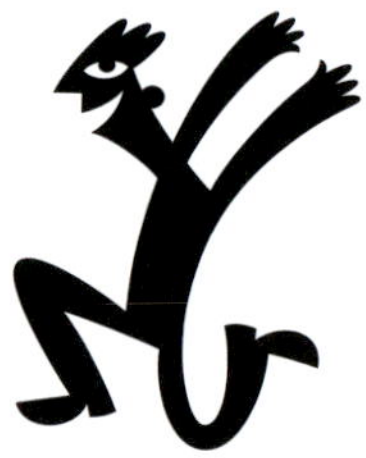

Frolic_**TM560**

Eco_Geek_**TM561**

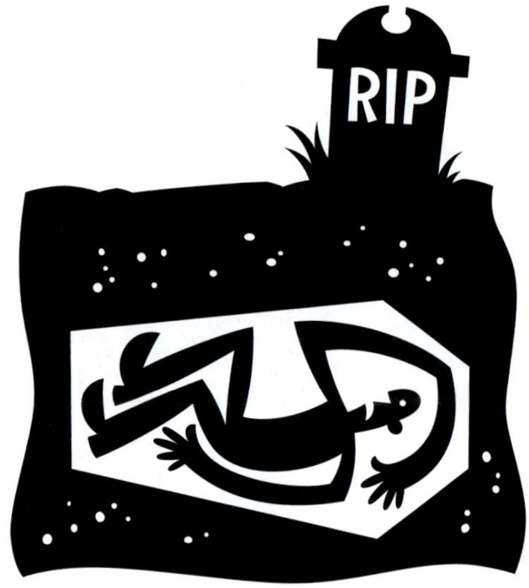

Buried_Alive_**TM562**

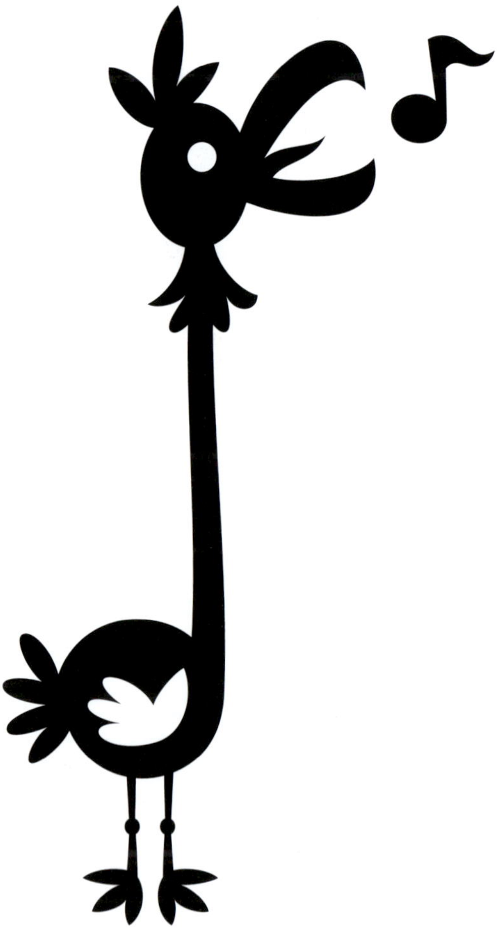

Elevate_Your_Voice_**TM563**

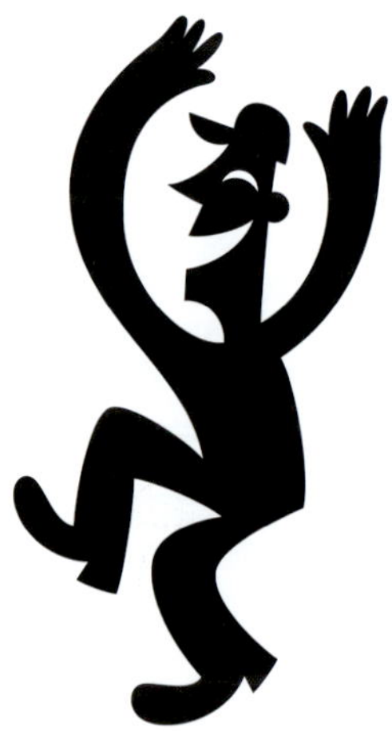

Happy_Dance_**TM564**

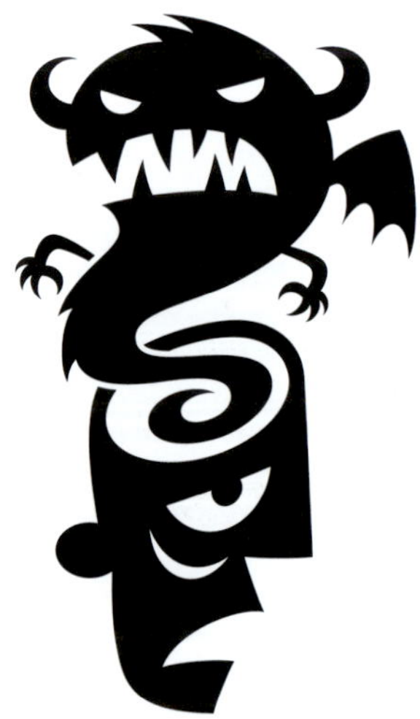

Demented_**TM565**

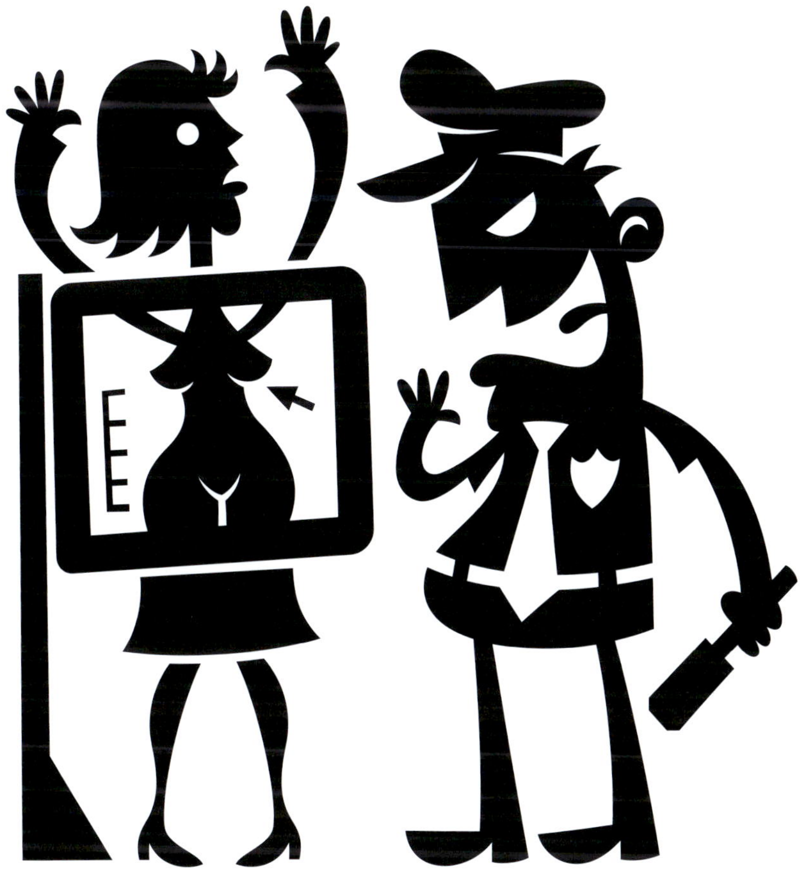

Fighting_Terrorism_**TM566**

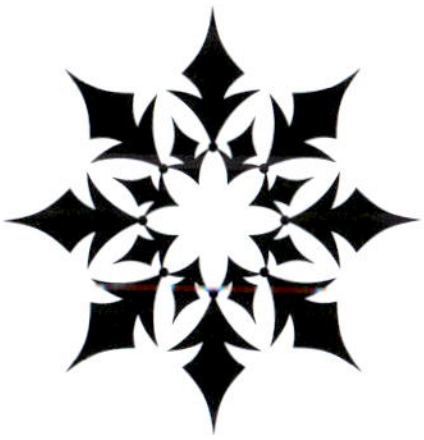

Dont_Be_A_Flake_**TM567**

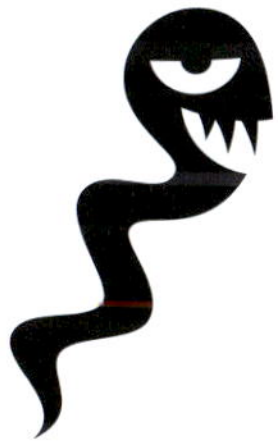

Dork_Worm_**TM568**

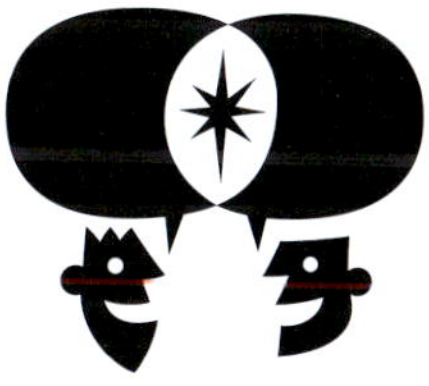

Conversation_Starter_**TM569**

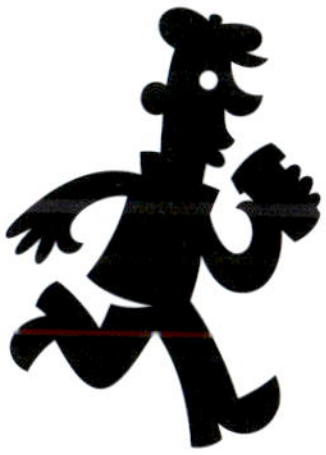

Daily_Grind_**TM570**

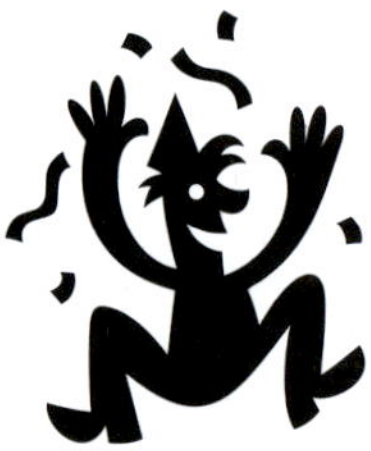

Get_Excited_**TM571**

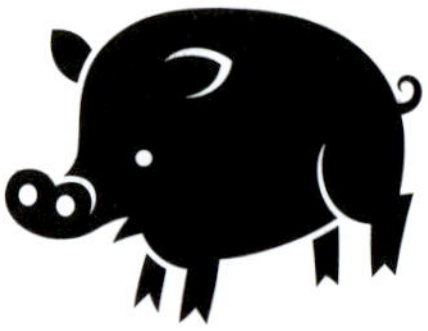

Future_Ham_Sandwich_**TM572**

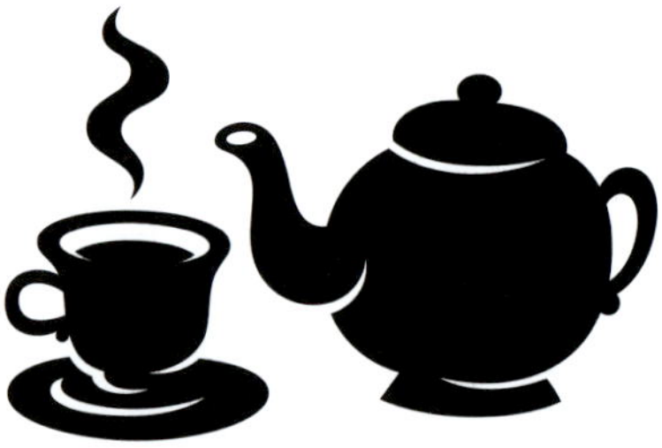

Earl_Grey_Make_It_So_**TM573**

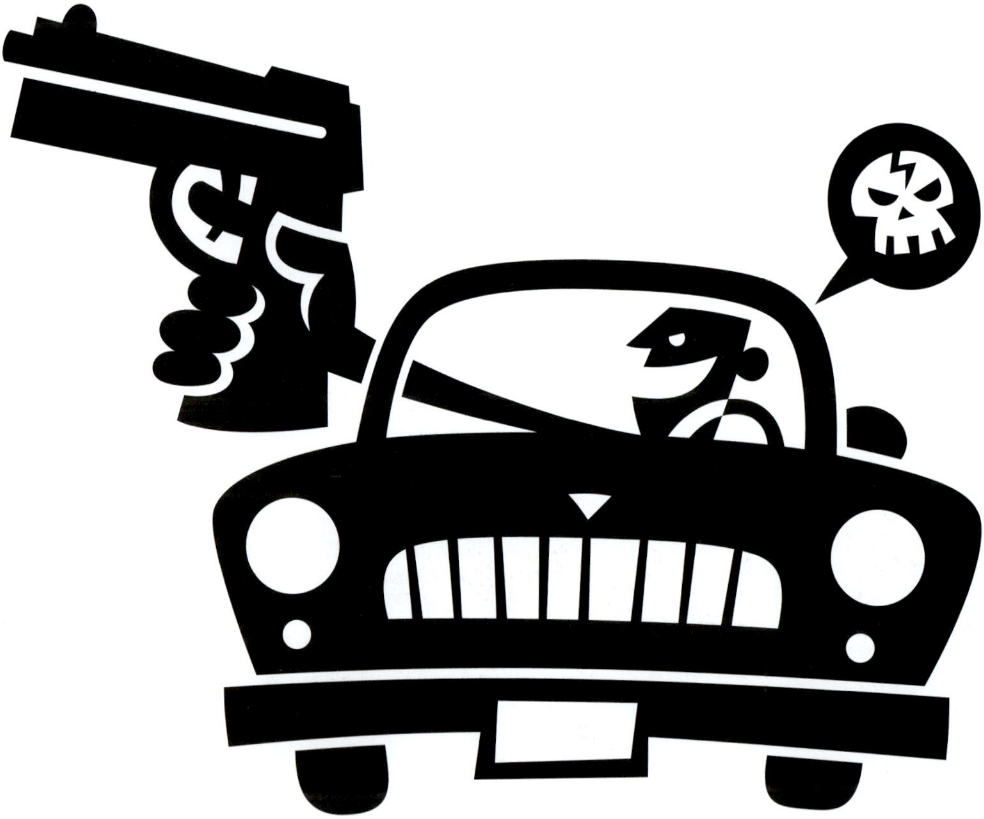

Drive_By_**TM574**

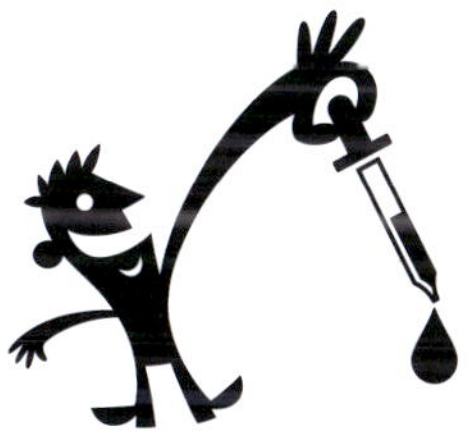

Last_Drop_**TM575**

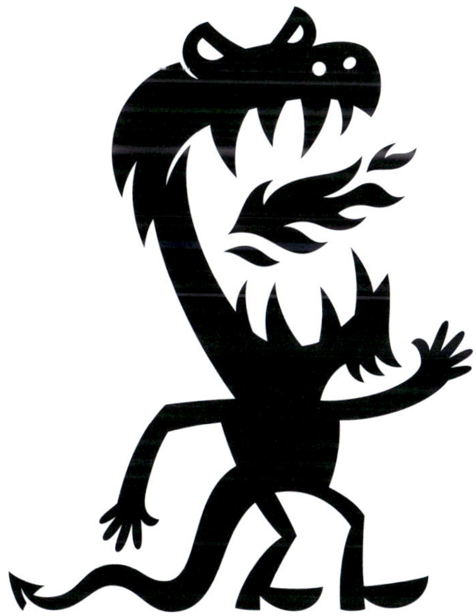

Dragon_Breath_**TM578**

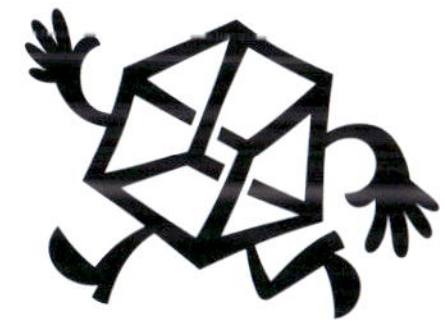

Multi_Dimensional_Personality_**TM576**

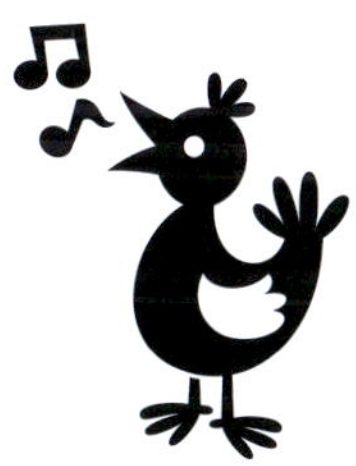

Make_A_Joyful_Noise_**TM577**

Happy_Talker_**TM579**

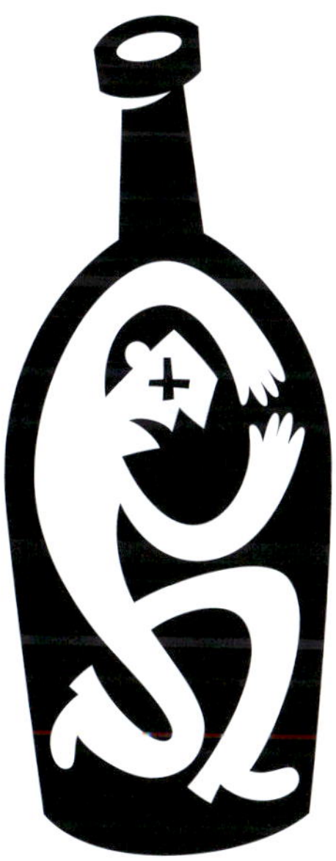

Bottle_Shock_**TM580**

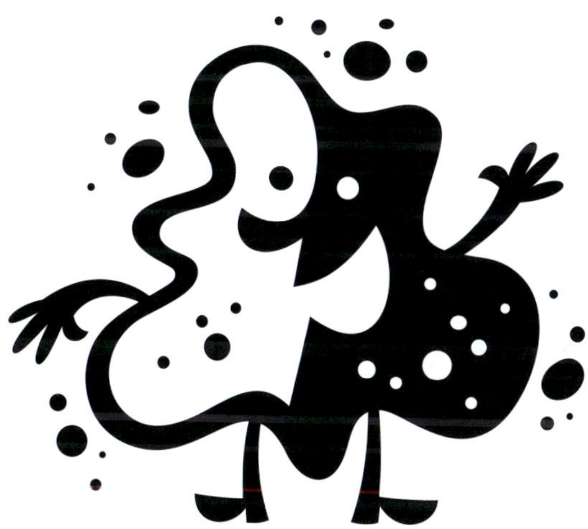

Go_Viral_**TM581**

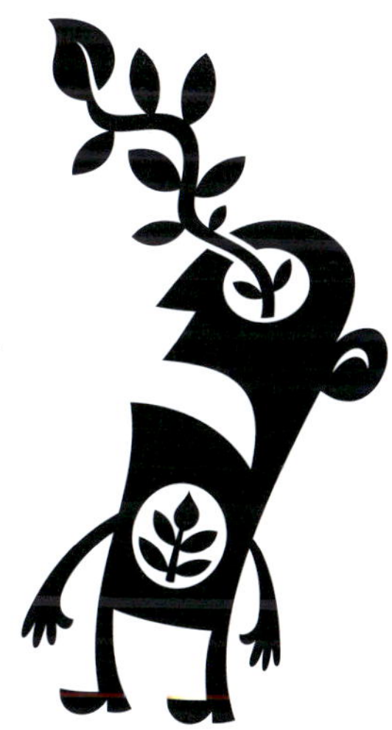

Environmental_Delusion_**TM582**

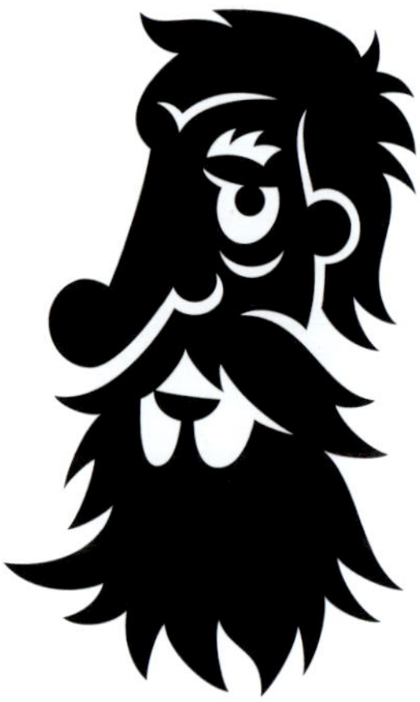

Time_To_Shave **TM583**

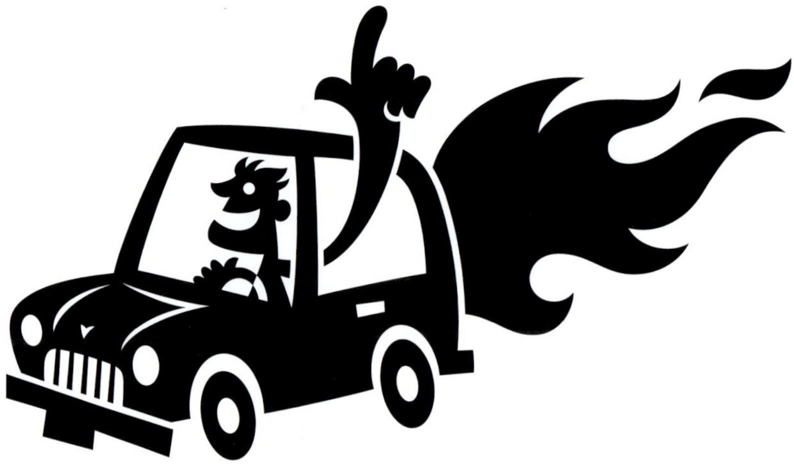

Burn_Out **TM584**

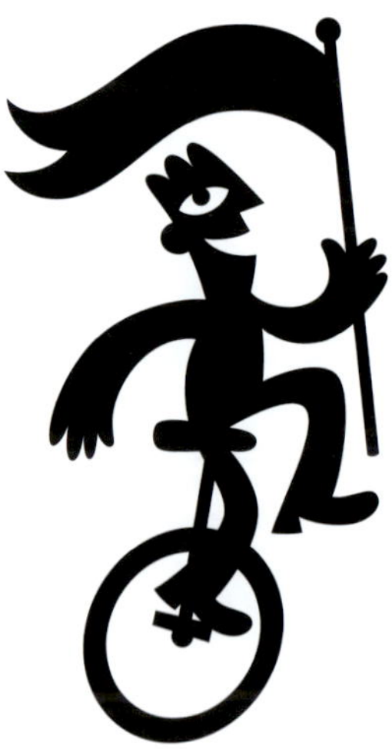

Unicycle_Dude **TM585**

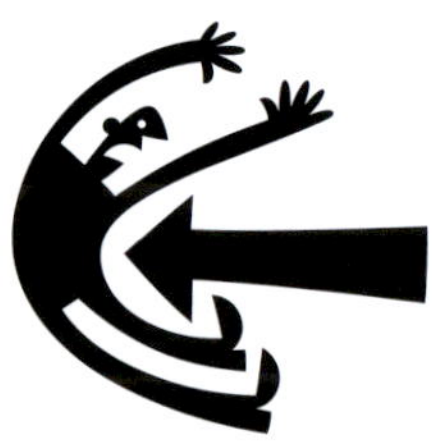

Going_Left **TM586**

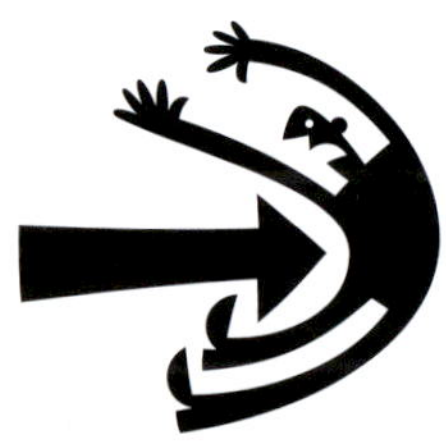

Going_Right **TM587**

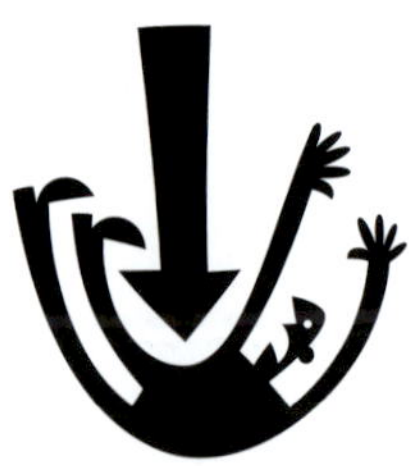

Going_Down **TM588**

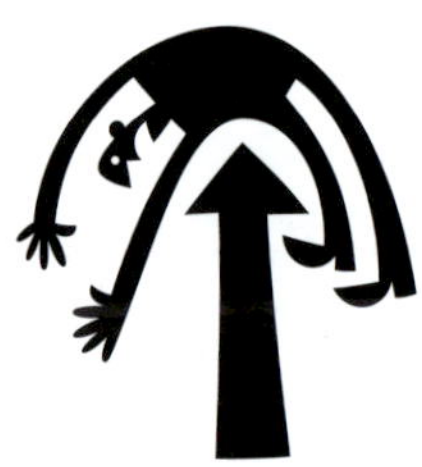

Going_Up **TM589**

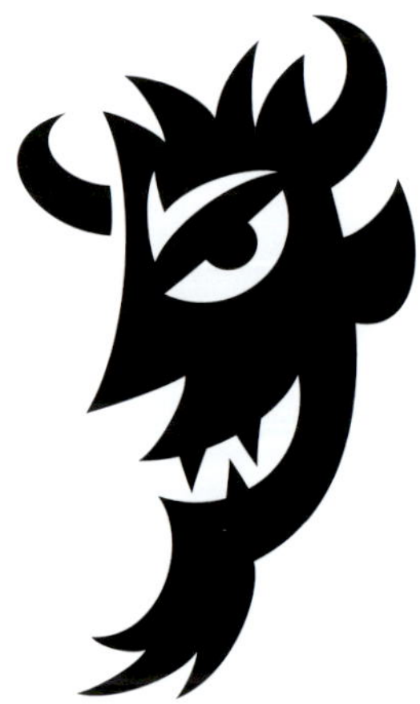

Louis_Cyphre **TM590**

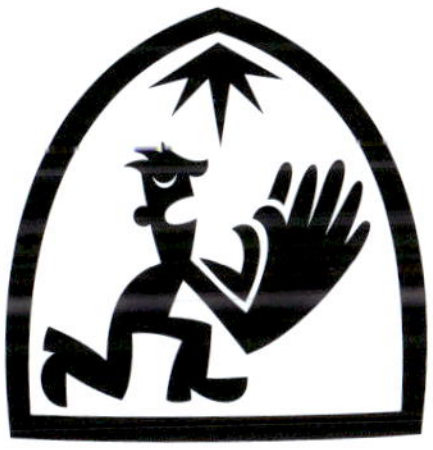
Who_Art_In_Heaven_**TM591**

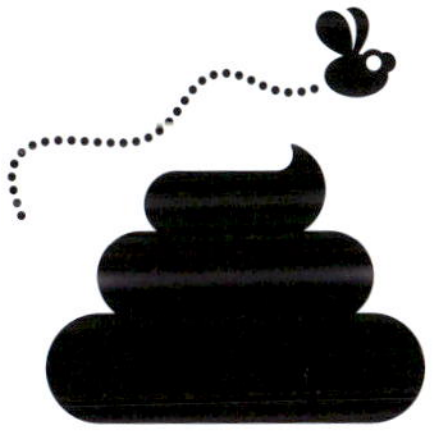
Craptacular_**TM592**

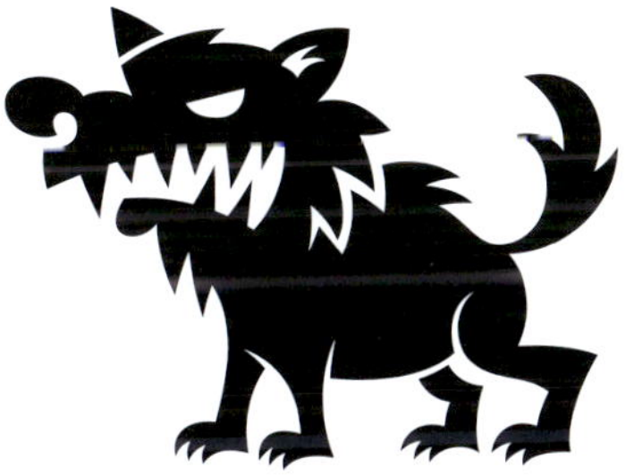
Feed_Them_To_The_Wolves_**TM593**

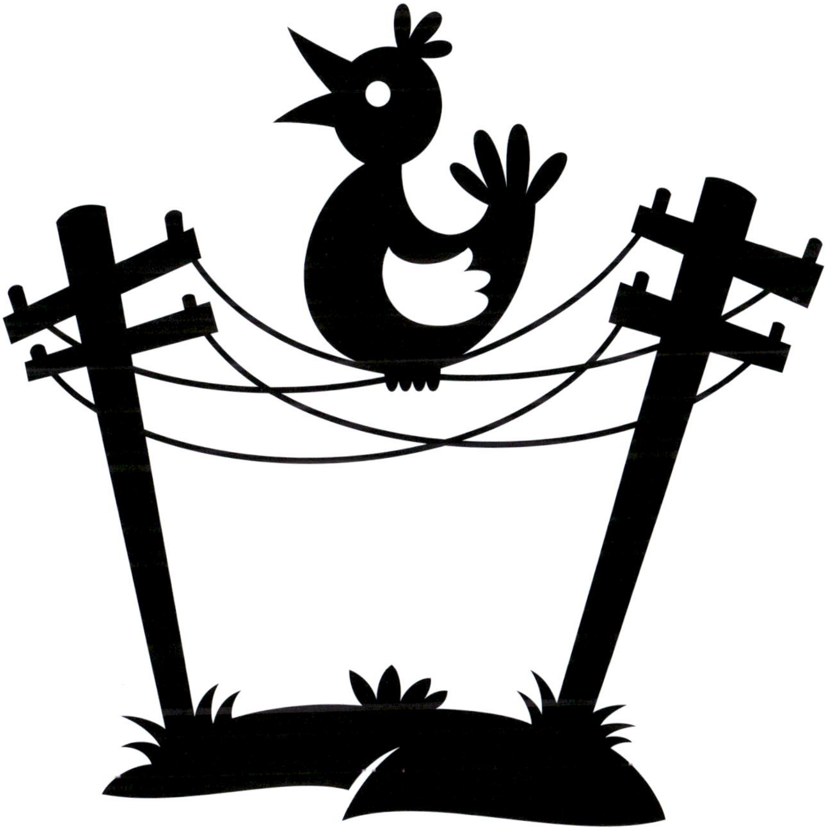
Hanging_Around_**TM594**

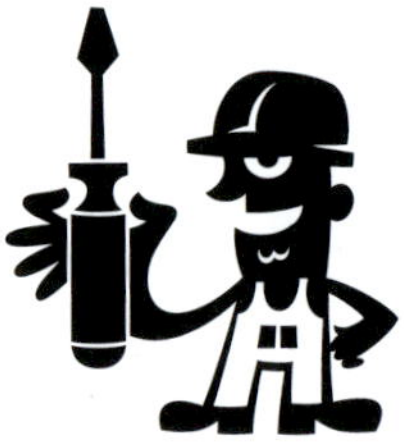

Screw_You_**TM595**

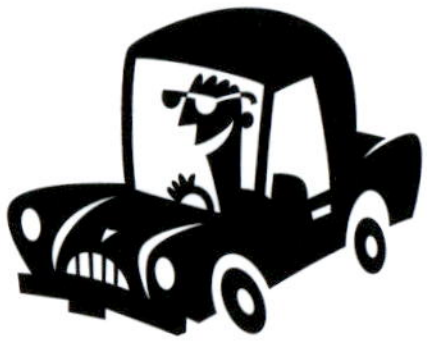

Commuter_**TM596**

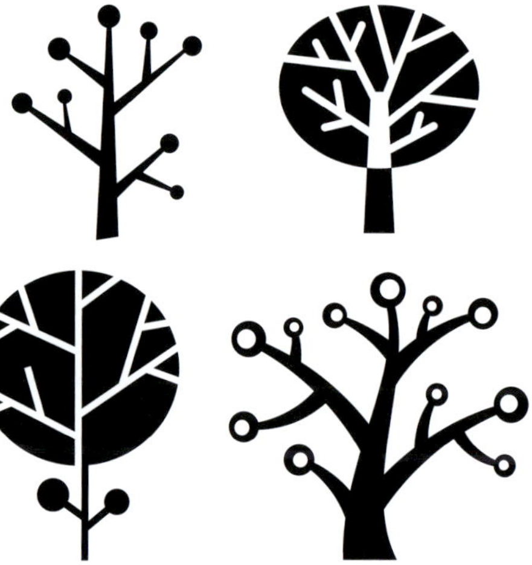

Funko_Forest_**TM597**

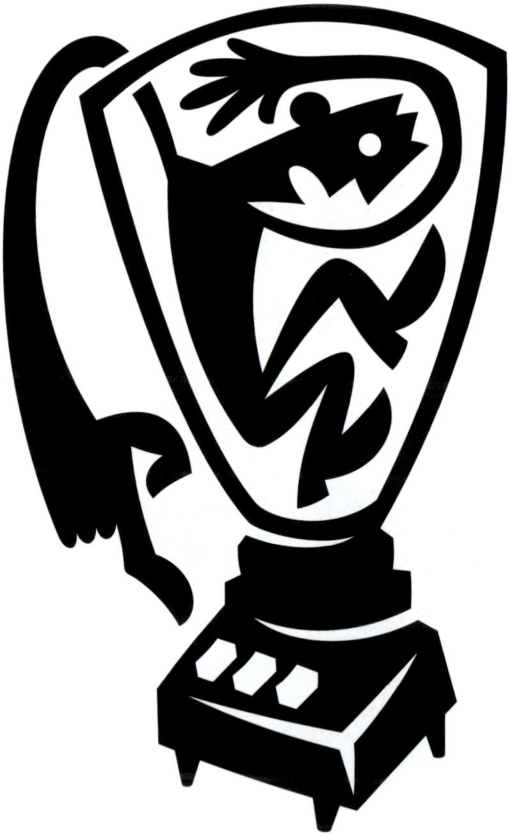

All_Mixed_Up_**TM598**

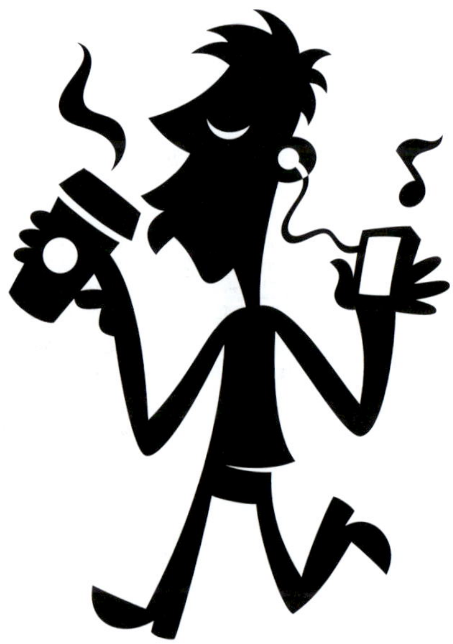

Imbibe_Life_**TM599**

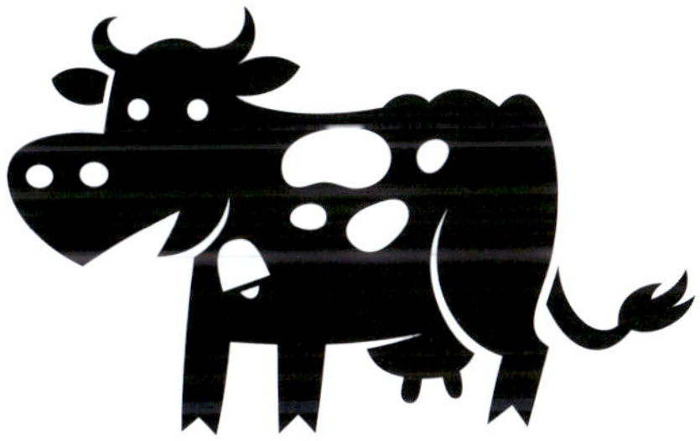

More_Cow_Bell_**TM600**

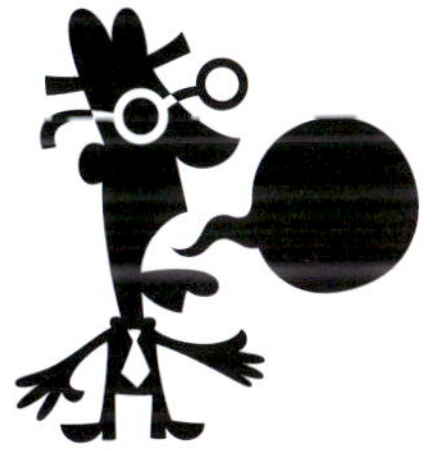

Speaketh_**TM601**

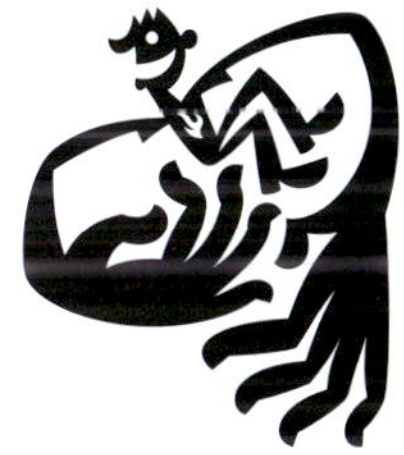

All_Encompassing_**TM602**

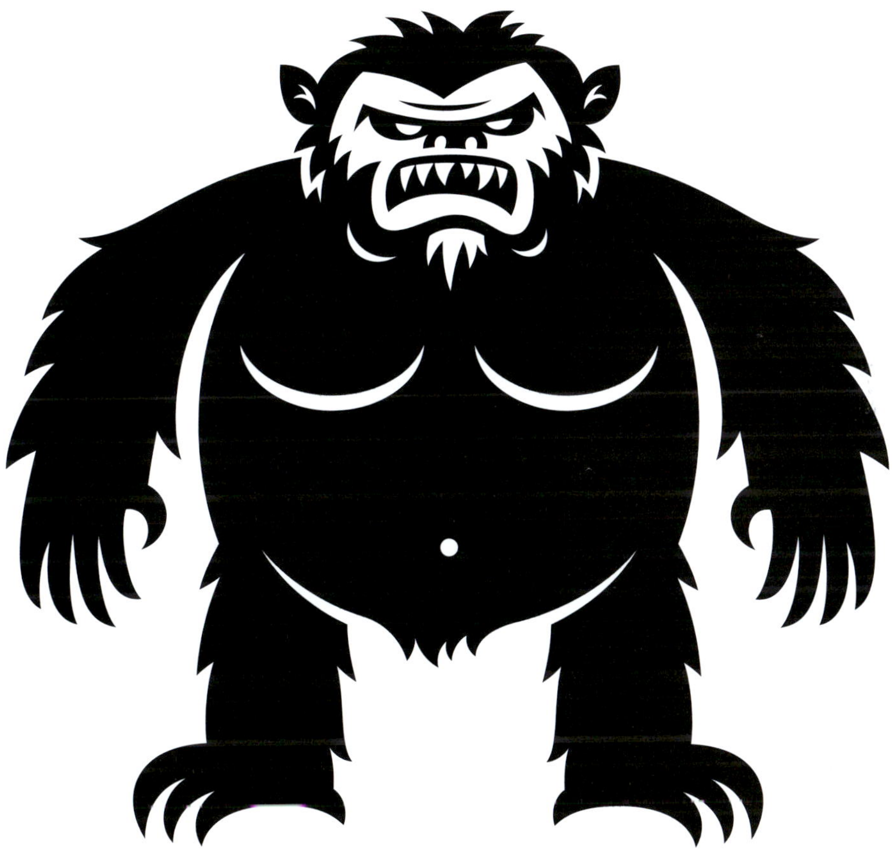

Angry_Yeti_**TM603**

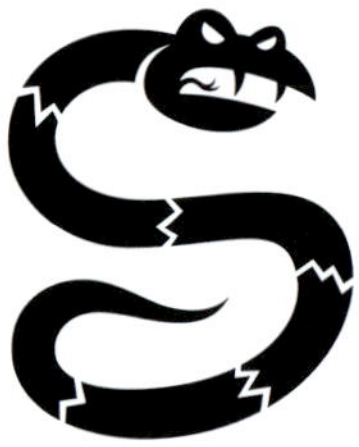

Dont_Tread_On_Me_**TM604**

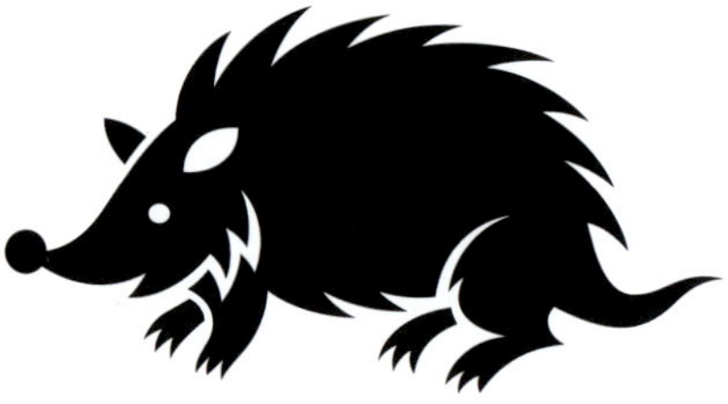

Varmint_**TM605**

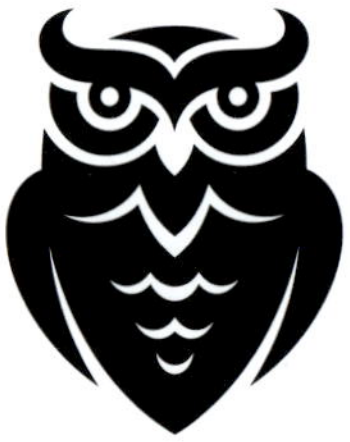

Bohemian_Bird_**TM606**

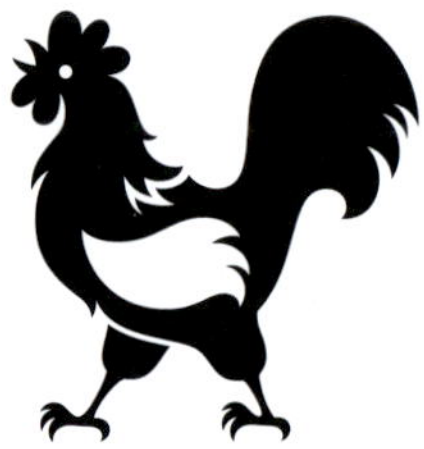

Cock_A_Doodle_Doo_**TM607**

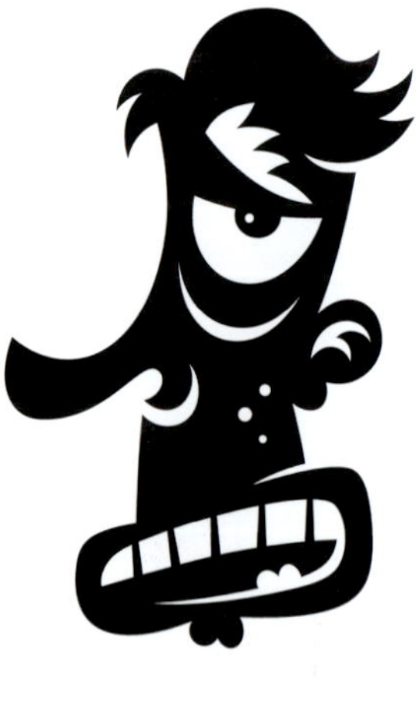

Pimple_Pubescent_**TM608**

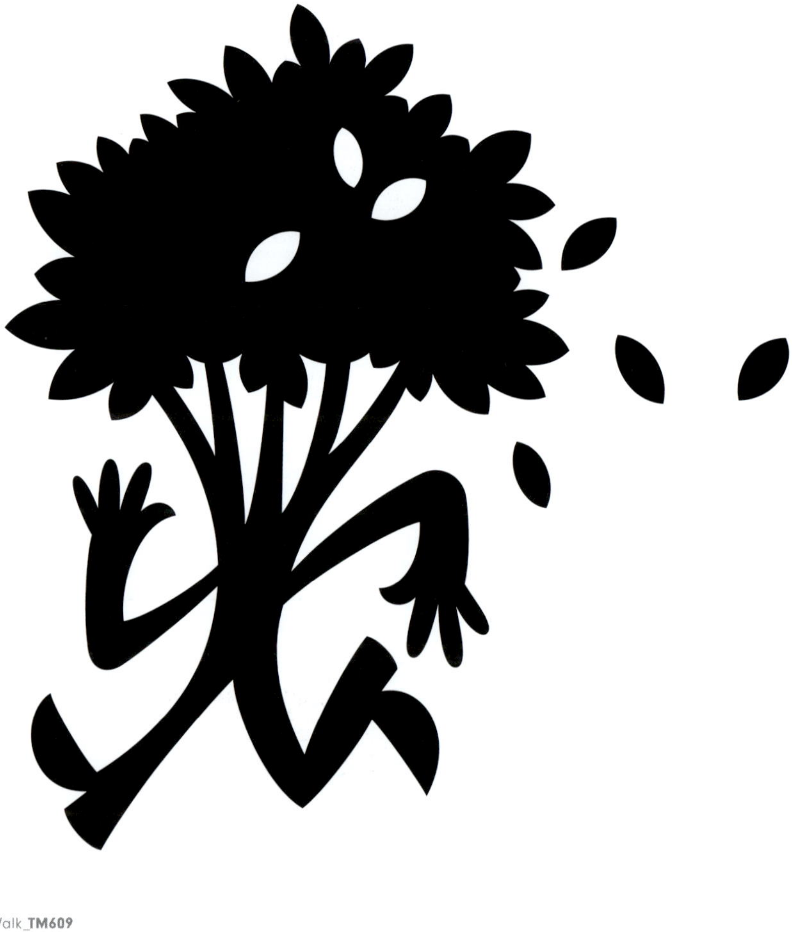

Nature_Walk_**TM609**

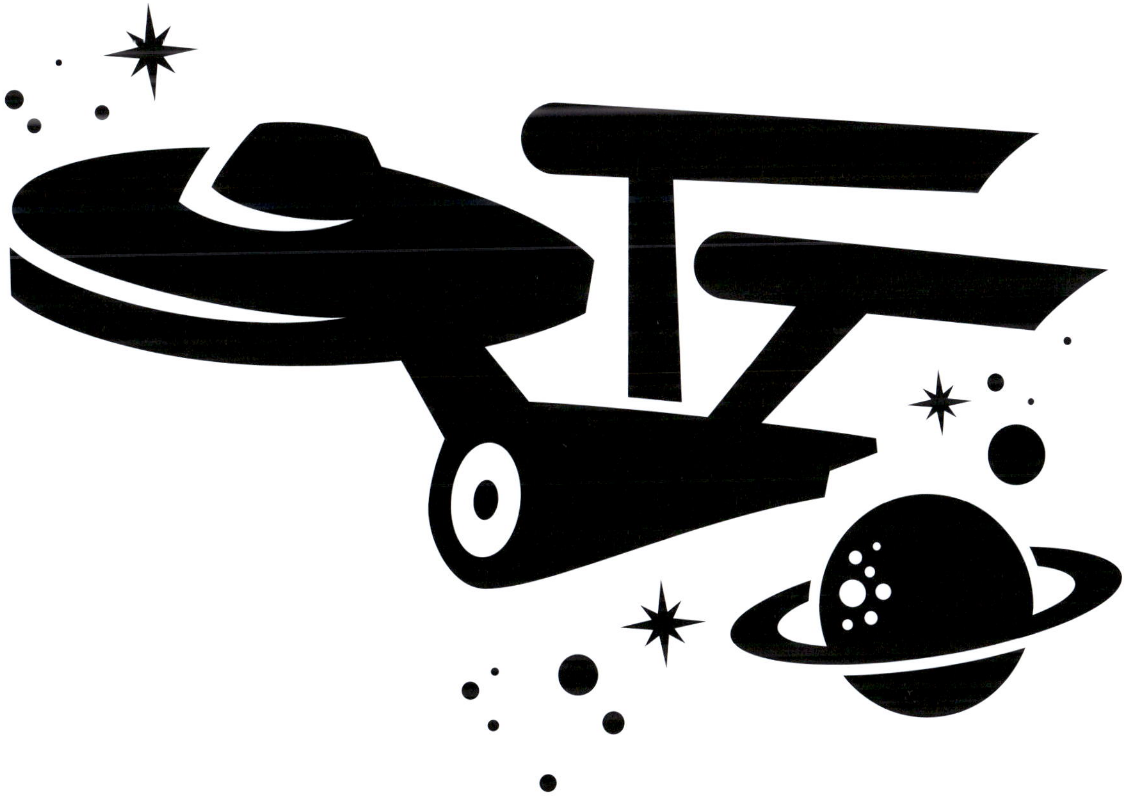

Boldly_Go_**TM610**

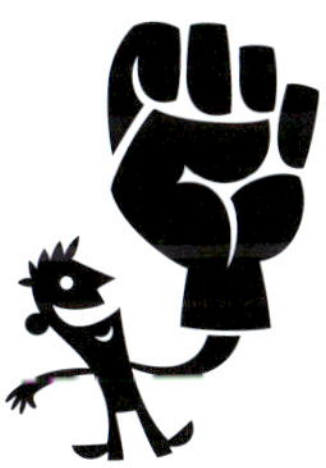

Be_Strong_**TM611**

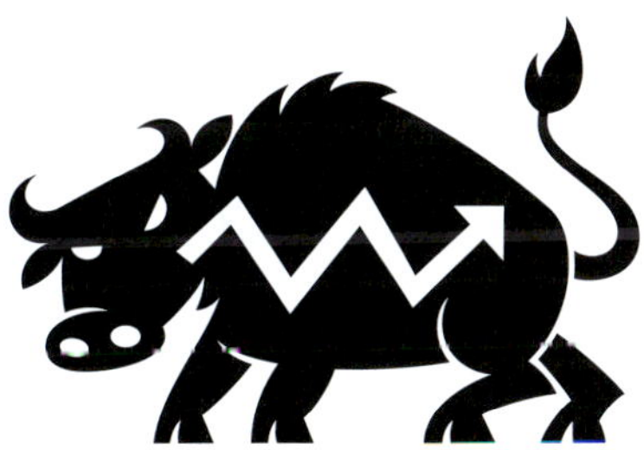

Bull_Market_**TM612**

Burn_It_**TM613**

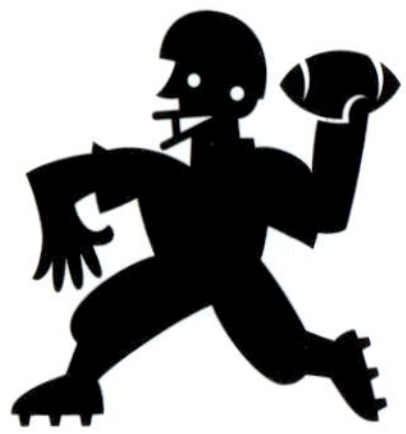

Grid_Iron_**TM614**

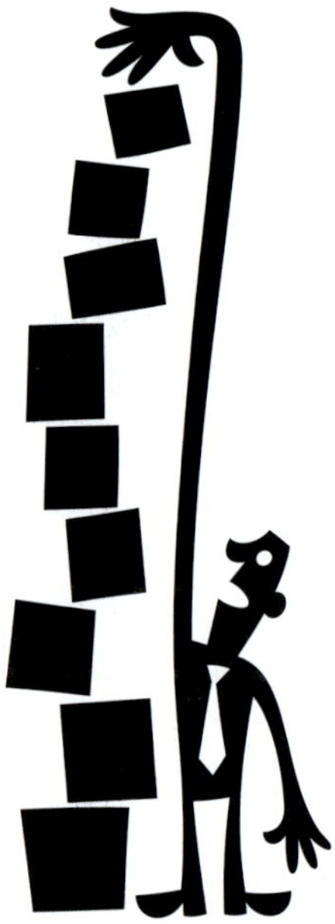

Its_A_Balancing_Act_**TM615**

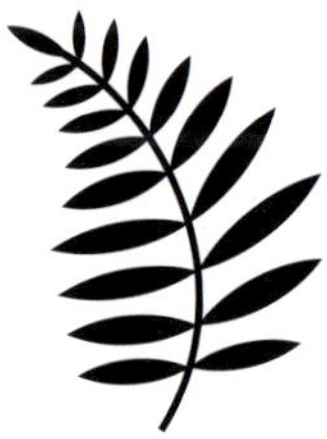

Fern_**TM616**

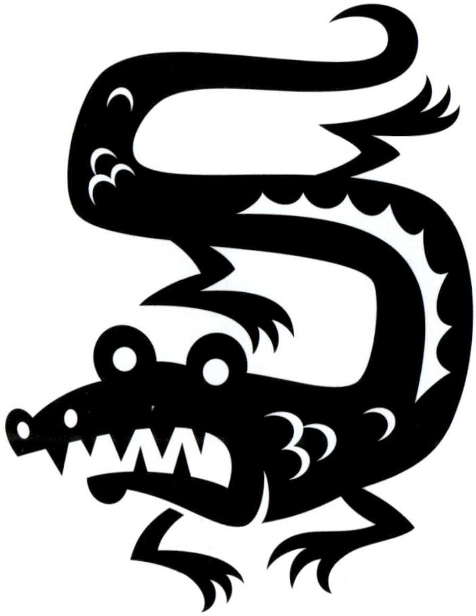

Lizzy_**TM617**

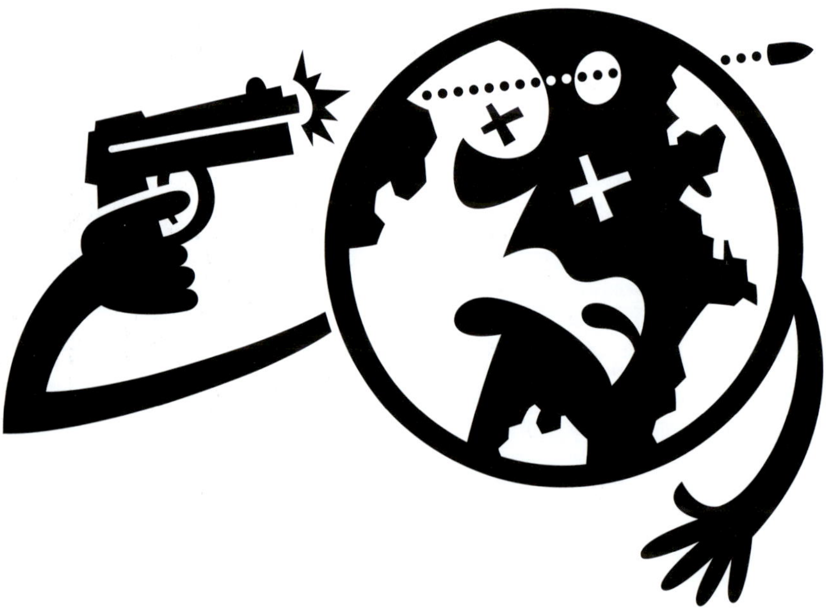

Ecocide_**TM618**

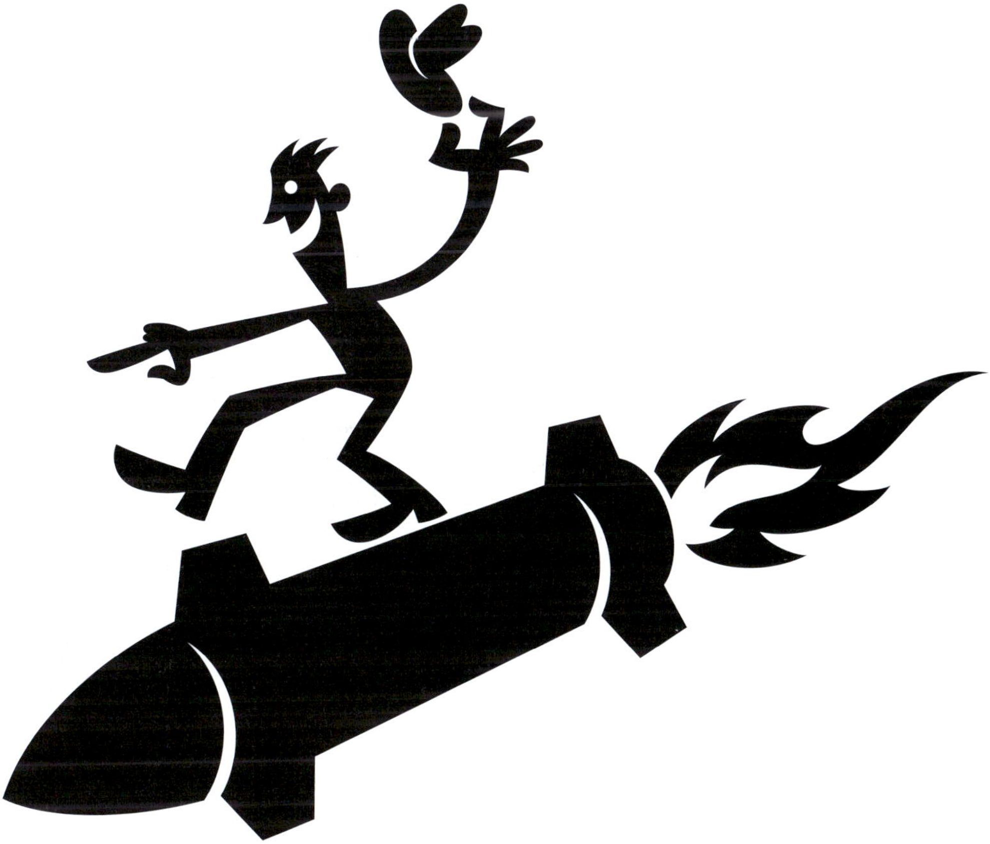

Dooms_Day_Rodeo_**TM619**

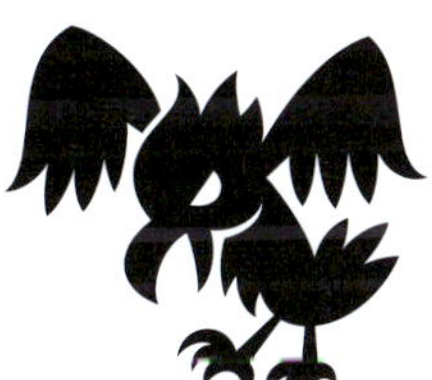

Bird_Of_Prey_**TM620**

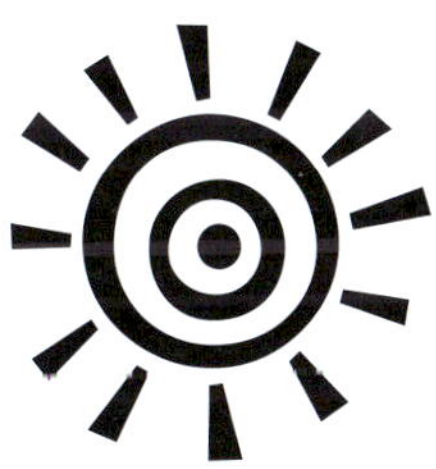

Brighten_Up_**TM621**

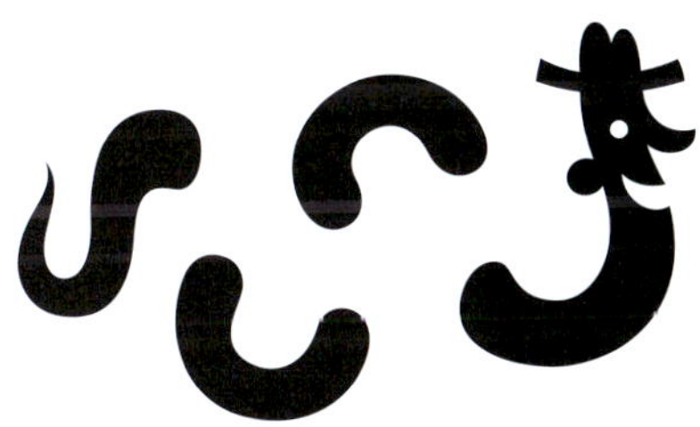

Do_The_Worm_**TM622**

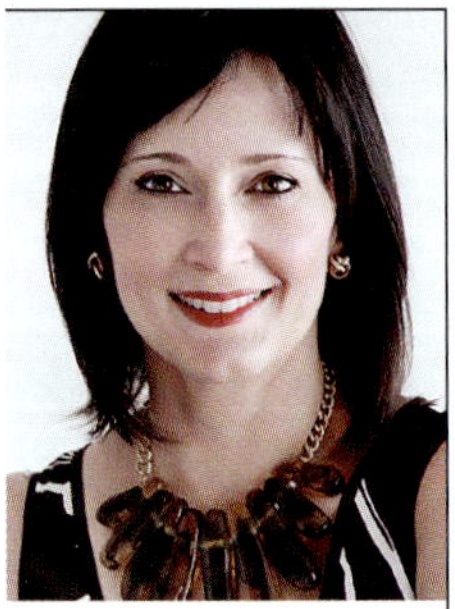

Sharon Nelson
Owner & Principal Designer
November + June • Naperville, Illinois
www.novemberandjune.com

There's something about creating a memorable identity that always puts my design skills to the test. It's a love-hate kind of thing, as I love the challenge but hate the "designer's block" that always seems to go along with it.

Take and Make Art's "Give a Hoot" was an easy choice. That little owl with his huge eyes was just begging to be turned into a logo. My intention was to bring life to this character through color and texture, so he became Mr. Hoot & Company.

The final logo and custom pattern is bright and cheerful...something that would appeal to parents and kids, with a slight feminine touch added through the selection of typeface.

Art Used: Give A Hoot TM997

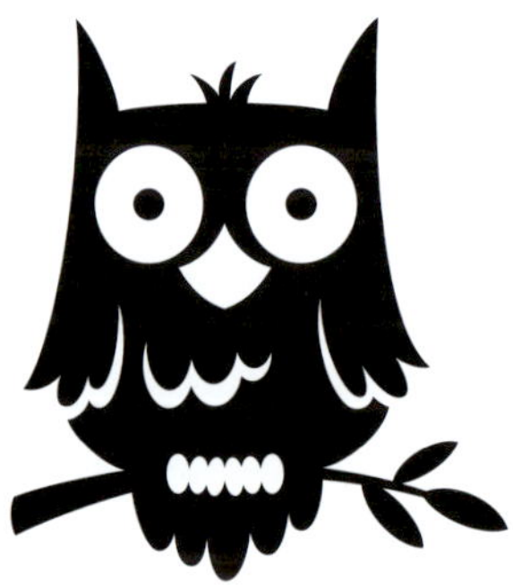

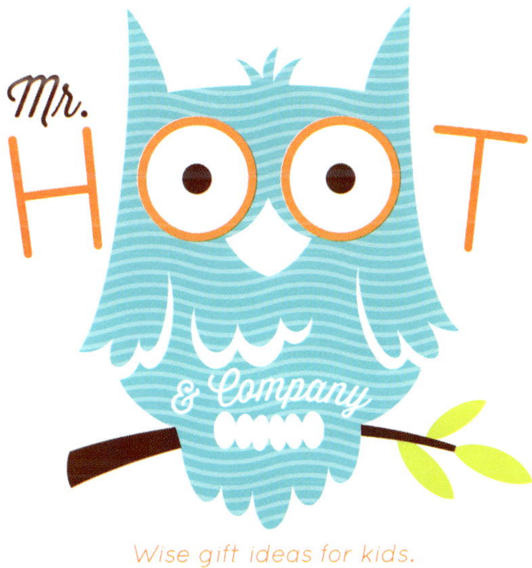
Mr.
HOOT
& Company
Wise gift ideas for kids.

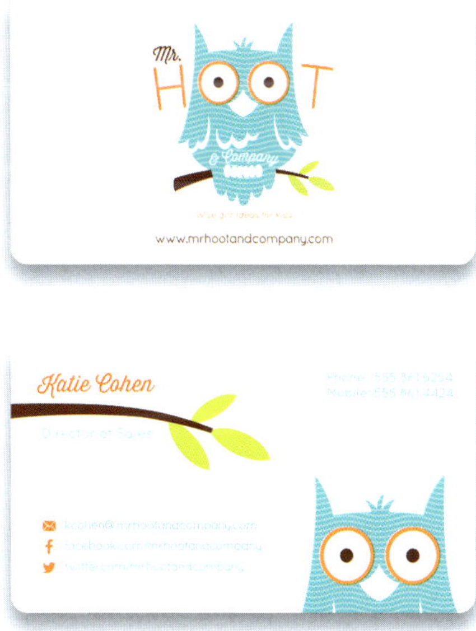
Mr.
HOOT
& Company
www.mrhootandcompany.com
Katie Cohen

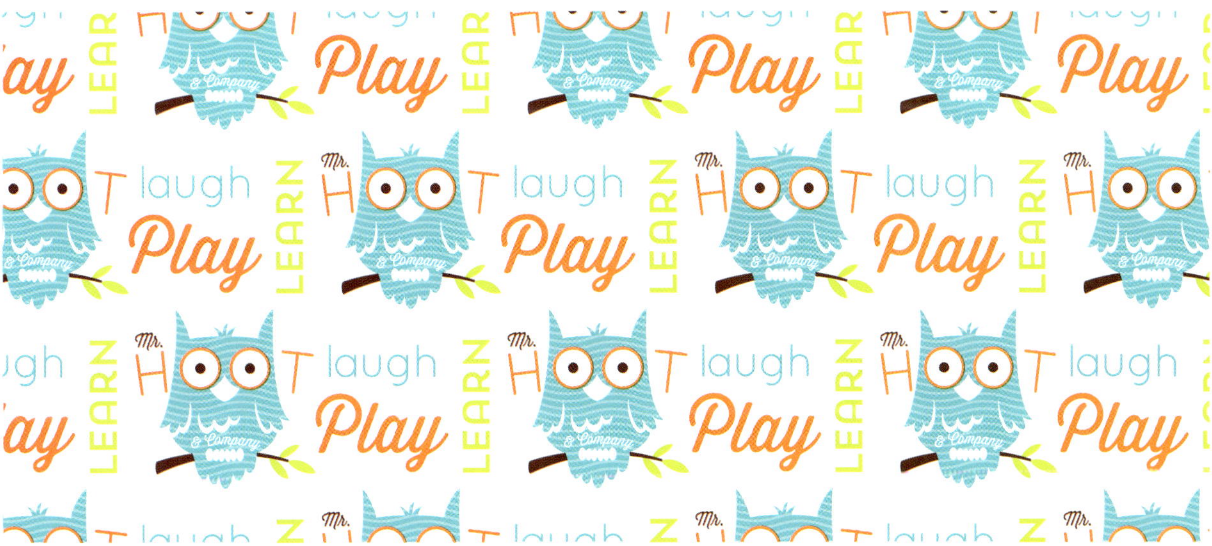
Mr.
HOOT
& Company
laugh
Play
LEARN

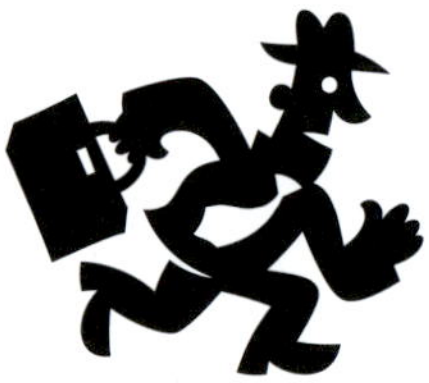
A_Real_Go_Getter_**TM623**

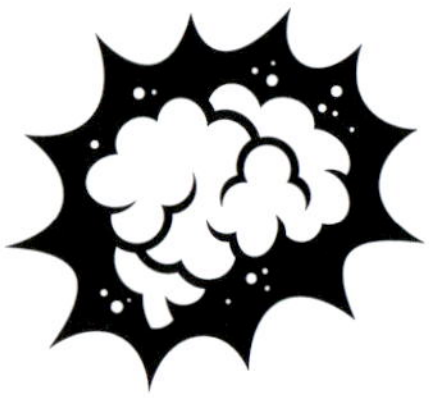
Brain_Power_**TM624**

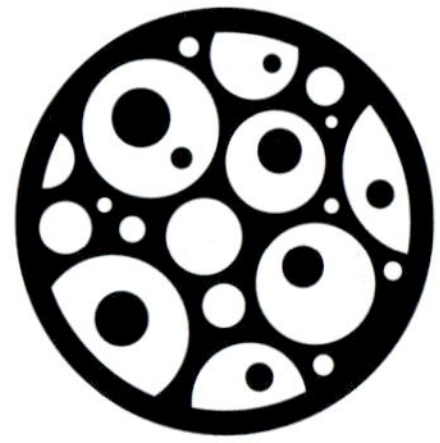
Cellular_Level_**TM625**

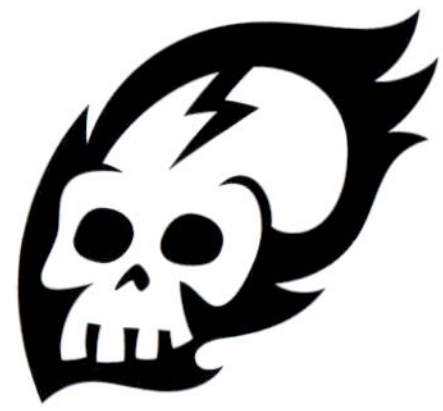
Hot_Head_**TM626**

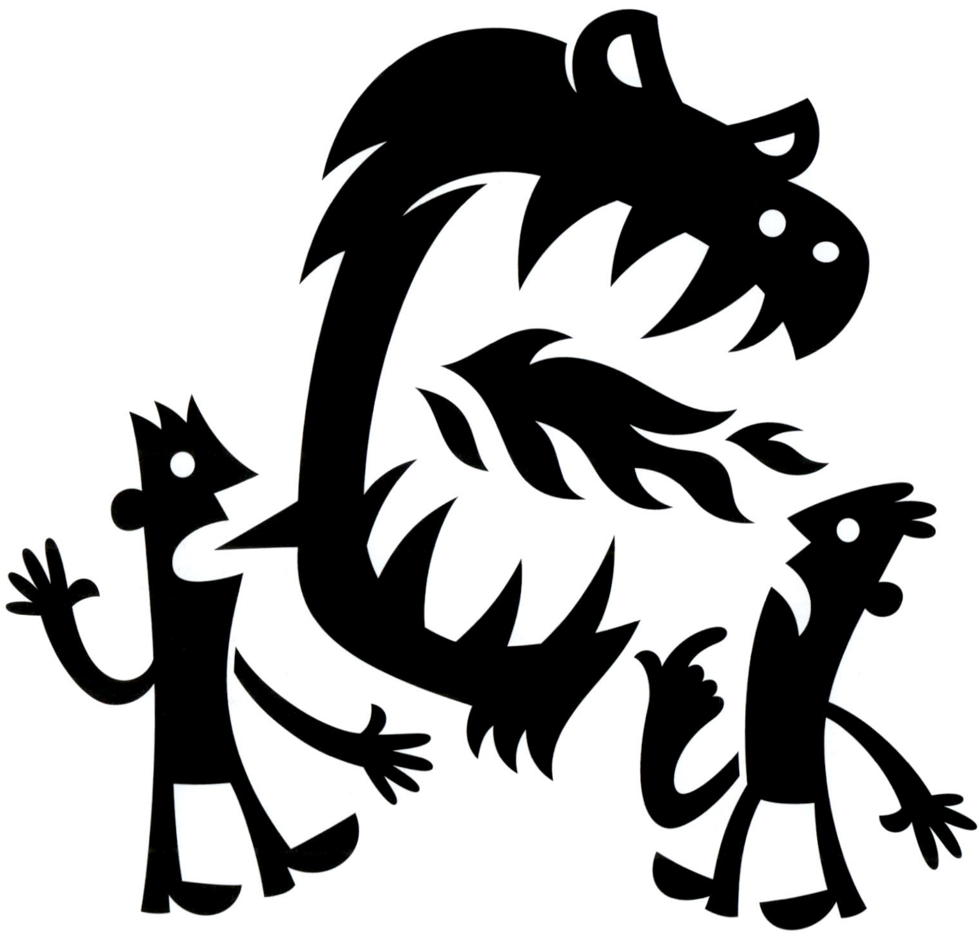
A_Discouraging_Word_**TM627**

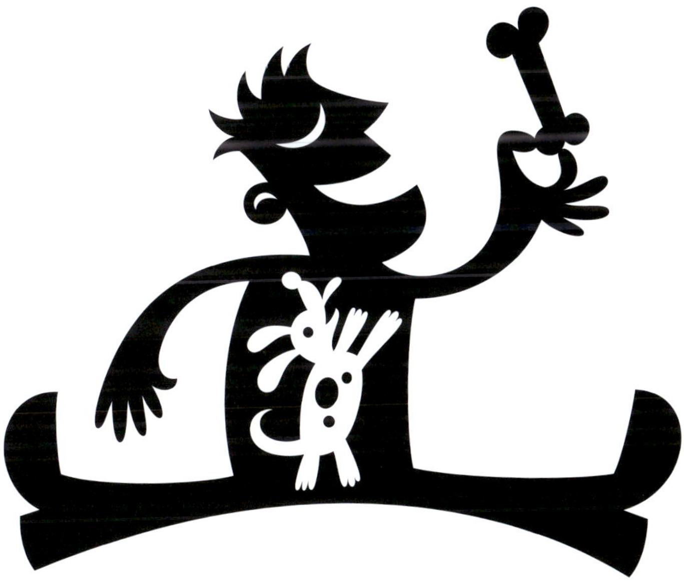

Begging_**TM629**

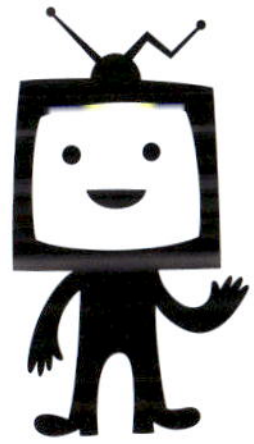

TV_Kid_**TM628**

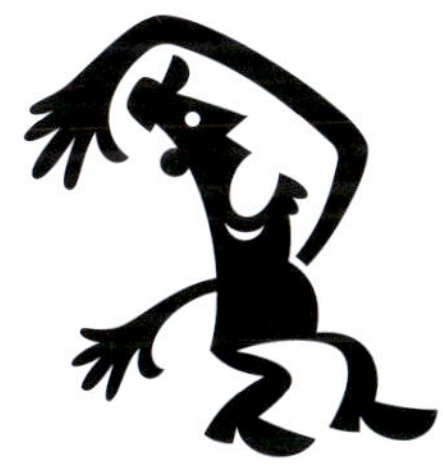

What_The_Frack_**TM630**

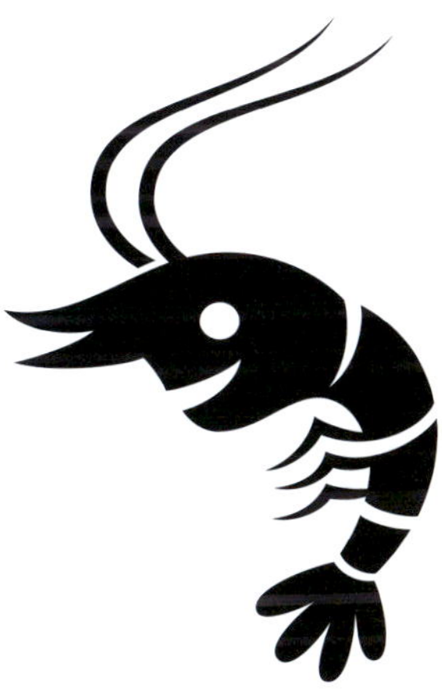

Lil_Shrimp_**TM632**

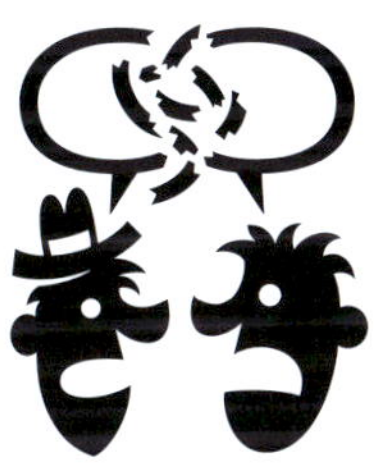

Not_Connecting_**TM631**

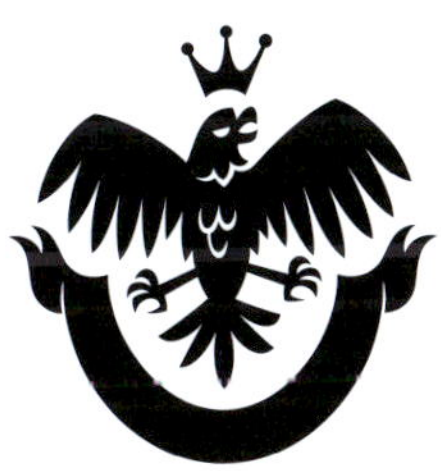

Reign_Of_Power_**TM633**

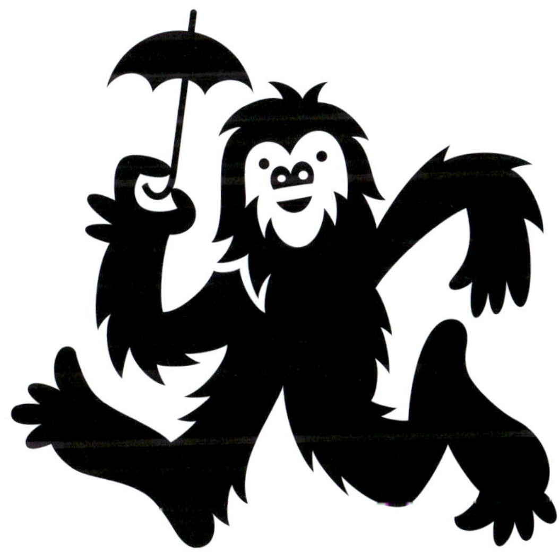

Bigfoot_**TM634**

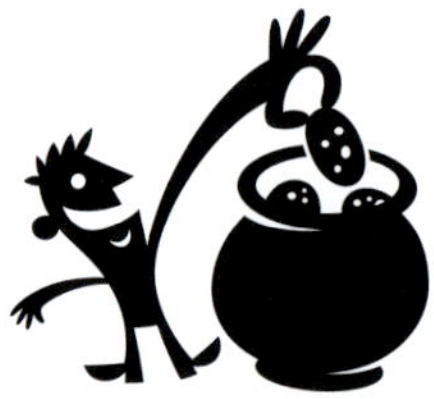

Cookie_Jar_**TM635**

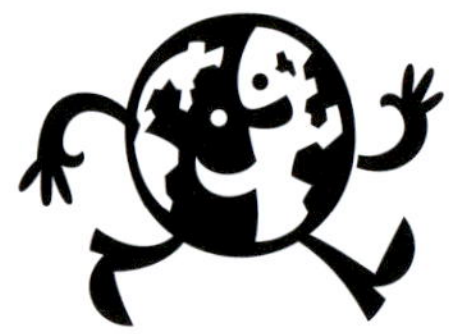

Globe_Trotting_**TM636**

Be_Careful_What_You_Say_**TM637**

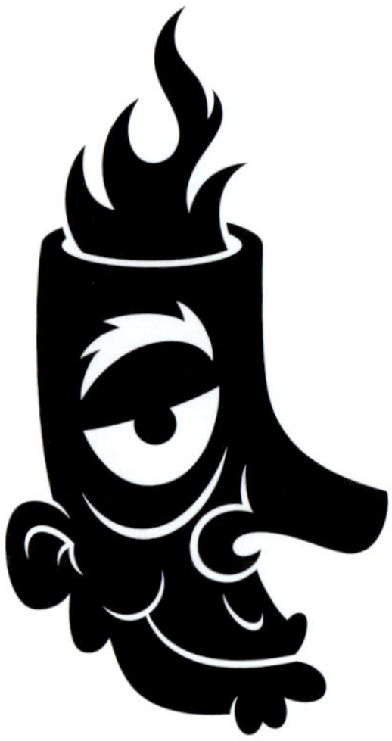

Baking_Ideas_**TM638**

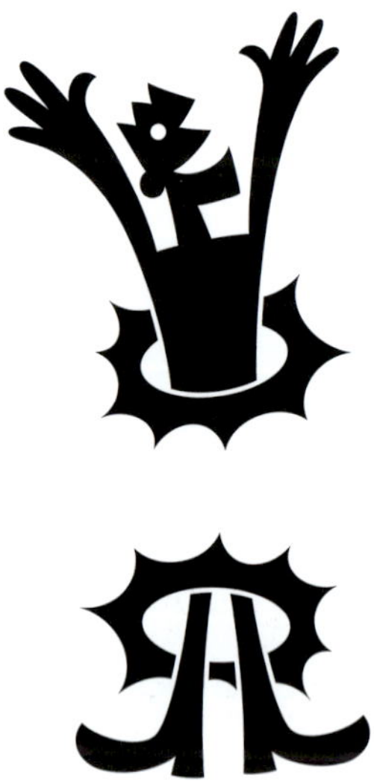

Wormhole_**TM639**

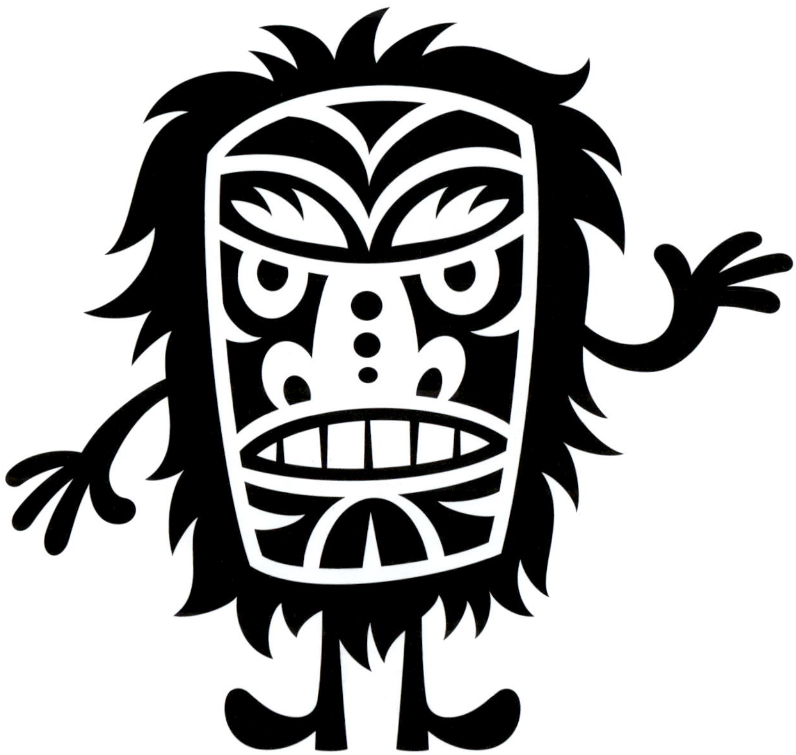

Witch_Doctor_**TM640**

Weenie_Roast_**TM641**

 Book_Runner_**TM642**	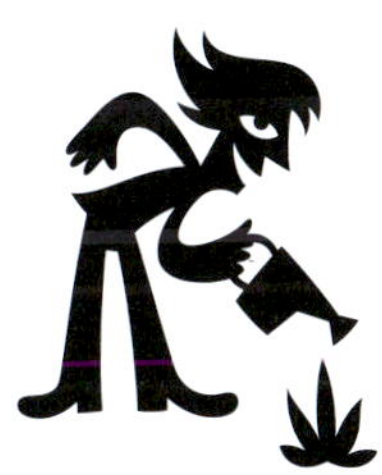 Watering_**TM643**	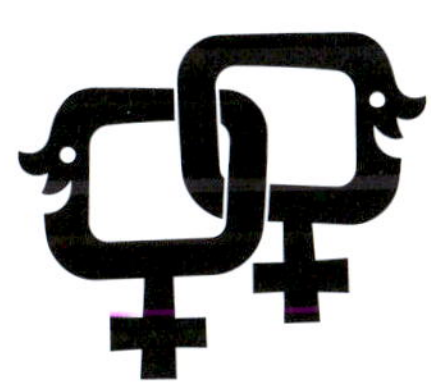 Same_Difference_**TM644**	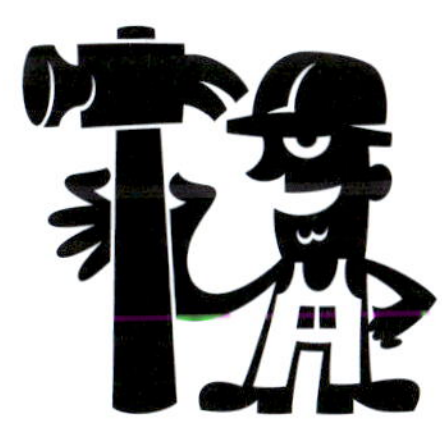 You_Nailed_It_**TM645**

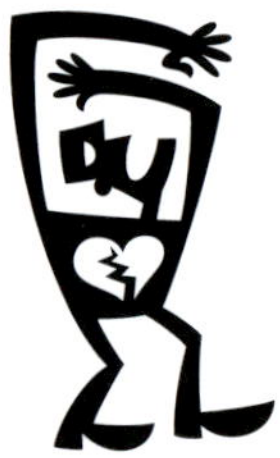

Sorrow_**TM646**

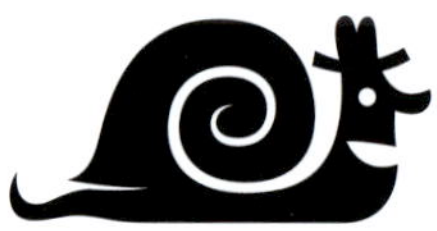

Life_In_The_Slow_Lane_**TM647**

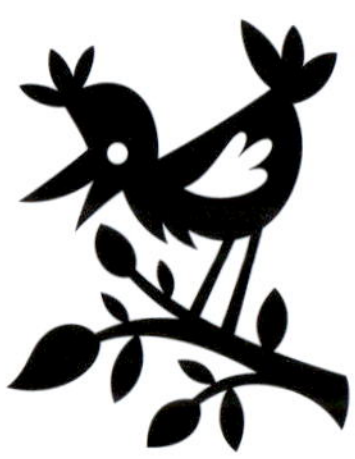

Perch_**TM648**

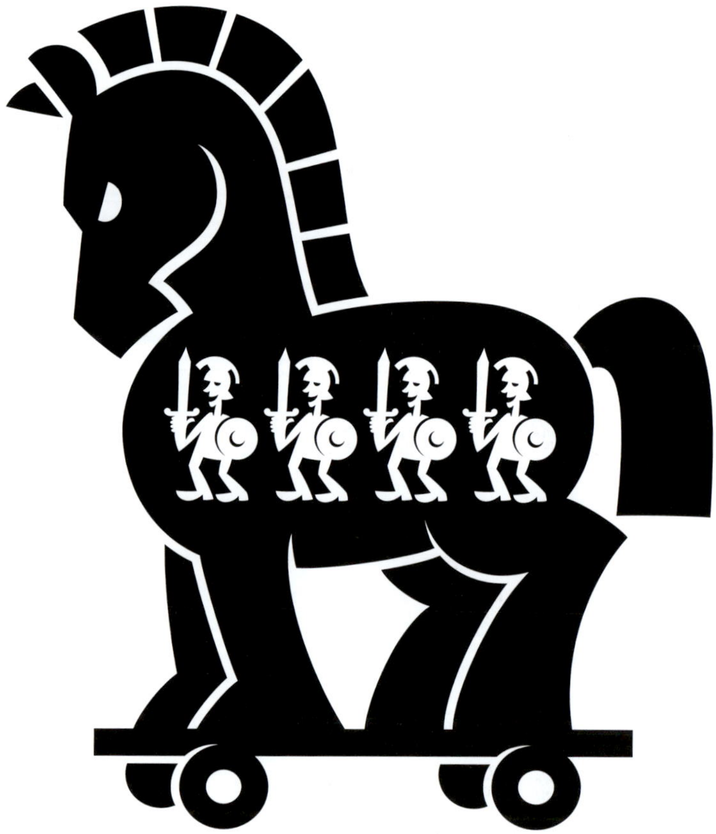

Ultimate_Deception_**TM649**

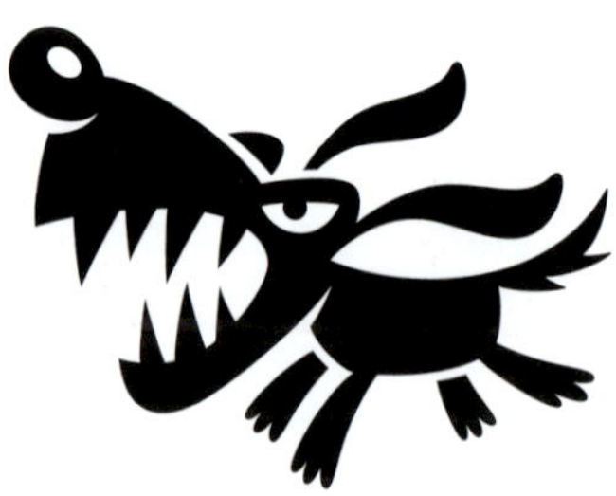

Chaotic_Canine_**TM650**

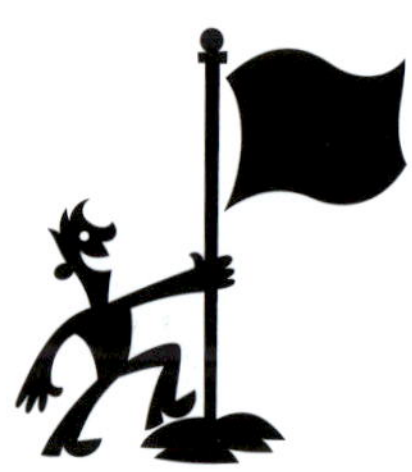

Stand_Your_Ground_**TM651**

Talking_Head_**TM652**

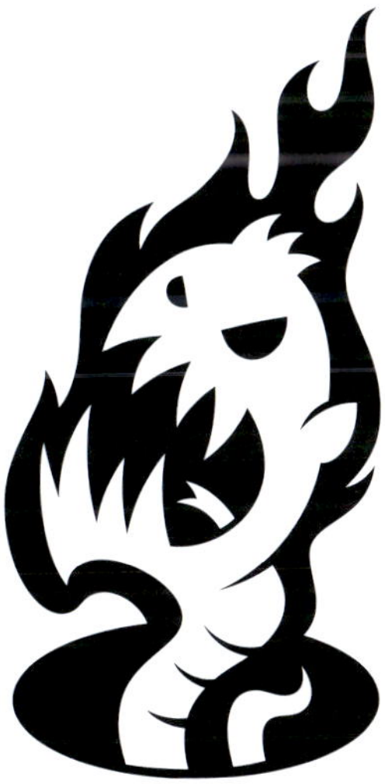

From_The_Pit_**TM654**

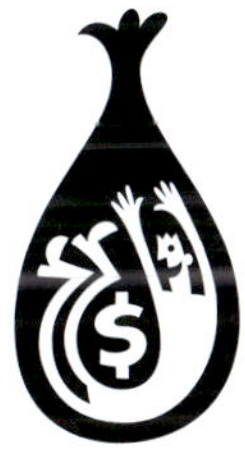

The_Money_Man_**TM653**

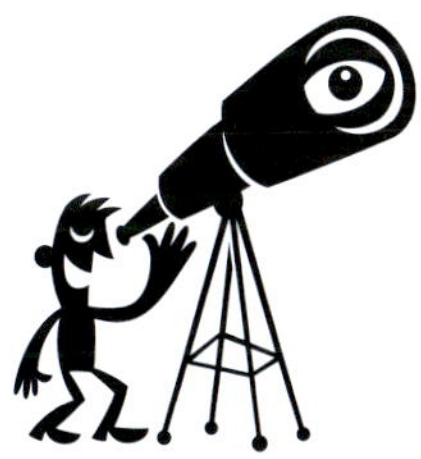

Keep_An_Eye_Out_**TM655**

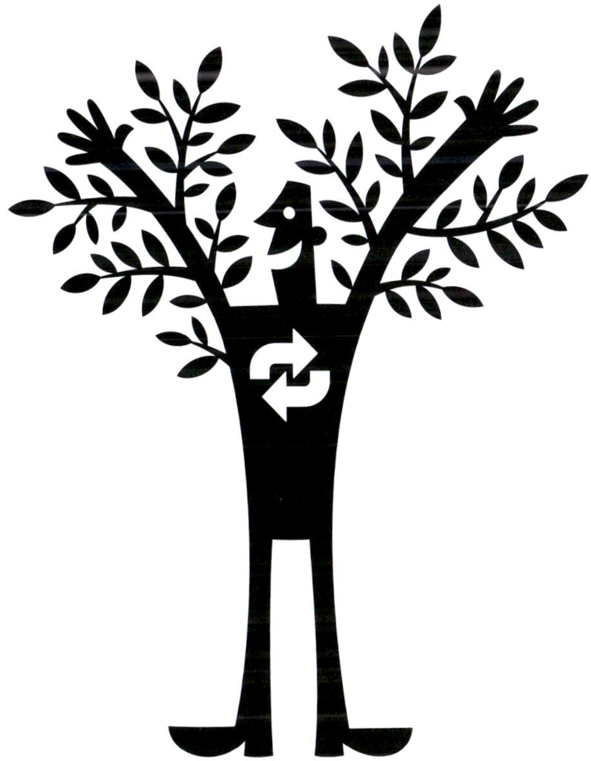

Embrace_Nature_**TM656**

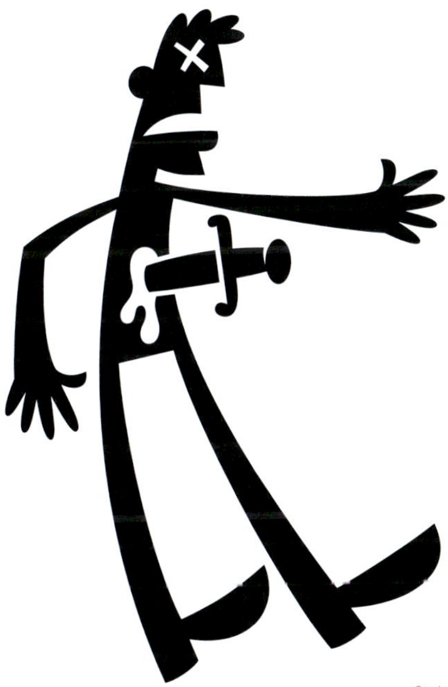

Stabbed_**TM657**

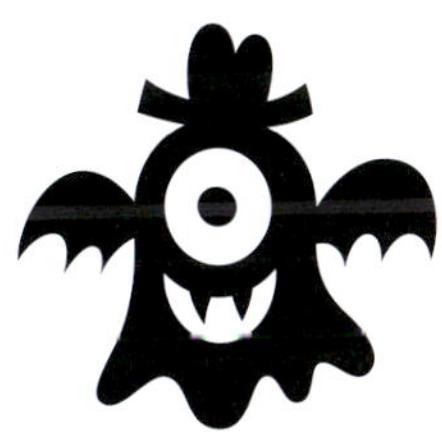

Bill_The_Ghoul_**TM658**

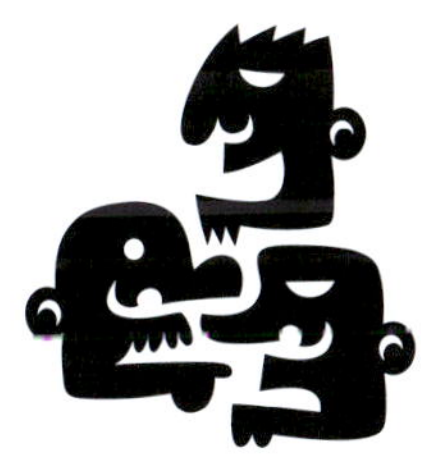

Three_Heads_Better_**TM659**

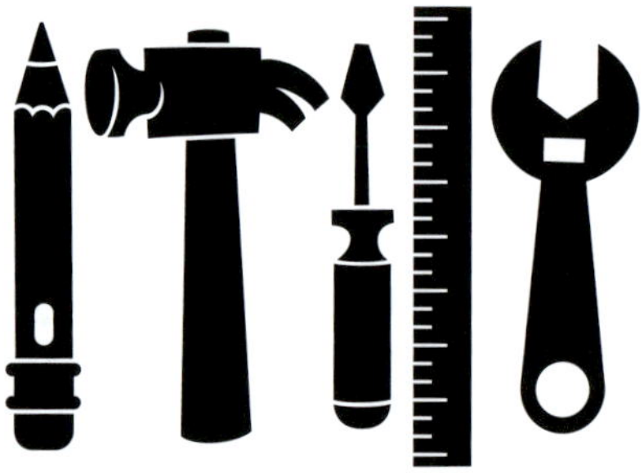

Build_Your_Dreams_**TM660**

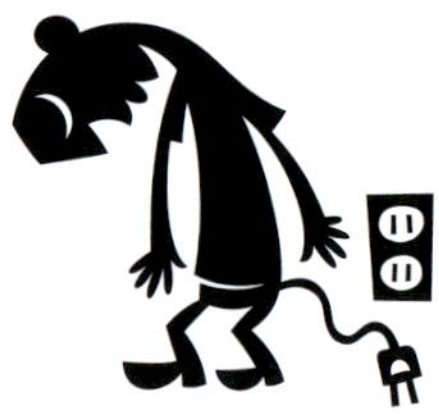

Low_Energy_**TM661**

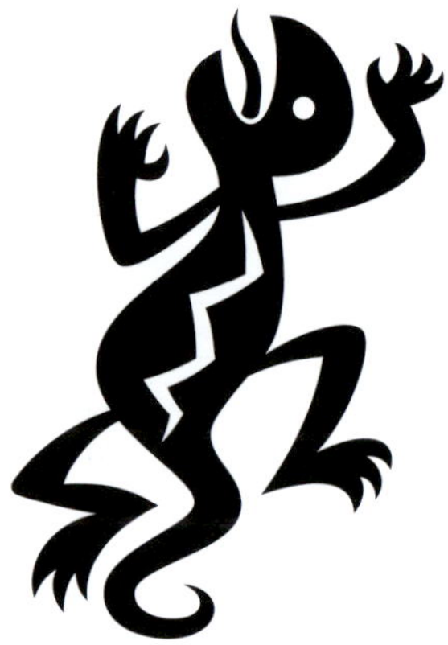

Gekko_**TM662**

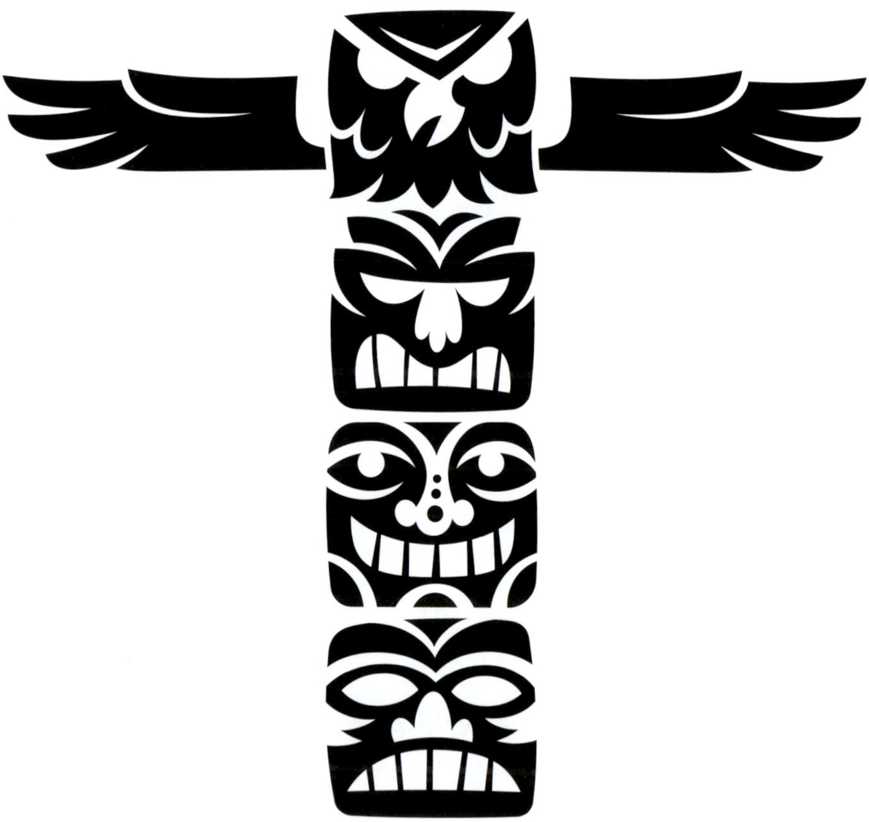

Totem_Pole_**TM664**

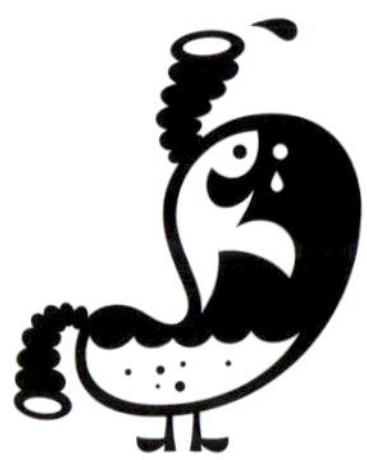

Cant_Stomach_It_**TM663**

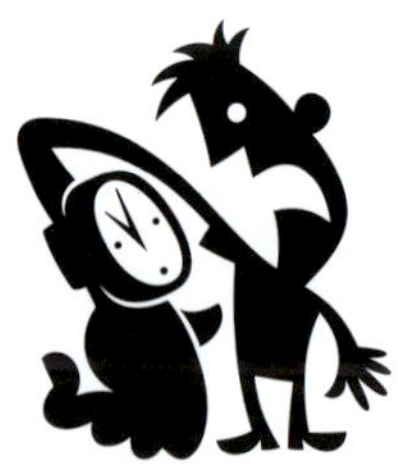

Time_Is_Running_Out_**TM665**

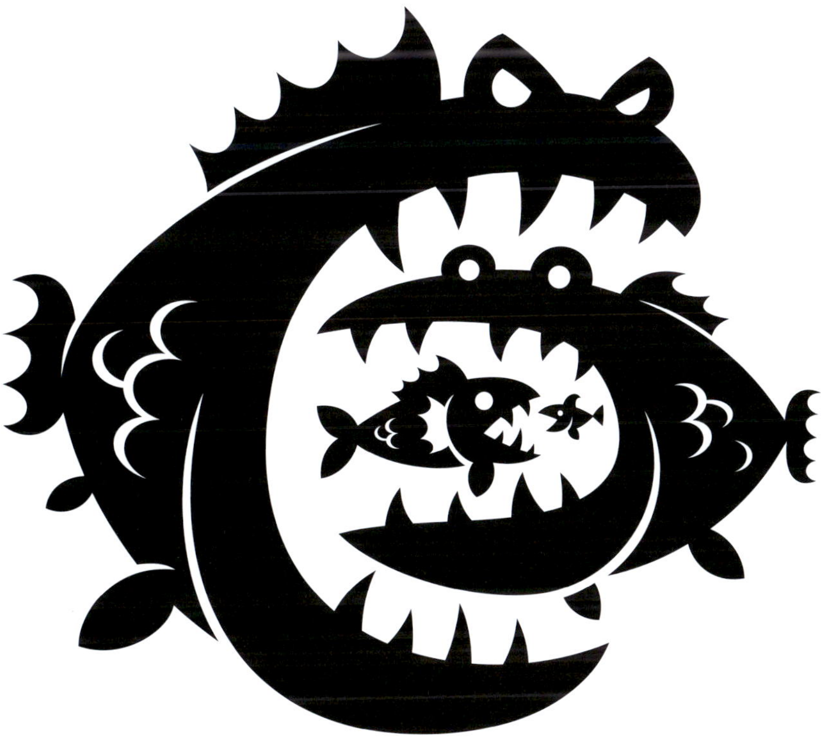

Always_A_Bigger_Fish_TM668

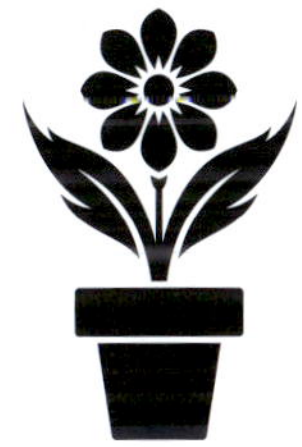

Potted_Plant_TM666

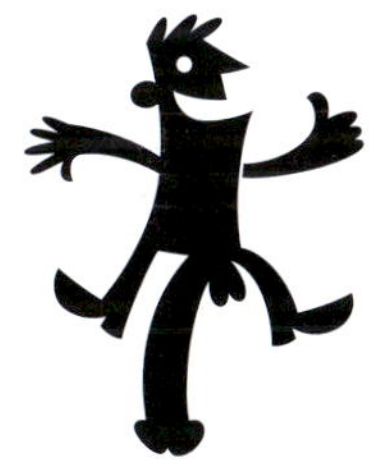

Well_Endowed_TM667

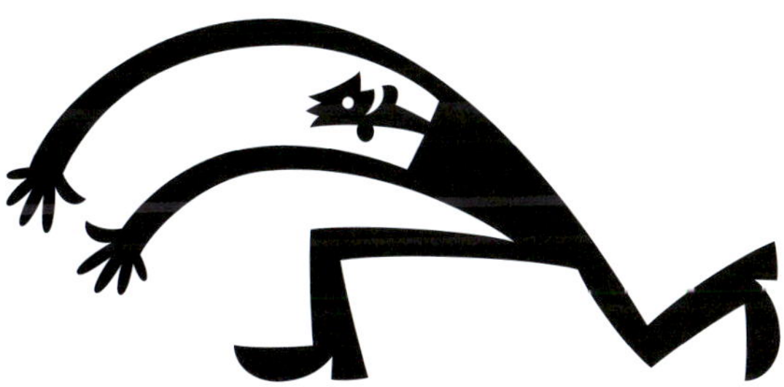

Be_Flexible_TM669

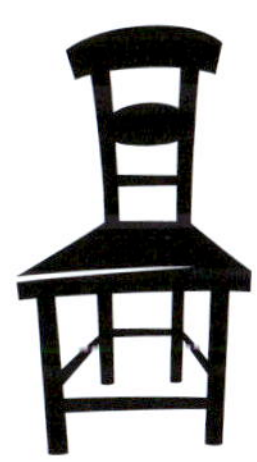

Amish_Wet_Dream_TM670

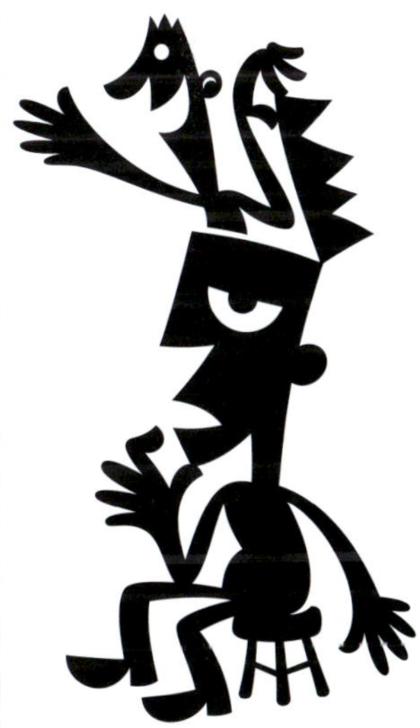

We_Welcome_Ideas_TM671

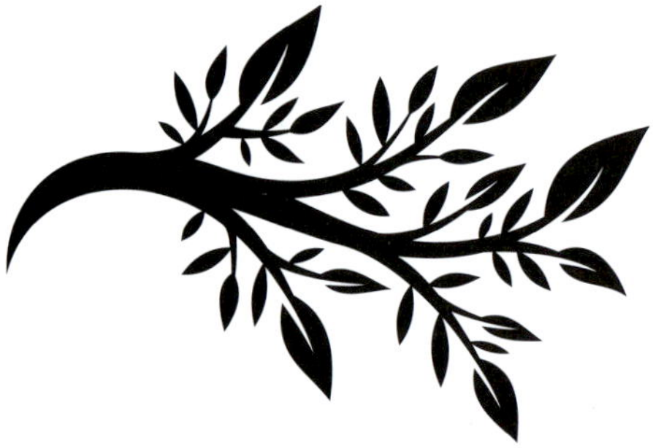

Branch_Out_**TM672**

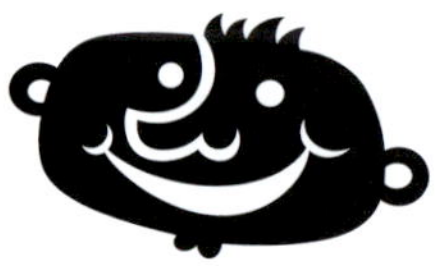

Charlie_**TM673**

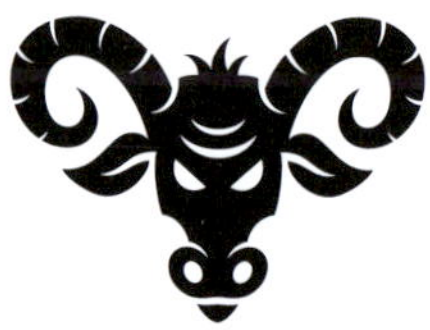

Bulls_Eye_**TM674**

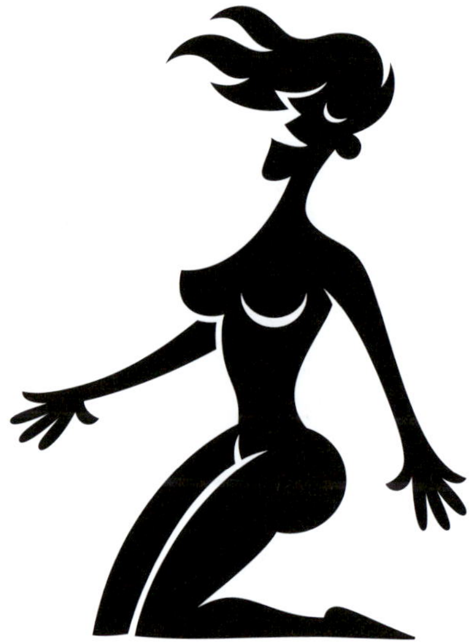

Pinup_**TM675**

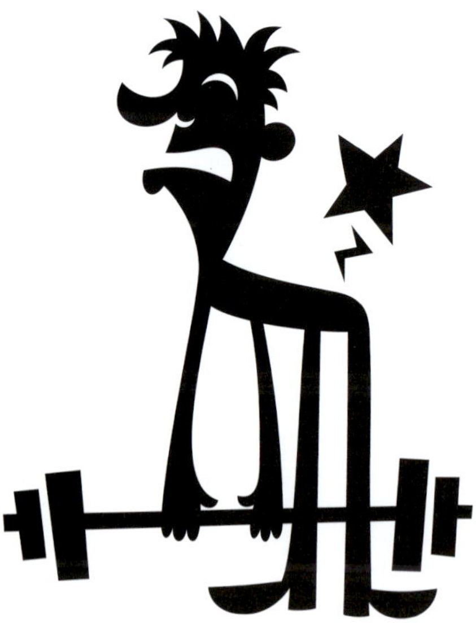

Weight_Break_**TM676**

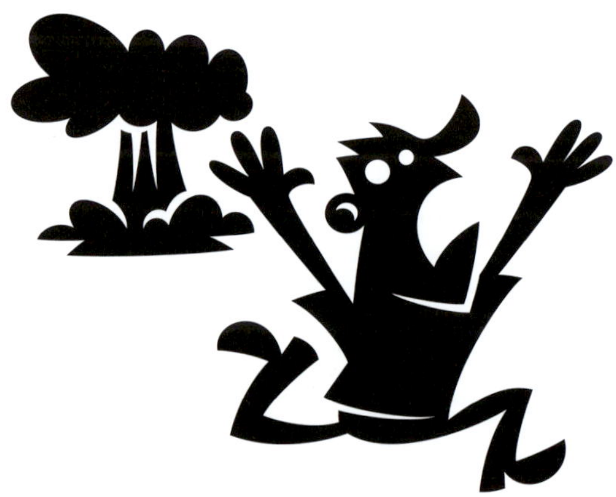

Big_Bang_**TM677**

Charbroiled_**TM679**

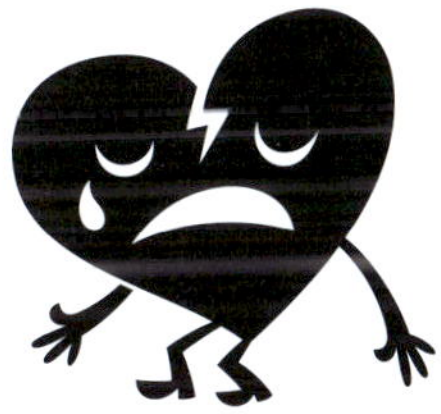

Broken_Hearted_**TM678**

Burning_Passion_**TM680**

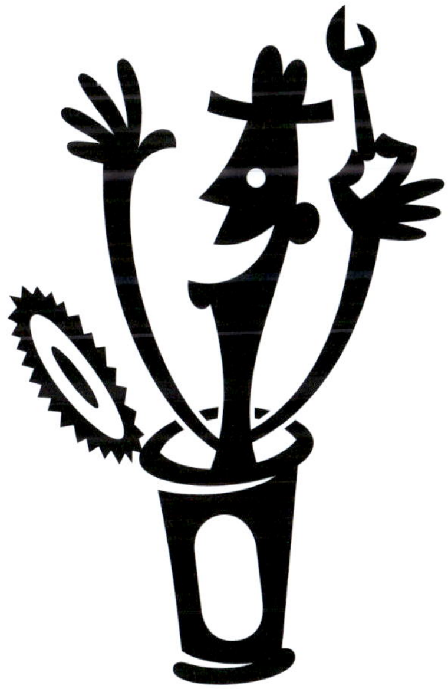

Canned_**TM681**

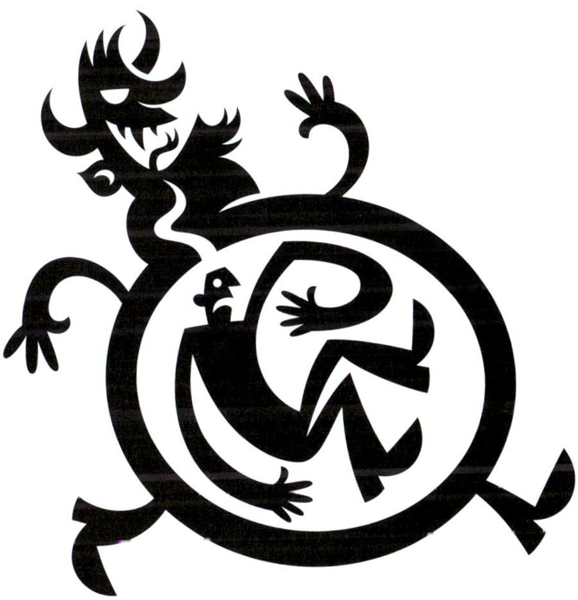

Devils_Food_**TM682**

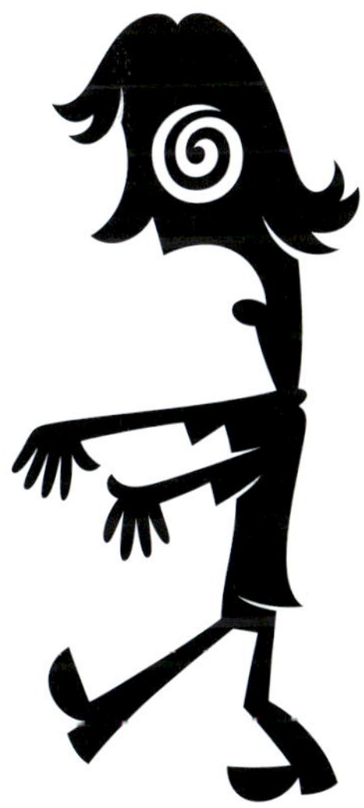

Bedazzled_**TM683**

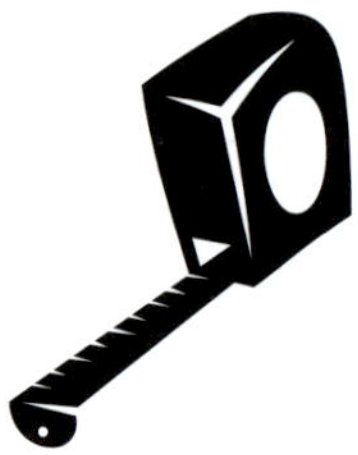

Screw_The_Metric_System_**TM684**

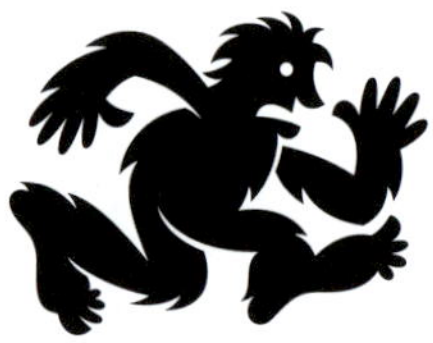

Yowie_**TM685**

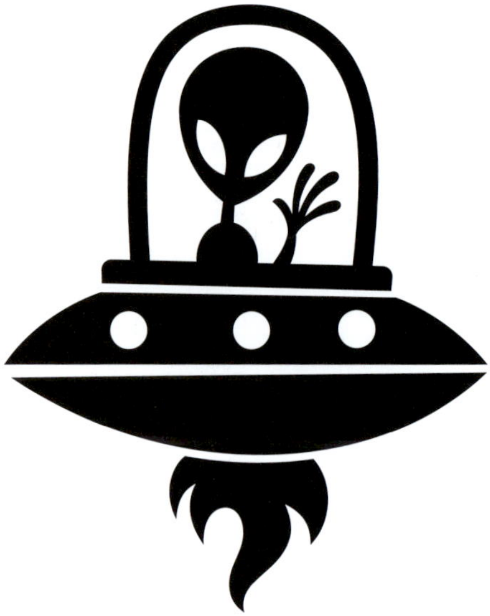

Hello_Earthlings_**TM686**

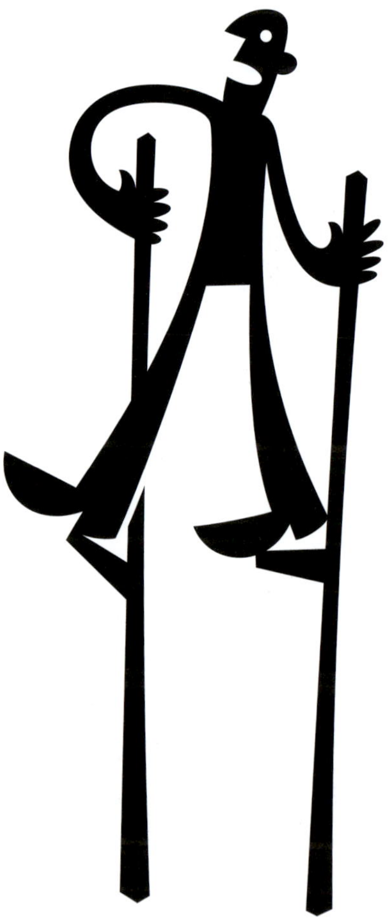

Walking_Tall_**TM687**

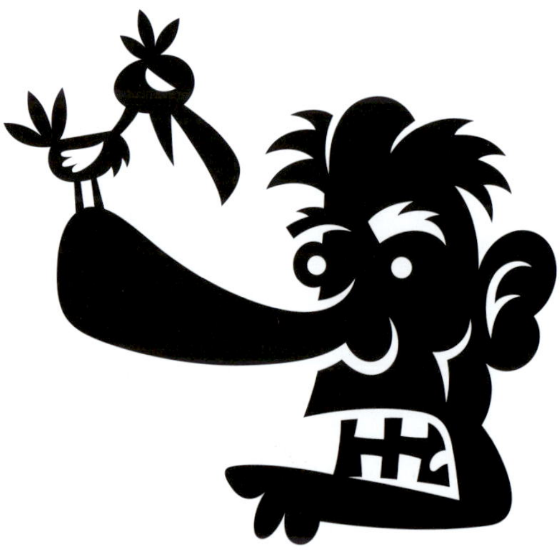

Birds_Eye_View_**TM688**

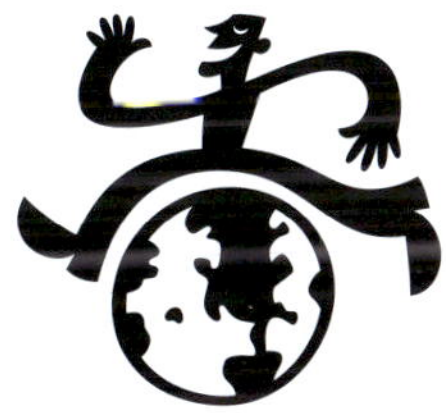

Sojourner_TM689

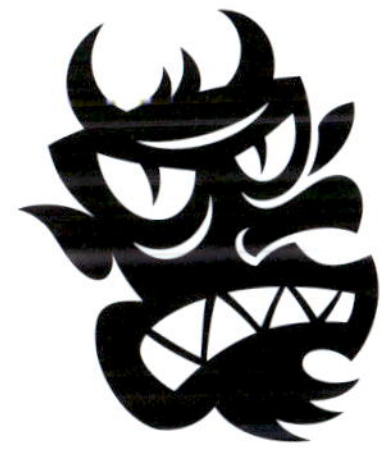

Devilish_Good_Looks_TM690

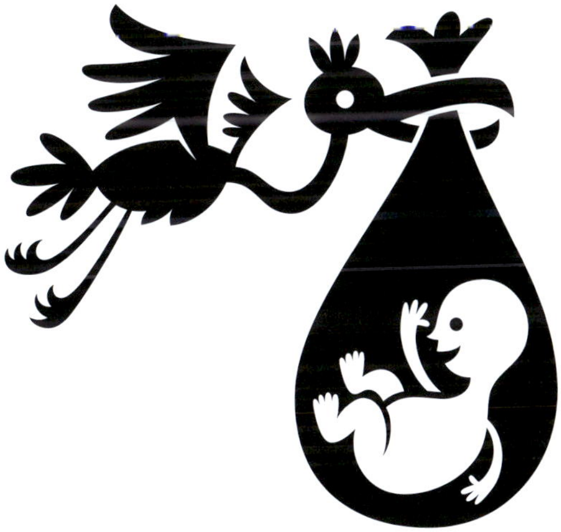

Where_Babies_Come_From_TM691

Overblown_Self_Esteem_TM692

Bad_Weather_TM693

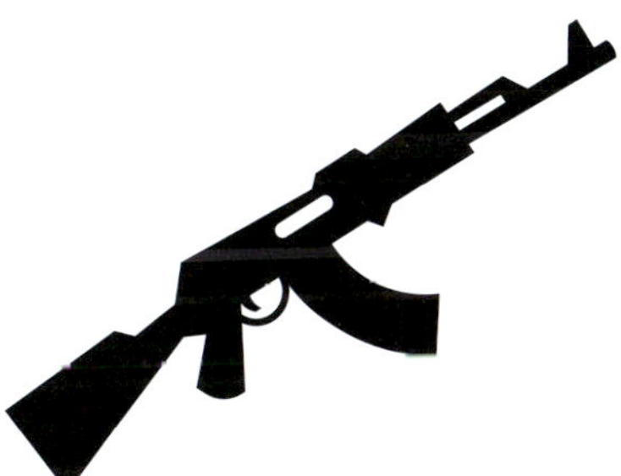

Lead_Diet_TM694

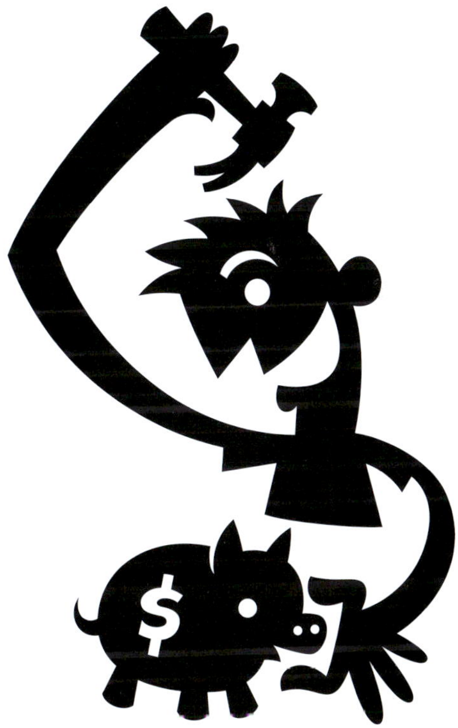

Breaking_The_Bank_TM695

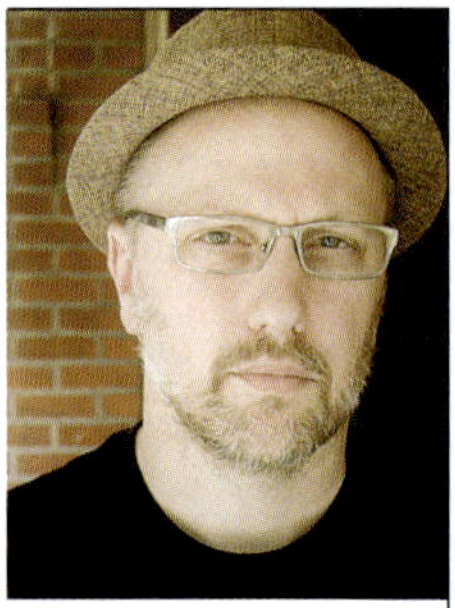

Keith Bowman

Designer & Illustrator

Amerikan Made • Philadelphia, Pennsylvania

www.weareamerikanmade.com

One of my favorite memories growing up in the 1970s was watching the TV show *In Search of...* with Leonard Nimoy, especially the episode on Bigfoot. It captured my imagination and made every camping trip as a kid just a little more exciting. When I saw *Take and Make Art's* "Bigfoot" character, I knew I had to use him for a new poster design.

I find it amusing that there are *still* shows on TV that are dedicated to "finding Bigfoot." So the concept came pretty quickly. I wanted to illustrate a Bigfoot documentary crew being photobombed by the real Bigfoot, who is out for a little moonlight stroll. I am not sure why he's holding an umbrella, but I feel it adds to the fun and absurdity of the scene. I originally designed this to be seven colors, but when I broke it into separations for screen printing I found that simplifying my design to three colors really gave it more visual energy.

Art Used: Bigfoot TM634

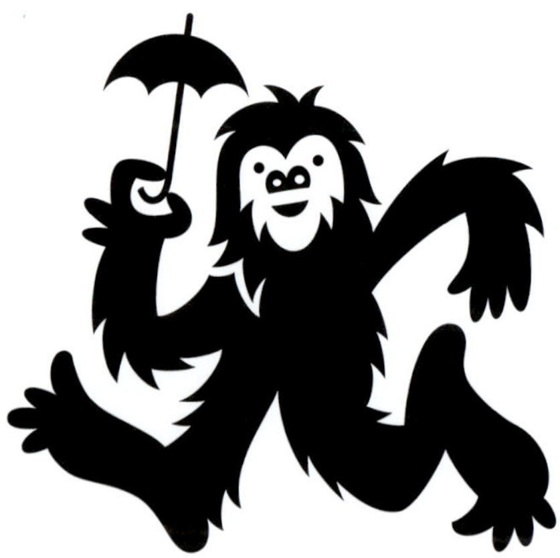

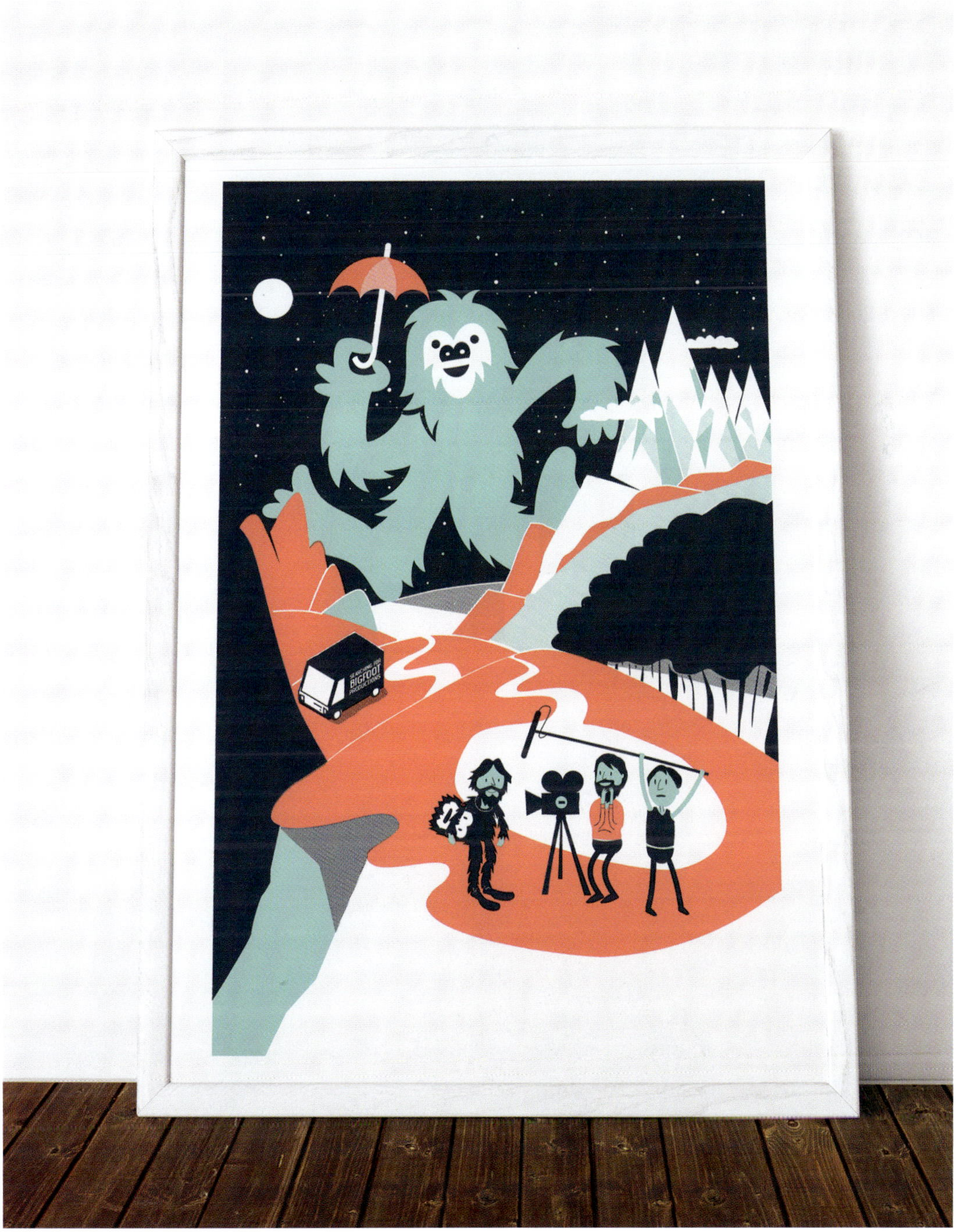
SEARCHING FOR
BIGFOOT
PRODUCTIONS

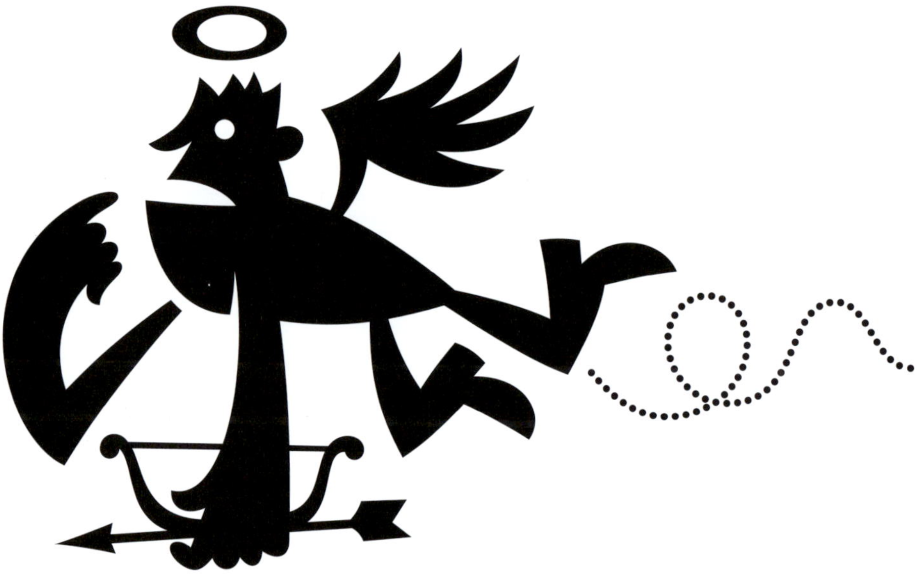

Hark_Harry_Angel_**TM696**

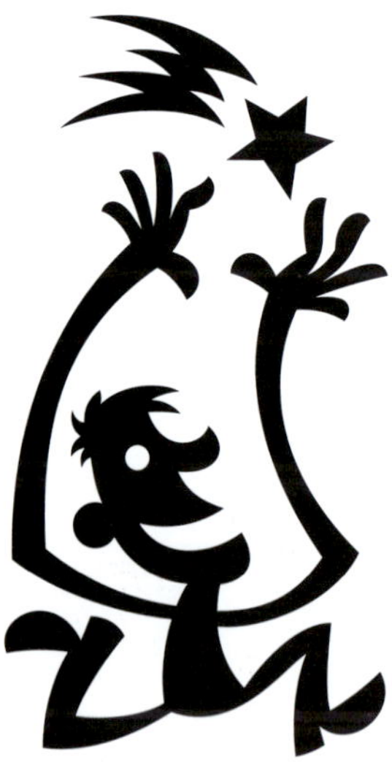

Chasing_Stars_**TM698**

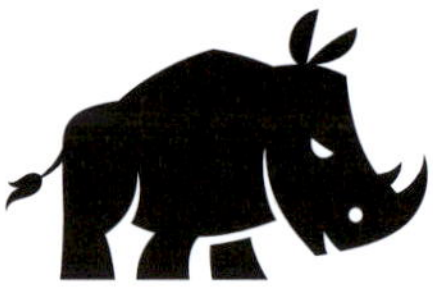

Bold_Rhino_**TM697**

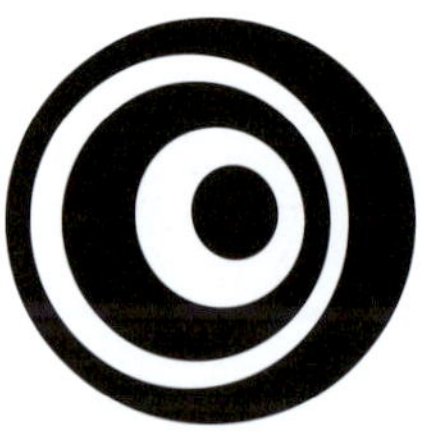

Cyclone_**TM699**

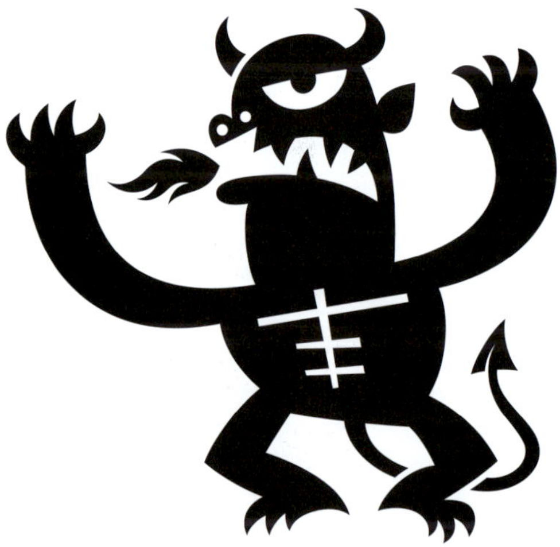

Personal_Demons_**TM700**

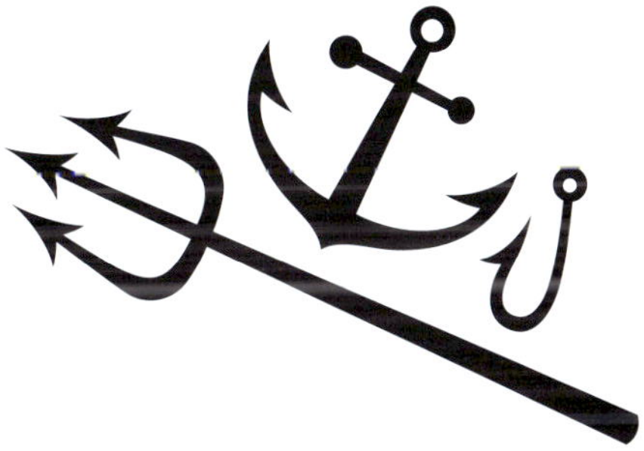

Pointy_Sea_Tools_**TM701**

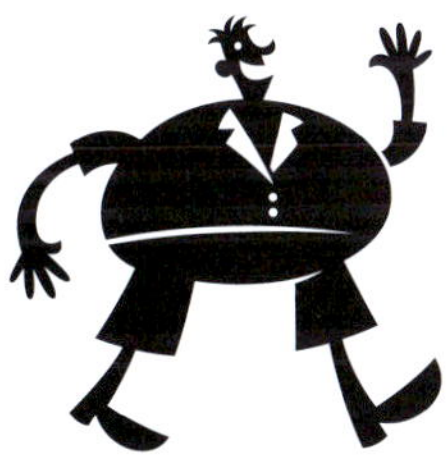

On_The_Move_**TM702**

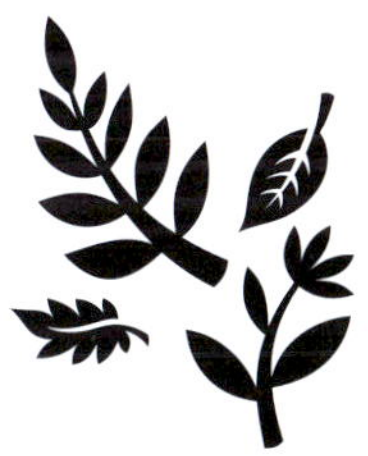

Yard_Clippings_**TM703**

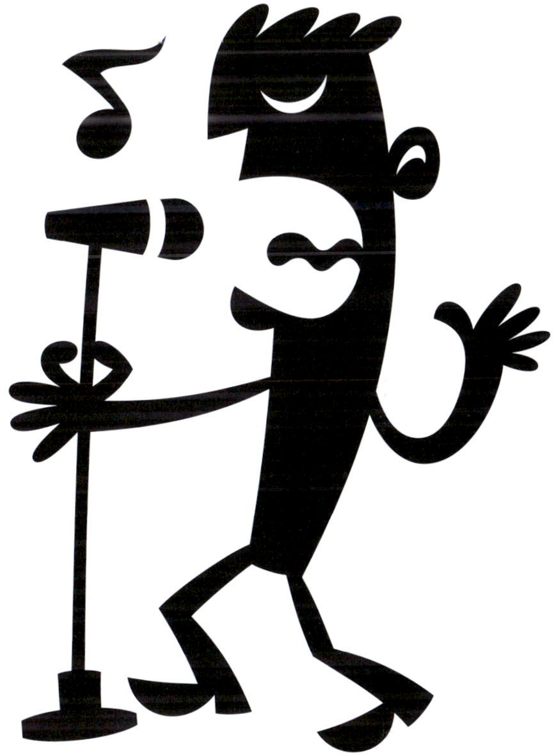

Belt_It_Out_**TM704**

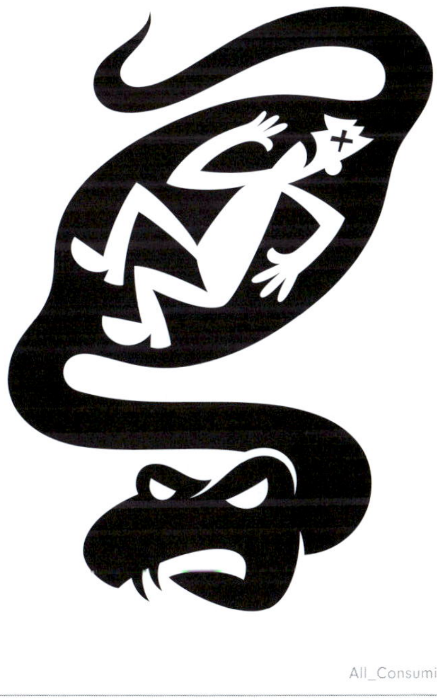

All_Consuming_**TM705**

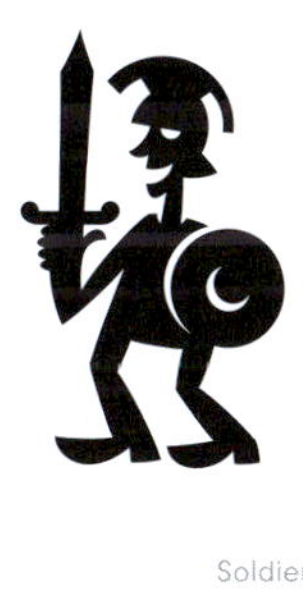

Soldier_**TM706**

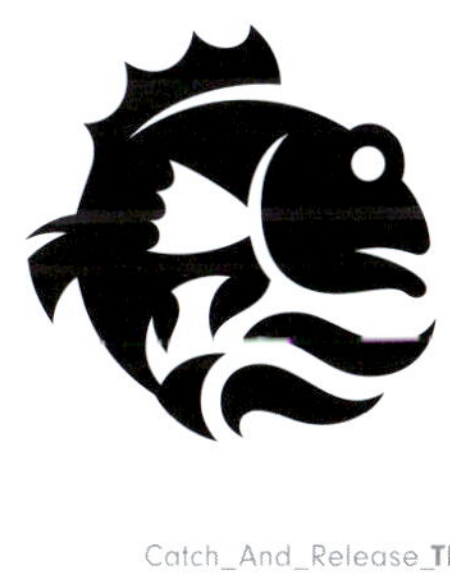

Catch_And_Release_**TM707**

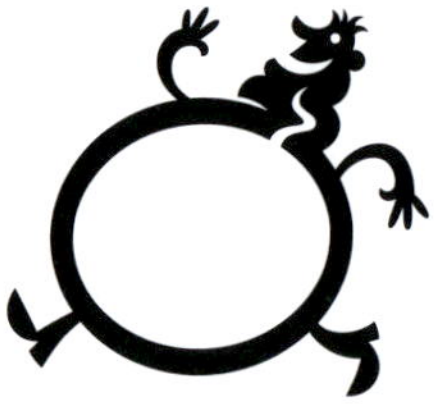

Bellyache_**TM708**

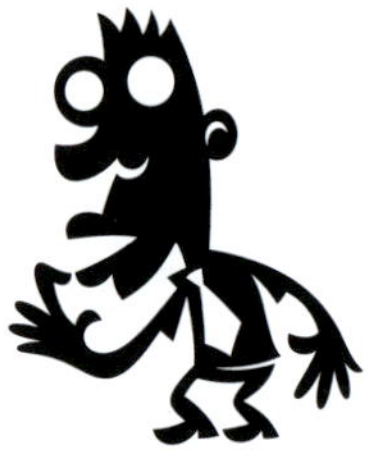

Dumbfounded_**TM709**

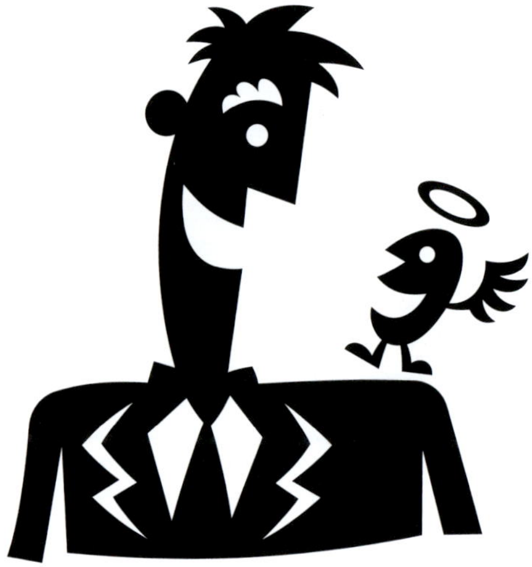

Shoulder_Angel_**TM710**

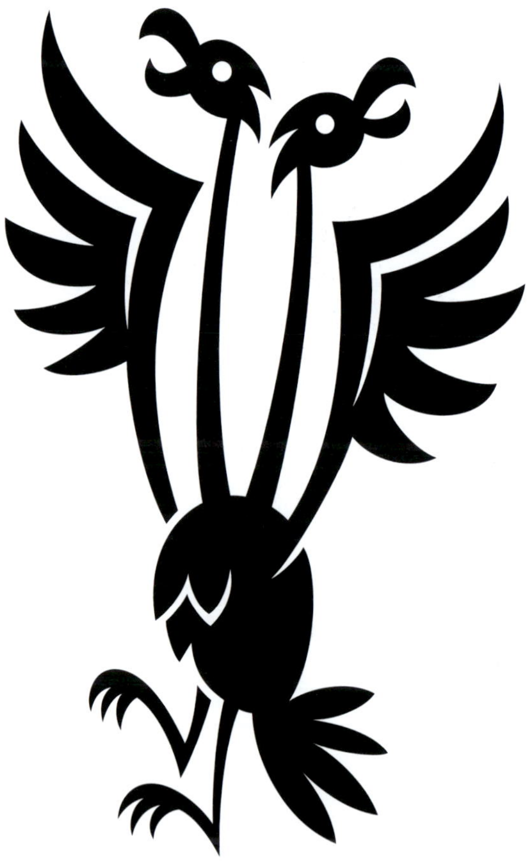

Duality_**TM711**

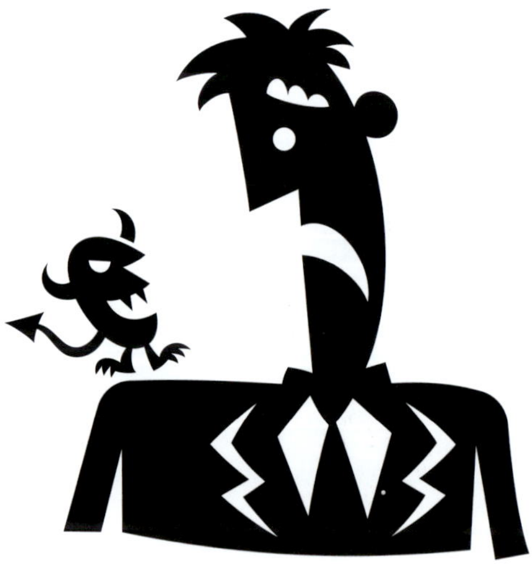

Devil_Made_Me_Do_It_**TM712**

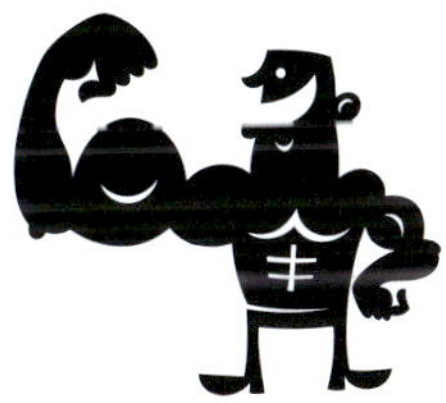

Stud_Muffin_**TM713**

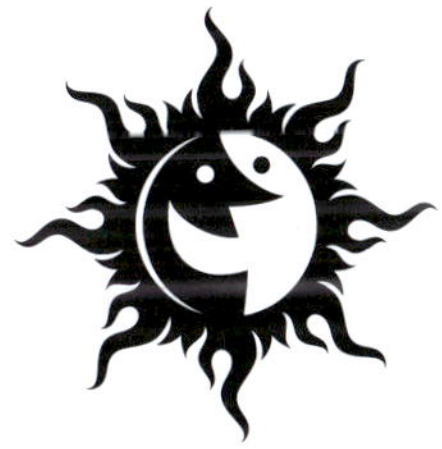

Sunshine_**TM714**

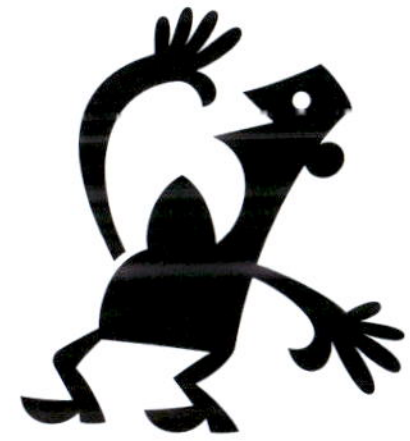

Cry_For_Help_**TM715**

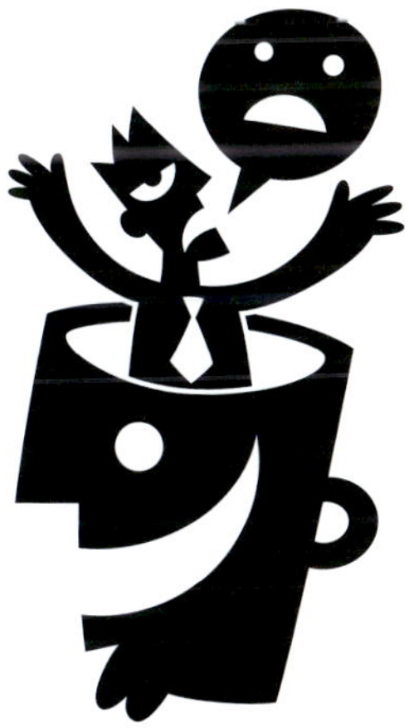

Dont_Speak_Your_Mind_**TM716**

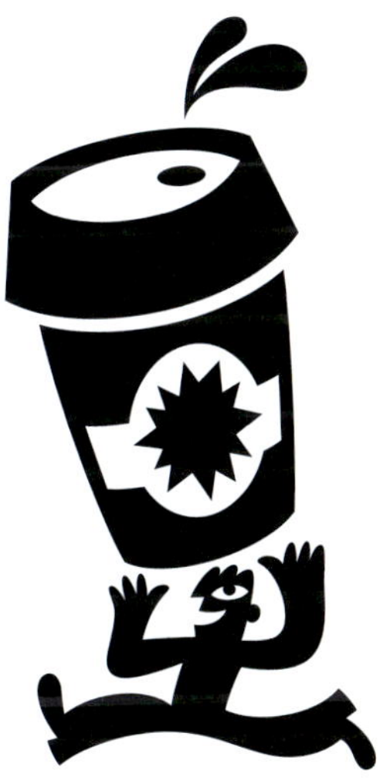

Coffee_Runner_**TM717**

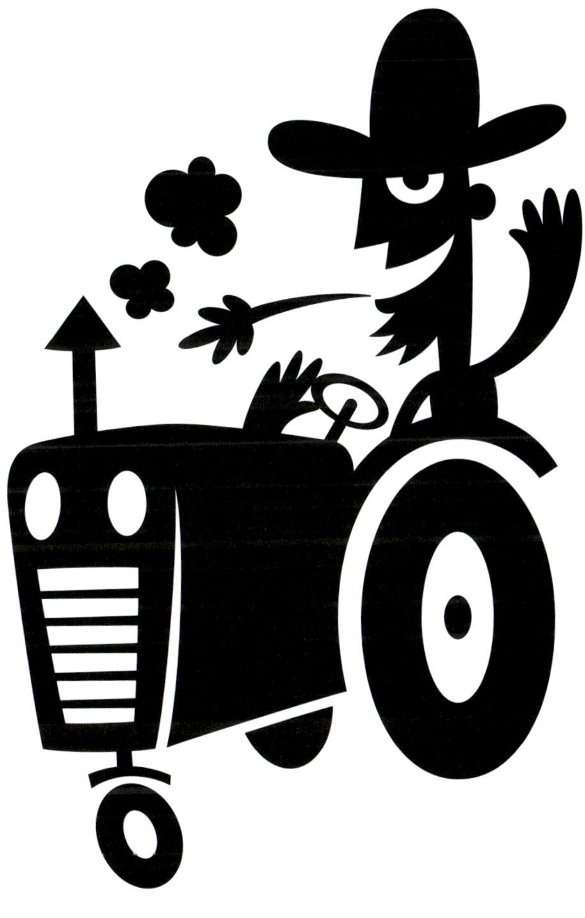

Furrow_Manager_**TM718**

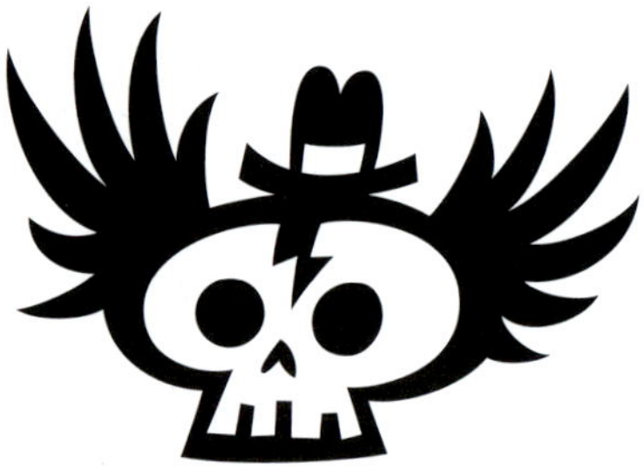

Flying_Skull_**TM719**

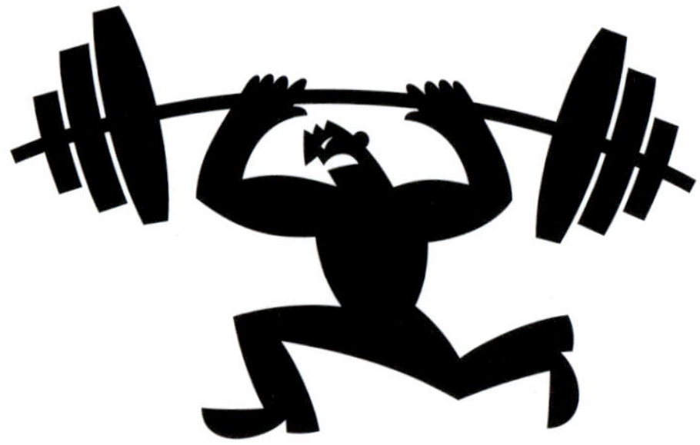

Power_Through_It_**TM720**

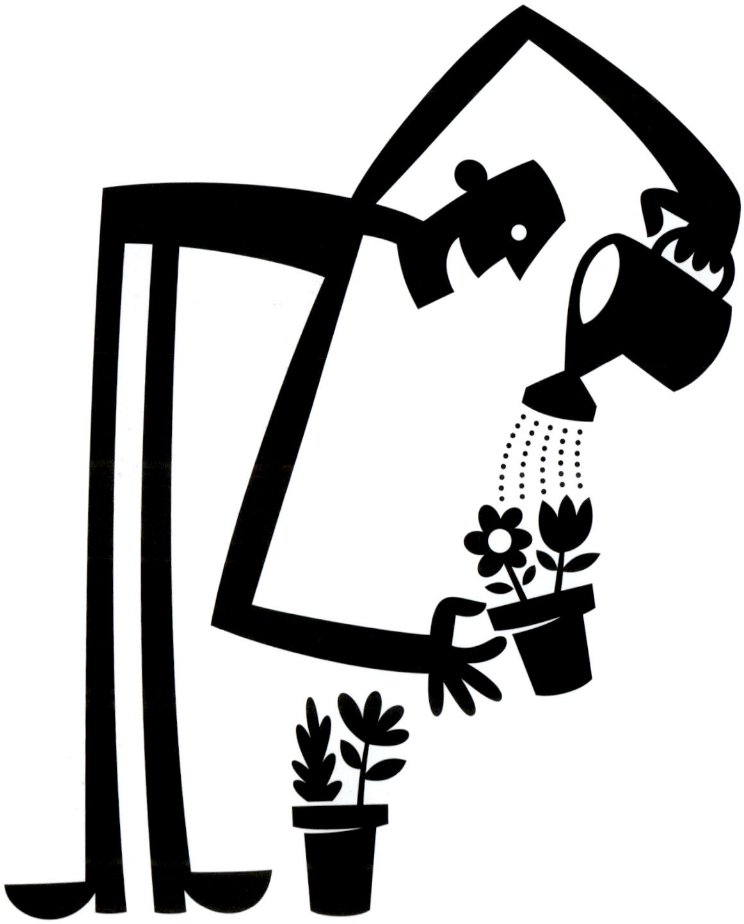

Green_Thumb_**TM722**

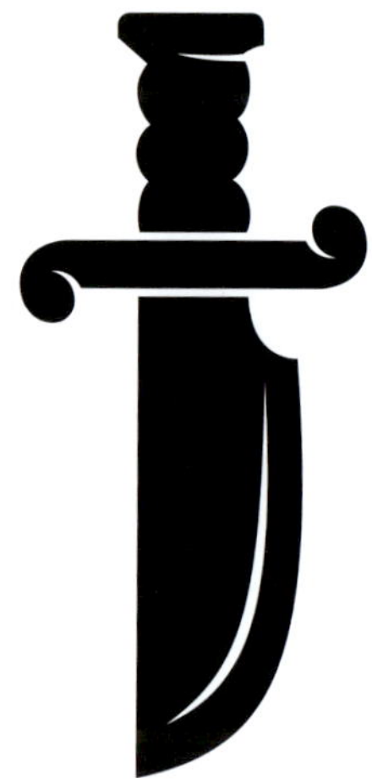

Cut_Throat_**TM721**

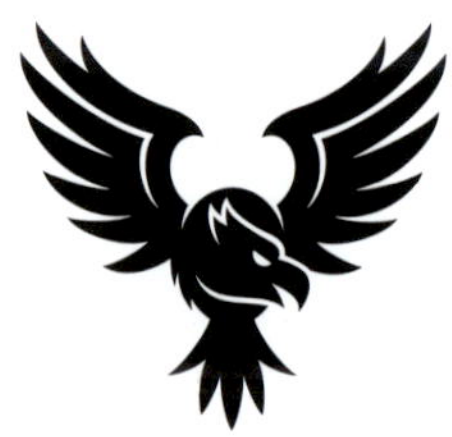

Black_Bird_**TM723**

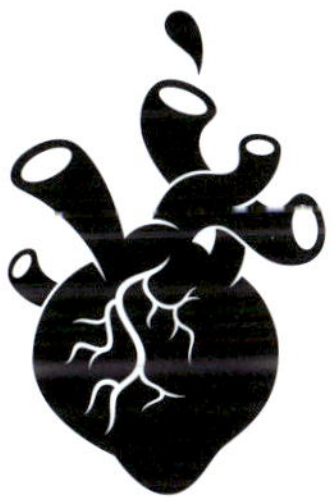

Do_Your_Cardio_**TM724**

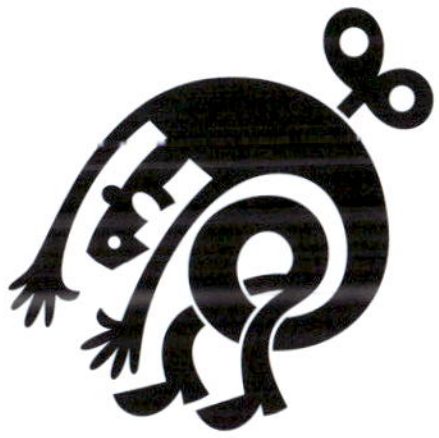

All_Wound_Up_**TM725**

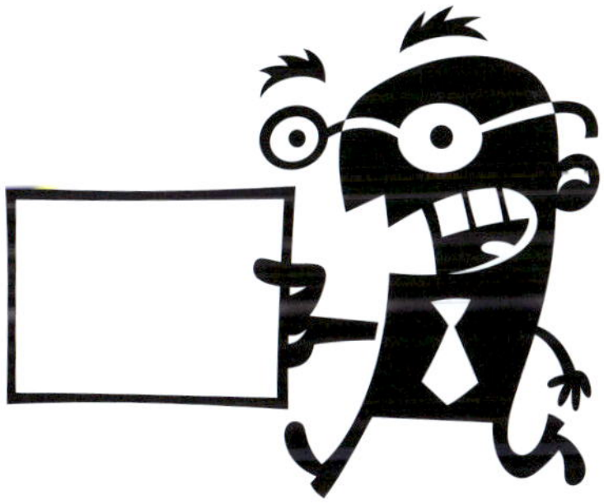

Special_Message_**TM726**

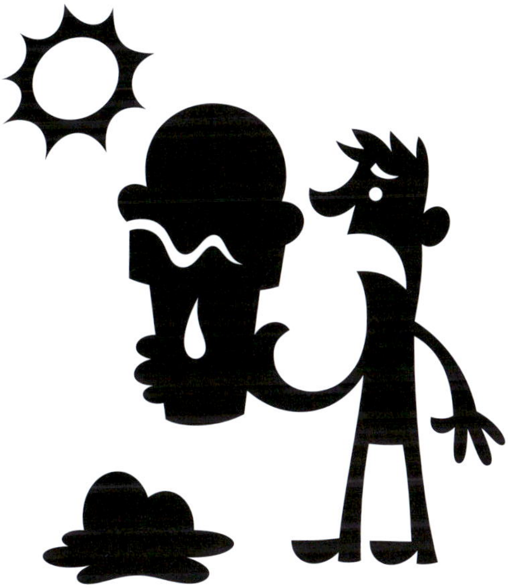

Blame_Global_Warming_**TM727**

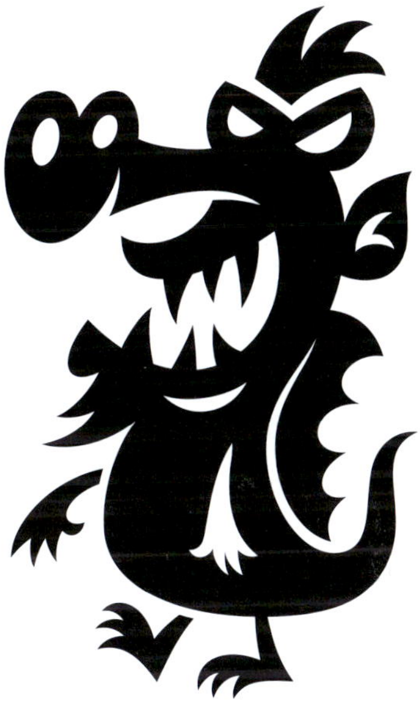

Beasty_Boy_**TM728**

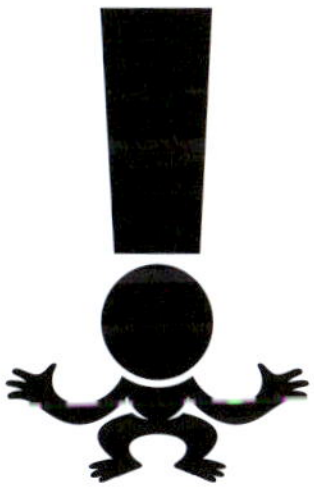

WTH_**TM729**

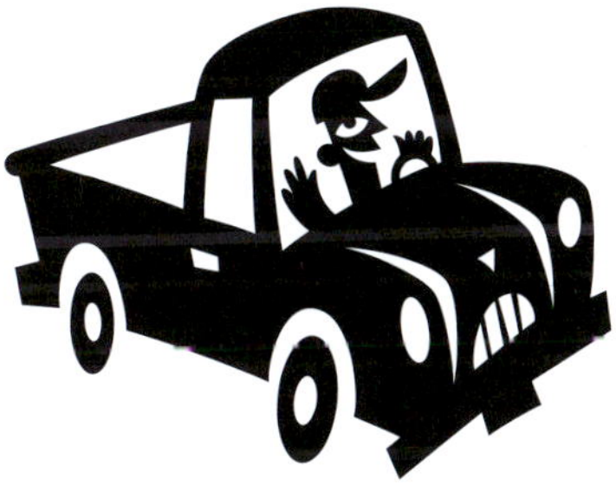

Pick_You_Up_**TM730**

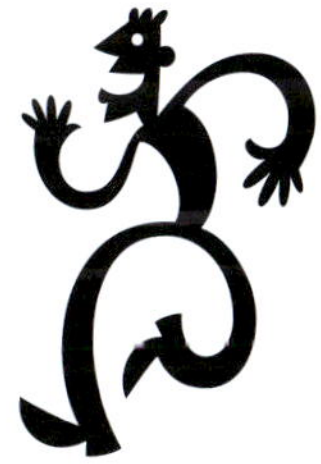

Do_A_Jig_**TM731**

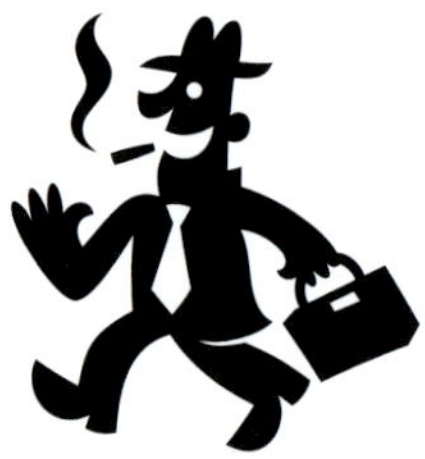

Business_As_Usual_**TM732**

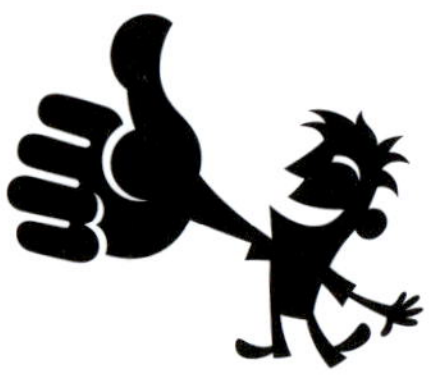

Yeah_Baby_**TM733**

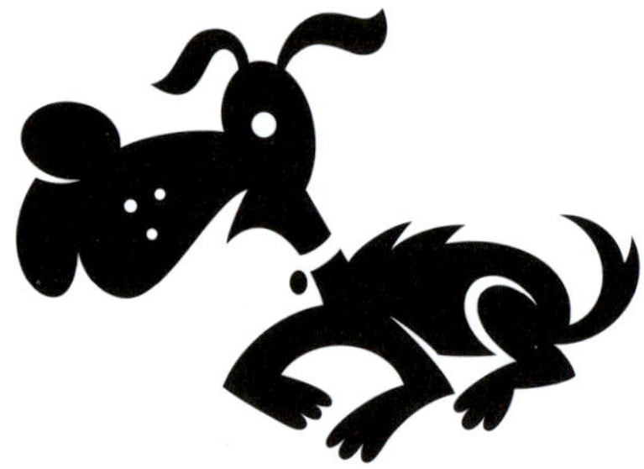

Dog_Day_**TM734**

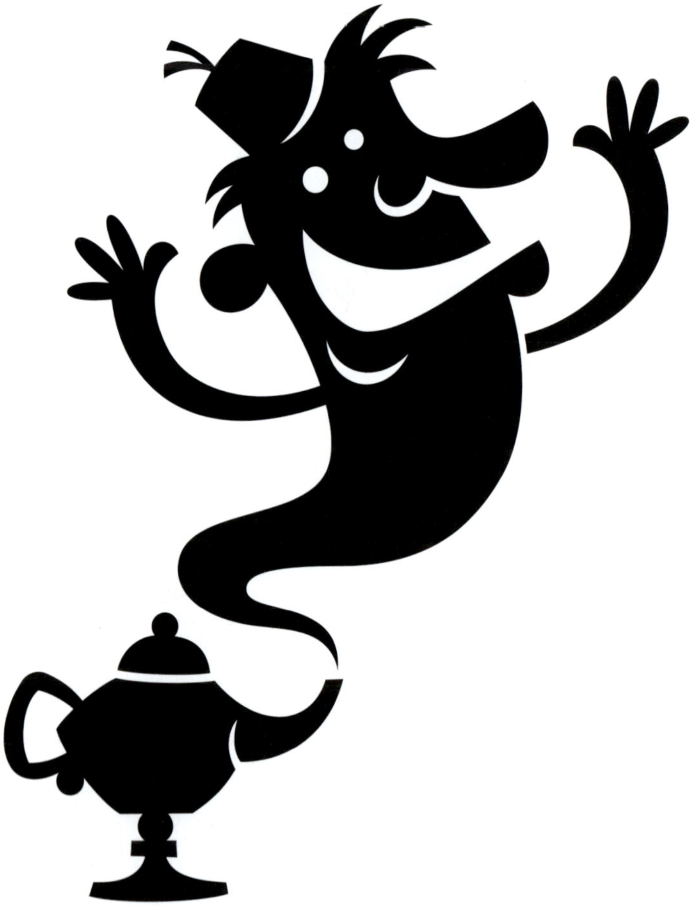

Your_Wish_Is_Our_Command_**TM736**

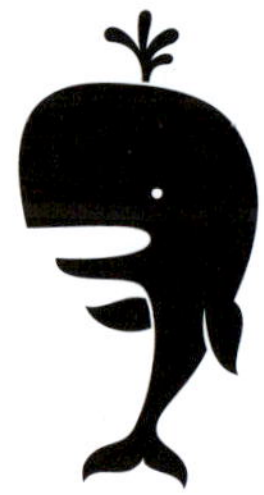

Whale_Of_A_Tail_**TM735**

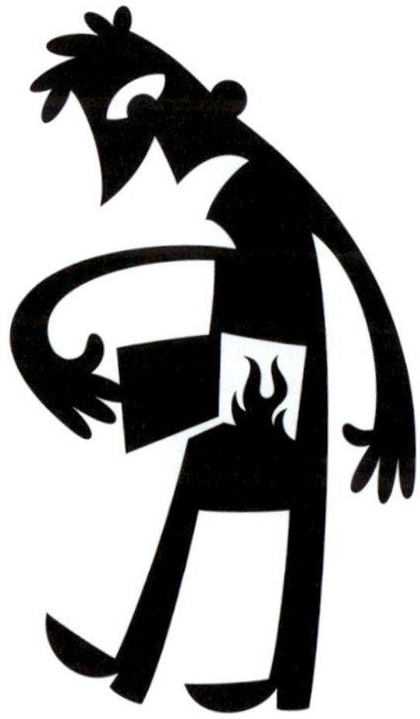

Burnin_Belly_**TM737**

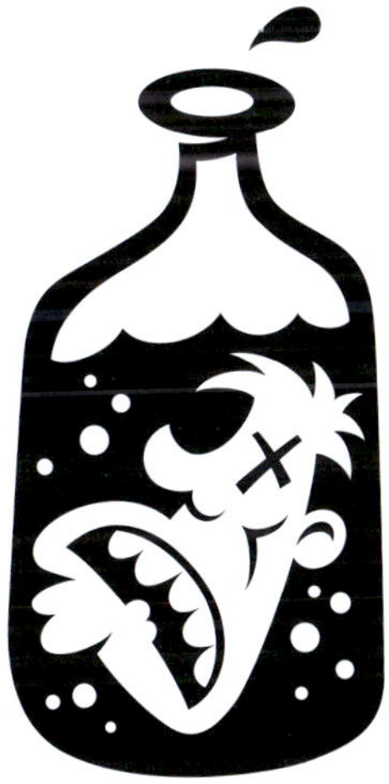

Jug_Head_**TM738**

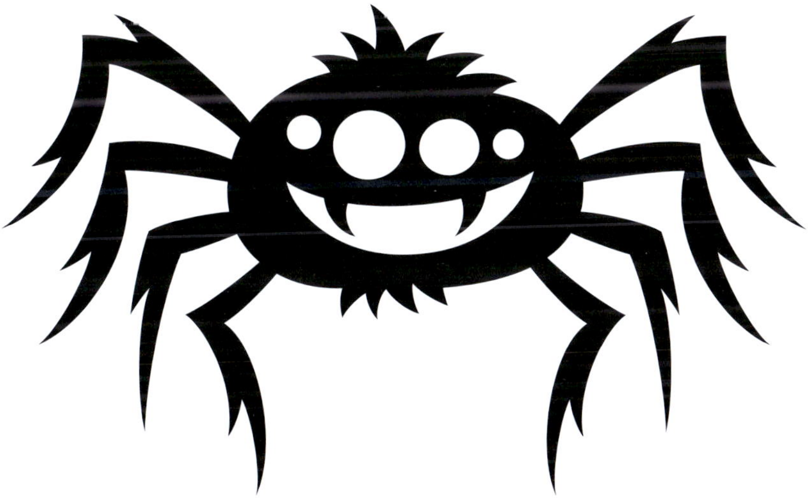

Harry_Spider_**TM739**

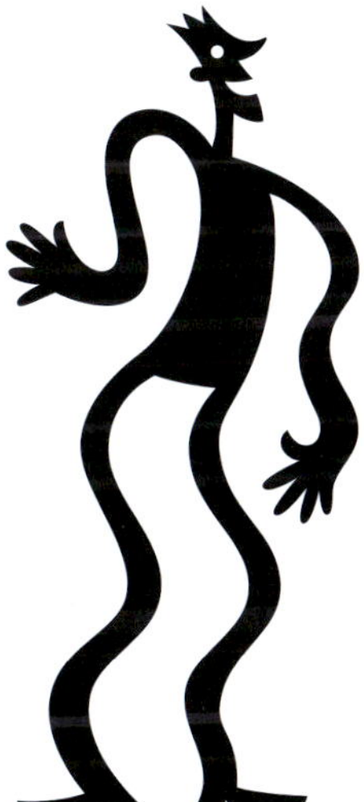

Heebie_Jeebies_**TM741**

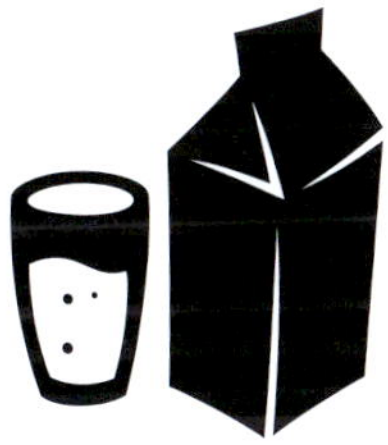

Cow_Juice_**TM740**

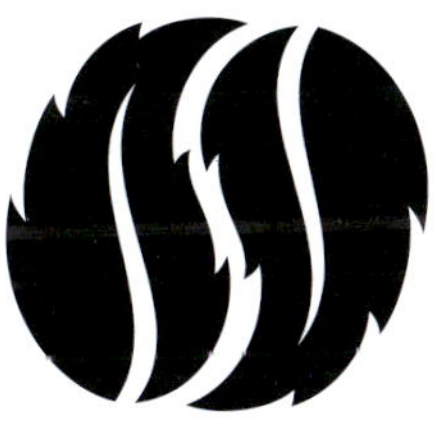

Leave_Me_Alone_**TM742**

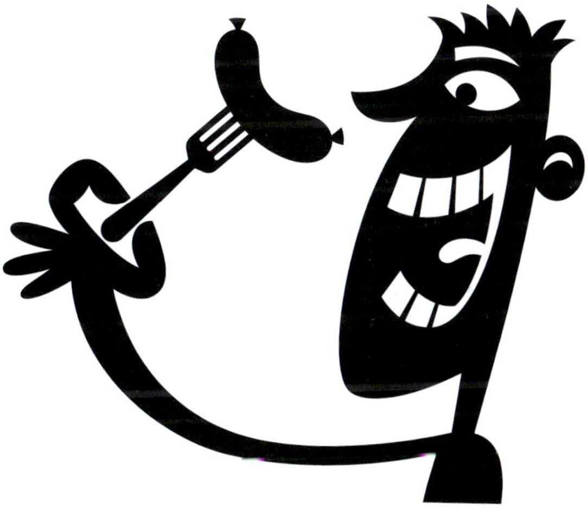

Chow_Time_**TM743**

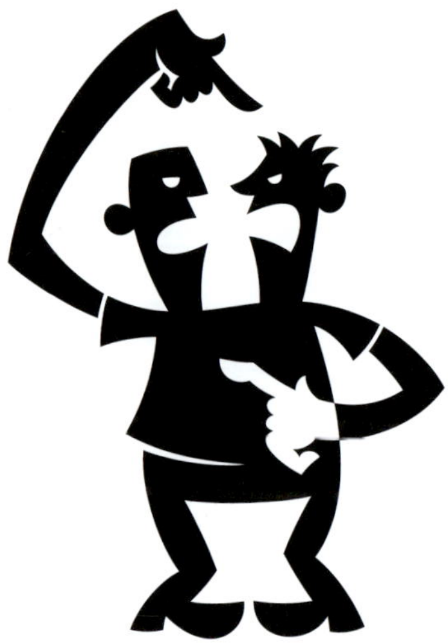

Inner_Conflict_**TM744**

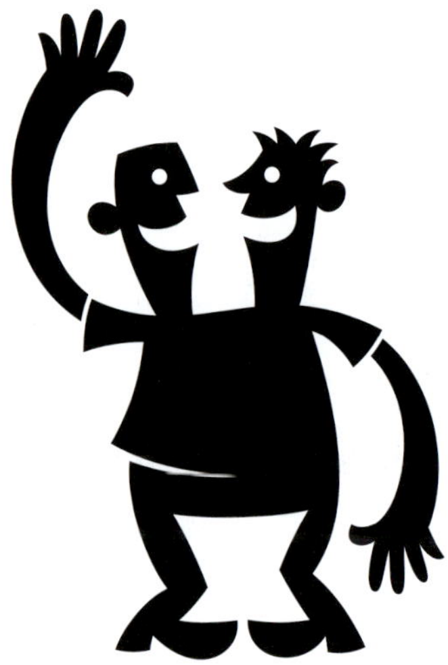

Inner_Peace_**TM745**

Group_Hangout_**TM747**

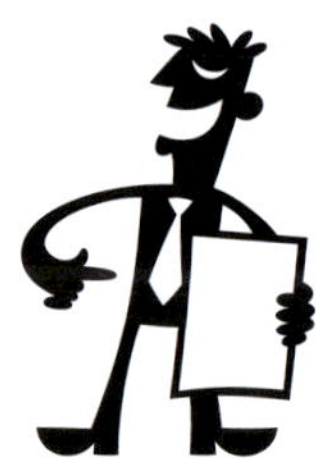

Be_Impressed_**TM746**

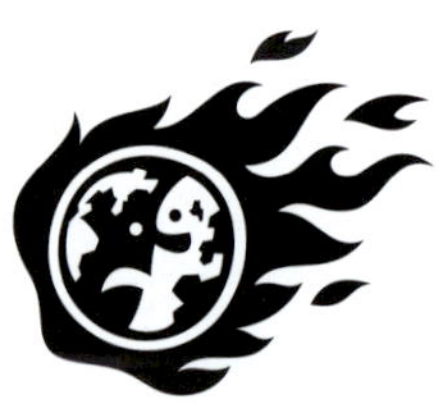

Global_Warming_**TM748**

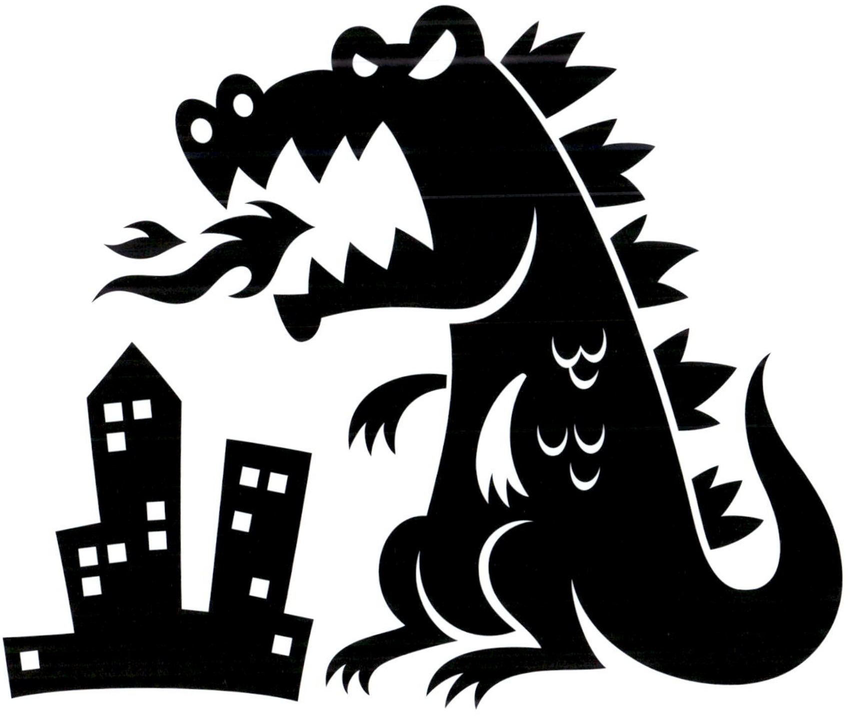

Go_Go_Godzilla_**TM750**

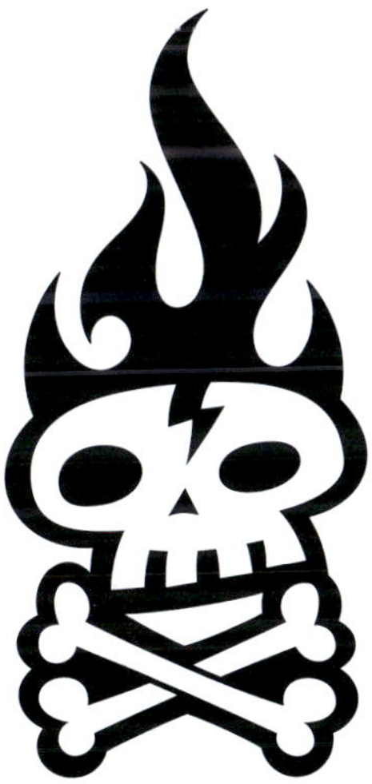

Scorched_Bonez_**TM749**

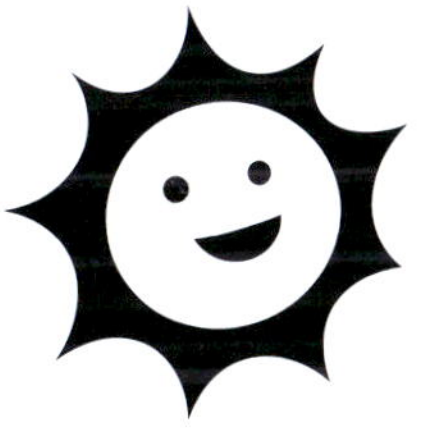

Sunny_Personality_**TM751**

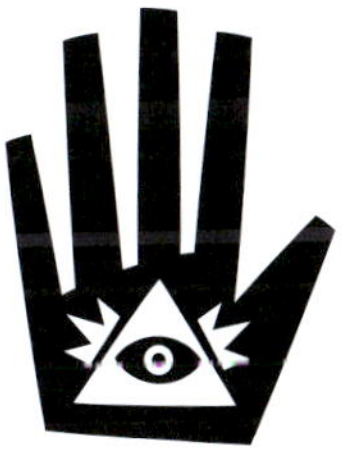

NWO_Handiwork_**TM752**

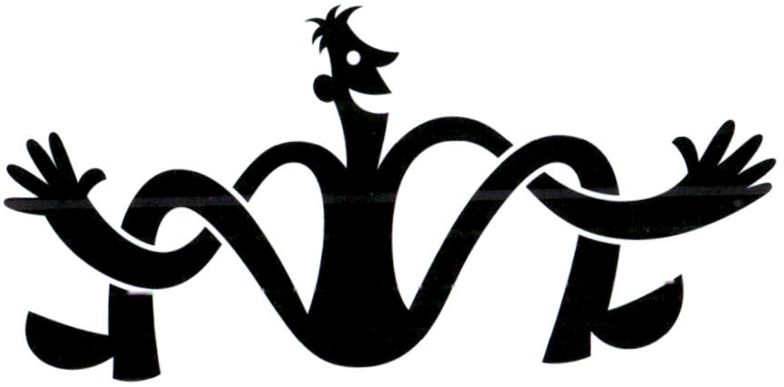

Good_Vibes_**TM753**

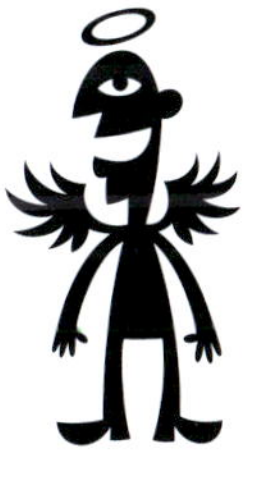

Heaven_On_Earth_**TM754**

Floraltasic_**TM755**

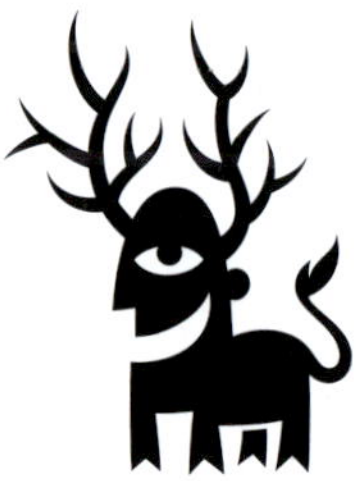

Bob_The_Antelope_**TM756**

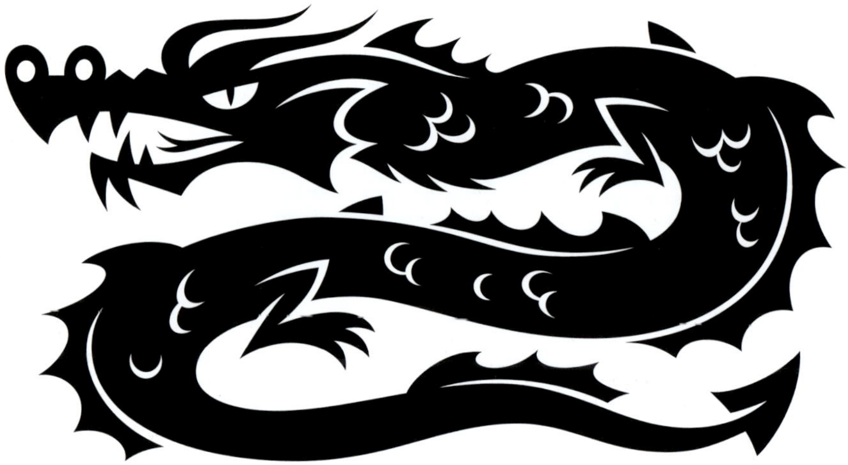

That_Ancient_Serpent_**TM757**

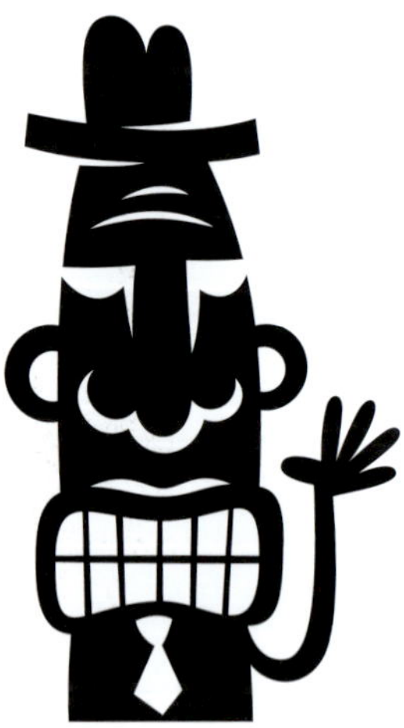

Im_Over_Here_**TM758**

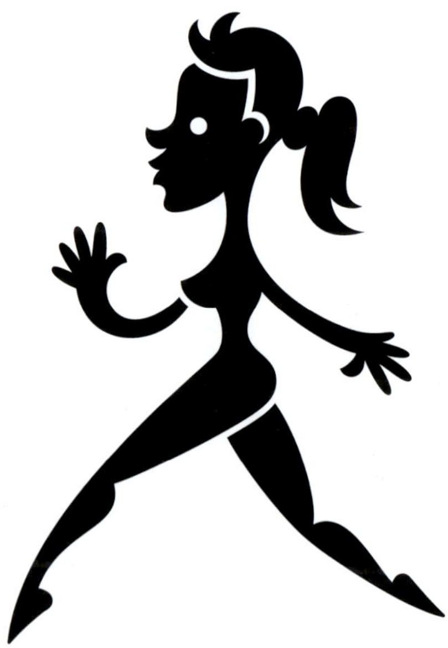

She_Knows_How_To_Use_Them_**TM759**

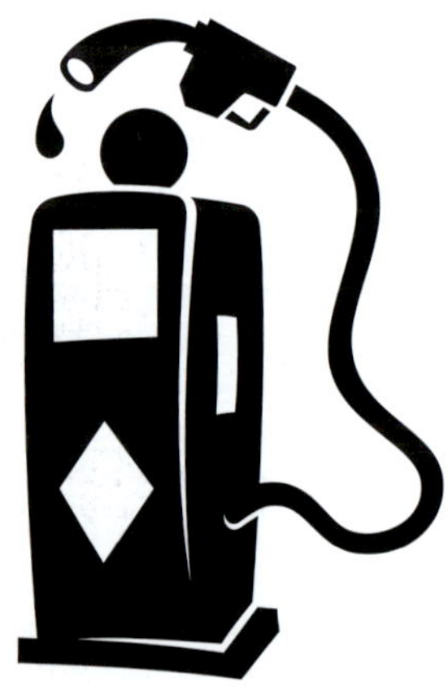

Fuel_Up_**TM760**

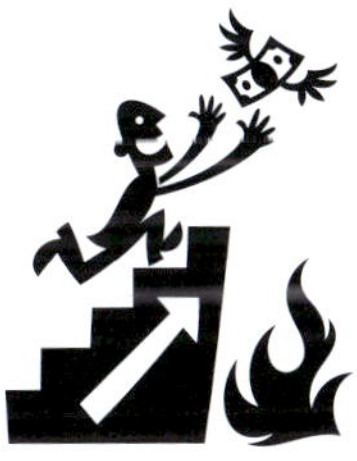

Chasing_Lucre_**TM761**

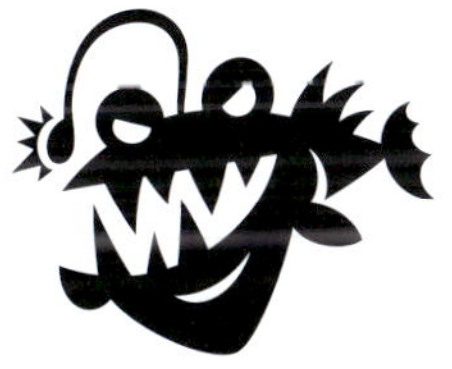

What_Lies_Beneath_**TM762**

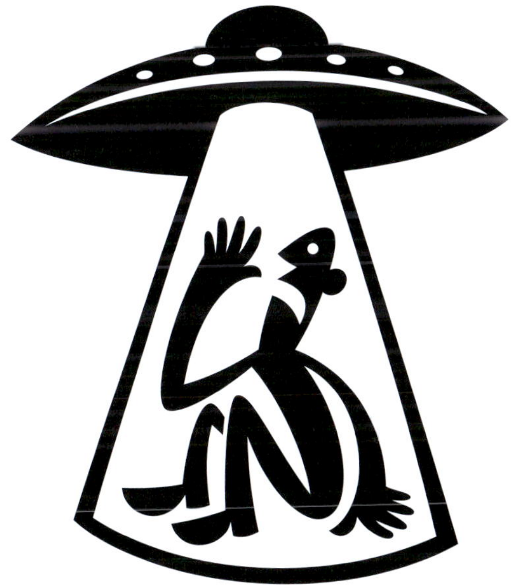

Take_Me_To_Your_Leader_**TM763**

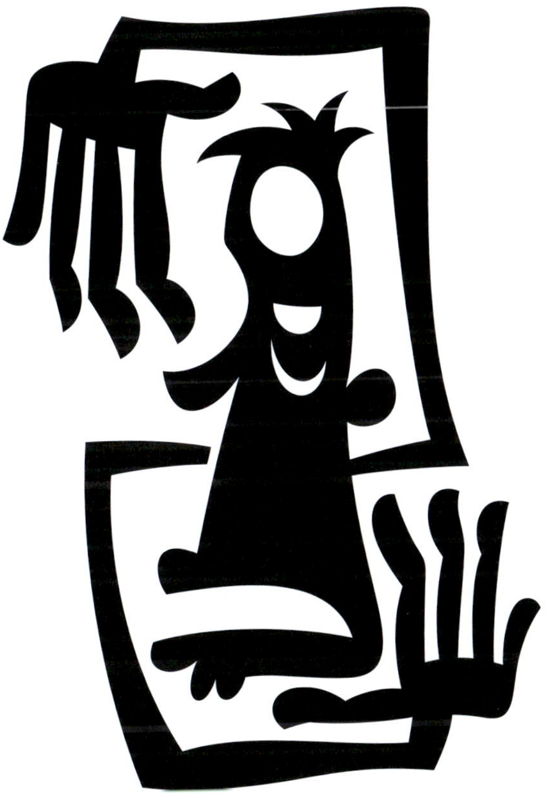

Fill_The_Void_**TM765**

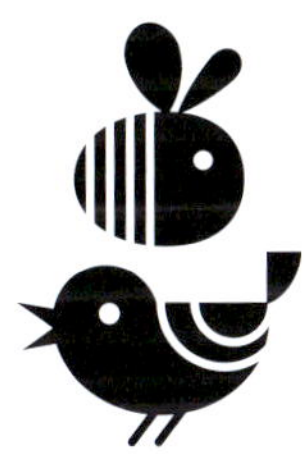

Birds_And_Bees_**TM764**

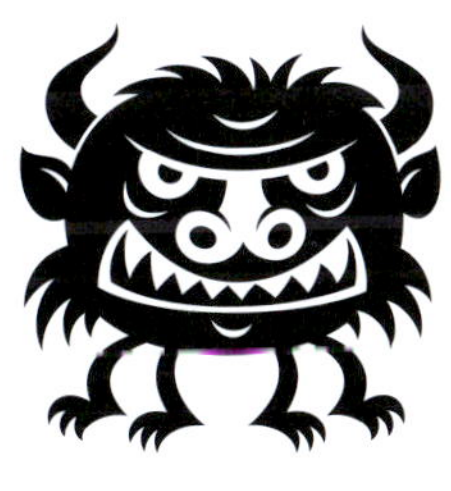

Creature_Comforts_**TM766**

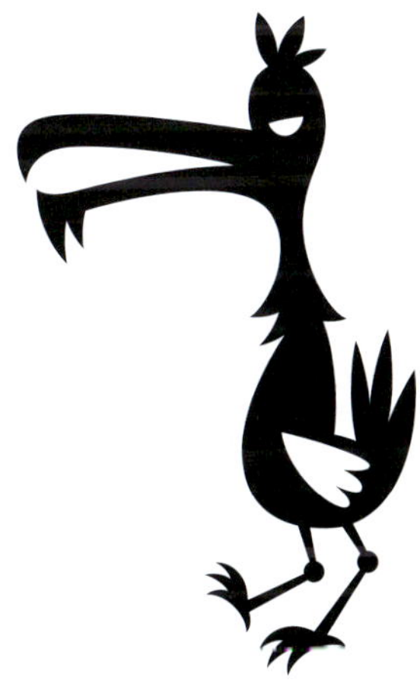

Strange_Bird_**TM767**

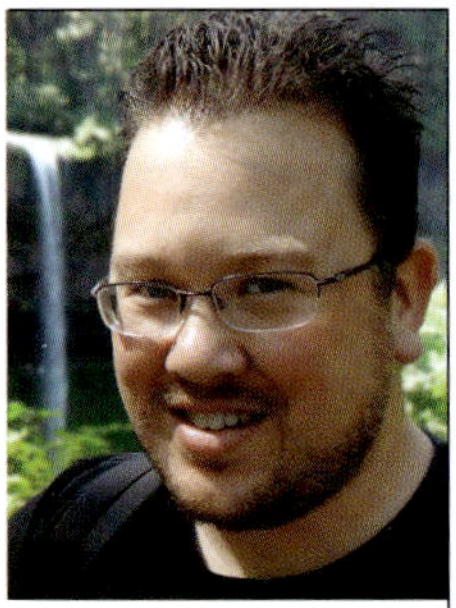

Josh Huhn

Designer

Design Point Inc. • Salem, Oregon

www.designpointinc.com

I used the Take and Make "Anchors Away" artwork as part the background for this book cover. The anchor illustration was a good fit for the book's theme and created some abstract visual interest in the positive and negative space of the background.

Combining textures with vector illustrations is a great way to add character and depth but still maintain the precise detail of a vector drawing. For this project, having quality vector artwork ready to use was a big time saver and made the final book cover design turn out great.

Art Used: Anchors Away TM818

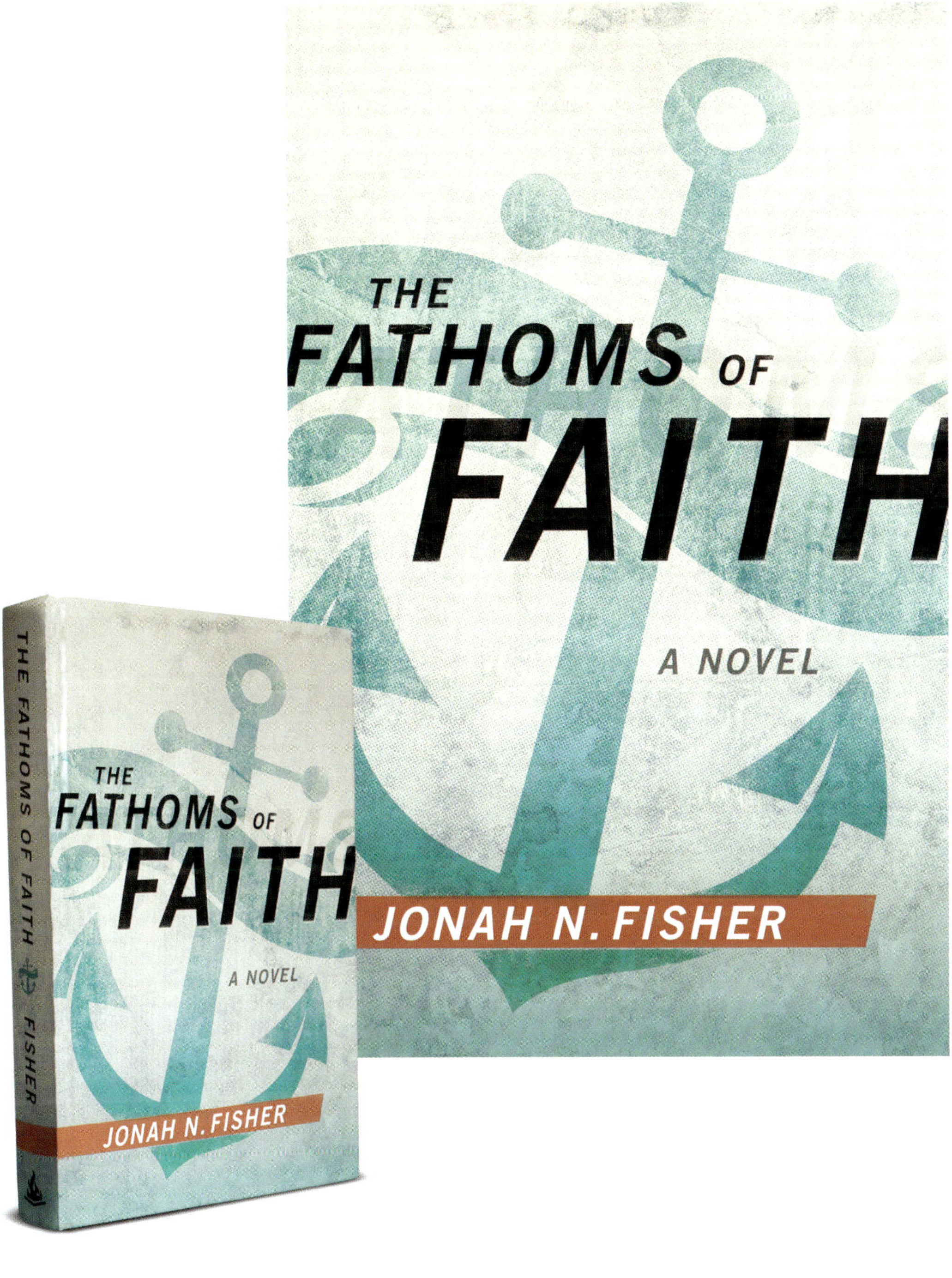
THE
FATHOMS OF
FAITH
A NOVEL
JONAH N. FISHER
THE FATHOMS OF FAITH FISHER

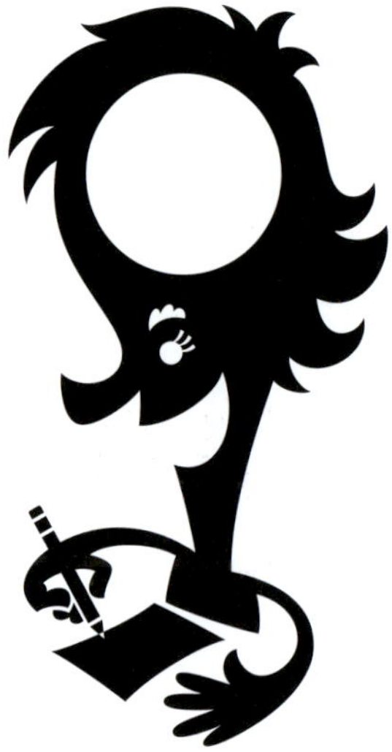

The_Write_Stuff_**TM769**

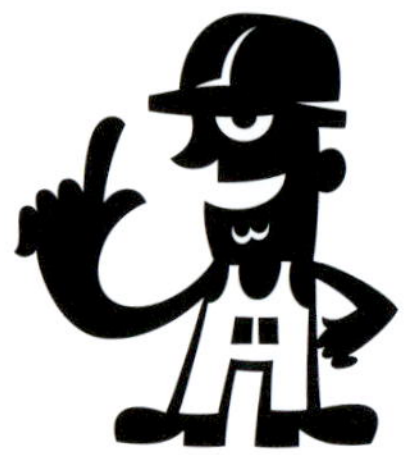

Be_Constructive_**TM768**

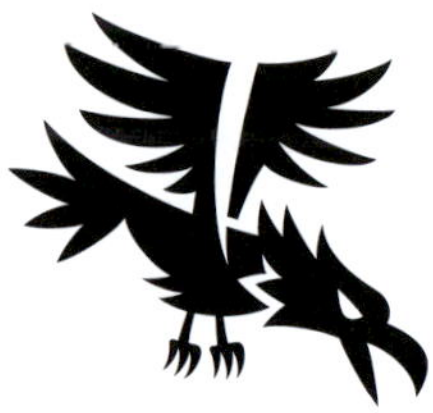

Crow_Of_Scorn_**TM770**

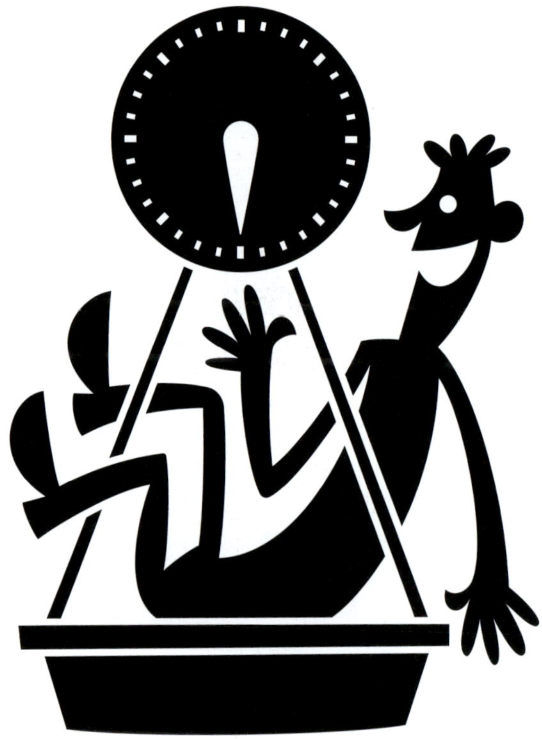

Carrying_The_Weight_Of_The_World_**TM771**

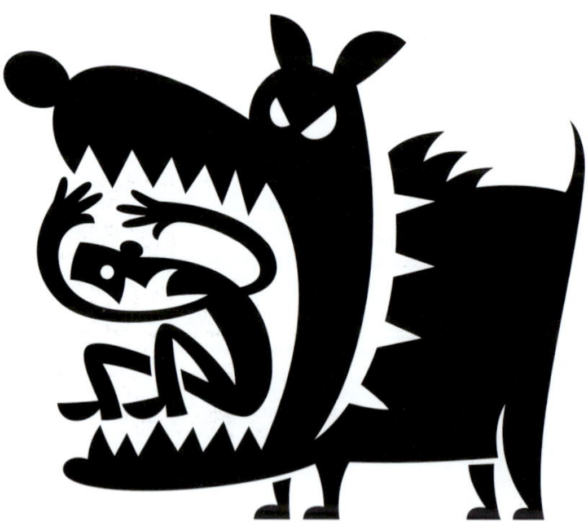

Dont_Be_Intimidated_**TM772**

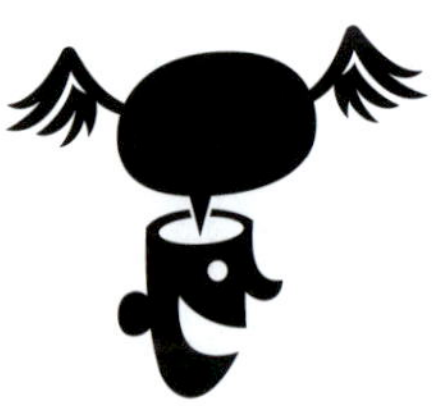

Conflicting_Thoughts_**TM773**

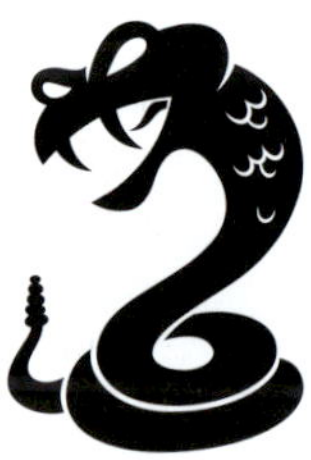

Brood_Of_Vipers_**TM774**

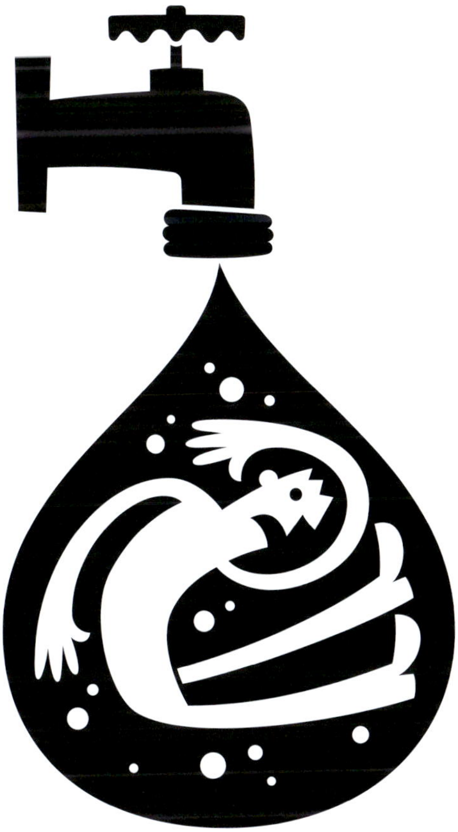

All_Washed_Up_**TM776**

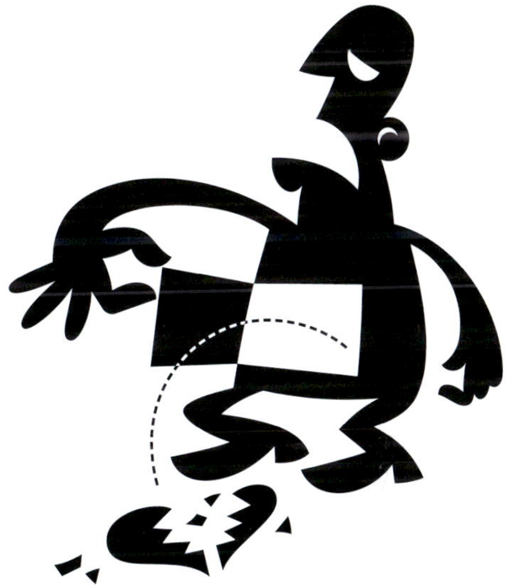

Broken_Heart_**TM775**

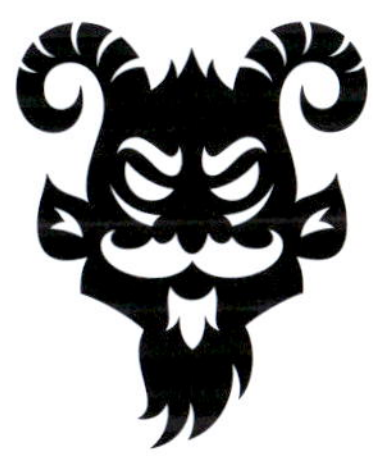

Diablos_**TM777**

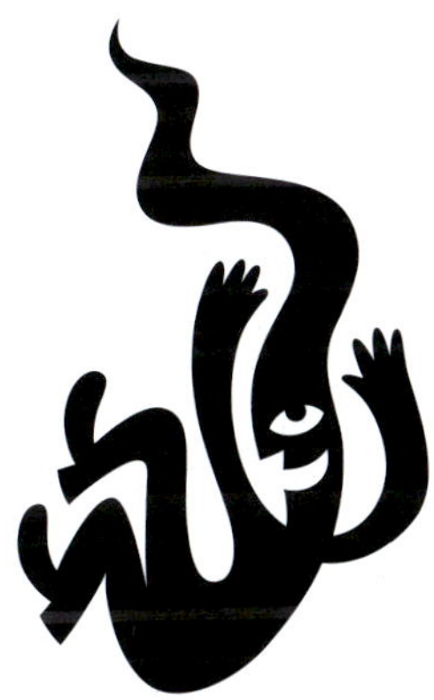

Elastic_Mind_**TM780**

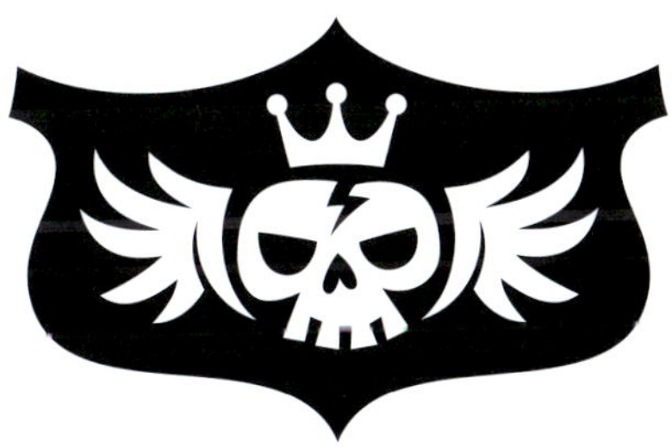

Guardians_Of_Reality_**TM778**

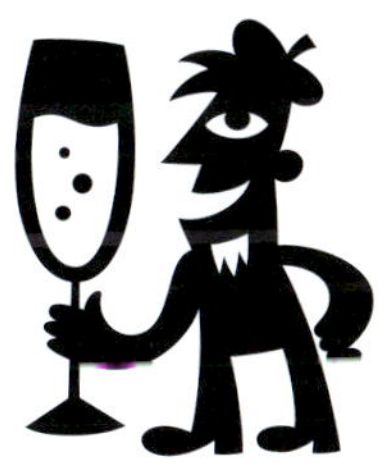

Wine_Lover_**TM779**

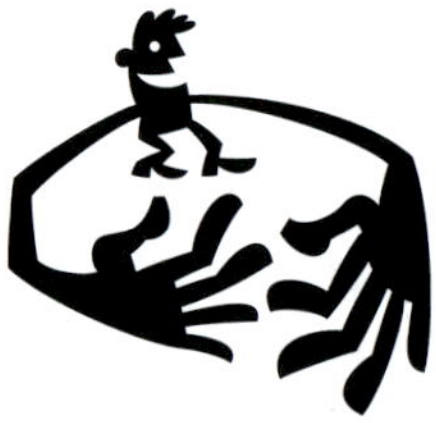

Huge_Hug_**TM781**

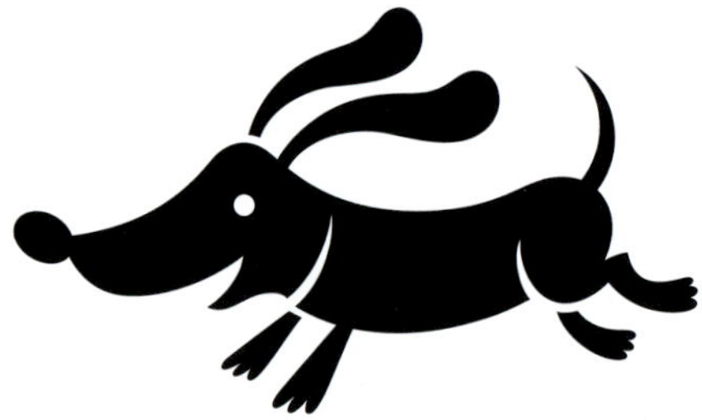

Weenie_Doggie_**TM782**

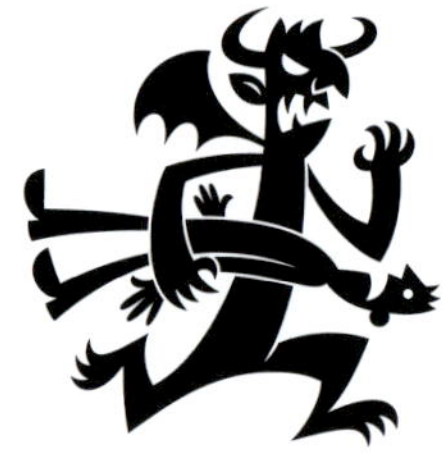

Dont_Get_Carried_Away_**TM783**

Let_Peace_Descend_**TM784**

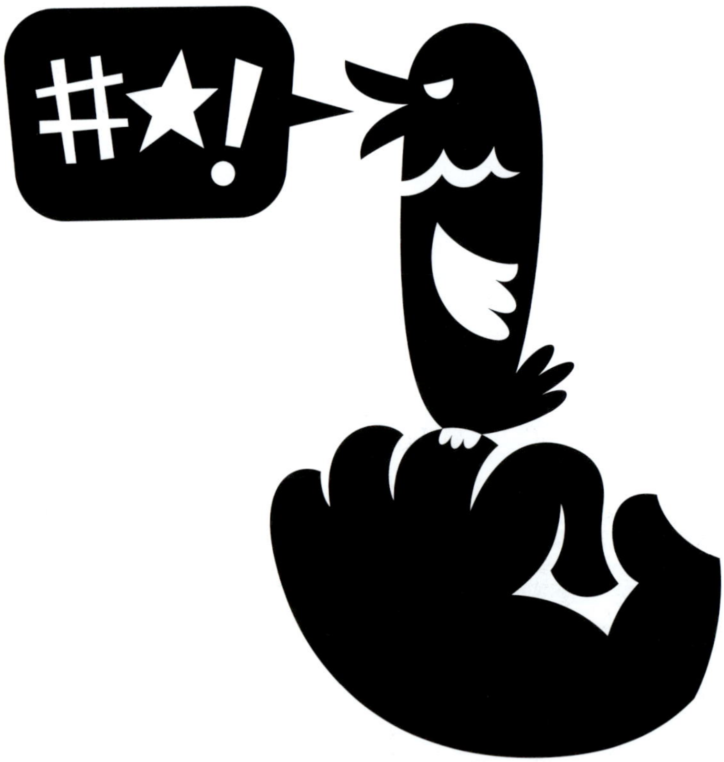

The_Original_Angry_Bird_**TM785**

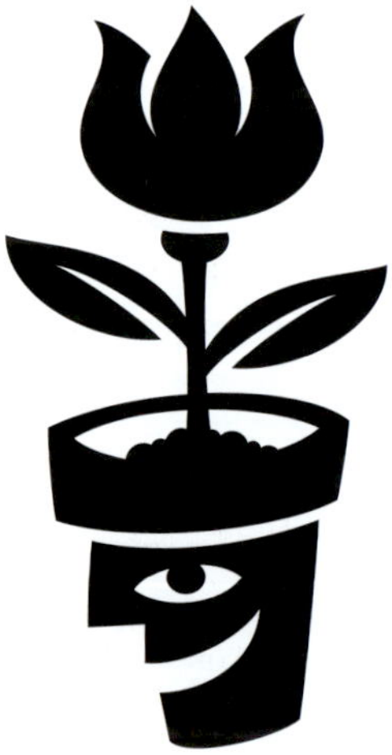

Fertile_Mind_**TM786**

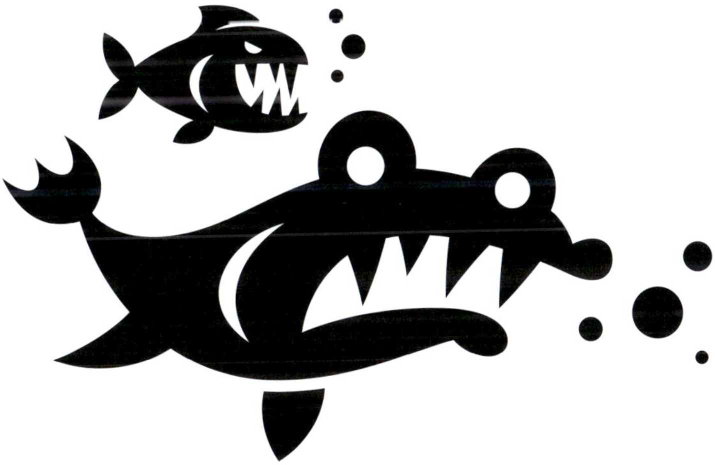

Bad_Fishies_**TM787**

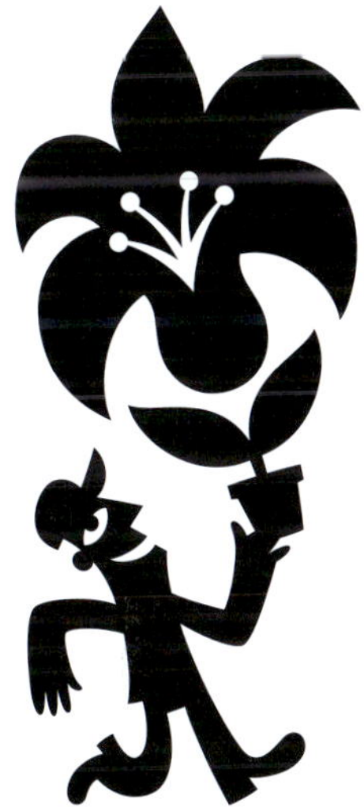

Tulip_Dude_**TM788**

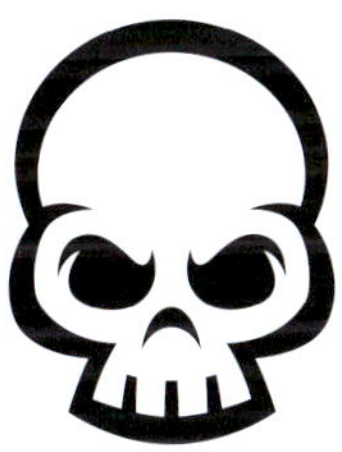

Cranium_**TM789**

Mutated_Gastropod_**TM790**

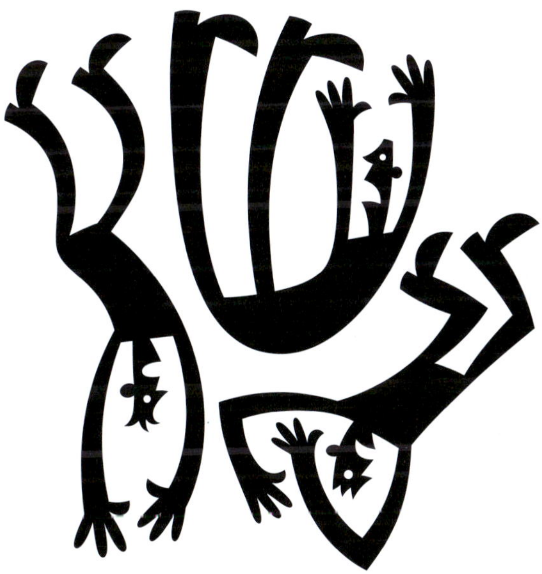

Falling_Away_**TM791**

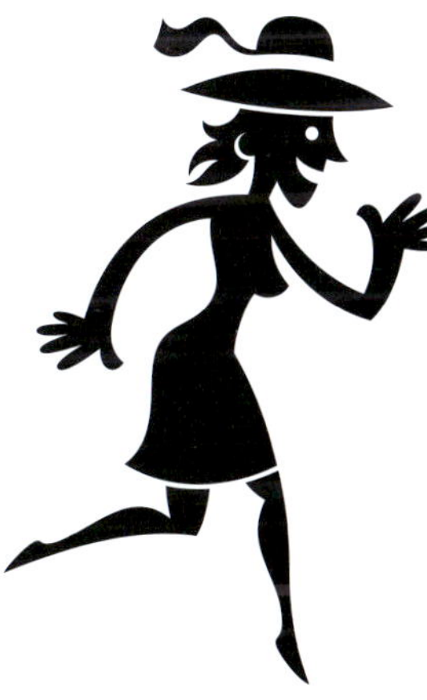

Shes_Got_Legs_**TM792**

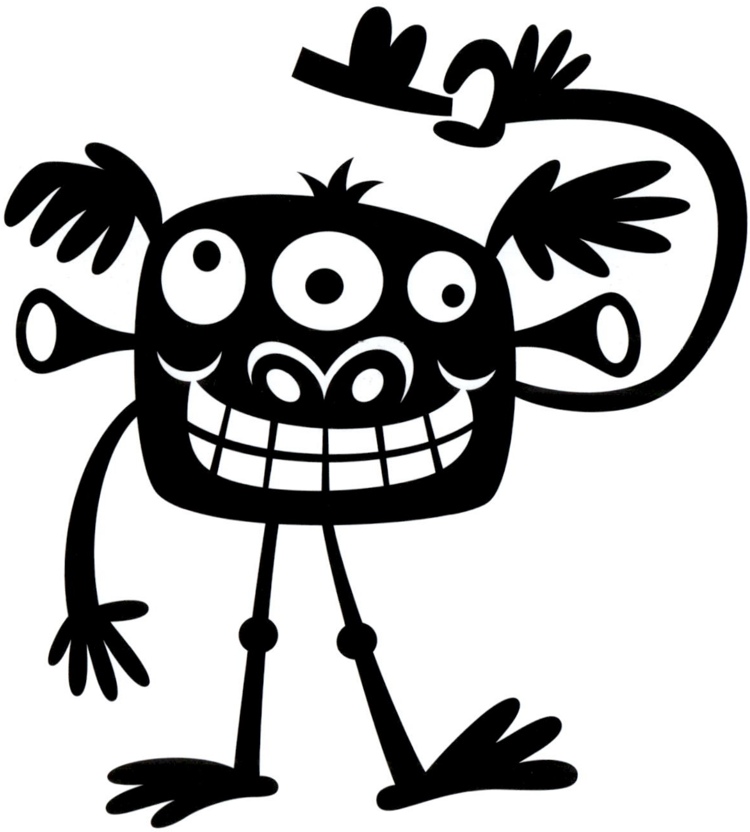

Greeting_Earthling_**TM795**

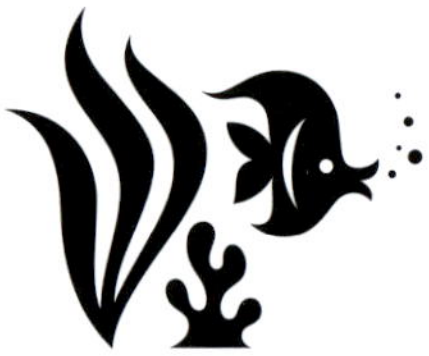

Aquarium_**TM793**

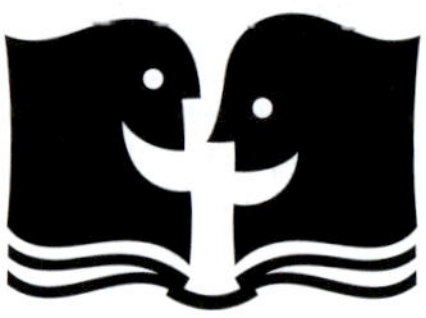

Facebook_**TM794**

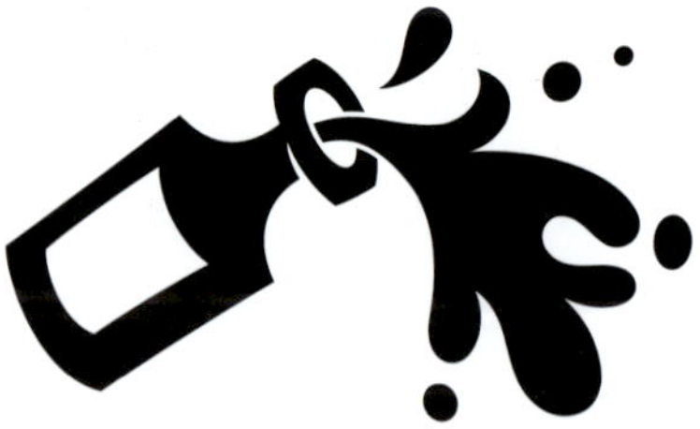

Dont_Cry_Its_Not_Milk_**TM796**

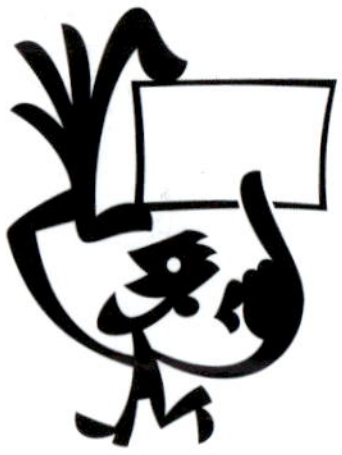

Check_This_Out_**TM797**

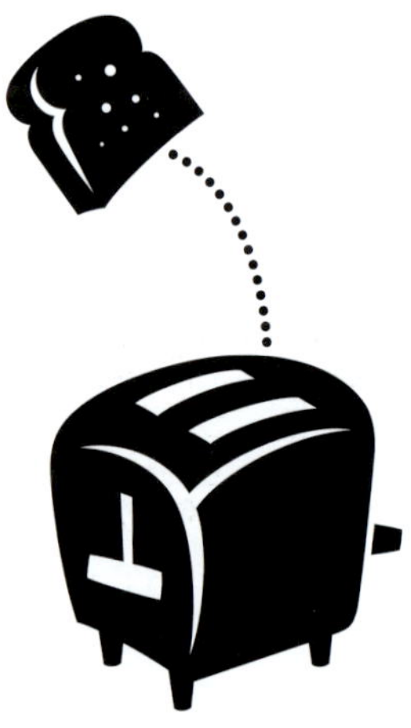

Burnt_Toast_**TM798**

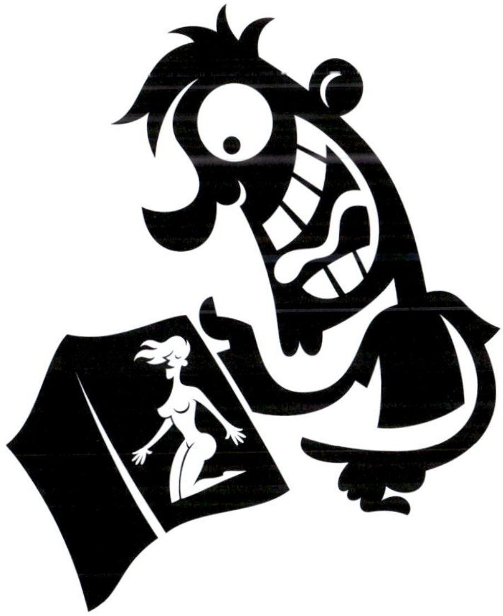

Horn_Dog_**TM800**

Woodnt_It_Be_Nice_**TM799**

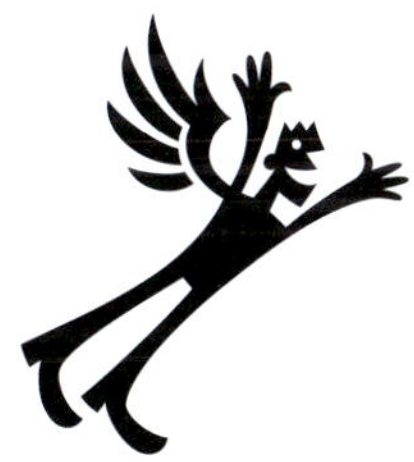

Take_Off_**TM801**

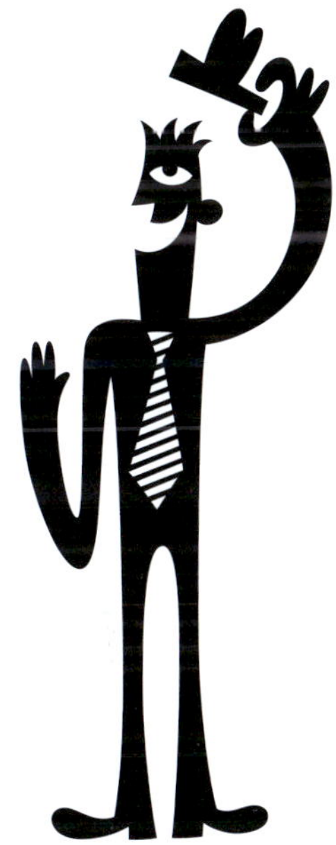

Good_Day_**TM802**

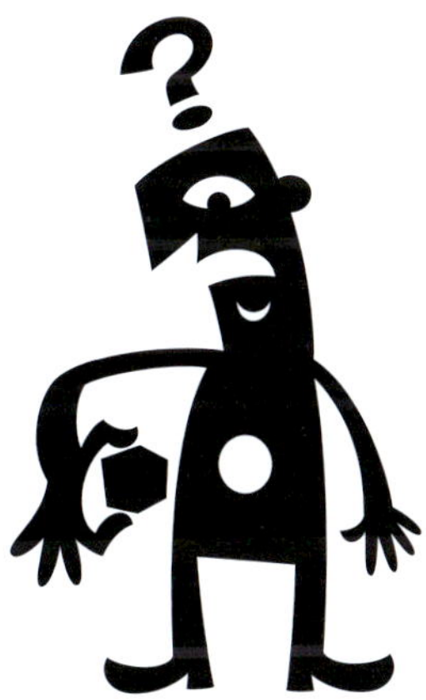

Wont_Fit_**TM803**

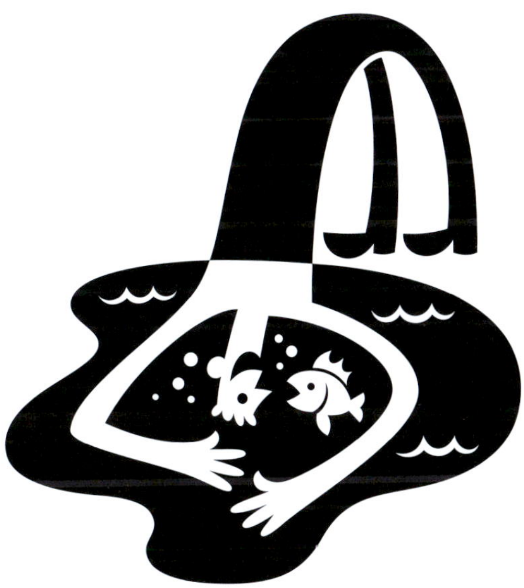

Change_Your_Perspective_**TM804**

Ghost_Arm_**TM805**

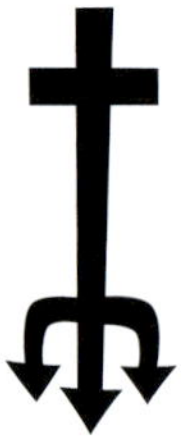

Devil_In_The_Details_**TM806**

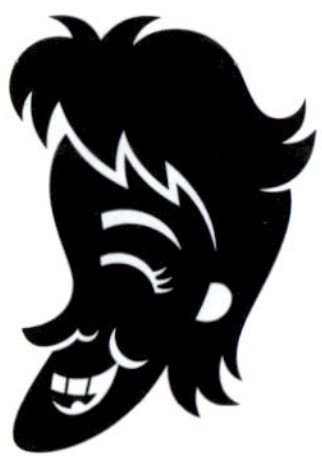

Giggles_**TM807**

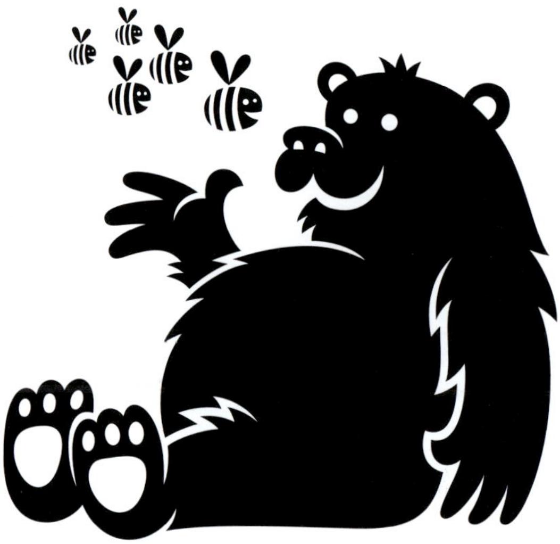

Sweet_Fellowship_**TM808**

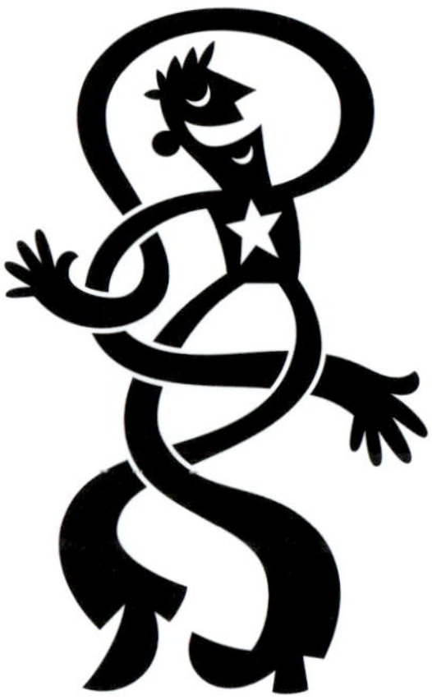

Dont_Get_Bent_Out_Of_Shape_**TM809**

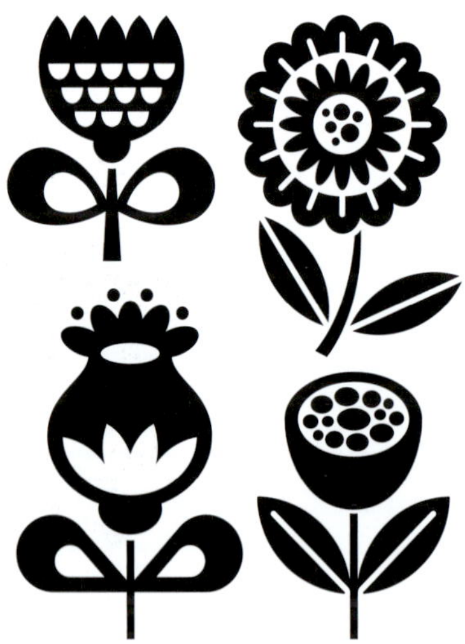

Nursery_**TM810**

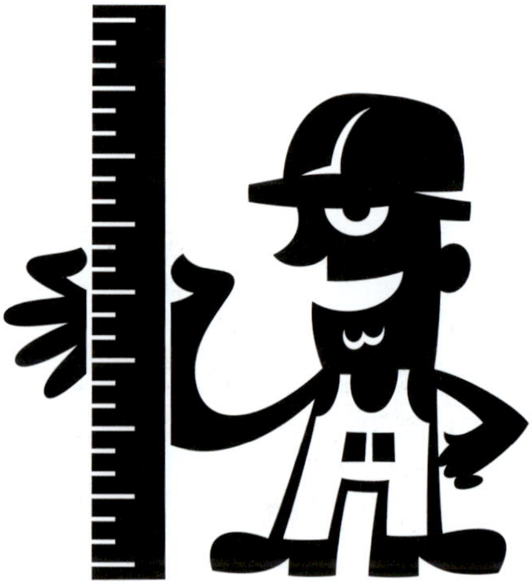

Do_You_Measure_Up_**TM811**

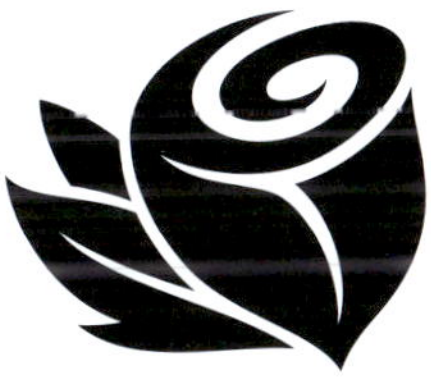

Rosey_**TM812**

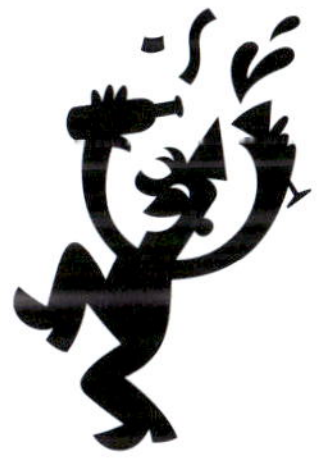

Reveler_**TM813**

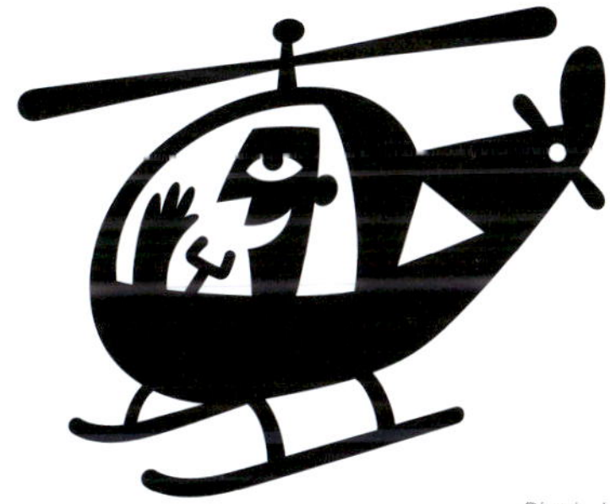

Black_Helicopters_**TM814**

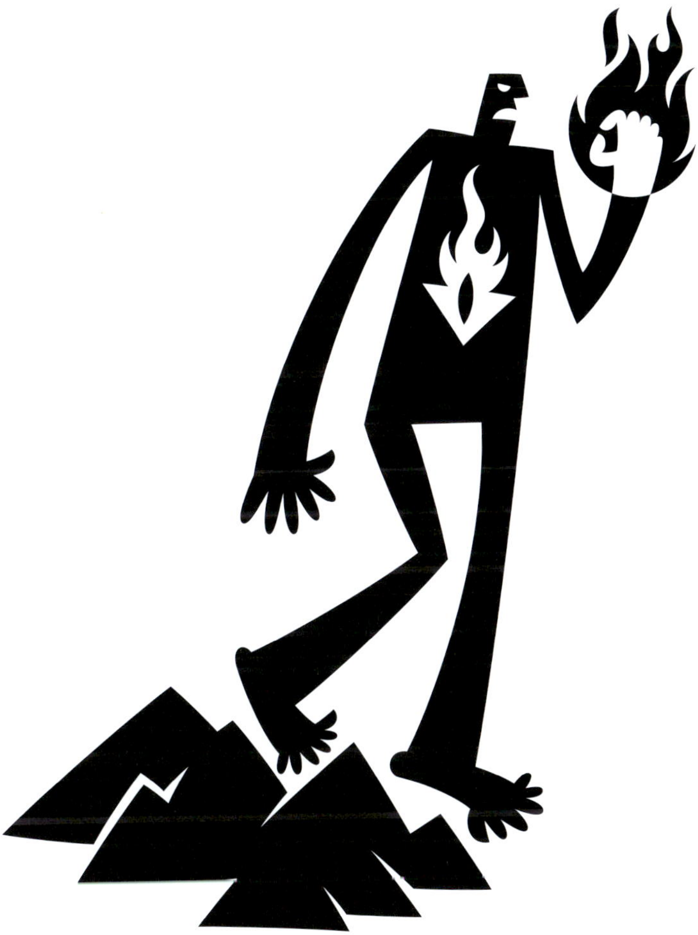

High_Places_**TM816**

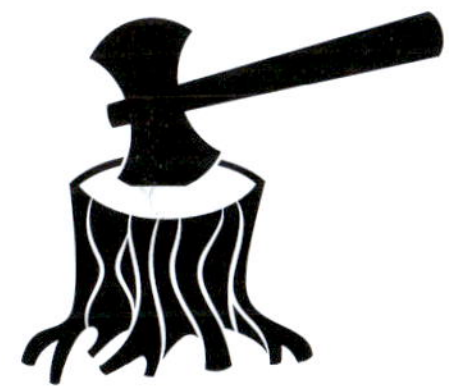

Getting_The_Axe_**TM815**

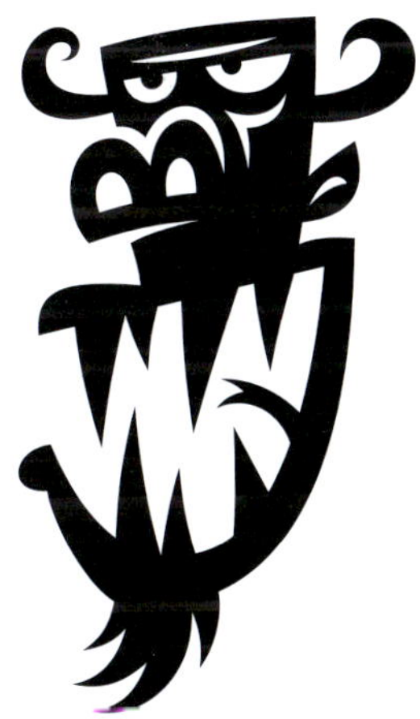

Goofy_Goblin_**TM817**

Anchors_Away_**TM818**

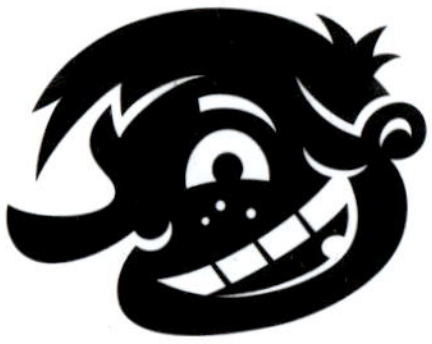

Glad_Child_**TM819**

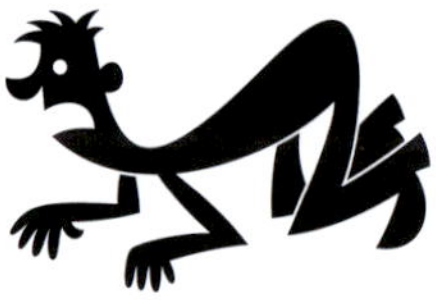

An_Ants_Perspective_**TM820**

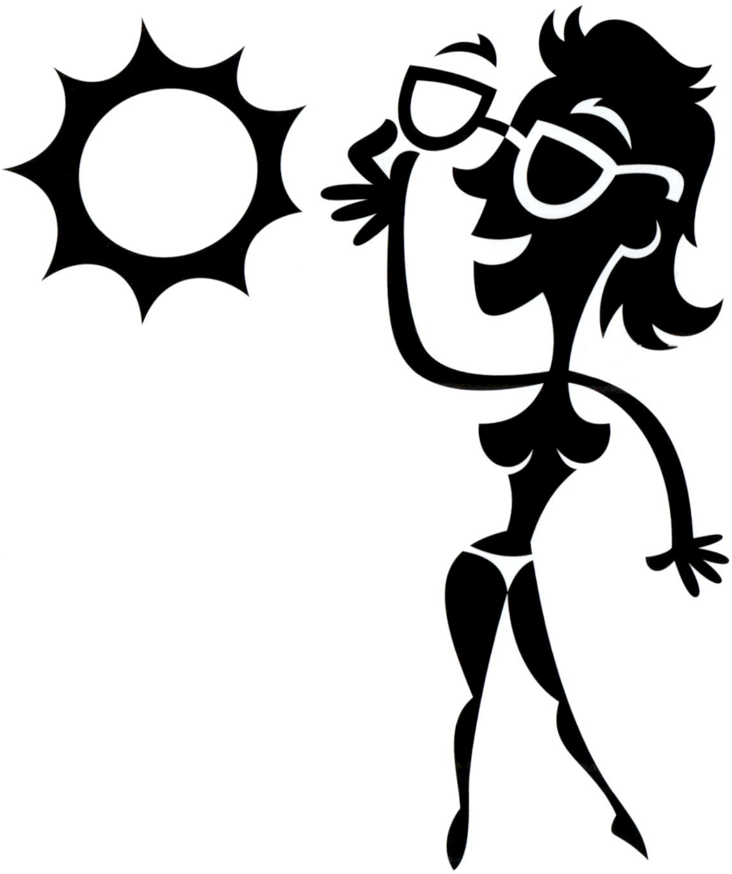

Sun_Bather_**TM821**

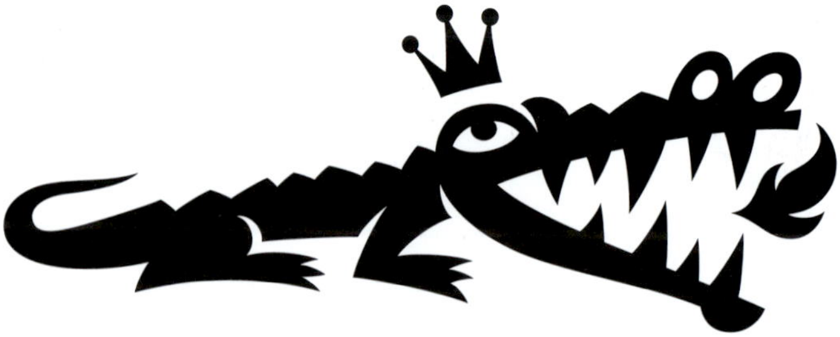

King_Gator_**TM822**

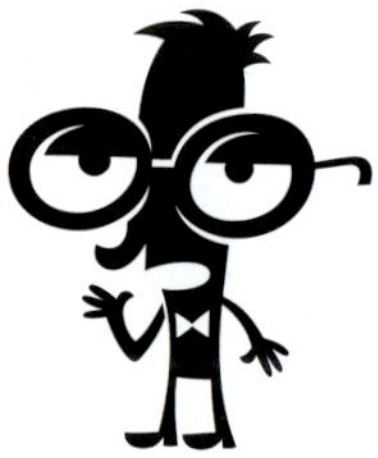

Dont_Be_A_Dweeb_**TM823**

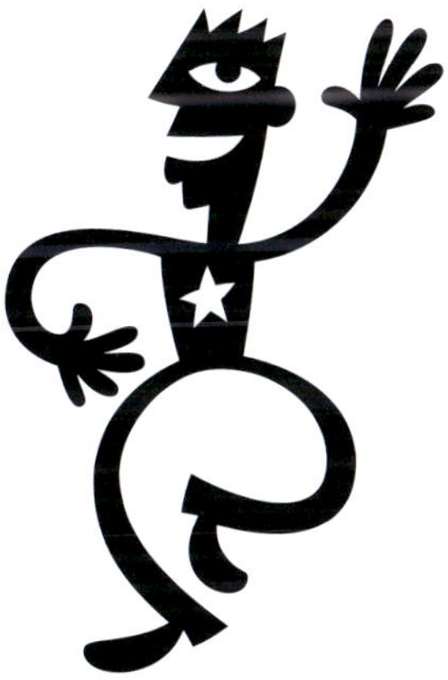

Prancer_**TM824**

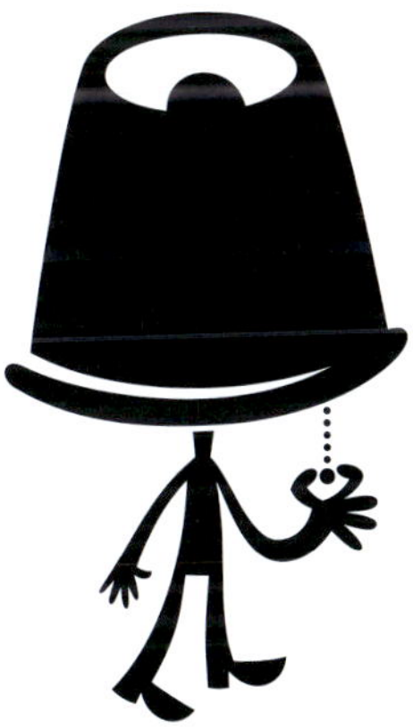

Light_Me_Up_**TM825**

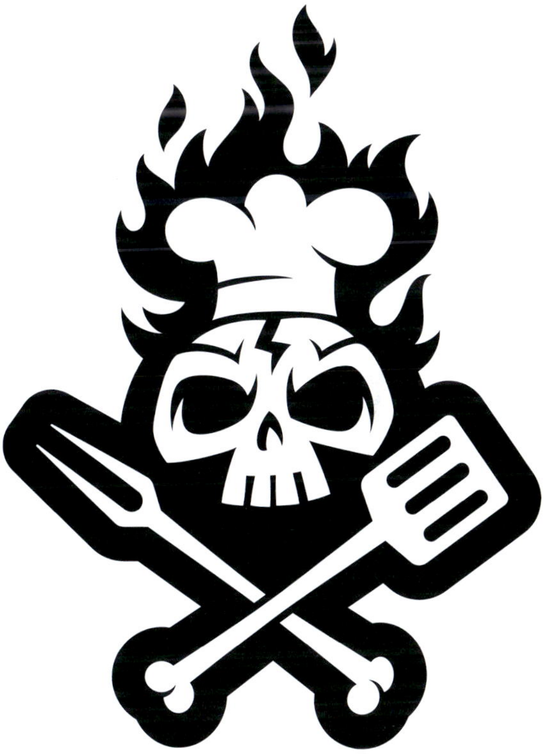

Killer_Food_**TM826**

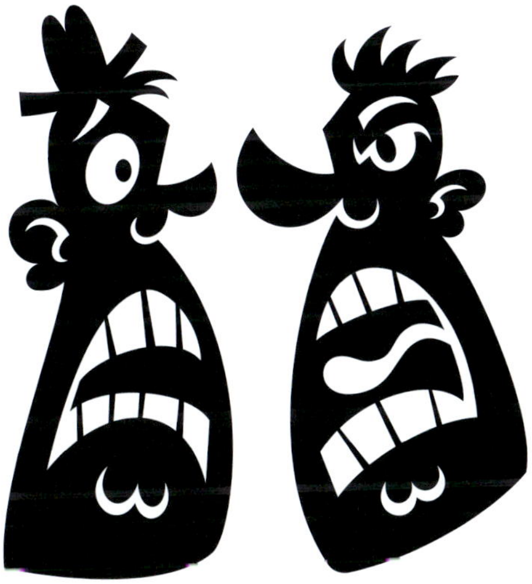

Arguing_**TM827**

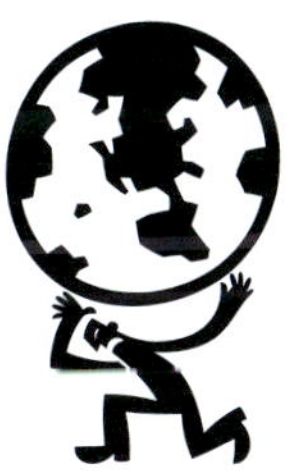

The_Weight_Of_The_World_**TM828**

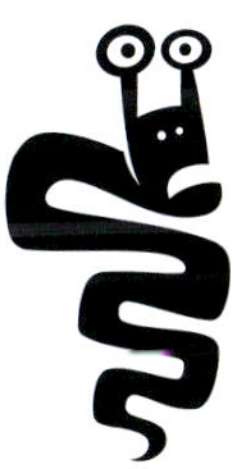

Worm_Of_Doom_**TM829**

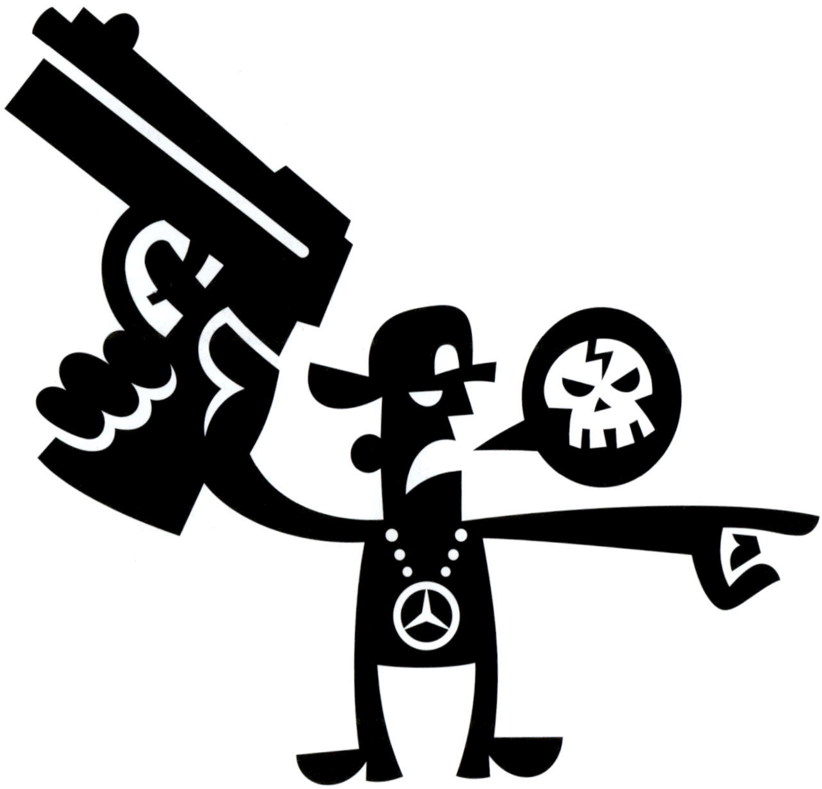

Thug_Life_**TM831**

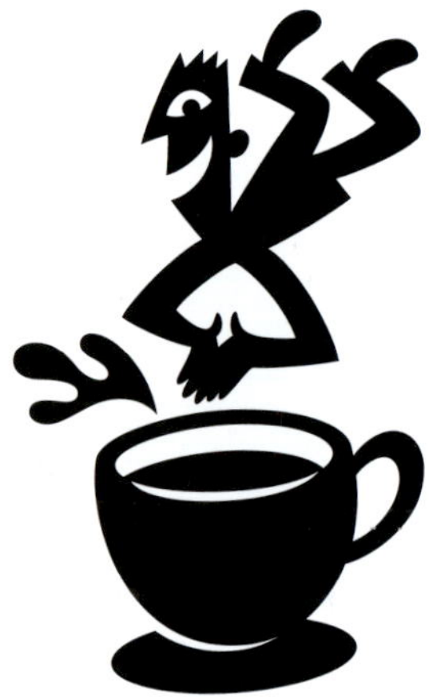

Morning_Swim_**TM830**

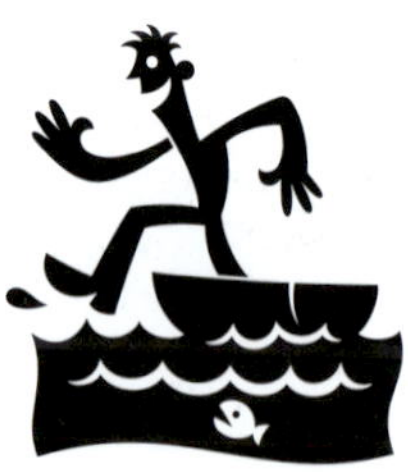

Take_A_Step_Of_Faith_**TM832**

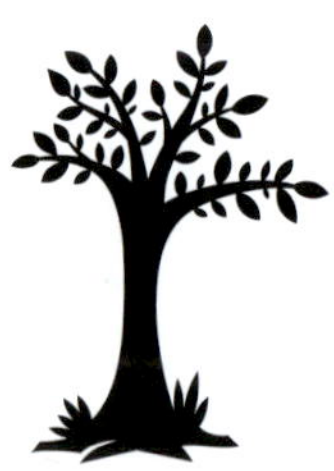

Spruce_Up_**TM833**

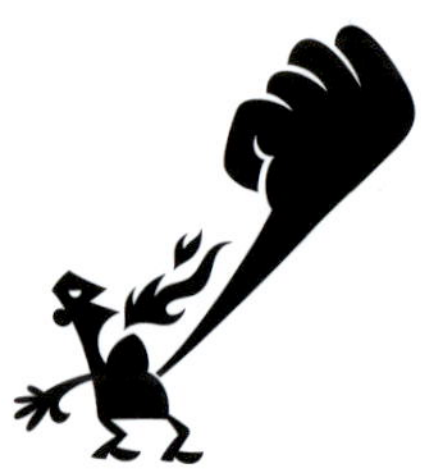

Rage_**TM834**

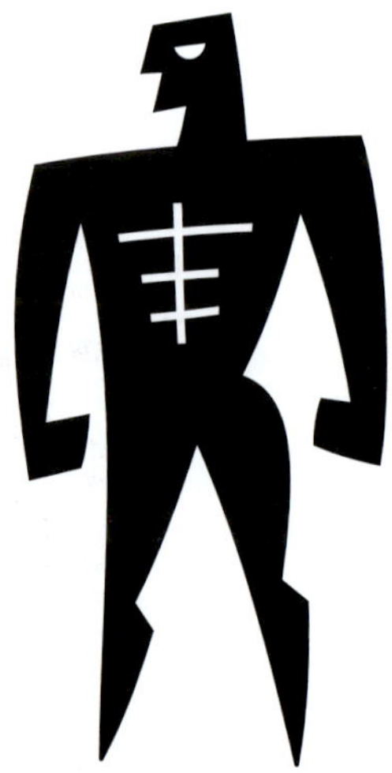

Heroic_**TM835**

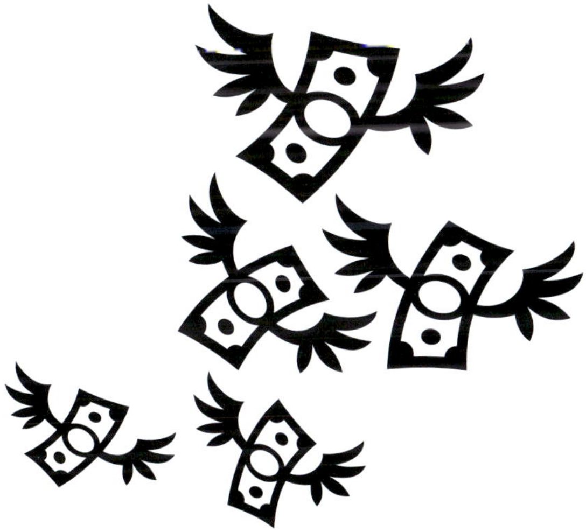

Flock_Of_Benjamins_**TM836**

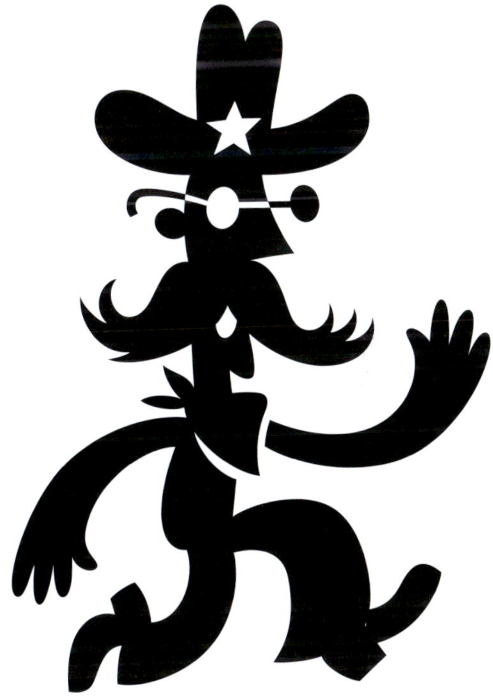

Giddy_Up_**TM837**

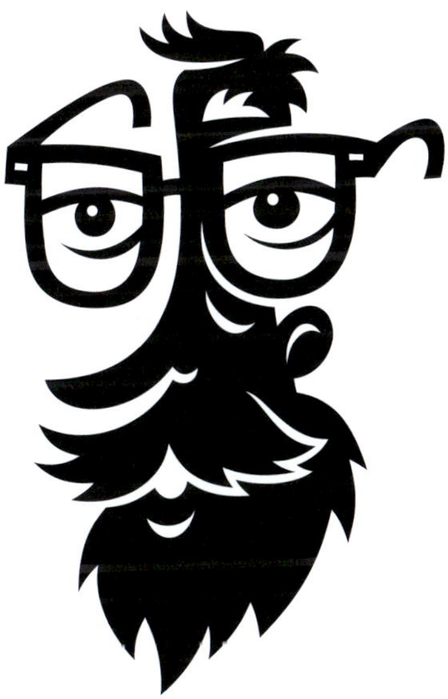

Four_Eyes_**TM838**

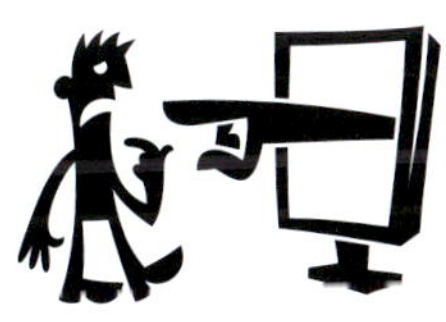

Social_Media_Trolling_**TM839**

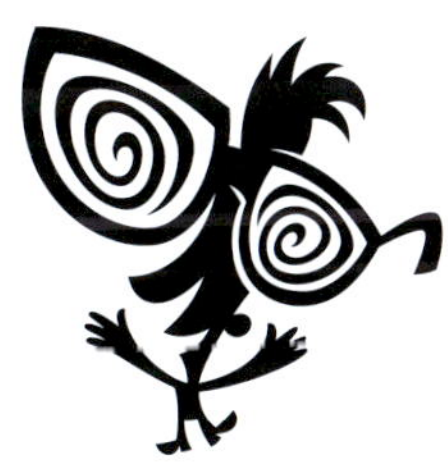

X_Ray_Vision_**TM840**

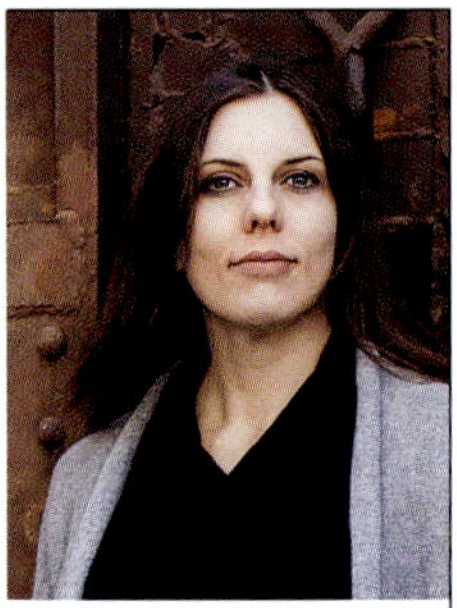

Amy Reyes

Designer and Illustrator

Chicago, Illinois

www.AmyReyes.com

Stock illustrations can come in handy if you're working with a small budget or just don't have the time to create something from scratch. When I was coming up with my concept, I was totally inspired by all of the fun and animated characters in this book. It was hard to narrow it down. I'm a big Sci-Fi fan, and the UFO theme kept jumping out at me...as well as a certain middle finger. I thought it'd be funny to tie the two together...then I added a few more elements to compose my final illustration.

Art Used: Take Me To Your Leader TM763, Road Rage TM857, An Uncomfortable Reality TM294, Branch Out TM672, Yard Clippings TM703

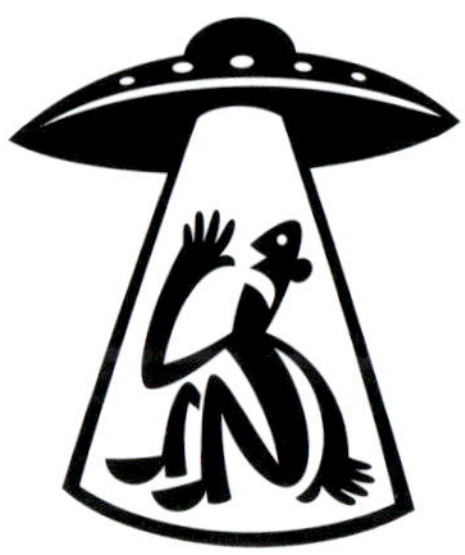

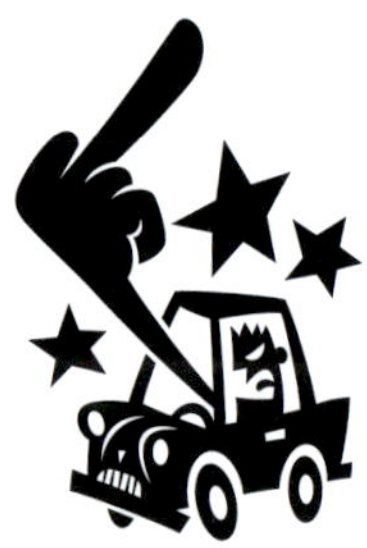

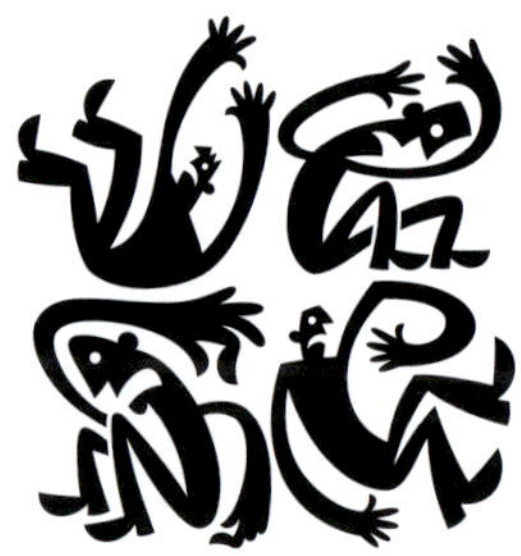

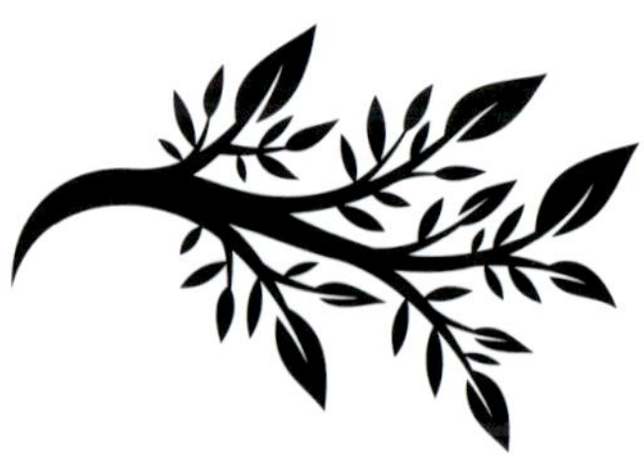

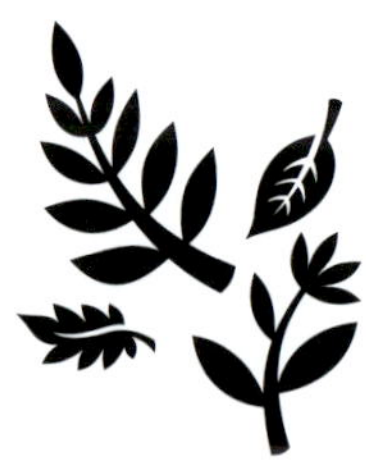

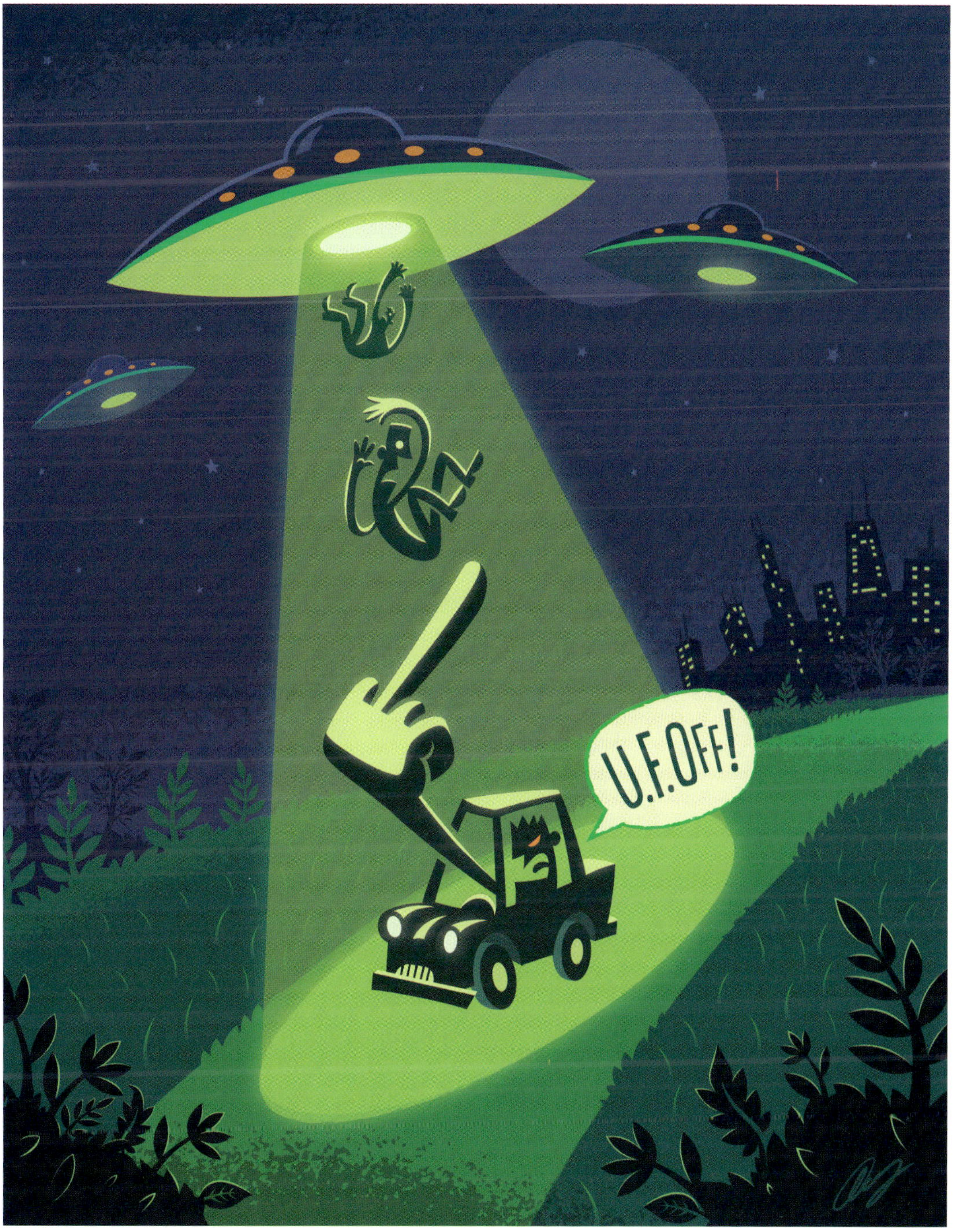
U.F.OFF!

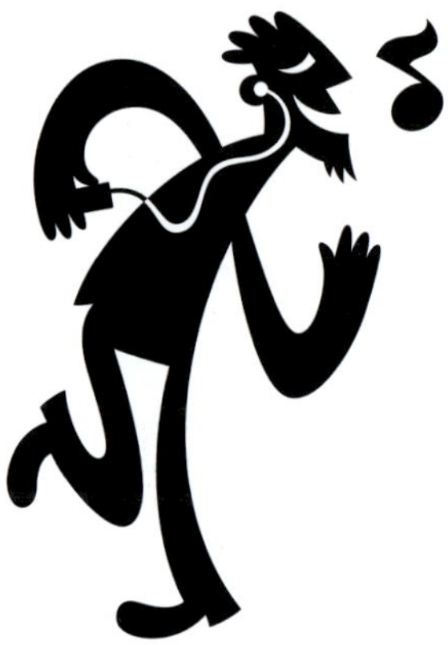

Cut_A_Rug_**TM842**

Whale_Of_A_Good_Time_**TM841**

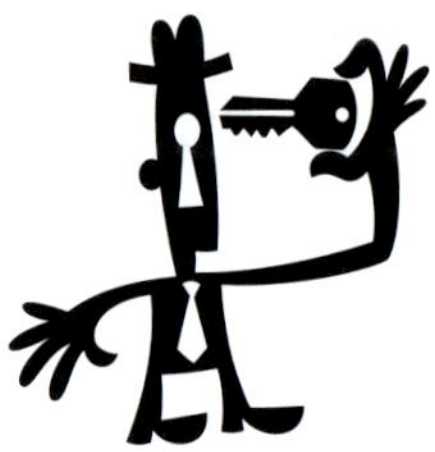

Unlock_Your_Potential_**TM843**

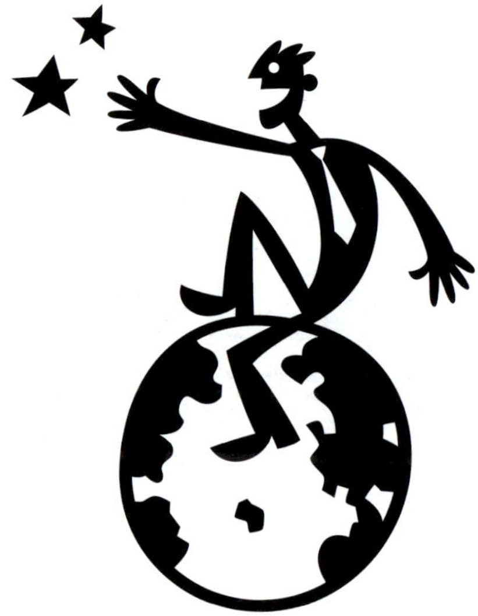

Star_Grabber_**TM844**

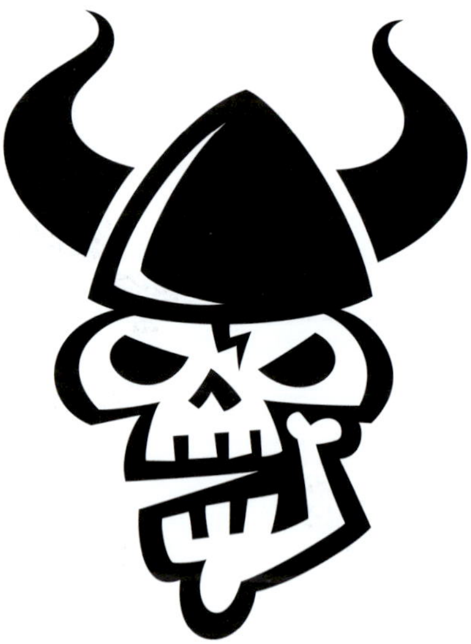

Helmet_Head_**TM845**

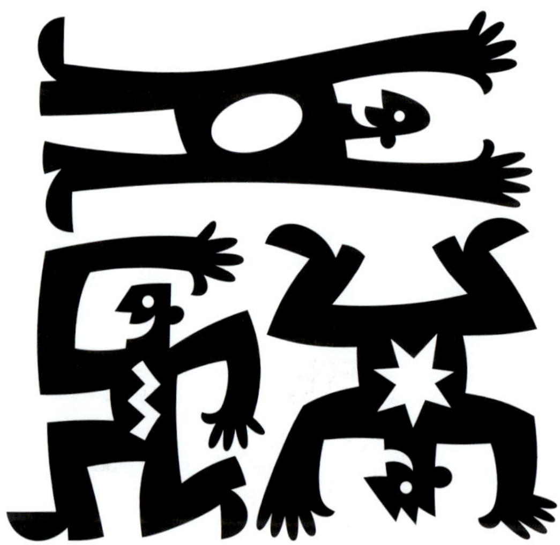

This_Way_And_That_Way_**TM846**

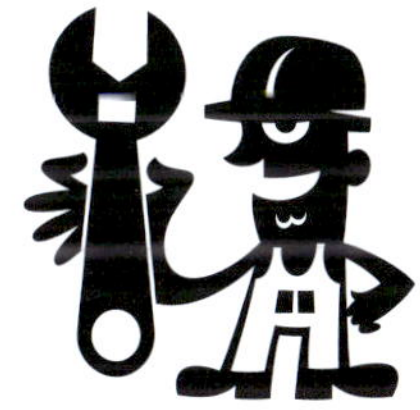

Dont_Be_A_Tool_**TM847**

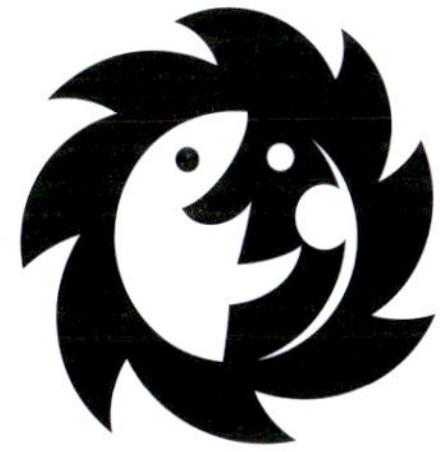

Morning_Sun_**TM848**

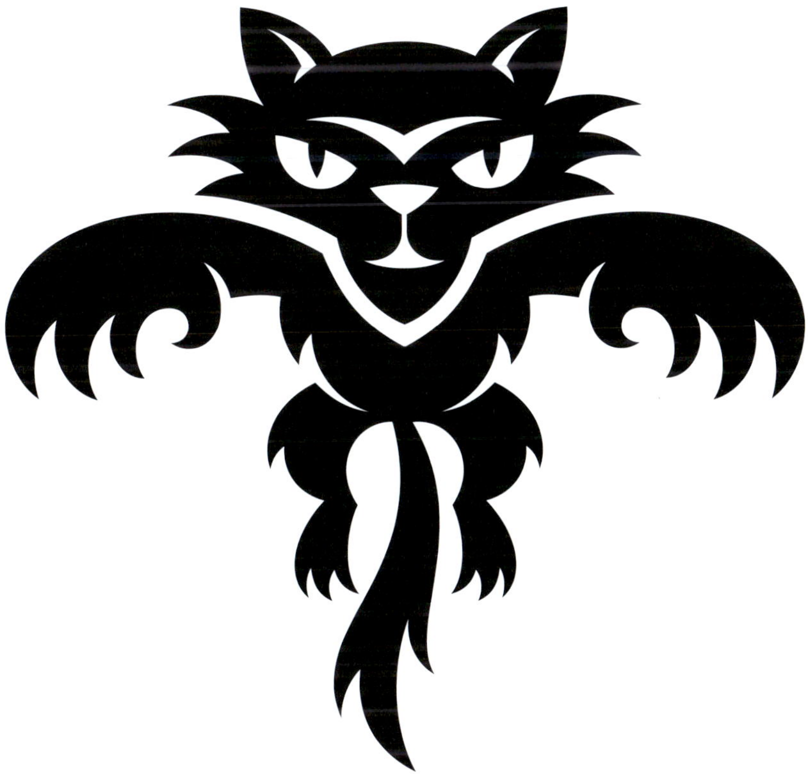

Attack_Cat_**TM849**

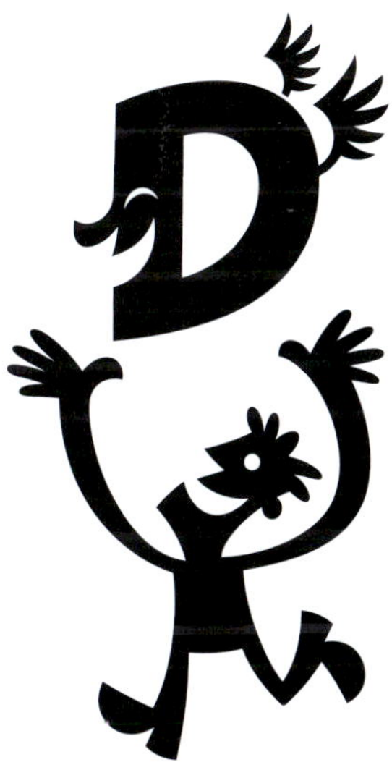

Chasing_Dreams_**TM852**

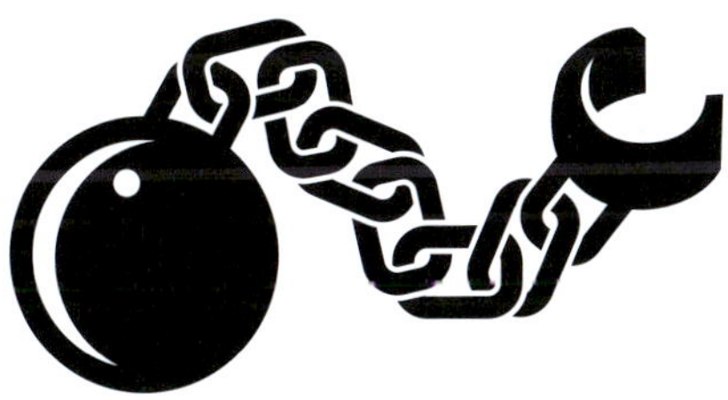

Set_Free_**TM850**

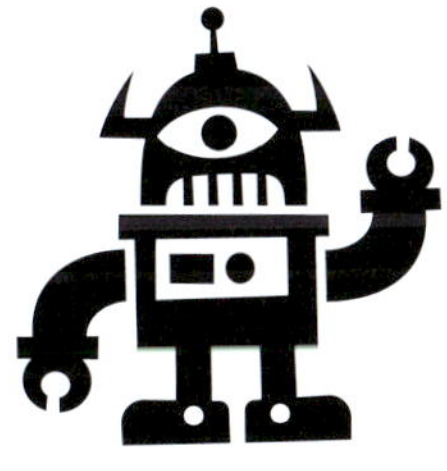

Robot_Clone_**TM851**

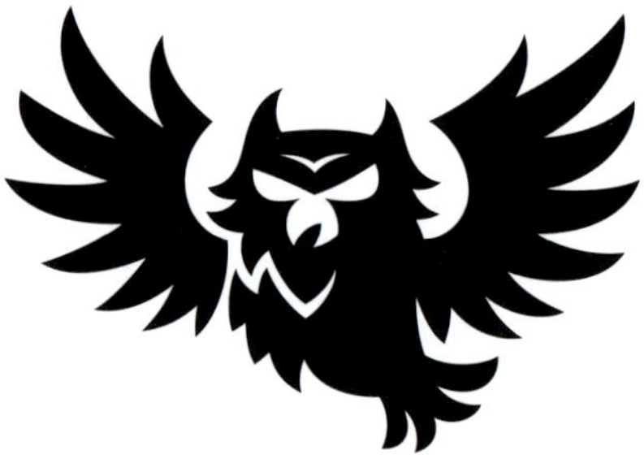

Night_Owl_**TM853**

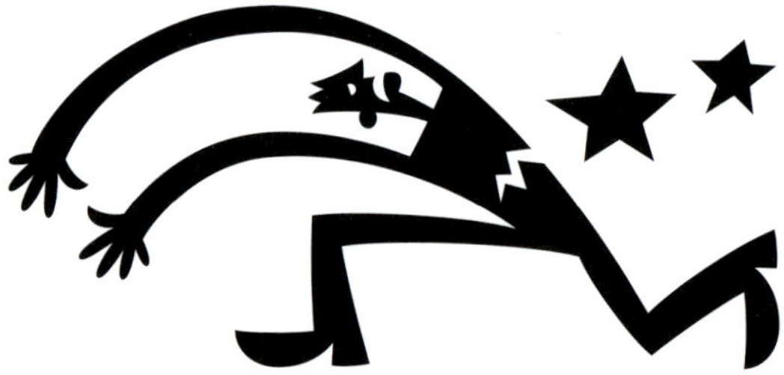

Reach_A_Breaking_Point_**TM854**

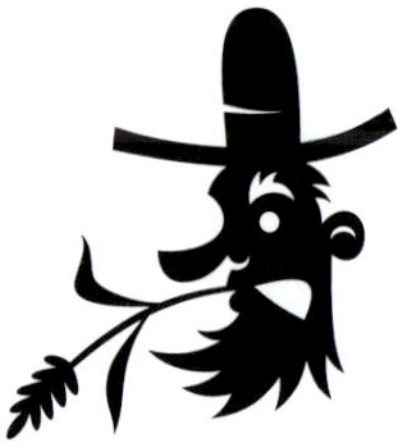

Country_Gent_**TM855**

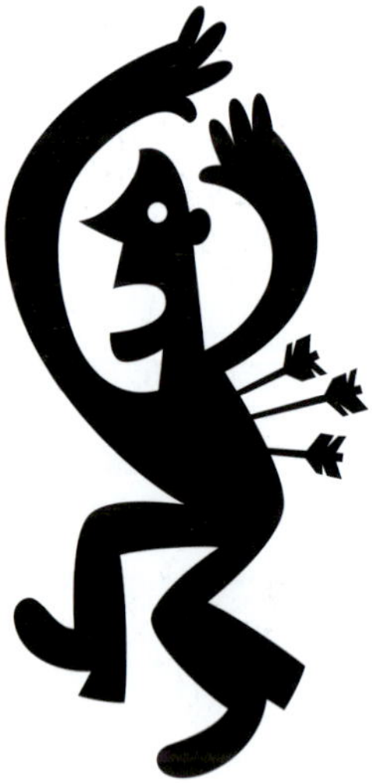

Watch_Your_Back_**TM856**

Road_Rage_**TM857**

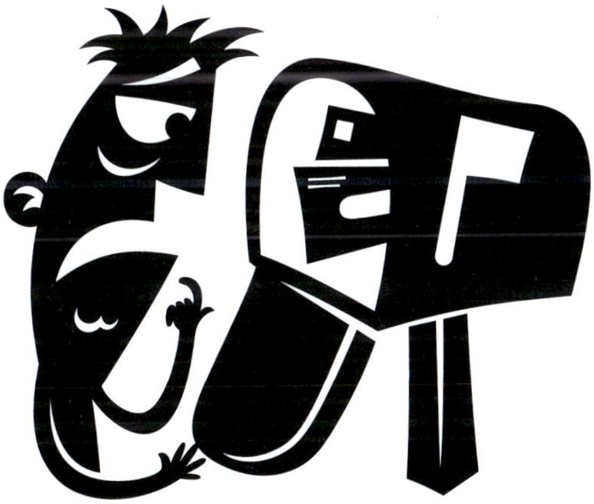

Mail_Bonding_**TM860**

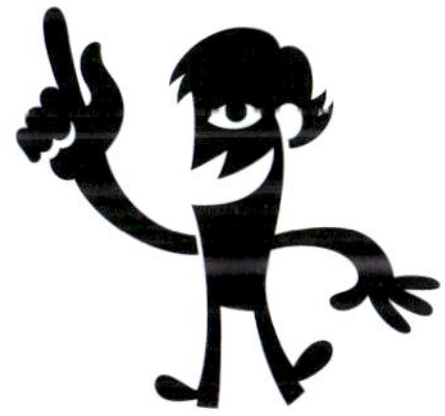

Make_A_Point_**TM858**

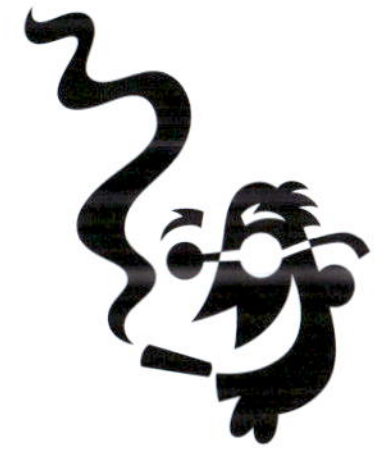

Big_Tobacco_**TM859**

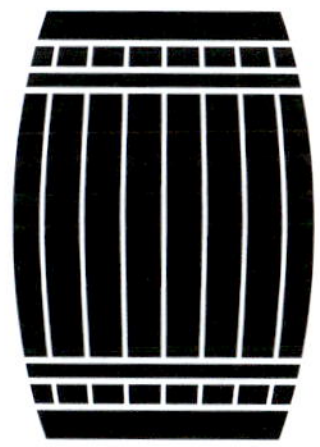

Roll_Out_The_Barrel_**TM861**

Honest_Abe_**TM862**

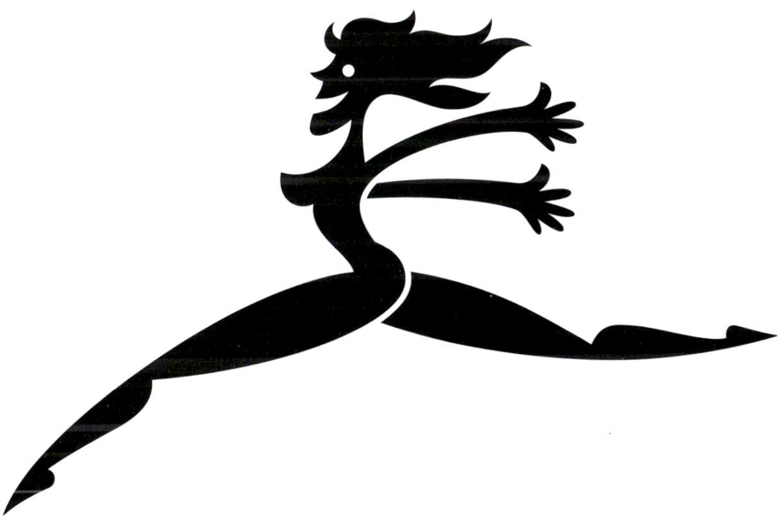

Free_Spirit_**TM863**

Gloomy_Daze_**TM864**

Green_Burst_**TM865**

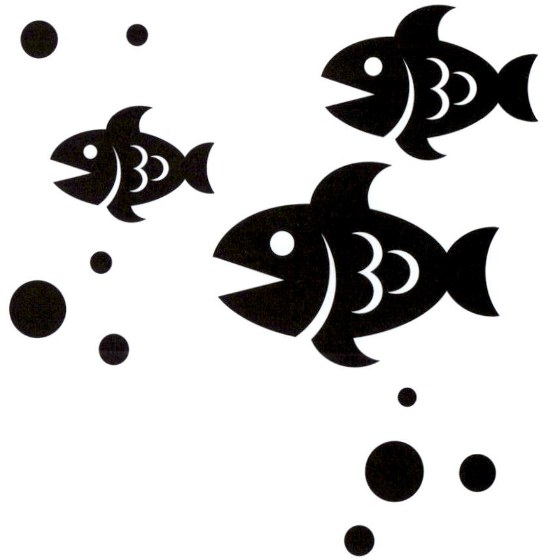

Go_With_The_Flow_**TM866**

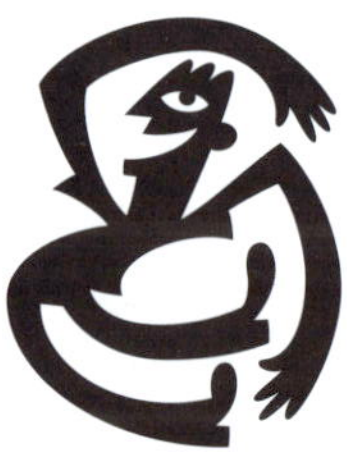

Dont_Wig_Out_**TM867**

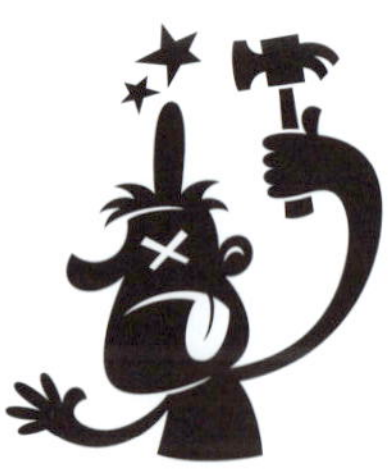

Duh_**TM868**

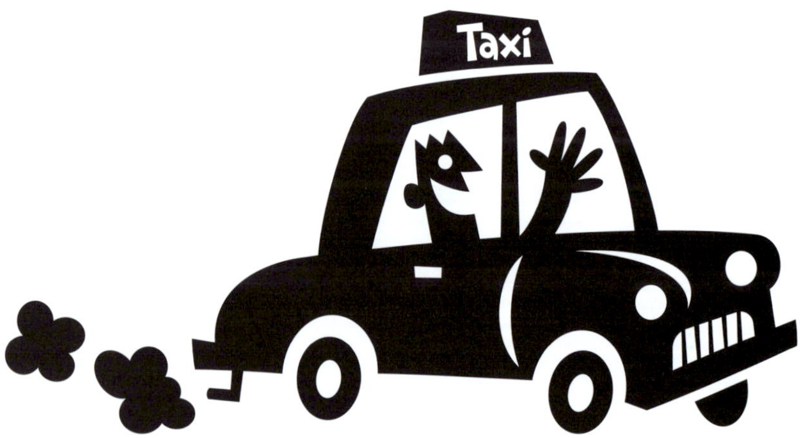

Taxi_**TM869**

Eat_Your_Greens_**TM870**

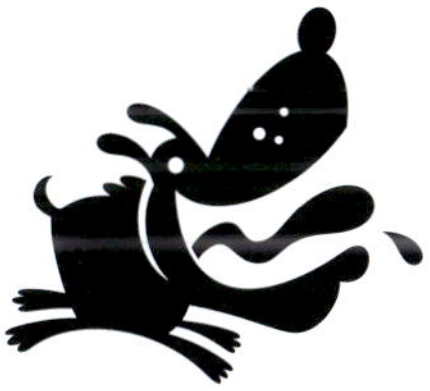

Happy_Doggy_**TM871**

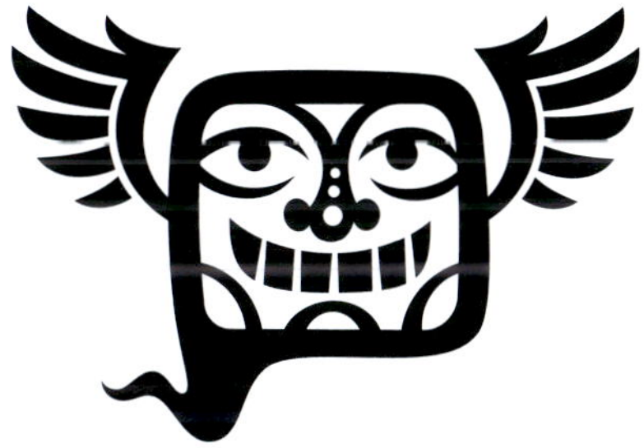

Spiritual_Freedom_**TM872**

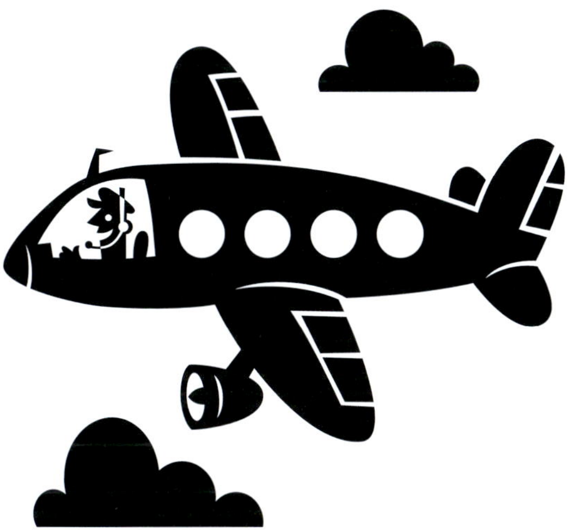

Frequent_Flyer_**TM873**

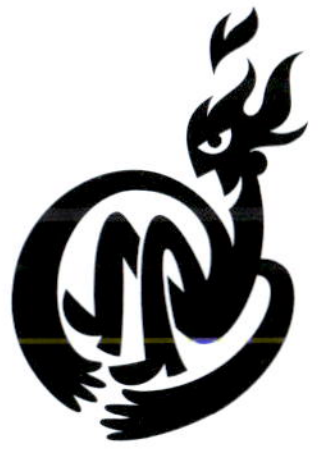

Flame_Jump_**TM874**

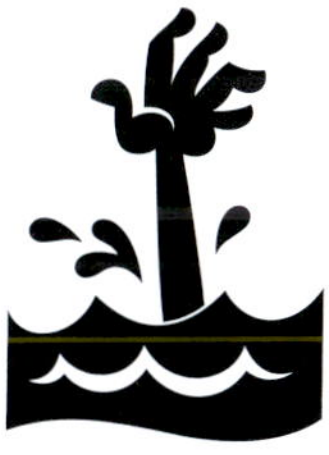

Drowning_**TM875**

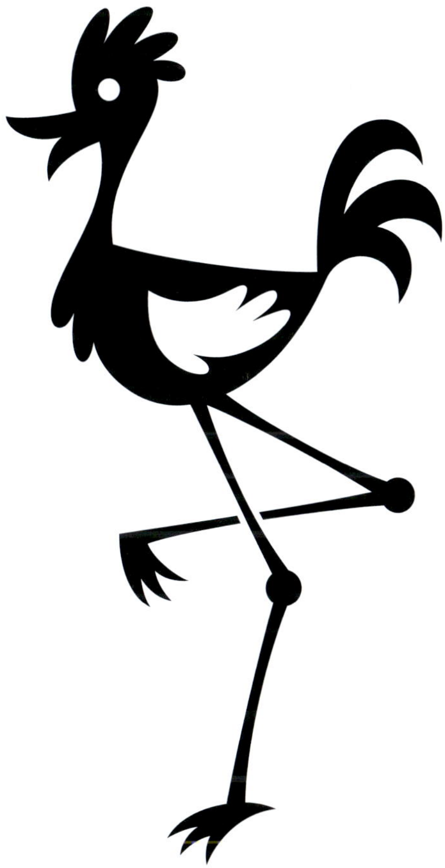

Strike_A_Pose_**TM876**

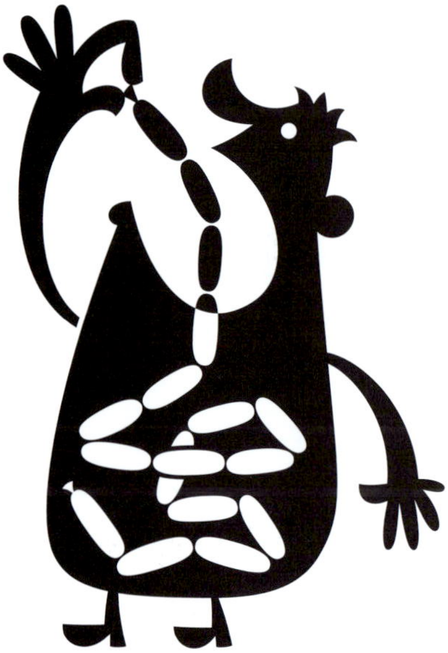

Sausage_Fest_**TM877**

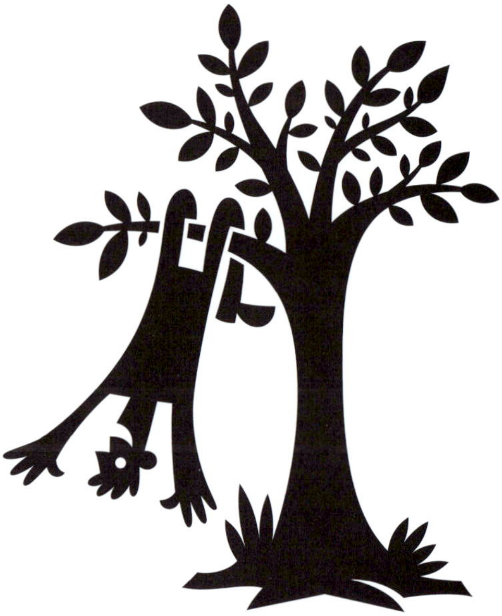

Swinger_**TM878**

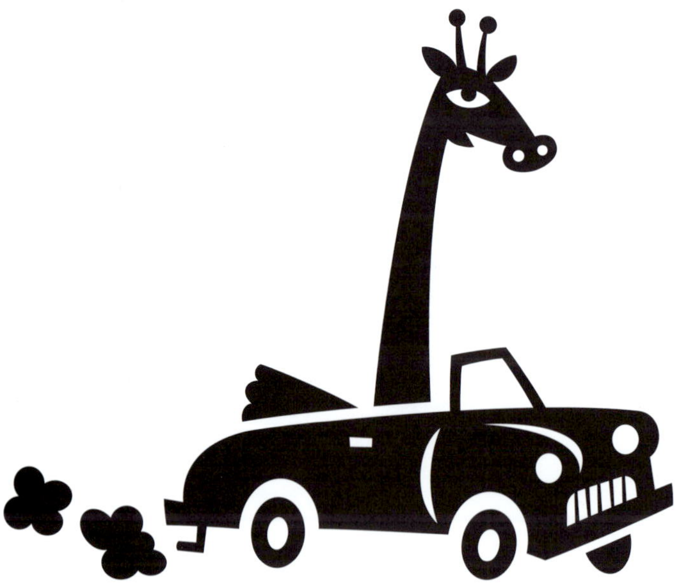

Jungle_Cruisin_**TM880**

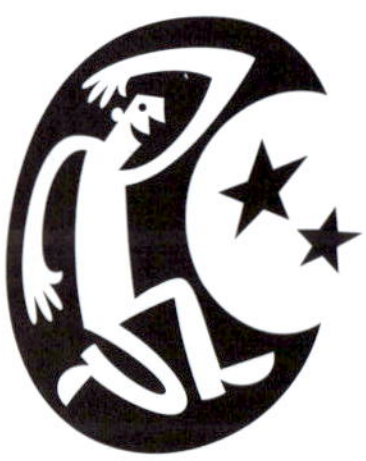

Man_In_The_Moon_**TM879**

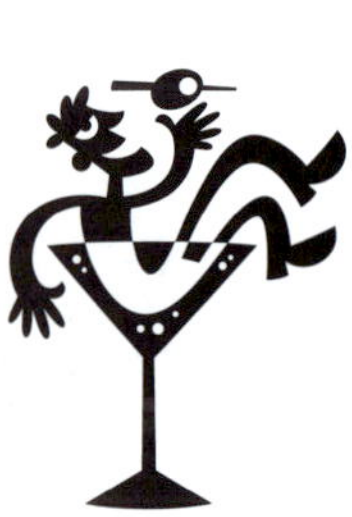

Lounge_Lizard_**TM881**

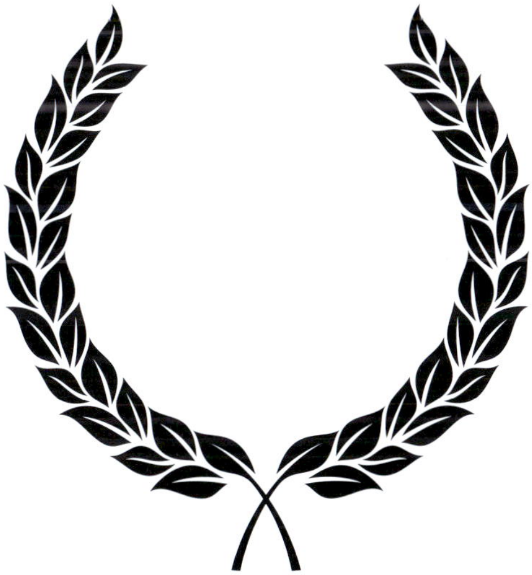

Rest_On_Your_Laurels_**TM884**

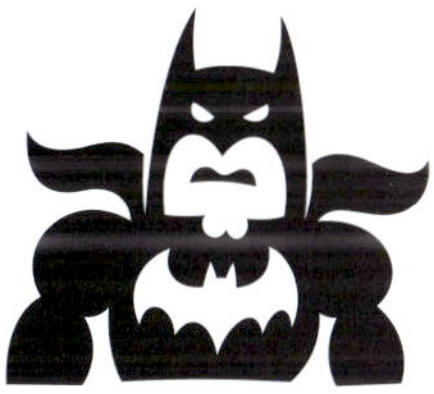

Nocturnal_Man_**TM882**

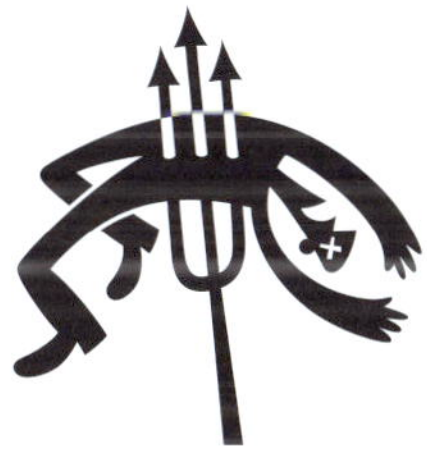

Tormented_**TM883**

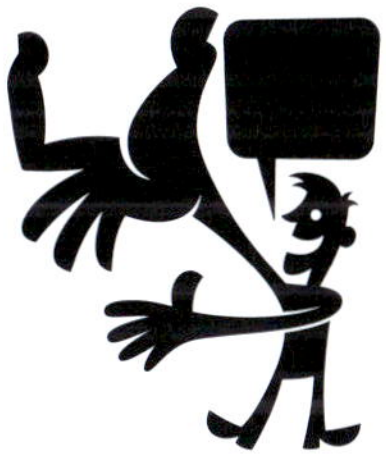

Get_On_Your_Soap_Box_**TM885**

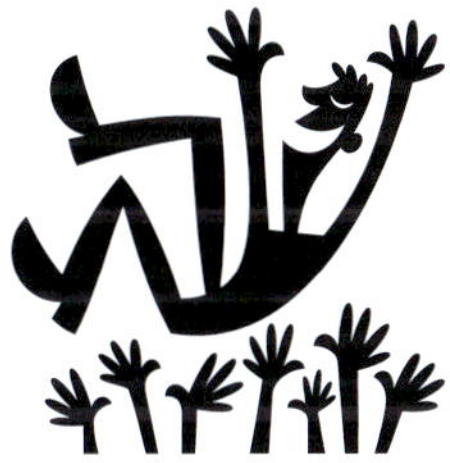

Celebrate_**TM886**

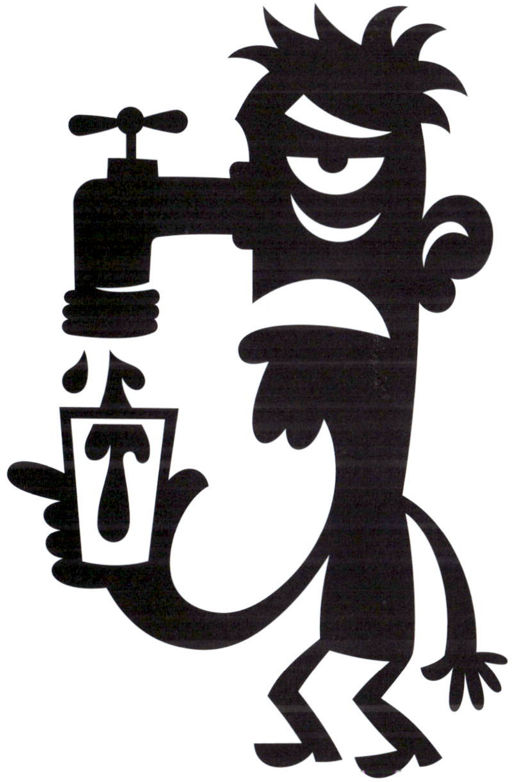

Post_Nasal_Drip_**TM888**

Hammerhead_**TM887**

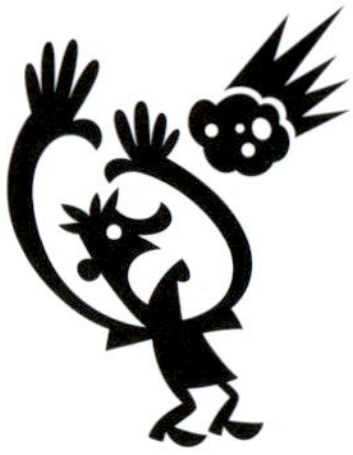

Bad_Luck_**TM889**

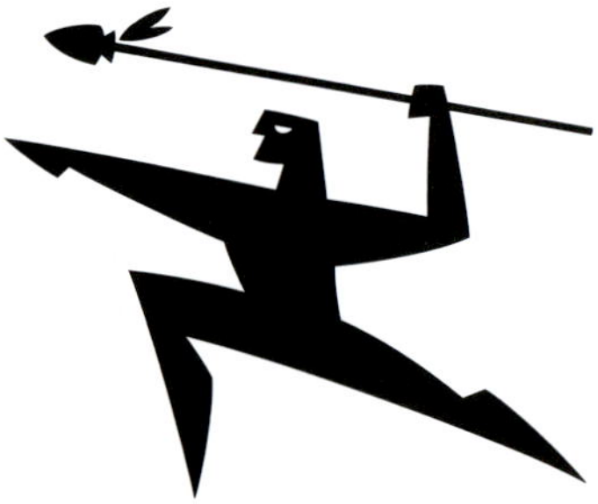

Go_Native_**TM890**

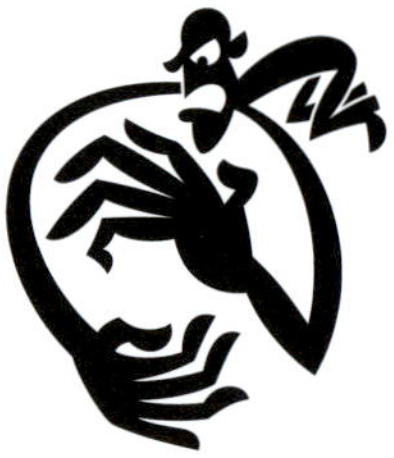

My_Precious_**TM891**

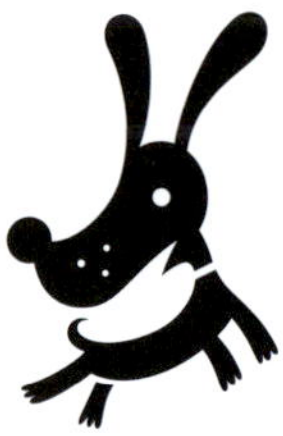

Hopping_Hound_**TM892**

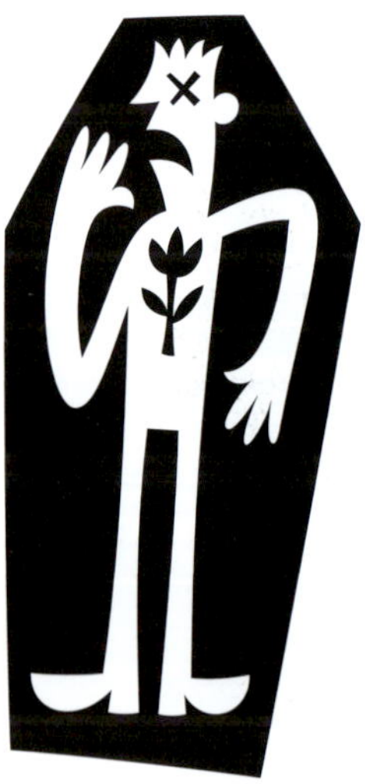

Our_Dearly_Departed_**TM893**

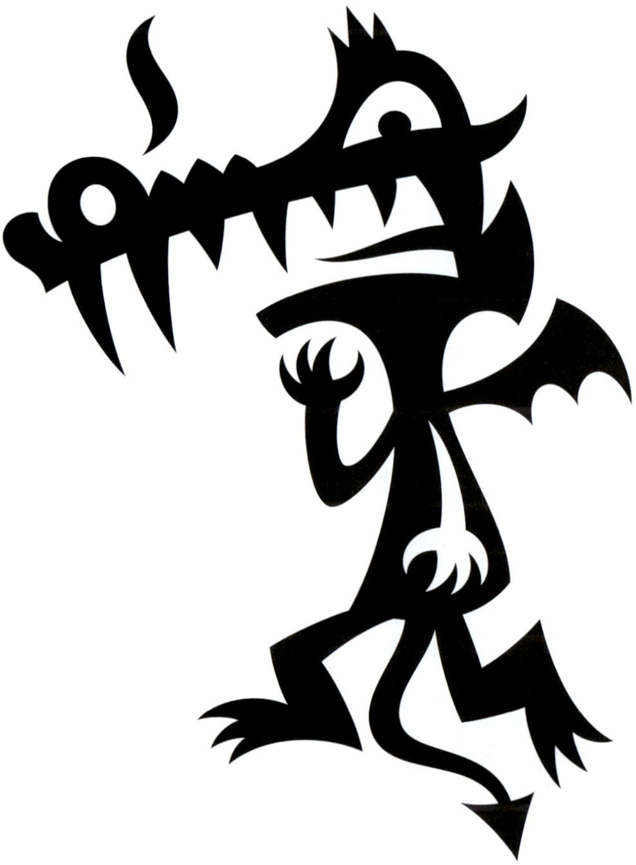

Dragon_Boy_**TM894**

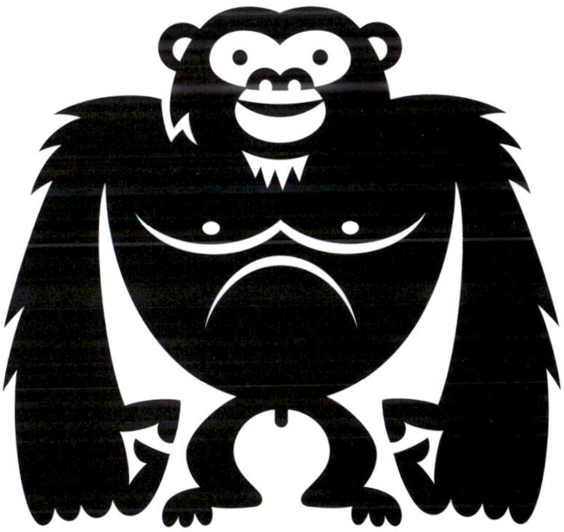

Funky_Monkey_**TM897**

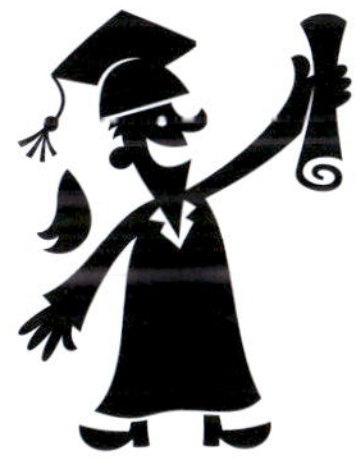

Future_Corporate_Drone_**TM895**

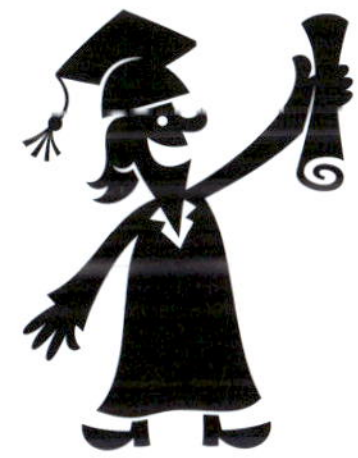

Future_Leader_**TM896**

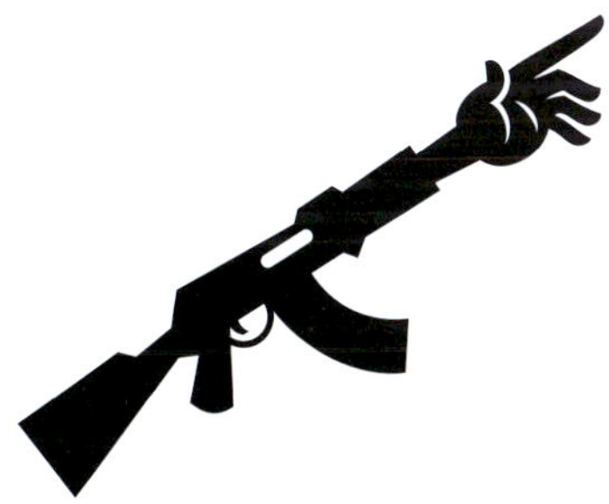

Fire_Arm_**TM898**

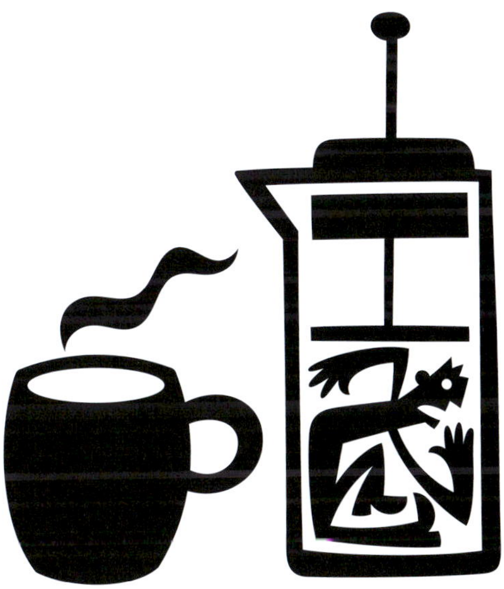

Pressure_Brewing_**TM899**

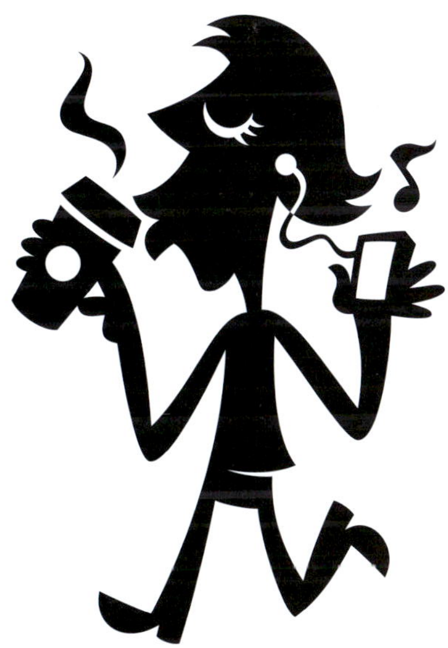

Gimme_Coffee_And_Tunes_**TM900**

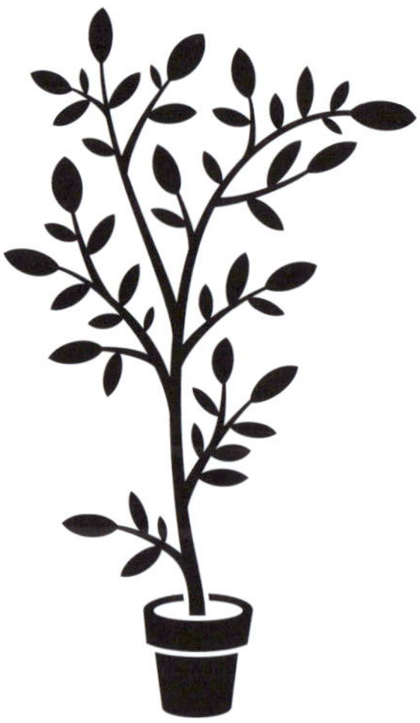

House_Plant_**TM902**

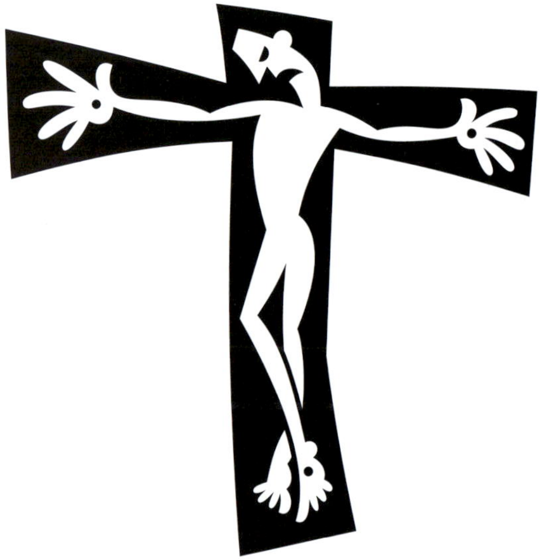

Paid_In_Full_**TM903**

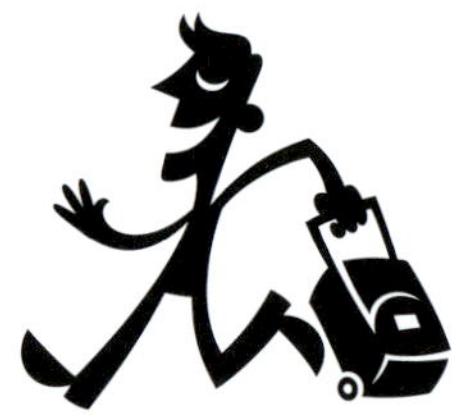

Jet_Set_**TM901**

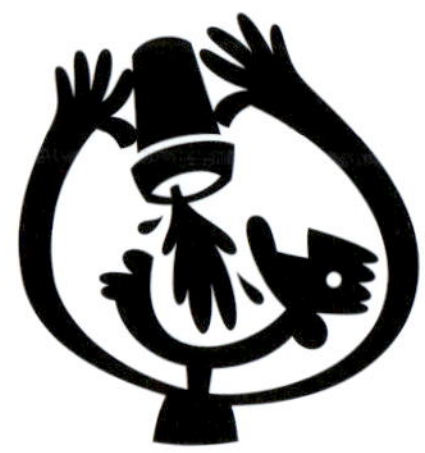

Caffeine_Chug_**TM904**

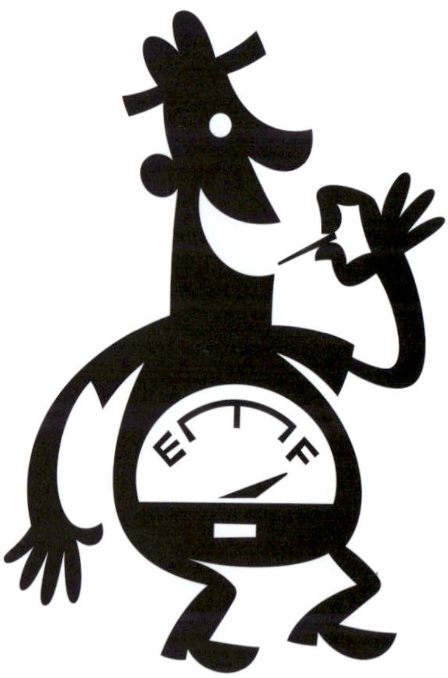

Im_Full_**TM905**

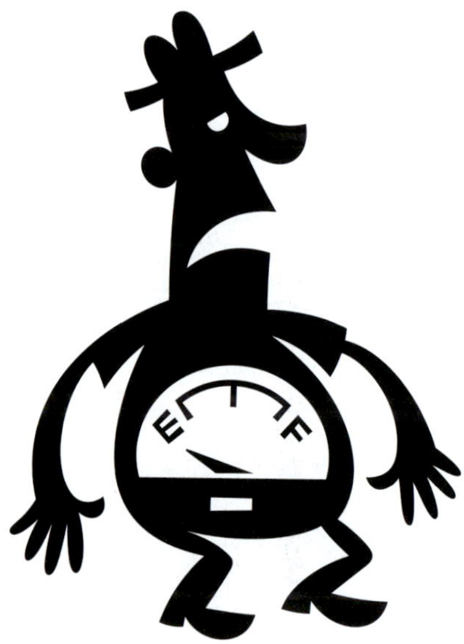

Running_On_Fumes_**TM906**

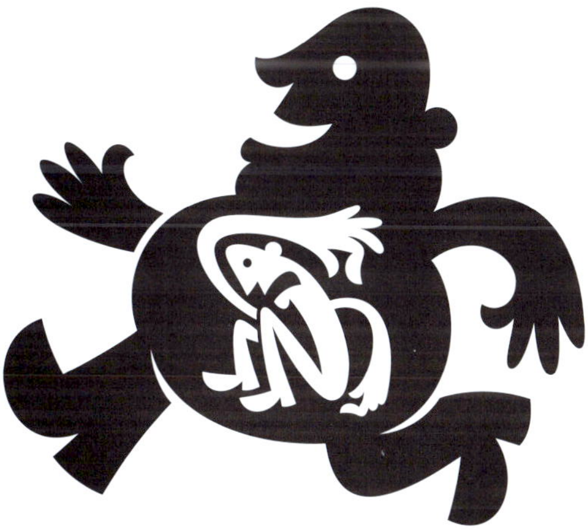

Have_You_For_Dinner_**TM907**

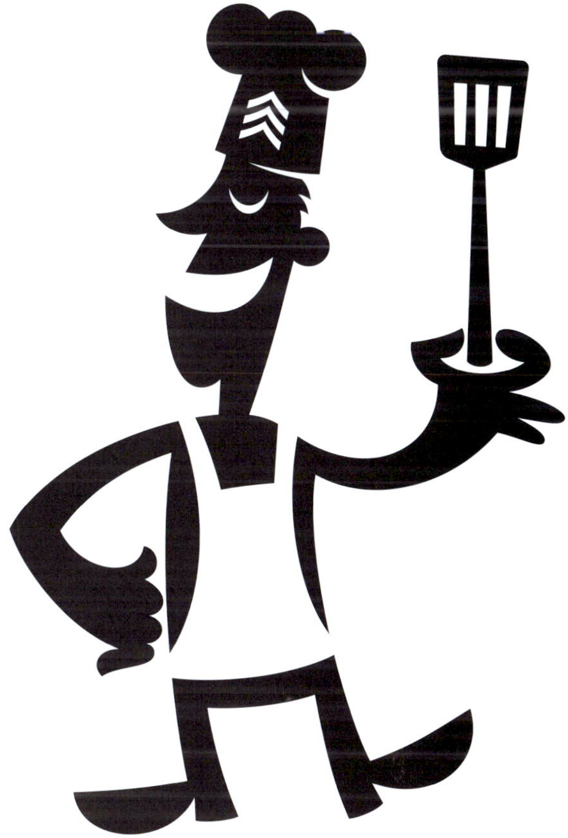

Grill_Sergeant_**TM908**

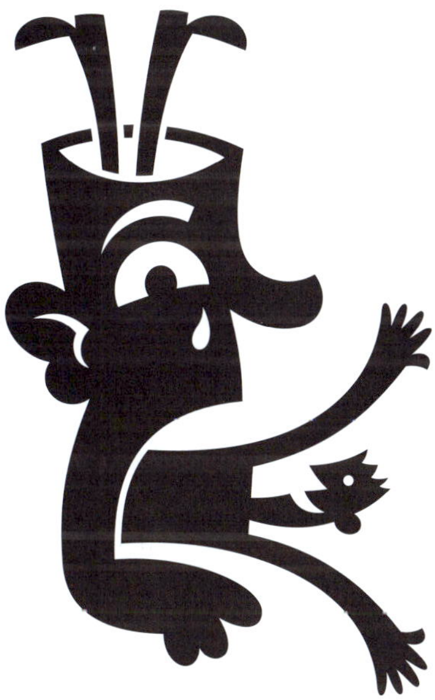

Eat_Me_**TM909**

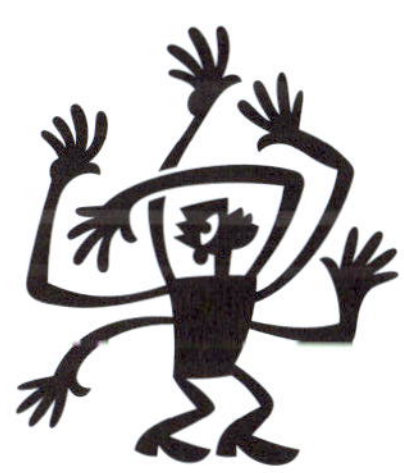

Gain_The_Upper_Hand_**TM910**

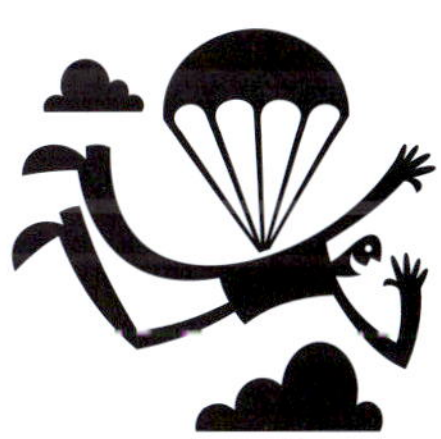

Golden_Parachute_**TM911**

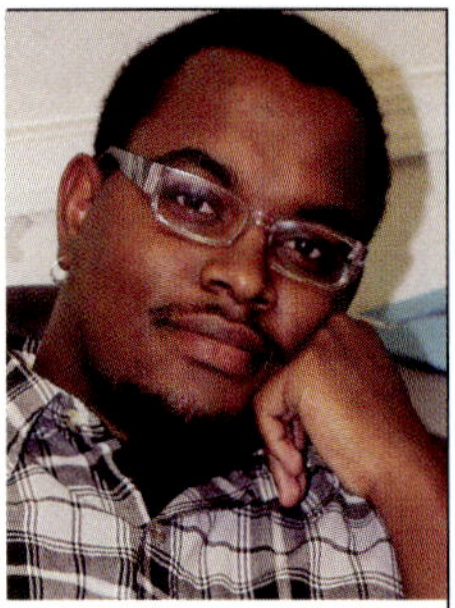

Quincy Washington

Brand Identity Designer

Albanus Design • Oregon City, Oregon

www.AlbanusDesign.com

Wairua Natural Energy was a fun project. I chose the Take and Make "Tiki" art because I wanted do something a bit outside of my element for this beverage design exploration. The Maori had a really cool culture so I started my research there. After some sketching I knew exactly what I wanted to execute for this organic energy drink design.

I began by making a subtle pattern using the Tiki to wrap around the mid section of the can. My use of color overlays and blending modes create a cool yet functional color scheme. The Tiki motif makes up the core identity in my design. Overall, I'm really happy with how the package design turned out, and the Tiki art was definitely a great choice.

Art Used: Tiki TM11

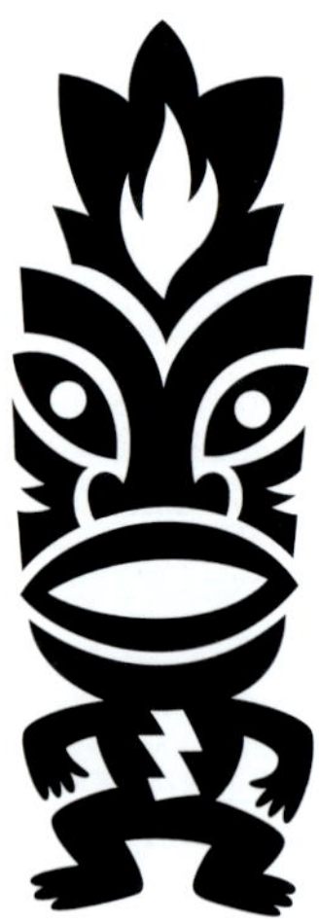

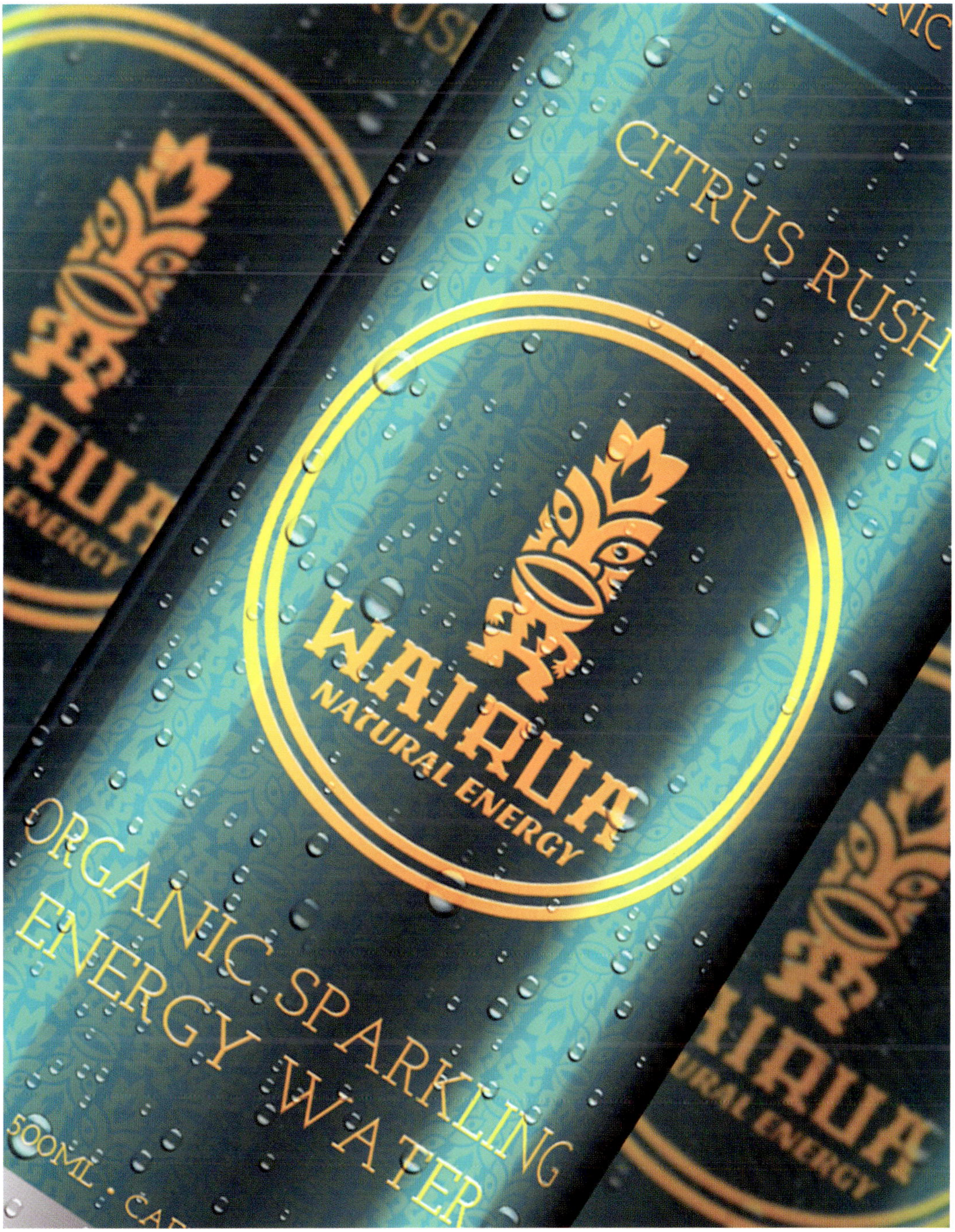
CITRUS RUSH
WAIRUA
NATURAL ENERGY
ORGANIC SPARKLING
ENERGY WATER
500ML

Gimme_**TM912**

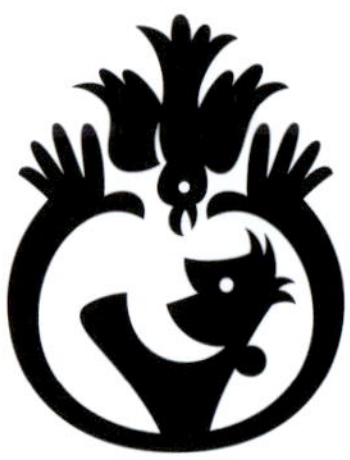

Embrace_Peace_**TM913**

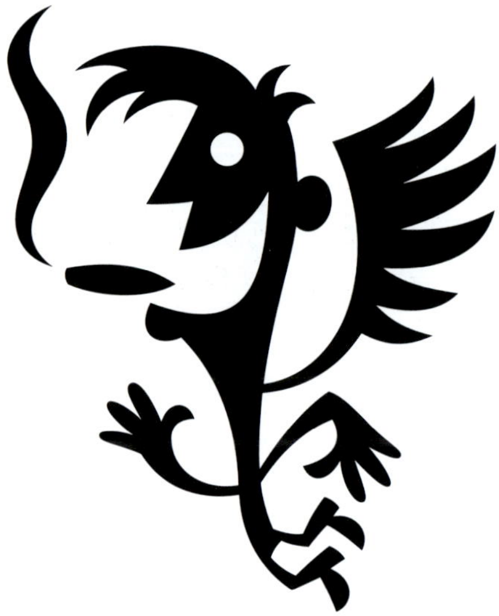

Holy_Smoke_**TM914**

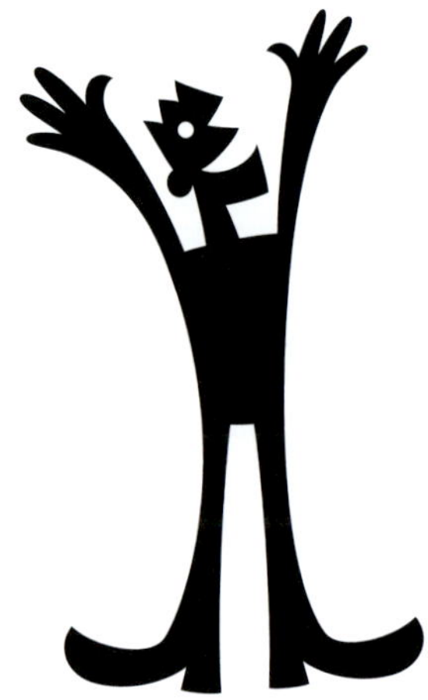

Wonderful_**TM915**

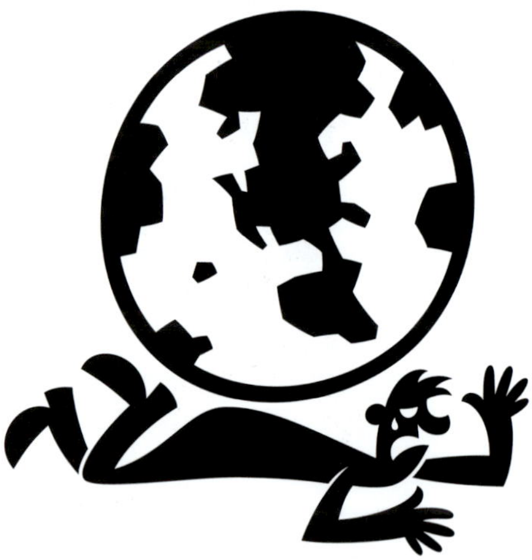

Dont_Let_The_World_Beat_You_Up_**TM916**

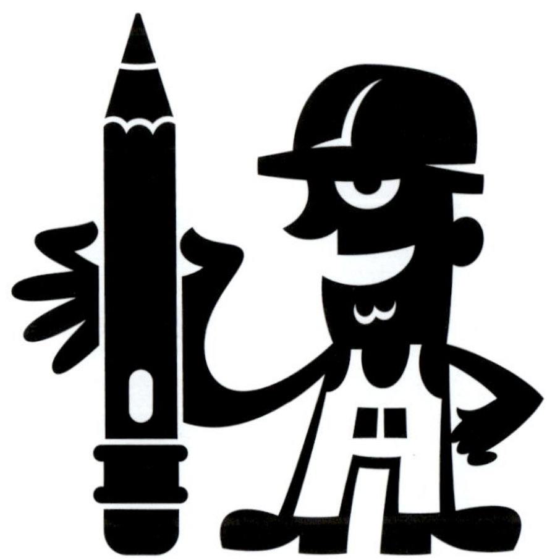

Drawing_Conclusions_**TM917**

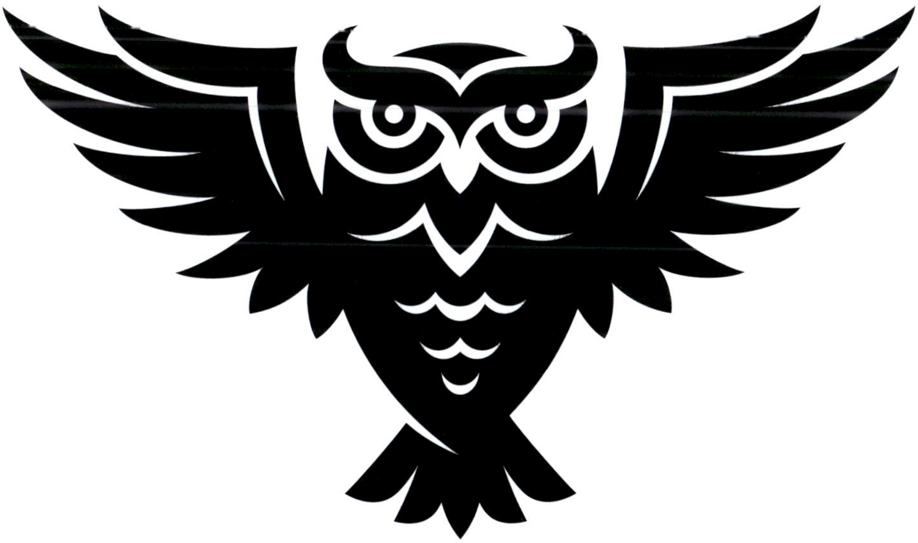

Take_Flight_**TM918**

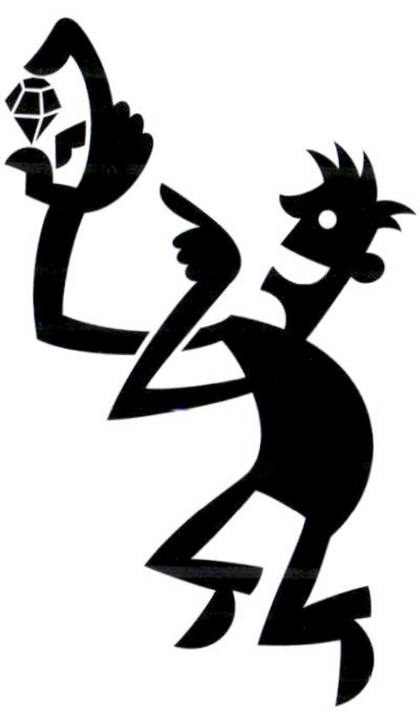

Thats_A_Gem_**TM920**

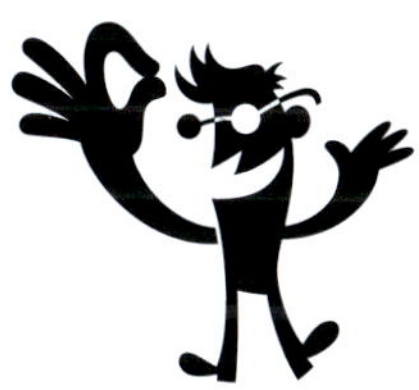

A_Ok_**TM919**

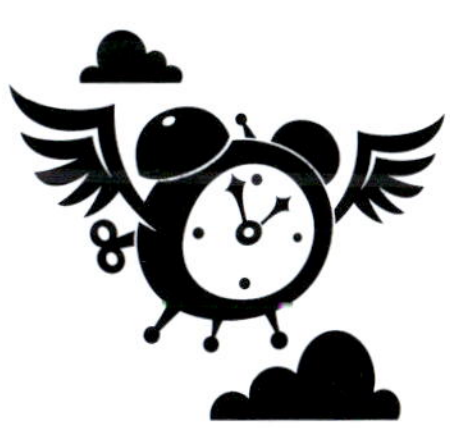

Time_Flies_**TM921**

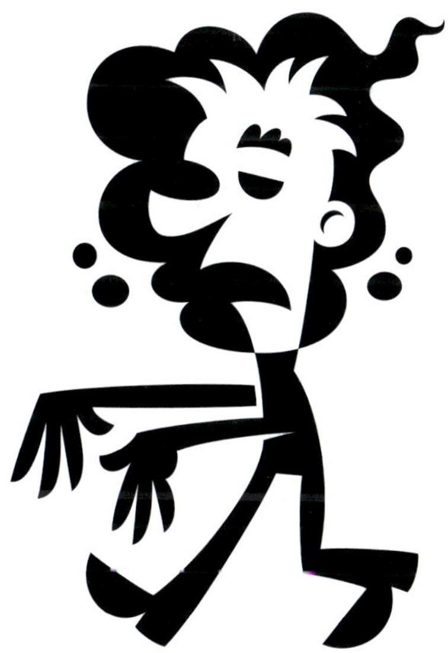

Fog_Of_Conscience_**TM922**

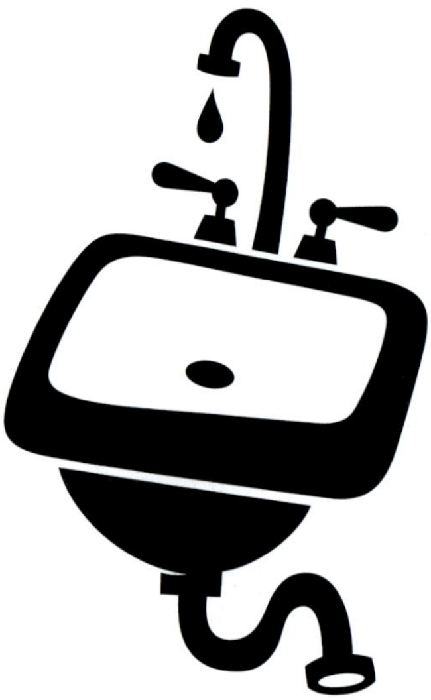

The_Kitchen_Sink_**TM923**

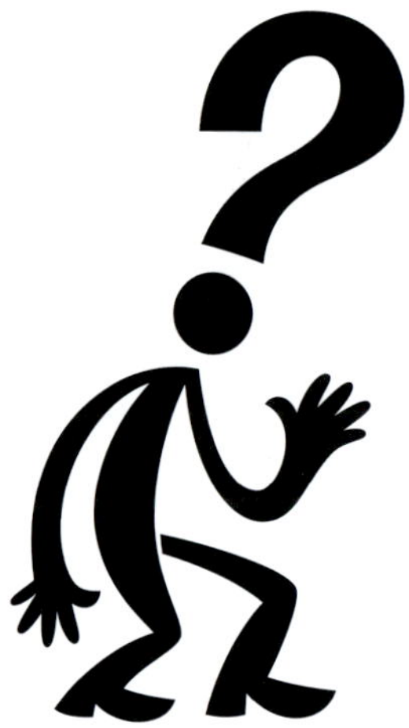

Wondering_**TM924**

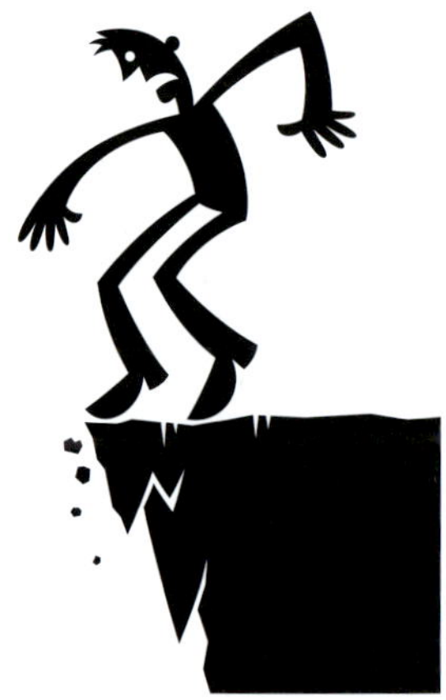

Life_On_The_Edge_**TM925**

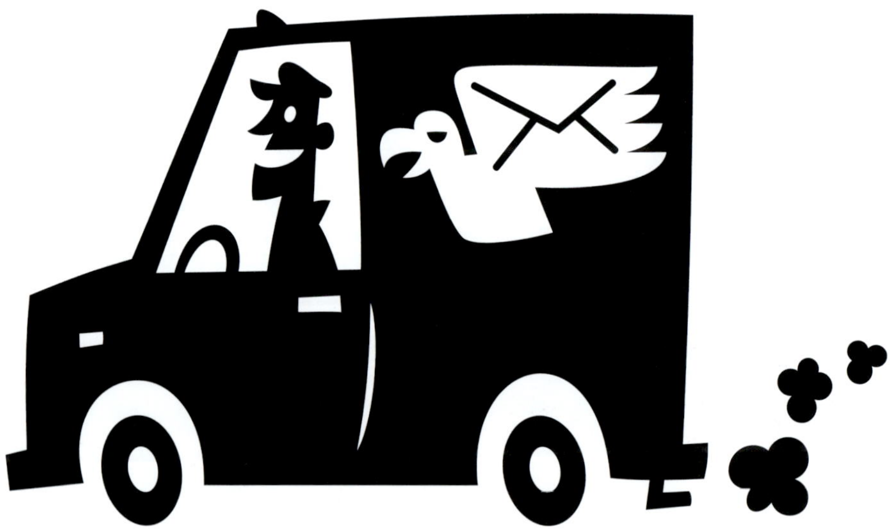

Snail_Mail_**TM926**

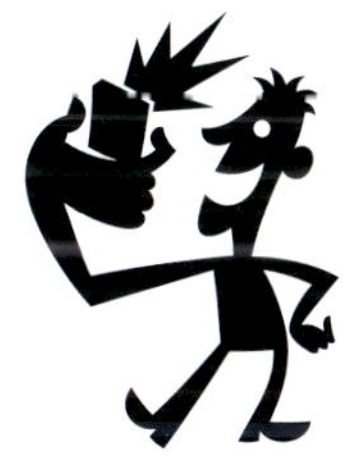

Narcissistic_Tendencies_**TM927**

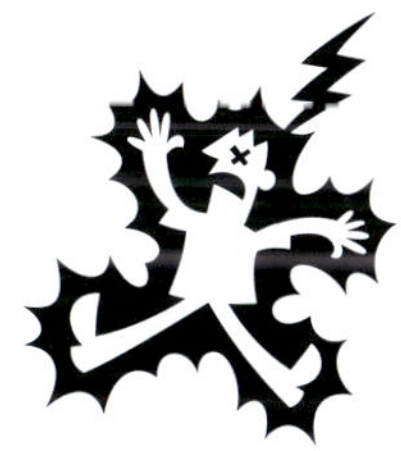

Im_Shocked_Shocked_I_Tell_You_**TM928**

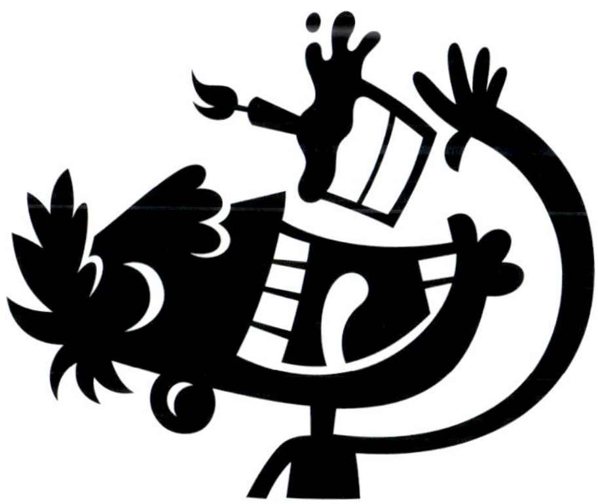

Junk_Foodie_**TM929**

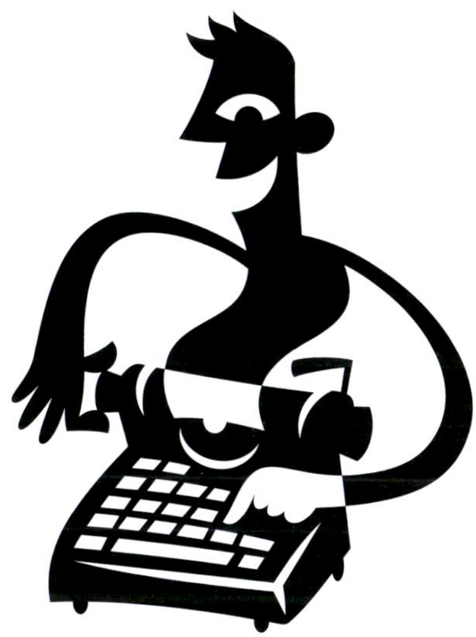

Type_A_Personality_**TM930**

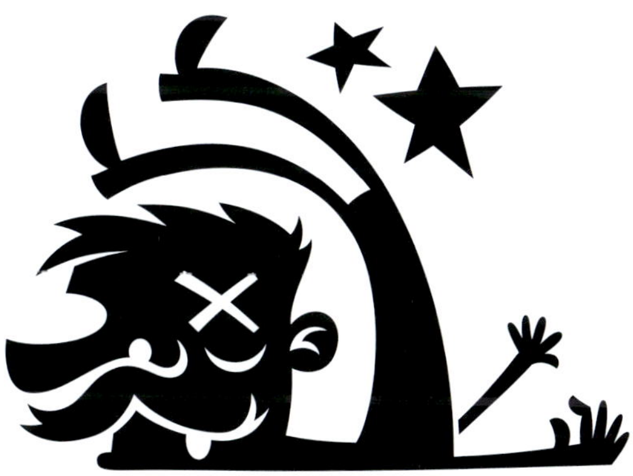

Motor_Skills_Failing_You_**TM931**

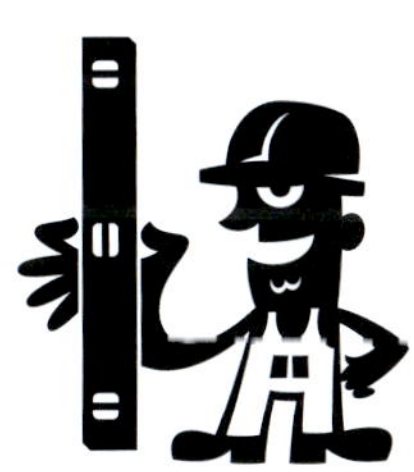

Are_You_On_The_Level_**TM932**

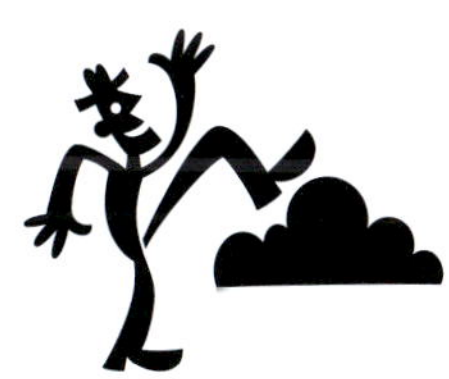

Cloud_Walking_**TM933**

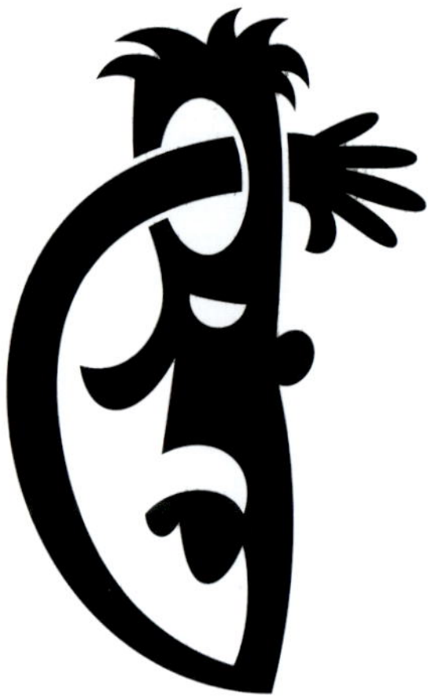

Nothing_There_**TM934**

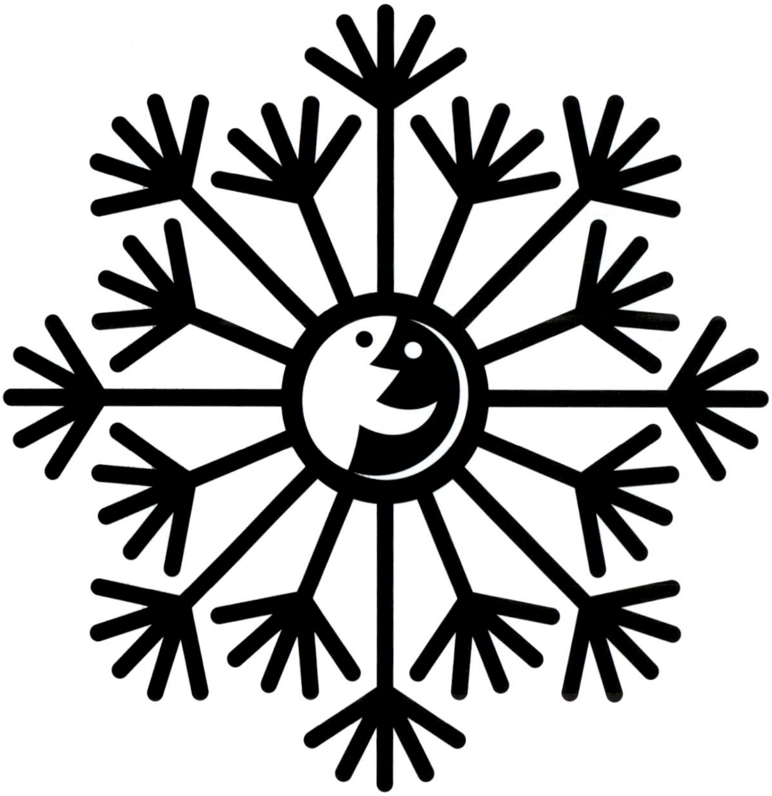

Dandelion_**TM935**

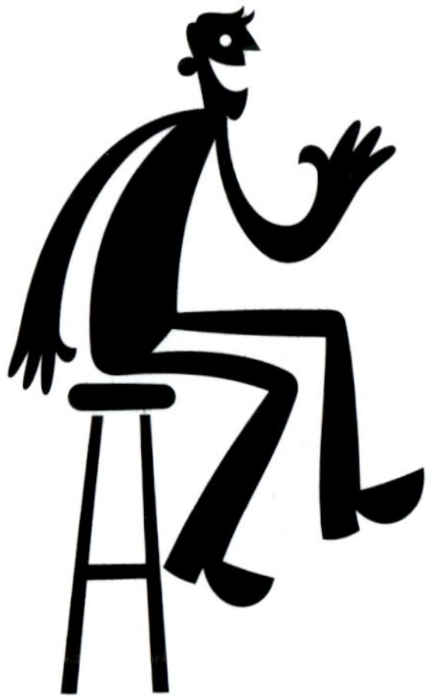

Casual_Conversation_**TM936**

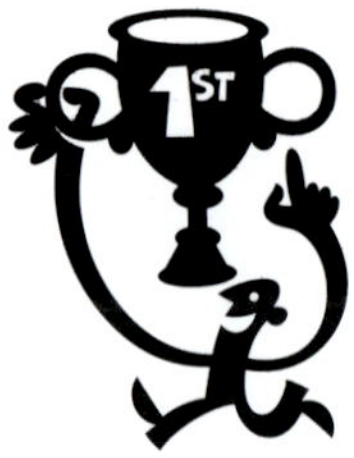

Trophy_Holder_**TM937**

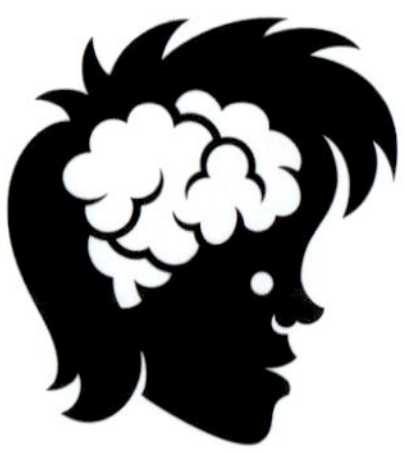

Girl_Has_Smarts_**TM938**

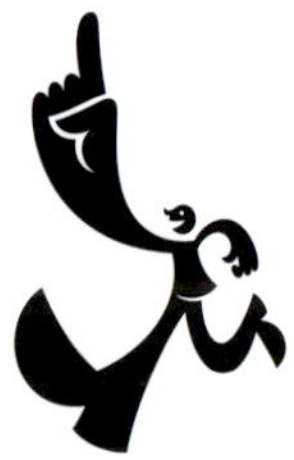

One_More_Thing_**TM939**

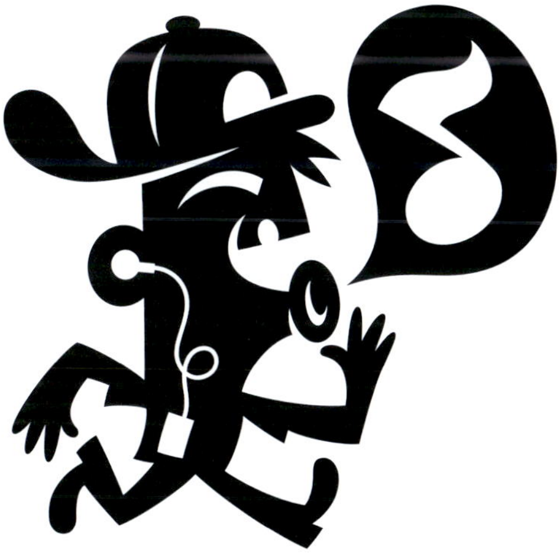

iWhistle_**TM942**

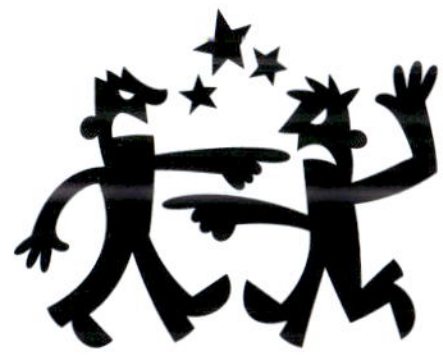

Finger_Pointers_**TM940**

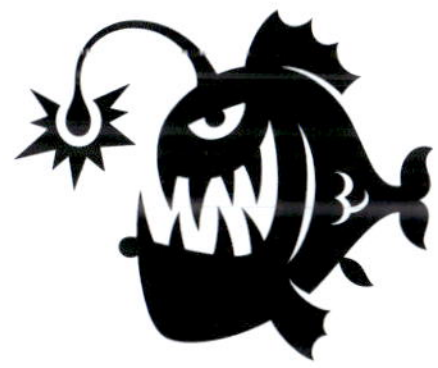

Deep_6_**TM941**

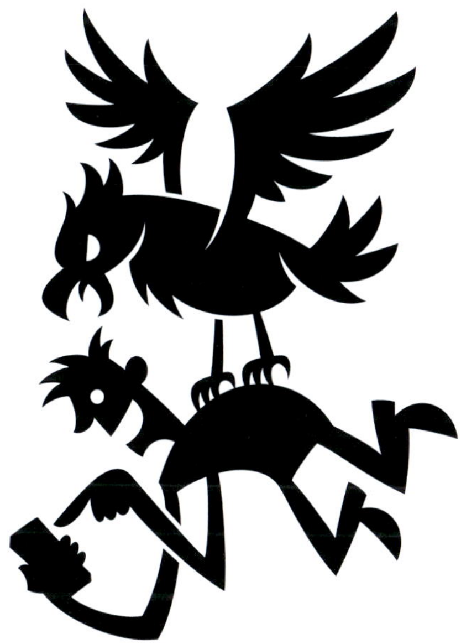

Too_Distracted_**TM943**

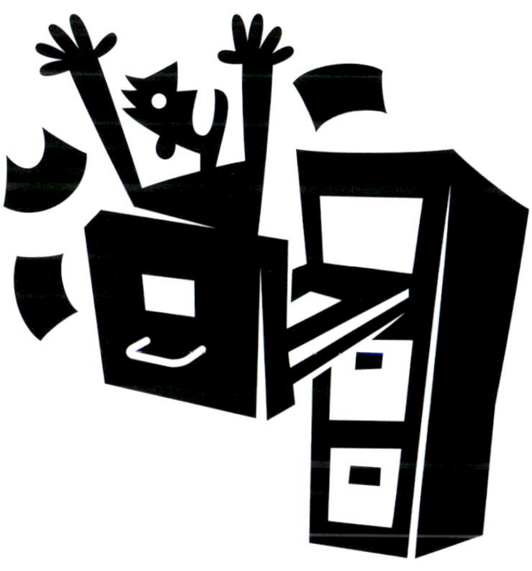

Victim_Of_The_System_**TM944**

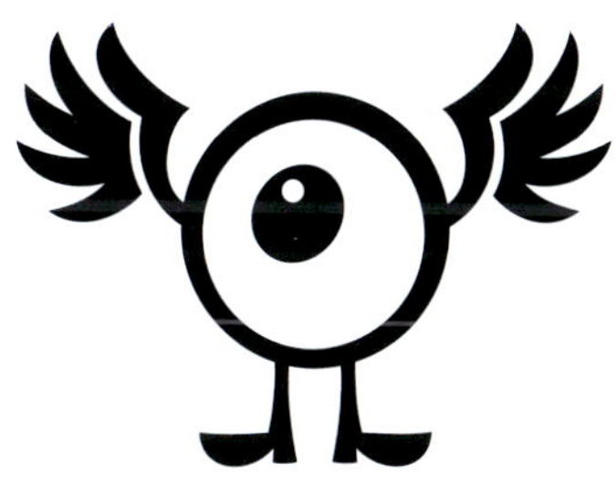

Elevate_Your_Vision_**TM945**

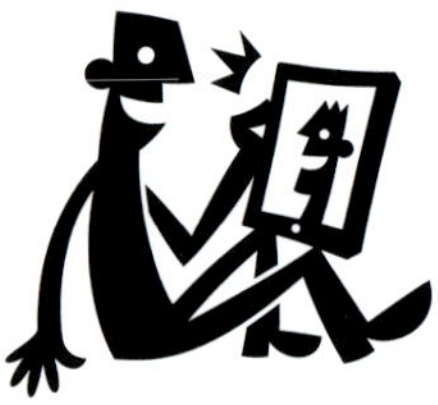

Virtual_Friends_**TM946**

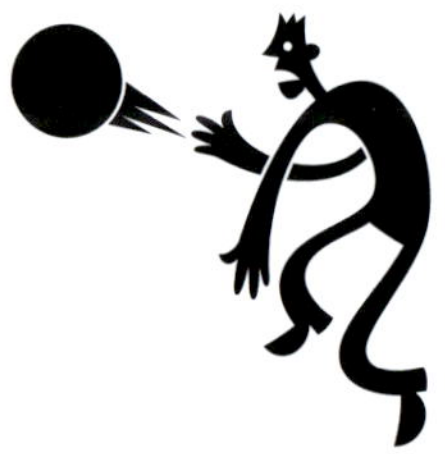

Throw_Away_**TM948**

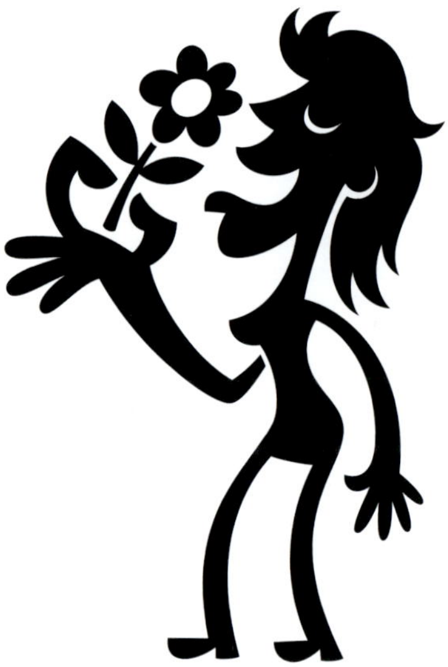

Precious_Interludes_**TM949**

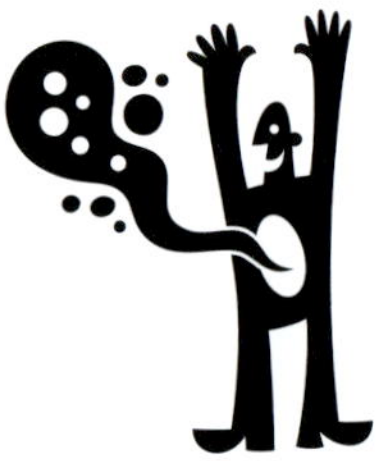

Inner_Spook_**TM947**

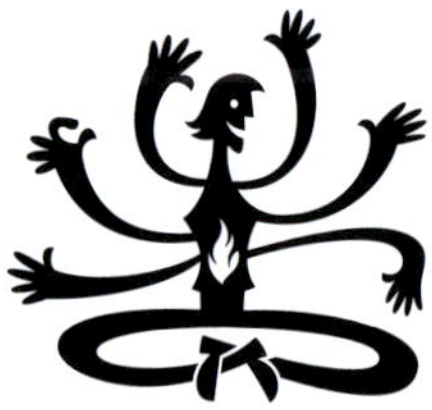

Goddess_**TM950**

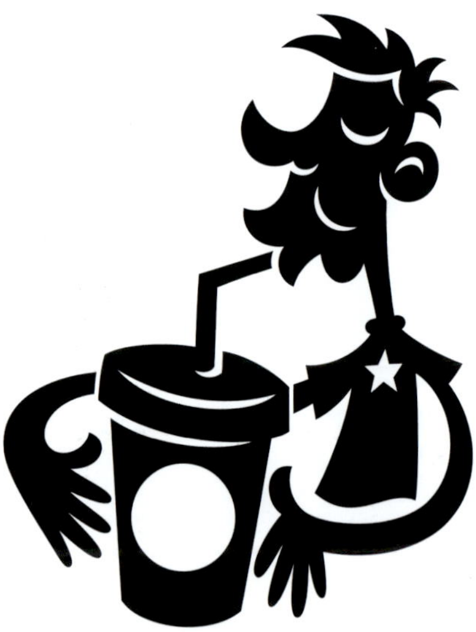

Drink_It_Up_**TM951**

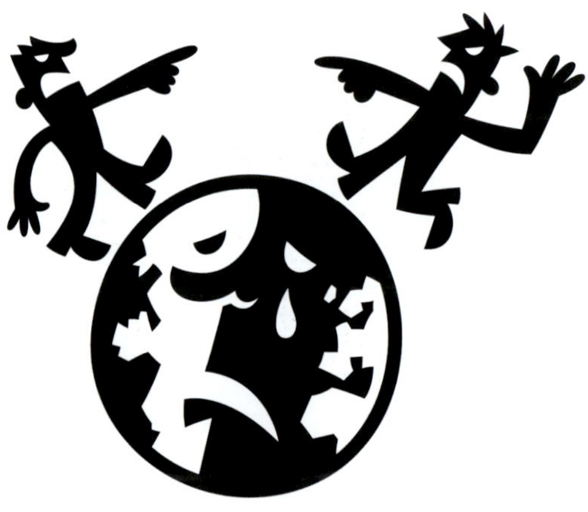

Global_Conflict_**TM952**

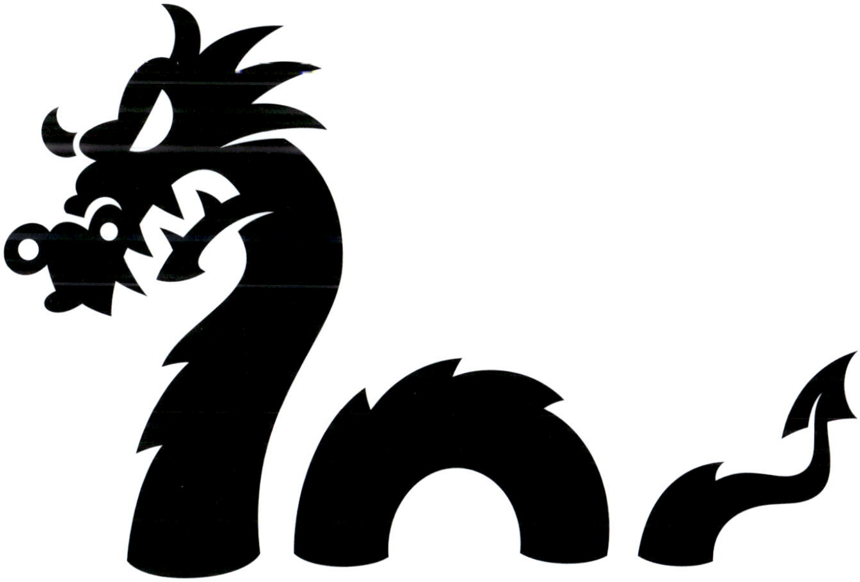

In_Search_Of_**TM953**

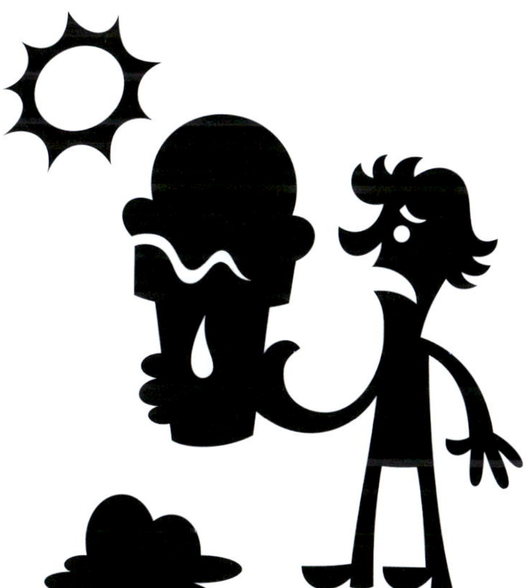

I_Scream_You_Scream_**TM955**

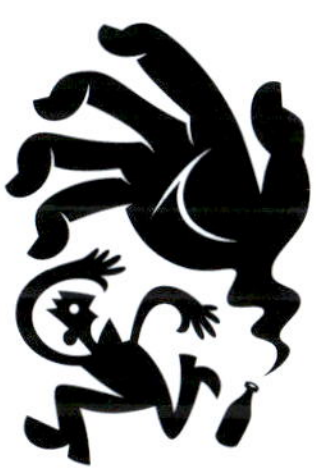

Liquid_Agony_**TM954**

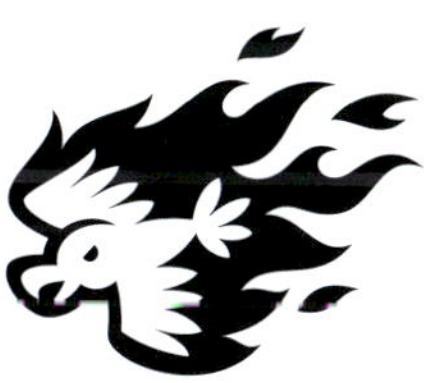

Fire_Bird_**TM956**

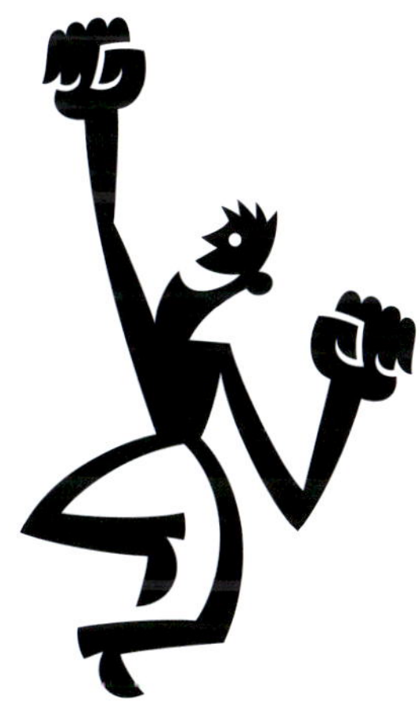

Victory_Is_Ours_**TM957**

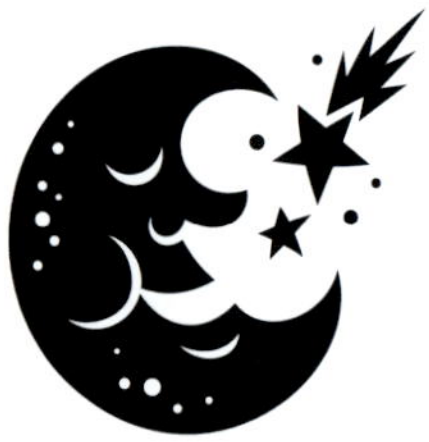

Fly_Me_To_The_Moon_**TM958**

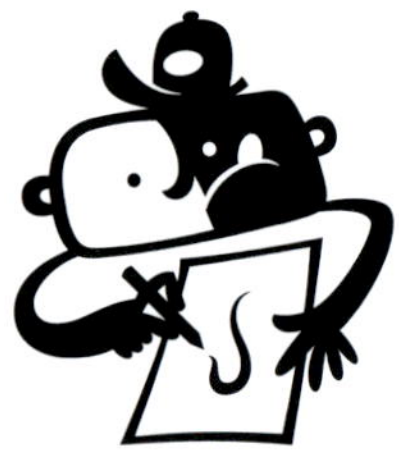

Scrawler_**TM959**

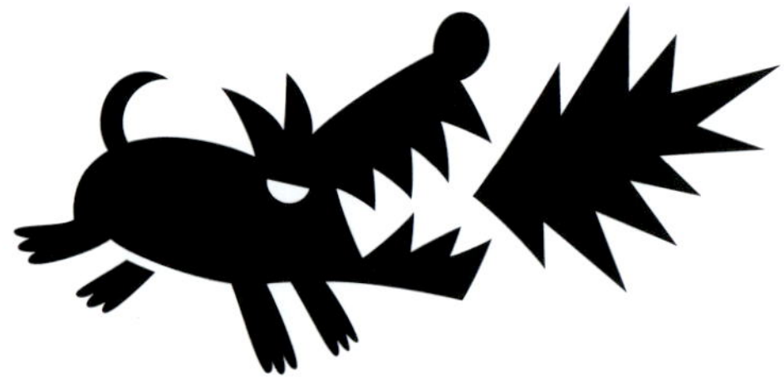

Riled_Rover_**TM960**

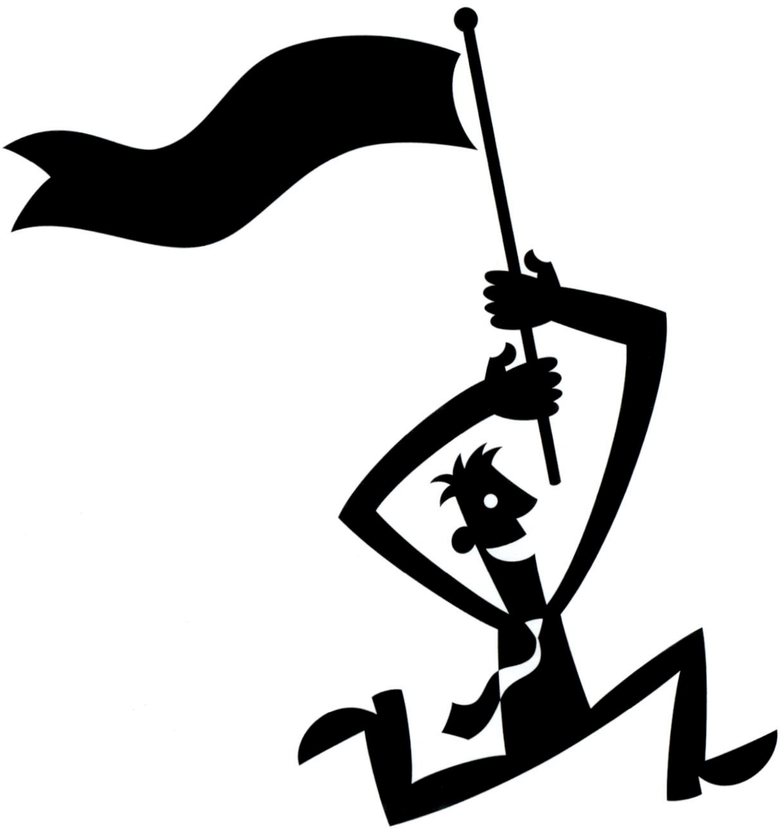

Its_A_Banner_Day_**TM962**

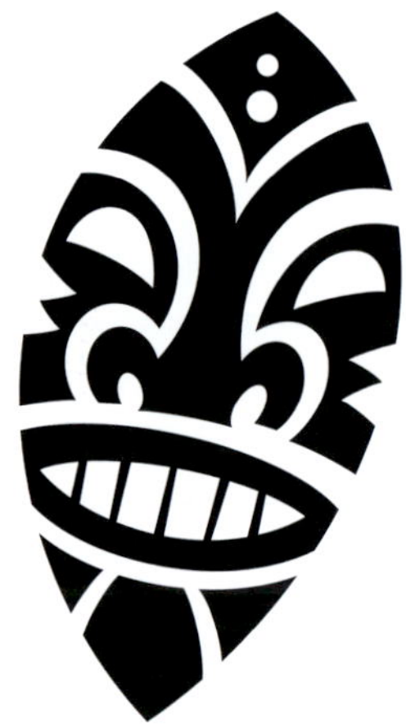

Dont_Mask_Your_True_Feelings_**TM961**

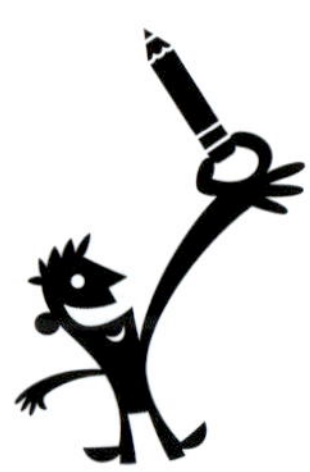

Mighty_Pencil_**TM963**

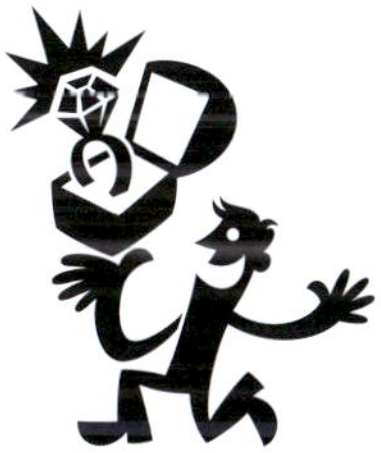

Will_You_Marry_Me_**TM964**

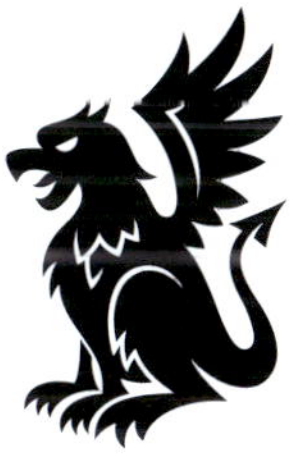

Gryphon_**TM965**

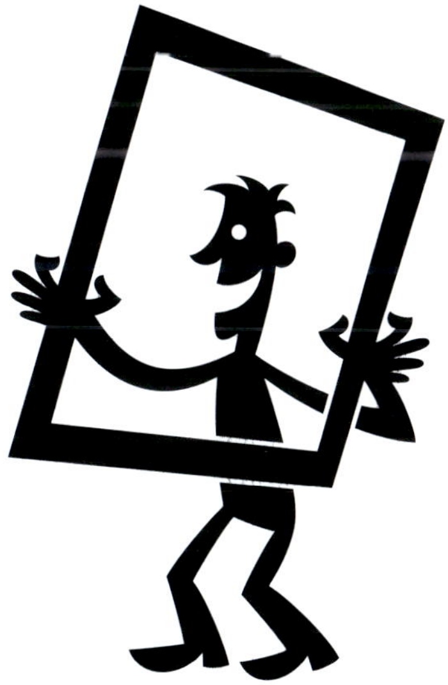

Framed_**TM966**

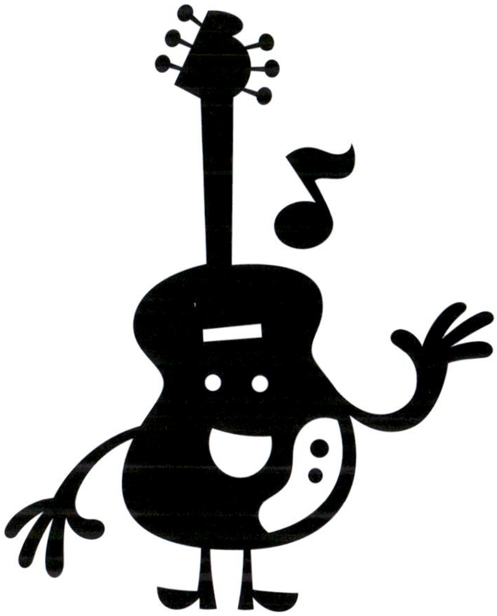

Guitar_**TM967**

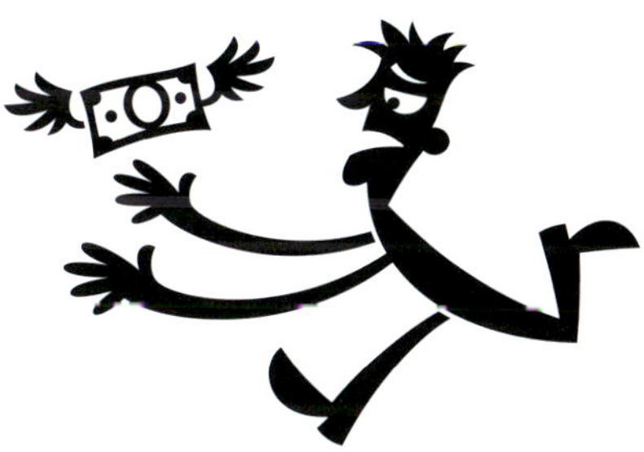

Chasing_Money_**TM968**

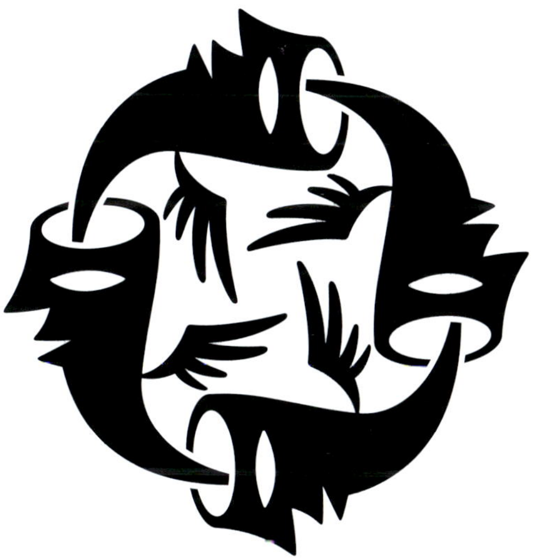

Eternal_Cycle_**TM969**

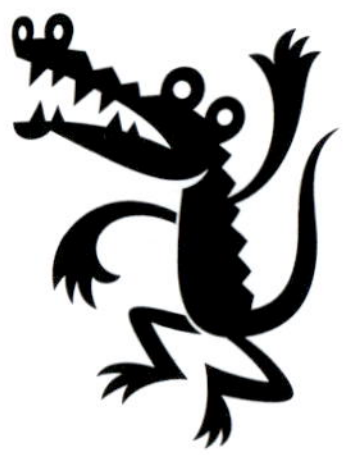

Gator_Dance_**TM970**

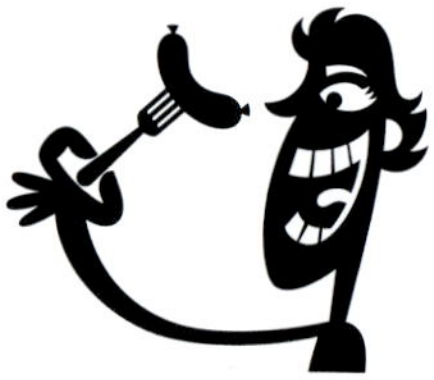

Scarf_Vittles_**TM971**

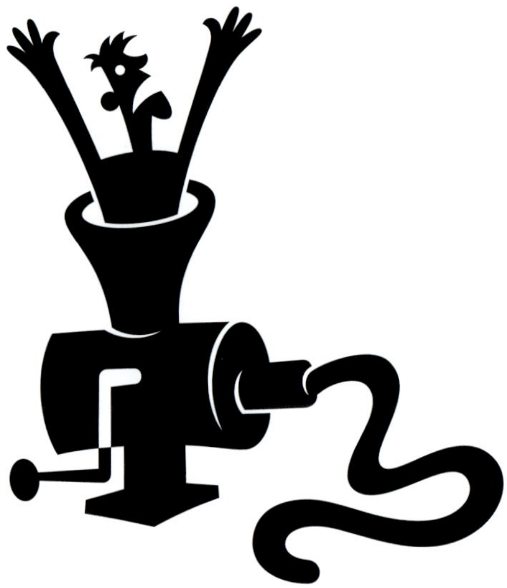

The_Daily_Grind_**TM972**

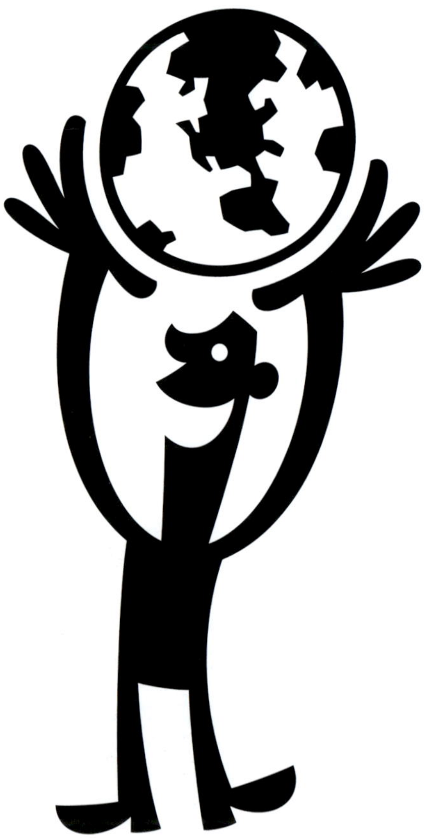

The_Whole_World_In_Your_Hands_**TM973**

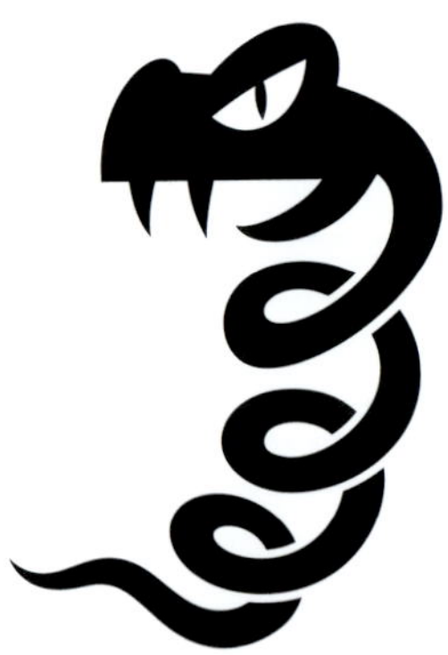

Coiled_To_Strike_**TM974**

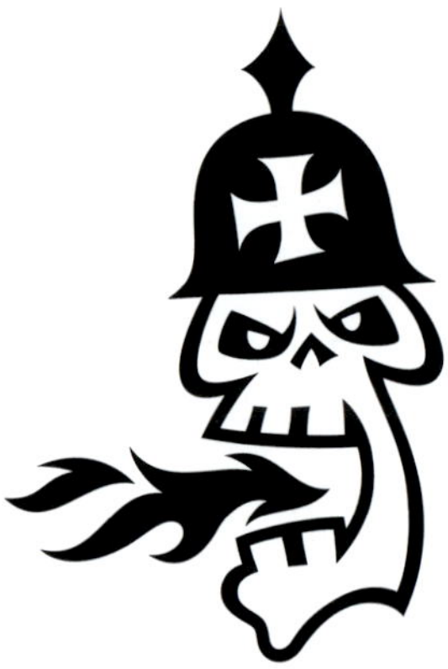

Hot_Talk_**TM975**

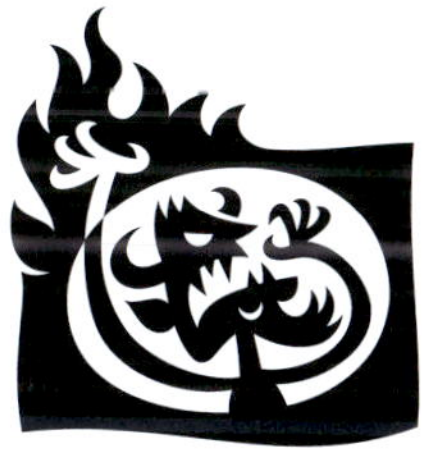

Keep_The_Devil_In_The_Hole_**TM976**

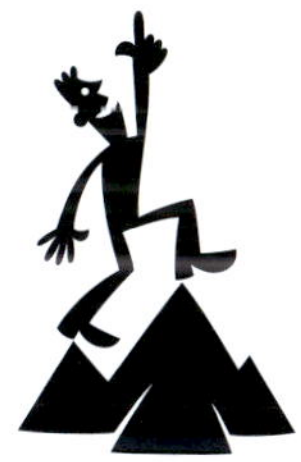

Go_To_The_Top_**TM977**

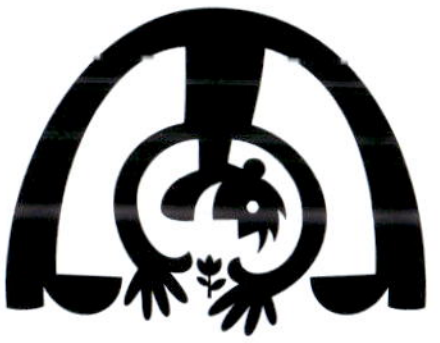

Appreciate_The_Little_Things_**TM978**

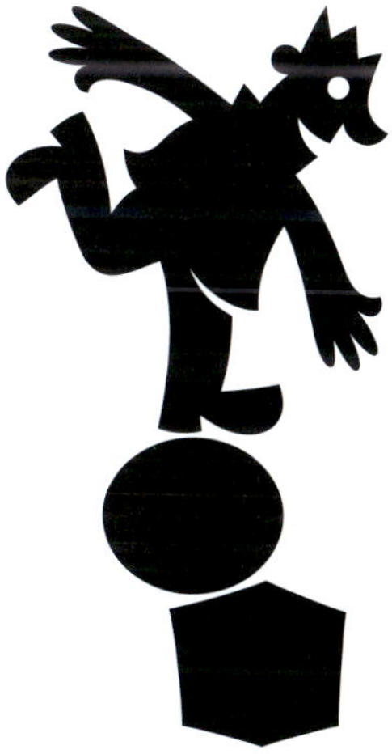

In_The_Balance_**TM979**

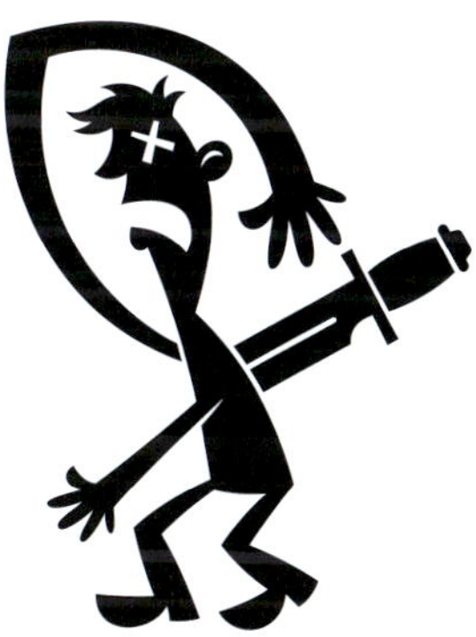

Back_Stabbing_Son_Of_A_Bitch_**TM980**

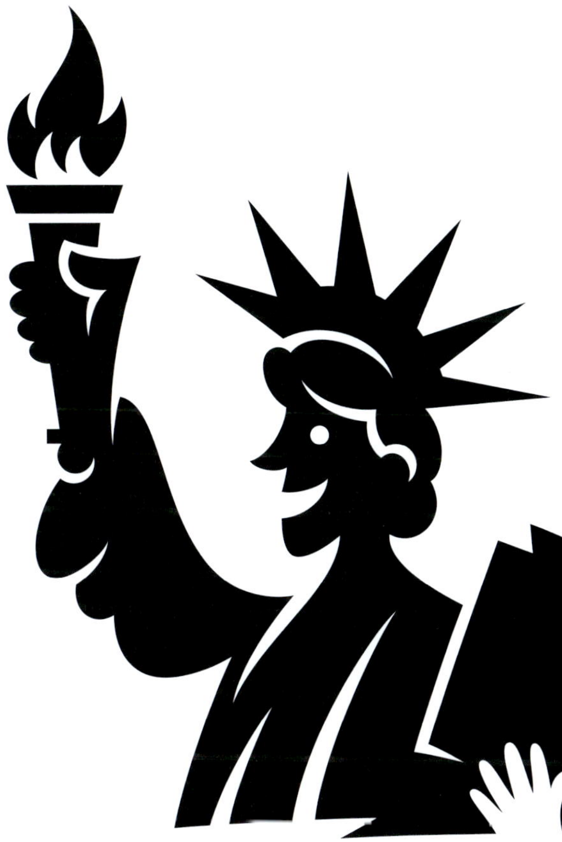

Liberty_For_All_**TM981**

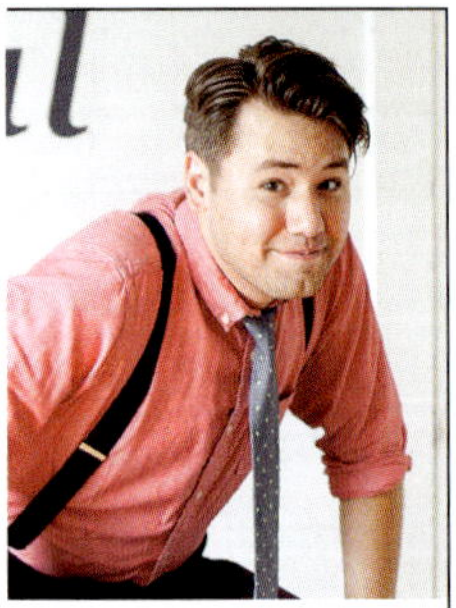

Ben Lueders

Owner / Designer

Fruitful Design • Omaha, Nebraska

www.fruitful-design.com

Differences explores the scary world of opposites from the eyes of a toddler—who is discovering that opposites can attract and deter at the same time.

Due to the wide array of illustrations in the *Take and Make Art* collection, I quickly hatched the idea of creating a piece that depicts the contrast between two separate designs. Being a sci-fi fan myself, the "Space Villain" Darth and "Boldly Go" were my obvious first illustration choices.

At first I played around with a lot of sketches and concepts for this illustration—but they always centered around two adults meeting for the first time while wearing conflicting shirt designs. It wasn't until one day when I watched my 3-year old son Jonah playing with his friend Charlotte that I became inspired to make this final piece.

Art Used: Space Villain TM35, Boldy Go TM610

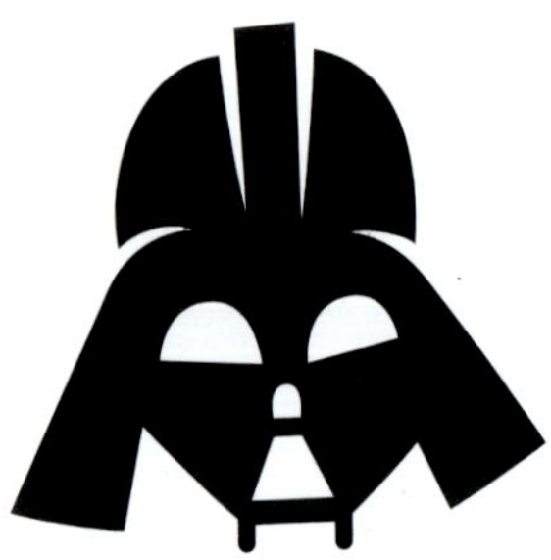

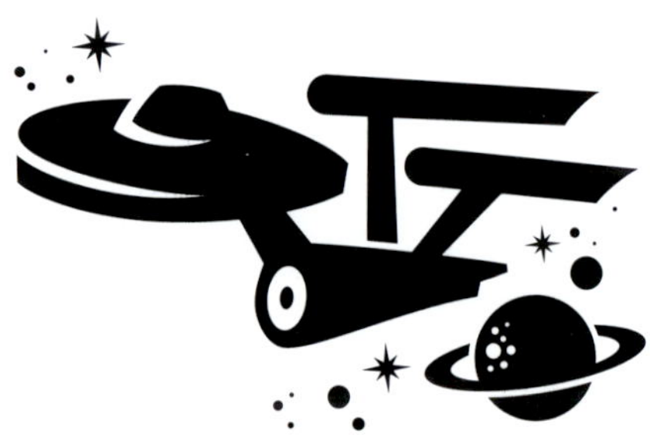

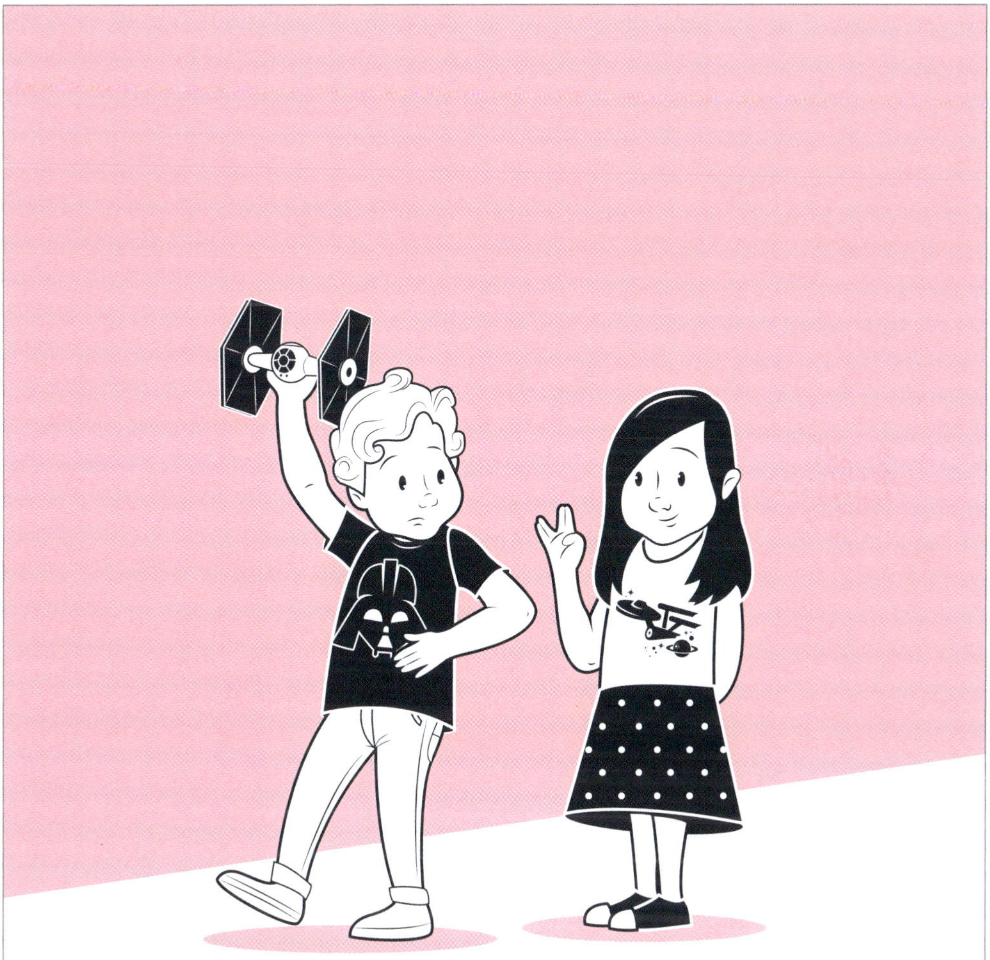

DIFFERENCES

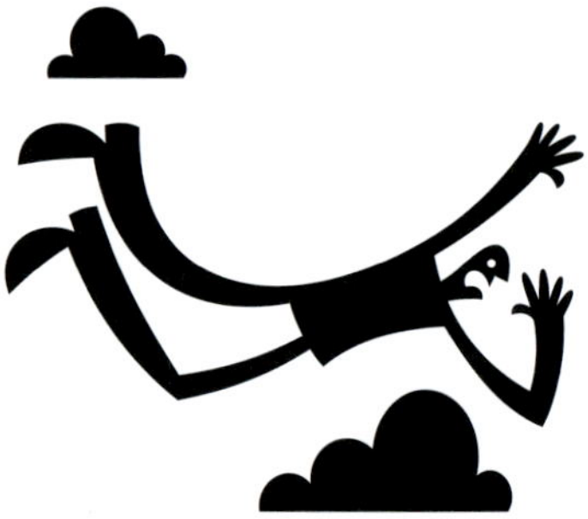
Free_Fall_**TM982**

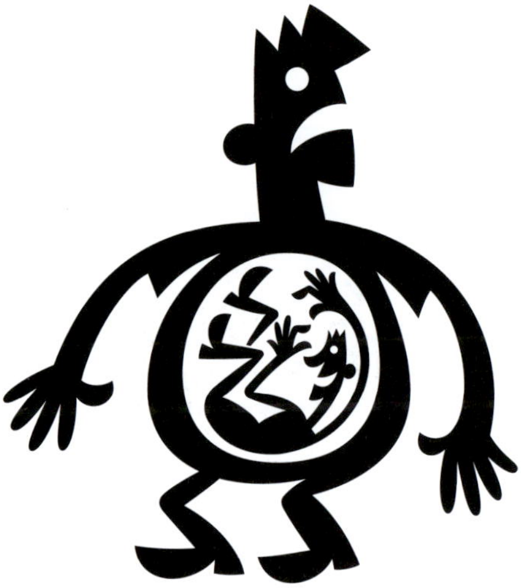
Inner_Happiness_**TM983**

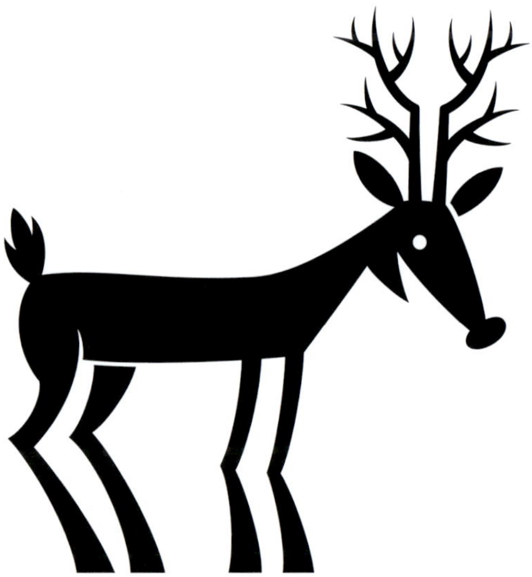
Stag_**TM984**

Lighten_Up_**TM987**

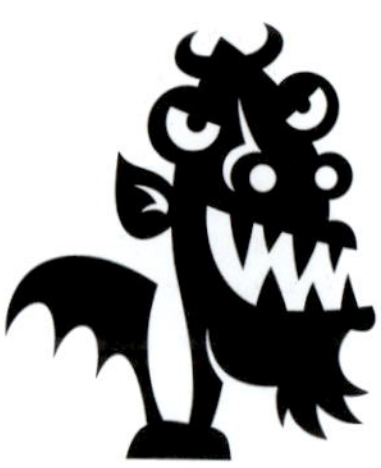
Diablo_Laughs_**TM985**

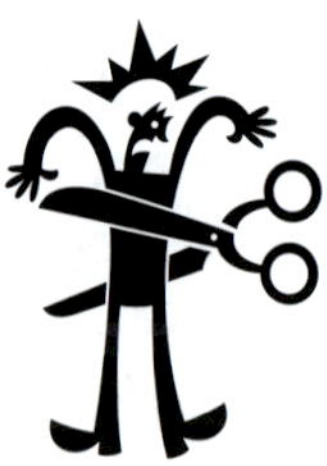
Cut_Up_**TM986**

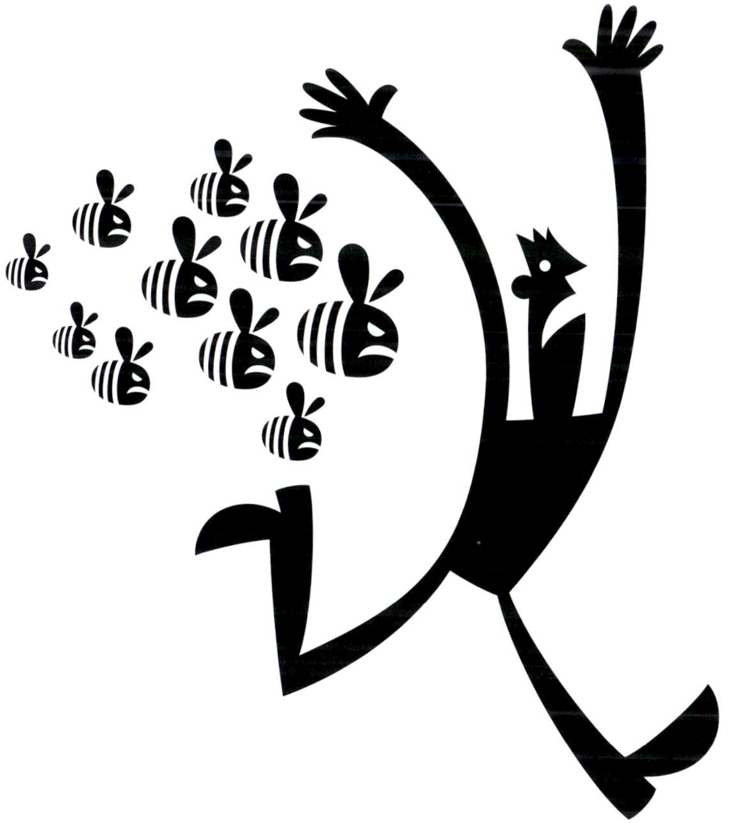

Killa_Bees_**TM989**

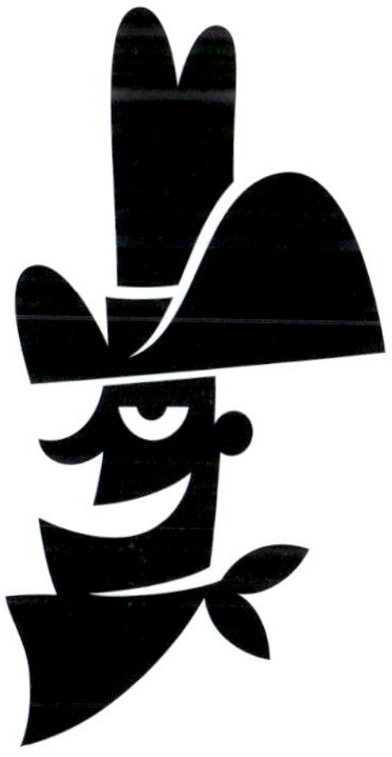

Howdy_Pardner_**TM988**

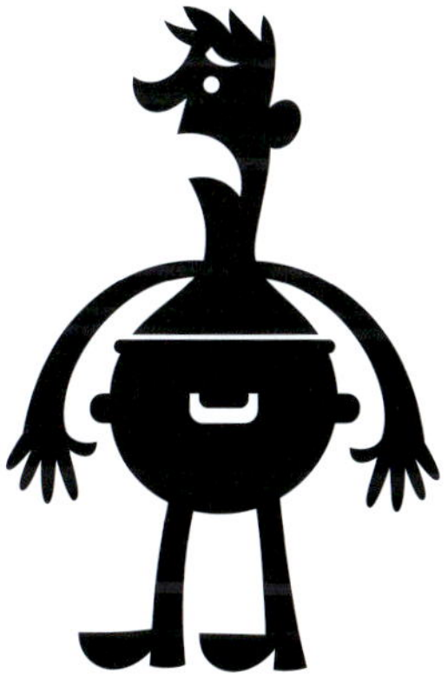

Pot_Belly_**TM993**

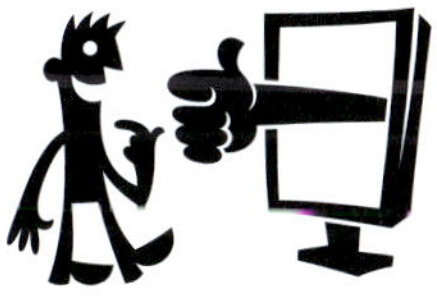

I_Like_You_**TM990**

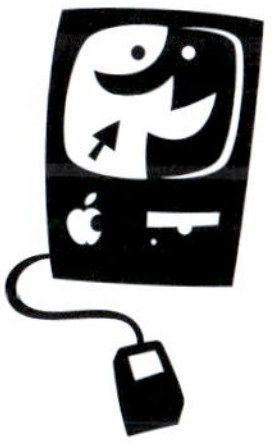

Hello_**TM991**

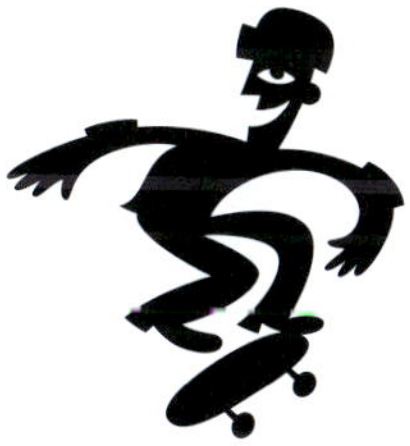

Rip_It_Up_**TM992**

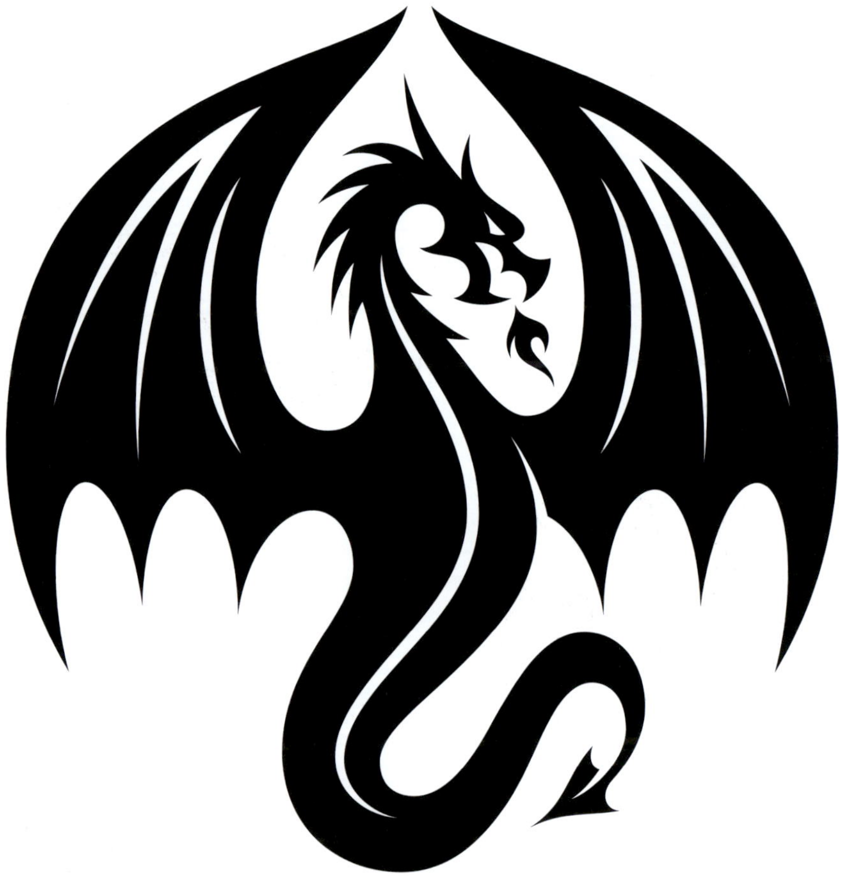

Great_Dragon_**TM994**

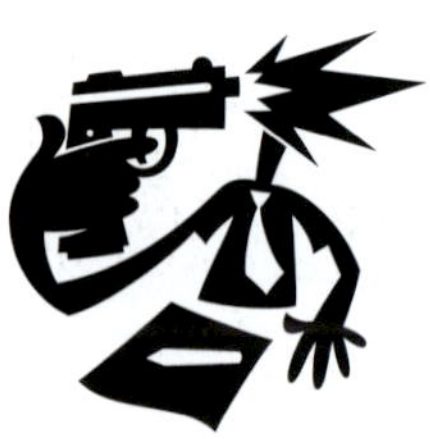

Cruel_World_**TM995**

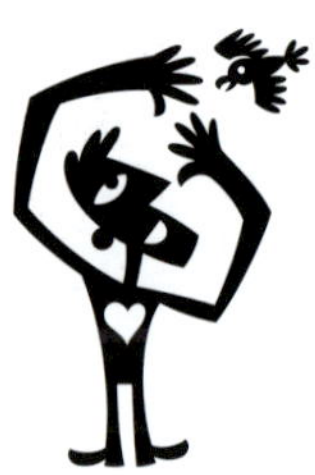

A_Little_Bird_Told_Me_**TM996**

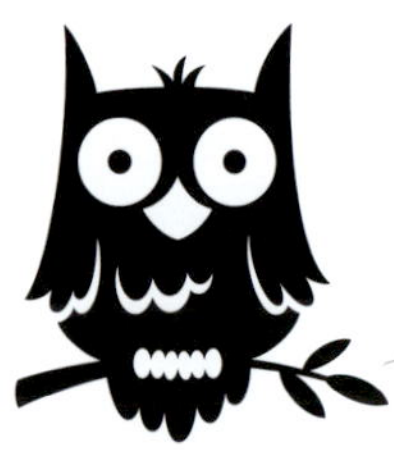

Give_A_Hoot_**TM997**

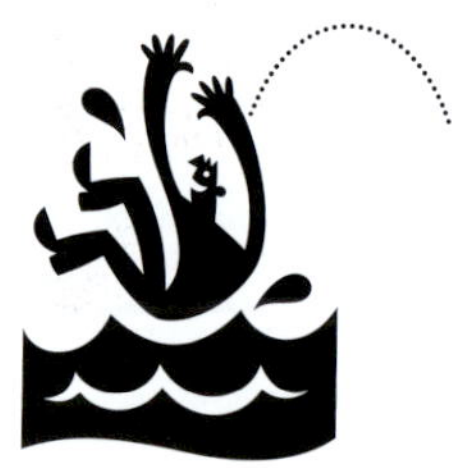

Jump_In_**TM998**

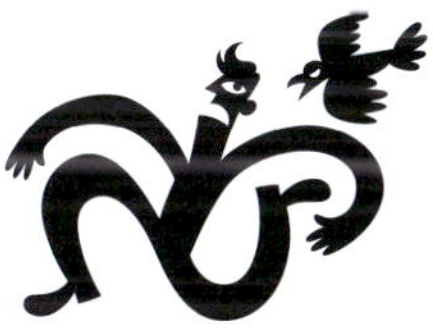

Mocking_Bird_**TM999**

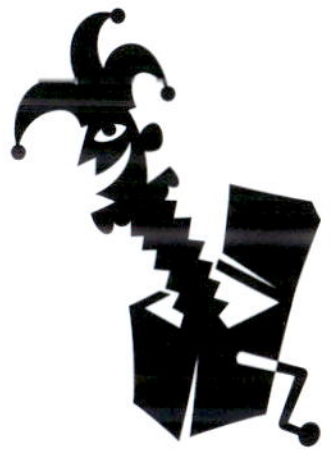

Jack_In_Box_**TM1000**

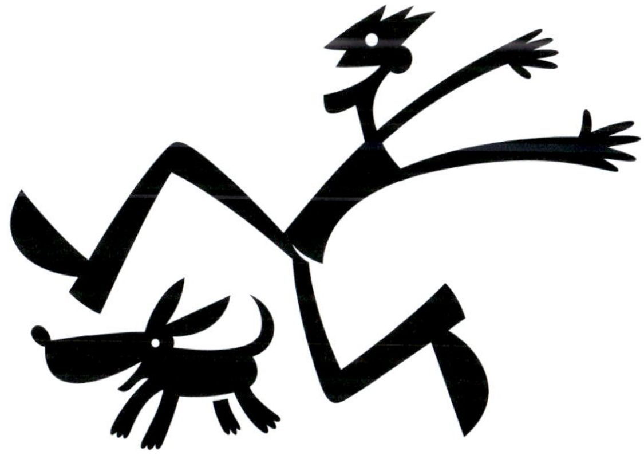

Best_Friends_**TM1001**

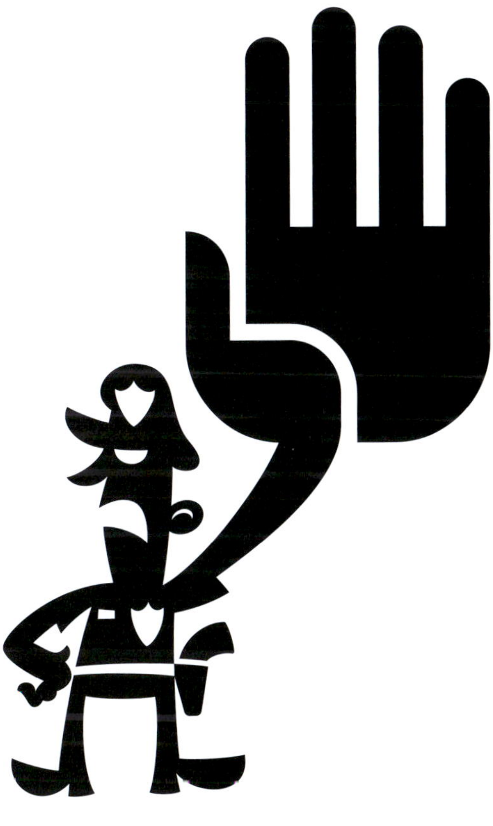

Stop_Right_There_**TM1002**

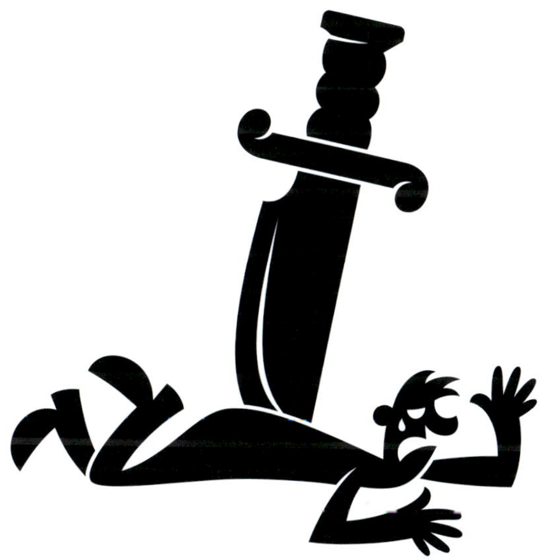

Feeling_Betrayed_**TM1003**

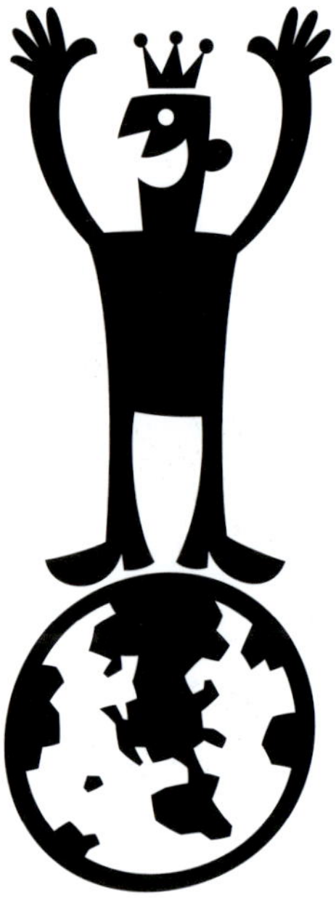

King_Of_The_World_**TM1007**

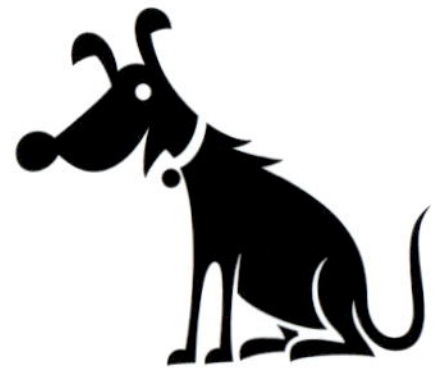

Good_Doggie_**TM1004**

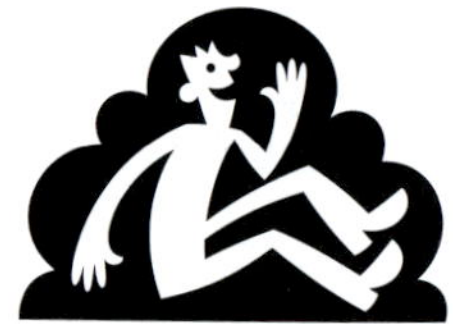

Living_In_The_Cloud_**TM1005**

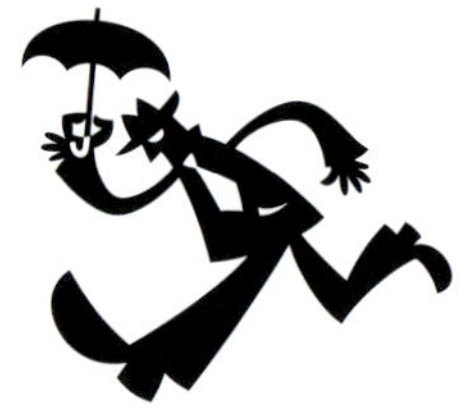

Bumbershoot_User_**TM1006**

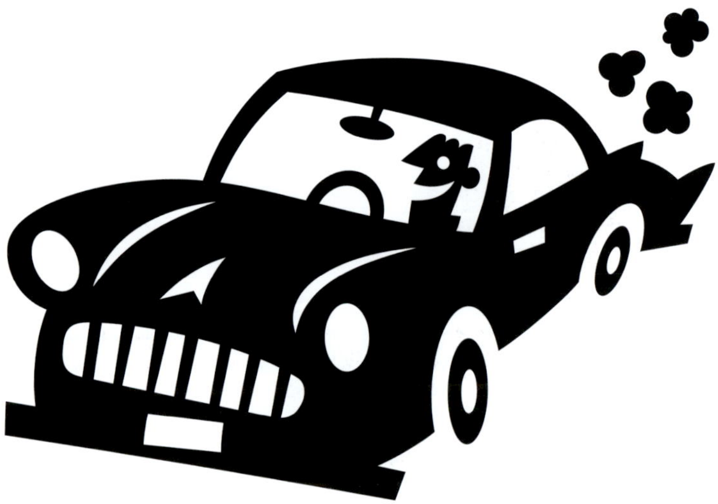

Cruizin_**TM1008**

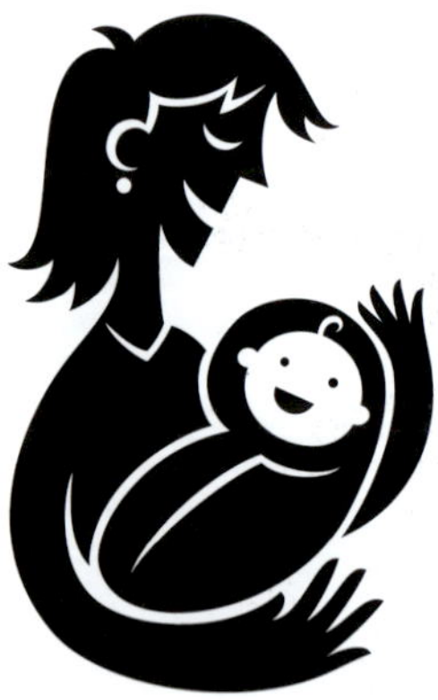

Holding_The_Future_**TM1009**

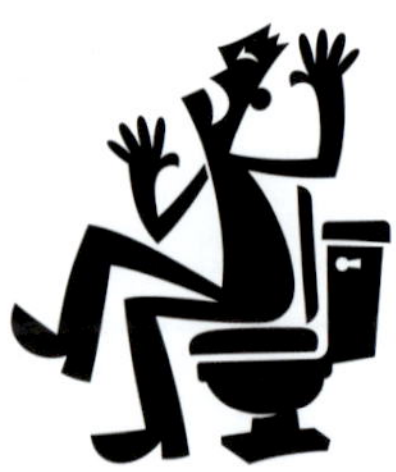

Oh_Crap_**TM1010**

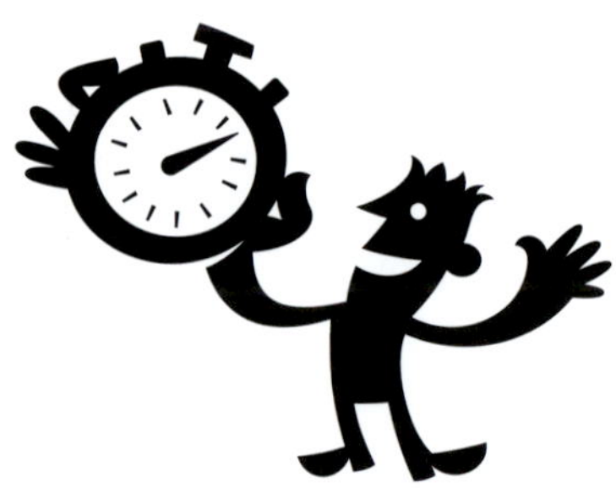

Ready_Set_**TM1011**

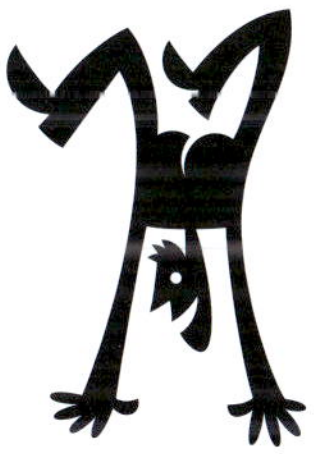

Where_The_Sun_Dont_Shine_**TM1012**

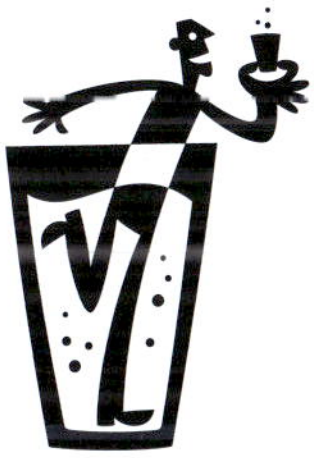

Sauced_**TM1013**

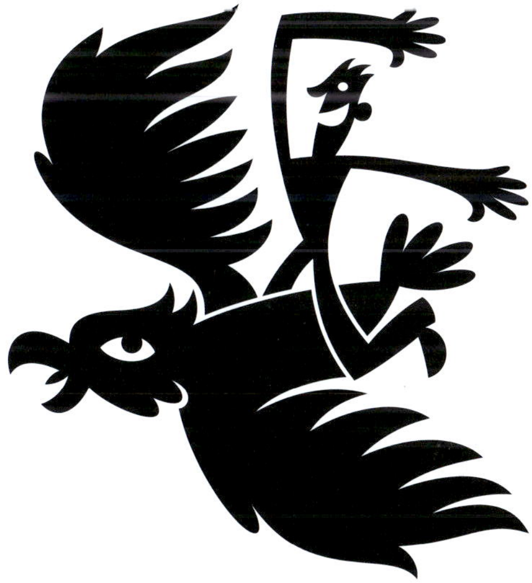

Soar_Above_Your_Problems_**TM1014**

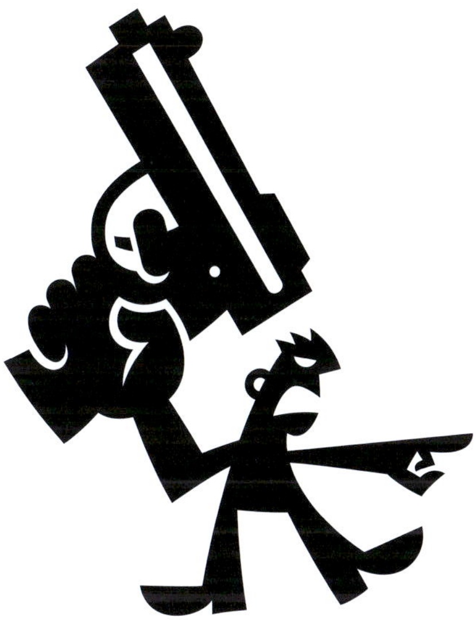

Gun_Show_**TM1015**

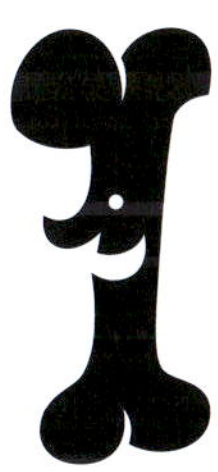

Funny_Bone_**TM1016**

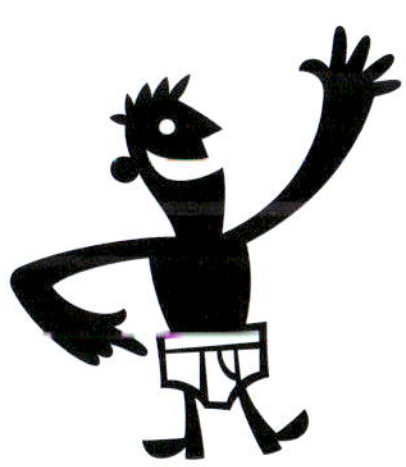

Brief_Encounter_**TM1017**

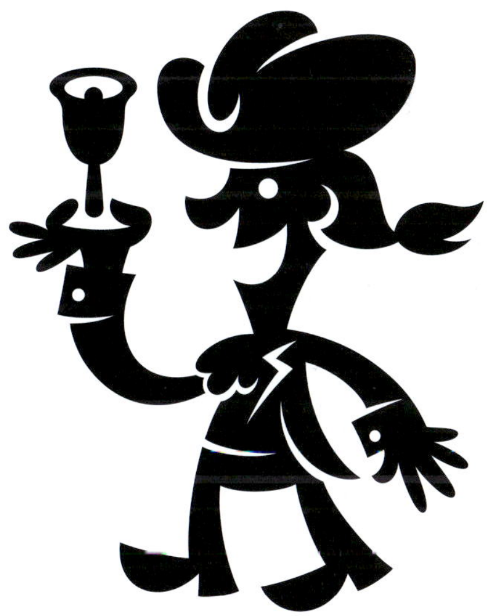

Yankee_Doodle_**TM1018**

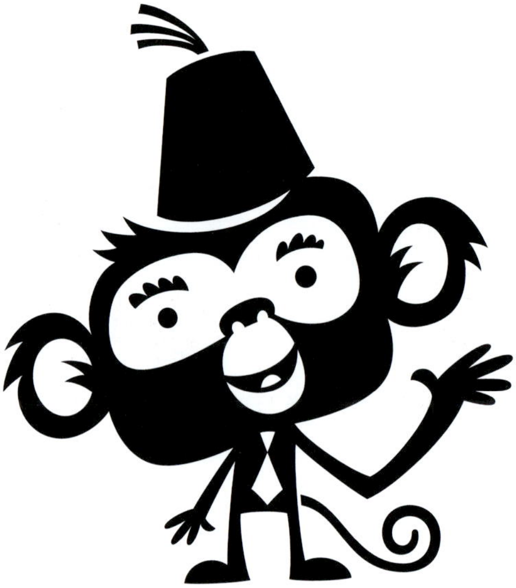

Monkeying_Around_**TM1021**

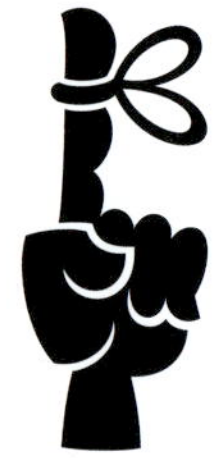

Remember_This_**TM1019**

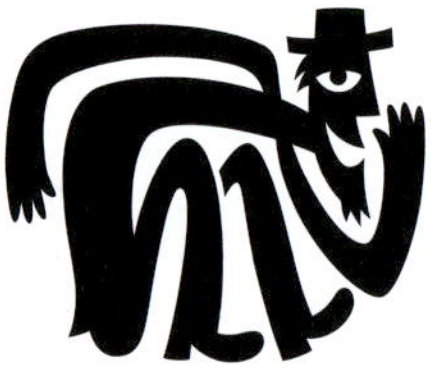

Get_Down_**TM1020**

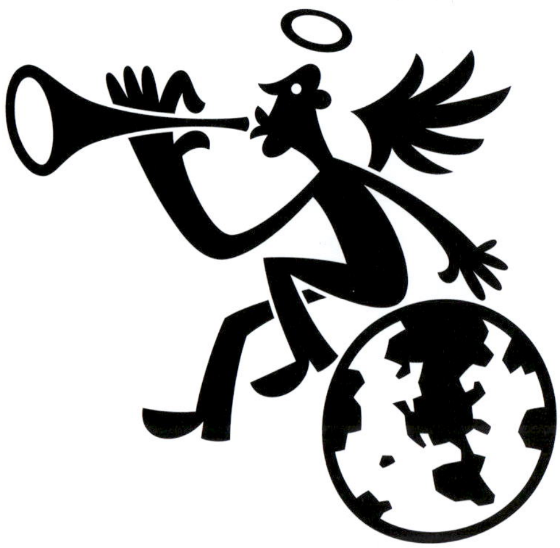

Hark_**TM1022**

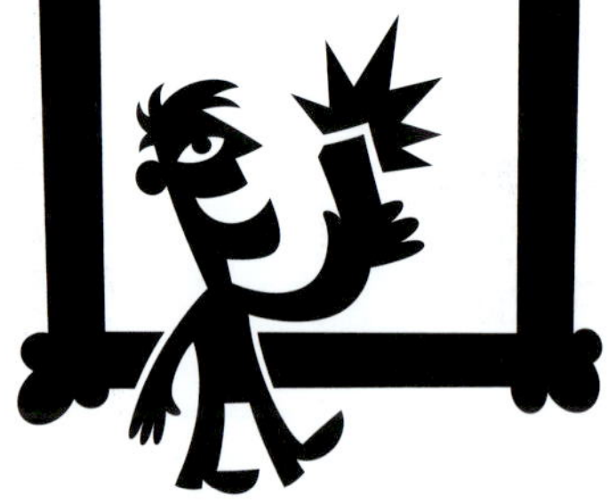

Gallery_Walker_**TM1023**

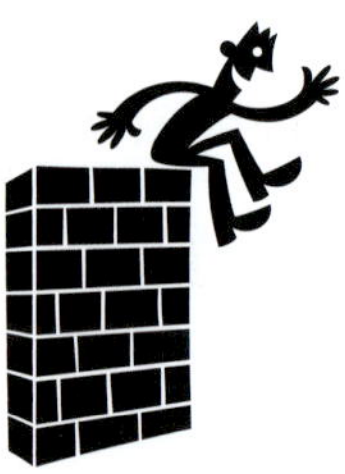

Off_The_Wall_**TM1024**

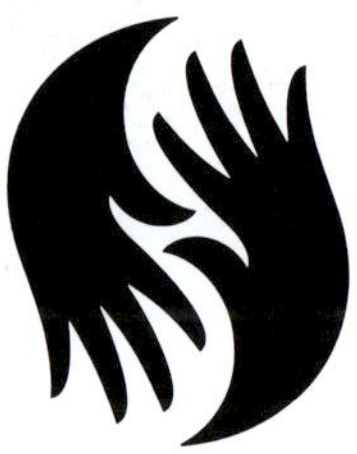

Eastern_Hands_**TM1025**

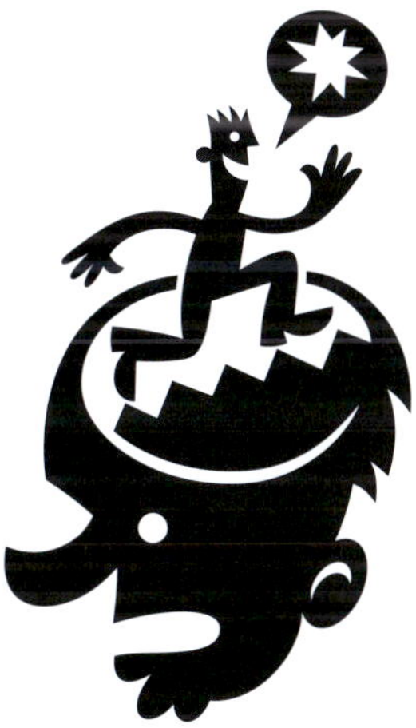

High_Level_Thinking_**TM1026**

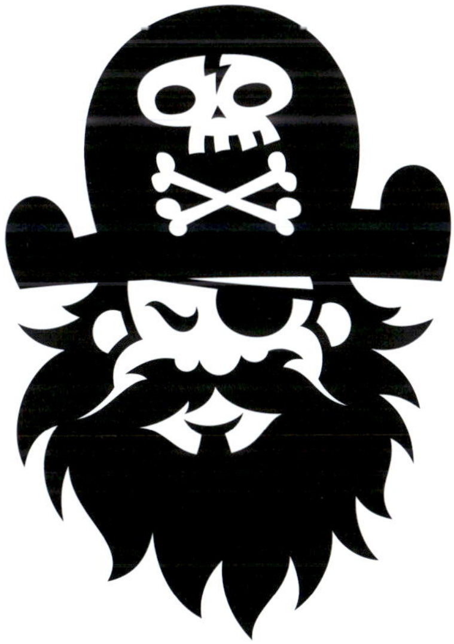

Black_Beard_**TM1027**

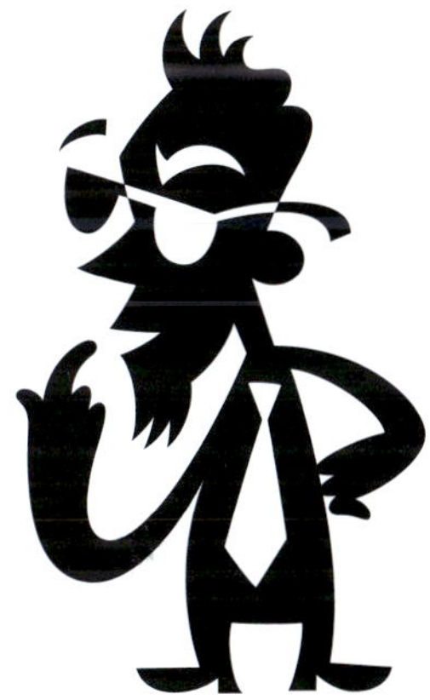

Ponder_This_**TM1028**

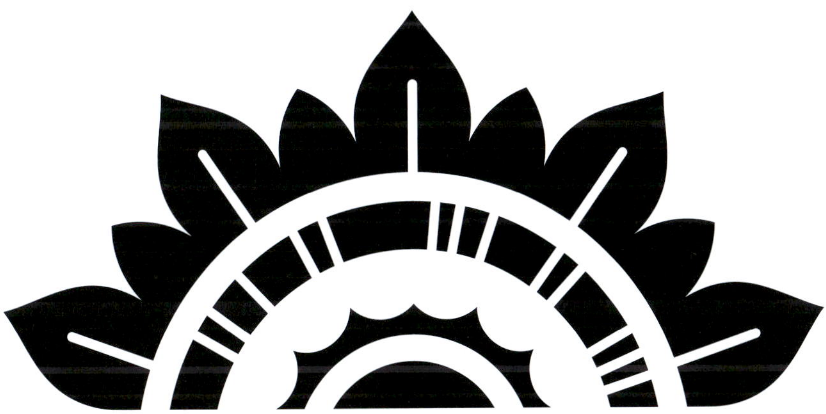

Sunrise_Floral_**TM1029**

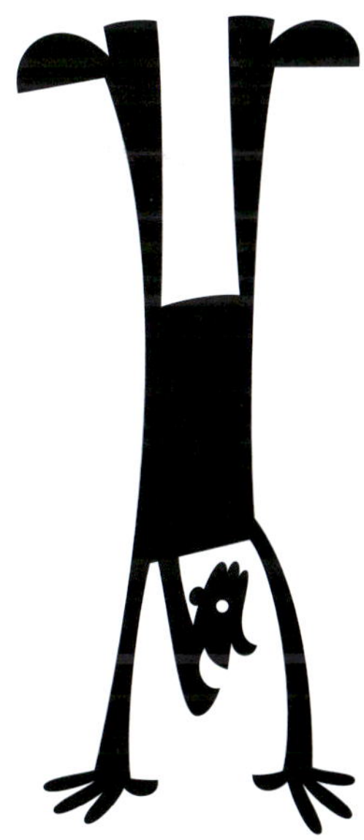

A_New_Perspective_On_Life_**TM1030**

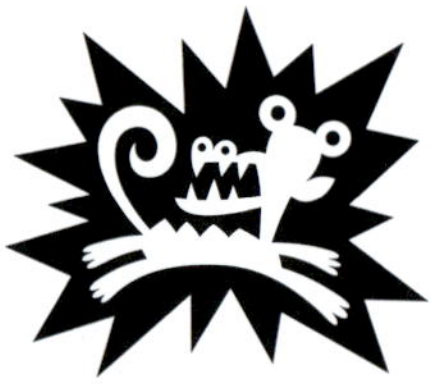

Flash_Of_Insanity_**TM1031**

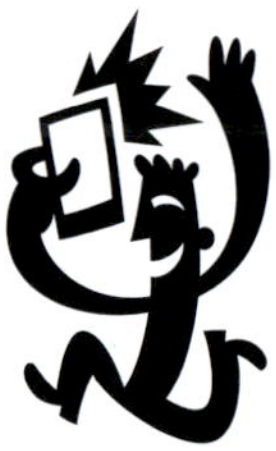

E-Joy_**TM1033**

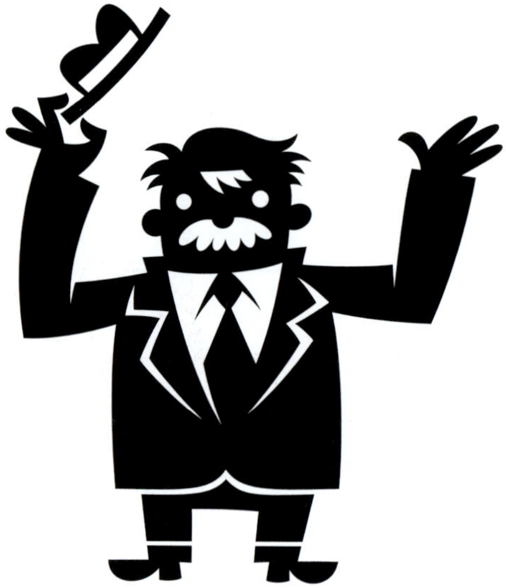

Good_Day_Sir_**TM1034**

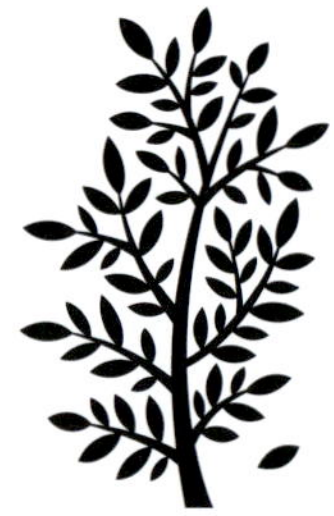

Flourish_**TM1032**

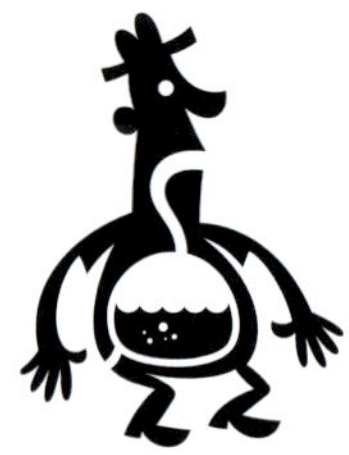

Digest_It_**TM1035**

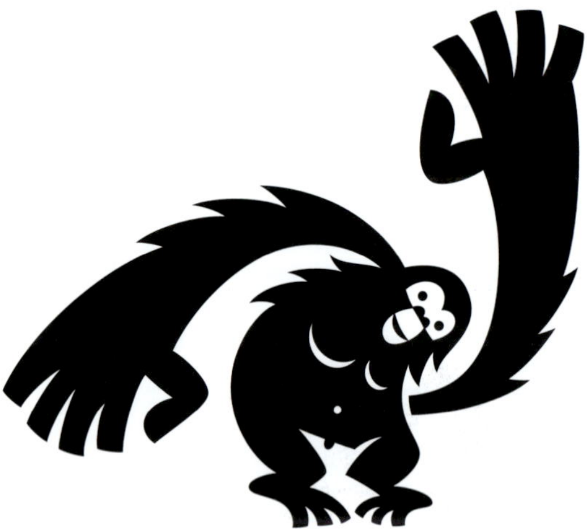

Gorilla_Hi_**TM1036**

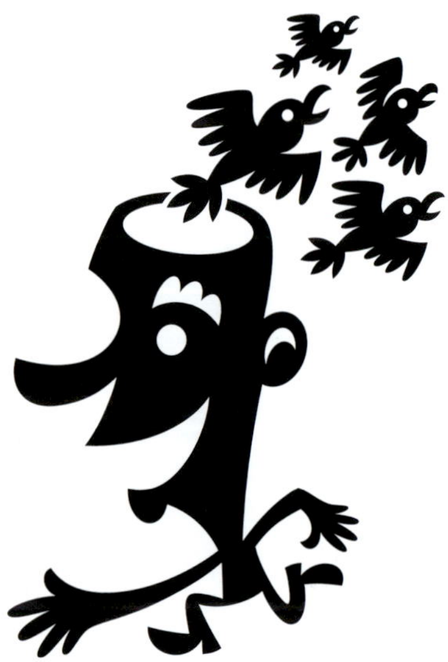

Bird_Brain_**TM1037**

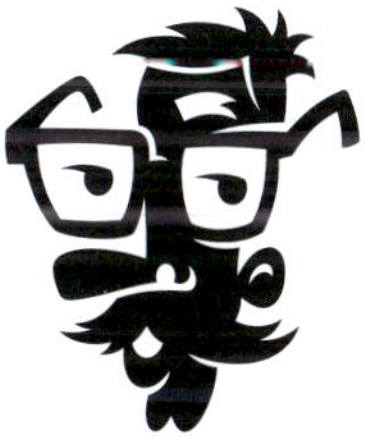

Dont_Look_Back_**TM1038**

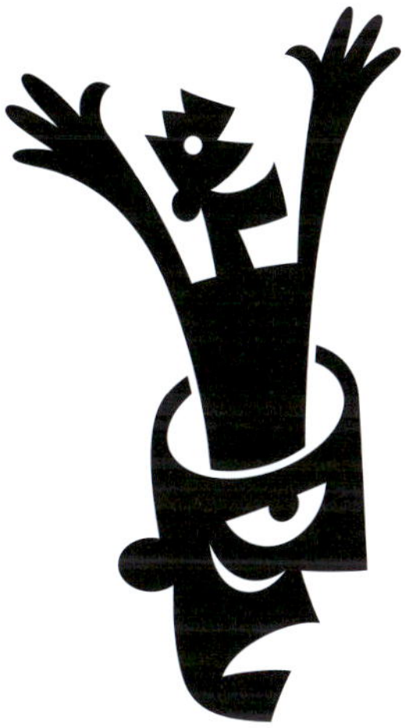

Renew_Your_Mind_**TM1039**

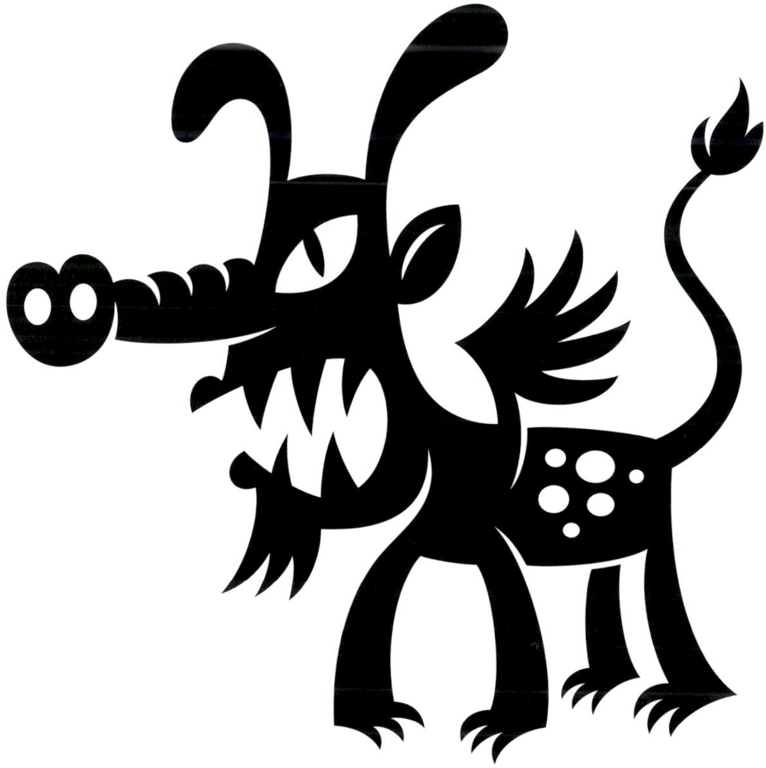

Monster_Dog_**TM1040**

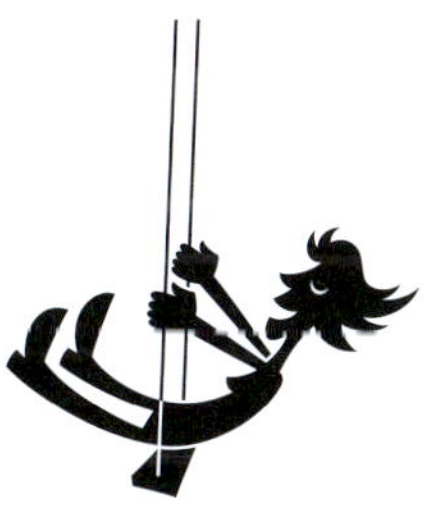

Dreaming_Of_Flight_**TM1041**

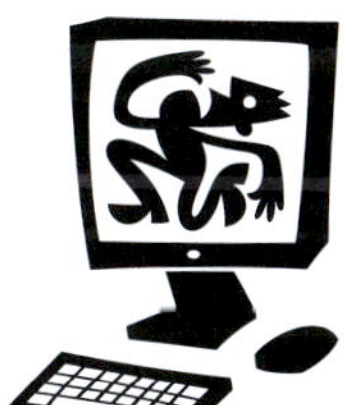

Screen_Capture_**TM1042**

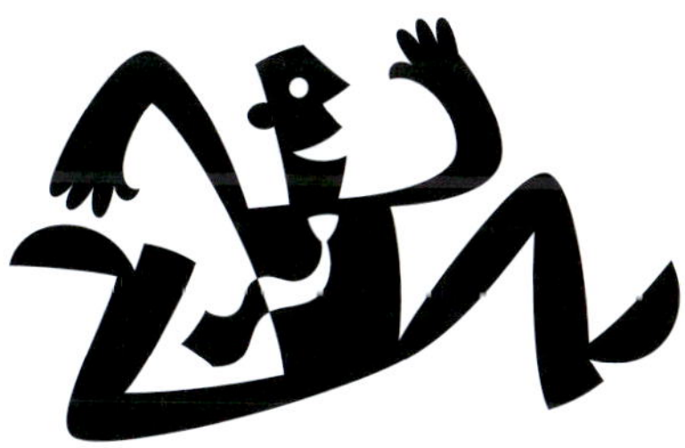

Running_Man_**TM1043**

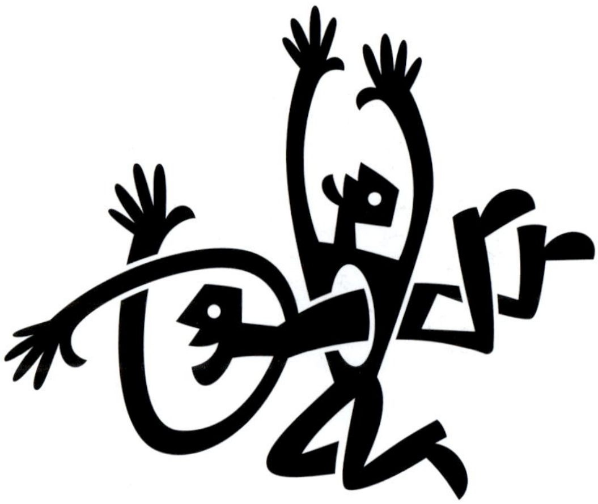

Inside_Out_**TM1046**

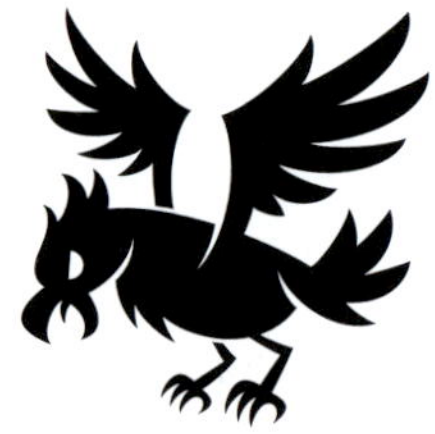

Attack_Mode_**TM1044**

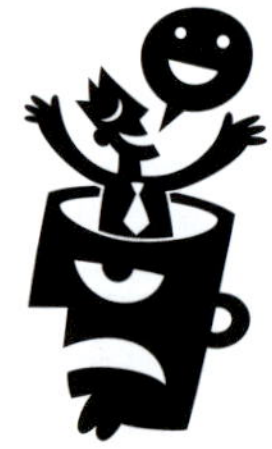

Speak_Your_Mind_**TM1045**

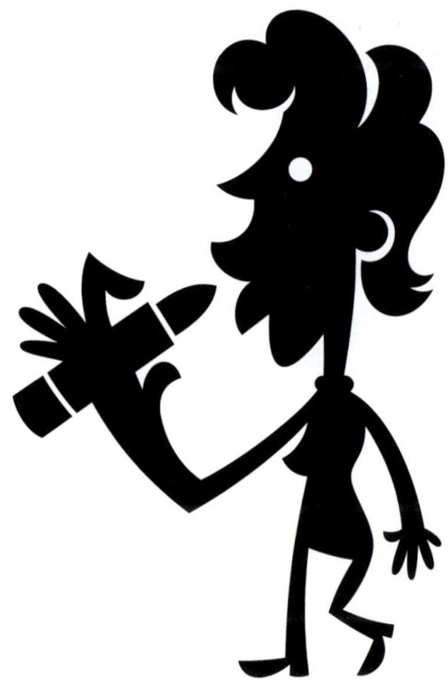

Pucker_Up_**TM1047**

Spirographtastic_**TM1048**

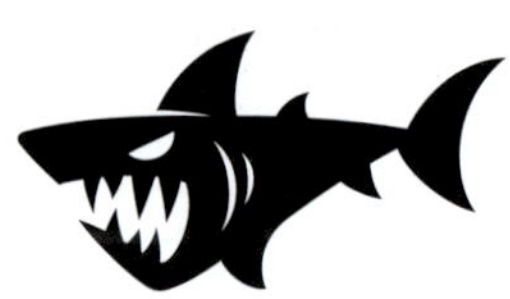

Chompy_**TM1049**

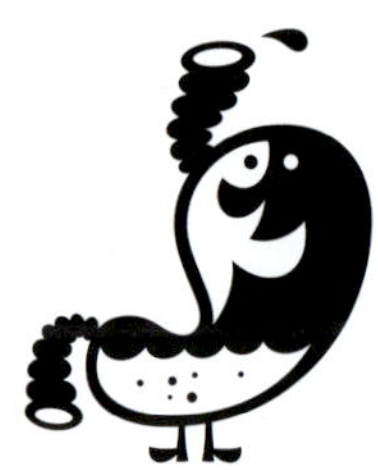

Go_With_Your_Gut_**TM1050**

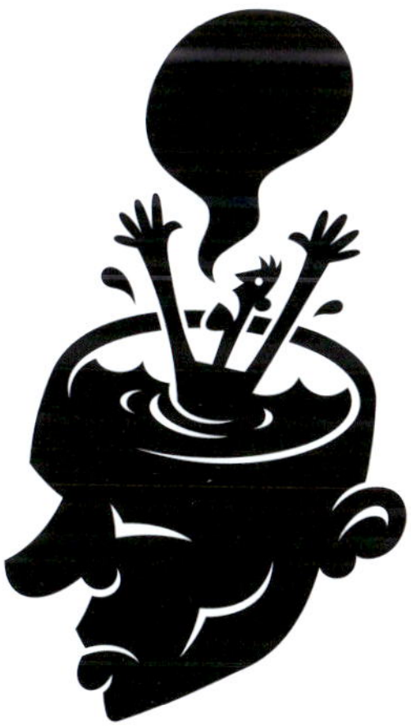

Depression_Kills_**TM1052**

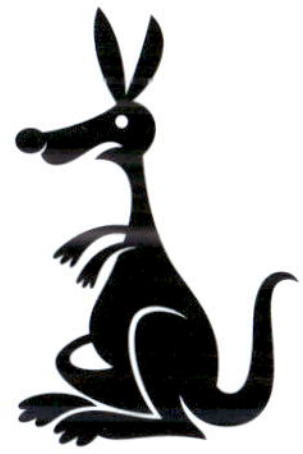

Jump_For_The_Chance_**TM1051**

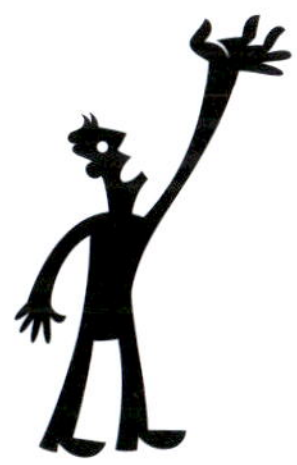

Why_God_**TM1053**

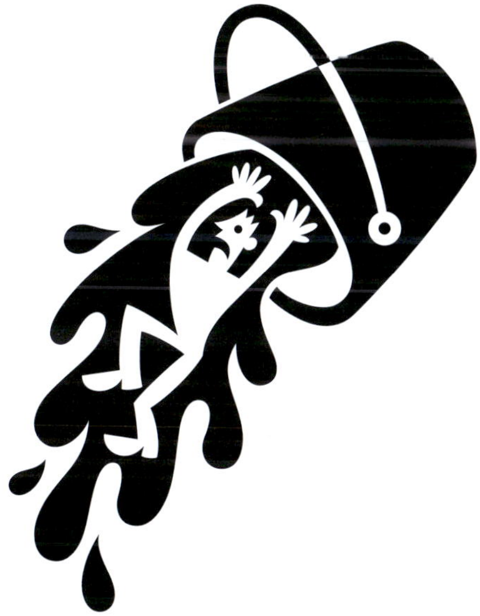

Dump_It_Out_**TM1054**

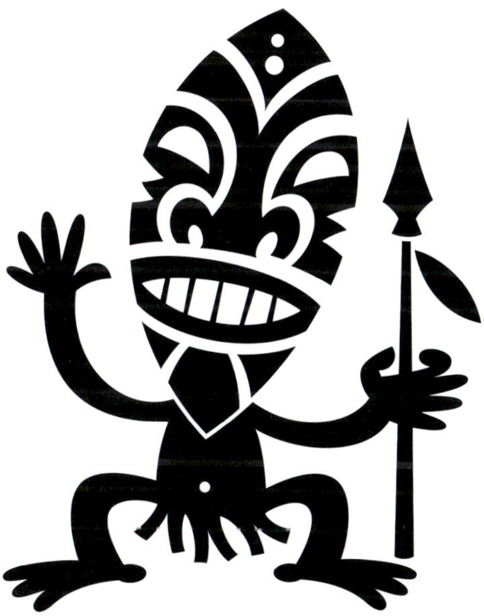

Primitive_Motives_**TM1055**

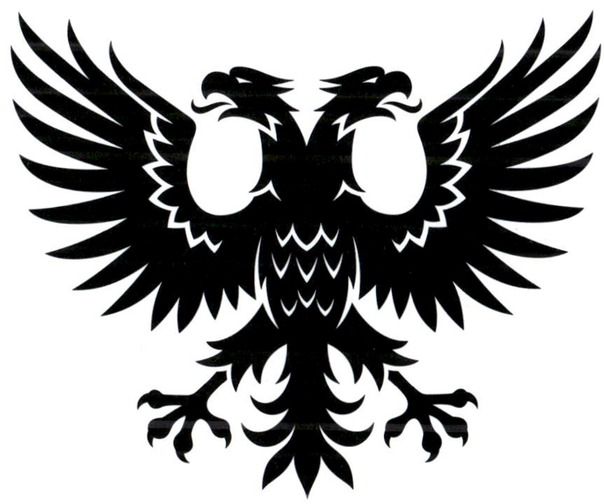

A_House_Divided_**TM1056**

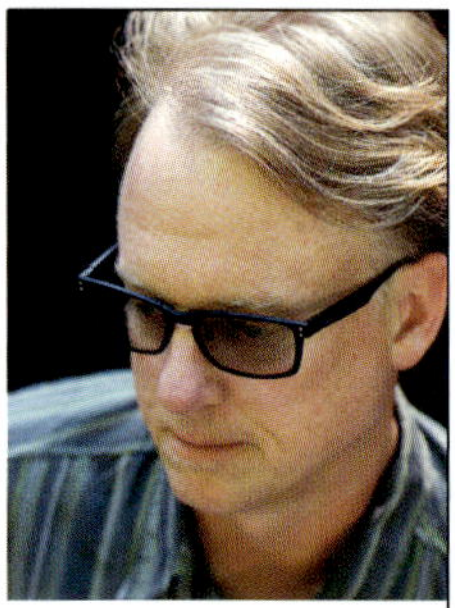

Greg Epkes

Illustrator / Designer

Epkes Creative Studio • Portland, Oregon

www.epkes.com

I chose three images from *Take and Make Art*, and used them to compose my layout and translated them using a textured painting technique. I'll also use this artwork for a mountain forest festival poster and beer labels for the same event.

Art Used: Happy Bloom TM430, Get Funky TM115, Spruce TM447

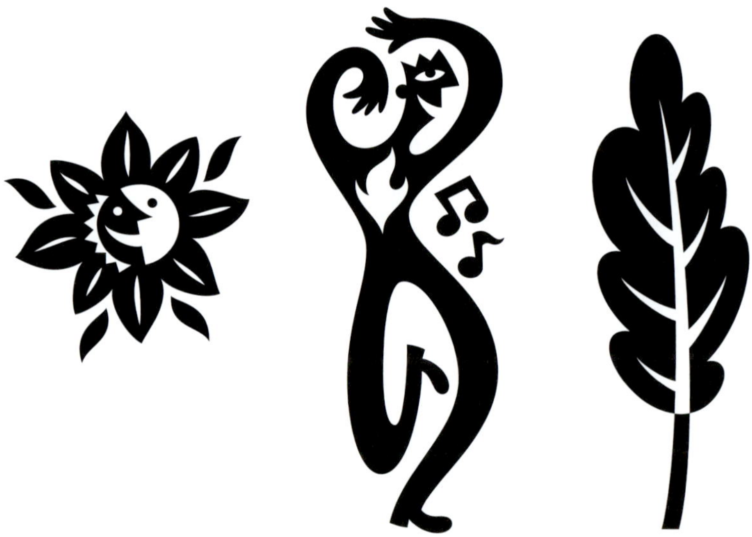

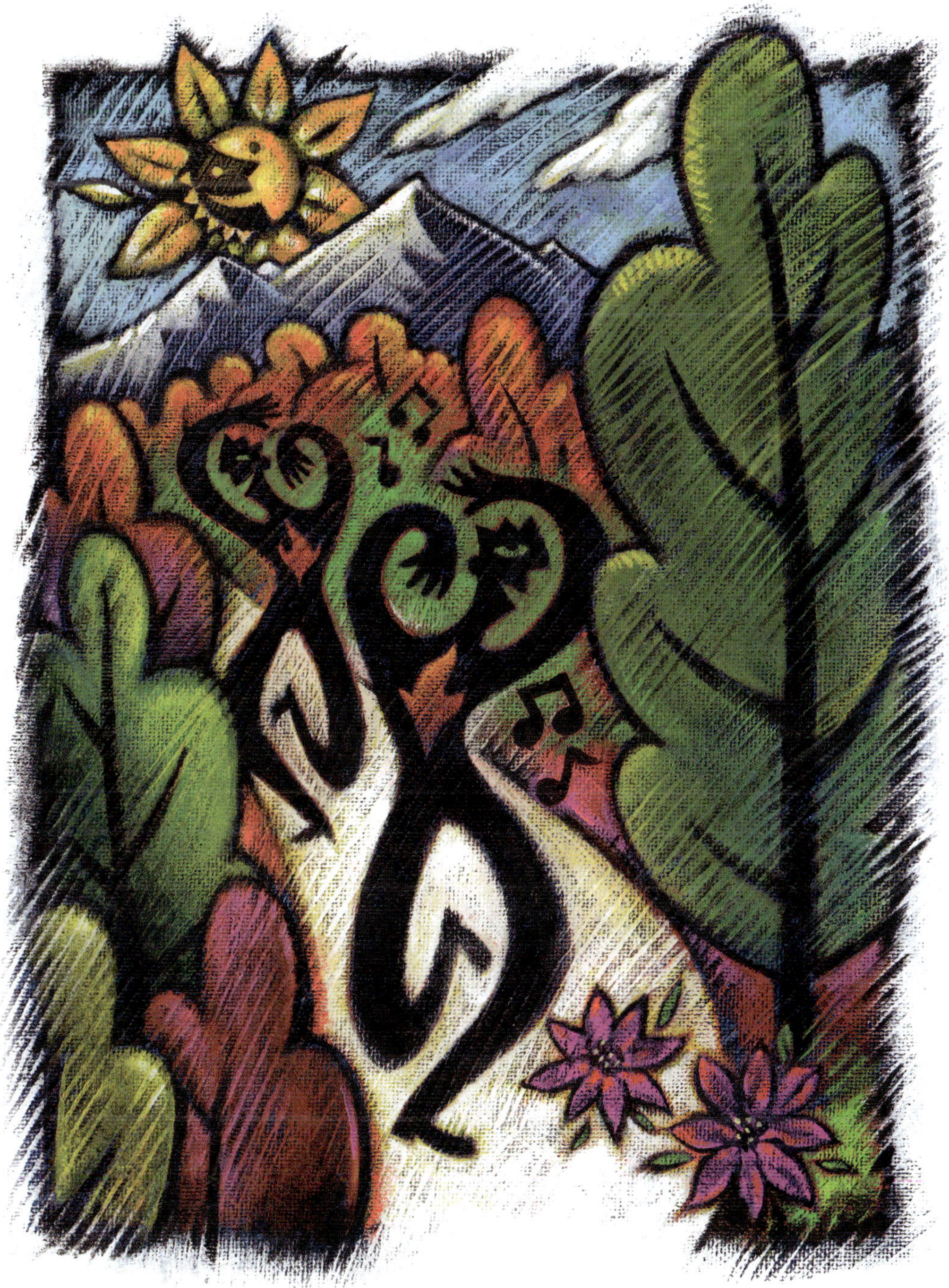

ARTWORK INDEX

ANIMALS & INSECTS

BUILDINGS

COMMUNICATION & SPEECH

DANGER, FEAR, STRESS, & ACCIDENTAL

ELEMENTS

FINANCE

FOOD & DINING

HANDS

HEADS & FACES

HEALTH, FITNESS, & STRENGTH

HOME & OBJECTS

ICONS & SYMBOLS

METAPHORS

MONSTERS

MUSIC, DANCE, & FESTIVITIES

MYTH, MYSTICAL, & FANTASY

NATURE

OFF-THE-WALL & STRANGE

PEOPLE & FIGURES

PLANTS & FLORAL

PRIMAL ART

RELIGION & FAITH

ROBOTS & TOYS

ROMANCE, HEART, & SEX

SECURITY

SCIENCE

SCIENCE FICTION

SKULLS & SKELETONS

SPORTS

TECHNOLOGY, DEVICES, & MACHINES

VEHICLES & TRAVEL

WAR, TYRANNY, FIGHTING, & PEACE

WHIMSICAL OR MISCHIEVOUS CHARACTERS

WORK

WORLD AFFAIRS, POLITICS, & GEOGRAPHY